STAN AND OLLIE

STAN AND OLLIE
THE ROOTS OF COMEDY
The Double Life of Laurel and Hardy

SIMON LOUVISH

faber and faber

by the same author from Faber

MAN ON THE FLYING TRAPEZE
The Life and Times of W. C. Fields

MONKEY BUSINESS
The Lives and Legends of the Marx Brothers

fiction

A MOMENT OF SILENCE
THE THERAPY OF AVRAM BLOK
CITY OF BLOK
THE LAST TRUMP OF AVRAM BLOK
THE DEATH OF MOISHE-GANEF
THE SILENCER
YOUR MONKEY'S SHMUCK
RESURRECTIONS FROM THE DUSTBIN OF HISTORY
WHAT'S UP, GOD?
THE DAYS OF MIRACLES AND WONDERS

First published in 2001
by Faber and Faber Limited
3 Queen Square London WC1N 3AU

Photoset by Agnesi Text Hadleigh
Printed in England by Clays Ltd, St Ives plc

A CIP record for this book
is available from the British Library

ISBN 0-571-20352-3

4 6 8 10 9 7 5 3

Contents

List of Illustrations vii
Prologue: 'No thoughts of any kind . . .' ix

PART ONE
Twice Upon a Time . . .

1 Once Upon a Clown 3
2 Fathers and Sons: Stanley 10
3 Sons and Fathers: The Road Diverges 22
4 Fathers and Sons: Ollie – War and Peace 30
5 Mother and Son: The Boarding House Boy 38
6 We Are Fred Karno's Army: What Bloody Use Are We? 49
7 In the Temple of the Magic Light Beams 59
8 Wow-Wows in Wonderland 69
9 Rum 'Uns a-Roamin' 79
10 Babe: 'All Broken Out with the Movies' 89
11 Vim and Vigour – or Straddling the Home Plates 101
12 The Laurel Wreath of Scipio Africanus – and Other Tall
     Hollywood Tales 113
13 Just Rolin Along – Commence the Hal Roach Story 119
14 Flips and Flops: The Larry Semon Show 128
15 Their First Kiss: 'Put 'em both up, insect, before I comb your
     hair with lead . . .' 140
16 The Handy Man 148
17 Somewhere, Over the Rainbow . . . 163
18 Into the Home Stretch: The Reluctant Suitors 177

PART TWO
The Glory Days – 'Tall Oaks From Little Acorns Grow'

19 The Fruits of Toil 193
20 From Babe to Ollie: The Metamorphosis 204
21 Running Frantically through the Streets 216

22 Full Supporting Cast: The Lot of Fun 228
23 Multiple Whoopee, or Wives and Woes 239
24 Unaccustomed As We Aren't 250
25 The Song of the Cuckoos 265
26 Chickens Come Home 280
27 A Very Good Boy 290
28 Busy Bodies and Devil's Brothers 295
29 The Exhausted Rulers 306
30 Babes in Toil-land 319

PART THREE
'We Faw Down': On the trail of the lonesome mimes

31 'Nice Weather We Had Tomorrow . . .' 329
32 Bohemian Girls 338
33 Believe It or Not – Stan and Hal Go Off the Rails 353
34 Hardy Without Laurel, Laurel Without Hardy 369
35 'Something wholesome, something tender . . .' 382
36 The Fox and the Huns 394
37 Nothing But Trouble 405
38 Any Old Port 421
39 Utopias and Unpromised Lands 432
40 Twilight of the Vauds 444

Epilogue: Going Bye Bye 456

Notes on Sources 463
Chronology 476
Filmography 479
Bibliography 499
Acknowledgements 503
Index 505

List of Illustrations

Frontispiece ii
Young Stan Jefferson 11
Arthur Jefferson 20
Oliver Norvell Hardy as a baby 31
Young Stan Jefferson – 'he of the funny ways' 58
Laurel and Chaplin with the Karno troupe aboard
  the SS *Cairnrona* 70
Early film antics of 'Babe' Hardy – a primal scream? 93
Babe in trouble again 102
Hal Roach with Harold Lloyd – early days 121
Stan Laurel – just rambling along . . . 124
The Lucky Dog – first contact 141
'Babe' Hardy and Larry Semon in *The Bellhop* 146
The Pest: Stan and Mae Laurel 149
Odd ruptures in *Mud and Sand* 151
Stan as Lord Helpus in *When Knights Were Cold* 153
Hardy and Semon in *The Perfect Clown*, with Dorothy Dwan 164
Leo McCarey 179
Laurel and Hardy with musical instruments 194
Stan and Ollie with Hal Roach 196
Prehistory: Cave Stan and Ollie with maidens in *Flying
  Elephants* 211
Ollie, Stan in drag and Jimmy Finlayson in *Sugar Daddies* 214
Whitewash in *The Second Hundred Years* 217
Stan and Ollie 226
Conflict resolution in *Big Business*, with Jimmy Finlayson and
  Tiny Sandford 234
Liberty – caught with their pants down, and on the high rise 236–7
'Stan starts to suffer . . .' – the Laurel cry 246
'Soda, soda, soda. And what will you have, Stan?' 255
Multiple wife trouble for the innocent spouse 263
Below Zero – in the Depression dumps 269

Modern transport in *Hog Wild* 271
In bed with 'Laughing Gravy' 276
Delivery accomplished – with Billy Gilbert and Gladys Gale in
   The Music Box 286
Gender-bending in *Their First Mistake* 296
Oliver Hardy as Mrs Laurel – *Twice Two* 299
Modern carpentry in *Busy Bodies* 304
Party time with Charley Chase in *Sons of the Desert* 314
Mounting silliness in *Babes in Toyland* 323
Ollie without trousers 330
Stan and Ollie in Scots Guards uniform 335
Perils of matrimony – Oliver and Myrtle Hardy, 1936 346
Carefree against the odds in *Way Out West* 351
The Laurel–Hardy Matrimony Case 360
Block-Heads – the walking wounded 367
Zenobia – Dr Tibbitt with Zeke, played by Philip Hurlie 372
A Chump at Oxford – Stan as Lord Paddington 379
The Flying Deuces 383
Reborn in the Fox-hole – *Great Guns* 401
Air Raid Wardens – 'Gone to fight the Japs' 408
Nothing But Trouble – two cooks with the wrong recipe 419
Ollie's last stand-alone – in Frank Capra's *Riding High* 433
Endgame – marooned on Atoll K 436
Endpiece 461

Illustrations courtesy of: Joel Finler, British Film Institute,
The Kobal Collection, John Cooper and the author's collection.

'No thoughts of any kind . . .'

I have forgotten more about my early life than I ever knew, and I am not going to invent a lot of anecdotes and thrilling escapes from fire and water and broken men. No: I might romance, but I will not do anything of the kind. I will go on telling the truth in my simple straightforward way, if it kills me.

Dan Leno, Hys Booke

Just before Christmas 1963, Mr and Mrs Short, of Bedlington, Northumberland, England, received a postcard from a famous friend living in Los Angeles, California:

DEC. 6, '63.

Dear Friends: Thanks your kind letter, 29th ult.

The tragic death of our beloved president Kennedy was indeed a sad & sickening shock – a great great loss to the U.S.A. & the Whole World in fact – why all this HATE in the world today? It's incredible and frightening – Mrs L. joins in wishing you both a very merry Xmas, continued good health, success & happiness in '64.

Take care – God Bless you –

As always sincerely,

STAN LAUREL

It is indeed a shock to think of Stan Laurel, partner, with Oliver Hardy, in the most successful comedy team of all time, co-existing with the violent events in Dallas, Texas, on 22 November 1963, the era of the Cold War, nuclear panic, the Cuban missile crisis, Che Guevara, Civil Rights protest in the American South, the first stages of US involvement in Vietnam. It is a far, far cry from the world of *The Music Box*, in which our two heroes struggle valiantly to carry a crated piano up the steepest steps in movie history, or *Big Business*, in which their failed attempt to sell a Christmas tree to their regular foil, Jimmy Finlayson, results in an epic battle of the mutual destruction of his house and their car, or *You're Darn Tootin'*, in which both Stan and Ollie seem unable to walk down an ordinary city street without falling down manholes. Or is it?

We live in a world of technological marvels, in which the century of quick transit, mass air transport, the motion picture, television and the telephone has given way to a new age of instant access and global chatter, to be defined by inventions yet to come, enabling men and women to rise above their limitations and reach out to brave frontiers. Or do we?

In 1900, too, when our heroes were both schoolboys, in different parts of the globe, rapid change was in the air. The motor car was still an exotic novelty, medical science was revolutionized by the X-ray, electric bulbs were replacing the gaslights, the phonograph was a novelty, not to speak of the new diversion of the moving pictures, which appeared on the vaudeville stages of New York City in 1896. These were the forces of the new age of modernity, and the magic lens that young Norvell Hardy was to embrace in 1914 and Stanley Jefferson (not yet Laurel) a few years later. What appears to us in our millennial turnover to be refreshingly quaint was the latest miracle of the day, with consequences that few could foresee.

Laurel and Hardy present themselves to us as the most familiar of images. For anyone up to the age of eighty, they have been with us since our childhood; wedded together, as in the scene in which they walk out of frame both encased in one pair of outsize trousers, tipping their hats, in *You're Darn Tootin'*; 'that sweet pair', as they were eulogized by comedian Dick Van Dyke, for whom 'the halls of heaven must be ringing with divine laughter'. And indeed they were known and loved throughout the world, under a bewildering variety of local names: Dick and Doof in Germany, Helan and Halvan in Norway and Sweden, Gog and Cokke in Denmark, Stan es Pan in Poland, Flip i Flap in Romania. In Portugal they were O Bucha and O Estica, in Italy Crik and Crok, in Greece Xonapoe and Aznoe, in Egypt El Tikhin and El Roufain, in Turkey Sisman ve Zaif. They have entered our unconscious thoughts, as primal beings, iconic figures to be used in advertising and cartoons, metaphors for a certain kind of chaos, a byword for confusion and incompetence, made to lampoon bungling statesmen, lunatic Pentagon generals, or captains of industry who reduce economies to the level of the unmade house in Stan and Ollie's *The Finishing Touch*.

But there is, of course, a difficulty with these all-so-familiar images, as we set out to seek the elusive reality behind the mask of the clowns. More than any other performers, Laurel and Hardy are idolized by an immense mass of active fans, organized (or more often dis-organized) under the general heading of the 'Sons of the Desert', the association formed by John McCabe with Stan Laurel's blessing in 1965. Since then 'Tents' of the order have proliferated on at least three continents, preserving the memory of 'The Boys' and their movies, publishing magazines, holding annual conventions, fairs and jamborees, imbibing celebratory libations, collecting memorabilia, and attending to the more serious business of preserving the duo's artistic heritage on film, video and new computer-age media. So large has this fan base become that it has developed within it fissures and feuds, conflicts of interest and theological disputes concerning the nature of the objects of worship. Issues that lie directly in the purview of your author's own cautious searches and divide tent from tent, fanzine from fanzine, founders from followers, lie at the nub of these arguments, and can become stumbling blocks for researchers who might enter the field in all blithe innocence but emerge covered in mud pies slung across the battleground much like the great pie fight of *The Battle of the Century*.

The essence of the argument is in the proposition, advanced by some of the more zealous of the fans who have spent lifetimes dedicated to their heroes, that Stan Laurel and Oliver Hardy were the warmest, most gentle human beings to grace the halls of comedy, both onscreen and off. This simple, straightforward assessment admits of some obvious flaws and exceptions, but is built to stand for posterity, a confirmation of the fans' tribute to the two men who gave such laughter to the world. And who would cavil? After all, Stan Laurel and Oliver Hardy were comedians, not politicians, nor soldiers, nor armaments salesmen, nor religious leaders, who spread disharmony and misery in the name of love, or God, or duty. They sought only to entertain us – and succeeded – creating featherlight diversions from the troubles and travails of everyday life. They never pretended to have discovered the Meaning of Life, nor to provide any spiritual guidance, nor to tell people how to live their lives, invest their money, or whom they might love or hate. The closest they came to any statement might be a formal letter by Stan Laurel, written from the Hal Roach Studios in 1934 in response to a query about his favourite 'funnies', suggesting that 'humor, in any form, is one of the finest tonics for depression, whether the depressed be an individual or a nation. The comic pages of America have done their part in lifting this country out of the dumps and bringing smiles to the haggard face of a worried world.'

And so, of course, had Laurel and Hardy. But profound thoughts were not their *métier*, even if one ratchets up their ambition from the opening intertitle of one of their 1929 shorts, *The Hoose-Gow*:

'Neither Mr. Laurel nor Mr. Hardy had any thoughts of doing wrong. As a matter of fact, they had no thoughts of any kind.'

Some critics, I might note, have approached the study of comedians in general in just such a blissful state. Who needs a biography of a comic, studiously researched, detaching fact from legend? Surely all that is enough is a happy picture book of the old vintage heroes, with jaunty captions and nostalgic tributes! Better to preserve the sledgehammer of research for our more sombre, 'serious' artists, our literary giants, painters, poets . . .

But what greater poets, singers of the eternal mischief of the human spirit, can we conjure but the clowns whose antics soothed us in this century past of social turmoil and bewildering challenges to our sense of personal identity and our individual contact to the world of never-ending flux and change? They sing an older song, when we examine it, with a deeper, more profound rhythm than first look, or cursory acquaintance, might suggest. In our more sceptical age, when knowledge of the past, and how we got here, tempers the moronic market's mass trumpeting of anything that can be traded as 'New', it is worth taking a closer look at the all-too-human narrative of the folk who kept us sane in the mêlée. It is not so much that our heroes have feet of clay, for it is perhaps our own clumsy footsteps in life that we cannot forgive, in an age that worships a mythical perfection, an easy path to material or even spiritual redemption that is belied by every actual life. But the comedians' own work, their art, onscreen or before the magic light beams made their art so available to the world, is nourished by the peculiarities of their own lives, convoluted, confused, contorted, full of strange twists and turns and indeed bizarre episodes as comic, or tragicomic, as any in their rich output.

For my own part, I confess to an initial reluctance to engage a subject on which, it seemed, so many books had already been published. The bibliography of Laurel and Hardy is indeed a lengthy list. John McCabe, aforementioned, has committed four books on Laurel and Hardy to print and is their 'authorized' biographer as well as the unchallenged founder of the 'Sons of the Desert'. As the father of Laurel and Hardy studies, his accomplishment stands in its own right. Two filmographies, Randy Skretvedt's *Laurel and Hardy: The Magic Behind the Movies* (1987, revised 1994 and 1996) and Rob Stone's *Laurel or Hardy: The Solo Films of Stan*

Laurel and Oliver 'Babe' Hardy, researched with David Wyatt (1996), are the definitive record of the duo's joint and separate film *œuvre* respectively. Glenn Mitchell's capacious *The Laurel and Hardy Encyclopedia* (1995), fills in whatever gaps remain. Given that Oliver Hardy appeared in over 270 films (almost all short subjects) on his own, Stan Laurel in over 90 solo short films, and that their work together comprises 106 titles, it is impossible (and distracting) to try to encompass them all in a biography, and these three books comprise essential companion pieces to any such project. A. J. Marriot's meticulously compiled *Laurel and Hardy: The British Tours* (1993) is also a peerless aid to the researcher.

But the project itself has proved – at least to its author! – well worth while. Despite the volumes preceding, the oceans of magazine ink, the harrying of every morsel of trivia concerning the duo's joint films, the forest has been mislaid, somewhere, among the trees. The questions of Who were Stanley and Oliver? Where did they come from? What were the origins of their particular comedy? How did their lives feed into their art? have remained open to a fresh examination.

What are the roots of comedy? We should not be afraid to dig, for the plant itself will not shrivel in our gaze. The work remains, to be enjoyed by new generations. Stan and Ollie's 1930 short, *Hog Wild*, is preceded by a title: 'Amnesia! Mr. Hardy was beginning to forget things, but Mr. Laurel had no fear of losing his memory – As a matter of fact, Mr. Laurel never had a memory to lose.' As a matter of fact, Mr Laurel had one of the best memories in the business, which just goes to show you shouldn't believe everything you see and hear at the movies . . . But Mr Laurel's memory, and Mr Hardy's too, is at the heart of the matter – the engine from which the magic tricks of comedy derive. Nothing creates nothing, and creativity is the endless churn of all that has been lived, absorbed, and learned.

So let us ignore, for the moment, the titles of H. M. 'Beanie' Walker, Hal Roach Studio's assigned writer, and settle down to what can really be recalled –

PART ONE

Twice Upon a Time . . .

CHAPTER ONE

Once Upon a Clown

The clown was always disreputable, once his ties with religion were severed. Although the old song tells us 'the things that we're liable to hear in the Bible, they ain't necessarily so', merry-making, as far back as we care to go, was associated with drunkenness and wine. The biblical archetype, Jubal-Cain, was said to have been 'the father of all such as handle the harp and organ', which places him perhaps dubiously as the ancestor of Harpo and Chico Marx. Nevertheless, by the time we got to Bacchus, the ties to divinity were getting a little shaky. The Greeks were supposed to have initiated, or defined, the art of the Pantomime, the development in dance of a language of gestures, in which emotions and ideas can be presented. The old Hellenes were said to have given us Tragedy and Comedy, although Chico Marx once quipped that 'You can't take anything from the Greeks; you can't even get your change back.' Tragedy was for the upper classes, the kings and queens and gods and princes. Comedy was for the common people.

The Romans stole all the Greeks' ideas, though their sense of humour was somewhat coarser. A good day out at the Colosseum might start with the jugglers and magicians but end with blood and guts on the sand. One of Stan Laurel's early stage acts, formed in a break from his stint with Fred Karno's road show, was entitled *Rum 'Uns from Rome*, but there were none so rum as the Romans themselves. The author of the *Satyricon*, Petronius, was said to be 'a man who spends his days sleeping and his nights working or enjoying himself. Industry is the usual foundation of success, but with him it was idleness.' One of the little ditties enclosed in his famous work goes like this:

> The Censor frowns and knits his brows,
> The Censor wants to stop us,
> The Censor hates my guileless prose,
> My simple modern opus.

My cheerful unaffected style
Is Everyman when in his humour,
My candid pen narrates his joys,
Refusing to philosophize.

An easy recognition. Out of the Roman *Mimi*, defined as 'an impudent race of buffoons who excelled in mimicry, and like our domestic fools, admitted into convivial parties to entertain the guests', emerged the gaudily costumed character of Harlequin – a clown of shaven head, sooty face, flat, unshod feet, and patched coat of many colours. Out of the same mould emerges the Italian Pulcinello, or the English Punch, with his long, hooked nose, his staring, goggle eyes and humped back. The generic name for this whole family of clowns has echoed down the centuries – in Latin *sannio*, in Italian *zanni*, in English zany. With the fall of Rome, and the rise of sombre-minded Christianity, these mimes were excluded from the rites of the Church, and their entertainments were frowned on. According to the Theodosian Creed, it was forbidden to administer the sacraments to actors except when death was imminent, and then only so that, if they recovered, they could renounce their calling. Rogues and Vagabonds, they wandered the earth, stubbornly laughing at tragedy. They were a worldwide phenomenon, in the Islamic and Oriental realms as well as the Christian. No culture was complete without its clowns. The élite among them became the court jesters, the fools with cap and bells who could laugh at the king when anyone else doing so would be doomed. But the truth, told behind the mask of the jester, could be only a joke: the proper 'truth' was still reserved by Church and State.

The old *zannis* continued to mutate, begetting a new family in the Italian theatre of the fifteenth century and on: Pantaloon, a merchant; Dottore, a comic physician; Spavento, a braggart; Pulcinello, the joker; and the blundering servant, Arlecchino. A description of Arlecchino–Harlequin, in R. J. Broadbent's 1901 *A History of Pantomime*, echoes, once again, with a close familiarity:

He is a mixture of wit, simplicity, ignorance, and grace, he is a half-made-up man, a great child with gleams of reason and intelligence, and all his mistakes and blunders have something arch about them. The true mode of representing him is to give him suppleness, agility, the playfulness of a kitten with a certain coarseness of exterior, which renders his actions more

4

absurd. His part is that of a faithful valet; greedy; always in love; always in trouble, either on his own or his master's account; afflicted and consoled as easily as a child, and whose grief is as amusing as his joy.

Sometimes Harlequin was just a simple booby or dolt, or a kind of Sancho Panza, travelling with a companion who was sharp-witted and smart, who played the part of his foil. These clowns developed in various ways, with different masks and costumes. One French observer of the eighteenth-century English clown type wrote:

[He] is an odd and fantastical being . . . His strange dress seems to have been taken from the American Indians. It consists of a white, red, yellow and green net work, ornamented with diamond-shaped pieces of stuff of various colours. His face is floured, and streaked with paint a deep carmine; the forehead is prolonged to the top of the head, which is covered with a red wig, from the centre of which a little stiff tail points to the sky. His manners are no less singular than his costume. He is not dumb, like our Pierrot, but, on the contrary, he sustains an animated and witty conversation; he is also an acrobat, and very expert in feats of strength.

The early nineteenth century saw a great inheritor of this old tradition: Joseph 'Joey' Grimaldi. Until his death in 1837 Grimaldi dominated the comedy scene in London. Before the days of the cinema, before the days of photography, it is difficult to gauge the particular qualities that made him so unforgettable to the audiences of his day. Whether in the simple way in which he stole a pie from a pieman, or in his many masks as a chimney sweep, a dandy, a tragic actor, a wet-nurse, he was a master of mimicry, who, in the words of a contemporary, 'uses his folly as a stalking horse, under cover of which he shoots his wit'. He also sang comic songs, 'infused with biting satire . . . poking fun at the vices of the age, getting laughs out of transforming everyday objects and gilding every situation with his inimitable and immortal comic gift'. Grimaldi was noted as well for his comic duelling, and the astute student of comedy might flash forward to Stan Laurel's solo two-reel short of 1923, *Frozen Hearts*, in which our hero, as a Russian swain, Ivan Kektumoff, duels with his rival, the equally well-named Lieutenant Tumankikine, for seven non-stop months until both are buried deep in snow. Clowns, if not their audiences, always know their history.

Grimaldi became a prototype for the clowns of the Circus, the Big Show sired by the eighteenth century's penchant for extravagance and spectacle. But as a stage performer, in the London theatres of Covent Garden and Sadler's Wells, he also set the mode for a generation of music-hall performers who were to follow, adopting his *mélange* of comic songs, patter, physical agility and multiple personalities expressed through a gallery of roles. The Harlequin coat of many colours dropped away, and a kind of genteel frock coat, with frayed pants and an often battered hat, reminiscent of the man about town who is somewhat the worse for wear, became a more common signature.

The story of music-hall is the story of the many individuals who were its featured entertainers. In the 'legit' theatre, the play's the thing, but in variety, it's the performer. Grimaldi established the idea of a 'style': it doesn't matter what you do, but how you do it, the manner it is that makes the clown.

Above all, music-hall was a popular medium; in the words of one of its chroniclers, Mr W. MacQueen Pope,

an entertainment of the People, for the People, by the People. It made no claim to Art, it made no claim to Culture, yet it was in its individual way a very highly skilled form of stage art . . . Music-hall was always very much larger than life. It ignored half-tones, it went out for highlights all the time. And it was right in doing so, because it dealt with a public which was itself surging with vitality. For music-hall was born on the wave of prosperity which came into being on the accession of the young Queen Victoria, it belonged to an era of prosperity and the people who welcomed it and supported it were the sons and daughters of an age of Beef, Beer and Peace.

Music-hall was a medium for the 'working classes' – or those of them who could afford the price of admission, as far from everybody shared in the benefits of the Victorian industrial boom that made Britain Europe's foremost empire. While this theatre thrived, Karl Marx (long before Groucho) formed his theories of the contradictions of Capital while nursing his carbuncles in Soho. But the audiences of music-hall seemed happy with their contradictions – at least while the show was on. Like their predecessors in the eighteenth century, who cheered at John Gay's *The Beggar's Opera* – the play that, by its boldness, galvanized the government of the day into instituting formal stage censorship – but also applauded war with France, so the people of Beef, Beer and Peace cheered on their Imperial Army when it went to war for Queen, Country and Commerce. Like the general public of the next century's mass-entertainment medium – America's moving picture industry – they could be supremely jealous of their own freedom from government, and less particular about the rights of foreigners, at one and the same time. This, too, would mark the nature of mass entertainment on stage and screen, and to our day.

The clowns knew all their moods and fears, their joys and their anxieties. In the last two decades of the nineteenth century, while the Great White Queen swallowed greater and greater parts of the planet in gobs of pink on the map, the great stars of the English music-hall strutted their stuff upon the stage: Arthur Roberts, 'a shrewd and knavish sprite'; George Robey, with his bowler hat, frock coat and cane well ahead of tramp Charlie Chaplin; Little Tich, diminutive mutant with five fingers and a thumb on each hand; Albert Chevalier, 'coster' singer, who knocked 'em in the Old Kent Road. And the women too. Major stars like Marie Lloyd, who sang 'a little of what you fancy does you good', Vesta Victoria and Vesta Tilley, the fabulous male impersonator, all had huge followings, spicing up an age that has presented itself to us as one of rigid conventions.

But the greatest of all was Dan Leno. Born as George Galvin in 1860, the son of itinerant actors, at an address that soon after became – according to legend – Platform 1 of Saint Pancras railway station, he was a child star by the age of eleven, billed as 'Dan Patrick Leno – descriptive and Irish Character Vocalist'. The family show was a simple slapstick act, much like that, one generation later, across the ocean, of the Three Keatons: Joe, Myra and little Buster. Leno wrote of himself, in a brief spoof autobiography entitled *Dan Leno, Hys Booke* (ghosted by one T. C. Elder): 'I came into the world a mere child, without a rag to my back, and without a penny in my pocket, and now I am a farthing millionaire.' (A primal echo of Groucho Marx's 'Years ago I came to this country without a nickel in my pocket and now – I have a nickel in my pocket.') 'I very soon displayed artistic ability,' wrote Leno, 'for having procured a large quantity of strawberry jam, I varnished all the furniture of a room with it, including the exterior of the cat, and the interior of a pair of my Dad's new boots, which he declared went on more easily next time he tried them.'

7

Leno's forte on the stage, after an early career as 'champion clog dancer of the world', won at a competition in Oldham, was his role as a variety of Christmas pantomime characters, frequently women, the famous 'Pantomime Dames' – Widow Twankey, Mother Goose, Fair Zuleika in *The Forty Thieves* – as well as a range of comic characters from real life – the Shop Walker, the Fireman, the Railway Guard, the Cobbler, the Ice-Cream Man, the County Councillor, the Hen-pecked Husband, the Chattering Wife, and One of the Unemployed. When people argue, nowadays, that vaudeville and variety are dead forms, remind them that the ubiquitous imitators and stand-up comics of present-day television derive their formulas from such as Dan Leno. For over ten years, he also performed a double act with another great variety man, Herbert Campbell. Campbell was large (nineteen stone) and rotund, and Leno was short and wiry. From 1891 they presented a series of notable double acts in Christmas pantos. In 1895, Campbell was the Baron and Leno the Baroness in *Cinderella*, assaying some vintage repartee:

BARONESS

Oh! That my first husband was alive!

BARON

Would that he were!

BARONESS

My first husband was the father of these girls, and do you know what he did?

BARON

He died, and I don't blame him.

In a sad serendipity, Herbert Campbell died in July 1904, and Dan Leno three months later, of a brain tumour, having been in failing health and mentally unstable for three years.

Leno's personal humour was quirky and eccentric, in a mode we would today call 'surrealist', a concept unavailable at the time, though this was an age that had already seen the publication of Lewis Carroll's *Alice* fantasies. He knew from experience that ordinary people's lives were odd and unpredictable, and had to be drawn in waves and curves, rather than straight lines. Marie Lloyd said of Leno:

Ever seen his eyes? The saddest eyes in the whole world. That's why we all laughed at Danny. Because if we hadn't laughed, we should have cried ourselves sick. I believe that's what real comedy is, you know. It's almost like crying.

Stan Laurel, a celebrated master of the comedy cry, always offered Dan Leno as his major influence among the English clowns. There is no evidence, however, that Stan ever saw Leno perform. Leno's last performances were in 1902, when Stan was twelve, and those were mainly in London, which Stan had yet to visit in his teenage years. But the influence of Leno, his gentle style, his formula of patter and songs, different characterizations and comic gags, spread through his peers and imitators.

Above all, the comedians of music-hall thrived on the characters they created on the stage. Whether you topped the bill, or 'opened' to a cold audience, or played down the bill to a sated clientele, or 'closed' the bill to the shuffle of seats as the patrons hurried to leave the hall, you had at the most fifteen or twenty minutes to wow the crowd and draw its interest. You had to be instantly recognizable. You had to be yourself in mask, a familiar face, a known commodity. In a business – for it was a very busy business at the turn of the twentieth century, with thousands of acts featured in hundreds of theatres throughout the country, and dozens of acts advertising in the stage journals' 'Variety Artists Seeking Positions' sections, seeking a venue for a magician, a vocalist, a serio-comic, a man with forty dogs, a living statue, a one-legged unicyclist or whatever – it was far from easy for a newcomer to command attention. But we must be mindful of the motto of Our Two Heroes, emblazoned on the cart on which they are bearing the crated piano they must deliver up the thousand and one steps to 1127 Walnut Avenue:

TALL OAKS FROM LITTLE ACORNS GROW.

And so, without further ado –

CHAPTER TWO

Fathers and Sons: Stanley

> There is nothing exceptional about being born. Birth is something which comes to all of us sooner or later . . .
>
> Dan Leno, *Hys Booke*

Ulverston, in north-west England, lies at the centre of a small peninsula which licks out towards the seaside town of Barrow-in-Furness. You might take a mainline train from London and change at Lancaster or Preston for a local two-carriage sprinter which rattles along the track past towns and villages that once were coal-mining communities. At Carnforth, you might spy the rusted carriages of old rolling-stock, or a small locomotive with a smile painted on its round face. Gouged hills bear witness to some quarrying, but soon give way to flat grassland, the sheer green of a golf course at Silverdale, pretty Olde Englishe houses at Arnside, and then, over the mouth of the River Kent, the stretches of a flat estuary leading to the aptly named Grange-over-Sands. The sea pokes in here, amid a flat bay, across whose shifting sands guides used to lead travellers before the railway cut across it in the late 1860s. The train speeds on, towards a low round hill with a peculiar and unique landmark, a lighthouse-like column known as the Hoad monument, constructed in 1897.

The town of Ulverston itself looks much, in outline, as it did in 1890, the year of Arthur Stanley Jefferson's birth. Old houses, rather than new developments, predominate, and some of the central shopping streets are still cobbled, with Market Street still sporting the old clock tower that was its landmark a hundred years ago. The adjacent houses all retain their original exterior, give or take a few layers of paint. The Wesleyan church and school that young Stanley attended can be recognized, as can even the old station road, though the trains have changed from the ancient steam puffers, and the old horse-and-carts no longer trundle leisurely up the path. The new town, having lost its old mining tradition, has prospered nevertheless, and sports a number of

reminders of its claim to world fame: the Stan Laurel Inn – 'Hot and Cold Food' – and Laurel's International Bistro, at 13 Queen Street, our heroes beaming from its large window. A simple plaque fixed to the brick wall of the modest terrace house at 3 Argyle Street (then named Foundry Cottages), states that 'Stan Laurel was born at this house, 16 June 1890.'

Ulverston's main memorial to its most famous son is, however, the Laurel and Hardy Museum, at Upper Brook Street, created and maintained until his death by local enthusiast Bill Cubin and now managed by his daughter Marion. The visitor enters through a low doorway into a tiny space crammed with memorabilia and photographs of Stan's and Ollie's lives, newspaper cuttings, dolls, books and artefacts such as a tin of Beers Treacle Toffee, supposedly wee Stan's favourite treat. A tiny theatre beside the entrance runs a constant stream of Laurel and Hardy films, a miniature world so far removed from the commercial hustle and bustle of Hollywood that enabled the Boys' celebrated careers. All is a paradigm of small-town cosiness and affection for the local boy who made good. This is old Lancashire, a region with its own laconic culture and down-to-earth populace, now recast in the maps as the southern part of

Cumbria, with Ulverston presenting itself to tourists as 'South Lakeland's friendliest historic market town . . . between the mountains of the Lake District and the waters of Morecambe Bay'. It has, apart from Stan Laurel, 'the world's shortest, widest and deepest canal' and 'a world-champion town crier', and it 'originated pole-vaulting as a competitive sport'!

In a corner of Bill Cubin's Museum an old document lies carefully preserved under glass. Arthur Stanley Jefferson's birth certificate, issued in the sub-district of Ulverston in the County of Lancaster, lists his father as Arthur Jefferson and his mother as Margaret Jefferson, formerly Metcalfe. The occupation of the father is entered as 'comedian', an appellation that has confused some later historians into seeing Arthur senior as a comic progenitor of his son, with his own act on the stage. But the title refers to his specialty as an actor of light dramatic parts – as opposed to a 'tragedian', who takes on the heavy roles such as King Lear, Othello or Hamlet.

This was a family with the theatre in its blood – not the music-hall, but the more 'legitimate' stage. Arthur Jefferson, known as 'A.J.' to many, claimed a relationship with the famous Joseph Jefferson of the American stage, but there is no verifiable connection. Old A.J. was a son of prim and proper Manchester parents and was said to have run away from home to go on the stage. His own birth date was 12 September 1862, but his early days are obscure. He first surfaces in dispatches in the memoirs of the theatre and screen star George Arliss, whose 1928 autobiography, *On the Stage*, describes how as a young actor he left London to join an Irish 'repertoire' company. This troupe toured the provinces, mainly Lancashire and Yorkshire, Durham, Northumberland and the small theatres of Scotland. Arliss notes 'Arthur Jefferson, who played the character parts (he afterwards became the manager of three or four provincial theatres), used to make everything. He made his own wigs and even his own greasepaints, and from him I learned many tricks of which I would otherwise have remained ignorant.'

A.J.'s multiple talents were the product of an extraordinary energy, packed into a man of medium height but strong frame, capped by flaming red hair inherited by his son. We do not know the date of Arliss's contact with him, but as Arliss was born in 1868, it cannot have been far from the date he married Margaret – Madge – Metcalfe on 19 March 1884. She was twenty-four years old and born in Askrigg, in the North Riding of Yorkshire, to George Metcalfe, a shoemaker, and his wife Sarah.

Oral history tells us Arthur was an actor–manager of a small theatre in Ulverston, the Hippodrome, also called Spencer's Gaff, or the Gaff, and he met Madge while she was singing in the local choir. Her parents, having moved from Hawes, in Yorkshire, lived at Foundry Cottages. Their second daughter, Sarah, born in 1863, was to be known to young Stanley as Auntie Nant, and would play a major role in his upbringing. Madge Metcalfe soon took up acting and toured in several of her husband's productions. Their first son, George Gordon Jefferson, was born in 1885, in Ulverston.

As was the case with Stanley, Madge's parents provided a base and haven at Foundry Cottages while Madge and Arthur continued to tour. Growing out of the acting profession, A.J. found his ambitions developing in two directions – theatre management and playwriting, two major roles into which he hurled himself with great vigour. This was not a man who did things by halves. Having become aware of the great thirst for drama in the northern part of England where he had made his home, he began in the early 1890s to renovate and reopen old theatres, beginning with the Eden Theatre in Bishop Auckland – across country to the east, near Durham – and continued with the Theatre Royal in Consett, in 1892. The local rag, the *Consett Guardian*, described the impresario's role at opening night, in August, when 'previous to the raising of the curtain, Mr Jefferson stepped to front and in a few brief words explained to the audience his intentions for the ensuing season, and having made up his mind that the comfort of his friends and patrons should be secured he had determined that on no account whatever would he permit smoking in the theatre'.

A prescient man, if a bit of a busybody, A.J. was concerned not only with the cultural level of his audience but also with their health and general well-being. His son Stanley remembered his acute concern with the plight of the poor, giving shoes and stockings to children and arranging special matinées for inmates of poorhouses, to whom he would hand packages of tea, sugar and tobacco. The main industry in most of the areas in which A.J. opened theatres was coal-mining, and the same newspaper that in 1900 reported the 'new theatre at Blythe, to open on Monday with the evergreen comic opera, *The Geisha*', carried an item on infant mortality in the colliery towns, which had reached 229 deaths per 1,000 births, a sombre sign of the depressed state of the region whose uplift Arthur Jefferson worked so hard to achieve.

As early as 1892, the *Auckland Chronicle* (28 October) commented on the impact of 'high culture' on the local audience, as witnessed by 'England's premier *danseuse*', Kate Vaughan, who appeared in the play *John Jasper's Wife*:

It seemed to have a profound effect on the miners and their families, showing . . . that the standard of taste in matters theatrical seemed to have risen considerably in that district. This, she thought, was in no small measure due to the spirited enterprise of Mr and Mrs Jefferson, who seem determined to secure thoroughly representative talent at a place of amusement which they have taken great pains to render comfortable and inviting.

By 1901 A.J. had opened theatres in Hebburn, Blythe, North Shields, Wallsend and Glasgow, as well as the Tynemouth Circus in North Shields, on the east coast by Newcastle-upon-Tyne. He was also, by that time, touring his own plays, *London by Day and Night* in Bury, Lancashire, and *The Orphan Heiress* at the Theatre Royal, again in North Shields. Throughout the northern counties of England, A.J. and his wife were a major force.

We are able, due to the ironies of censorship, to have an even closer insight into the second string to A.J.'s bow – his prolific playwriting career. Deriving from powers granted since the furore over *The Beggar's Opera* in the eighteenth century, every play or stage sketch produced in Britain had to deposit a copy with the Lord Chamberlain's office (a censorship that did not end until the 1960s) and these texts are now available at the British Library. A.J.'s first extant play, *The World's Verdict*, dated 1893, covers a 200-page handwritten notebook. It is a vintage piece of Victorian melodrama, in which an errant nephew, Jasper, returns from Melbourne in Australia begging to be received under the roof of good Sir Geoffrey, who muses:

I told him never to darken my doors again. But he has touched a tender chord, his dead father, my poor brother. Heaven knows how I loved that man. For his sake I will revoke my harsh decision. He was young and . . . when the news reached me that he – my nephew – had absconded from the Union Bank with close upon £500 in his possession. The old story – horse racing, gambling, bad companions . . .

The old story indeed. We must consider young Stanley Jefferson, growing up with the timbres of this archetypal model of a soon-to-vanish stage tradition, not only in performance but in the experience of a father spending late nights in his study scribbling away in his notebooks before the typewriter arrived to save his labours in the last years of the century . . .

The Orphan Heiress, following in 1895, with characters such as Lord Warwick Ainsley, Mabel the heiress and George Garden, lowly bank clerk in love with Mabel, persevered with the old tradition, as did *The Bootblack* in 1896, and *London by Day and Night*. These texts can be quite turgid, as A.J. never used one word where eight could suffice. But his melodramas almost always included, for variety, a comic sub-plot involving the hired help. In *The Orphan Heiress*, it is a love affair between the cook, Betsy Buggles, and the policeman, Jack:

JACK
I love you as I have never loved. I have a big heart.

BETSY
Yes, and Big Feet.

JACK
You are joking. My feet are not so big as my heart.

BETSY
No, but they're wider.

In the earlier *World's Verdict*, the comic stuff is between Sammy Carrot, the rebellious servant, and Sally Jenkins, chambermaid. Sammy enters in comic livery, with a tray piled with plates, covered with cloth, rehearsing his role as waiter for the Squire's dinner:

SAMMY
Yes sir, bring the macaroni, yes sir.

Re-crossing falls over chair, breaks plates, etc. Bus. – Sally laughs. He looks savagely at her.

SALLY
Now what are you doing?

SAMMY
I've spilled the macaroni.

15

Yes, and a nice mess you've made of the carpet.

Both pick up pieces.

SAMMY

It wasn't me! It was you!

SALLY

It wasn't!

SAMMY

You're another.

SALLY

You're an idiot.

SAMMY

So am I.

SALLY

You're no gentleman.

SAMMY

And you're no gentleman.

Readers who cry out at the similarity to Laurel and Hardy's classic dinner-party waiters in *From Soup to Nuts* (1928), need claim no prizes. Old influences do run deep. But can we surmise from the first sighting of the phrase 'a nice mess' an even older echo – some primal infant trauma? Let us not get carried away too soon . . . But it is clear that A.J. became more and more fond of his comic interludes, and as the pressures of his entrepreneurial activities allowed him less time for his long-winded plays, he switched, in the early years of the new century, to shorter, pure comedy sketches. A local press item of 9 February 1900 etches in the timbres of the age and reveals the impresario in typically harassed form at the opening of another of his new theatres, the Theatre Royal at Blyth:

The vestibule gives one the first real idea of the new theatre's beauty and wealth of structure. A massive chandelier sheds over it the glamour of gaslight. A mosaic floor, a marble staircase, finely proportioned mahogany pillars, and artistic wallpaper make up a very pleasing scene. A small crowd surrounded the pay box, and up and down the stairs and through the hall there was a gathering, ceaseless hum of excitement. A man in a cloth cap and tweed suit came rushing down the steps – spoke for a moment at the pay box – and then almost unconsciously wheeled round in our way. Mr Jefferson, of course.

'Ah! So glad to see you!' he said with an air of preoccupation and hurry he tried politely to hide. 'Fact is, I scarcely know where I am. It's such a difficult thing to be in every place at once. I'm dreadfully worried, you know. Best wishes! Thanks, thanks.'

By this time, 1900, Stanley was ten years old, and had a six-year-old sister, Beatrice Olga, born 16 December 1894 in Bishop Auckland, and a baby brother, Edward Everitt, born 1 April 1900 in North Shields, to add to elder brother Gordon. Another brother, christened Sydney Everitt, had been born on 30 April 1899, in North Shields, but lived less than five months.

Stanley himself had not been a healthy baby and fears about his well-being on the road were said to have prompted A.J. and Madge to leave him in the care of the elder Metcalfes, while they continued their theatrical work. The Metcalfes were a somewhat sombre lot, ardent Methodists and stern but loving to their growing brood. Family lore told that Granda George Metcalfe would banish errant children to the washhouse in the backyard. Young Stanley was said to be a frequent and enthusiastic sinner, as he had a secret hoard of matches, candles and hidden comics which could keep him occupied in the dark. When in favour he had a fair number of playmates, mainly the sons and daughters of Auntie Nant and her husband John Shaw, who had six children.

For a late Victorian childhood, it was a happy one, far from wealthy but detached from the poverty that still afflicted even the smaller towns and villages, let alone the larger northern cities. Stanley remembered fondly, in his autumn days, the family's many outings to surrounding beauty spots in the nearby Lake District. He wrote in 1955 from California to Nancy Wardell (Aunt Nant's granddaughter) of 'many happy memories of my holidays there with your grandparents. I can see the old grocery shop and the apple orchard opposite very vividly when your mother (Mary), Jack, Charlie, Nellie and poor Elsie were all kids together and full of mischief . . .' (Cousin Elsie had died relatively young, aged thirty-nine.)

The Jeffersons' permanent move from Ulverston and Bishop Auckland to North Shields, closer to A.J.'s east-coast theatres, took place in 1897. The new family home was at 8 Dockwray Square, in the centre of the town. From here Stanley was sent to a boarding school at nearby Tynemouth, a decision taken, he later claimed, because of his incorrigible naughtiness: 'Setting fire to the house (accidentally of course) & falling into a barrel of fish guts in my best Sunday suit . . .' It was more likely due, however, to both A.J.'s and Madge's continued absences attending to their many stage affairs.

Despite its veneer of normality, this was an era of high patriotic fervour and anxiety. The cause of this was the real-life drama of the Boer War, which broke out in 1899 across the ocean, in South Africa. The Empire was fighting to subdue the bearded Boers and their uncouth leader, President of the Orange Free State, Paul Kruger, who had already humiliated the British by defeating an expeditionary force launched against him in 1896 from Rhodesia. No child was too small to uphold the Imperial flag in this battle of Virtue against Villainy. The Relief of Mafeking – the lifting of a savage siege in which the rebels had almost starved the British garrison to death – was marked by celebrations throughout the realm. In North Shields, a hasty jamboree was mounted, as set out in the local *Shields Daily News* of 21 May 1900:

Work in the shipyards and engineering shops in the district seemed to have been entirely suspended, for the streets were crowded with working men in their best and flaunting the red, white and blue. There was scarcely a single individual, from the smallest child to tottering old age, to be met with who was not adorned with some sort of decoration . . . Flags flew from every window ledge . . . There were a great deal of effigies, President Kruger's being most prominent . . . (At three o'clock) the band of the *Wellesley* . . . and the whole ship's company under arms came ashore and paraded in Dockwray Square. Patriotic songs were played and sung during the march, and the route of the procession was densely thronged with people, who seemed deeply interested. Master Roland Park, attired in full regimentals representing Lord Roberts, and mounted on a pony, was the central figure; he was attended by Masters Jefferson, Walton and Davidson attired in the uniform of the Imperial Yeomanry, and they made a perfect little picture, which excited much comment among the spectators . . .

This is the first mention of Stan Laurel, young Master Jefferson, in printed annals. His very first performance, to the admiring crowd. A surviving snapshot catches him standing, holding the reins of his pal's horse, quite the little yeoman, with an ammunition belt over his coat and a bugle dangling above his tightly wound puttees. He looks a little fatigued, as well he might, by the rigours of the day. To the end, Stanley Jefferson would maintain his bemusement at the strange activities and conflicts the human race got entangled with outside the happy world of show business. Like all his great, cavorting predecessors, he only ever wished to entertain . . .

A.J. recalled his second son's burgeoning interest in show business in a memoir penned towards the end of his own life, in 1939, which was unearthed and published by John McCabe:

As Stan grew older, it became increasingly apparent that his young mind was obsessed with the idea of one day 'following in father's footsteps'; spending all his pocket money on toy theatres, Punch and Judy shows, marionettes, shadowgraphs, magic lanterns etc. . . . When about nine years of age, Stan begged me to convert the attic of our home in North Shields . . . into a miniature theatre, to which I agreed . . .

Stanley, with help, A.J. wrote, from his local theatre staff, created a small hall with

seating for twenty to thirty people: in brief, a perfect replica of the average small theatre of the period. Stan, assisted by several 'dying to act' boys and girls, was hard at work inaugurating the 'Stanley Jefferson Amateur Dramatic Society' – featuring said S.J. as Director, Manager, Stage Manager, Author, Producer, and Leading Man.

A perfect re-creation of A.J.'s own growing empire.

In January 1901, an advertisement in *Shields Daily News* announced, at Arthur Jefferson's Theatre Royal, a special New Year attraction to accompany the featured play:

Living Pictures by the Royal Randvoll. A thousand feet of Film. New subjects will be shown, including the most marvellous Film of the present day, specially recorded for the Holiday Season, and the first duplicate secured for the provinces, entitled 'THE CHILDREN'S DREAM OF CHRISTMAS' – 'IN YE OLDEN TIMES' (20 scenes).

A.J. became the proprietor of something called 'The North British Animated Company', Chief Operator and Photographer: Harry Parkinson, 'at present with the Edison Company, Manchester'. A.J. was not one to neglect the latest gadget enhancing the show-

Arthur Jefferson, in a later incarnation as an old-style comedian

business world. (There is an even earlier mention, in April 1900, of
something called 'Jos. Poole's Myriorama', at the Theatre Royal,
Blyth, featuring 'The New and Improved Cinematograph', screening

'General Buller's March and Lord Dundonald's Dash to the Relief of Ladysmith, the Fighting Fifth Crossing the Modder River' and 'Blowing Up of the Colenso Bridge across the Tugels'.) But his son, he later claimed, was not impressed. 'And did the North like it?' A.J. told an interviewer for *Picturegoer* in 1932. 'Not a bit. Not even when I put a singer at the back and tried to synchronize her with the film. And did Stan get excited? Not a bit. I don't remember a single display of enthusiasm on his part. In that black box lay his future fortunes, and he wasn't even interested.'

Perhaps. At age ten, was it likely that Victorian Dad Arthur Jefferson would have let his son anywhere near his new state-of-the-art machine? The year 1901 was, however, somewhat early for the motion picture, still marked by the sheer excitement of its capture of reality in tableaux on celluloid. The close-up was an exotic rarity, not to speak of D. W. Griffith's revolutionary editing techniques . . .

In August 1901, A.J. expanded his empire to its furthest, taking over the Metropole Theatre in Glasgow, once the famed Scotia music-hall, which he was converting to straight drama. This earned him a full-page accolade in the splendidly named *Victualling Trades Review*, praising both his own efforts and that of 'his good lady, under whose supervision the decorations have been so handsomely carried out in the Metropole this summer . . . Of Mr Jefferson, it may truly be said: "He came, saw and conquered", but, like Peter the Great, his unimpaired energies are still seeking for further outlet and other worlds to conquer.'

CHAPTER THREE

Sons and Fathers: The Road Diverges

By 1902, twelve-year-old Stanley was trying to conquer his own worlds at a new school, King James I Grammar School in Bishop Auckland. This was probably the school at which, he fondly recalled in later years, he was recruited by a master, Mr Bates, to amuse him and his fellow teachers after hours. Stanley performed 'jokes, imitations, what have you', while the teachers partook of their tipple (a scene one cannot imagine in our enlightened day and age, when the constabulary would have been summoned to cart Master Bates off to durance vile). Imitating the pompous German teacher in his presence, however, did not go down so well. After about eighteen months of such scholarly pursuits the young Stan was extracted by A.J. from this convivial berth and he was enrolled at the nearby Gainford Academy.

The next three years were more settled for the growing boy, and one can assume he absorbed at least some standard learning. But in 1905 the Jeffersons moved again, to Glasgow, to be closer to A.J.'s mainstay, the Metropole, leaving his other theatres to be run by local managers. Madge was, by this time, in failing health. From an initial address at Buchanan Drive, Rutherglen, the family moved to 185 Stonelaw Road. From Stonelaw High School to Queens Park Secondary School, Stanley continued sampling the educational system, still playing truant, he later claimed, when inclined.

At this time A.J., fatigued by his entrepreneurial whirlwind, gave up writing full-length plays and discovered his penchant for shorter, funnier sketches. Four of these titles have survived: *Home from the Honeymoon*, registered with the Lord Chamberlain's office in 1905; *Her Convict Lover*, registered in 1906; and *Amateur Fire Brigade* and *For His Sake*, both dating from 1907. A fifth title, *An Unwilling Burglar*, does not seem to have been registered, and perhaps was not performed. As these sketches were to play, in the fullness of time, a vital role in young Stanley's development of his own comic style, it is worth taking a closer look at these artefacts of a long bygone age.

In *Home from the Honeymoon*, two newlyweds, the Honourable Percy Fitzhuggins and wife Lydia, arrive in London after their honeymoon and seek a country house to let. (Waiter in swell London coffee house: ''Oneymooners! Poor deluded creeter, 'ow pretty she are – reminds me of my Mathilda Anna before she poisoned 'erself with chloride of lime . . .' A.J.'s rendition of the local Cockney argot – he was a lifelong northerner – left something to be desired.) The newlyweds find a country house to let at number 47 The Cedars, Kingston Park. But the house they arrive at turns out to be inhabited by two burglars, Flash Harry and Lightfoot Jim, who have broken in and fortuitously found a note on the table revealing that the true owner, Colonel Pepper, is absent, and his servants have gone off on a binge. When the couple knock at the door, the crooks masquerade as owner and servant. So enamoured was young Stanley with his father's confection that it turns up twice as a Laurel and Hardy film comedy, once as *Duck Soup* (1927), and then as the classic *Another Fine Mess*, shot in 1930.

In the original, several pages of banter ensue between the innocents and the crooks, with Flash Harry explaining that the maid, Semolina (Lightfoot Jim in drag), has been with him since she was adopted by his first wife, and stayed with him through the second:

PERCY

Are both gone?

HARRY

Only too true – one died in –

JIM

Jail.

HARRY

One died in Calcutta!

JIM

Yes, he 'cut 'er' throat.

Well, it went down pretty well in Newcastle, on the Stoll and Moss tour of summer 1908, when young Stanley was said to have joined the company to act in an unrecorded role in the play. At the end of the sketch, Colonel Pepper turns up, shouting apoplectically, as the burglars have convinced poor Percy that he's a deluded intruder:

COLONEL

You consummate ass! You blithering dotard! You dummy! You brainless nincompoop! I'm Colonel Pepper – owner of this house!

PERCY

Good gracious, he's simply raving, takes himself for another man – what shall I do? He'll murder me, I must try and humour him I've heard that's the proper thing. (*Aloud*) Of course you are – I knew you at once – I've seen your photograph in the papers – read about your heroic actions on the field of battle. I knew your father and your mother – and – I used to nurse you when you were a baby . . .

COLONEL

Shut up, you wizened-faced kangaroo – come here – surrender or I'll murder you!

PERCY

Help! Help!

A situation readily recognizable from so many Stan and Ollie routines . . .

As the sketch was first performed at the Metropole, Glasgow, in October 1905, might not young Stanley have joined the cast earlier than recorded, and might this have been his first turn on the stage? Stan Laurel's own account dated his first formal appearance as an actor rather vaguely, in 1906, at amateur night at Glasgow's Britannia Theatre (alias Pickard's Museum), the oldest music-hall in the city. A.J., in his 1939 account, tells of his amazement at walking into the theatre and being told by his friend, the proprietor, Albert Pickard, that his son was due on in five minutes, having rehearsed his act secretly for weeks:

Very soon Stan's number, billed as an 'extra turn', went up. On he came wearing a pair of baggy patched trousers (new trousers of mine, cut down, patches added) and also my best frock coat and silk hat . . . He did his act, the details of which I cannot now remember, and he got a very good reception and scored a genuine success, finishing up to loud laughter and applause and even shouts of 'Encore!' The shouts brought him back, and he beamed the now popular Laurel smile, but, in bowing his acknow-ledgements, he spotted me!

According to A.J.'s account, Stan then rushed to escape, catching his father's frock coat on a steel hook and tearing it and losing the top hat to a member of the orchestra, who stepped on it, a neces-sary slapstick move. Young Stan returned, tearful and fearful of Dad's vengeance, only to receive his heartiest congratulations. Stanley himself described the scene thus:

I removed my make-up and rushed back to the Met to hide from my father's wrath, but he was already there. He called me into his office where, for what seemed like several minutes, neither of us spoke. Finally he glanced at me and said, 'Not bad, son, but where on earth did you get those gags?' Fearfully, I told him the whole story and waited for the storm to burst. Slowly, he rose to his feet. 'Have a whisky and soda?' he asked quite casually. At first I could not believe my ears. But when it dawned on me, I seemed to grow six inches in as many seconds. My boyhood was behind me – Dad was accepting me as a man! Then I did the silliest thing – I burst out crying.

A nice old tale, and possibly true. But it would have been obtuse of A.J., given all the razzmatazz about young Stan's home and school theatrics, to expect his mercurial son to choose any other path in life. The eldest brother, Gordon, was already involved in the man-agement of his Dad's theatres, and Stan's sister Beatrice would soon follow in the same mode. Dad might have hoped that Stanley would take up the more legitimate drama, rather than the uncer-tain music-hall life. But his own sketches show that A.J. was quite happy to dabble in music-hall routines himself. Be that as it may, he did his best to facilitate his son's ambitions, and soon found him his first proper job with a theatrical juvenile company, Levy and Cardwell, specializing in Christmas pantomimes.

The seasonal offering in 1907 from Harold B. Levy and J. E. Cardwell was *The Sleeping Beauty – or The Prince with the Golden Key*. A copy of young Stanley's first proper contract shows him signed on with the company for the princely sum of one pound five shillings per week. The tour to run from 19 August to Easter 1908 inclusive. Stanley Jefferson to 'provide all dresses wigs tights and shoes as the management desires', although Mr and Mrs Harold B. Levy do agree 'to pay all train and boat fares (third class only)' for the duration. Rules and Conditions include: no play, no pay; no intoxication under pain of instant dismissal with no pay; and a final clause specifying that 'addressing the audience, without the permission from the management, subjects the offender to instant dismissal'.

Levy's *Sleeping Beauty* was an extravaganza anticipating the Disney Corporation's *Toy Story* by ninety years, with a tale of automaton toys that come alive in a boy's playroom. The boy, Bertie Dalrymple, was played by Wee Georgie Wood, a child star five years younger than Stanley billed as 'music-hall's little boy who never grew up'. A fellow northerner, born in Jarrow, he excelled in later years in a nursery sketch in which he performed imitations of various music-hall artistes to his teddy bear. No wonder one critic said of him, 'He's so clever, I could smack his face.' (He lived to the ripe old age of eighty-four.)

Stanley Jefferson is billed in the cast as Ebeneezer, 'Golliwog Number Two'. His first printed line in the playscript comes as the Good Fairy blesses the baby who will in the next act become the Sleeping Beauty:

EBENEEZER
Ya! Ya! Ya! What are those in the sardine tins?

Not, perhaps, the most auspicious start to an illustrious career, but everyone has to begin somewhere. In scene 5, set at the Tower Ruins, the Golliwogs enter to Ebeneezer's question, 'I say, Julius Caesar, where has our young master gone?', to be told, 'Let us wait and amuse ourselves. He is sure to find us.' Ebeneezer: 'All right, let us have one of our old plantation songs and dances.' Which, one assumes, follows.

The *Sleeping Beauty* tour, despite its six months' length, was limited to north-country theatres. There followed bit parts for Stanley in two more northern toured plays, *The Gentleman Jockey*, a 'musical comedy drama' by Edward Marris, and another Levy and Cardwell pantomime, *The House That Jack Built*, in 1908. In the first, a piece of vintage flimflam concerning stolen diamonds and an 'American crook' named Frank Snakeworthy, Stanley's name cannot be found in the primary cast list and he must have featured in a small role, possibly in the 'Pierrot entertainment' set up for the swells. In *The House That Jack Built*, Stanley was one of a brace of motorists, who enter to ogle girls in the buffet of the Hotel Metropole:

> HAROLD (FIRST MOTORMAN)
> I say, Percy, this is a dismal place . . . I declare it gives me the pip.

> PERCY (SECOND MOTORMAN)
> (*Looking at barmaid*) Ha, jolly fine girl, about the best thing we've seen in the village.

How perfectly spiffing.

Earlier in 1908, in the summer, Stanley toured with his father's sketches and, although it is not in the annals, he may well have played in several of them, not only in *Home from the Honeymoon*. The most lavish of these sketches, *Her Convict Lover*, was distinguished by a final act played in 'animated pictures' projected on a cloth dropped on the stage. These included movie scenes at a railway station, in the carriage, and in an office at Scotland Yard, featuring a flurry of crooks and cops. By now A.J. had graduated from the primitive projections of 1901 to the greater sophistication of producing his own mini-motion picture, although there is still no evidence that this greatly impressed young Stanley. The Scotland Yard sequence, nevertheless, was quite complex:

SCENE 3
Scotland Yard office. Inspector writing. Policeman on duty at door. Frank hastens in, followed by Dennis – momentarily barred by policeman. Inspector pantomimes directions to let them pass. Questions them as to their business. Frank explains himself and removes wig and beard. Policeman at door, joined by another policeman, immediately arrest him. Dennis steps forward, produces document, Inspector reads it – gives satisfied expression and orders men to release Frank, which they do – shakes hand with him. Policeman enters, conveys message to Inspector. Inspector motions Frank and Dennis to stand back. Desborough and Leach enter hurriedly, point to Frank Atherton denouncing him to the Inspector. Inspector beckons policeman to come forward and arrest them both, while Inspector produces document and shows it to Leach and Desborough. Leach goes on knees for mercy. Policeman kicks him, he gets up, both led away. Change of picture.

A.J. as a pioneer Hitchcock . . . But the theatre, not the movies, remained Arthur Jefferson's medium. A third sketch in his repertoire, *Amateur Fire Brigade*, aka *Firefighters of Frizzlington*, provided a classic play of crazy antics with firemen who can't get a grip on their hose. Could it have been Stanley, at some point, who played the comic mayor's son:

SON

Bring me a ladder quick.

Men bring him a ladder.

MAN

It's not long enough, captain.

SON

Then cut it in two, you idiots, and splice it.

A sentiment that would have gone down well at Hal Roach's studio. At the finis of the sketch, the mayor is hauled up on a rope to save a girl at a window, but as her shawl comes off he sees she's ugly, pushes her out of the window and calls for help. As the crowd cheers, the son and firemen haul the mayor out on the rope; he stands on a hogshead of beer, whose top collapses depositing him inside, beer splashing up, curtain down and up again showing the mayor hauled out of the keg.

This, too, will have its echoes. *The House That Jack Built* toured until April 1909, and in the summer of that year Stanley joined the last of his touring company plays, an American import entitled *Alone in the World*, scripted by one Hal Reid and presented by impresario Percy Williams: 'A Beautiful and Pathetic Story of Child Life' said the billing, adding, 'Over 3 tons of new Scenery carried'. Stanley is credited as a policeman, P.C. Stoney Broke, of whose performance the local *Todmorden Herald* declared, 'Mr Stanley Jefferson . . . is a first-rate comedian and dancer, and his eccentricities create roars of laughter.'

The play was about a New York mother whose newsboy son has vanished, and who looks for waifs in the city in the hope of finding her boy. A glance at the text shows that it also contained a pair of outrageous (but standard for the time) racial stereotypes, Angel and Jezebel, who turn up on the city wharf and explain themselves:

I come from Arkansas, suh, but my wife she's a quality
nigger – yaas suh, she comes from Old Virginny . . .

In his reminiscences to John McCabe, Stan described himself playing another role in this farrago, a tramp fishing on the banks of a
levee in the Deep South, intoning, as a choir sang 'Swanee River' in
the background, 'Wal, I guess 'n' calculate I can't ketch no fish with
that tarnation mob a-singin'. Gee whizz!'

Glasgow was a long way from the 'Swanee River', but Stanley
was not to know that, in the fullness of time, destiny would close
that gap . . . The tour of *Alone in the World* was, however, ill-fated,
hobbling from Manchester to Leeds to Todmorden to Kidder-
minster and then cancelling before its scheduled gig in Newcastle in
October, as the manager allegedly made off with the proceeds.

Young Stanley's career appeared to be stalled. But this was merely
a hiatus before the next move. The most significant event in Stan's
life was about to occur.

A fitting place, perhaps, to leave him, cooling his heels, fishing
for bookings, and humming about the imaginary Swanee, while we
veer off, across the ocean, to visit the real, authentic Deep South,
and seek there for the roots of our second hero – a somewhat
heavier waif . . .

CHAPTER FOUR

Fathers and Sons: Ollie – War and Peace

The town of Harlem, Georgia, lies on the old cross-country route that runs from Georgia's second city of Augusta to its capital, Atlanta, though today the road peters out at Covington and joins the interstate highway. The railway track runs across the main street, and houses with neat lawns line the few roads that meander about the flat, green, pleasant countryside. The local histories relate that the town itself was founded by one Newman Hicks, who resigned from the railroad when required to work on Sunday and vowed to build a town of his own where no hard liquor would be sold. The name of Harlem was chosen deliberately to reflect the then fashionable – and very white – New York suburb of that name.

Today, it is still a quiet haven, akin in some ways to the mythical Scottish town of the musical *Brigadoon*, in that it seems to slumber through most of the year and then come alive in a sudden burst of dynamism for one day a year, the first Saturday of October, to celebrate the annual Oliver Hardy Festival.

The first sight of Harlem from the road tells you all you need to know – emblazoned on the white water tower, the smiling face of Our Hero and the legend:

HARLEM – BIRTHPLACE OF OLIVER HARDY

As you slow down for the traffic lights at the turn into Main Street a great multi-coloured mural on the side of a brick wall greets you: Stan Laurel and Oliver Hardy wearing their signature bowler hats, and beside that a smaller picture of the duo leaning against the grand-piano crate as seen in their classic movie short, *The Music Box*.

A memorial plaque, marked as a 'Georgia Historic Marker', is set up outside the police station. It proclaims the official tale:

OLIVER NORVELL HARDY
HARLEM BECAME THE BIRTHPLACE OF ONE OF HOLLYWOOD'S GREATEST COMEDY TEAMS WHEN OLIVER HARDY WAS BORN JANUARY 18, 1892. AFTER HIS FATHER DIED AND WAS BURIED IN

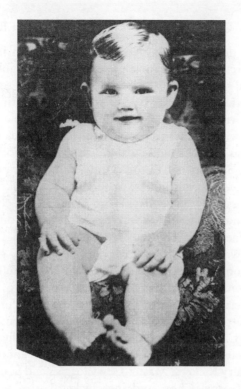

THE HARLEM CEMETERY THE YEAR OF OLIVER'S BIRTH, MRS
HARDY TOOK THE FAMILY TO MILLEDGEVILLE WHERE SHE
BECAME THE MANAGER OF THE BALDWIN HOTEL. YOUNG OLIVER
WAS ENTHRALLED BY THE VISITING TROUPES OF PERFORMERS
WHO STAYED THERE. LATER, AS MANAGER OF THE TOWN'S FIRST
MOVIE THEATRE, HARDY PERFORMED REGULARLY.

AFTER ATTENDING GEORGIA MILITARY ACADEMY, THE
ATLANTA CONSERVATORY OF MUSIC, AND, FOR A SHORT TIME,
THE UNIV. OF GEORGIA, HARDY LEFT GEORGIA IN 1913 FOR THE
NEWLY ESTABLISHED FILM COLONY IN JACKSONVILLE, FLORIDA.
AFTER WORKING AT VARIOUS STUDIOS ON THE EAST COAST, HE
LEFT FOR HOLLYWOOD IN 1918.

When the legend becomes truth, print the legend. In fact,
Harlem is a little embarrassed that the house Ollie was said to have
been born in was one of the few in the area to be torn down completely, some decades ago, and replaced with the local automatic
laundry. At 125 South Hicks Street, it proudly proclaims –

– and boasts (let no one say your author stints on his research) three commercial washing machines, thirty-five regular washing machines, and four driers.

I attended the festival day of 2 October 1999, getting lost in the unexpectedly vast crowds that descended on the place on a fine sunny day. Twenty thousand people had visited the festival the year before, and this year the figure was closer to thirty thousand. There was a regular old-time small-town American parade: vintage cars, the fire brigade, Georgia cadets, majorettes, stilt-walkers, the Civil War re-enacters, Boy Scout Pack 105, Evans High School ROTC, Thomson Shriners, school bands, clowns, the mayor on a float with Santa Claus, the works. The Stan and Ollie professional lookalikes – Messrs Dale Walter and Dennis Moriarty, two merry gentlemen of Ohio – were on hand to entertain the children, as well as a strong contingent from an assortment of tents of the 'Sons of the Desert'. Then there were craft booths, Laurel and Hardy T-shirts, non-stop movies in the police station's conference room, memorabilia displayed at the City Hall, the lookalike competition, the Miss Oliver Hardy Scholarship Pageant, Grovetown Elementary Jumping Jaguars, Country Kickers, Master City Cloggers and Square Dancers, G. R. Dean Gospel Choir and the chicken barbecue held in the local fire station, with generous portions piled on paper plates.

Ollie would certainly have been tickled pink. It was his kind of South that was being celebrated – open-hearted, fun-loving, friendly, with a warm welcome for strangers who came from far and wide to honour the Favourite Son. It was an inclusive crowd, black and white – if predominantly white – comfortable in its present prosperity in a buoyant state that not long ago gave a progressive, if short-lived, president, Jimmy Carter, to the US of A.

But the stronger the sunshine, the deeper the shadows. This was not always a happy place . . .

Standing in the Harlem graveyard, among green lawns, and good brown earth. In a neat plot, with fresh-laid gravel, there are urns of flowers beside two tombstones. The inscription on the stones is faint, and only just readable:

OLIVER HARDY
BORN DECEMBER 5 1844
DIED NOVEMBER 22 1892

And beside him:

CORNELIA E. MAGRUDER
1846–1888

In 1861, before Harlem town was founded, the lands west of
Augusta were farming lands, mainly plantations. The Confederate
States had declared their independence in February, and in April a
Confederate Army had fired on Fort Sumter. President Lincoln
called for volunteers for the Union. All over the South, volunteer
companies were being formed. In Columbia County in Georgia,
Company K, the 'Ramsey' volunteers, was set up by Captain
Joshua Boyd from planters and their sons, farmers, plantation
overseers, a number of goldminers and sawyers. It was to be part
of the Sixteenth Georgia Regiment. A memorial book, compiled by
Thomas Earl Holley, of Thomson, Georgia, from contemporary
records, lists the following:

Captain Joshua Boyd
Second Lieutenant George Ramsey Magruder
Third Sargent Edwin C. Magruder
Fourth Sargent Oliver Hardy

Thirteen further officers, one surgeon, and eighty-seven soldiers are
listed. When recruited, Oliver Hardy joined as a private. He was
seventeen years old. He was the son of Catherine and Samuel
Hardy, a planter, the third of eight children. The Hardys were of
English stock, but established in Georgia. Researcher Leo Brooks
has traced the Hardy family tree back to Jesse Hardy, a soldier who
accompanied the founder of the Colony of Georgia, General James
Oglethorpe, from the Old to the New World, in 1733, claiming
lands for King George II. One of his sons, John Hardy, was a
captain in the Revolutionary War and received bounty land for his
services, in Warren and Columbia Counties, in the 1780s. His son,
also John, begat Samuel Hardy, who, in 1840, was listed as owning
thirteen acres and nine slaves. By 1860 his personal property is valued
at $10,700, and his eldest son, Oliver Hardy, is listed as 'overseer'.

It is no wonder then that Hardy and his compatriots mustered a year later for what they saw as a sacred cause – not only their way of life, but their livelihoods and their commercial interests. The two Magruder boys who volunteered with him were the sons of the local plantation owner, George Milton Magruder, registered in 1860 as owning an annual wealth of $25,000, and described as 'one of Columbia's most prosperous planters and best citizens'. Joining the tens of thousands summoned for the South, they went off to war.

Holley records:

Of the 102 soldiers mustered, at least 21 were killed in action. At least 22 others died of disease or from wounds, 42 per cent of those who fought. In addition, 21 soldiers were captured or exchanged at some point – some twice, 4 came home amputees.

Both the Magruder brothers died in the war. In 1870, the lucky survivor, Oliver Hardy, was to marry their sister, Cornelia.

Holley quotes an extract from the diary of one young soldier of Company K, Wave Ballard, who served in General Lee's army:

Sunday, 28 June 1863
Lying on the bank of a large creek a half-mile north of Chambersburg, Pa. Black and dirty. Low-spirited thoughts wandering far away to those I love so much at home. How strange it makes me feel to see so many faces and not one familiar or friendly one among them. I often think and say to myself, 'Only suppose the Northern Army should pass through our own country, our own dear homes, our property and everything we hold most dear, destroyed by a craven foe.' I know it must appear equally as hard to them, and for this reason, I scrupulously abstain from every encroachment upon private property.

7 August
Had orders to move but heavy rain came up so waited a more favorable day. This day have resolved never to swear another oath.

The soldiers of Company K fought in sixteen battles of the Civil War, culminating in Appomattox on 9 April 1865. Oliver Hardy was wounded at Sharpsburg, Maryland, on 17 September 1862, in what has become known as the Battle of Antietam.

The survivors of Columbia County's volunteers came back to a ruined country. Their part of Georgia had, at least, been spared the horrors of Sherman's March, which decimated the South in the winter of 1864. Their houses still stood, and their abandoned fields, but their cause was lost. The following years were full of despair and fury over the liberation of their former slaves. We do not know the deeds of Oliver Hardy, twenty-one-year-old veteran of a defeated army, in the dark period of the late 1860s and early 1870s, the years of the Night Riders, the early Ku-Klux-Klan. We do know that he lost no time in marrying – eligible men were at a high premium in November 1865 – a Columbia County girl, Miss Sarah E. Olive. But she vanished from sight, possibly died of disease, not long after, leaving Oliver to marry the daughter of the plantation owner, and thus become part of the Magruder clan.

Local Madison historian Marshall Williams unearthed two children born to Oliver and Cornelia: Lillian, born in 1871, and George M., born in 1875. A third daughter, Mamie L. Hardy, pops up in 1880. The rest is fuzzy. The memories of an old railroad man, Ed Adams, place Oliver as a line foreman for the Georgia Southern Railroad in the 1880s, putting down track between Augusta and Madison. Marshall Williams, however, found only evidence of a farming venture, followed by a partnership in a retail store. By 1877, Hardy had emerged as a local politician and Tax Collector for Columbia County. In this capacity his first mention in dispatches comes to light, contributed by local Harlem historian Charles Lord from the pages of the *Columbia Sentinel*, 25 April 1885, reporting the musings of one Dr H. R. Casey:

. . . Oliver Hardy, Columbia's active and efficient Tax Collector. If there is a man in the county that Oliver does not know, I might almost say that man is not worth knowing, for he is bound to exercise a sort of pastoral care over his flock . . . It is hard to resist that good open, jolly, funful face, round as the full moon, and covered all over with smiles, and a form as far from the idea of consumption as one ever saw, but evincing a very decided penchant for the consumption of the good things of the table. I think I have heard the boys say that Oliver was a good feeder. I do not know whether he 'lives to eat or eats to live', but I do know that, with all this avirdupois, this Falstaffin figure, he is as polite and graceful as a French dancing master, a popular ladies' man and is quite sure to kiss the babies about voting time; and, as he is standing candidate for life, as he says till he gets beat, he intends to take in a quantum s(u)ffiet of rations, to the end that he may never be off of foot or feed and the last end may still find him in harness . . .

A startling image, indeed a spitting image almost of the son that he would never see grown. The only known faded photograph of Oliver senior shows a bluff round face, balding, white-haired and whiskered, with a disconcerting resemblance to the iconic Colonel Sanders. A wounded veteran of the Confederate cause, son-in-law of the richest man in town, Oliver Hardy seemed to have found his station, and was ensconced at the South Hicks Road address in Harlem that now boasts so many fine front-load washing machines. Local lore, however, recounted by Charles Lord, has it that Hardy lost popularity by his reluctance to oppose a law that required farmers to fence in their animals to prevent them grazing freely on other people's property (presumably the property of the Magruders), and was voted out of office some time in the late 1880s. At about this time, he also lost his wife, Cornelia. But he was not long alone. On 12 March 1890, he married Emily Norvell Tant, a widow, former wife of T. Sam Tant.

The multiple marriages and genealogy of the Hardys, Tants and Norvells can become quite confusing. The Norvells, like the Hardys, were a prominent local family, and their graves dot the cemeteries in Harlem and nearby Grovetown. Emily's father, our hero-to-be's grandfather, Thomas Benjamin Norvell, was also a Confederate veteran, having been wounded and captured at Gettysburg in 1863. He later became a schoolteacher, which was also the profession of his daughter. Her mother, Mary, was from South Carolina. Leo Brooks, applying his magnifying glass to the Norvell family tree, uncovered records showing that both Emily and her father were fired by the Columbia County School Board in 1879, and this was promptly followed by Emily's marriage to T. Sam Tant, an unschooled labourer. Legend has it that T. Sam Tant later worked for Oliver Hardy senior on the railroad. He did not last the course. He died at about the same period as Cornelia Hardy, and his tombstone has recently been found in Grove Baptist cemetery, marked only with a barely legible name. Emily was left a widow with four small children, who now became the family of Oliver Hardy senior and were to be the siblings of Our Hero.

Rumours circulating at the new couple's next port of call, the town of Madison, reported to Leo Brooks by an extremely aged local resident, appeared to suggest that Emily's first child, Elizabeth, had been born out of wedlock, and this was the cause of the termination of her teaching appointment and her first marriage to the unschooled Sam Tant. Oral history being fragile, no one can confirm this, and the gossip did not deter Oliver Hardy, who took the entire Tant brood under his capacious wing. Within a year, a new child was conceived.

Thus, on 18 January 1892, sired of Oliver and Emily (née Norvell) Hardy, our second waif arrives in this world. He was named Norvell Hardy, to preserve the memory of both these families scarred by the Civil War. The surviving baby photograph, presenting him propped on a cushion, is without the shadow of a doubt the Ollie we know. The charming moon face, the eyes gazing out at us, cheerful but a little quizzical, not quite 'here's another nice mess you've gotten me into' but a lively intimation of things to come.

By the time of Norvell's birth, his father had left Harlem and Columbia County for Madison, in Morgan County, about eighty miles to the west. Oliver Hardy, having lost his Tax Collector's office, and sold the family farm, was seeking a new business to support his wife and stepchildren. In 1891, he had found a new *métier* – as a hotelier, taking over the proprietorship of a hotel in Madison, the Turnell–Butler. He moved with his family but for some unrecorded reason Emily returned to Harlem to be with her family in the latter stages of her new pregnancy. Thus it was that baby Norvell was born in the family house in South Hicks Road and then carried back, by his mother, to Madison.

Within months of this return, however, tragedy struck the widow, as her new husband, the ebullient and food-loving ex-politician, dropped dead, 'in the twinkling of an eye', on 22 November 1892, just three days short of Thanksgiving.

CHAPTER FIVE

Mother and Son: The Boarding House Boy

The spirit of the gay nineties was contagious in town and country. A bandstand stood on the old courthouse square, where local musicians and the Wray Brothers Band rendered concerts. Young ladies, in summer dresses, sauntered down to the soda fountains of the drugstores, for these were favorite vantage points from which to hear the concerts. They were invariably joined by the young swains of the town . . .

From *Rambles Through Morgan County*, by Louise McHenry Hickey
(Morgan County Historical Society, 1971)

A Bloody Fight Between the Races in Florida. One Young White Man Shot and Instantly Killed. The Murderer Caught and Swung to a Tree. The Excitement Subsiding.

From the *Augusta Chronicle*, 13 January 1892

The best of times, the worst of times. It all depends on your point of view. A century later, the wounds of the Civil War still bleed, as is demonstrated by current passionate arguments about the use of the Confederate flag. The newspapers of the day bear witness to the divided world of white and black, winners and losers. The *Madisonian* of 23 December 1892, one month after Oliver Hardy's death, recounts that:

Mrs Emmie N. Hardy, having applied for a year's support out of the estate of Oliver Hardy, dec'd, and appraisers having been appointed to set aside the same, and said appraisers having made and filed their report to this office: This is therefore to cite all persons concerned to file their objections to said report, if any they can, on or before the first Monday in January, 1893, as said application will be passed upon that day . . .

T. H. Baldwin, Ordinary

The *Madisonian*'s issues for the week of Oliver Hardy's death are missing, thus raising a question about the precise circumstances of the event, but had it been anything out of the ordinary, such as foul play, this would have echoed in the columns for months. Madison was, then as now, a small place with a town centre the size of a postage stamp, marked by elegant buildings built after the Civil War following the fire of 1869. The same issue of the *Madisonian* that printed Emmie Hardy's citation also noted that 'a monstrosity on the street yesterday was a young negro with a deformed foot as large as a fifteen-pound ham. The thing had only three toes, and was a dime museum in itself.' Madison had its harsher spirit behind the elegant façade.

Hardy's death, most probably of a heart attack, perhaps brought on by pre-Thanksgiving gourmandizing, left the twice-widowed mother with five children and an uncertain legal situation. She had had little more than a year's taste of prosperity with her new husband, but there was no time to build up any proper wealth. The Turnell–Butler hotel had been built by local Madison merchants Steve and Jack Turnell, together with the mayor, Butler, after the mode of the fashionable Kimball House hotel in Atlanta. It was a three-storey affair of brick and stone, with a ballroom on the third floor, 'where real balls were given, and at which formal evening clothes were worn'. A surviving card from the hotel, which stood on the corner of Hancock and Jefferson Streets, proudly presents:

THE TURNELL–BUTLER – OLIVER HARDY, PROPRIETOR.
RATES $2 AND $3 PER DAY – SPECIAL RATES FOR
PERMANENT BOARDERS
EVERY MODERN CONVENIENCE
THE MANAGEMENT BESTOWS ESPECIAL ATTENTION TO
PLEASING ITS GUESTS.
THE CUISINE OF THE TURNELL–BUTLER IS NOTED
THROUGHOUT THE STATE –
COME AND SPEND A DAY AND BE CONVINCED.

The project was ambitious, but the new proprietor did find some difficulty in balancing the books. Town records, dug up by Marshall Williams, include a complaint in Morgan County Court against Oliver Hardy, ordering him to appear on the first day of October 1892, to pay an outstanding sum of $143.25 for 'use of Electric Lights' at the hotel. The sum was settled, but within weeks Oliver Hardy was dead, leaving no proper will. Thus Emily had to apply to the Ordinary (Probate) Court for guardianship of baby Norvell, promising to 'maintain him in drink, clothing, lodging, and . . . cause him to be educated in such a manner as to be suitable to his interest'. The appraisers set aside $628 for Emily for one year's support out of the deceased's property, listed as 'cigars, bedding, crockery, lamps, silverware, coal and a showcase', as well as cash owed by a number of debtors and enough furniture allocated for her use.

Messrs Butler and Turnell would not allow the widow to take over their hotel, whether due to her aforementioned stigma or just standard prejudice we do not know, and so Emily was left high and dry. It is clear, however, that she was a determined woman, who took hard knocks in life and came out fighting. She resolved, after losing two husbands, to strike out in business on her own, advertising, in April 1893, a new venture:

THE HARDY HOUSE, MADISON, GEORGIA –
MRS EMMIE HARDY, PROPRIETRESS
CENTRALLY LOCATED. FIRST CLASS FARE. POLITE ATTENTION.
RATES MODERATE. SAMPLE ROOMS CONVENIENT AND FREE.

The new hotel was situated on West Jefferson Street, near the railway depot. This served Emily and her children well for four years. The *Madisonian*, 24 December 1894: 'The Hardy House enjoys a splendid patronage . . . Mrs H(ardy), the genial landlady, needs a more roomy building, and we hope she may soon procure one. Her house is the travelling man's home, and one and all speak highly of its management.'

It was here, legend and fact agree, that young Norvell Hardy sat in the lobby of his mother's hotel, watching the guests come and go, observing their diversity and their gestures, picking up the small details of behaviour, subterfuge, anxiety, that he was to draw on in the distant future. There was also Aunt Susie, Emily's sister, Susan Norvell, a lady of refinement from whose manners Norvell was able to pick up and retain such etiquette as the proper way of holding a teacup.

In November 1894, Emily had put a down payment of $40, out of a total of $435, a princely sum, for a piano purchased in Augusta. Young Norvell's interest in and love of music begins here. He was a sweet singer, encouraged by his mother, who had her hands full with her Tant children, noted in the town for their wild antics. They stuffed newspapers in their pants, set them alight and ran about playing at Indians. Little Norvell sat at the piano and sang.

From the outset, Norvell was fat. There is no avoiding the word. This boy growed and growed, his big bones taking on solid flesh. It was as if he had internalized the image of his dead father, and willed himself to swell to his size. More likely, he was doomed by genetics to be a chubby child, who grew into a fat boy, over two hundred pounds in weight by the age of fifteen. Very different in temperament as well as physique from the Tant children – Elizabeth, Emily, Sam and Henry – he appeared to do well at school. Only one record of a year's attendance at Madison Public School – which is today the Madison–Morgan Cultural Center – is extant:

1st Grade, 1898–99: Norvell Hardy, Parent Mrs E. A. Hardy
Attendance: 95
Deportment: 90
Reading: 50
Spelling: 80
Writing: 80
Arithmetic: 80

As the fat boy sang, Emily struggled to hold her business together. In October 1898 she sold up the Hardy House and leased a hotel in nearby Covington from one Mrs Pitts. But in the New Year 1899 she was back at the Hardy. By May, however, she had to give it up again, to the ubiquitous Turnell. Her next venture was a boarding house in a cottage on South Main Street, where the family lived for a year. In 1900 Emily leased a hotel north in Oconee County, in Athens, but after just one day she left for Atlanta. With this precipitate move we lose her trail, and next pick her up with her family in Milledgeville, way to the south, in Baldwin County.

And still, the boy continued to sing . . .

Milledgeville, in central Georgia, is an important, if sometimes neglected station along the Antebellum, Old South trail. Planned at the turn of the nineteenth century as the state capital, it hovers today between the cultural heritage of local writer Flannery O'Connor and Uncle Remus fabulist Joel Chandler Harris, who was born a few miles upwind, in Eatonton. Between the decaying, religiously obsessed South, and the perky antics of Brer Rabbit, lies this elegant and leafy town, which is today the home of Georgia

College and State University, as well as Georgia Military College – early nemesis of our hero – whose entrance gates were built in the late 1860s from the bricks of the arsenal destroyed by General Sherman. A Georgia Historical Marker on the old Statehouse Square proclaims: 'On this corner in 1860 stood the public market where slaves were sold and local sentences were executed.' But the only sentences executed nowadays are those of the sophomore students, and the only public market is the College Book Fair selling the Speeches of Martin Luther King junior.

In the 1890s, before Emily and Norvell Hardy got here, there were a bare 3,300 inhabitants, mostly sharecroppers. The old glory had gone, with the state capital removed to Atlanta back in 1868. Segregation was in full swing; black Georgians were firmly put in their place and the shadow of violence was never far below the surface. Nevertheless, by the first decade of the twentieth century, electricity had come to Milledgeville. Occasionally, an automobile could be seen in the streets, driven by those rich and bold enough to drive one. This was a land where the black majority was desperately poor and many of the whites not much better off, despite the glorious columned buildings in the centre of their towns.

In Milledgeville, Norvell Hardy passed his teenage years, while his mother ran the Baldwin Hotel, on the corner of Greene Street, today the location of the First Federal Bank, opposite the First Presbyterian Church. The boy could not fail to be deeply shaped by the surroundings he grew up in. A recurring legend has it that he was nursed in his first years by a black 'mammy', a common experience for a white child in the American South of the nineteenth century as in the apartheid South Africa of the twentieth. There is, however, no corroborating evidence of this, nor has a name come down to us. An apocryphal tale tells of a black retainer, named Sam, killed in a fight with one J. W. Bearden, who took over the Turnell–Butler Hotel from Emily. But none of this has echoes in the archive.

There is no doubt that the image of the father he never knew was a central part of Norvell's being. His mother must have told him endless stories of the popular and prominent citizen of Harlem, the ebullient hotelier and socialite, the wounded hero of the War to save Our Vanished Way of Life. Did he nurse a primal memory of that great moon face poised over his not so tiny frame in those first ten months of his life? Certainly the sentiment was strong enough for him to decide, as a teenager, to add the name of 'Oliver' to his given name, and to become known as Oliver Norvell Hardy.

Unlike his later partner, Stan Laurel, Ollie rarely spoke about his past. Where Stan Laurel was a living, walking heritage of music-hall, Oliver Hardy presented himself as a *tabula rasa*. He was a self-made man, a creature of the burgeoning technology of motion pictures, a man with roots, but roots that turned more languid and vague the more they reached into the undergrowth. It took a long time before he was to rediscover and make his own the source that, in his early adult years, he put aside for the solace of hard work.

The most extended interview that Oliver Hardy ever gave was to author John McCabe, in 1954, published in McCabe's *Mr Laurel and Mr Hardy* in 1961. 'There's very little to write about me,' he said. 'I didn't do very much outside of doing a lot of gags before a camera and play golf the rest of the time.' McCabe, however, persevered, and was told by Hardy that his father was a lawyer descended from an English family close to the famous Admiral Nelson. The genealogy, as we have seen, is false, though it may well have been part of the story Emily told young Norvell. Of his educational record, Hardy told McCabe, 'I went to school at Georgia Military College . . . Oh, I forgot to tell you that when I was eight years old, I joined Coburn's Minstrels for a while. We were on tour all over the South but I was really too young for that life so I came back home.'

There is no factual record of this event, which could hardly have occurred when the boy was still at grade school. Of his years in Milledgeville, Hardy says very little, jumping from his mother's move there to 1910, when 'I opened the first movie theater ever to be built in town.'

The tale of young Norvell's minstrel venture is told in greater detail in McCabe's later biography of Hardy, *Babe*. The Coburn Minstrels, so the story goes, stayed at the Baldwin Hotel in Milledgeville, and so captivated the lad that he ran away with them to the next town. Coburn wrote to Mrs Hardy and suggested she allow the boy to remain until he got homesick and came to his senses. And so it was, after a few weeks on the road.

It is a nice tale, so why spoil it with researcher's doubts? Leo Brooks, however, interviewing Norvell's niece, Mary Sage, in 1988, was told by her that the entire Coburn Minstrels adventure was made up by a publicity agent on the Hal Roach lot one day, well into the 1930s, when Babe Hardy was reminiscing to his film crew about the theatrical groups who used to stay at his mother's hotel. Hardy, ever easy-going, went along with the invention, and adopted the tale from then on. Ma Emily always hated the story, as it suggested she was such a bad mother she would allow her son to 'go on the road with that kind of trash'.

An intriguing picture, of Emily Hardy as the traditional hard-nosed landlady, much akin to the angular Mrs Wendleschaeffer in W. C. Fields's *The Old-Fashioned Way*, who offered no quarter to the towel-stealing riff-raff who took refuge under her roof. By all accounts, Emily Hardy ran her business in Milledgeville with an iron hand, intent on turning a profit for the hotel owners and so confound the meanness of Messrs Turnell and Butler, back in Madison. As a husbandless widow with five children, Emily, like the Red Queen in Lewis Carroll's Alice tales, had to run twice as fast in order to stay in the same place. By the time she had reached Milledgeville, however, she could afford to slow down, as the family sojourn in Atlanta had yielded a wealthy husband for her eldest daughter, Elizabeth, in the shape of railroad contractor Ira Yale Sage.

Idle hands were frowned on at 'Miss Emmie's' Baldwin Hotel, and local witnesses recall young Norvell being sent out with a sandwich board to trudge about advertising the 'evening special'. This was terribly embarrassing for the boy, who needed no extra encumbrances to draw attention to himself in the streets. Other tales of Milledgeville, from long-gone witnesses, are contradictory. Some said that young Norvell was popular in the town for his singing prowess. Others that the entire family were looked down on – those uncouth, wild Tants. Emily, according to this view, was 'low class', and 'left town leaving many debts'. One old Milledge-villite remembered 'Fatty' Hardy as distinctly odd, effeminate, perhaps 'queer'. But this may have been much later, when, as an eighteen- or nineteen-year-old, the boy was still struggling with his self-image.

There can be little doubt, despite kind souls remembering the past through rosy spectacles, which picture young Norvell as 'always happy and singing', that the boy endured a harsh rite of passage. It cannot have been easy to be an obese teenager in a small, racially divided town, where any trace of 'otherness' would be rejected. Lucille Hardy, Oliver's third wife, spoke in her twilight years of his abiding sense of the burden of his corpulence: 'Kids used to tease him at school – he was a head taller and bigger and he looked like he was several years older than his classmates and they used to tease him and call him Fat Boy and Fatty and things like that, and it really hurt.'

In such common circumstances for a boy who was different, he responded as 'outsiders' have done from time immemorial. He did everything and anything to be popular: he sang for his school-mates; he told jokes; he offered to umpire the baseball games. He tried to be, at all times, the life and soul of the party. Happy to encourage his singing, Emily arranged for lessons, reputedly with a Professor Adolph Dahm Patterson, of the Atlanta Conservatory of Music, although there is no record of Norvell ever attending the conservatory as a regular student. The story goes that the teacher gave up on the boy, as he failed to turn up for his tutorials, com-menting that the lad may have had a fine voice, 'but no damned ambish'!

Nevertheless, he sang on. Two songs from the repertory became standard, well into his adult years: 'Silver Threads among the Gold' and 'When You and I Were Young, Maggie'. Somewhere along the line Norvell had indeed succumbed to the lure of the stage, the travelling players who penetrated everywhere. Even Milledgeville had its own opera house, a vaudeville theatre featur-ing the acts of the day, headlining even luminaries such as Lillian Russell. Legend has it that, when acts were cancelled, Norvell would take the stage and sing. Again, this may have occurred much later, when he was well known as the operator of the Electric Theater, from the year 1910.

Music remained an abiding passion. The story goes that the boy saved his pennies to travel into Atlanta, to see the more lavish musical revues and operettas that played in the big city. Some tales have him spending his last coins and walking most of the way back home. (Atlanta is over eighty miles from Milledgeville!) His greatest thrill, he related, was to hear the great tenor Enrico Caruso sing. At one point, the stories tell, he was stuck in Atlanta during a race riot, in 1906. McCabe dates this event as 17 April but it would more likely have been 22–24 September, when a white mob,

45

thousands strong, killed at least twenty-five black Atlantans and wrecked and looted black and white stores alike. Between white violence and black retaliation, it would have been a terrifying education for the kid who only wanted to hear Caruso.

Emily, ever fearful of her boy being footloose in hard times, was determined that he should receive an education that would enable him to fit into society, as hard a squeeze as that might be. Despairing of the Atlanta Conservatory, Emily enrolled him at Milledgeville's sternest school, the Georgia Military College.

The year is 1907. Pity the fifteen-year-old, dragging his 200 pounds plus along the drill field, trying to mount the obstacle course. Singing and performing sketches for the fellow students could take him off the hook – for a short while. Eventually the terror set in again, the common taunts of 'Fatty Hardy'. On the other hand, it might have been his physical training at the college that gave the fat boy the unexpected agility that marked him in later years. Even at his largest size, in his solo Florida movies, in 1915, one marvels at the capacity of young 'Babe', as he had become by then, to leap over fences, take pratfalls and otherwise cavort with speed and grace. It was during his stint at the military college that Norvell was first noted for his participation in baseball games. Initially posted as umpire, he was later to play shortstop, with ample width to stop the ball. And yet this was a period of torture for Norvell. Even if he could master the physical aspects of the course, the rigid discipline of the military life was definitely not for him. Eventually, his mother bowed to his pleas to be released from bondage, and sent him to a 'progressive mountain school', Young Harris College, way up at the border with North Carolina, north-east of the Chatahoochee National Forest. Anything rather than have the boy learn his manners from the rough travellers who graced the Baldwin's spittoons.

We may presume that Norvell learned something at Young Harris, though he would later bemoan to his wife Lucille the lack of a proper education, and express regret that he hadn't studied as he should have. A photograph sent by an old boy of the college to John McCabe showed Norvell among his classmates, as members of a 'smoking club'. Emily, it seems, was doomed to disappointment, and later events would bear out her probable assessment that she had done what she could, but the boy would go his own way.

One anecdote of this period relates how Norvell, returning home from the 'mountain school' and taking a detour to visit family members in Columbia County, met up, on the train to Augusta, with a young man with whom he was soon deeply engaged in an enthusiastic discussion about baseball. This turned out to be the famous batsman Ty Cobb, who invited him to a game that he would remember long afterwards. The record shows, however, that the memorable Ty Cobb game was in Milledgeville, in April 1913, where 'more than 2000 fans saw Cobb hit the first ball thrown to him with such force that it carried far over the fence'. Oliver Hardy dined out on this tale for decades, relating it with relish on the Hal Roach lot in Culver City, California.

Another oft-told tale set during his Young Harris tenure, at another home visit, has Norvell diving into the Oconee River to try to rescue his stepbrother Sam. Despite Norvell's efforts, Sam drowned. Although there is no public record of this event, Oliver Hardy related it with such regret, years later, that we may take it on trust.

Hardy's official biography, put out by the studios, had him grad-uating from the Law School of the University of Georgia, as part of Emily's plan to lead him in Papa's footsteps. Neither Hardy, in fact, ever studied law. The boy's sights were already set, not on estab-lished professions, but on the open terrain of show business. Singing in local venues could be a stopgap, but it was a precarious voca-tion. Then, in late 1909 or early 1910, a business opportunity came up in town. The first motion picture theatre in Milledgeville was to be opened, opposite the opera house. It was named the Electric Theater.

And so we are back in the realm of facts. The National Census of 1910 finds our lad ensconced in his new post, formally listed as 'Electrician, Electric Theater' – i.e. the projectionist. Old locals remembered that he ran the whole show, taking tickets, sweeping the hall, and acting as day-to-day manager. Here he began his apprenticeship in the maturing art of the magic-picture light beams. Oddly enough, the census lists him as living apart from his mother, now named Emmie Jackson (a new husband had been swept up somewhere along the way), in the household of one Roy J. Baisden, together with Henry L. Jante (probably Tante, his brother). Although listed on a separate sheet, the address, in fact, at 205 North Wayne, is the same address as Emmie's hotel. So perhaps this was some kind of tax dodge. The name entered is Oliver M. (*sic*) Hardy, so he has already taken on the name that immortalized his long-dead, but far from forgotten, father.

Here, then, we may leave him for a while, eighteen years of age, goggling at the screen of the Electric Theater, poised on the brink of a new life, and the very latest show-business medium, as we return to twenty-year-old Stanley Jefferson, embarking on his own great leap forward into his stardust dreams . . .

CHAPTER SIX

We Are Fred Karno's Army: What Bloody Use Are We?

On 1 December 1908, Madge Metcalfe-Jefferson died. This blow descended on young Stanley Jefferson just days before he was due to go on tour with the Christmas pantomime *The House That Jack Built*. Madge had lived in the shadow of her entrepreneur husband, borne his sons and daughters, acted in his plays, aided him in the management of his theatres and advised him on his designs and décor. 'Her most important part', wrote her Glasgow obituarist, 'was Olga Snake in *The Bootblack* in which she excelled, and beautifully gowned made a most imposing appearance . . . [Her husband] attributes much of his early success to her artistic taste . . . as well as her business tact.'

One could say that the self-effacing element of the character Stan Laurel was to develop, twenty years later, derived in large part from his mother. It certainly didn't come from his father, A.J., who soldiered on with his many enterprises. For Stanley, too, the show went on. The loss of his mother probably strengthened, as such events do, the sixteen-year-old boy's feeling that he was a man now, able to strike out on his own. After the Levy pantomime, and before his brief sojourn on the city wharf of Hal Reid's *Alone in the World*, Stanley tried a short run as a solo comedian, billed as 'Young Stanley Jefferson – He of the Funny Ways'. This was, he later confessed, an imitative act, mimicking the routines of Harry Randall, a third partner of the legendary Dan Leno, who had himself soldiered on on his own after both Leno and second partner Herbert Campbell died in 1904. There were also lesser-known, northern-circuit comedians as potential models for the beginner. Morny Cash, 'The Lancashire Lad', specialized in playing old men. Robb Wilton, 'The Confidential Comedian', had his own fireman sketch, with the catchline: 'Keep the fire going until we get there.' Wee Georgie Wood was and remained a close friend, but young Stanley could not decide whether he wished to stick to juvenile roles or branch out and find an adult voice.

He later said of this period, 'I just didn't know what kind of comedian I was. I guess I was at an awkward age. All I know is I enjoyed being in front of the footlights.'

And who would gainsay him? It was still the great age of music-hall. George Robey, he of the pre-Chaplin bowler hat and cane, dominated the stage, specializing, like Leno, in pantomime dames, which he presented all over the northern theatres. In fact the battered top hat, umbrella and silly smile of 'He of the Funny Ways' looks very much like early Robey. Little Tich, Wilkie Bard, the Scots star Harry Lauder, Marie Lloyd, Vesta Tilley *et al.* were all in their prime. The 'legitimate' theatre of Arthur Jefferson was still a force on the stage, but to a young man, full of pep and vigour, the old styles of the Victorian melodrama were things to mock, not to emulate. It is worth noting that this was already the age when the dramas of George Bernard Shaw and Oscar Wilde were catapulting the British stage towards modernity. But, outside the intellectual middle classes, it was comedy that was king.

And the king of comedy was Fred Karno.

When Stanley Jefferson met Fred Karno in November 1909, Karno had been a name in British music-hall since 1895. He is mentioned often, as an early discoverer of Stan Laurel, but mainly as the power behind Charles Chaplin, Stan's senior contemporary. However, the significance of Karno in both these actors' inheritance goes deeper than merely that of a mentor, the man who set them forth on their careers.

His life is a legend, but also a mystery. Only two books, in the entire twentieth century, exist that purport to tell his tale. The first, Edwin Adeler's and Con West's *Remember Fred Karno? The Life of a Great Showman*, was published as long ago as 1939, and the second, J. P. Gallagher's *Fred Karno – Master of Mirth and Tears*, was published in 1971. The first relies heavily on the reminiscences of the showman's son, Fred Karno junior, and the second on the memories of Fred junior's wife, Olive, friends of Karno's wife, Edith, and show-business people, Stan Laurel among them.

As legends go, Fred Karno's was a self-made affair. He said of himself, in an early interview in 1908, 'I was originally one of the "submerged" and that I am not today one of the "won't works" I attribute to the fact that good Old Dame Nature gave me an energetic disposition and a taste for athletics of any kind.'

Fred Karno's taste for athletics was in fact slow in coming. Born Frederick Westcott, in Exeter, on 26 March 1866, he was the eldest of seven children of a cabinet-maker who then settled in Nottingham in 1875. From his father he inherited a ferocious work ethic, the familiar 'no work – no food'. Sent to work in a lace factory at the age of fourteen, young Fred tried to make money on his own, cleaning the local barber's shop, or renting a small workshop to garage milkmen's carts. This did not bring in much cash, and Fred accepted an apprenticeship in the plumbing trade. It was here, sent for a job at a local gymnasium, that Fred discovered his penchant for athletics.

'At all events,' Fred related in 1908, 'I soon became one of the "star" performers at the gym and used to be engaged to give exhibitions at fêtes and galas . . . until I came under the notice of Mons[ieur] Alvene, a well-known gymnast and equillibrist in his day.'

The abiding characteristic of Karno was his fanatical perseverance in any field of activity that he set his mind and body to. Graduating from Alvene's patronage to Harry Manley's Circus, Fred became schooled in the ways of clowns and mimes. The circus took him on a tour of the mining towns and villages of South Wales, carrying his food in a 'peck tin', sleeping in miners' cottages, and gaining a close knowledge of the grim conditions workers in the Victorian era had to endure. This brush with real poverty appeared to scare him into leaving the showmen's world for a time, and trying the craft of a glazier. He and a lad named Mike worked the towns and villages of England, breaking a few windows on the sly, at night, so they could come and fix them in the morning. The record doesn't reveal whether this tall tale was told before or after Charles Chaplin's window-breaking film, *The Kid*, in 1921.

Glazing proving unattractive none the less, he returned to Nottingham and took a job at a 'ponging booth', a mobile booth or tent in which jugglers and gymnasts performed to festival crowds. These wandering jobs led Fred to a trapeze act named 'The Four Aubreys', with whom he travelled to the Continent. After an accident on the high wire, he returned to London, scrabbling for jobs at 'Poverty Corner', a hang-out for out-of-work actors and actresses just outside Waterloo Station, where the bookers from nearby theatrical agencies would call to dole out occasional work. Many of the stars to be – Dan Leno, Harry Lauder and Marie Lloyd among them – were said to have served their time on the 'Corner'. It was here Fred met two other unemployed gymnasts, Ted Tysall and Bob Sewall, and eventually these three were offered a position to replace an act called 'The Three Carnoes', which had been booked at a music-hall in Edgware Road but had failed to turn up.

And so The Three Karnoes were born. Initially busking around the West End, Bob Sewall singing 'Funiculi Funicula', and Ted Tysall and Fred accompanying on mandolins, they eventually toured the provincial music-halls, and then played the Continent: Naples, Paris, Lyons, Dieppe. In 1888, while playing the Christmas pantomime in Stockport, Cheshire, Fred met a seventeen-year-old girl named Edith Cuthbert, whom he eloped with to London and married, despite the vehement objections of her parents.

Fred Karno's personal life was stormy and his treatment of his wife, who bore him eight children, five of whom died in infancy, was brutal and violent. In many ways he epitomized the double life of the showman, the schizoid nature of the performer and clown. He would beat his wife, leaving her permanently scarred, and flaunt his many mistresses before her with a sadistic flair. And yet he became the master of so many shows and acts that would delight thousands, and later, through his protégés, millions of men, women and children. The archetypal self-made showman, once he discovered that he could make more money getting others to work for him than risking his own life on the high wire, he pursued the notion to its limit. An early wheeze, in 1889, was his adoption of a relatively new invention, the phonograph, which could record and replay sounds and voices. Redubbing it the 'Karnophone', Fred approached music-hall stars, later to include Dan Leno and Herbert Campbell, and persuaded them to sing into the mouthpiece. No one thought to charge him for this service, which enabled the showman to add this business to the Three Karnoes' act, and amaze the music-hall audience. His first break as a full-fledged producer came at the Bell Theatre in Portsmouth, where, legend has it, he put on, at a day's notice, an old pantomime sketch, *Love in a Tub*, performed entirely in mime, so as to save the actors learning their lines.

Enter an unsung contributor to the art of twentieth-century comedy, a pantomimist, Rick Klaie. Karno recruited him to devise an entirely original sketch in mime, to be entitled *Hilarity*, and to be presented in the first-run London music-halls. Tested on a provincial tour in the autumn and winter of 1894, it opened at the South London Palace on Christmas, and proceeded to play the halls for several years.

No 'text' of Karno's pantomimes has survived, though scripts of his later shows can be found. The shows appear to have been highly planned, with a great deal of physical 'stuff', including, in *Hilarity*, Karno himself performing above the stage on the high wire. An item in the stage journal the *Era*, in April 1897, records that

Mr Fred Karno . . . during a performance of his sketch *Hilarity* at the Washington Theatre of Varieties on Thursday, 15th inst., narrowly escaped a most serious accident. During the rally he is suspended in an inverted position high up on a house piece. The house piece was just about to fall on the stage, the braces having given way, when Mr Marshall Rhodes, the popular secretary and treasurer of the establishment above-mentioned, who happened fortunately to be in the wings at the time, with great presence of mind rushed to the help of Mrs Karno, who had also discovered that the scene was falling . . . Mr Karno was safely released . . . from his dangerous position . . .

Indeed, this may have been his swan song on the bars. Quite what *Hilarity* was is unclear. It featured 'a humorous donkey possessed with a receptive and reflective mind, an actively funny footman, impervious apparently to hard knocks, a couple of lovers, a grumpy guardian and a domestic', living in 'rural retirement'. The *Era*'s reviewer (9 January 1897) notes that 'the farce will not bear analysis. It is built simply for laughter making purposes, and fulfils its object admirably.'

Karno's next production, *Jail Birds*, provides us with a little more detail:

The first scene represents the quarry at Portland. Blasting operations are in progress. The convicts shoulder their pickaxes and begin work, but most of their time is spent 'larking' and playing practical jokes on the warders and visitors . . . A red-faced official is ignominiously hoisted aloft by a crane employed for lifting the blocks of stone, which are also freely used for pelting inquisitive visitors. The scene closes with a tremendous explosion of dynamite, which shatters a wooden bridge and does other damage.

53

The next scene reveals a corridor of the prison. Dinner time comes, and the inmates of the several cells have their basins filled with an unsavoury looking liquid labelled 'paste'. Batches of loaves arrive, but are so hard that it necessitates the use of a carpenter's saw to divide them, and much fun is made out of the active pursuit of their charges by excited officials . . .

Era, 1 February 1896

Sounds familiar? We are looking at the 'missing link' between the grotesque antics of clowns such as Grimaldi and the crazy tricks of the future silent cinema. At the end of the sketch, 'walls and floors open as if by magic, to make way for pursuers and pursued, and finally the curtain falls on an effective tableau'.

Karno's antics offstage to publicize his shows were no less bizarre than his onstage inventions. He would send four of the players to a nearby town, two dressed as cops and two as prisoners. They would travel thus accoutred on the train to the town the show was playing at and then stage a mighty tussle, the 'cops' chasing the 'crooks', together with hundreds of flapdoozled townspeople, till they would enter into the doors of the theatre, and people would realize: "Eee! It were just Karno's Jail Birds. Coom on, Bill, lets 'ave a sup o' ale.' Or so Adeler and West tell the tale. Another wheeze was a Black Maria police van, decked out with banners of 'Fred Karno's Jail Birds'. In some quarters of London, apparently, where the police were not fancied, the wagon was pelted with rubbish.

Nothing could stop Karno now. He had found his formula. *Jail Birds* and *Hilarity* played regularly around the country for six years. It has been rarely realized how unusual Karno's shows were for their time. The music-hall was a verbal medium; its forte was songs, patter and dialogue. Some chroniclers of the period have mistakenly assumed that, due to censorship strictures, dialogue was not allowed in music-hall sketches. The situation was different: the performance of full-fledged plays was permitted only in 'legitimate' theatres, subject to special licences, and the control of the ubiquitous Lord Chamberlain. Sketches were tolerated in the less strictly regulated music-halls providing they were limited in length, and these too had to be screened by the Lord Chamberlain's office. Sketch writers and producers continually transgressed these restrictions, as is borne out by massive coverage in the *Era*, in 1904, when a sketch, accused of being in fact a play, and licentious to boot, led to the prosecution of the Oxford Theatre in London. The 'music-hall sketch problem' continued to be an issue until 1912, when a new law brought the music-halls in line with the 'legitimate' theatre, in both status and obligations.

But if you wished to escape censorship altogether, pantomime was the only solution. No dialogue – no obligation to send your script to the Lord Chamberlain's office. And thus there are no Karno texts in the present British Library collection until *Saturday to Monday* in 1903, and Karno's speechless comedians ruled.

To argue that Karno had any specific political or social agenda is to fly in the face of both tradition and evidence. But it can be noted that, in early 1896, when Karno was opening the anti-authoritarian *Jail Birds* in London, many other theatres, including the Paragon, Mile End, in which the sketch played, were inundated with patriotic plays and sketches echoing events in South Africa. This was the period of the Jameson Raid, the failed attempt by Cecil Rhodes's colonial administrator and sidekick, L. S. Jameson, to invade and take over the Boer Orange Free State (an early precursor of the full-scale Boer War). The German Emperor Wilhelm sent a telegram congratulating Boer President Paul Kruger, thus igniting hysteria in Britain about imminent war with Germany. A hastily mounted monologue, exhorting British troops to fight 'for the honour of Old England', preceded *Jail Birds* at the Paragon.

It was not that Fred Karno did not care for 'the honour of Old England', but that he cared far more about making money for Fred Karno by making whoopee on the stage. In finance a conservative, in domestic life a brute, anarchistically apolitical, Fred Karno was 'Old England' in effigy. The satirical sediment of Karno's numerous spoofs shows up in the song sung by soldiers in the First World War of 1914–18:

> We are Fred Karno's army, what bloody good are we,
> We cannot walk, we cannot fight, what bloody use are we?
> And when we get to Germany, the Kaiser he will say,
> Op kop my wop what a bloody fine lot, Fred Karno's infantry!

In Karno's 1903 *Early Birds*, Karno added complicated mechanical scenery and effects to 'an original pantomime burlesque' of life in London's Whitechapel, a spoof of Dickensian degradation, representing 'the life mostly of the loafer, the thief and the dosser'. Fred himself played a Fagin-like Jew, a travelling glazier, who has a knife fight with a 'brutal-looking blackguard hiding from justice' (*Era*, 10 January 1903). 'The contriver of this clever sketch', raves a later *Era* scribe, has

caught the very essence of the hopeless gaiety, the gruesome jollity of English poverty, wretchedness and crime . . . How vivid is the picture; how it reeks with life and reality! And in this twilight where virtues are vices . . . looms large the typical ruffian, the 'sponger' on women, the brutal, remorseless 'rough'. Anon night falls, and we are transported to the horrible lair where the human animals fling themselves down in their rags and tatters at the close of the day.

It is not difficult to discern in this the origin of Chaplin's 1917 *Easy Street*, down to the ending in which the young hero beans the 'rough' with a table.

In 1904, Karno presented the sketch that was to launch both Chaplin and Laurel into orbit, the eternal *Mumming Birds*. Noted as the most successful music-hall sketch of all time, this piece of drollery, performed in America as *A Night at an English Music Hall*, was recycled on the stage for over twenty years. Chaplin biographers have made it globally famous. *Mumming Birds* derived from an idea originally titled *Entertaining the Shah*, which had been sparked by a visit of the Shah of Iran to the Empire and Hippodrome Theatres in the summer of 1902. Musical blacksmiths, comic jugglers and Burton's Leaping Dogs amused the monarch, who left to the strains of the Persian national anthem and 'God Save the King'. The legend goes that one day, rehearsing Karno's Persian delight, Billy Reeves, a young comic first starred by Karno in *Early Birds*, made derisory noises offstage. Challenged by Karno, Reeves allegedly said, 'Surely, guv'nor, you don't seriously intend to do this rubbish! They'll never stand for it, take my word for that.' Thus was born the idea of a self-referential stage comedy in which the acts on the stage are continually interrupted by comments and arguments going on in the wings.

To make this work, the scenery for the sketch included a stage within the stage. '*Mumming Birds*', wrote Adeler and West, Karno's biographers, 'was based on an idea as old as the hills – the essential cruelty of audiences . . . The characters have no names. There is the inebriated swell, originally played by Billy Reeves . . . the bad boy in the box, originally played by Charley Bell; the dear

old uncle, played by George Craig; the conjurer by Billie Ritchie . . .'
The acts on stage included Can Can Girls, a comedy lady singer, a
reciting actor, a comedy quartette, a girl singer doing 'Old Tyme
Songs' and the *pièce de résistance* – the wrestler Marconi Ali, or
'The Terrible Turk'. This was the show Sydney Chaplin, Charlie's
elder brother, joined in the summer of 1906, just in time for
Karno's first American tour.

By this time, Fred Karno was not only an institution but an
industry, having bought two large houses in Vaughan Road,
Camberwell, and expanded them into 'The House That Karno
Built', at which, Fred himself boasted, 'we'll turn you out anything
theatrical, from a pantomime, cast, scenery, dresses, everything
complete, down to a property periwinkle'. Covering Karno's
autumn 1906 tour of the United States, the *New York Morning
Telegraph* enthused, in a long article on 7 October:

When the companies set out from 'The House That Karno Built', it is very
much in the nature of a pageant. First comes a succession of motor cars,
followed by a four-horse coach, with the Karno driver and the Karno footman gaily uniformed and lending a holiday air to the streets through which
they pass. Then come the Karno buses, more four-horse teams, and the
drays holding the scenery and properties.

An idea of the extent of the business conducted from the Camberwell
district may be had when it is known that Mr Karno is constantly treating
with managers for entire productions, including scenery, costumes, properties, stage management, rehearsals, engagement of artists and booking
the tours of dramas, musical comedies, pantomimes, etc. Each department
has a first-class principal and a full staff of competent assistants . . .

Meanwhile, back in northern England, Karno's many enterprises
were a theatrical staple from the turn of the century, playing,
among other venues, in Arthur Jefferson's own houses, such as
the North Shields Boro' Theatre, which advertised Karno's *His
Majesty's Guests* (a *Jail Birds* spin-off), in October 1902. Without
doubt young Stanley Jefferson – then twelve years old – grew up
with Fred Karno's 'army' as a familiar part of his youth. By 1909,
'The Guv'nor', as Karno was known to all, was presenting up to
ten different acts at any one time in theatres up and down the land.
In November, he was presenting the pantomime *Mother Goose* at
the Grand Theatre, Glasgow, where Stanley, after the fizzling out of
Alone in the World, presented his card backstage.

Young Stan Jefferson – 'he of the funny ways'

'A gentle-voiced little man came forward to meet me,' Stanley later related,

'Well Mr Jefferson Junior,' he said, 'What can I do for you?' I told him I wanted to see Mr Karno. 'You're seeing him now,' he replied quietly. It was quite a shock and such a relief to find him such a pleasant, friendly man. Briefly I explained that I wanted a job as a comedian. 'Are you funny?' he asked. I told him of my youthful experience. He nodded. 'Very well,' he said, 'I'll try you out at £2 a week. Report to Frank O'Neill, who is running my *Mumming Birds* company in Manchester. Push yourself forward, and I'll see you in London in a few weeks' time.'

Of such small moments is history made. Stan was to appear in four Karno sketches during his tour with the company – *Mumming Birds, Skating, Jimmy the Fearless* and *The Wow-Wows* – before embarking, together with Charles Chaplin and a company of fourteen, on 22 September 1910, *en route* to the United States . . .

58

CHAPTER SEVEN

In the Temple of the Magic Light Beams

The year is 1910. The place, the Electric Theater, Milledgeville. Or any other of the several thousand small theatres or nickelodeons that had sprung up all over the cities and towns of America since 1905. The eighteen-year-old theatre manager has taken the tickets and waited for the noisy patrons to settle down. Then, turning off the lights, he either cranks up or switches on – some movie projectors did work off the electric power by then – and the cone of light shoots out across the dust of the hall . . .

What were the movies that Oliver Norvell Hardy watched in the three years in which he showed films at Milledgeville's only cinema? Imagine the boy, not long demobilized from Young Harris 'mountain' College, memories of his dreadful stint at the Georgia Military College still fresh in his youthful memory. Claims that he was well loved wherever he went are not borne out by facts or logic. 'Fatty' Hardy, if not quite the town freak, was notable as being different in a world of tight conformity. He found an outlet in his outward-going good humour, his joking personality, his consistent attempts to amuse his peers. A Hardy among Tants, he might have been remembered by his sister, Elizabeth, as 'adored by all of us', but it cannot have been any easier then than now to be the fat boy with a doubtful future.

And then the magic light beams arrive . . .

The cinema, in 1910, might appear pre-historical to most of us, but was, in fact, in the midst of a period that would see it shoot from the status of a curiosity to an industry that would shake the world. Already in January 1909, the *New York Times* reported, the capital invested in moving pictures totalled 40 million dollars, with an estimated 45 million persons attending shows weekly. The number of 'picture shows' totalled ten thousand, with receipts per week of 3 million dollars. 'A well-equipped picture exhibition', reported the *Times*, 'requires the service of ten people . . . This includes a piano player, a drummer [i.e. someone who drums up business outside the theatre], a man at the lantern and his assistant, and two ushers only.' (Of course if you have 'Fatty' Hardy, one will suffice, though it's safe to assume there must have been a helper or two, as well as someone tinkling the ivories.)

These picture shows were entertainment for the masses, costing 5 or 10 cents as against the 40 or 50 cents you had to pay for a top-rated vaudeville show, or a dollar for a 'legit' musical comedy. The *Billboard*, in its Christmas 1910 issue, announcing that 'the motion picture . . . has come to stay', revealed that 'the manufacturing end of the industry is represented now by some twenty-five or thirty companies, each of which releases from two to three reels of film per week. More than half of these manufacturers are members of the Motion Picture Patents Company.' This was the association of the movies' earliest moguls, who claimed the sole right to control the use of camera and exhibition equipment, manufactured by the Edison company. Norvell Hardy might well have used the Edison Projecting Kinetoscope, advertised in the same issue of the *Billboard* as 'The Machine You Will Eventually Buy' (if you knew what's good for you!): 'constructed of the best materials . . . projects the brightest and steadiest pictures, yet is the simplest to operate. You don't have to send it to a repair shop. Every part is inter-changeable . . . All you need is a Screw Driver. Think of the saving in time and money.' Aaah! Of course, there was the American Lifeograph company, touting a different machine further down the page, but they were at a distinct disadvantage.

In 1910, a standard show would include a two-reel (twenty-plus-minute) drama or adventure, a one- or two-reel western, a one-reel comedy, and educational reels, showing 'historical and geographical subjects, current events, scenes of commercial and industrial life, and occasionally literary subjects'. As old vaudeville traditions still prevailed, audiences were far from passive at these exhibitions, and expressed their opinions forcefully or added their own dialogue to the scenes. 'Illustrated songs' would be projected, to get everyone more convivial. This was very much a socially – though not racially (especially not in the South) – mixed audience. Women, from an early stage, found these theatres congenial places to go with girl friends or work mates, and social guardians were already protesting that these theatres had become dens of vice, which should be closed down, or at least closely controlled. *Déjà vu* sets in when one reads the press reports from July 1911 regarding the problem of unaccompanied children being in the dark with unsavoury adults:

'I always asked a man to get my ticket because I'm not old enough to go in alone,' said a child who explained how she gained admittance . . . It was not that the pictures were bad, but that the men took the children to the dark balcony, where they could begin their vicious work . . .

So what were the movies that were projected in these insalubrious conditions? Westerns, of course, had been eternally popular since movies had begun – in fact they were practically contemporaneous with real life. While Buffalo Bill Cody was still touring Europe with his *Wild West Show*, a series of 'Buffallo Bill Wild West and Pawnee Bill Wild East' movies were released by the American Film company. The Éclair company shot films with members of the Buffalo Bill show, directed by the splendidly named William Haddock. In July 1910, an ambitious actor named Max Aronson, who had renamed himself Gilbert Anderson, learned to ride and re-invented himself again as 'Broncho Billy' Anderson, shooting films for the Essanay company in Niles Canyon, California. Titles such as *Broncho Billy's Cowardly Brother* and *Broncho Billy's Christmas Dinner* heralded a slew of one-reelers, featuring daring acts of horsemanship and gunplay, and leaping on and off stage-coaches. Tom Mix, who at least was a genuine cowboy (he claimed to have been born in a log cabin and to be part Cherokee Indian on his mother's side), made his first film for the Selig Polyscope company in the summer of 1910.

For the Biograph company, D. W. Griffith was already shooting westerns such as *Ramona* and *Song of the Wildwood Flute,* portraying the injustice done to the Indians. By 1910, Griffith had been making films for two years for Biograph, mainly on the East Coast, but he moved to California for the winter sunlight early in January, making *A Romance of the Western Hills*, *The Way of the World*, *The Two Brothers* and several other titles, before returning east. In all, in 1910 Griffith shot over eighty films! Norvell Hardy would have screened many of these.

Melodramas were rife, in 1910 as always, and most movies were yet to learn from Griffith's experiments with camera placement, the direction of actors, and editing – how to make an art from silent artifice. An advertisement in the *Billboard* offers the Lubin company's *The Dead Letter*, a Civil War picture: 'The story of two lovers, united after many years of misunderstanding because of a letter that was lost. A beautiful drama that begins shortly after the Civil War time, and has its happy ending about twenty-five years later.'

The same company, which was to play a crucial part in our hero's story, released in the same week of 19 December four more movies – another drama, *An Exile's Love* ('an unusual story of the love of an exiled Prince for an American Girl. Deep heart interest and the acme of Lubin acting throughout'), and three comedies: *The Musical Ranch* ('a delightful comedy in a western setting'), *An American Count* ('another of Lubin's screaming comedies'), and *Reggie's Engagement* ('a howl from start to finish. Poor ballroom Reggie gets into all kinds of trouble while trying to make an impression at the home of his wealthy sweetheart. He wins her too.').

Lubin's slogan was suitably frantic: 'A Comedy Every Tuesday and Saturday – A Drama Every Friday – A Two Reel Feature Every Wednesday and Thursday.' Everyone else was churning 'em out as fast, if not faster. On 9 April, the week of Oliver N. Hardy's registration as 'Electrician of Electric Theater' in the Census form, the *New York Dramatic Mirror* reviewed over forty new films: *Gold Is Not All* from Biograph, *The Little Vixen* and *Polar Bear Hunt* from Pathé, *The Treasure Hunters* from Selig, *Red Hawk's Last Raid* from Kalem, *The Indiscretions of Betty* from Vitagraph, *The Capture of the Burglar* and *Michael Strogoff* from Edison, *The Flower of the Ranch* from Essanay, *The Cowboy Preacher* from Nestor, and on and on and on. Even ancient times were featured: *The Kiss Was Mightier than the Sword*, from Gaumont, was praised as 'a real novelty, being a classical comedy adapted from the *Lysistrata* of Aristophanes. The scenes are laid in ancient Athens, and the story tells of the efforts of the wives of the Athenians to prevent the latter from continuing their warlike excursions, which for twenty years have proved disastrous.'

Comedies too, naturally, were staple fare. D. W. Griffith made his quota of these as well. In 1909, he shot *The Curtain Pole* for Biograph, a 'French chase comedy of the old style', featuring Mack Sennett, no less, as a drunken Frenchman who tries to carry a curtain pole through the streets, with comic results. This was similar in style to the films of Max Linder, the screen's 'Chaplin before Chaplin', who made his first film in 1905. In 1907 Linder shot a short film, *At the Music Hall*, which was a direct pinch from Fred Karno's *Mumming Birds*. His creation of the dapper man about town with hat and cane, a jaunty air, and a great belief in his ability to surmount the setbacks of life, was a crucial influence on the young Charlie, and his comic gags were stolen (or imitated) by everyone. One of his films even has a familiar twiddle, as he sets his hat on his cane instead of his head, which was made a trademark decades later by W. C. Fields. Mack Sennett was yet to form his own Keystone company, in September 1912.

In 1910, a since forgotten actor, Augustus Carney, in a double act with one Victor Potel, was making a series of 'Hank and Lank' comedies for Essanay. These were turned out so quickly they some-times had no titles: an ad from 5 October 1910 simply proclaims, 'Oh Joy! Hank and Lank Again! – They Get Wise to a New Scheme!' In 1911, Carney and Potel made a film called *Alkali Ike's Automobile*, which led to a series that was successful in Europe as well as the US. Fame is fleeting however, as an ill-judged move to Carl Laemmle's Universal company plunged Carney into such obscurity that even his date of death cannot be found.

One major movie comedian would have commanded the attention of young Oliver as he sat by his 'lantern'. John Bunny, the first proper American comedy star, left a promising career on the stage to become an actor at Albert Smith's and Stuart Blackton's Vitagraph company, for $5 a day. The comedies he made – as the hen-pecked husband of harridan Flora Finch in *Father's Flirtation* or as the daughter-pecked father of *The Troublesome Step-daughters* – became immensely popular. A large, rotund and jolly figure, he could not fail to have excited in Oliver the feeling that he, too, could perhaps dream of the movies, of passing from behind the lantern to before the camera. In 1954, Hardy told John McCabe, 'I saw some of the comedies that were being made and I thought to myself that I could be as good – or as bad – as some of those boys.'

This feeling must have welled up as time went by and the movies of 1911, 1912 and 1913 hit the screen. The cinema was progress-ing in leaps and bounds, and comedy was finding new stars. Key-stone's first films, directed by Mack Sennett, *The Water Nymph* with Mabel Normand, and *Cohen Collects a Debt* with Ford

Sterling, were released in autumn 1912. Sennett had decamped with his two stars – Mabel (already his lover at that time), and Fred Mace, from Griffith's Biograph – to set up shop in California. Keystone was the first film company to be dedicated purely to comedy. In 1913, newcomers included Charlie Murray, Mack Swain and another overweight actor who was to be a star, Roscoe 'Fatty' Arbuckle.

Roscoe Arbuckle and his wife, Minta Durfee, had begun, like many others, in vaudeville. He first appeared in some relatively obscure films for the Selig company in 1909 and 1910. Certainly Oliver Hardy would have become aware of 'Fatty' Arbuckle as a Keystone regular by late 1913. His boyish charm, his agility and the dynamism that belied his girth could not fail to have excited young Ollie. To be still smarting over the nickname of 'Fatty' Hardy, and to see a young man who flaunted the epithet of 'Fatty' become so successful in the medium he had grown to love was to see an image of his future.

By this time, however, oral history tells us that Oliver Hardy had already quit his job as projectionist–manager of the Electric Theater and had journeyed south, to Jacksonville, Florida – though we might safely assume that he continued seeing movies as a paying patron. The story goes that a local Milledgeville friend who had vacationed in Florida came back with tales of a new movie-making colony growing there, in Jacksonville, only two hundred miles distant. Ollie upped sticks, left for Florida and found a job singing in vaudeville theatres and night-clubs, billed as 'The Ton of Jollity'. His first jobs were at Cutie Pearce's Roadhouse and at the Jacksonville Orpheum. At the Orpheum, the tale goes, he met a young woman he had encountered before, at the Milledgeville Opera House, a virtuoso piano-player. Her name was Madelyn Saloshin, and, on 17 November 1913, at Macon, Georgia, they were married.

The tale of Madelyn Saloshin has hitherto been the vaguest and least documented element of the story of Oliver Hardy – 'Babe', as he was said to have been named due to a Jacksonville barber who patted his chubby face down with the soothing words, 'Nicee bay-bee . . .' (Or 'Babe' might have been chosen precisely to preclude 'Fatty'.)

The story as it has been known so far goes that Madelyn, having met Oliver at the Jacksonville Opera House, got him a job in the vaudeville company she was touring with, around the South, thus accounting for the marriage at Macon. Later the couple returned to Jacksonville, where they worked the vaudeville halls by night, while Ollie hung about the movie studios by day, waiting for his chance to join their crews.

New research, by our genealogical bloodhound, Dave Rothman, in family history archives, provides a much less tidy, more complex trajectory for Oliver and Madelyn Hardy. The City Directories of Atlanta for the years 1913–14, when both Oliver and Madelyn are supposed to be in Florida, reveal one 'Oliver H. Hardy' listed in 1913 as 'manager, Montgomery Billiard Hall', and one 'Oliver N. Hardy, singer', listed in 1914. (We may assume the dates refer to residence in the previous year.) The first Hardy may not be our Ollie, but the second definitely is. We can note that his address, in 1914, is 41½ Peachtree, a mile or so downwind of Ira Y. Sage (and Ollie's sister Elizabeth), who were living at 800 Peachtree.

Atlanta was also Madelyn Saloshin's home town, and she too can be found in the Atlanta Directories, listed in 1912 and 1913, as 'saleslady'. In 1914, she is still resident, listed as 'pianist, Montgomery Theater'.

The record suggests, therefore, that Oliver and Madelyn first met, neither at Milledgeville's nor Jacksonville's opera houses, but at the Montgomery Theater in Atlanta. Ollie was singing and Madelyn played the piano, and the wooing and plighting of troth duly followed. Madelyn was several years older than Oliver, but the young man was smitten by her lively manner, and, we can safely deduce, she cared not at all that her young swain was large in more than the spiritual sense.

According to the family accounts, Oliver and Madelyn eloped to Macon due to Ma Emily's fierce objections to her son marrying a much older woman. Emily was 'in a rage for days' after the marriage. But what has, until now, been missed are the full implications of these particular nuptials, at this time, and in this place.

Madelyn Saloshin was Jewish, of a working-class family. Her parents, Louis and Tillie Saloshin, both American-born children of immigrants from Prussia (now north Germany), had moved from Ohio to Fulton County, Georgia. The 1900 Census locates them in

Atlanta, with two boys, Milton and Samuel, and a daughter, 'Madaline', born in 1885 or 1886 (the handwritten entry is smudged). This would make Madelyn twenty-seven or twenty-eight years old when she married Oliver Hardy.

Louis Saloshin was by trade a printer, though there were other members of the family who later worked in the song-publishing business in New York. In 1913, Louis and Tillie are still registered in Atlanta, though the entire family seems to be now in 'saleship'.

But 1913 was not a good year for Jews in Georgia. It was, as the sad history of the Deep South reveals, the year of the arrest and trial of a Jewish pencil-factory owner, Leo Frank, for the murder of one of his young female employees, Mary Phagan. The Leo Frank case became famous as the most significant anti-Semitic event in the history of the United States. Throughout the trial, which took place in Atlanta in August 1913, the ethnicity of the defendant was noted. Frank was a prominent member of Georgia's Jewish community centred in Atlanta. In October 1913, the Jewish organization B'nai Brith was moved to set up an Anti-Defamation League, noting that 'for a number of years a tendency has manifested itself in American life toward the caricaturing and defaming of Jews on the stage, in moving pictures'. The Frank trial was the biggest event in Georgia at the time, making front-page news throughout August. On the 26th, Frank was sentenced, on flimsy and questionable evidence, to death by hanging on 10 October. Attorneys' motions for a new trial dragged out the legal process for almost two years.

We can understand, I think, why Oliver and Madelyn chose to be married – one month after the Frank verdict – neither in the bosom of his family in Milledgeville, nor in the bosom of her family in Atlanta, but instead eloped to Macon. The chronology of the previous years might have to be revised accordingly. It may well have been that Oliver left Milledgeville and the Electric Theater earlier than previously thought, in 1912 or early 1913, tried his luck at the Jacksonville studios, failed to find a job there first time around, and earned his living as a professional singer. (We might insert the 'Ton of Jollity' and Cutie Pearce's Roadhouse here.) Not wishing to return home, he moved on to Atlanta, where his sister Elizabeth was comfortably ensconced and could provide an appropriate safety net. There he met Madelyn, and Cupid's arrow struck.

Seven years later, Oliver Hardy's divorce petition versus Madelyn

Hardy provides a completely different slant on Cupid's weapon, but this revision is best left to its own time. Suffice it to say, the matching of Oliver and Madelyn, in 1913, was highly significant. All previous accounts of Oliver Hardy's life have elided the issue of his racial attitudes. A terrible embarrassment overtakes the fans whenever the Southern element is highlighted. A 'good son of the South', scion of a Civil War veteran, how could Oliver Norvell Hardy fail to be a product of his environment? But here is evidence of an act of personal rebellion, which has to be seen in light of the surrounding miasma of prejudice, soon to bear familiar 'strange fruit' chillingly close to home.

Twenty-two months after Frank's trial, in June 1915, Georgia Governor John Slaton, convinced of Leo Frank's innocence, commuted his death sentence to life imprisonment. This sparked a campaign by populist leader Tom Watson, whose newspaper, the *Jeffersonian*, whipped up a froth of virulent incitement against 'the Jew who raped and murdered the little Gentile girl, Mary Phagan'. For his safety, Leo Frank was moved from Atlanta to the state penitentiary in Milledgeville. But there, on the night of 16–17 August, a lynch mob broke into the prison, removed Frank, drove to nearby Marietta, location of Mary Phagan's girlhood home, and hanged him, amid scenes of bloodcurdling hysteria and enthusiasm of a crowd estimated at close to a thousand. Postcards depicting the lynching were on sale for years. On the back of this triumph, Tom Watson revived the Ku-Klux-Klan in Georgia.

By 1915, Oliver and Madelyn Hardy were well clear of Milledgeville, and of Georgia, and the record suggests that he never returned there. One need not plead a keen political or social awareness on behalf of Oliver to state that he could not have been ignorant of these events, or the social consequences of marrying a Jewish woman in the autumn of 1913, particularly if we realize, as the archive shows, that he was actually living in Atlanta at the time of the Leo Frank trial. His marriage to Madelyn can therefore be seen as a message, to Georgia, to Milledgeville, and to his own family, that, as an outsider, he picked an outsider's mate. As an individual in his own right, he would choose his own personal path.

We may also deduce something about Oliver's actual isolation – the sense he had, and that continued all his life, of being imprisoned in a body that required him to set up a mask to deal with the world around him; the yearning for companionship beyond the family circle that could offer him only an anchor at a familiar harbour and from which he wished to sail on to new and unknown horizons. In other words, we should never underestimate the desperation of the fat.

A contemporary photograph of Madelyn and Oliver shows a lady of plain if pleasant features dwarfed beside the looming Ollie, dressed in his good suit, waistcoat, bow-tie and chequered flat cap. She is clutching a small, rather crushed-looking terrier, whom they had named Babe Junior. This was clearly not a marriage expecting offspring. But Oliver looks calm and content, and the tensions that would, in due course, blow this marriage apart, appear to be a distant prospect. The marriage to Madelyn provided him a structure, and some peace of mind, as he continued to pursue the goal set by his months and years watching the silver screen from behind his projector.

It may well be that Oliver and Madelyn did not return to Atlanta after their marriage but proceeded directly to Florida. It would have made sense for them to head straight for Jacksonville, so that Oliver could have another go at the studios.

And indeed, his perseverance paid off. For in April 1914, Oliver Norvell Hardy appeared, for the very first time, before the camera, in a Lubin production. The movie was entitled *Outwitting Dad*. But it might more serendipitously have been called 'Outwitting Mum'. Because, although Oliver Hardy insisted, to the end of his life, that he adored and worshipped his mother, they rarely met again, and the maverick son of the old politician of Harlem, who had departed the scene almost as soon as his son entered it, began to construct a new life, and a new identity, both on screen and off.

CHAPTER EIGHT

Wow-Wows in Wonderland

But we have galloped ahead, much like Broncho Billy, who will play a further role in our saga. Let us return to 1910, and join the good ship *Cairnrona*, which sailed from Southampton, England, on 22 September, bound, not directly for New York harbour, but for Montreal, which she reached after eleven days of rough seas.

This ship, a converted cattle-boat, was carrying a cargo that, unbeknownst to anyone on or off board, would transform the face of American show business and stamp the twentieth century's entertainment culture with an indelible Fred Karno dye. The main conduits, the carriers of this comedy bacillus, were two of the cast of fifteen members of the Karno company aboard – Charles Chaplin and Stanley Jefferson. Charlie was already the star of the show. Stanley was the freshest recruit. The other members of the cast were: Albert Austin, Fred Palmer, Bert Williams (not, I hasten to add, the famous African-American star of that name), George and Emily Seaman, Frank Melroyd, Muriel Palmer, Amy Minster, Arthur Dandoe, Charles Griffiths, Alf Reeves and Fred Karno junior, the latter two in a managerial role.

Chaplin, in his autobiography, has described the scene when the cast finally arrived in New York City after the exhausting train ride via Toronto:

At ten o'clock on a Sunday morning we at last arrived in New York. When we got off the streetcar at Time Square, it was something of a let-down. Newspapers were blowing about the road and pavement, and Broadway looked seedy, like a slovenly woman just out of bed. On almost every corner there were elevated chairs with shoe lasts sticking up and people sitting comfortably in shirt sleeves getting their shoes shined. They gave one the impression of finishing their toilet in the street.

Chaplin added to this somewhat prim judgement:

Many looked like strangers, standing aimlessly about the sidewalks as if they had just left the railroad station and were filling in time between

Laurel, bottom left, and Chaplin, in lifebelt, with the Karno troupe
aboard the SS *Cairnrona*

trains. However, this was New York, adventurous, bewildering, a little
frightening . . .

Chaplin saw himself, by that time, as a 'man of the world'. He
had been in Paris, with Karno, in 1908, and sampled the marvels
of the *Folies Bergère* and the offerings of the *habitués* of its
promenoir, the brothel ladies of the *belle époque*. But for nineteen-
year-old Stanley, this was his first taste of the world outside Britain.
He described, to John McCabe, the antics of Chaplin on the boat,
rushing to the railings and crying, 'America! I am coming to
conquer you! Every man, woman and child shall have my name on
their lips – Charles Spencer Chaplin!' As he was addressing the
shoreline of Quebec rather than the US, we can imagine young
Stanley standing by puzzled, perhaps scratching his head in what
would become a world-famous quirk. But Stanley was a far less
ebullient character then than his senior, though he told McCabe:

We had a lot of fun in those days. Charlie and I roomed together and I can
still see him playing the violin or cello to cover the noise of the cooking of
bacon I was doing on the gas ring (forbidden of course). Then we'd both
take towels and try and blow the smoke out of the window.

The difference between the two can be gauged by their memories. Chaplin's account is self-aggrandizing, observing all through his self-conscious prism. Not a peep about rooming with Stanley. Chaplin did not like to give others credit. Stanley, on the other hand, revels in little anecdotes, like the night he put his shoes outside the door to be shined as he would in a regular British hotel, only to find they'd been stolen, and, of course, they were his only pair. Or his search, together with Chaplin, both caught short with full bladders, for a public convenience in New York – an experience that has obviously not changed for ninety years – and the discovery that they had to ingest more liquids, in a saloon, before they could be allowed to expel them. 'We must have been funny-looking chaps,' Laurel told McCabe, 'what with our English style of dress and speech.' This sense of strangeness remained with Stanley and never left – but it took him almost twenty years to realize it could become the core of his own act.

The sketch Fred Karno had chosen to tour with was his latest pride and joy, *The Wow-Wows*. This was a kind of spin-off of an earlier, 1909 piece, *Skating*, which had introduced a cast of upper-class English youths, featuring a 'broken-down swell', Archibald, who enters stage to ask:

ARCHIE
Has the last train gone for Waterloo?

ATTENDANT
What! Do you take this for a station?

ARCHIE
What is it?

ATTENDANT
A skating rink!

The rest of the piece consists of much tit-for-tat dialogue familiar to anyone acquainted with English music-hall humour from time immemorial, and a spate of physical action which informed Charlie Chaplin's short, *The Rink*, in 1916. Stanley played a small part, with Chaplin starring, in Karno's run of *Skating* from January to April 1910, switching immediately to another Karno show, *Jimmy the Fearless*, from April to September. Stan Laurel later claimed that he had been promoted to play the lead part in the latter play, for a few early performances, due to a spat between the star, Chaplin, and Karno, over Charlie's interpretation of the role.

Jimmy the Fearless was the story of a miner's son who lives what would later be called a 'Walter Mitty' life, imagining himself into the derring-do exploits of his 'Penny Dreadful' comics. He becomes a gun-totin' cowboy, defeating the outlaws led by 'Alkali Ike' (Augustus Carney's character must have crossed the ocean pretty rapidly), and then defeating a horde of pirates on the high seas. 'We were appearing at two theatres,' Stan said, 'Willesden and Ealing . . . the show was a terrific hit. I had to take five curtain calls. You can imagine how I felt. I was a "star comedian" at last, and a Karno one at that.'

Chaplin, of course, would not have liked this at all, and quickly got himself reinstated. One need not doubt Stan's word to feel that there was a fair amount of wishful thinking here. Chaplin was Karno's established star, and perhaps Karno wanted to teach him a lesson by replacing him with his rawest new man. Still, it gave young Stanley the confidence that, one day, he could play the lead. But that day would be long in coming.

In *The Wow-Wows*, which played only four performances in England before being taken abroad, the character of Archie – the Honourable Archibald Binks – returns, this time as part of a whole slew of 'I say, confound you, old man' English 'swells', who decide their friend Archie is a proper bounder and should be taught a hard lesson. They decide to pretend to initiate him into a secret society, the Wow-Wows, torment him with their silly rites, and then unmask themselves. The piece is full of banter such as:

ARCHIE
I'm going to have a bath. I say, Jimmy, what have you for breakfast?

JIMMY
There's two eggs for you but they're quite rotten.

ARCHIE
What, that one bad and that one bad? That's too bad. I am a devil when I crack these little jokes.

Indeed you are. We are not sure which of the supporting idiots Stanley played, in this or the later scene in which the members of the supposed secret society dress in grotesque clothes and hoods to intone:

BRUNTON

Most high and mighty master, our abject slave No. 6 craves initiation of our order of Wow-Wows!

BOYS

(*Solemnly*) Wow wow!

BRUNTON

(*To Archie*) Say Yes! Yes!

ARCHIE

Yes! Yes!

It should have been no surprise, except to Karno himself, that the audiences for his new sketch, when it opened at the Colonial New York City, were not amused, and saw it rather as a 'collection of blithering blathering Englishmen', though Chaplin was still singled out for praise. Chaplin claims he had begged Karno not to play this sketch in America, but the Guv'nor, as usual, had his own way. *Variety*'s reviewer wrote, on 8 October:

Chaplin will do all right for America, but it is too bad that he doesn't appear in New York with something more in than this piece. The company amounts to little, because there is little for them to do . . . The genuine fun in *The Wow Wows* is not quite enough to stand off the half-hour of running time . . . The Colonial audience laughed at the show Monday night, but not enough. An act of this sort, erected solely for comedy, should register a bigger percentage of laughs . . .

In their third week in New York, Chaplin reported, the company played to an audience of English expatriate valets and butlers who laughed so hard the act picked up and got them a six-week booking on the minor Sullivan–Considine Midwest circuit. But the record seems to show that the Karno company remained in New York throughout the winter of 1910 honing the act and working to make *The Wow-Wows* funny. All this time Stan remained loyally in the shadows, playing his minor roles and frying bacon on the old gas ring. While Chaplin discovered the streets of New York, their

73

tumult and their vast contrasts of rich and poor, building up his intellectual assets in pursuit of his towering – if at that time elusive – ambitions, Stan settled down to be the trouper, to do his job with the team.

By January 1911, Karno had clearly realized that there was a limit to how funny his Wow-Wows could be in the eyes of an American audience, and changed the act for the cross-country tour his manager Alf Reeves had finally booked. Thus *A Night in a London Club* opened at the American Music Hall in Chicago on 30 January:

SHOW WORLD – FEB 4 1911:
FRED KARNO'S LONDON COMEDIANS
A Night in a London Club (pantomime farce)
American Music Hall, Chicago, Jan 30 1911
(place on bill – 11th in 15-act show)
Fred Karno's London Comedians began a three weeks' stay at the Music Hall with *A Night in a London Club, or the Amateur Entertainers*. The plan is to produce a different farce each week. There are ten men and three women in the company. The offering somehow suggests Dickens. Seeing it one is reminded of the gatherings of the Pickwick club. The caricatures of the individual members of the club are with a graveness that makes the comedy stand out. The comedy is rough but the characters are well drawn . . . Various members of the club are called upon to entertain. There is a woman singer who gets her key repeatedly but cannot strike it when she begins to sing, a precocious daughter of one of them, who offers a childish selection to the plaudits of admiring friends and among others an ambitious tragedian who, after reminding the master of ceremonies several times, is at length permitted to start a scene of a play, only to be interrupted by the 'drunk' (played by Charles Chaplin) which has come to be recognized as the leading comedy character of the Karno offerings. As seen Monday afternoon the only shortcoming of the farce was the lack of a big laugh at the finish.

Alf Reeves and the cast had segued Archibald and the 'swells' into a version of the ever-popular *Mumming Birds*. This was already familiar to American audiences since the first Karno company to tour the US, in 1905, presented it as *A Night at an English Music Hall*. Now it was revived full blown for the tour, which opened in March at the Empress Theater in Cincinnati. It moved back to Chicago, then played Milwaukee, and hit the Unique,

Minneapolis, and the Empress, Duluth, in a split week commencing 27 March. On 21 March 1911 a local Minneapolis newspaper reviewed the show thus:

ENGLISH MUSIC-HALL HUMOR

Broad English humor is very broad indeed. It smacks even more of the slapstick than our old friend, the burlesque comedian. Yet there are always moments of unexpectedness. Where the American would do the obvious thing, the Englishman does the unusual. Fred Karno's *Night in an English Music Hall*, now headlining at the Unique, is one of the funniest of all the skits. It is elaborately staged, showing several boxes and a miniature stage, with all the habitués of that place of entertainment. There is the inebriated swell, the fresh young chap from Eton, his dignified uncle, and then the typical turns – the topical extemporist, the ballad vocalist, the magician, the village choir singers, the saucy soubrette, and, finally, 'The Terrible Turk', the whole ending with a wild rough-and-tumble burlesque wrestling match. There is just enough of truth in the whole to make it entertaining, despite some far-fetched comedy and the fact that the company is not especially strong . . .

It is worth loitering a bit around this opinion, to look at the perceptions of the form of pantomime that Karno brought to America. Mime was as old an art in the US as in England, but, as elsewhere, most comedy was played in words. American vaudeville comedy was resolutely ethnic, leaning strongly on stereotypes ranging from Irish to Jewish, German, or the eternal black caricatures of Minstrel. Karno himself noted, on his first personal trip to New York, in 1906, addressing the assembled press:

This class of pantomime must not be confused with the spectacular pantomime such as has been produced in this country by large musical organizations, but is the outgrowth of circus-clown work. In my younger days I was a circus performer and conceived the idea of carrying the development of the 'dumb act' beyond the limited field of acrobats, trained animals and so on. I have been in this line now for about twelve years, and have achieved a success which has exceeded my most sanguine expectations. Although this is my first trip to America, and I am only going to remain about a month this time, it is by no means to be my last, and I intend to give American vaudeville audiences a line of entertainments entirely new to them.

I have discovered that, contrary to the prevalent idea in Europe, Americans are not slow to understand pantomime, but heretofore they have never had pantomime offered to them as a vehicle for real comedy, and I find that comedy is what they want. It was with this idea in my mind that I sent my A *Night in an English Music Hall* company over here about a year ago to play one month as an experiment. They have been here ever since, and are booked in the United States until next May. This certainly speaks for itself.

Karno was noted for the rigorous training he gave his actors in developing a sense of timing and pace. Some credit him with developing the famous 'take', the reaction, often delayed, of the comedian to some startling behaviour or event. Mime, however, as we have seen, was not a new art form. It is a moot point how much Karno himself had to do with the creative processes of his companies of actors and how much was due to unsung heroes. All histories, and archival texts, credit Fred Karno with the authorship of the sketches he produced. But nothing we know about Karno suggests a creative writer, or even a master of gags. Essentially he was an entrepreneur, who, like a very different impresario, Florenz Ziegfeld, in America, knew how to pick the right people and then enable them to give of their best. His major stars, Fred Kitchen, Harry Weldon, Billy Reeves, had a great deal to do with the way the sketches were played to the applauding public, and probably co-wrote their own lines. The great success of Karno's Speechless Comedians was an ensemble accomplishment, actors learning from each other. All this was fully acknowledged by Stan Jefferson, always ready with credit for his peers, as against Chaplin, who eagerly built his own myth as a *sui generis* genius. Even his costume, which derived from George Robey, Fred Kitchen, Little Tich and others, was claimed to have been adopted in an inspired accident in Mack Sennett's prop room.

Chaplin was to become, however, the primary conduit through which the Karno company's style of pantomime flowed into the bloodstream of American silent comedy, transmitting that peculiar 'unexpectedness' the reviewers of Karno's acts wrote about: 'Where the American would do the obvious thing, the Englishman does the unusual.' Where the American comedian exaggerated and lampooned real life, the English comedian explored the 'surreal' aspect we encountered with Dan Leno. Chaplin's tramp was not modelled on the way real tramps looked or acted, he was a type, a character developed out of old music-hall traditions. Chaplin adapted these with elegance, charm and finesse, and understood how the old characters could relate to the new medium, to the camera, in a completely new way. It was this that made Chaplin such a key figure in the history of both mime and the movies. Many of his followers, including Stan Jefferson, took a long time to discover their own relationship with the magic lens, how to make it reflect their emotions, their inner self, and their ideas.

ECFK – Everything Comes From Karno – may not be a mathematically provable theory – both Buster Keaton and Harold Lloyd found their own voice their own way – but one can see a quantum change in silent-film comedy before Chaplin's ascendancy in 1914–15 and after. Stan Jefferson, as he was to call himself in his American vaudeville life up to 1917, is a prime example of the difficulty any comedian had in moving out of Chaplin's shadow. Most of Stan's history, on stage and on screen, well into the mid-1920s, is the story of this process.

Back to 1911 – and the Karno company's continued tour on the Sullivan–Considine circuit. Much of the time they played split weeks – three days in one city and three in another – hopping from train to train, without respite. In April, from the Empress Duluth straight to the Bijou in Winnipeg, Canada. Then back across the border to the Majestic in Butte, Montana, the Washington Theater in Spokane, Washington, then to the Majestic, Seattle. Back across the border to Vancouver, Canada, then to the Grand in Victoria, British Columbia, and back to Tacoma and Portland Oregon. All this in less than two months.

Stan has not left us a detailed record of this period, but Chaplin's autobiography provides vivid vignettes. On staying in Chicago:

We lived uptown on Wabash Avenue in a small hotel. Although grim and seedy, it had a romantic appeal, for most of the burlesque girls lived there. In each town we made a bee-line for the hotel where the showgirls stayed, with a libidinous hope that never materialized. The elevated trains swept by at night and flickered on my bedroom wall like an old-fashioned bioscope . . . Chicago was full of [burlesque] shows, one called *Watson's Beef Trust* had twenty enormously fat middle-aged women displaying themselves in tights. Their combined weight went into tons, so it was advertised. Their photographs outside the theatre, showing them posing coyly, were sad and depressing . . .

And on going on the road:

Living was cheap. At a small hotel one could get room and board for seven dollars a week, with three meals a day. Food was remarkably cheap. The saloon free-lunch counter was the mainstay of our troupe. For a nickel one could get a glass of beer and the pick of a whole delicatessen counter. There were pig's knuckles, sliced ham, potato salad, sardines, macaroni, cheese and a variety of sliced sausages, liverwurst, salami and hot dogs. Some of our members took advantage of this and piled up their plates until the barman would intervene: 'Hey! Where the hell are you tracking with that load – to the Klondike?'

Shades of the café scene in Chaplin's *Modern Times* . . . The troupe did not end up in the Klondike, however, but in San Francisco, where, at the Empress, they wowed the audience for three weeks: 'The big draw was Fred Karno's *A Night at an English Music Hall*, which was one continuous scream of laughter' (*Billboard*, 24 June). The company then doubled back, across the Rockies, to Colorado. A surviving photograph in Chaplin's own collection shows him beside a dapper Stanley, standing in front of some rocks and under a sign saying 'CONTINENTAL DIVIDE – ELEVATION 6350 FEET ABOVE SEA LEVEL'. It was at this point, in Colorado Springs, so the tale is told, that not only the continent, but the group, divided, and Stan Jefferson and another trouper, Arthur Dandoe, decided to leave the company and head home. The story goes that the pace was so tough and the pay so low, given that periods of travel were not covered by salary, that both downed tools, as it were, and demanded a salary hike from Karno's manager, Alf Reeves. It was not forthcoming and so the two left, and headed back east. This is another one of these tales for which there is only Stan's account to rely on, but we can safely assume that the break was at the actors' initiative, as Stan was able to rejoin the Karno troupe later. We do know, however, that Stan Jefferson and Arthur Dandoe embarked on the liner *Lusitania* in New York, and travelled, steerage, back to Blighty.

CHAPTER NINE

Rum 'Uns a-Roamin'

Photographs of Stan Jefferson at this period show a young man, of smart appearance, rather handsome in fact, with hair slicked back and parted towards the left, confidently facing the world. He was quite a tall person. People assume Stan was small when he stood beside Ollie, but Oliver Hardy was a very large man, six foot one even in his carpet slippers.

Stan's early confidence, however, was to face a hard test on his return to England from the United States, in the late summer of 1911, with little money, and few prospects. Apart from the dispute over pay, Stanley never mentioned any other reason for leaving Karno's show so abruptly. But it is not difficult to see the uncertainty behind the dapper boy's assured front. Unlike Chaplin, he did not feel at this point that his future lay in America. He may well have felt simply homesick. Perhaps, too, he was still remembering the brief moment he had taken over from Chaplin back home, in *Jimmy the Fearless*, and his hope that he might be promoted up the Karno ladder to something better than a lowly supporting role in the cast was dashed by Chaplin's clear hegemony as the star of the show.

But no stardom awaited Stanley in England. Once again, we are in the realm of oral history: Stan and Arthur Dandoe developed a sketch, entitled *The Rum 'Uns from Rome*, and set themselves up as 'The Barto Brothers': 'Ridiculous Romans and Grotesque Gladiators – Barmicuss and Silicuss – an Original Broad Burlesque Absurdity – Brutus, the Only Filleted Horse in Existence, and Titus, the Famous Banana Eating Lion'.

The only description we have is from John McCabe:

The setting is a city square in Rome of the golden age. A column containing a trap door stands center stage near a dais. A comic two-man horse enters pulling a chariot. Stan is riding the horse in full Roman regalia, brass helmet, shield, and huge ax. Dandoe is represented as riding the chariot but actually walks it across stage with his feet showing below.

And so forth. We do not know how many performances were given or where this ramshackle event took place, but it appears to have made no dent in the listings (unless it mutated into something called 'The Two Britons', who appeared in a 'gladiatorial act' at the Empire, Hull, on 23 November 1911). Even A. J. Marriot, chronicler supreme of Stan's and Ollie's sojourns in Britain, has found no trace of the 'Rum 'Uns'. He quotes Stan as recalling, 'Then, like a couple of silly schoolgirls, Dandoe and I had a slight difference of opinion – and our partnership fizzled out . . . After that I was out of work for a year.' Which invites the question of what he did in that interim. All the signs are that Stan, already in his father's bad books for joining the music-hall, rather than the 'legitimate' theatre, remained away from the family home, determined to make his own way.

In 1912, A. J. Marriot reports, picking up the trail again, Stan joined a production named 'The Wax Works', and then re-formed the Rum 'Uns with a new partner, Ted Leo. Stan and Ted then joined another group of out-of-work actors, consisting of one Bob Reed, his wife, daughter and son, Jim, and a couple of other foot-loose youths. This group became 'The Eight Comicques'. In the spring of 1912 they set off for a Dutch tour, playing the Circus Variété in Rotterdam with a sketch called *Fun on the Tyrol*. This occurred in the week of 25 May, and non-stop rain on the tin roof was said to have disrupted their acting. Laurel and Hardy fan Bram Reijnhoudt, however, took the trouble to check the weather for that week in May 1912 and discovered that there had been no rain in Rotterdam. So much for memory. A temporary solo job as a funny waiter in Rotterdam, and an unverified gig at the Palace, Liège, saw the Eight Comicques wilting fast. Their act, reported to consist of the comedians walking on stilts with huge papier-mâché heads, did not amuse even the Belgian audience. This was the last straw, and Stan returned to England.

It was only at this point that Stan swallowed his pride and fell back on the Jefferson family. 'Tired, travel-stained, shabby', he turned up at the door of his brother Gordon's flat in High Holborn, having walked penniless from Waterloo station. Gordon had followed in old Arthur Jefferson's footsteps and was the manager of the Princes Theatre in London. Stan was taken in and given a small, unlisted part in the production of *Ben My Chree*, a nineteenth-century Manx family melodrama about two brothers who quarrel lethally over a girl, playing at the Princes from 3 to 7 July.

After five years on the stage, Stan seemed to have reached the point he had started from – unbilled bit parts in 'legitimate' plays. It appeared that he might have to sink into the family business and take up the managerial side of the theatre. A small item in the *Era*, on 3 August, reveals that another Jefferson offspring was now being groomed for the stage – Stan's sister Olga, Beatrice Jefferson, who, according to the piece,

has just completed her education on the Continent, and in obedience to the call of the blood she has embraced the stage as a career. She starts at the Grand Junction Theatre, Manchester, in the new play that Mr Walter Howard, the well-known dramatist and theatrical entrepreneur . . . Mr Howard has engaged her for a small part, but . . . she will also understudy . . .

In other words, she would proceed along the proper theatrical path as set by Dad, Arthur Jefferson.

In the event, nothing much was to become of sister Beatrice's stage career, and her big brother soldiered on his own way. Not for the last time, a deep dip in Stan's fortunes was followed by a stroke of good luck. At the end of July, Karno's Comedians' American touring group returned to England. Stan, as A. J. Marriot tells the tale, 'bumped into Alf Reeves . . . In Leicester Square, Reeves inquired of Stan, "What are you doing nowadays? Starring in the West End?", to which Stan quickly replied, "Starving in the West End, more like it."' On the spot, Reeves offered Stan his old Karno job back, and a place in the company's resumed US tour. They sailed again, on the SS *Oceanic*, on 2 October 1912.

Stan's homecoming disaster must have convinced him that, this time, his future did lie elsewhere. The autumn 1912 Karno tour opened at the Empress, Cincinnati, at the end of October. On 2 November the *Billboard* reported, of the show at the Empress: 'One of the best things ever seen at this house was Fred Karno's London Comedy Company in *The Wow Wows*, presented by Alf Reeves. Charles Chaplin, who assumes the role of a souse, is exceedingly funny.' Since there is no souse in *The Wow-Wows*, the company must have rehearsed and changed the original witless sketch to an amalgam with the usual *Night in a London Club*. This travelled along the Sullivan–Considine route from Seattle to Vancouver, Tacoma, Portland, and down to San Francisco at the end of January 1913. And on to Sacramento, San Diego, Salt Lake City, Denver, Pueblo and Colorado Springs. This time Stan stayed put at the Continental Divide, heading east, to the more prominent venues of Philadelphia and Washington DC. The new tour included some new members of the cast: Ted Banks, the nicely named Billy Crackles and Whimsical Walker, and a music-hall couple, Edgar and Ethel Hurley. Whimsical Walker, a famous Drury Lane clown, became ill in Seattle and stayed there. Several other members of the company were not well either, and, Chaplin wrote, the audience did not always get the jokes:

We were playing A Night in an English Music Hall during which a quartette renders a song in the most awful manner possible – the worse it is sung, the greater the fun . . . We had returned to the hotel and were compelled to listen to many uncomplimentary remarks. 'What do you think of the big act?' one Pennsylvania man asked another Pennsylvania man . . . 'Absolutely rotten,' snapped the other. 'Why,' he added, 'that quartette couldn't sing for four apples. In fact our local quartette could beat them in seven different ways!'

The legend goes that, when in Philadelphia, a telegram arrived for manager Alf Reeves which read: 'IS THERE A MAN CALLED CHAFFIN IN YOUR COMPANY OR SOMETHING LIKE THAT STOP IF SO WILL HE COMMUNICATE WITH KESSEL AND BAUMAN 24 LONG-ACRE BUILDING BROADWAY.' This was the historic summons for Charles Chaplin to join Mack Sennett's Keystone film company. Groucho Marx, who met Chaplin in Winnipeg during the tour that summer, claimed that Chaplin had told him he was being wooed by Sennett at $500 a week but was not sure the job would last. Nevertheless, in August, he wrote to his brother Sydney in England to confirm that he was taking the Keystone job, at $150 a week starting salary. 'They are very funny,' he wrote. 'They also have some nice girls ect.' Chaplin's spelling would improve with the years. But the nice girls were too good a prospect. In November, while the tour was still playing the Rocky Mountain Empresses, Chaplin left the Karno act for good.

Chaplin's desertion was the last straw for the Karno US company, though it soldiered on through the winter and into 1914, playing Kansas City, Philadelphia, Quebec and New York State, where it is last sighted on 9 May at Shea's Theater, Buffalo.

The reader will have noticed that our hero, Stan Jefferson, appears to be taking a back seat in the story of his own life, the tale being told through the records of others. This is inevitable, given the lowly position Stan was forced to take during both Karno tours of America. When Chaplin left, Stan nursed hopes that he might be chosen to replace him in the lead part. Stan himself told John McCabe:

The company proceeded to Philadelphia, our manager informing the Nixon–Nirdlinger people [the theatre owners] that Chaplin wasn't with the company any more but also advising them that I was equally as good as Chaplin. They didn't agree to this arrangement . . . It ended up with them agreeing to accept the contract if Karno would bring over from London the principal comedian from the London Karno company named Dan Raynor. He came, we opened, but the show was a flop, and after we played a couple of weeks, the contract was canceled and the troupe disbanded.

It is extremely unlikely, however, given the way the company functioned, that Stan would have been given the Chaplin role. But he felt, once again, humiliated and passed over. Given the economic circumstances, and his bad brush with poverty back home, it seems likely that Stan remained with the Karno troupe till at least the spring of 1914. It was at this point, logic suggests, that he joined up with two other Karno orphans, Edgar and Ethel 'Wren' Hurley, to try to market their own act. Stan recalled having a day's work, before that, 'doing a shadowgraph act called *Evolution of Fashion*, about a drunk in a café. It was almost like a movie – acting in shadow pantomime before a white screen.'

Appearing as a shadow before a screen is a good metaphor for Stan's situation at this time. For, as Chaplin rises, performing in thirty-four short films in 1914 alone, before decamping from Keystone to Essanay to appear in *His New Job*, *The Champion*, *A Jitney Elopement*, *The Tramp*, etc., which catapulted him to the status of a world star and icon, Stan Jefferson falls below the level at which the standard vaudeville route listings in the stage journals keep track of him, playing small halls in out-of-the-way places, and barely holding body and soul together.

In his recollections, decades later, in retirement from his great fame as Stan Laurel of Laurel and Hardy, he made light of those days: 'I wrote this act which I called *The Nutty Burglars*,' he told John McCabe. 'We produced it in Chicago and played there and around there for several months.'

Neither McCabe, nor the hordes of Laurel and Hardy zealot searchers, nor your humble author, have been able to find hair nor hide of the first version of this act in the archives, though it was said to have been labelled 'The Three Comiques'. A photograph of Stan and the Hurleys, Stan in crushed cap, tattered jacket, and a bag marked 'Waffles & Co., Berglars, Merders Dun', wielding a mallet and chisel, is reproduced in McCabe's *Mr Laurel and Mr Hardy*. The only archival sighting, in the listings of the *Billboard*, is on 13 June 1914: '4 Comiques' at Lake Nipmuc, Milford, Massachusetts. Who the fourth 'Comique' might have been is a mystery. Or it could be that this entry refers to some other group of comic unfortunates, plying their trade in the utter boondocks, scrabbling for survival in the lower depths of vaudeville, just one step up from amateur night.

These are, we can imagine, tough and toughening months for Stan. One character trait the young man no doubt carried from his father and from his Lancashire background was a stubborn determination to stick it out. If the London boy Chaplin could make it, so could he. 'I'm just as good as him' is a refrain that echoes through the later Laurel's amiable recollections. But, for the moment, there was also a blind spot. The moving pictures, which Arthur Jefferson had embraced so enthusiastically in their infancy, still did not appear to Stan Jefferson as the medium in which his future lay. He was still, 100 per cent, a son of the stage.

The Nutty Burglars, which was to serve Stan, in various permutations, for the next six years, was – we can be as sure as it is possible to be without documentary evidence – a version of Arthur Jefferson's missing 1908 sketch, *An Unwilling Burglar*. Stan and Edgar Hurley break into a house and are interrupted in their safecracking act by the maid, who doesn't believe they're the icemen. One of the burglars flirts with her while the other prepares a bomb to blow the safe. The bomb is thrown from hand to hand; it gets thrown offstage; explosion; cop enters (this may be the fourth 'Comique'); arrests them. End of sketch.

In Cleveland, John McCabe reports, a colleague, the illusionist Kalma, introduced them to two big-time booking agents, Claude

84

and Gordon Bostock. This led to a series of better bookings and a change in the title of the trio to 'Hurley, Stan and Wren', transformed into a more commercially viable act which would capitalize on the growing Charlie Chaplin craze. Bostock realized that Stan, who knew Charlie inside out, had understudied for him and could retrace his every gesture, was an ideal mimic. And he was English too – what could be better? They would call the act 'The Keystone Trio'. Edgar Hurley would imitate Chester Conklin and 'Wren' would be Mabel Normand, two other Keystone stars.

'The Keystone Trio' first appears in the annals at the Orpheum, Altoona, Pennsylvania, on 20 February 1915, and played Proctor's 125th Street Theater in New York on 3 April. Despite Stan's recollections that it was 'a bloody sensation', it did not register very highly in stage annals, although the *Albany Evening Journal* reported, when the act opened at the Proctor Theater in town on 16 April, that 'Mr Jefferson impersonates Charlie Chaplin to the letter.' The oral recollection has it that Edgar, wishing to play the Chaplin part, supplanted Stan in future performances and the act died the death of a thousand recriminations in Newark a short while later.

Despite the thought that any act might die in Newark, the record shows the Keystone Trio struggling on through October, when it again played a New York theatre, the American: 'The Keystone Trio: two men and a woman, in a comedy "burglar" set, went fair. The set depends mostly on the man doing Chaplin,' wrote the *Clipper*, on 9 October. Not a heart-tingling vote of confidence. The *Albany Evening Journal*, however, clocking in to confuse us, reports on 2 October that, again at the local Proctor's, an act called the 'Stan Jefferson Trio will present a comedy skit called *The Nutty Burglars*'. Same show, same act, but under different headings, in two places at once – both booked for the entire week in question.

What seems to have happened, as Stan told John McCabe, was that Edgar Hurley had replaced him in the act with another fellow Karno fall-out, Ted Banks. The bookers soon discovered the act had been changed, and dumped it. The record shows that the Keystone Trio, presumably without Stan, continued touring, playing the Colonial, Logansport, Indiana, on 16 October 1915, followed by Topeka, Kansas, in November, and ending up at the Majestic, Houston, on 13 December, sharing the bill with 'Miss

U.S.A.' and 'The Sultanas'. Then it disappears off the lists, thus verifying Stan's tale.

For the next eighteen months, Stan Jefferson vanishes from recorded history, a period that reflects his continuing tale of woe, masked by rose-tinted memories.

In the autumn of 1915, the story goes, in Toronto, the Keystone Trio had shared the stage with another husband-and-wife act, Alice and 'Baldy' Cooke. Alice was of a veteran show-business family, as her father had been a noted circus press agent and a manager of Buffalo Bill Cody's *Wild West Show*. She had married Baldwin Cooke and gone on the road with him together with her sister and another young man. By 1915 their quartet had become a duo. The account of their new alliance with Stan relies on the recollections of Alice Cooke, who lived to a grand old age, as related in one version to John McCabe and in another to Stan biographer Fred Lawrence Guiles.

The gist of Alice's tale to Guiles was that, rather than being dumped by the Hurleys, Stan dumped them, having become dis-illusioned with their demands and their talents. As Stan was later to 'dump' the Cookes, Guiles concluded that

We are faced with a hero of shifting loyalties, whose eye was on the main chance and whose nimble feet were moving heedlessly over a number of dead bodies. Some of the same callousness that stained Chaplin's character throughout his career had crept into Stan as well.

The reader might note the many angles from which one might watch the same event and see different things. We might reflect that, if Stan were a ruthless schemer, he would hardly have been appearing with Edgar and Ethel Hurley in the also-featured list at Toronto in the first place. The more likely picture is of a drowning man clutching at straws.

Alice Cooke remembered the venue of their meeting, when inter-viewed by John McCabe, as Saint Thomas, Ontario, and Stan's split with the Hurleys occurring some months later, which, given the Albany sighting, sets the meeting back to the late spring of 1915. 'We all got together to do our own three-act,' she said,

the Stan Jefferson Trio . . . I think we were the three happiest people in the world, doing that act . . . We rented a darling cottage near the Atlantic Highlands in New Jersey. Stan wrote an act which he called *The Crazy*

Cracksman, and we rehearsed hard every day and had it ready for our fall showing which Claude Bostock, brother of Gordon, Stan's old agent, got for us.

Alice's tale as related by Fred Lawrence Guiles is more colourful, a picture of offstage saloons and hard drinking. Baldy, it was said, had a high capacity for the sauce, and Stan's name for Mrs Cooke was 'Alice, the Bar Fly'. He too took to the libation, and much merriment ensued into the night hours.

As they say, seeing is believing. The myopic researcher, poring over the documents, can only state that the 'Stan Jefferson Trio' registered even lower than 'The Three [or Four] Comiques' on the Richter scale, achieving not a single mention in the stage bibles – *Variety*, the *Billboard* or the *Clipper*. Presumably it played all the usual boondocks. One does wonder why, given this apparent dead end, Stan did not throw in the towel and return home to England. But this would have been only to risk the fate of all eligible young men, subjects of King and Country, who might be marked for slaughter in the trenches.* The boondocks were the better option, and this was still America, land of opportunity. And thus, *Variety* informs us, on 27 April 1917, another new act kicks into being: at the Hippodrome, San Diego, 'S. & M. Laurel'. A week later, at the Hippodrome, Los Angeles, a second-rate theatre playing continuous vaudeville from 1 p.m. to 11 p.m. every day (matinees, 10 cents; evenings, 15 cents), the *Los Angeles Times* logged: 'Other bright features of the bill will be Stan Laurel – regarded as the only legitimate imitator of Charlie Chaplin – and Mae Laurel, in *Raffles, the Dentist*, one of the laughing hits of the season.'

A new act, and a brand new name, though the notice quoted above suggests it has been on the go for some time. Somewhere along the cheesy route of the lower depths of variety, fate had intervened, yet again, in the shape of a somewhat husky and vivacious Australian woman, named Charlotte Mae Dahlberg. According to Alice Cooke, she had been appearing in an act called 'The Hayden Sisters', of which, too, no trace can be found. Dahlberg was her maiden name; legally she was Charlotte Mae Cuthbert, having left a husband behind in the Antipodes. By the spring of 1917, just

* I am grateful to A. J. Marriot for relieving my myopia in this regard.

after the United States entered the First World War in Europe, Stan Jefferson had changed both partners and monikers, becoming the Stan Laurel whom we know from then on. And then, within a few weeks, another earth-shaking change was noted: the first appearance by Stan Jefferson in a short moving picture, co-starring Mae Dahlberg, shot in Hollywood, California, entitled *Nuts in May* . . .

CHAPTER TEN

Babe: 'All Broken Out with the Movies'

> Jacksonville is all broken out with the movies. The whirring of
> cameras resounds over the state like the humming of locusts,
> and the wails of directors when the sun goes under a cloud
> fairly rattles the windows for miles around . . . It is an empty
> train, indeed, that brings no star and her cortège to 'Jax' as the
> people who live in Jacksonville call it. And Jax takes good care
> of them too.
> Quoted in *Journal of Popular Film and Television*, fall 1980

The movie companies that came to Florida in the first decade of the
twentieth century found a congenial country and almost year-
round sunshine closer to the financial hubs of New York and
Chicago than the growing colony in California. Many production
companies had offshoots that toured and opened branches in
various locations. The Kalem company had come to Florida from
New York in 1908, and was the first to open a studio in
Jacksonville, which at that time was the largest city in the state, the
south-east's main financial and manufacturing centre. The city lay
by the wide St John's River, with many scenic opportunities near
by, from the Okefenokee swamp just over the state line in Georgia
to the forests in the south-west and the sandy beaches to the east.
The Kalem crews, led by director Sydney Olcott, settled in
Roseland House, a small boarding hotel, and began shooting the
first 'Sunny South' pictures. These one-reelers were popular and
profitable, and other film companies soon followed suit. The Selig
company arrived and set up shop in 1910. The Lubin company's
principal director, Arthur Hotaling, first shot films in Florida in
1909, and the head of the company, Siegmund Lubin, sent him
back to establish a more permanent branch in the autumn of 1912.
By 1914 it was claimed that there were more movie units making
pictures in Jacksonville than in Los Angeles, and Lubin's southern
operation was producing 4,000 feet of film – four one-reel films –

per week. This was the company the newly married Oliver 'Babe' Hardy joined in the spring of that year.

The Lubin company was a prominent example of the kind of film studio that was flourishing in the days before Griffith's epic *Birth of a Nation* of 1915 and other 'feature-length' films transformed the movies into the industry we know today as Hollywood. Lubin's operation was industrial enough. The company's main, purpose-built studio, nicknamed 'Lubinville' and completed in 1910 in north Philadelphia, was an extraordinary achievement. Like the other studios of the period it was a greenhouse, but on a grand scale, with special prism glass to diffuse the sunlight that would be the primary source for even the indoor cameras. The electrical lighting, to aid shooting on cloudy days, was state of the art, with over a hundred four-foot mercury-vapour tubes and twenty large arc lights. Special machine shops manufactured and maintained the cameras on site; the property rooms were vast warehouses; the processing laboratories could turn out 1.5 million feet of film a week, and dozens of women worked at the assembly benches editing the exposed films. This was a factory that, by 1912, boasted some of the most progressive labour practices in the country, maintaining a cafeteria with free lunches, seeing to the workers' health and safety, and encouraging special Lubin athletic teams. By 1915 the factory had over seven hundred employees.

All this was the dream-child of a German Jewish immigrant who settled in Connecticut in 1876, married, and travelled as a maker and salesman of eyeglasses. Siegmund Lubszynski set up a business in Philadelphia as 'Prof. S. Lubin, Eye Doctor and Optician' in the 1880s, under the slogan: 'The eye is the mirror of the soul.' By the early 1890s he had an optical factory, and in 1895 his scientific curiosity in the field of lenses led him to the Atlanta Exposition and the 'Projecting Phantoscope' of two ingenious inventors, C. Francis Jenkins and Thomas Armat. By 1896, this machine was being marketed by the Edison company, as the 'Edison Vitascope', and the original inventors were forgotten. By 1897, Siegmund Lubin was marketing the Lubin 'Cineograph and Stereopticon Combined', which you could buy, with four demonstration films, for just $100. A list of 1,000 film titles was available for projection by May of that year. Lubin's first films were images of his horse, a passing train, and an indoor pillow fight between his daughters. But he soon found it cheaper simply to copy Edison's own films and sell them as his own. This did not please Edison, and was the beginning of major rivalry between the competing pioneers.

In 1901, Lubin advertised that 'Life-Motion pictures may be given in your drawing room by yourself. A rubber hose attached to the gas burner will operate my new CINEOGRAPH, specially adapted . . . A child can operate this machine.' (Reader, do not try this in your own home.) Lubin specialized in short films of re-enacted real events, such as *Beheading the Chinese Prisoner* set during the Boxer Rebellion of 1900. *The Dreyfus Court Martial Scene* was another example. Of such stumbling beginnings was the twentieth century's greatest art form born. A special gallery for producing these pictures followed, and then, even before the age of the nickelodeon dawned, special Lubin theatres in Philadelphia. By 1909 Lubin was one of the major participants in the Motion Picture Patents company, who met to sew up the growing picture business.

Lubin's operation was markedly oriented towards technicians, rather than creative artists. He knew that he had to have actors and artists to design and prepare the costumes and sets. But for a long time he clung to the belief that the important thing in cinema was the person who physically shot the film – the cameraman. The actors, or the director, were just like everyone else in the factory, cogs in the wheel. Unable to ignore the developments in the rest of the industry, such as Griffith's increasingly bold work at Biograph, Lubin reluctantly decided that real talent had to be paid for with real money, and set about recruiting experienced actors and actresses from the stage. The director's work began to be properly recognized. One of the earliest of Lubin's collaborators was Arthur Hotaling, who had worked with him since 1897, as projectionist and all-round doer of things. By 1912 Hotaling had become Lubin's senior director, and was chosen to run the Jacksonville, Florida, arm of the empire. This was the man who would produce all the films featuring Lubin's new 1914 recruit, Oliver Norvell Hardy.

On 21 April 1914, the Lubin Company released *Outwitting Dad*. Produced and directed by Arthur Hotaling, it featured Billy Bowers, Frances Ne Moyer, Raymond McKee and O. N. Hardy. Hardy played Reggie, whose brother Bob wants to marry his sweetheart Lena but her Dad doesn't approve. Bob comes up with a wheeze to disguise Reggie as a gun-totin' desperado so he can scare Dad and lock him in the stable, while Bob and Lena rush off to get married. But Reggie falls asleep at the stable door, and when Dad sneaks out and discovers his real identity, he gives Reggie a beating, then goes to beat up Bob but meets the newlyweds coming out of the church. Lena's tearful pleas win the old man over. The End.

The *New York Dramatic Mirror*'s review of this film concluded, 'Overacted at times, and not especially funny, this offering begins the reel with *The Rube's Duck*.' This refers to the custom of the 'split reel', i.e. two films contained in the same twelve to fifteen minutes (depending on projection speed), which means the movie was pretty brief.

Rob Stone, stubborn chronicler of Laurel's and Hardy's solo films, reports on the rumours of a previous Hardy film, shot by director C. Jay Williams for the Edison company late in 1913. The Edison studios were across the river from Lubin, and Ollie might have tried his luck there, possibly during his first time round in Jacksonville. There is, however, no actual evidence that such an early film featuring Hardy ever existed.

Moving Picture World was not impressed with *Outwitting Dad* either, deeming it 'a comedy that's about on the par with the also-rans of the pioneer days of animated pictures'. But Oliver Hardy, the movie actor, had been born.

The film has not survived, as is the case with most of the staggering number of 270 short films Oliver Hardy appeared in without Stan Laurel. Only about one hundred of these are extant. The silent cinema was, to the studios, an expendable element, and thousands of feature films, let alone short subjects, were either allowed to rot or literally melted down for their materials even before sound came to sweep them away. Zealous – at times fanatic – detective work by archivists and historians, collecting forgotten prints from the Yukon Territory to Prague, has uncovered many lost treasures, some of which have survived in amazingly clear prints while others look as if they have been dragged through a mincing machine after having been recopied in amateur film labs. Of the Lubin films, only a handful survive in any decent shape, as periodic fires in the Lubin vaults depleted the inventory. Most exist only as summaries in Lubin's Film Bulletins and a selection of stills.

Early film antics of 'Babe' Hardy – a primal scream?

A typical exemplar would be *They Bought a Boat*, written by J. A. Murphy, released on 15 August 1914, and described in the Bulletin thus:

Jack Burns and Billy Hale buy a motor boat. Swelled with the importance of ownership, they invest in uniforms and engage a cabin boy weighing three hundred pounds. They are about to make a trial when the Government Inspector warns them that they are lacking in necessary equipment, such as life preservers, fire apparatus, fog horns, lights, etc. They buy enough equipment to sink a battleship and when it is all loaded on it comes near to swamping the boat. They put 'out to sea', however, and their friends watch them from the shore. The boat leaks and a panic ensues. They try to bail the water out with tin cups while the cabin boy puts the pump hose overboard and pumps water into the boat. They yell loudly for 'Help.' An old sailor wades out to see what is the matter and tells them they are aground in ten inches of water and had better walk ashore.

CAST
Captain Burns – Roy Byron
Captain Hale – C. W. Ritchie
Government Inspector – Ed Lawrence

Ancient Mariner – James Levering
Jack Kedge – Billy Bowers
Cabin Boy – Babe Hardy

'Babe' was the name Oliver now adopted for most of his Florida films. Although Roscoe Arbuckle might have revelled in the name 'Fatty', it was certainly not one by which Hardy wished to be even temporarily hoist. Our Milledgeville historians report that old witnesses remember being told to see one of the Lubin films because the local boy, 'Fatty' Hardy, was in it.

These Lubin one-reelers or split-reelers followed each other in rapid succession, one per week, sometimes one every four or five days. *Casey's Birthday, Building a Fire, He Won a Ranch, For Two Pins, The Particular Cowboys, A Tango Tragedy, A Brewertown Romance* – all take us barely into June 1914. Ollie plays a cop in four of the above, one of the cowboys in two, and 'person at dance'. Many of the stories were written by one Epes Winthrop Sargent, a columnist for *Moving Picture World*, whose scripts revelled in easy stereotypes and ethnic caricatures. One of his dubious masterpieces, *He Wanted Work* (August 1914), roped Babe Hardy – playing the foreman – into a tale of a black man who dresses up as an Irishman to get work but is found out when a hose is turned on him, and is chased off. This was one of a series of thirty 'Colored Comedies', directed by Arthur Hotaling, caricaturing blacks as happy-go-lucky idiots. The Irish, for Sargent and Hotaling, were violent drunks, the Italians sex-crazed buffoons, the Germans beery dummkopfs, and so on. Hotaling is also credited, by Lubin expert Joseph P. Eckhardt, with introducing the stereotype of the black mammy, later humanized by actress Hattie McDaniel in *Gone with the Wind* and other classics, to the American screen.

Whatever his views on the prevailing racist ethos, which are demonstrated by his own marriage, Oliver Norvell Hardy kept them to himself, and embraced any and every character that he was called on to play. Cop, cook, cowboy, grocer boy, sailor, jailbird, bartender, outraged father, unlikely lover, hotel boy, giant baby, even women's roles in traditional drag – all were grist to the mill of the movie-struck young man. By November 1914 the popularity of his presence, even in minor roles, was noted by Lubin in advertising that stated, after a list of titles: 'Babe Hardy, the funniest fat comedian in the world, is in all these subjects. – He's a fair knockout.'

The first full extant Oliver Hardy film that we can see is *The Servant Girl's Legacy*, released on 28 November 1914, produced and directed by Arthur Hotaling with a script by the ubiquitous Sargent. This is a 'split-reel' short, with Mabel Paige as Mandy Spragg, the servant girl, and Babe Hardy as Cy, the gardener, who loves her. He enters frame left, as she sits on the step of a mansion, peeling potatoes into a pan. He sidles up to her, almost popping out of his shirt and pants, smiling under his cloth cap. This is Oliver near his maximum weight, carrying nearly three hundred pounds by now, far larger than he will be at his time at Roach. He whispers in the servant girl's ear, but she empties the pan of water on to his head. Shoving him back to his garden, she pushes him down and kicks him in the bum. The postman brings her a telegram, which says: 'YOU INHERIT UNCLE'S ENTIRE FORTUNE. WILL WIRE AMOUNT WHEN SCHEDULES ARE COMPLETE, JAMES DOUGLAS, EXECUTOR.' She throws the pan out again in her joy, once more hitting Hardy on the head. He still pleads his case, getting down on his knees, but gets laughed at. Meanwhile, the young blades who have been out with the mansion's two gals in their motor car return to find Mabel slacking on the veranda, reading a magazine. She shows them her telegram, and the girls lend her clothes and a hat to go shopping.

Cy appears again, this time uncomfortably clad in an ill-fitting suit with a tiny waistcoat stretched to bursting over his tummy and a tiny hat, a 'boater', perched on his head. He brings flowers but is rejected again. He looks woeful, and gulps, the first view of that Ollie gulp when things are not going too well. Meanwhile the young swells have seen another telegram for Mandy, stating that she has only inherited $25. They mock her and send her back to work. Nevertheless Cy woos her as she beats a carpet, only to get whacked for his pains. But Mandy relents and admits she loves him after all. Delighted, he puts a ring on her finger. The postman arrives again, with a third telegram that reveals the previous sum was a mistake, the inheritance is $250,000. The young men gather round to woo her, but she chooses Cy – and they embrace.

Ollie, at twenty-two, is already set up for on-screen rejection, a rube who doesn't know when he's licked. He perseveres. For the first time we can see a trait that will be built on much later – the eternal attempt to maintain his dignity. He straightens the hat on his head with an instinctive gesture that we shall come to know. Already his acting is a little more restrained than that of his fellow actors, particularly the gesticulating Mabel Paige. The endearing clumsiness is apparent, although he indulges in some rural spitting which has lost its charm for our day and age.

While Stan Jefferson learned his techniques from the stage, Oliver Norvell Hardy, from the start, learned from the camera. The one favours and responds to the audience, the other to an intangible sense of distance and space from the lens and the artificial proscenium that different focal lengths and camera position relative to the actors creates, which is, to use a current term, 'virtual'. The stage actor has the dimensions of his platform, its physical restrictions and limitations. The camera, which can be set anywhere, appears to set no limits, but imposes strictures nevertheless. Lubin and other pioneers might have known only a crude set of options compared to the practically unlimited ways in which today's cinema relates to actors, space and the very bounds of reality, but it was a magic world none the less. Its characters, though taken from life, were larger than life, more like the newspaper cartoons and funnies than anything then known on the stage.

It should be noted that both in England and America, any kid growing up at the turn of the century would know the comic strips of the newspapers such as the 'Happy Hooligan' or Britain's 'Comic Cuts' magazine. 'Mutt and Jeff' premièred in print in 1907, Windsor MacCay's 'Little Nemo' in 1905 and George Herriman's bizarre 'Krazy Kat' made his début in 1913. Most of these fed into animated cartoons, and their ethos was part of popular consciousness in an age of frenzied change. Oliver Hardy himself recalled, in later years, that he modelled his on-screen persona on a cartoon character popular in his youth, which he named as 'Helpful Henry', who got into scrapes by trying to help people. There was no such cartoon character, but the description fits the Hearst-syndicated Happy Hooligan, who, in one 1905 strip, gets into trouble as he tries to catch a lady's muff which has fallen from the gallery of the British House of Lords, only to land on top of the speaker who happens to be lauding 'Our American Brothers', causing a ruckus and ending up in the Tower of London.

By 1915 Roscoe 'Fatty' Arbuckle was established at Keystone as the screen's most popular comedian next to Chaplin, often in collaboration with Keystone's third great asset, Mabel Normand. The flirtatious fat man had been a comedy staple since John Bunny, we might recall. Fat or thin, or shaped like a shoehorn or whatever, these were great times to be in comedies.

There was no looking back for 'Babe' Hardy. *He Wanted His Pants, Dobs at the Shore, The Fresh Air Cure, Weary Willie's Rags* (December 1914 to January 1915) – the titles evoke the spirit of anything goes at Lubin's. Babe would star, support, or just appear in a flash – in *They Looked Alike*, a tale of two interchangeable tramps who enrage a bamboozled cop, he is simply a man walking in the park who is entangled and brought down by the chase, a sequence of just ten seconds. In *Spaghetti and Lottery* (released on 16 January 1915), he is a cook in an Italian restaurant who prepares a big dish of spaghetti for Antonio and Pasquale, who throw it at each other and the customers. In the next film, released three days later, *Gus and the Anarchists*, he is 'Tom Dreck' the owner of a seedy café, presumably the previous restaurant with lingering spaghetti stains. Nothing goes to waste in Papa Sig's factory. Only *They Looked Alike*, of the above films, has survived.

Another extant film of this period, *Shoddy the Tailor*, has Babe as one of a Keystone-like group of cops whose clothes are stolen by a tailor with a grudge against them for beating him up for flirting with one of their girlfriends. This leads to an excellent intertitle: 'Girls go out! The officers have no clothes!' The cops, who are drunk and generally incapacitated, salute their commanding officer by placing their thumbs to their noses. Babe loses his pants, for one of the first times but certainly far from the last time in his career. The tailor, having hidden the policemen's clothes in a well, has his revenge, as they all dive into it in the finale. Law enforcement was never so shriven.

Soon after this film was released, in February 1915, Lubin closed his Jacksonville studio. The home operation, in Philadelphia, was in fact growing, and Lubin recalled producer–director Arthur Hotaling to direct a new series of comedies starring ex-Karno comedian Billy Reeves, the original *Mumming Birds* drunk. During 1915 and 1916 the company released a further twenty shorts featuring Babe Hardy that had already been shot. These included another extant, surviving title, *A Lucky Strike*, in which Oliver Hardy (so billed) is a miner who puts an ad in the paper for a young lady to correspond with: 'object – matrimony'. As he sends out the ad, a dream sequence finds him in a palatial residence, with wife and kids around him. Two women in the city, aunt and niece, are amused by the ad and decide to play a trick, answering it in the name of their cook, Nora. Meanwhile Oliver has another reason to go to the city, as he is negotiating to sell his mine to a big company. He arrives with flowers to his correspondent's home to press his suit, and the ladies persuade Nora to pose as the bride-to-be. Oliver's performance has subtlety and charm, as he delicately picks the right chair to sit in. There is already the awareness of how small gestures have a significance the camera will notice. When the mine owners turn up with their offer of a million dollars for his mine, the tricksy ladies almost faint, and reveal to him that it was they who responded to his ad. Nora slumps back into the kitchen, but Ollie follows her, seeing a pie on the table and sampling it. 'Did you make this pie?' he asks. Nora nods coyly. He embraces her, as the two rejected ladies faint in each other's arms.

A number of Lubin's Florida crew, including Babe, leading man Raymond McKee and director Will Louis, travelled to New York, expecting the suspension of the Jacksonville operation to be a temporary break. McKee and Louis, soon realizing that this was not the case, joined the Edison company in New York, while Babe headed back to Florida. From March to May he spent time with Madelyn, and may have looked for work with other Jacksonville companies. In New York, McKee and Louis were given the running of a subsidiary Edison production unit to make their own comedies. Babe and Madelyn travelled to New York but Babe appeared in only four short films for Edison. In one of them, *Clothes Make the Man*, a vehicle for Raymond McKee, he appears, of all things, as a black janitor, Rastus, who takes the lead's pants down to the tailor's. In the next film, *The Simp and the Sophomores*, Hardy plays a boxing instructor who beats up his students. Clearly McKee was not allowing his colleague much leeway.

Babe's next berth was with the brothers Leopold and Theodore Wharton, two more Edison refugees who had begun to make films for the Pathé company. He participated, again in minor parts, in four episodes of a series called the *New Adventures of J. Rufus*

Wallingford, a film version of a popular Hearst newspaper serial, starring Burr McIntosh. A still from the second of these shows Babe in a traditional clown's make-up and costume. In the last he plays a luckless burglar. There follows a pot-pourri of New York films shot in locations such as Flushing and Yonkers. *Ethel's Romeos* was shot for Gaumont/Mutual at about the same time (October 1915) that W. C. Fields was making his second Gaumont/Mutual short, *His Lordship's Dilemma*, raising the intriguing thought of an early, unchronicled, crossing of paths. Neither Fields nor Hardy made much headway with this company. *Fatty's Fatal Fun*, filmed for the highly obscure Mittenthal Film Company (directed by Unknown, story by Unknown, notes the zealous Rob Stone with unabashed thoroughness) at least gave Babe a starring part as a practical joker whose friends decide to play a joke on him on his wedding day – kidnapping and dressing him as the 'wild man' who has been reported to have escaped from the circus. The *New York Dramatic Mirror* said, 'Fatty is married while still garbed only in a small piece of fur and a smile.'

Babe's next film, *Something in Her Eye*, produced and written by more unknowns for the obscure Novelty/Mutual Film Corporation, has become the best preserved of Oliver Hardy's early films due to a 35mm print being discovered in 1984 in the cellar of an English collector. A woman who has been choked with dust from a building site wanders about winking uncontrollably at the men she comes across. One, an intellectual type, is seen reading a large book marked 'IBSEN'. Another is a man about town who climbs out of his car to woo her, and the third is Babe Hardy, a grocer, who throws off his apron and rushes after her. Much mayhem ensues between the suitors and the girl's father, followed by a fist fight for her hand which Babe would win easily had his rival not put a crab in his pants. Nevertheless, the girl decides he is her man.

Rob Stone comments about this film, 'While Babe generally disliked New York City, he must have found some agreement with the local cuisine since he is considerably heavier in this comedy than he had been earlier in the year while at Lubin.'

The legend that Babe disliked the Big City and yearned for Florida and the South can be only partly true, as his next major career move still occurred within the New York companies. Another one-off film, *The Crazy Clock Maker*, saw Hardy working in

99

another small role for Louis Burstein's Wizard Comedies. These featured a duo, 'Pokes and Jabbs' – Bobby Burns and Walter Stull – who had first appeared for Lubin. Apart from other ex-Lubin actors such as Mabel Paige (the 'servant girl') and Billy Bowers, this vanished film put Hardy beside Charlie Ritchie, another ex-Karno trouper. But Louis Burstein, a veteran producer by then, had grander plans, and was about to form a new company, to shoot films in a revamped studio in Bayonne, New Jersey. The company was to be called Vim Comedies, and, in an irony of fate, it would relocate, early in 1916, back to the same studio lot vacated by Lubin a year earlier, in Jacksonville, Florida.

The South was not yet through with Babe Hardy.

CHAPTER ELEVEN

Vim and Vigour – or Straddling the Home Plates

Babe Hardy made sixty-five films at Vim, between November 1915 and March 1917. An average of one film per week, of which, again, only a handful are extant. They flash by us like blurs, these ephemeral chimeras, with their strange antics and grotesque characters, artefacts of a frenetic age. Who was the projectionist at the Electric Theater in Milledgeville who took over from Norvell Hardy, and watched the bouncing energy of the town's fat boy making his mark on the world? There is no trace of any homecoming visit, any attempt by the boy who once sweated on the parade ground of Georgia Military College to flaunt his fame before his teenage companions, or his family. We know only that his mother Emily moved, at an unspecified date, to Atlanta, to be near her daughter-in-law, Elizabeth Sage.

John McCabe reports, of Babe's and Madelyn's return to Jacksonville, that she became the director of a ragtime orchestra at the Burbridge Hotel Cabaret, where Babe joined her in the evenings to resume his singing with a quartet, variously named 'The Twentieth Century Four', 'The Half Ton of Harmony', or under the old moniker of 'The Ton of Jollity', presuming that the three other partners were as well fed. The Hardys stayed, with the rest of the Vim troupe, at the Atlantic Hotel, a moderately priced apartment complex in the town. After adopting Babe junior, their doggie, they also acquired Babe III, a capuchin monkey. The space for real babies was rapidly disappearing. One thing missing in the account of this second sojourn in Florida is any mention of contact with Emily Norvell-Hardy-Tant-Jackson, or her children in Georgia. One might deduce that Madelyn Hardy was still not persona grata with 'Miss Emmie'. But Babe was now very much his own man, and more confident both in work and play, as an unsourced cutting from this period, in Hardy's second wife Myrtle's scrapbook, reveals:

PLAY BALL: SOME BASEBALL LIKE FATHER USED TO PLAY
*Will happen today at Barr's Field at 2 o'clock – The Grudge Participators
Will Be the Gaumont-Vim Movie Actor Men, and I Understand They Are
Going to Fight it Out Some How –*

They will have two umpires, one for each team, and Dominick Mullaney
will be the head of the trio. Inasmuch as every base will have a sandbag, I
expect to see some extra slugging just the same . . . The admission is
NOTHING, which is very reasonable to all concerned . . . I didn't get much
detail on the line-up of the game but one big feature I know of and that
will be 'Babe Hardy'. He's going to act as shortstop. Personally, I don't
think they could have selected a better man for that position. I know there
won't be any balls passed while he's at his post. I guess you know the width
of 'Babe'. I understand he can straddle first, second, third and home plates.
What chance is there for any ball to pass? . . .

Trusting it will be a very close game – say 44 to 45.

Oh, somewhere bands are playing, and somewhere hearts are light.
Somewhere men are laughing, and somewhere children shout, but there is
no joy in Mudville, mighty Casey has struck out.

This local column is signed, 'with much anxiety . . . GOLDY',
whoever he or she might have been.

Another local cutting in the scrapbook, also unsourced and undated, gives us a rare eyewitness view of the Vim crew at work in Jacksonville's streets:

MOVIES CAUSE A STIR WITH SHOTS

. . . [spec]tators in [illegible] saw a man leap – the fire escape of the Waverly Hotel quickly followed by two others, one a colored porter. It did not take long for a big crowd to gather as the excitement kept up at fever heat for several thrillers, they being put on by the Vim Photoplay Company.

Babe Hardy, the big boy of the Vim Company, was the hero who made the daring leap, while onlookers gazed with abated breath expecting to see some terrible tragedy, which resulted in real comedy when the true situation was realized. The scene was pulled off in realistic form and when the erstwhile boarder re-entered the hotel by means of the fire escape, the crowd gave approval by their applause of the excellent execution of the scene which will be another 'Made in Jacksonville' feature to be produced by the Vim Company.

Other loose cuttings suggest that Hardy was presenting himself in Jacksonville as 'an Atlanta boy', omitting Milledgeville from his biography completely, although the anonymous reporter who described him thus had an interesting take on his subject's chronology: 'Babe Hardy, prize heavyweight comedian with Vim comedies . . . His unique sense of humor, which used to make his comedy work the feature of a local quartette, has lost nothing in its transmission on to the screen.' Either a case of journalistic confusion or verification of a previous Hardy sojourn in Jax.

Much talk of Babe's famed generosity at this time filtered through old memories, as fellow trouper Bert Tracy, English-born actor, assistant director and gag man, remembered, 'He spent more money on more damned deadbeats than anyone you ever heard of. He was the original Mr Soft Touch.' Lucille Hardy, too, recalled tales of old-timers who told her how Babe had helped them out when work was scarce.

Jacksonville was good to Babe Hardy, at last a citizen of standing at the age of twenty-four, and standing on his own two, formidable feet. The Vim crew and actors maintained a friendly, family-like atmosphere, and functioned in a less industrial manner than was the case at Papa Lubin's lot. He retained his fond memories of this period, as his prompt reply, in 1934, to a fan letter from a Mr Halle Cohen, of Cohen Department Store, Jacksonville, Florida, from Culver City, can show:

Dear Halle,
Received your letter of June 15, this morning, and I was awfully happy to know that my old friend, whom I have never forgotten, still thinks of me.

I don't know when I will find time to get down that way, although I often think of and wish that I could be there again. Even though I am in California, my heart is in Florida as the best times of my life were spent in Jacksonville . . .

I appreciate your offer to spend a few days with you, and in the event I do come, I am going to accept. Please write me when you find time and tell me more about yourself. In other words, don't be so damned formal!
   Your friend

                                                          OLIVER HARDY

The first pictures Babe Hardy made at Vim in Florida were continuations of the 'Pokes and Jabbs' comedies developed by Louis Burstein in New Jersey. In most of these one-reelers a diminutive, unhandsome comic named Billy Ruge featured as a character called 'Runt'. Babe's role in many of these films was, unsurprisingly, 'Fatty'. It was only a matter of time before the old itch of producing double acts would team them together, and this occurred in a film entitled *This Way Out*, released in January 1916. Bobby Burns and Walter Stull, as 'Pokes' and 'Jabbs', still starred, but Babe and Billy Ruge were prominent as two street cleaners, billed as 'Plump and Runt'. Ruge, however, was not teamed with Hardy in Vim's next film, the first Vim known to have been shot in Jacksonville, entitled *Chickens*, whose plot bears quoting from the ever thorough text of Rob Stone:

Ethel, Hiram Gothrock's daughter, is ordered by her father to marry Count Chasem in an attempt by the newly rich Gothrocks to enter high society. Jabbs, Ethel's true love, has been banished from her presence. He goes to his friend Pokes, the village barber, for advice. Pokes advises him to impersonate the Count. On his way to the Gothrock's home, the Count and his valet are held up by two chicken thieves and forced to exchange clothes. The Count and his valet are then immediately arrested as the chicken thieves. Meanwhile, Pokes and Jabbs in disguise have laid ruin to Gothrock's house. When the chicken thieves arrive dressed as the Count and valet, Gothrock has them arrested for doing the damage. At the station house, Gothrock learns the real Count is already married and he gives his blessing to Ethel and Jabbs.

Chickens, however, did not pass muster with the Censor Board in Ohio, which feared an epidemic of imitative fowl-poaching. We do not know if this had anything to do with the separation of Babe and Ruge from Pokes and Jabbs but by the end of January 1916 'Plump and Runt' were launched on a life of their own, with titles such as *Frenzied Finance, Busted Hearts, A Sticky Affair* and *One Too Many*. The last named, released on 17 February 1916, is the first Plump and Runt film to survive. It is a bizarre tale of switched babies and swooning mothers in an apartment house where Plump is leading a carefree life on money sent by his uncle to support his non-existent wife and child. Runt is the janitor, to whom Plump turns with the panic call, 'Here's $50! Get me a baby!' Eventually Runt steals or buys several babies, from their nannies, including one black child. The panicking mothers retrieve their babies and Plump is left with Runt in a pram, smoking a cigar. Laurel and Hardy fans may note that this idea of having to keep up a façade of proper family life to keep the moolah from a rich uncle or aunt is a theme that echoes far down the canon, and we shall rendezvous with it again in due course . . .

In another extant movie in the series, *Hungry Hearts* (June 1916), Plump and Runt are starving artists with a pretty model for whose portrait an art dealer (played by the aforementioned Bert Tracy) offers $5,000. But Plump, who loves the model and can't stand anyone else owning her image, destroys the painting. Desperate for funds, he finds a rich widow who gives him the eye. Cue Plump to Runt: 'Help me to choose between the widow with the dough and the model whom I love!' Runt betrays him and marries the widow, but the model then receives a message from 'Attorneys Skin & Flint' revealing that she is the true heiress of the widow's estate. Runt and the widow return from their honeymoon to find their supposed home repossessed, with a notice: 'THIS PROPERTY CLOSED FOR DISINFECTION BY ORDER OF MR & MRS PLUMP.'

There is a great deal of general mucking about and good fellow-ship in these movies, and more than anything they reveal a group of people having a really good time. Another extant Plump and Runt, *The Battle Royal*, is a hillbilly comedy of the feud between the Plumps and the Runts, with much leaping about in forests, and a 'romantic' plot in which 'Peter Plump goes courting with his shotgun' and 'Robert Runt loves Polly Plump'. One intertitle anticipates a future classic: 'Battle of the century'. Eventually both families are attacked by the hated 'revenooers', and fight them off together.

None of these comedies appears to team Babe and Billy Ruge in any sense of acting in concert. They are simply two separate characters in the same film, with none of the business that would make them any kind of template for the Laurel and Hardy that will emerge, more than a decade down the line.

All in all there were thirty-five Plump and Runt movies, all one-reelers. The last, *The Precious Parcel*, was released in October 1916. Billy Ruge soon migrated to Jaxon Films and starred in his own series, but his trail goes cold in the early 1920s and even the indefatigable film historian Glenn Mitchell has found no clue as to his later fate. It appears that he never left the Florida studios and was a victim of their eventual decline. He may have been of limited talent as a character actor, but his physical agility and prowess were an asset to the Vim troupe. In the partly surviving *An Aerial Joyride*, Runt buys a car to impress a girlfriend but can afford only an old two-seater, and hires Plump to be his chauffeur. When the girl is in the car, Runt has to ride on the axle, and is thrown off in a magnificent pratfall. He then runs after the car in a chase that provides us with a fascinating, if blotchy, view of Jacksonville's main streets in 1916. In scenes frustratingly missing from the extant print, the car eventually takes to the air, and is shot out of the skies by the rampaging police.

The loose jack-of-all-trades system at Vim appeared to work to Babe Hardy's advantage as he graduated from acting to directing towards the end of the year. Titles cited by Rob Stone as directed by Babe Hardy include *The Guilty Ones*, *He Winked and Won*, *Fat and Fickle* and *The Boycotted Baby*. Babe's involvement behind the camera, however, turned out to be a mixed blessing, as he discovered irregularities in the company accounts while checking expenses in his capacity of head of one of Vim's production units. This caused a major stir, which contributed, at least in part, to the collapse of the company at the end of 1916, at the instigation of its parent company, Amber Star. Executives slithered hither and yon and Vim ceased to be, although the company's films continued to be released into March 1917.

The last Vim release appeared to be *Wanted – A Bad Man*, an unfortunate title in the circumstances. One of the many vanished films, it starred Babe as 'Giant George', the bad guy of Hicksville. It was one of his early roles as a heavy, though not the first, as he had played a full-fledged rat with bushy moustache and heavy brows – Shifty Mike – in *Ups and Downs*, in December 1915. But this was a mask that would soon serve him well.

Another role Babe had experimented with at Vim was the vaudeville standard cross-dresser. In *Busted Hearts*, shot late in 1915, he had been Peggy Plump, daughter of old farmer Plump who has always discouraged her suitors. This was a Pokes and Jabbs comedy, and Pokes eventually elopes with Peggy. In the end, bizarrely, Peggy Plump is reunited with her original boyfriend, who else but the ubiquitous Runt! In a later film, *A Day at School*, Plump follows his girlfriend to a boarding school and ends up impersonating one of the girls. In *Maid to Order* (October 1916), the unemployed Plump dresses up to get a job as a maid. Zealots will recognize a budding theme that will return in such classic Laurel and Hardy movies as *Twice Two*, *Why Girls Love Sailors*, *That's My Wife* and *Another Fine Mess*. While doctorates have been advanced concerning cross-dressing, female impersonation and gender-bending in Laurel and Hardy movies, it should be noted at this early point that this is an ancient music-hall tradition – men dressed as women, women dressed as men. The world of mime, indeed of theatre, abounds with conventions turned upside-down. Every male comedian in the movies, including Chaplin, got into the ladies' combinations, at one time or another. The unique aspect of this trend in Stan and Ollie's films is the way in which they played with this tradition in the light of their own 'special relationship'. But we shall get into these frisky folds later . . .

The only extant 'drag act' by Babe in Vim comedies is in *A Warm Reception*, in which Babe's sweetheart's mother banishes him from her house because she wants her daughter to marry the horrendous but suave Count de Appetyte, played by Joe Cohen. Babe gets his friends to kidnap Mother and impersonates the daughter to the Count. At their first meeting, he kicks the Count playfully in the rear, then, at a reception, flounces down the stairs with a fan and falls over. Having scared the Count, Babe changes back into his own clothes, and rushes off to 'rescue' Mother, who is so impressed by his heroism she reinstates him as her daughter's beloved. In the change-over, as Hardy begins to disrobe, the camera irises in, and Babe, noticing our gaze, looks back at us, shyly. The camera irises out, and Babe is dressed as a man again. This is, in the surviving solo films, Oliver Hardy's first look in the camera, a subtle awareness of the presence and power of the lens, the glass eye representing the audience that can be drawn into such intimate play.

By the end of his fifteen months at Vim, Babe had emerged as a performer of experience and confidence, with a solid working knowledge of his medium. Rob Stone records that he appeared at the Screen Club of Jacksonville's annual ball, leading the grand march through the ballroom, an event recorded at the time by newsreel cameras – although the footage has not survived. Coburn's Minstrels, the same group Babe had been rumoured to have run away with aged eight, were guest performers at this bash. By this time, Babe had also strengthened his position as a solid citizen and member of a professional trade by joining the local Masonic Lodge. According to Glenn Mitchell, he petitioned the Jacksonville Solomon Lodge Number 20, F.A.M. (Free and Accepted Masons) on 20 March 1916, giving his address as 725 May Street. He remained affiliated to this Lodge all his life.

The Masonic ideal of a secular communal spirit and charitable works for the needy was perfectly attractive to a man of a mixed marriage who had no high regard for religious rigidity. The Masons remained a force and a value in Ollie's life even though, as we can see on the screen, he would be happy to poke fun at their esoteric rituals, as Stan and Ollie's feature masterpiece, *Sons of the Desert* of 1933, will demonstrate with consummate skill.

The collapse of Vim did not retard Oliver Hardy's career for more than a few weeks. The company's studios were almost immediately taken over by a new film company, Caws, named for its founders, businessmen Samuel Cummins, Charles Abrams, Arthur Werner and Nat Spitzer. Since this was a lousy, if ingenious, name for a film company, it was soon renamed the King Bee Film Corporation, with Vim's Louis Burstein, Nat Spitzer and Louis Hiller as its principal owners. Their star was a twenty-two-year-old actor of Russian origin named Roy B. Weissberg, who had appeared in vaudeville as 'William B.' or 'Billy West'. Around the same period that Stan Jefferson was appearing with the Keystone

Trio as an imitator of Charlie Chaplin, West too took up this role. But if for Stanley it was a reluctant response to the need to earn money, for West it became his entire career. Although Billy West did make movies in which he played other roles, it is as a Chaplin imitator that he has entered film history. By the time he arrived in Florida, signed by Caws to a five-year contract at $25,000 per year, he had been playing Chaplin on the screen for a year.

Producer Louis Burstein had his own ex-Vim troupe ready to co-star in Billy West movies. In retrospect, it seems obvious that Babe Hardy would be cast in the role of Chaplin's bulky foil, Eric Campbell. But this took time to develop. In two of the early West films for King Bee, he repeats his cross-dressing role, as a real Babe, and as West's mother-in-law. The first Billy West film in which Babe is the traditional villain, with moustache and beetle brows, is *The Chief Cook* (alias *The Star Boarder*), in which Billy boards at a theatrical hotel where the employees have gone on strike. Babe is the jealous husband of Billy's flame, Dolly, who beats up the ersatz Chaplin with his cane. The film was shot in Bayonne, New Jersey, to which King Bee migrated, with all its crew, rather abruptly, in June 1917.

This may have seemed a temporary move for Babe, who had done an earlier stint at Bayonne, with Vim. But it in fact represented a final farewell to Florida and a stepping stone to a new location. For, after only seven films in New Jersey, King Bee upped stakes again, and travelled west, to California. The crew of nineteen – director Arvid Gillstrom, actors Billy West, Budd Ross, Babe Hardy, Ethlyn Gibson, Martha Dean, Leo White, Jackie Jackson, cameramen and grips – boarded a special Pullman carriage on the Santa Fe Sunset Flyer.

On 24 October they arrived in Hollywood, to put up their tent at 1329 Gordon Street, location of the Al Christie Studios. They left behind on the East Coast a split-off company, which starred Raymond Hughes as a back-up Billy West, imitating the imitator of Chaplin.

Babe's first film in Hollywood was *The Slave*, an *Arabian Nights* spoof, with Babe Hardy as the Sultan of Bacteria and Billy West as the eponymous rebel servant. It laid claim to be the first film to be shot without any intertitles. The female lead was Leatrice Joy, who was to become a major silent star in Cecil B. de Mille features. This film has not survived. One of the pre-Hollywood batch that has, *The Hobo* (released in November 1917), gives us a vintage view of Babe Hardy at a lunch counter, scoffing a huge string of sausages and demolishing a plate of pancakes. Billy West, as the cook, flips the pancakes into Babe's mouth, one by one. But the cakes are spiced, and Babe does a devilish dance and begins to throw food and crockery. This is a dapper Babe, in jacket and flat straw hat, a man happy in his time and place.

The Billy West films are part of the nine-tenths of the iceberg of silent-comedy shorts that lie concealed under the top strata of the famous stars in their apprenticeship period. While Chaplin thrived, and Arbuckle gambolled, with vaudeville kid star Buster Keaton learning the ropes in his shadow; while Harold Lloyd pursued his experiments with his embryonic 'Willie Work' and 'Lonesome Luke' characters, the bread-and-butter business of shoot-'em-quick comedies sparked and fizzled like a continuous fireworks show. Larry Semon, Billy Ritchie (another ex-Karno stalwart), Jimmy Aubrey, Billy Bletcher (another Vimite), and a host of Mack Sennett's Keystoners cavorted.

Among them, young Charles Parrott, soon to become Charley Chase, was enthusiastically learning the ropes. He was first to cross the path of one of our heroes as a newly hired director of Babe's and Billy West's Hollywood shorts in spring 1918. He also appears with them before the camera in *Playmates* as, of all things, a homosexual dope fiend whom Billy tries to reform, but only to steal his cocaine. (The censors had yet to sweep this kind of stuff off the screen.) *Playmates* is a curious precursor, also, of another film in our ambit, Stan and Ollie's *Brats* (1930), with its early scenes in which Billy West and Babe, as two lifelong friends, are seen as kids among oversize sets. Another figure who was crucially to affect the future of our heroes and screen comedy in general, Hal Roach, had by 1918 formed his first film company, Rolin, with actors Harold Lloyd and 'Snub' Pollard.

In the world outside, war had come and was about to go. The trenches of Europe had swallowed up millions of young men, among them three hundred thousand Americans. The world was drowning in blood, but Billy West was still imitating Chaplin. In one of the best of the series, *He's In Again*, released in December 1918 and directed by Charles (Charley Chase) Parrott, Billy runs into a saloon from which the head waiter, Babe Hardy, evicts him again and again. Unlike the Plump and Runt films, the scenes with Babe and Billy display real teamwork and comic timing, as Billy rushes through Babe's legs, turning up at the table from which Babe first pulls him by the legs, then by the scruff of the neck, finally picking him up bodily and throwing him out in the street. Billy West has all of Charlie Chaplin's gestures and movements down pat, but he lacks the grace and that split-second Karno-trained timing that made the real Charlie a star. In close-up, the eyes do not shine with the inner glow of the Tramp, they are too busy concentrating on the gags. And this is a gag-rich environment, courtesy, one suspects, of Parrott, one of the greatest of all constructors of comedy. The seedy bar, the drunks and freeloaders, the muscular six-foot dancing lady, whose biceps Billy uses to work his cocktail shaker – all are painted in with panache.

In a previous Parrott–West movie, *Bright and Early* (May 1918), Billy West is the bellhop and Babe Hardy is the villainous boss of the hotel–flophouse, all Eric Campbellite forked beard and black eyebrows. The boss has a bunch of crooks in the basement who rob the guests. The guests in any case are freeloaders, listed in the great book marked 'UNPAID BILLS'. There is a great deal of leaping up and down stairs, and a guest who keeps spitting on the floor despite Billy setting spittoons all over the lobby and even providing a washbucket. (The role of spitting in early silent comedy might rate a monograph of its own . . .) Another customer's wig keeps falling off till Billy nails it down with a hammer. This is the training ground where gags are born. Some are old; some are new. Parrott himself, as Charley Chase, defined the principles in an interview he gave in 1926 to *Motion Picture Magazine*:

A public is supposed to last seven years. At the end of that time, you can give them stuff that was too old to show them when they began. So the really valuable gag man is the one who has lots of experience and can dig into his memory for what is funny to the last generation and vary it so that it's funny to this one.

From the horse's mouth – and confound all the theories. Charley Parrott, and his brother Jimmy, who will also play a major part in our story, had been in Los Angeles since 1911, before even Keystone was born. But by the time Oliver Norvell Hardy was ensconced in Hollywood, another gag man had already reached the city of dreams and made his first halting, hesitant steps there as a motion-picture comedian. These two had yet to meet, but by the end of the Great War in Europe they were, for the first time in their lives, at last in the same line of business.

CHAPTER TWELVE

The Laurel Wreath of Scipio Africanus – and Other Tall Hollywood Tales

How Stan Laurel Got His Name. Mae Dahlberg, interviewed in her old age by John McCabe, told the tale she had always told all-comers:

> I can remember just how Stan got the name Laurel. It was not long after we were teamed together, and we were travelling as a double act sometimes called Stan and Mae Jefferson, or mostly Stan Jefferson, with me as assistant. Stan had been thinking for some time that Stan Jefferson had thirteen letters in it, and it began to prey on his mind a bit . . . Well, one night after the show, I was in the dressing room at whatever theatre we were playing, looking at an old history book that someone in the previous week's show must have left there in one corner of the dressing table. I opened it up casual like, and I came to an etching or drawing of a famous old Roman general. Scipio Africanus Major. I'll never forget that name. Around his head he wore a laurel, a wreath of laurel. I learned later that laurel leaves are really bay leaves . . .

Well, Stan Bay Leaf would hardly have done. Since this kind of story was also told about 'Babe' Hardy changing his name from Norvell for the same superstitious reason (although Norvell Hardy has only twelve letters), we must toss a ton of salt around this one. A recent alternative tale, proposed by a native of Sunderland, England, Thomas Cowley, recalled that Cowley's father had toured the Shields district of the north of England as Laurel of the double act Leonard and Laurel, back in 1910. The suggestion was that, when the other Laurel ceased using that name, the younger actor took it on. But as Stan Jefferson did not become Laurel until 1917, that too requires a little seasoning. We may be back with Scipio Africanus after all, that brutal imperialist who destroyed Carthage.

In fact, Stan was not to change his name formally to Laurel until August 1931, in a petition to Marshall F. McComb, Judge of the Superior Court of Los Angeles. Nor did he ever, like fellow Karnoite Chaplin, become an American citizen. But it is not difficult to figure why a name change was necessary once Stan began touring with Mae Charlotte Dahlberg as his companion in bed and board, since he could not legally confer on her the name of Jefferson, due to her status as Mrs Cuthbert, of the aforementioned Australian hitch. Stan and Mae Laurel, however, could travel as man and wife and sit nicely in the vaudeville route lists. However Laurel surfaced, Laurel remained, to leak its way into posterity. The act that Stan and Mae introduced to the determinedly low-brow Ackerman and Harris variety circuit, and then transferred to the more lucrative Pantages period, was yet another version of the perennial 'Nutty Burglar' sketch. A detailed review can be found in the *Los Angeles Times* of 25 November 1919 – almost three years after the act's début, and clearly playing on unchanged:

The exceptionally funny sketch by Stan and Mae Laurel is a feature on the bill at the Pantages this week . . . Stanley Laurel's work classes him as an able character actor . . . Mea [*sic*] Laurel appears in an elaborate parlor scene as a distressed damsel with a toothache and telephones for the doctor. Enter Stanley Laurel as the comic burglar with some nimble dancing, character songs and a plenitude of comedy. The girl takes him for the doctor, and he silences her dread toothache with a large mallet which knocks out the girl. Her grateful recognition of his 'skill' results in some happy situations.

The great advantage of this act, as we can read here, was that it could be performed *à deux*, with no complicating extra factors. It seemed to chop and change its name, too, having begun as *Raffles the Dentist* and then mutated into *No Mother to Guide Her*, a spoof reference to a well-known tear-jerking drama of that title. The *Spokesman-Review*, of Spokane, Washington, wrote on 22 September 1919, 'Stan Laurel as "honest, I'm a burglar" and May [*sic*] Laurel as the girl with "no mother to guide her" provide laughs galore, the vamping of the male Theda Bara being especially hilarious.' This hint of cross-dressing in the vaudeville show is intriguing, and we will come across this familiar phenomenon quite markedly in some of Stan's solo films.

It certainly seems, though, that at this crucial juncture in Stan's life and fortunes, Mae was a saving grace. She is also the first of Stan's helpmates whom we can glimpse, in moving pictures, co-starring with him in a number of his early films. Stan's penchant for women of some fleshly substance was to be a feature of his future married life, as well as a source of conflict, as these independent, strong-willed as well as strong-bodied women demanded their proper place in the sun. But all this lies ahead, for, in the spring of 1917, as Stan and Mae first hit Hollywood, their first chink of movie light opened up.

Film archaeologist Rob Stone recounts that the opportunity was provided by a former general manager at Universal Studios, Isadore Bernstein, who was already producing dramatic short films but announced his intention to form two comedy units. The lore has it that another manager, Adolph Ramish, owner of the Los Angeles Hippodrome, arranged the meeting between Stan and the man from Universal. The formation of 'Stanley Comedies' was announced in late June 1917, with Stan Jefferson and Mae Dahlberg signing on for the comedy series.

In the event, one film was shot, previewed at the Hippodrome, and promptly vanished from sight. It was not formally viewed by the censor board, nor released, nor noted apart from a small item in the *Los Angeles Times*, quoted by Stone, relating to Isadore Bernstein Productions:

Last week a harmless steamroller . . . was sighted about the studio grounds. An eagle-eyed member of the Stanley Comedy outfit passed the good word along. Before the roller could make its lumbering escape it was boarded by a group of film pirates, the driver walked the plank, and Stan gave himself a star performance in the 'cab'. After which the scenario writer sat on the curb and wrote the story.

This hint of one of the gag points of *Nuts in May*, Stan Laurel's alleged first movie, is all that remains on the record, though some scenes in the film, according to the archaeologists, were incorporated into its remake, *Mixed Nuts*, in 1925. Careful analysis by Rob Stone has shown that the latter film contains scenes in which the actors are dressed discontinuously, and Stan himself looks a little younger. The steamroller scene, in which Stan takes the vehicle over to crack some stubborn chestnuts, seems disconnected from the rest of the film.

To extrapolate from the remake, Stan's first role in motion pictures was that of a book salesman obsessed with Napoleon who is hit on the head and becomes convinced he is *l'empereur* in person. The cast, apart from Stan and Mae Dahlberg, included Lucille

Arnold, Owen Evans and Charles Arling, all of whom disappeared with their product into the black hole of history.

According to the story, as passed down from scribe to scribe, persons invited to the preview of the film at the Hippodrome included Universal's boss Carl Laemmle and Stan's ex-colleague Charlie Chaplin. Rob Stone's calculation of the periods these luminaries were in Los Angeles narrowed the date of the screening to August or September 1917, which is problematic, given that the film would have been completed in a few days, at the end of June. Rumours that Stan would sign a deal to appear with Chaplin are part of this legend, which cannot be verified.

Once again Stan, having taken one step forward in his attempt to climb out of the doldrums of vaudeville, had to step back, and return to the stage. Back to Stan and Mae Laurel and Raffles, Baffles or Waffles, the name-changing orthodontist. His Universal début, however, was not wasted. Carl Laemmle must have seen *Nuts in May* at some point and liked the brash young comic with his strange and manic ways. For in July 1918 the L-KO Motion Picture Kompany, one of Universal's comedy units, released the first verifiably shot Stan Laurel film, entitled *Phoney Photos*.

This film has not survived either, but a review in *Motion Picture World* tells its tale:

A two-reel comedy number by Edwin Frazee featuring Rena Rogers, Stanley Laurel, Neal Burns and others. The action takes place in a girls' school and concerns the efforts of two young men to marry the same girl. One of them succeeds by palming off a colored girl on his rival in a double elopement. The action is of the nonsensical, farcical sort and while not extremely laughable has numerous funny spots.

What this has to do with phoney photos, beyond the fact that one of its working titles was *The Photographer's Story* (another was *Skidding Hearts*), is a mystery. Rob Stone has established that this film was shot in late September or early October 1917 at Universal City and therefore predates Stan's next film, *Hickory Hiram*, which was shot in October 1917 but in fact released before *Phoney Photos*, in April 1918. Pre-Stone accounts of Stan's film career fingered this as the first of a series of 'Hickory Hiram' pictures, but in fact it was the only one. Stan played a hired farmhand who dreams of life in the big city, takes his girlfriend Trixie and heads for the metropolis, only to land up in jail, and then wakes up to find he's been dreaming.

Hickory Hiram was made by the second Universal comedy unit, Nestor Comedies, but it, too, like Stan's next two pictures, is a lost film. The two subsequent titles, *Whose Zoo?* (for L-KO) and *O, It's Great to be Crazy* (for Nestor), sound tantalizing, but not a frame has survived to whet our appetite for Stan's earliest movie *œuvre*. *Whose Zoo?* had Stan as a head waiter in a swank hotel and co-starred one Rube Miller as the zoo-keeper. The second short put Stan in the role of a job-seeker who takes a job supervising a lunatic asylum whose previous manager had allowed all the inmates to escape.

After shooting this first tranche of four short films, Stan returned with Mae to the stage. There is no record of Mae having played a role in the L-KO–Nestor pictures, but without the evidence we can't be certain. She may have had a small role. Stan himself would say only that 'the films were pretty bad, and were released, so I understand, to all the best comfort stations'.

The problem was, as becomes clearer when we get to the early Stan Laurel films that are available for viewing, that it was difficult for producers, directors and writers to figure out what character this newcomer to the movies might be playing. He was known, to American audiences, either for his one-track 'Nutty Burglar' act or his previous role as a Chaplin imitator. The latter mask had already been donned by Billy West, and in any case Stan wished to strike out on his own. He had said of his English début, as a teenage actor, that 'I wasn't sure what sort of comedian I wanted to be', and this hesitancy was still dogging him ten years later.

We are so familiar with the character Stan Laurel came to be, in the classic movies with Ollie, that it is something of a challenge to imagine him striving so hard to be someone else. But this is, in fact, a mark of all the pictures that Stan was to make until the penny actually dropped, another ten years on, and the partnership that charmed the world was – very reluctantly on Stan's part – born. In fact, Stan's embrace of the movies was in itself very hesitant at the beginning, and he was very careful not to give up the night job, the stage act with Mae, until well into 1921. Stanley Jefferson was still very much a child of the stage, the son of his father, a theatre brat. This was a lure that lingered, despite the fact that it had hardly led him to fame and fortune. Like his nagging wives, the theatre was as much a burden as a boon to Stan, but it remained in his blood, a part of his soul.

Ploughing the Pantages circuit, he continued, with Mae, playing the central plains and the American West. But the movies continued to beckon. Returning to Los Angeles in May 1918, Stan was scouted, so the story goes, by director Alf Goulding, who saw his vaudeville act at the Main Street Theater. Proceeding to the Portola Theater at Santa Barbara, Stan was followed by an urgent telegram. A major new Hollywood producer of comedies had been caught short when one of his featured actors, the famous clown Toto, whose real name was Arnold Novello, was not able to fulfil his contract to star in a series of two-reelers. The producer urgently needed a substitute, and Stan Laurel was invited to shoot a screen test. The test was shot, with Stan as an eccentric waiter and 'Snub' Pollard as his foil. The distributors, Pathé, approved the test reel. And so Stan headed back to the cameras, and to his first encounter with the second most important mentor of his artistic future: producer, director, writer and all-round human dynamo, Hal Roach.

CHAPTER THIRTEEN

Just Rolin Along – Commence the Hal Roach Story

From an interview with film historian Anthony Slide:

A.S.: How did you get into the film business?

HAL ROACH: In Los Angeles I saw an ad in the paper, 'Dollar car fare and lunch to work in motion pictures in western costume.' Well, like any boy from New York I had cowboy boots and a stetson hat and a bandana handkerchief, which I went to put on, and stood in front of the post office – only to see how movies were made like any person would.

Anyway they had a gambling scene with a roulette table, and from my experiences in Alaska I knew all about a roulette table. Knowing nothing about pictures I breezed up to the director and told him, 'What you want to know, I know.' Well, he says he wants the leading man to win at the start and eventually to lose everything, but you're too young to be the croupier, so you stand next to him and tell him what to do. So about four o'clock the assistant came to me and said, 'Be here at eight o'clock in the morning.' I said, 'Why?' He said, 'To continue the scene.' 'Well,' I said, 'I came from the post office this morning.' He said, 'I don't care where you came from this morning. Tomorrow you're an actor, and you get five dollars a day.' Well, five dollars a day in 1911 is pretty big money.

A.S.: Which company was this?

HAL ROACH: This was the Bison company, afterwards became Universal. So I went the next day, and a couple of more days, and I got to know something about studios and I liked them. All you had to do was stand in front of the studio and they picked you . . .

Hal Roach lived so long, refusing to kick the bucket until he passed his century in 1992, that he was able, by dint of countless interviews, given over a span of sixty years, to establish a version of his own history that could stand for posterity. To students of California's 'Long Long Ago' history project, in 1982, he gave an entertaining vision of his youth in Elmira, in New York State, at the Pennsylvania border, where his mother, like Oliver Hardy's Emily, ran a boarding house at the turn of the century. He related:

When I was very young my grandfather, who was a Swiss watchmaker, had cataracts in both eyes and became blind. My grandfather had a big white beard and was sort of ferocious looking but he really wasn't. He smoked a corncob pipe with a long stem so that he wouldn't burn his shoulders. When he was blind, he allowed me to invite the children from around the neighborhood over after supper or dinner, and he would tell them a story. He would make a little squeak in the pipe and that was supposed to be the fairies coming to tell the story . . . I never knew until years later but he would take grown-up stories and tell the kids these grown-up stories in the way that they would understand . . .

Shifting from school to school, the young man soon went to work, and claimed his father sent him to Seattle to learn to be an engineer on the Leigh Valley railroad. But from Seattle Roach took ship for Alaska, where he worked, so the legend goes, as a mule-skinner, a fish-wagon driver, a saloon swamper – whatever that is – and a prospector in the Yukon gold rush. Arriving back in Seattle, he drove an ice-cream truck and was then hired to truck pipes and supplies down to southern California. Leaping on from job to job, he became a superintendent for a freight company: 'I had six hundred mules and horses and long-line skinners.'

In this version of the tale the first encounter with the movies took place in 1912. (In other versions, it gets pushed back to 1913.) Roach progressed from an extra to the role of a heavy opposite the western star J. Warren Kerrigan. Another bit player performing at Universal for his dinner at the time was the twenty-year-old Harold Lloyd. Lloyd's biographer, Tom Dardis, recounts the tale of the two young men's reacquaintance while acting in a series of cheap 'Wizard of Oz' sequels (the very first *Wizard of Oz* was a 1910 one-reeler starring a very young Bebe Daniels, who was to be Lloyd's first on-screen female partner). In the intervals of cavorting in Hottentot costumes, Hal and Harold took their breaks in the park and began to talk about producing comedy films. A year later, in 1914, using an inheritance of $3,000, Roach teamed up with a business partner called Dan Linthicum, to form a company named as a combination of the first letters of their last names – Rolin. Roach said:

When I started my own company, we had no studio, no camera, nothing. We bought a second-hand car, we picked the actors up on street corners.

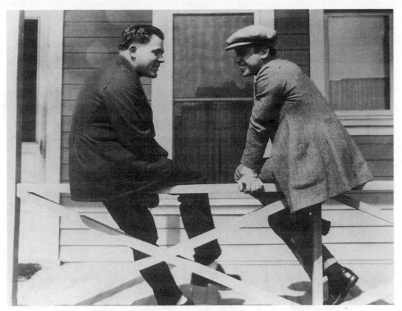

Hal Roach with Harold Lloyd – early days

The first picture I made was at the beach, the second I made in a street car, and the third I made at a park. We never had any scripts until we starred Harold Lloyd with glasses.

Before that, of course, there was Harold Lloyd without glasses, as Willie Work. This was the second coming of Rolin, for the first films the company made were released into obscurity, and the principals parted, only for Roach to reconstitute the company later in the year, with a new partner, Dwight Whiting. Willie Work was, like Stan Jefferson in his American vaudeville act, a Chaplinesque character, slightly disguised in a battered top hat rather than a bowler, a cat's-whisker moustache and a long coat. In a prevision of Stan's first film, Lloyd's was entitled *Just Nuts*. Lloyd recalled to Tom Dardis, 'We'd go out in a park like Echo Park or Hollenbeck Park, with no script, no idea, just characters, and we'd make up our comedy as we went along . . .'

Happy times indeed, but five dollars a day soon palled, especially as Roach began paying another actor, Roy Stewart, ten bucks to star in dramatic two-reelers. In a pay spat with Roach, Lloyd moved across town to Mack Sennett's Keystone Studio for a while, but soon returned to Rolin, at $50 a week and with a new character – Lonesome Luke. This was an even closer variation on Chaplin, and Lloyd was soon teamed with another young actor Roach had snapped up along the way, Harry 'Snub' Pollard, a diminutive Australian who had breached American waters as part of a vaudeville touring company. With his 'Kaiser Wilhelm' moustache, mistakenly applied upside down one day and left that way for posterity, 'Snub' was to be one of Roach's long-lasting stalwarts. Between 1915 and the end of 1917 over seventy Lonesome Luke shorts were produced.

Roach released his films through the Pathé company, which was voracious for new material. By 1917 Lloyd was getting pretty tired of Lonesome Luke, and was looking for a fresh character to escape the shadow of Chaplin. The Pathé company was not happy to abandon a profitable franchise, but Roach, already a shrewd judge of what actors, left to their own creative devices, might produce, allowed him to try out the new 'glasses' character, while he attended to his own new idea of luring the clown Toto from the New York stage. The result of that failed detour by Roach, ironically, gave two classic clowns to the screen and posterity: the 'glasses' Harold Lloyd, and Stan Laurel.

Roach was always at pains, in his interviews, to give himself maximum credit in developing the kind of comedy that made his studio successful. In a 1987 interview with *Screen Actor Hollywood*'s Harry Medved, asked to differentiate his brand of comedy from Mack Sennett's Keystone, Roach said:

Mack was almost 100 per cent physical. In the early days, everybody used slapstick. I mean, you kicked a character out of the scene and they fell on their rear end into the next scene. You'd hit them over the head with an anvil – something that would kill them – and they'd only get up mad. That's what was funny about it. But . . . Mack had two things that were wrong. The first was that there were a lot of cartoons that could do slapstick better than you could do it with actors. And the other was the Mack Sennett Bathing Beauties . . . When you put the Bathing Beauties in a movie . . . people stop laughing and you have to start your comedy all over again. That's when we passed Sennett. The exhibitors started paying us more than they paid him, because our movies were funnier. Instead of slapstick, we had stories and tried to work out funny ideas and situations.

The major emphasis, of course, was not only on stories and situations but on characters. Here Roach, like Fred Karno before him, was at his best, as an enabler of comedians. As he had done with Lloyd, he continued with the kid group 'Our Gang', featuring a motley crew of little rapscallions and originally devised around the black child, Ernie Morrison, aka 'Sunshine Sammy'. The first of these to be released was *One Terrible Day*, in 1922. Charley Chase, Will Rogers, Earl Mohan and Billy Engle in 1924; Clyde Cook, Arthur Stone, Glenn Tryon, Mabel Normand, Mae Busch and others followed before the big whammy of Laurel and Hardy. Writers and directors too were given wide leeway to develop gags and stories – George Marshall, Leo McCarey and the brothers Charles (Charley Chase) and James Parrott were among many who flourished at Roach's 1920s Culver City Studios.

But all this was yet to come, in 1918, when Stan Laurel planted his tiny crop of five one-reelers in the Rolin allotment. The first of these was *Do You Love Your Wife?*, shot in mid-June 1918, with Stan as the harassed janitor of an apartment building, involving mix-ups with wives and husbands. The cast list is a roll call of stalwarts who would feature, with or without Stan, in the silent pantheon for years to come: Bud Jamison, Marie Mosquini, Noah Young, William Gillespie, Jimmy Parrott. Rob Stone has also noted that one supporting player is named as Lois Neilson, most probably the same Lois who would become Stan Laurel's second wife, in 1926. A still survives, of Stan administering a vacuum-cleaner hose to a jowly guest, surrounded by maids and onlookers, but not much else to cast light upon the goings on, apart from a tart *Moving Picture Review* notice which says, 'This contains some fairly amusing burlesque touches.'

Stan's second film for Rolin, *Just Rambling Along*, is the first Stan Laurel picture that is readily available for viewing. Our first glance at our hero in motion: he is twenty-eight years old, rather tall and lanky, with an ill-fitting jacket, pants and spats, an untidy bow-tie and a frayed straw hat. We first see him standing by an alley beside a soft-drinks booth, where a small boy has just picked up a wallet Stan has spotted on the sidewalk. Stan and the kid wrestle over the wallet. Cut to burly cop Noah Young, watching this from a beachfront with the sign 'VENICE POST OFFICE STATION ONE' clear in the background. The cop walks over and the

Stan Laurel – just rambling along . . .

kid says (intertitle): 'Oh Daddy! look what I've found.' Stan rubs
his hand and turns away in a huff, as the cop and his son gleefully
paw over the bills in the wallet.

The scene already reveals Stan's attempts, like Lloyd's, to detach
himself from Chaplinesque mannerisms. The twitching of the head,
the coy glance at the wallet and the push and pull with the boy are
still Chaplin, but this is no tramp but a young man about town,
either fallen on hard times or simply out of funds, as young men
are. In the next scene, a young woman, the classical 'vamp', played
by Clarine Seymour, passes by a row of men on a bench who rise
as one and follow her come-on look. Passing by Stan she vamps
him too and he rushes after, ahead of the line. The men, resembling
nothing so much as escapees from the loonie bin featured in one of
Stan's earlier pictures, led by a leering bearded maniac in a long
bathing suit, enter a café, from which Stan is kicked out due to lack
of cash. He sees the kid again, fingering a coin, presumably his

portion of the moolah expropriated by the law. Pretending to hold the boy up by poking him in the back, Stan snatches the coin and re-enters the café, emitting his first line of intertitle dialogue: 'Tut tut; I am with money!'

There follows a lengthy sequence at the food counter with the chef, played by Bud Jamison. After wiping his dirty food tray on the chef's cap, Stan prances up and down the line, sampling and then refusing each dish, until he accepts a cup of coffee and repairs to the vamp's table. Some of the exchanges with the chef, stealing pies while his back is turned, mirror a similar scene between Charlie Chaplin and his brother Sydney in *A Dog's Life*, released only two months earlier. Another gag, in which Stan's efforts to enter the café with his hat on are frustrated by the busboy whipping it off and putting it on the hat stand, until Stan takes two hats off the stand and remains with the one he entered with, is repeated in Stan's later *Mixed Nuts* (and may have been in the original *Nuts in May*), as well as in a couple of Harold Lloyd movies. As *Just Rambling Along*, like the preceding and next of Stan's Rolin pictures, was directed as well as produced by Hal Roach, this gag might have come from the director, rather than the star, loath as we are to doubt Stan's authorship of every trick in his *œuvre*.

Stan's attempts to vamp the vamp result in her switching the bill on him, so that his original 10 cents becomes a tab for $1.25. Great consternation and panic at the cash till; Stan crawls his way out; only to encounter the cop and his kid outside; crawls back in; is caught by the chef and waiter (Jimmy Parrott), shaken and thrown out, to be snatched by the cop and beaten about the head with his truncheon. The End.

A cruel punishment for one of life's little *faux-pas*! In Roach's little kingdom, as in Sennett's, violence, albeit cartoonish, is always visited on the innocent who transgress without guile or malice. The early screen comic cut-ups were made long before the age when the cinema was thought worthy of the attention of intellectual critics, sages and psychiatrists. But viewed today, in an era top heavy with theories of representation, they echo with a kind of savage abandon. 'We shot a film on the beach,' says Roach, and there is California's Venice seafront, today's 'Muscle Beach', with its ice-cream booths and diners, its benches and awnings and the strange dance of the passing beauty and her putative swains. Ordinary life is fraught with peril, not only for Chaplin's down-and-out tramp, but for the youth who slides between the sunbeams, street smart perhaps, but always short of the stroke of luck that will give him a break in the hustle.

Stan's next two Rolin films are missing again: *Hoot Mon!* and *No Place Like Jail*. The former is the first of Stan's occasional flirtations with Scottish whimsy, which would find its place in history with *Putting Pants on Philip*, a decade down the line. Stan is a Yank who goes to buy a pub in Scotland. Rob Stone quotes the *Exhibitors Trade Review*: 'Much of the attraction centers around Ye Blue Coo Inn . . . full of laughs as it is of kilties.' In the next film, Stan and a pal are let out of jail and consent to kidnap a young college girl, but grab the headmistress by mistake. Shades of later Laurel and Hardy jail jinks.

The fifth and last Rolin film, however, is extant. *Hustling for Health*, filmed in July 1918, was produced by Hal Roach but directed this time by one Frank Terry (aka Nat Clifford), who also co-starred as the friend who offers young Stan a quiet time at his rural home when Stan misses the train for his vacation. 'He longs to smell the salt air of the pine woods,' reads a loopy title. The locale of this first scene is the Santa Fe station, also to occur in a future Stan and Ollie film, *Berth Marks*. While Stan is loaded up with his friend's parcels and heading for his peace and quiet, the friend's home is echoing to the timbres of a suffragette meeting hosted by his wife: 'The question before the house – are husbands human beings or microbes?' (A matter still hotly debated in today's post-feminist culture.) At their destination, a cart draws up, but the horse ambles offon its own, and Stan is left to haul the cart up a steep hill, a trick shot with a heavily tilted camera. Arriving at the house in the midst of the ladies' debate, Stan is roughed up and thrown out of the window. He and the friend hide in the bushes while the women exit, and then enter to set about cleaning the house. Meanwhile, the fussy neighbour, Mr Spotless (Bud Jamison again) (title: 'He originated the barbless rhubarb' [?!?]), has enlisted the local cop to get the folks next door to clean up their own filthy garden. Stan sets to with a hose, dousing his friend and wrecking his neighbour's garden, in a scene that clearly prefigures Stan and Ollie's future *Helpmates*.

This is a slightly different Stan from the beachfront rambler – a bit of a country bumpkin, with a squishy cap and a helpless *shlemiel* demeanour, who never kicks against the pricks but eventually gets to cavort with the next-door neighbour's frisky, if somewhat top-heavy, daughter. *Moving Picture World*, oddly, wrote, 'Stan Laurel . . . appears in this as a hen-pecked husband who goes to the country to recuperate. He makes with some funny misadventures. There is no very definite connecting plot and the number is on the whole only fairly strong.' There is no hint of the 'hen-pecked husband' in the available version, which might have survived in a truncated form.

The reviews reveal no great critical enthusiasm. Nor was there, apparently, great public clamour for more Stan Laurel comedies, and so Roach failed to renew his new star's contract. Harold Lloyd's 'glasses' character was doing great business, featuring in over thirty short films in 1918. (In all, Lloyd made just over ninety one- and two-reelers for Roach before his first feature in 1921.) Stan Laurel was a struggling artist who had not found a central focus, and all five of his Rolin films were in fact held back for release until early 1919. Nevertheless, Stan's movie run of summer 1918 was not yet over. Balked in his attempts to become the featured player, he took a gamble and accepted a series of supporting roles in short films starring an up-and-coming comedy star, signed with the Vitagraph company, named Lawrence 'Larry' Semon. Within a short while, Semon would be producing a number of films co-starring another, already established, supporting actor, Oliver 'Babe' Hardy. Our heroes were converging, slowly, towards their very first meeting, a serendipitous moment that would, ironically, pass unnoticed and unmarked by either of them, engendering only business as usual.

A 'missed link' for both Stan and Babe, Larry Semon was, none the less, a vital influence on the next stage of the evolution of our heroes' comedy style.

CHAPTER FOURTEEN

Flips and Flops: The Larry Semon Show

In 1920, the publicity for the in-house journal *Vitagraph News* declared:

Larry Semon, star comedian, smiles down upon New York's gay White Way from a spectacular signboard on the top of the Putnam Building facing two ways at Broadway and 46th Street. It is the most conspicuous sign on the Great White Way these days. The comedian's face and the slogan of The Comedy King in letters four foot high are visible for ten or fifteen blocks north on Broadway and Seventh Avenue.

And this was no mere studio puffery. In 1916, Mississippi-born Lawrence Semon, son of a magician who toured the country with his wife and boy as Zera the Great, began directing comedy one-reelers for the Vitagraph company, initially starring Hughie Mack, another fat lad in the mould of John Bunny. The young Larry had begun his own career as a graphic artist and a cartoonist on the *New York Sun*. In 1917 he moved in front of the camera and began acting, appearing as a white-faced boob, a kind of American Punch. This echo of the ancient clowns served him well in Europe where he became known as Jaimito or Tomasin in Spain, Zigoto in France, and Ridolini in Italy. In America, too, his star rose, with twenty-seven short films released in 1917 alone. In 1919 he was signed to a new Vitagraph contract at the dream salary of $3,600,000 for the next three years. This put him on the same stratospheric level as Chaplin, and he was just thirty years old.

Semon's is another salutary tale in the long series of Hollywood's 'Where are they now?' Only silent-film buffs and archivists remember Larry Semon, the Comedy King of the early 1920s. His films were renowned mainly for the spectacular stunts that influence many people's primal memories of what a silent film comedy is. The speeding motor car is chasing the speeding steam train. The crooks climb on top of the train. The hero fights with the crooks on the carriage roofs. At a crossing, a driver hauling a mobile house stalls on the tracks. The train, still carrying the fighting men, smashes the house to matchsticks, and everybody on the carriage roofs tumbles to a fall. This is a Larry Semon movie, *The Show*, made in 1922, with Babe Hardy as a villainous stage manager.

In *The Sawmill*, Larry's preceding picture, also co-starring Babe, a series of gags involving log-riding, rope-swinging and villains falling into vats of water from a great height are capped by the finale, in which Larry and the heroine are caught up a redwood tree by the minions of the villainous foreman – Babe. As they chop it down, Larry swings over the adjacent lake by a rope attached to a wooden tower, which, chopped off, deposits both in the water. Only Keaton could rival Semon's stunts, which were, in his first films, performed by himself, but later were acted out by stunt doubles, notably Richard Talmadge or Bill Hauber. One early Semon stunt-man was Joe Rock, who was soon to play a vital part in the Stan Laurel saga.

Stan's first film with Larry Semon was *Huns and Hyphens*, shot in the summer of 1918. Larry stars as a waiter who pretends to be a rich man to impress a girl. Stan is one of a group of thugs, presumably the Huns of the title, though who the Hyphens were is anybody's guess. His only solo scene is standing by the bar, stealing eggs and putting them down his trousers, only to have them hatch as chicks who crawl out of the turn-ups. There is a great deal of down-to-earth tavern humour, with a washerwoman on the roof of the diner squeezing soap into the beer below, followed by a stocking in the soup and the rotund lady herself, crashing down on to the tables. A thuggish client is dispatched with a vase on the head by Larry, who then attaches a calendar and hat to the man's body like a sail, and turns on a fan which propels the oaf out of the diner, down a flowing gutter and into a manhole. Stan just has to wave a gun and stumble about, while Larry chases his stuntman, Bill Hauber, up a building on to a protruding plank swinging over the busy main street. Larry obligingly saws himself and his opponent off to the finale fall.

This penchant for featuring the most apparently dangerous gags for no organic reason except the fun of it is typical of many of these routine two-reelers. The humble pratfall was no longer enough, at the tail end of World War I, to amuse an audience who knew that, in real life, young men were being blown sky high by real gunpowder. Stuntmen performed the most amazing feats for a few dollars a day, leaping off buildings, even if the subsequent twenty-storey fall was completed by a dummy.

Larry's next movie, *Bears and Badmen*, seemed to cement his reputation, though it appears today as one of the weakest in his *œuvre*, a farrago of country-bumpkin caricatures and ridiculous exits pursued by a bear. Stan is fishing unsuccessfully in the river when Larry turns up with his tin of fish food and a club to stun the trout. They have a couple of brief scenes together, then it's off to the cabin for some skylarks with rampaging bad men, the heroine and somebody, possibly Bill Hauber, in the costume department's worst bear suit.

In the following film, *Frauds and Frenzies* (everything had to be called *This and That*, a trend followed by Stan in future solo films until it ran out of steam a few years later), Stan Laurel was for the first and only time playing as an equal partner with Semon. They appear as two convicts, old buddies – or 'hammock hounds' as the intertitle suggests with more than a hint of forbidden frolics – who prance about outdoing each other in their chain-gang antics. Their business together has a strange whiff of partnerships to come, though they are too physically similar, and seem not to have worked out who is the foil to whom. Eventually they escape, and appear in the city having switched their stripes for ill-fitting civvies, after an eerily prescient title:

> Two souls with but a single thought,
> Two brand-new suits which they have bought,
> Two heads each filled with naught but naught,
> Both hoping that they won't be caught.

Proceeding to the park in the pursuit of a flirtatious girl with a parasol who hands them both cards that read 'Dolly Dare, 32 Followme Street', they end up at her house, only to discover she is of course the daughter of the prison warden. Their attempt to crawl out of trouble is confounded by a phalanx of cops who seem to be loitering in the garden. Recognized by the warden, they sit on either side of him as he cuffs himself to Stan, allowing Larry to escape and proceed with a classic Semon chase – prefiguring Keaton's 1922 *Cops* and his later feature, *Seven Chances* – with the policemen chasing Larry in and out of pipes on a construction site and Larry hoisted by a crane way up in the air. Lowered by the crane into a car, he kisses his pursuers goodbye only to find he is seated again with Stan and the warden, who handcuffs his two charges properly.

Stan was said to be miffed at Larry leaving him in handcuffs for the climactic scene, a ruse rumoured to have been caused by crew comments during rushes that Stan was funnier than Larry. The fact that no more Stan and Larry films followed might indicate that Semon wanted no on-screen rivals, but historian Rob Stone has also noted that the great influenza epidemic of autumn 1918 temporarily closed all the Hollywood studios, including Vitagraph, soon after the film was shot. As Stan had no long-term contract with the company he had to return to vaudeville, not that it was faring any better, as stage theatres were closing too. Be that as it may, Stan was not to work with Larry Semon again, and Babe did not begin working with the 'Comedy King' until September 1919.

We are therefore back with Stan and Mae, returning to the vaudeville grind in November 1918, hitting Springfield, Illinois, with *No Mother to Guide Her*: 'One of the best laugh producers seen at the Majestic this season.' In December, they played Michigan and Indiana, swinging back to Illinois in January 1919. February: Indiana; March: Iowa and Nebraska; April: Minnesota and Wisconsin, and so on. This time, the movie option seemed really to have run out for Stanley, and the only stage he could rely on was the old variety stomping ground, which was to maintain him throughout the next two years and more, while the cinema proceeded to grow in leaps and bounds, but, as yet, without Stan Laurel.

The relationship between Stan and Mae was tempestuous. Both were strong-willed, and often stubborn. Eyewitnesses of the time, such as the Great Survivor, George Burns, told consistent stories of how Stan and Mae seemed the essence of comradeship on the stage, but as soon as the dressing-room door was closed the arguments began within. A great deal of controversy has surrounded allegations that this was a period in which Stan hit the bottle. If he did, he would only have been following the example of many, in and out of show business, who felt that Prohibition, which came into law at the beginning of 1920, was a challenge to consume as much intoxicating liquor as the human body could survive. Stan's biographer,

Fred Lawrence Guiles, made great play of the alcoholic binges our hero was said to indulge in. The record, and common sense, suggest that, in his profession, Stan would have been a saint not to drink, but that his problem was that a few drinks were too much for him, rather than that too much was his standard.

Rumours persisted that Stan and Mae had undergone some sort of quasi-legal ceremony, to formalize her position as 'common-law wife'. There is no documentation to prove this, but sixteen years later in 1936, as Stan was entwined in a divorce wrangle with Virginia Ruth Laurel, his second wife, Mae turned up in Los Angeles, claiming maintenance on the basis of a common-law arrangement made in New York in 1919. Explaining matters to the judge, the ill-named Dudley S. Valentine, Stan admitted that 'he lived as man and wife with the auburn-haired actress until 1925'.

'You introduced her as Mrs Mae Laurel, didn't you?' the *L.A. Examiner* reported the query by Mae's attorney, S. S. Hahn. '"Naturally, I had to," was the comedian's reply. "You didn't tell people she wasn't your wife, did you?" Hahn inquired. "That wouldn't be the gentlemanly thing to do," Laurel snapped back.' After a year of such bandying about of the comic's woes, Mae settled out of court for an undisclosed sum and agreed that she had never been Stan Laurel's wife, a charge that, if proved, would have branded Stan a bigamist. All this, and more, will be recounted in due course.

Another old survivor who remembered Stan and Mae on the stage was Joe Rock, who had begun his career as a stunt double for Mary Pickford. A short-lived career with Vitagraph as a comedian teamed with one Earl Montgomery was followed by a more successful run as an independent producer. Joe Rock told film historian Randy Skretvedt, in an interview conducted in November 1979, when Rock was eighty-eight:

ROCK: He [Stan] always wanted Mae to be in the picture. Well, she wouldn't play a character part. Had she had played the character parts, she'd have been the best in the business.
SKRETVEDT: She did have some talent as a comedienne, then?
ROCK: On the stage, she was as good as Stan. They did rockabout, knockabout acrobatic stuff that was terrific. She'd take better falls than he would take . . . I gave him the idea of doing a fanny flop, by falling flat on his fanny with his feet sticking out – and bounce, see? And it's a

funny fall . . . It hurts you a little bit more, but it's a hell of a good fall. And she used to do that. Under her skirt, you see, she'd put a pad. And for his pair of pants. He'd put a pad on it. And then, they would act, you see, and then they'd turn around to go, he was supposed to go this way, not that way – and they'd meet, and they would both . . . bounce back. They'd get good laughs. A lot of good laughs. And they sang, not too bad . . . and they became very very good.

But not good enough at that point to return to the movies, so they were absent when Oliver 'Babe' Hardy joined the Vitagraph company early in 1919. Before that, Babe had wrapped up his partnership with Billy West's Chaplin imitations in the summer of 1918 – though Babe and West were to return to a new teamwork a few years later. The summer and autumn of the last gasp of the Great War in Europe were spent by Babe at another studio which Stan had passed through – L-KO. Together with young Charley Parrott, who was continuing his first run as director, Babe appeared in eight shorts whose titles seem more interesting than the films: *Business Before Honesty* (Babe as a 'blind' con man), *Hello Trouble* (Babe as a devoted husband), *Painless Love* (Babe as a dentist, Dr Hurts), *The King of the Kitchen* (Babe as a German customer), *The Freckled Fish* (Babe as chef Solomon Soopmeat in a 'Charlie from the Orient' series with a Chinese Charlie Chaplin, Chai Hong, a black mammy and the eponymous fish, of which *Moving Picture World* said, 'The action is too indefinite to hold the attention closely'), and so forth. But L-KO was going nowhere, with or without Babe, and he soon crossed the road to join the more solid Vitagraph crew and cast, working alongside both Larry Semon and another of the company's main stars, Jimmy Aubrey.

Aubrey was another Karno leftover, who had cut his teeth in the seminal *Mumming Birds* sketch, as the wrestling 'Terrible Turk'. His first film position was as part of a double act, 'Heinie and Louis', for Starlight Pictures in New York. By 1918 he had reached Vitagraph's Los Angeles studio, and Babe Hardy's first appearance as his foil was in the two-reeler *Soapsuds and Sapheads*, released in February 1919. Babe made twenty-six short films with Jimmy Aubrey, mostly playing the heavy-set villain he had built up with Billy West. In a typical sample, *Squeaks and Squawks* (here we are with those *This and That* titles again), c. March 1920, Jimmy is the repair boy for the local blacksmith but spends his time schmoozing his boss's daughter. Babe is the evil landlord who threatens to take the girl in lieu of the mortgage. At one point Babe, all top hat and tails, thick villain's moustache and beetle eyebrows, is stuck in glue poured on the ground by Aubrey, who dances round hammering him from all sides. Babe eventually works himself free of his shoes and chases Aubrey all over the scenery.

Aubrey was another comic with a signature moustache of his own, but he was notoriously ego-ridden and jealous of anyone else taking his laughs. Joe Rock said, 'He would go to the cutter, and he'd say, "Now look, the only way to cut this picture – it'll be easy for you – just follow me . . . all through it. Never mind about anybody else, just follow me all the way through it."' This was not a recipe for a happy time, but there was never any sign that Oliver Hardy resented it. The quintessential acting professional, he always gave his best performance as a part of the ensemble. Learning, all the time, gaining experience with the camera eye.

Hardy's first film with Larry Semon was *Dull Care*, in the autumn of 1919, in the midst of his run with Jimmy Aubrey. Larry played a detective and Babe a flirtatious janitor. A few weeks later Babe played a cop alongside Larry as the lead in *The Head Waiter*. In September 1920, he had a tiny role as a restless member of the audience in Larry Semon's *The Stage Hand*. But it was not until the spring of 1921 that Babe left the Jimmy Aubrey unit at Vitagraph and transferred for a long-term stint as Larry Semon's regular heavy.

Babe, too, was having to navigate his personal life through increasingly stormy waters. Little has been hitherto revealed about Babe's married life with Madelyn, after the first, apparently happy days at Jacksonville. Lucille Hardy, Oliver's third and final wife, recalls that all that Babe told her about his first marriage was that 'I was very young, and she was a singer.' Those were 1940s memories, washed in bucketfuls of thankful amnesia. Behind the curtain of easy domesticity, however, all was not well, and by the move to California in 1917 serious tensions were building up. Within three years, events would follow that would stretch the marriage to its breaking point.

The National Census of 1920 finds Oliver N. Hardy resident at 4401 Clayton Avenue, Los Angeles, which is in Los Feliz, at the end of Hollywood Boulevard. He is listed as boarding with two sisters, Marie and Myrtle Reeves (twenty-four and twenty-two years old respectively) both listed as 'Actress Motion Pictures'. And therein lies the tale. A new Mrs Hardy was on the horizon, and this time the lady was five years younger than the gentleman, rather than the other way around.

Myrtle Reeves was in fact a fellow Georgian, having hailed from Atlanta. She had been a jobbing actress at least from the age of eighteen, since a letter to her survives from the Balboa Feature Films company, dated 3 May 1916, which indicates either her value to the company or a company ethos so alien to our current era that it deserves quoting in full:

Miss Myrtle Reeves,
C/o The Studio
Long Beach, California.

Dear Madam,
This is to advise that beginning Monday, May 8th, your salary will be increased Five Dollars ($5.00) per week.

This is in accordance with our policy, for faithful and loyal services rendered The Balboa Amusement Producing Company.

We sincerely hope that we will have the pleasure of giving you many more increases in the near future.

With very best personal regards, I beg to remain,
Yours very truly,

H. HORKHEIMER
President and General Manager,
The Balboa Amusement Producing Company

The Balboa company was another of the mushrooming 'teens companies that did not survive them, having to close in 1918. Myrtle Reeves continued as an actress, together with her sister, just two of the thousands of young women hoping against hope to climb the fragile ladder of Hollywood success, which, alas, failed to support them.

Later studio puffs claimed Oliver Hardy and Myrtle had been childhood sweethearts in Atlanta, a clearly impossible tale. Myrtle had been sixteen when Oliver married Madelyn Saloshin, in 1913, and her acquaintance with him could not have predated the Hardys' move to Los Angeles. Once established, however, the acquaintance quickly ripened, and, on 1 March 1920, Oliver Hardy initiated a petition of divorce against Madelyn.

This petition, dug up by our zealous sleuth, Dave Rothman, does not make pretty reading, apart from casting further doubt on the accepted chronology of Oliver Hardy's life in 1913. Both dates and claims in the petition, constructed in the blood-chilling language of American divorce suits, have to be taken with the usual amount of sceptical seasoning, but the degree of rancour and hostility in the document is a sad window on the home life of the clown.

Babe presents his marriage to Madelyn as a complete sham from the start. She treated him, the petition claims, in a 'cruel, inhuman and barbarous manner'. She had demanded letters she had sent him when he was in New York (he claimed he was acquainted with her for four or five months before marriage) insisting that he return to Georgia and marry her, which he wouldn't have done if she had not claimed to be pregnant, thus taking advantage of a youth who had not yet attained his majority (not true, as Oliver was twenty-one in January 1913). When not given the letters by Oliver or by his mother, she thereafter was abusive throughout the marriage on this subject. 'Excessively jealous and suspicious nature,' claims Oliver.

The plaintiff alleged that Madelyn was jealous after a kissing scene in a movie (not specified). They had a noisy row on this subject; she attacked him with a knife, and they were forced to vacate their apartment. In March 1916, they had a blow-up in a Jacksonville cabaret where he was earning $50 per week and she was earning $47 per week (an interesting take on events at the Burbridge Hotel which the oral accounts painted as a harmonic idyll). In the summer of 1916, they had a blow-up about a young unnamed actress in New York. This kind of behaviour continued after their move to Los Angeles. In the words of the petition, Madelyn told Oliver 'she had put a "Jew curse"[!] upon plaintiff'. In August 1919, when they were living at 4633 Vermont Place, she kept him up all night with her nagging one time after he was 'wrestling all day with a cow' on the set. (Might this refer to *Yaps and Yokels*, filmed in summer 1919, a Jimmy Aubrey film set on a farm?)

If he came home even a few minutes late, Oliver claimed, she would ask what was it this time: gambling or a woman? When Madelyn's father Louis died, in January 1920, she left for Atlanta, and her husband gave her a one-way ticket and a money order for the same value. When she got to Atlanta, he wired her not to come back.

It is difficult to reconcile the petition's version of Oliver and Madelyn Hardy's marriage with the strong evidence that, at least until late 1916, it was, on balance, a happy one. The past, however, is a moral maze, and one often finds oneself ducking and weaving along deceptive roadmarks and competing versions of the same facts. There is no greater fury, though, than a divorce between two people who once loved each other and then ferociously battle to apportion the blame – even to the extent of wielding the same racial insults that would have been hurled against them both at the start. We should bear in mind, too, the legal struggle, in these suits, to avoid liabilities and alimony payments by painting the opponent in devil's hues. It is the lawyers, after all, writing the scripts.

In the event, the court granted Oliver Hardy a temporary restraining order, which was later contested. A deposition was taken from two people in Atlanta, Babe's mother and Mrs Maggie Lee Reeves, mother of Myrtle, who was clearly already in the picture. Madelyn counter-sued for divorce in August.

In November 1920 the Superior Court of the County of Los Angeles issued an interlocutory judgment in the divorce case brought by Madelyn Hardy. A year later, on 17 November 1921, the Final Judgment of Divorce was entered. A week after that, Babe and Myrtle Reeves were married, on Thanksgiving Day, at the Church of Christ, Hollywood.

The Vitagraph company, for whom Babe was working at the time – he had just completed *The Show* with Larry Semon – issued a report that was duly reprinted in the Los Angeles press, as an undated cutting in the Skretvedt archive reveals:

COMEDIAN MARRIES – BABE HARDY WEDS PRETTY MYRTLE REEVES
By Grace Kingsley

The song about nobody loving a fat man is all wrong, take it from Mrs O. N. Hardy, Myrtle Reeves that was. To prove it, Miss Reeves went so far, on Thanksgiving Day, as to wed a fat man, said chubby person being the fat comedian, O. N. Hardy, usually called 'Babe' Hardy, who helps make for the gaiety of nations in Larry Semon Vitagraph comedies. The wedding occurred on the above date at the Church of Christ, in Hollywood, and the pair are now at home at 2425 Russell Avenue, Hollywood.

As Myrtle Reeves, Mrs Hardy is well known to the screen, having appeared in various Vitagraph dramas and comedies. She is a very beautiful

137

young woman, the daughter of Mr and Mrs W. D. Reeves of Atlanta, GA. The groom also was a resident of Atlanta before coming west and entering on his career in pictures, three years ago.

The romance is of some time standing, since the bride and groom knew each other back in Atlanta when they went to school together. The first Valentine the bride ever received, she says, was from her youthful admirer, when she was ten years old. She thought he was making fun of her, and wouldn't speak to him for a week. Then he managed to waylay her, and explain.

'Well, I thought you'd lots rather have a nice funny Valentine than one of those silly things!'

Apparently Miss Reeves was convinced, and stayed convinced, since she has wed a comedian rather than a handsome young leading man, who was paying court to her for some time.

Thus was Madelyn Saloshin-Hardy airbrushed from history, only to emerge almost two decades later in even sadder circumstances, which will, in due course, be unveiled.

To recover from the miasmas of the divorce, Babe and Myrtle departed on an extended honeymoon. The filmography shows, indeed, a long gap between *The Show*, completed in November 1921, and Babe's next Semon vehicle, *A Pair of Kings*, shot in the spring of 1922. In the interim, Rob Stone has noted a curiosity, a western feature, *Quicksands*, produced by Howard Hawks and directed by Jack Conway, starring Richard Dix, Helene Chadwick, J. Farrell MacDonald and Jean Hersholt, which was co-written and assistant directed by Babe, though he does not appear in the credits. As Howard Hawks is the credited writer for the movie, one does have the fond image of the young Hollywood macho man and our hero chewing the cud together in the creative field, while Myrtle buzzed about in the sun.

Before this, however, there was another landmark, a curiosity that has caused much confusion in the ranks of Laurel-and-Hardians. Between his stint with Jimmy Aubrey and his promotion to Vitagraph's 'A' company with Larry Semon, Oliver Hardy took a part in a one-off picture with G. M. 'Broncho Billy' Anderson's Amalgamated Producing company, directed by Jess Robbins. It was a film conceived as a vehicle for another actor whom Broncho Billy had long admired and whose stillborn movie career he wished to kick-start. For a long time this movie was assumed to have been made far earlier, in 1917 or 1918, but Rob Stone (adding to research by Swedish film historian Bo Berglund) has convincingly demonstrated it must have been shot in January or February 1921. It was passed by the censorship board of New York in October 1921.

The star actor was Stan Laurel, and the film was called *The Lucky Dog*.

CHAPTER FIFTEEN

Their First Kiss: 'Put 'em both up, insect, before I comb your hair with lead...'

The Lucky Dog is a strange artefact, a somewhat nondescript two-reeler, an odd start to the double act of the century, particularly as neither Stan nor Oliver regarded it as anything but a chance encounter.

Stan is thrown out of his boarding house by his landlady, who flails at him with a broom and the tart comment, 'Pay your bill – it's beginning to look like the war debt.' Knocked silly by her broomstick, he falls in the road, and imagines nymphs dancing about him, till he wakes to find a stray dog nuzzling his face. He adopts the dog, and moons about the streets, almost getting hit by a streetcar, whose conductor dusts him down with the reprimand, 'If you want to be a headlight come around when you're lit up.'

Reeling from this, and finding that the dog, inside his carrying case, is trotting off with it, Stan runs after the dog, and pins it down at a fence by which a hefty thief, with a flat cap and black moustache, is robbing a stranger. Back to back, their behinds touch as Stan bends over to tend to the dog, and the thief stuffs the wad he has stolen into Stan's pants pocket, not his own.

Thus do Stan and Babe finally meet, cheek to cheek, and of such moments is history made. Swinging round, the thief confronts Stan with the first words (albeit intertitled) said by Hardy to Laurel, 'Put 'em both up, insect, before I comb your hair with lead.'

This first exchange is already in perfect physical synch. Stan can't put his hands up without handing Babe the dog. Babe takes the dog with one hand and searches Stan for the cash. The bewildered Stan looks at the cash, grabs it and runs. Babe follows, getting stuck in a hole in a fence, prompting Stan's first thought about Ollie, 'You can't get a truck in a Ford garage.' Then Stan kicks the thief in the bum and runs off. Scene One.

The next scene has Stan trying to get rid of the dog so he can go into a diner. The thief turns up again, but slinks away on seeing a cop. The cop also foils Stan's attempt to stuff the dog in a garbage

The Lucky Dog – first contact

can. Stan then becomes entangled with a poodle which is being entered by a young lady in a nearby dog show. Eyeing the girl, Stan tries to enter the show, but it's for thoroughbreds only, and he is thrown out, followed by more dogs – another sample here of Stan's vaudeville 'fanny flop', as described by Joe Rock. Chatting up the girl in her car, which is parked by a fire hydrant, Stan is told to move on by the cop, so he drives the car off, to the rage of the girl's pompous beau.

Next scene: Stan at her upmarket house, bantering with her side-whiskered Dad, who enquires, when Stan gets his finger caught in the whisky flask, 'Are you always in the same good spirits?' – the liquor jokes marking the movie quite clearly as Prohibition era.

Meanwhile, the jealous beau has recruited Babe to foil Stan – 'He plans a revenge that's worse than the telephone service,' runs the timeless title. Babe has turned up with two guns in his belt, and a stick marked 'DYNAMITE, 100%', commenting, 'I have this Bolsheviki candy.'

Cue the second major scene between Stan and Oliver, who is introduced by the beau to Dad as 'the Count de Chease from Switzerland'. Stan and the thief are left on the sofa, as Babe pokes his gun in Stan's eye with the promise, 'You and the world are going to separate.' Once again the moves, the gestures, the rapport, the well-meshed timing is evident, though Babe was fitting in with Stan only in the same mode he worked with Larry Semon. Just another acting job. Stan puts his fingers in his ears but Babe's gun jams. Stan: 'What have you got in there, rubber bullets?' Followed by: 'I'll fix it, I used to open shells in an oyster house.' Not the greatest dialogue, but H. M. 'Beanie' Walker, Stan and Ollie's later stalwart, was honing his own craft elsewhere.

The gun goes off, shooting the beau in the bum, causing much rushing about, as Babe kidnaps the girl and the beau sets the dynamite by the sofa. The dog, of course, picks up the dynamite. Stan faces the villainous Babe with the gun, but it fails to go off again. Babe picks Stan up and beats him pretty thoroughly, till the beau alerts him to the dog with the dynamite. They run out to the lawn, pursued by Lucky Dog, who is coaxed back by Stan and the girl, leaving the dynamite to blow the two villains up in the shrubbery, making them most dishevelled. The End.

All Stan ever said of this film was:

We had no studio, so we rented space at the Selig Zoo Studio. We were making this picture so Mr Anderson could take it to New York to show them back there, to get a release for twenty-six comedies. So Jess Robbins brought his cameraman over, and also Babe, as we affectionately called him, to play the heavy. That's the first time I met Babe. So we made the comedy and I didn't see him again for probably two or three years.

In fact this film, once again, lead Stan nowhere, and he returned with Mae once more to vaudeville, while Babe returned to his new bride, and to Larry Semon. It was not till the end of the year, winter 1921, that 'Broncho Billy' Anderson finally made money out of *The Lucky Dog*, and returned to the project of producing a comedy series with Stan Laurel.

Of all the mentors in Stan Laurel's life, 'Broncho Billy' was perhaps the most crucial: he kept his faith in Stan's individual talent and put his money down when there were few signs that Stan had any future as a viable screen comedian. Karno and Roach were more influential people, but Stan was only one of their ensemble, initially just a cog in their machines. G. M. Anderson, old Max Aronson, pioneer of a very different genre, had ambitions in the comedy field, and was a stubborn fan. Before Laurel, he had tried to enable Ben Turpin and Billy Armstrong in a series of 'Jolly' comedies, but the financiers failed to share his zeal. Amalgamated Producing was his second comedy venture, and this time, when he persevered, he succeeded.

The Lucky Dog, and the subsequent films Stan made for Anderson, show our Stan still perfectly hesitant in his long-term quest for a comic character. The world of *The Lucky Dog* is a kind of chaos of clashing cultures, of a constant transition: on the one hand, the dangerous world of the streets, where rent-poor hustlers wander about looking for the essentials, food and sex, where thieves rob with practical impunity and the police totter about ineffectively, looking for someone to whap over the head with their clubs. Just beside it, the effete world of the thoroughbred dog fanciers, the vampish girls, the pretentious young men, and their old-world papas living in gilded homes, vulnerable only to the odd stick of dynamite, the con-man burglar on the settee.

The dog itself is a perfect metaphor, trotting happily between the milieux. But, of course, this is bred in the bone of the movie comedy of the times. There is every sign that *The Lucky Dog*, for example, never had a script, and was put together from the bits and pieces of experience of its directors and actors. There was no *auteur* here, not even Stan's relentless search for gags, which would have been only one element of the largely improvised stew.

This is, in fact, America itself in transition, the uneasy cusp between a pre-existing hierarchy of rich and poor, *faux* aristocracy and soup kitchens, newcomers and *arrivistes*, the forward march of technology – telephones, motor cars – and the backward tug of lost rural idylls, with the suffragettes scheming in the backyard. All is uncertainty and flux, as would be apparent in the serious dramas that would define mainstream Hollywood in this period – the crippled soldier played by John Gilbert returning to his rich parents after the horrors of war, in King Vidor's *The Big Parade*, or Stroheim's insistence on dragging MGM's moguls into the lower depths of society with *Greed*. Money may be the root of all evil, but to Charlie Chaplin, Harold Lloyd or Stan Laurel the difference between a ten-cent or one-dollar bill in a diner is the difference between bliss and being beaten up by a coterie of thuggish waiters.

This was, as I have noted in writing about W. C. Fields, also the period in which popular culture, variety, vaudeville, nickelodeons, the newspaper funnies and their celluloid outgrowth, animated cartoons, were having an impact on mainstream writers, dramatists, critics, the world of Broadway and its aficionados in America's big cities. In music: the jazz age, young white men and women dancing to the syncopation of black sounds. This, too, is an indelible part of the silent screen, the tinkling accompaniment that marks even the most basic tracks put on prints or videos of the era's films.

Speed and mobility: the silent comedies exemplify 1920s America, the breathless pace, the churning dynamo of life. Harold Lloyd captured the essence in his 1923 feature classic, *Safety Last*, desperately climbing the tall building floor by floor, hanging by the clock arm above seething traffic, a perfect metaphor of the times. It was, perhaps, part of Stan Laurel's problem that, as a foreigner, an Englishman in America, he was slow to grasp these underlying themes, which seem so obvious to us in hindsight, eighty years down the line. Chaplin, who had the keenest social sensibility and insight of all show people, understood both medium and society, and seized his moment with the tramp. Lloyd took time to find his 'glasses' character, the all-American boy, but then clung to him and reaped the benefits. Keaton found his quiet zone in the storm, and captured the spirit of the eye of the hurricane, the still point around which everything swirls – until he too is thrown into action, with unparalleled force.

To the end of his life, Stan insisted on being an apolitical being, a showman compleat, a universal clown. Of course, he had opinions about the issues of the day, about humanity, about war and peace, about racial divisions, about the sorry plight of the poor. He was, in this sense too, his father's son, scion of Arthur and Madge Jefferson, who brought theatre to the working classes of their area and supplied barefoot children with shoes. Unlike his father, who did his stint as a local Tynemouth councillor in 1901, he had no desire for any influence other than that of entertainment. In a 1934 letter from the Hal Roach Studios, answering some general query sent to show people asking them to name their favourite newspaper comic strips, Stan cites Popeye and The Little King: 'Humor, in any form, is one of the finest tonics for depression, whether the depressed be an individual or a nation. The comic pages of America have done their part in lifting this country out of the dumps and bringing smiles to the haggard face of a worried world.' (Though even that statement may have been ghosted at the time by the studio.)

Getting a general opinion out of Stan Laurel was like pulling teeth. To the end of his life, faced with questions such as, on the Laurel and Hardy British tour of 1932, 'Do you want to play Hamlet?', he would answer doggedly, 'No . . . I am quite satisfied with my job as a comedian.'

Babe would easily give the same answer. It was his job, a stock in trade. You pay me a salary, and I'll act. Although Babe clearly did harbour thoughts of doing more serious stuff, as his brief forays into writing and directing indicate. His third wife, Lucille, confirmed that he had such ambitions, but often lamented the lack of education which, he believed, rendered him unfit for the more lofty spheres. But for Babe, in fact, acting was far more than a job, it was his life, his salvation. It was the way the fat boy turned his fleshly prison into a liberating force. The schoolboy taunts of 'Fatty' were eventually turned into the plaudits of the world. But, unlike Stan, Babe Hardy was less concerned about the nature of the mask.

Thus Babe could return, without much anxiety, to his position as Larry Semon's heavy: the villainous boss, the hotel manager, the angry foreman, the bootlegger 'Don Fusiloil', the father of the bride, 'Dangerous Dan McGraw' the racing driver, and the unshaven, hiss-worthy 'Killer Kid', in *Her Boy Friend* (a later film, of 1924, which also featured another silent film heavy, the even fatter Frank Alexander).

The Semon films were becoming more and more elaborate, with ever more spectacular stunts based on ever more expensive sets, which would stretch the shooting schedule beyond that normally associated with short films. Instead of a film a week, or every two weeks, Semon's films came at monthly intervals, then every two months, or more. Eighty thousand dollars could be spent on a two-reeler. This was making the Vitagraph company's financiers more and more nervous. For *The Sawmill*, Larry spent three months of the summer of 1921 on location in forests five hundred miles north of Hollywood living in log cabins built for crew and cast. A fire in the Sequoia National Forest delayed production and the entire crew of seventy-five joined the firefighters. It was good copy, but a financially sombre time.

Babe enjoys himself in all the Semon pictures, strutting his stuff

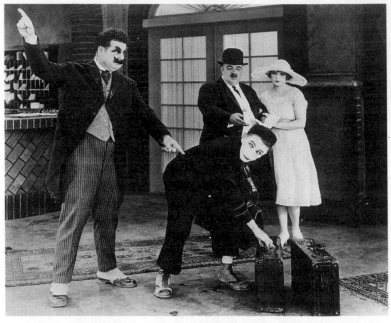

'Babe' Hardy and Larry Semon in *The Bellhop*

and beetling his massive brows. In *The Fall Guy*, a 'modern' western, he plays Black Bart, alias Gentleman Joe – 'WANTED FOR EVERY-THING' according to the poster – who escapes from the law in a racing motor car and then, trapped by Larry in the car in a cabin, drives the entire cabin down the road at high speed until it goes over a cliff.

In *No Wedding Bells*, shot in late 1922, he is the father of a girl who is abducted by a Chinese gang who want to try out their new sleeping potion. The inevitable stereotypes are lightened somewhat by the endless succession of ingenious stunts, falling in and out of secret manholes, being tossed out of windows on to an ambulance only to fall right through a hole in the ground. One of the gags in the film raised the hackles of New York censors, who noted:

Father throws suitor out of house. He goes to trolley track and puts head on track. Car goes by but parts at switch and goes on another track. Man goes over and puts head on second track and car goes on regular track. Man gets disgusted and leaves. Eliminate scenes as 'inhuman and tending to incite crime'.

Babe used some of the gaps in Semon's filming to try two supporting roles in mainstream features. He appears as 'Chief of Police' in Vitagraph's five-reeler *Fortune's Mask*, starring Earle Williams in a South American drama, and as 'Bull Mulligan' in a lost five-reel western, *The Little Wildcat*, starring Alice Calhoun as 'Mag o' the Alley'. 'Bull' was, according to the synopsis, a tough thieves' tavern-owner, who turns out to have a heart of gold.

Both films were shot in the spring–summer of 1922, but Babe then returned to Larry Semon films. In *Lightning Love* (October 1923) he plays Larry's rival for the love of a girl whose father is wheelchair-bound but cantankerous. Much throwing of people out of windows ensues, followed by a major storm sequence in which lightning, marked as animated zigzags on the action, follows the protagonists all over the house and eventually blows the whole building on to a ledge. Larry steps out into empty space and falls down the cliff, on his head. In *Horseshoes* (December 1923), Babe is 'Dynamite Duffy', a fighter who challenges all-comers for $50, but is beaten by Larry with a horseshoe in his glove. In *Trouble Brewing* (released March 1924), Babe is a bootlegger who puts dynamite in the liquor to get rid of troublesome police agent Larry. This was the last of Larry Semon's films for Vitagraph, before he reopened for business as an independent producer in the summer of 1924.

Larry's ever more desperate measures to keep falling on his head from great heights would continue, with Babe at his side, throughout the year. Meanwhile, Stan Laurel, having fallen on his feet, was beginning, at last, to make his mark.

CHAPTER SIXTEEN

The Handy Man

Stan Laurel's first two films for 'Broncho Billy' Anderson were *The Weak-End Party* and *The Handy Man* (filmed early 1922), in both of which he plays a gardener. Neither is particularly distinguished, but there are signs that Stan is beginning to work out a coherent screen character, much akin to the mischievous, amorous servant in the traditional Harlequin mode. In *The Handy Man*, he flirts with the cook, the rather outsize Mirta Sterling, who is also being wooed by the overseer. There are echoes here of Arthur Jefferson's Victorian plays, with their sub-plot affairs between the downstairs help. In one scene Stan and the cook dance into the circle of rich guests, as Stan's tray of garden plants unleashes a plague of poorly animated rats in the ballroom. The film also features a 'Mysterious Stranger', who loiters about under a superimposed question mark, only to be revealed at the end as the cook's lawful wedded husband.

Stan began here in earnest his habit of recycling gags and trying situations that would be repeated, sometimes confusingly, in later films. Rob Stone, in his archaeological excavation of the Stan and Ollie solos, has shown how Stan might re-use scenes from one film in another, or insert out-takes from a previous work. This enabled Stan eventually to resurrect his lost 1917 first movie, *Nuts in May*, to be remade as *Mixed Nuts* by the Anderson company in 1922. Once again, Stan is a book salesman who is so obsessed by Napoleon he becomes Napoleon and wanders in the streets ordering people about after getting away from the asylum. The new movie not only used segments from *Nuts in May* but also some out-takes from Stan's previous short, *The Pest*, which also had him as a stubborn book salesman. The obsession with finding ways to crack nuts – putting them under a judge's gavel, or under a steamroller, is carried over from *The Handy Man*, in which Stan used the gavel of the Justice of the Peace to whom he had repaired with the cook for their disrupted marriage.

There is a clear taste emerging in these movies for highly eccentric

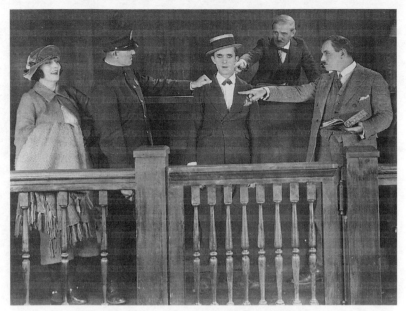

The Pest: Stan, centre, Mae Laurel at far left

gags, which we would today call 'surreal' and which involve ordinary ideas and gestures carried to literally lunatic extremes. Even the titles can go off the map: the introduction to *Mixed Nuts* provides a shot of 'Napoleon' on a rock overlooking the sea and the legend, 'Unknown to the world lives a youth whose great-great-grandmother-in-law washed dishes for Napoleon (which makes him an Elk). Work and money were strangers to him.'

When Stan snatches the steamroller, to crack his nuts, he also rolls forward flattening a row of workmen's lunchboxes and then a row of cars – one of the scenes probably recycled from *Nuts in May*. But this soon proved a dead end. *Mixed Nuts*, in fact, was rejected by Metro, the company releasing G. M. Anderson's films, and it did not in fact get distributed until 1925, by Samuel Bischoff Inc. Still, Stan could not settle on a character. Instead, he veered off in another direction entirely, towards a long-established comic staple – burlesques of mainstream features. The first of these, *Mud and Sand*, ran to three reels. It was Stan Laurel's longest film to date, and his breakthrough to critical acclaim.

Rudolph Valentino, the silent screen's latest and greatest star,

had just released *Blood and Sand*, a smouldering tale of bullfight-
ing and romance. In his own version, Stan plays Rhubarb Vaseline,
a brash young man of rural España whose parents are distraught.
'Mon Dios! I sent Rhubarb for a sack of flour at sunrise! Where can
he be?' moans Mama, while Papa rages, 'Ever since he met that
bullfighter Sapo all we get out of him is bull! bull! bull!'

Rhubarb and Sapo are in fact cavorting down a country road
when they spot a bullfight at the local ring. It's amateur day. The
young blades go into the ring one by one and are carried out on
stretchers. Even Sapo is stricken. But when Rhubarb finally goes in
the ring the first two bulls come flying over the gateway, stunned,
and the third is carried out on the stretcher.

Proceeding to woo his schooldays sweetheart, Caramel (after the
obligatory balcony and pratfall scene), Rhubarb marries her and
rides off to Madrid, where he becomes 'the idol of Spain', and
hangs out at 'The Café Espanola – a famous rendezvous for
picadors, toreadors, matadors, Floradors, Commodores and –
cuspidors'. Here he is spotted by the vampish 'Filet de Sole – who
could put her fins around any poor fish in Spain'. But before she
can snag him, he catches the eye of 'Pavaloosky – the premio
dancer of Madrid'.

Here is our first proper glimpse of Mae Dahlberg-Laurel, as
Pavaloosky, flouncing round the courtyard with Rhubarb. It is a
brief scene, with a tantalizing demonstration of the way the two
move together. Stan wiggles his hips and legs as Mae prances, and
then lets her fall in the fountain as he succumbs to the glad eye of
La Filet sitting on the balcony above the café courtyard.

Mae's presence in the film, and in subsequent ones, was a problem
that was to dog Stan for the next two years. Having been a double
act on stage, the vaudeville act abandoned, and Stan determined to
stick with screen comedies, Mae required her quid pro quo. Stan
and Mae Laurel should be a double act on screen as well, and
Stan informed all his producers of this condition. As Joe Rock,
who would produce his own series of films with Stan in 1924, commented, 'Had she played the character parts, she'd have been the
best in the business.' But Mae insisted on playing *femmes fatales*.

This proved more *fatale* than either would have wished. Even as
Pavaloosky the Rooskie, Mae is carrying a fair deal more body
weight than you might expect in such a role. Unfortunately, she

Odd ruptures in *Mud and Sand*

was no movie beauty. That elusive, intangible quality required by the camera was not part of her gift. The movie audience was still in love with Mabel Normand, Mary Pickford, Lillian Gish. The statuesque woman was, long before Margaret Dumont, a comic foil, but not a leading lady. Behind the scenes, this clash of wills, and Mae's delusions of stardom, ate away at the foundations of the non-marriage, the 'gentlemanly' deal between Mae and Stan.

On screen, the fun and mayhem continued. Rhubarb is seduced by Filet de Sole, but is caught out in her apartments by his wife, Caramel, to whom he makes the feeble, and very modern excuse, 'I didn't mean anything wrong – I just wanted to see her gowns!' Deserted by his wife, he fights the last bullfight of the season, an opportunity for a lot of on-screen bull. Pavaloosky, desiring revenge, persuades her matador admirers to spike Rhubarb's rag with ether, which puts the bull to sleep and Rhubarb too, out cold in a cascade of hats. And the moral: 'If you want to live long and be happy – cut out the bull!'

The anonymous critic of *Motion Picture News* wrote:

Every now and then there comes to the screen a young man who 'carries on' idiotically, who appears – casually observed – a mere clowning fool, but who, more thoughtfully considered, shows himself that rarest of artists, a true buffoon, gifted with the power of bringing laughter which is strangely close to tears. Such a man is Charlie Chaplin; and such a man Stan Laurel is by way of becoming fast.

Such praise was all the sweeter to Stan because the writer gave no sign of knowing that Stan Laurel was Stanley Jefferson who had shared boat and board with Charlie Chaplin just over a decade before. For the first time, he had been recognized and placed at the same level as his Karno colleague of yore. *Kinematograph Weekly* could only have added to his pleasure: 'Stan Laurel is a slapstick comedian who really can act . . . He occasionally copies little actions used by Charlie Chaplin, but does not literally imitate him.' Out of the shadow at last.

It must have been a good Christmas for Stan, in 1922. He already had another 'burlesque' in the can. *When Knights Were Cold* was a pastiche of *When Knighthood Was in Flower*, which starred Marion Davies, and had opened earlier in the year. Stan was Lord Helpus, a Slippery Knight, and Mae was Countess Out, a Classy Eve. The characters' names – Earl of Tabasco, a Hot Knight; Duke of Sirloin, a Tough Knight; Rainy Knights, Foggy Knights and Knights of Pity-Us – look eerily forward to our contemporary Monty Python's *Holy Grail* exploits, as does the scene, described by Stan in later years, in which the knights advanced on paper-basket horses, much as the horseless Pythons of our day.

Despite the critical acclaim of *Mud and Sand*, which was not matched by the response to the second burlesque, this was the end of Stan Laurel's stint with 'Broncho Billy' Anderson. It is not clear whether the distributor, Metro, abandoned the series or whether Stan was satisfied to end the deal because he had found another berth. However the chips fell, by the time the 'Knights' were released to the screen, Stan had signed, for the second time, with Hal Roach, in March of 1923.

*

Stan as Lord Helpus in *When Knights Were Cold*

The Hal Roach Studio that Stan joined in 1923 was a very different enterprise from the belt-and-braces operation of the Rolin company of summer 1918. Roy Seawright, who later became head of Roach's optical and special-effects department throughout the entire Laurel and Hardy period, described those earlier days when the studio 'consisted of one little open-air stage, and in those days nothing was covered up. They just had the draw cloth . . . [to] cut out the sun. And at night-time all the furniture had to be moved in, under cover, in case it rained.' But in 1919 Roach, along with several other film producers, took the opportunity of an offer by real-estate developer Harry Culver to provide free land to build their studios on acreage he had bought south of Los Angeles, previously orange groves and soy-bean fields. Producer Thomas Ince moved in and built a studio which was later to become the mighty Metro Goldwyn Mayer. Roach, having freed himself of former partners, bought nineteen acres to set up the Hal E. Roach Studios, in what was soon to be called Culver City. Roy Seawright's father was Roach's chief architect, but died tragically in a work accident before the studio was completed. The buildings were ready in 1920, and Roach began to gather around him the coterie of crew and actors who would become his regular stock company. Harold Lloyd was still his main star, though he worked with his own autonomous unit, and when Stan joined Lloyd was riding the crest of his wave with his feature masterpiece, *Safety Last*. 'Snub' Pollard was still going strong and Roach had already launched what would become his most lucrative franchise, the 'Our Gang' films, in 1922.

Two key players in the early Hal Roach saga were, as we have mentioned before, the brothers Charley and Jimmy Parrott. Jimmy, as noted, had a small role in Stan's first extant Rolin movie, *Just Rambling Along*, as the waiter who helps throw Stan out at the end. By 1921, he was starring for Roach in a series of one-reelers under the moniker of 'Paul Parrott', his lugubrious long-faced visage advertised as 'The Doodlewit of Screen Comedy'. It was to alternate with the 'Paul Parrott' series that Stan was signed on by Roach. James Parrott was, it seems, an epileptic, and this led to his being switched eventually from acting to directing, as Roach figured the director was easier to replace at short notice. Later on, there would be other, compounding problems, with both Parrott brothers, of the familiar intoxicant kind. James's brother Charley began his career with Roach exclusively as a director, mainly for the 'Snub' Pollard series, from February 1921. In December 1921 Charley was appointed director general of the Hal Roach studio, making him the most important figure in the shaping of the studio's style of comedy, long before he turned to full-time acting and became Charley Chase, in the autumn of 1923.

Apart from the Parrotts, Roach had a full menagerie of animals, dogs, monkeys, ducks and larger beasts, who would even have their own short-lived series, under the rubric of 'The Dippy Doo-Dads'. The most dangerous of these animals were the ostriches, which, in another studio, Fox, put paid to the career of another Karno exile, Billie Ritchie, the only comedian to have been kicked to death by a bird. (This too occurred in 1921.)

From the beginning, there was a great deal of raucous fun at the Hal Roach lot, and 1922 inaugurated an annual Christmas dinner and show in which most of the actors took part. The 1922 show was a spoof Civil War drama, with Jimmy Parrott and 'Snub' Pollard dressed as Honolulu hula dancers, climaxing in a drag beauty contest. The record does not reveal who took the trophy . . .

By 1923, the studio was expanding again, and Roach found new investors to put several hundred thousand dollars into his enterprise. In July, Charley Parrott and Robert MacGowan, director of the 'Our Gang' pictures, opened a school for comedy directors, meeting every Monday.

Stan Laurel, however, had his own ideas of comedy, and from 1923 on he finally had the freedom to develop and enhance them. Although Stan's second phase with Hal Roach was interrupted by a series of films he made for Joe Rock, we can take Stan's solo movies from now on as a fairly seamless progression and experimentation in search of his own comic style. With twenty-four films shot in the first year of his contract, twelve for Joe Rock from early 1924 to summer 1925, and a further twenty-four – some of them as writer and director – for Hal Roach, before his first teamed appearance with Oliver Hardy, Stan Laurel was busy exploring his art.

To Stan, of course, art was not the issue so much as work and the remuneration thereof. The move to Joe Rock, like the move back to Hal Roach, was caused by business conflicts arising from issues such as the percentage the actor would retain from the producers' take on each movie. Twelve and a half per cent from Roach, fifteen from Joe Rock, and various arguments about advances. The most prominent witness to this, producer Joe Rock himself, exhibits the selective memory common to many old-timers, claiming that Stan Laurel was down on his luck at the time, short of funds, and badly advised by his manager, Percy Pembroke. In fact, actors always had good reason to fight for their cash with producers, and documents from the Hal Roach Studio reveal that payment to Stan Laurel, in the year 1925, when Stan was already a minor star in his own right, totalled $5,695, at a salary range of $125 to $200 per week. These were not, even for 1925, hot figures, even though Stan made only six movies for Roach that year. In 1926, when Stan made seventeen movies for Roach, he was paid $12,050, or an average of about $700 per film.

The other persistent wrangle, according to Joe Rock, was Stan's continuing insistence on Mae as his co-star. The record shows, however, that Mae was not listed in the cast, and was certainly not co-starring, in most of the 1923 batch of Roach comedies. She was present in the first of those films, *Under Two Jags*, a Foreign Legion burlesque, as Cheroot, dancer at the Café D'Joint, who falls for a dashing young stranger. But Stan had a cuter leading partner here in Katherine Grant (as 'Princess') a Roach regular with a much sweeter screen presence.

The next Stan vehicle, *The Noon Whistle*, was Mae-less, but chock-full of Roach regulars such as Noah Young, Sam Brooks and William Gillespie, and another recent Roach recruit, who would play an enormous part in shaping the comedy that would lead to Laurel and Hardy. Playing the foreman to Stan's clumsy lumber worker, here is our first peek at Jimmy Finlayson.

Who can forget Fin, the balding, moustached and often seething Scot, master of the double and triple take, whom many would regard as the third member of the Laurel and Hardy team – the indispensable foil, the vengeful home-owner who would rival them in mutual destruction in their Christmas tree sales saga, *Big Business*, and countless other episodes?

He was born James Henderson Finlayson in Larbert, Scotland (near Falkirk, often recorded as his birthplace), on 27 August 1887. Laurel and Hardy fan Bill Cappello, with the help of a Finlayson offshoot, John Armstrong of Dundee, has traced the family back to one Malcolm Finlayson, 'iron-grinder' at the turn of the nineteenth century. Fin's father, Alexander, was a blacksmith. His mother, Isabella Henderson, hailed from Stonehaven. James had three sisters and two brothers, one of whom, Robert, became a cameraman. Little is known of his childhood and early life, which involved an apprenticeship as a metal worker, abandoned for the more congenial life of an actor. The oral tale includes a stint at Edinburgh University (possibly apocryphal), and dramatic work with Alex Lauder, brother of the famous Harry, in plays that included *Rob Roy*. He first surfaces in the verifiable record as part of a repertory company that came to the United States in late 1911 or early 1912, playing a role in a short, 'curtain-raiser' drama called *The Great Game*, at Daly's Theater, New York.

This was another of these rather common English sketches concerning spoof detectives and cod burglars, not a million smiles removed from Arthur Jefferson's own *Unwilling Burglar*. 'It has three characters', wrote the *New York Herald* (17 May 1912),

and its one scene is in a Tilbury docks house. Two criminals are dodging the police in this hiding place, which has a secret outlet. They expect a young Scotchman, an innocent country relative of the landlady. He comes and proves as innocent as a lamb and a great bore. The thieves get some of his money at cards and then proceed to unpack his valise. Of course, anybody who has read the programme knows that the Scottish country bumpkin is a detective. How these English hate a joke or a secret! So this braw laddie from the Hielands lets the thieves unpack and when they find a pair of handcuffs in his bag he 'covers' with a revolver and orders the other to put the 'irons' on the main robber. Then he marches him out of doors, manacled, and, revealing his detective personality, shouts over his shoulder to the gaping criminal: 'It's a great game.'

The *New York Tribune*, on 12 May, sniffed that 'the piece seems better suited to be used as a sketch for the varieties rather than as a curtain-raiser to a drama. It has, in fact, been used in the London halls.' But, the paper averred, it was 'well enough done by James Finlayson as the detective, Frank Woolfe as the burglar and Lewis Broughton as the thief'. The *New York Dramatic Mirror* was, as ever, more generous, commenting, 'James Finlayson had an excellent opportunity, which he did not miss, for developing two characters in his one role – the simple, naïve Scotchman and the artful, determined detective. The remarkable thing is he managed to do them both at the same time.'

There's our Fin, ready made. His next incarnation was in a more substantive piece, Graham Moffat's three-act Scottish comedy *Bunty Pulls the Strings*, a character piece of village life, with James Finlayson as Rab Biggar, spouse of the eponymous Bunty. This had a long, successful tour, which clearly convinced Fin, like Stan Laurel and Chaplin before him, that America was the place for him. He was said to have toured across country with Alex Lauder in a sketch called *The Concealed Bed*, which was so well concealed that no trace of it can be found.

Arriving in Los Angeles in 1916, James found work at L-KO and Thomas Ince's studio in films of which there is no record. Official statements that he was one of the original Keystone Kops are the usual froth of legend, though he acted in several post-1917 Mack Sennett comedies. At Sennett, however, he always played 'second banana' to Mack's established stars – Ben Turpin, Ford Sterling, Louise Fazenda, Billy Bevan. He left Sennett in 1922, but a short sojourn at Metro and Universal did not lead to better prospects. His move to the Hal Roach Studios coincided, give or take a month or two, with Stan Laurel's, and was part of Roach's expansion plans.

The Noon Whistle is an inspired twinning of Stan and Fin in an antagonistic combination. Finlayson's outraged sideways glance and the emphatic fury at Stan's incompetence are both present from their first scene together. Fin is foreman O'Hallahan of an ailing lumber company, whose boss rails at him, 'The men are so lazy they lean against each other when they loaf.' The prime loafer on site is Stan as 'Tanglefoot – doesn't know what it's all about – doesn't even know it's going on'. Much mayhem ensues with piles of wood and planks which Stan carries, scurrying about and behind Fin, twisting and turning to catch him. A gag with Stan carrying a long plank past Fin with it extending seemingly for ever until Stan appears carrying its other end will be repeated in Stan and Ollie's *The Finishing Touch*. The whole ethos of the piece will re-emerge in *Busy Bodies*, ten years down the construction line. Stan's character, albeit more brash and deliberately obtuse than he will be with Ollie, is heading in a familiar direction. Some destructive business hauling a bag of cement up with a rope leaves Finlayson dangling with his feet caught in a barrel of glue. At the end, the boss decides to fire the foreman for failing to get his men to work properly, handing him a slip that reads:

NOTICE OF DISCHARGE
Name: T. O'Hallahan
Complaint: Dumb-Bell
Time due: 3 Days
5–11–23

The Noon Whistle inaugurated a series of Roach one-reelers in which Stan parodied and explored gags about various forms of work. *White Wings* had Stan as a street cleaner; *Pick and Shovel* had him working in a mine; in *Kill or Cure* he was a door-to-door salesman; in *Collars and Cuffs* a laundry worker; in *Gas and Air* a petrol-station boy; in *Oranges and Lemons* a citrus-grove hand; in *Short Orders* a cook and waiter. Some of these were directed by his manager, Percy Pembroke, and others by Roach regular George Jeske. Jimmy Finlayson appeared in the first three of the series (and was to return later), and most of them feature a new Stan Laurel regular-to-be, the cross-eyed innocent played by George Rowe. Katherine Grant appeared in all but the last of them, and Mae Laurel appeared in none.

These films are typical of the Roach ethos of characters and situations that would be recognizable to the ordinary man in the street. Though thin on plots, they were certainly a gag-rich environment. In *White Wings*, Stan's white-suited cleaner – a character both Chaplin and Harry Langdon were to play at some point – is positively manic in his disdain for hard work and sheer relish in getting himself chased by his foe, the fat cop, played by Marvin Lobach (who would later co-star with 'Snub' Pollard in a short-lived Hardy-and-Laurel-like series). Stan takes all setbacks in his stride, being swept away in mid-job by a car, picking up a baby to admire from its pram, only to end up carrying it off in panic when its nurse alerts a policeman. A gag that will be repeated much later in the Laurel and Hardy feature *Block-Heads* has Stan, perched with his right leg folded on a fire hydrant, handed a coin by a compassionate passer-by, cross-eyed George Rowe, who mistakes him for a crippled war veteran. When Stan straightens his leg, Rowe alerts the policeman, and the chase resumes, leading to a 'PAINLESS DENTISTRY' booth, at which Stan gets mistaken for the dentist. 'YOU HAVE THE TEETH, WE HAVE THE PULL,' says the notice. Stan proceeds to administer anaesthetic with the aid of a mallet – shades of the old Stan and Mae dentist sketch – but when his last patient is the cop, he is the one who gets bashed on the head and knocked out.

In *Pick and Shovel* Stan picks up the old Larry Semon *Huns and Hyphens* gag of arriving at work dressed in top hat and tails only to disrobe to reveal himself as a worker. In *Collars and Cuffs*, every laundry joke in the book is pulled, climaxing in Stan shutting a fellow worker in the washing machine and flooding the workplace with an ocean of soap suds. The climax of slipping, pratfalling workers and policemen looks forward to the mass mutual destruction of the early silent Laurel and Hardys, the great pie fight of *Battle of the Century* or the mass pants-ripping of *You're Darn Tootin'*.

Following the 'job' series, *A Man About Town*, filmed in May 1923, is another characteristic Roach confection of city-street gags, with Stan asking a conductor which streetcar he should transfer to for his destination, and being told to 'follow that girl, she's going in that direction'. Endless wrong turnings shot in the streets and shops of Culver City ensue as Stan follows the wrong girl, with Keatonesque tenacity, and is followed in turn by Jimmy Finlayson's store detective, in and out of streetcars and to a barbershop graced with not one but two cross-eyed barbers. Jimmy Finlayson exhibits his growing capacity to be funny simply by appearing on screen. His air of exaggerated zeal and misplaced energy made him an indispensable second-stringer, though his ambition to have his own series was still thwarted by Roach.

Stan and Fin starred next in *Roughest Africa*, a return to the pastiche, spoofing popular documentaries highlighting the 'dark continent'. There are bathing beauties, apes, lions, a rhino, an elephant and native bearers, but this is one genre that fails to bridge the gap to our times. The trade magazines of the day, however, loved it. Stan continued the trend with *Scorching Sands*, another oriental flimflam, and, the same summer, *Frozen Hearts*, an elaborate satire set in Tsarist Russia.

This Russian two-reeler marked the return to the screen of Mae Laurel, as a haughty princess, alongside Jimmy Finlayson as General Trobounikoff and Stan as the peasant lad, Ivan Kektumoff. Discussing this film prompts thoughts of the experience of viewing many of these old, rediscovered solo movies, often found in European archives, in French, Spanish or Dutch versions. The names of the characters often changed depending on local titlers' fancies. Some of the Larry Semon films have survived only in Spanish versions with a soundtrack consisting of an infuriating narrator noting smugly every fall and gesture of 'Jaimito'. A batch of the Stan Laurel Roach solos come from Holland, with the non-Dutch speaker having to wrestle with the intertitles: 'In dien tijd deef de Rusland onder en militaire terreur . . . Menschen mit borstelig haar werden naar Siberie gezonden.' I think we can get the drift.

Stan, as Ivan, is 'de aanbidder van Naphtaline en zoon van een vroeger Wolgaschlepper', which sums Stan up pretty thoroughly. One early gag has Ivan saying his farewells to his girl, Naphtaline ('Sonia' in the original), retreating to open door after door and return for another kiss, the final opening being a window through which he pratfalls to be caught by the guards of the villainous Lieutenant Tumankikine, who snatches the lass off to bondage in St Petersburg. Ivan follows, becoming enmeshed in the lechery of Fin the General and Mae as Princess Sodawiski. There are further cross-eye-ist gags with George Rowe as a soldier who, ordered to shoot Stan, shoots the guards either side of him. A duel in the snow between Stan and Fin is the centrepiece of the action. They fight to a standstill, and a title good enough for Buñuel's *L'âge d'or* proclaims, 'Seven maandes later', with Stan and Fin buried chest high in snow, still feebly pawing each other with broken swords.

Stan appears very assured in this spoof, donning a false beard to dance a kazatski with Mae, and peeling off a most effeminate corset for his duel in undershirts with Finlayson. The duel continues with pistols, everyone getting shot but the duellists, until Stan/Ivan and his girl are reunited under a ton of snowflakes.

Another spoof, *The Soilers*, also included Mae Laurel as a saloon girl and Fin as the shady businessman, Smacknamara. Stan's next two films abandoned pastiche for a while. *Mother's Joy*, the tale of a reluctant bridegroom, burlesques Stan's own real-life relationship with Mae. Stan doubles as Magnus Dippytack and his son Basil, Magnus being the seducer of Baron Buttontop (Finlayson)'s daughter, and Basil is the Baron's now adult grandson. The Baron wants to marry Basil to rich heiress Flavia de Lorgnette (Mae), but Basil likes the maid (Ena Gregory). There is an early precursor here of the posh dinner party in Stan and Ollie's *From Soup to Nuts*, and a return to Stan's more surreal moments. When a whistle interrupts the wedding, Stan rushes into the bathroom to feed a horse hay. (Horses in strange indoor places will also figure in the future Laurel and Hardy *œuvre* . . .) There is the first instance of Stan dissolving in tears, though it is still not a 'proper' Laurel cry. Stan's offer to sing empties the room of all guests, and prompts the title about Mae, 'She accepted him on one condition – that he died young.'

The wedding ceremony is constantly interrupted by the obvious reluctance of both parties to go through with it. Pastor: 'Do you take this awful man to be your awful wedded husband?' Mae: 'No, I've taken a dislike to him.' Stan, asked the same question after she has been calmed down: 'No, I've taken a dislike to her.' And the climax – Pastor: 'I refuse to marry them! I've taken a dislike to the whole outfit!'

A keen, if unconscious foresight of Stan's marital life as it would unfold. But for the moment he was still journeying through life and work with Mae, difficult as this would be for the producers who wanted Stan to stick to prettier screen-mates. This conflict would slowly simmer and eventually come to the boil during Stan's stint with Joe Rock in the latter part of 1924. Stan did not rejoin Hal Roach until the spring of 1925. But by that time our Dance of the Two Separated Heroes had begun to end, as Oliver Norvell Hardy was recruited to the Hal Roach studios between January and April of 1925.

Laurel and Hardy were finally in the same studio – but still, as performers, apart.

CHAPTER SEVENTEEN

Somewhere, Over the Rainbow . . .

Babe Hardy's long stretch with Larry Semon climaxed with Larry's most ambitious project to date, a feature-film production of Frank Baum's classic *The Wonderful Wizard of Oz*, released in 1925. This was not the first 'Oz' feature, as Frank Baum himself had produced *The Patchwork Girl of Oz* back in 1914. The 1925 film was Larry Semon's second feature – the first, *The Girl in the Limousine*, was shot in the summer of 1924. Chaplin had produced *The Kid* in 1921; Lloyd had shot six features, including *Safety Last*, by 1924; Keaton had made four features, including the ambitious *The Navigator*, by then. Semon considered his time had come, but he misfired. Oliver Hardy, shorn of his villain's whiskers, and playing a young man about town, joined Larry faithfully in his limousine, but the film disappointed both critics and audiences, who judged it an artificially padded two-reeler.

Semon's *Wizard* was given the full luxury Hollywood opening, and picked up a mixed bag of reviews. Some, like the *New York Evening World*, praised 'one of the best comedies seen on Broadway in a long time'. Semon still had his fans, but the film does not stand up to the test of time. Where Chaplin, Keaton and Lloyd were mastering structure, plot and character, Semon was stuck in a doll's house of slapstick antics, animated lightning bolts, and sneering villains with names like Prime Minister Kruel, Ambassador Wikked and Countess Vishuss. The familiar 'Oz' tale was thrown overboard and replaced with a long Kansas prologue in which Dorothy, winsomely played by Semon's wife Dorothy Dwan, is revealed to be the real ruler of Oz, who will come into her inheritance on her eighteenth birthday if only the plans of the Kruels and Wikkeds can be thwarted. Semon and Babe were farmhand rivals for her favours, Semon the good innocent country bumpkin and Babe the corruptible one. The storm sequence in which they are both swept up with Dorothy in a cabin swept along the sky is the film's best moment, a spectacular use of giant wind-machines. But

Hardy and Semon in *The Perfect Clown*, with Dorothy Dwan

the script has them dressing up as the Scarecrow and Tin Woodsman merely as a ruse to fool the Ozites. Babe lumbers about semi-amiably with not much guidance – the dead giveaway is the credit for Semon as writer, director and producer. The worst aspect of the film is the casting of Spencer Bell, toe-curlingly credited as 'G. Howe Black', as the Cowardly Farmhand cum Lion, a depressing Jim Crow type. The film totters towards an inconclusive chase in a tackily constructed dungeon before reverting in exhaustion to its framing device of an aged Larry reading the book to his little granddaughter.

Oliver Hardy appeared in two more Larry Semon features, *The*

Perfect Clown in 1925 and *Stop, Look and Listen*, released in 1926. The latter is a lost film, and in the former Babe has a small role as a bullying landlord chasing Larry for his rent. Once again there are some good slapstick gags, but Larry's career was already edging downwards. Although in 1923 he had signed with Truart Pictures for a million dollars a year, by 1927 he could hardly get paid to be buried. His entire output for the year was two shorts and a failed independent feature, *Spuds*, with Dorothy Dwan but without Babe Hardy. Later in the year he even tried returning to vaudeville. In March 1928 he filed for bankruptcy and, his health broken by his sudden fall from grace, he died on 8 October 1928, at the age of thirty-nine.

Like Harry Langdon soon after him, Semon was the victim of the dizzy boom and bust of movie acclaim. The addled memory of Hollywood assured his oblivion, and it is ironic that today he is remembered, and his films rediscovered, mainly because of Babe Hardy's presence in them. He was a man who sought harm for no one and wished only to amuse and entertain. If he was brought down by his own delusional faith in his star, he was only following the American Dream, which rocketed him to the skies, and then allowed him to fall to his doom. Perhaps we should leave him flying in his storm-tossed cabin, midway between Kansas and Oz.

Babe Hardy, on the other hand, plodded on, still content in his supporting roles. Life with Myrtle, and the long periods waiting for Semon to make up his mind about his productions, allowed him some leeway to develop a new interest in life – a lasting passion for golf, a pastime to which Semon had introduced him. Now that he had joined the world of Hollywood's denizens, he might as well play their game, and look back fondly, but distantly, on the days of proletarian baseball. Since 1922 Hardy had moved home twice, first to 4425 Russell Avenue, not far from his former home in Los Feliz, and then, in 1924, to 1719 Talmadge, also near by, just off Sunset Boulevard. At some later point he joined the Lakeside Country Club, which was, alas, restricted to non-Jews.

Babe's loyalty to his collaborators was expressed in his tribute to Larry Semon, quoted by John McCabe:

Larry was second only to Stan and Chaplin when it came to creating gags. The thing that kept him from staying at the top was that at heart he was never really an actor. I felt very bad about his end because when I worked for him, he gave me every opportunity to shine, and that wasn't usually Larry's way with other comics . . . He wanted the action to concentrate on him, and why shouldn't he? I lost a good friend and a very kindly boss.

A handsome tribute, but what does Babe mean about Semon not being an actor at heart? There is some puzzlement here at people who reach for more than just the professional satisfaction of a job well done. Naked ambition was an alien trait to Babe Hardy.

In the intervals between Semon features Babe returned to shorts, finding a new berth at a company called Arrow Pictures, which had signed on Babe's old partner, Billy West, and another young performer, Bobby Ray. Their first film together, with Billy West producing, was *Stick Around*, released in March 1925, and often known today to fans under a later retitle, *The Paperhanger's Helper*. It is an intriguing two-reeler, in which Bobby Ray and Babe present an embryonic Laurel and Hardy routine, with Bobby as the new gormless recruit to Blatz and Blatz Interior Decorators and Babe Hardy as his frustrated boss. Both are dressed in the overalls and bowler hats characteristic of *The Finishing Touch* or *Busy Bodies*. Babe even has the little smudge of a moustache that would remain for most of his next Arrow films and his solo run at Roach.

From the start, Babe is taking control from Bobby: 'Leave everything to me and see what happens.' He tips his hat forward, with that determined look. Bobby proceeds to make a Stan-like mess of papering the sanitarium they're contracted to decorate, while Babe snoozes on a chair. Paint spills, falls occur from ladders, and a patient's long beard is accidentally glued and cut off ('Remove the shredded wheat, Santa Claus!') to the plaintive cry of: 'You've ruined my beard! Now I've got to wash my neck!'

Stick Around is a seminal film, because it demonstrates that the on-screen relationship and routines of the Laurel and Hardy movies derive as much from Oliver Hardy's experience of teamwork with his range of comedy collaborators, from the days of Lubin and Vim through to Billy West and Larry Semon, as from Stan Laurel's workshop of gags. What appears unique, or *sui generis*, to the casual observer, is revealed so often as the consequence of a long string of development which has been obscured by the amnesia of passing time and the disappearance, except to a band of zealous restorers, of so much work that danced and sparkled in its day. And so much that has been rediscovered, in movies, suffers from the often terrible state of surviving prints, the fuzzy images of old dreams vanishing into a chemical entropy.

At the end of *Stick Around*, the hapless decorators get drunk, due to booze spilled into the water supply, and, when the head shrink tells them, 'You're fired!', Babe replies, 'You can't fire us! We quit!', linking arms with Bobby and backing gracefully out to the balcony, only to fall over, one floor down, into the street. The old, once again, prefigures the new.

Babe and Bobby Ray were teamed again in Babe's next-but-one Arrow film, *Hey, Taxi!*, in which they work for rival cab companies and steal each other's customers. Despite being a 'Mirthquake Comedy' it is not very mirthful, featuring a fair amount of falling out of windows and hiding in barrels. Babe reverts to his role as a heavy, which he plays in three out of the four remaining shorts in this series. Billy West, who stars in three of the Arrow films, has abandoned his Chaplin imitation and tries to find a new role as a tearaway. The presence of many Semon-like gags suggests that Babe had a great deal to do with the planning and staging of these films, despite playing second fiddle again.

The short-lived Arrow productions could only be a stopgap for Babe in his search for a new long-term engagement. But he was now an established and well-known asset, a character actor of proven value and versatility. With the small production companies wilting under the pressure of Hollywood's big battalions, and Mack Sennett's comedies a pale shadow of their former glory, there was only one place for the jobbing comedian with an eye to the future to go. And so it was that, in May 1925, the first film of the Hal Roach Studio featuring Babe Hardy was released by Pathé Exchange.

Called *Wild Papa*, it was part of a now obscure comedy series featuring the 'Spat Family', with Frank Butler and Sidney D'Albrook as scatty brother-in-laws. Babe played a gun-toting country bumpkin. The film has not survived, nor has Babe's next effort, *Neptune's Stepdaughter*, for the Fox Film Corporation. But Babe's next short established him firmly as a Roach company player. The vehicle was a Charley Chase comedy, *Isn't Life Terrible?* Babe co-starred with a cast of studio regulars already familiar to us from Stan Laurel's

Hal Roach films – Katherine Grant, the optically challenged George Rowe and Sam Brooks. It also introduces into our tale another major player, and crucial fulcrum in the development of Laurel and Hardy – director Leo McCarey.

Meanwhile, back in the domestic arena, things were not turning out so well for Stan and Mae Laurel. Biographers are often expected by readers to follow their subjects into their most intimate places, breathlessly wielding the negatives of speculation and required to produce positive facts. It is bad enough to place trust in the recollections of living witnesses, or to try to interpret the poisonous language of divorce petitions, but when one deals with events stretching back eight decades, the reader should be wary of the results. In this case, the memories are those of Joe Rock, to whom Stan turned after his percentage spat with Hal Roach, early in 1924.

A letter from Stan to Warren Doane, Roach's manager at Culver City (sent from Stan's residence at Sommerset Apartments, 6075 Franklin Avene, Hollywood – not far from Babe at Russell Avenue), provides a little background to this switch and shows his growing irritation with Roach's handling of his work:

Dear Mr Doane,
I shall be pleased if you would give me some information regarding the participation due me, also as to whether 'KILTS' and 'RUPERT OF HEE HAW' have been accepted or not.
    Awaiting your favour, best wishes,

                                             STAN LAUREL

The letter is written on paper headed 'Stan Laurel Comedies, Under the Personal Management of Percy Pembroke; European representative: Arthur Jefferson, Esq., 49 Colebrooke Ave., West Ealing, London W.(13)', an interesting insight into the reconnection of the Jefferson clan. Stan's letter refers to the last two of his 1923–24 films for Roach, the first another spoof, of *Rupert of Henzau*, still featuring Mae Laurel, as the Queen, with Stan in a double role as both the king and the impostor. The second title, *Short Kilts*, a tale of thrifty Scotsmen, can best be described as: 'The inhabitants of Brigadoon wake up on the wrong day.' Jimmy Finlayson at last gets to play a 'real' Scotsman, beside one of Roach's 'Our Gang' regulars, young Mickey Daniels. There is no sign, mercifully, of Mae. The film may have been a follow up to a previous offering, *Near Dublin*, a tale of cod Irishmen hitting each other over the head with bricks. Stan's next short, *Smithy*, was another 'Noon Whistle' tale, with Fin and Stan reprising a set of building-site jokes – another dry run for *The Finishing Touch*.

Both the films referred to in Stan's letter were not released till the summer of 1924, but by then Stan had jumped ship to Rock. Joe Rock claimed to have signed Stan for a five-year contract, but this, too, was contested later. Rock recollected, in his rambling interview with Randy Skretvedt of 1979,

I had given Stan, even before I signed him . . . $1,000 before I went to find out if they'd take him – nobody wanted him. I couldn't sell him . . . Because, Educational said, 'Joe, you're never gonna deliver twelve pictures with Stan. Now we know that.' . . . Because of Mae . . . Because, you see, he never could finish with anybody else . . .

There follows a great deal of confusing information in which details of Stan's first stint with Roach, and his decision to go back to the stage with Mae, are mixed up with the second, two years later. Then Rock remembers, again out of sequence, days shooting with Stan at Arrowhead Lake, in the San Bernardino mountains, which must refer to the eighth of the Rock-produced films, *The Snow Hawk*, another spoof:

ROCK: We couldn't get accommodation up in Arrowhead, so there's a little spot before going up to Arrowhead, where there was an inn, and bungalows . . . [it was] on location . . . Perce Pembroke, I think, was doing the picture then . . . [Percy Pembroke directed ten of the Rock films, Harry Sweet the other two.] He had a bungalow, Stan and Mae had a bungalow, I had one . . . the rest of the people stayed in the inn. Ten or twelve, fifteen, whatever number it was . . . And I don't know whether it was when I first came down, and parked, and going towards my bungalow and there comes Mae.
SKRETVEDT: Stan had brought her with him?
ROCK: Oh, yeah . . . But I'd never allow her on the set, you see. And I talked to her. I said, 'I didn't know you were up here.' 'Oh, yes.' 'Fine.' So I went to the inn, and whatever the meal was, so, I got into my bungalow, and . . . my wife was there, see. Nobody knew she was up . . . So the next morning, Stan gave me the [?]. And I said, 'What the hell is the matter?' He said, 'You know what the matter is, you know what the

matter is.' I said, 'What is the matter?' So he took me aside, and he said, 'What did you do with Mae?' He said, 'You came into the bungalow, and you tried to make her . . .' I said, 'Oh, come on, did she tell you that?' He said, 'Yes, she told me that.' I said, 'Stan, you must be kidding.' I says, 'Come here.' So we walk up to the inn, we walk in and there's Louise [Rock's wife]. He says, 'Louise, when did you come up?' She said, 'Last night.' He looks like this, and when we walked out, he said, 'Joe, I'm sorry. Mae has pulled that on Roach, she's pulled it on Jack White, she's pulled it on . . .' I said, 'Stan, look. After all, she's your girl. She's not mine.'

Mae was trying, Rock claimed, to use her wiles to get into the pictures, a pretty counter-productive ploy, given the availability, one might think, of younger and more attractive ladies. In the fog of time, it is impossible to verify Rock's tale, but there can be no doubt that Stan's and Mae's fights were grinding both of them down, as well as affecting their friends and colleagues and impacting badly on Stan's career. Rock even claimed that Stan began appearing to work, in the mornings, with the scratches of Mae's nails on his face.

The solution, Rock maintained, was to pack Mae back home, to Australia:

I said, if she does want to go, Stan, I'll put up the money. Would $1,000 cover it?' He said, 'Oh, yes. I've got to get out some jewelry . . .' I said, 'Give me a list.' The jewelry was about $200 or $300, and the boat maybe $200 to 300, so on and so forth. I said . . . 'There's transportation up to San Francisco', because the boat leaves from there . . . So that was agreed. She would have close to $300 in cash. And she'd have a new hat, new coat, all that kind of stuff, and the ticket. So then Stan came to me, and he says, 'Joe, Mae is not gonna go until she gets the jewelry.' I said . . . 'She's gonna go, or else . . . she's gonna get it when the purser gives it to her a hundred miles out in the ocean. [Rock had planned to pay the purser $10 for this service.] She's gotta be on that boat.' And then there was a stand-off for about a day or two, then they came. Because she had no money, you see, and she could have made money on the ticket, and all that kind of business . . .

Another tale, that had Stan and Joe Rock plotting to have Mae deported from the country as an illegal foreigner, only to face the apathy of the US Immigration Service, sounds even stranger than the account above. There is, in fact, no hard evidence that Mae ever left the US, as she was back in the story in 1936, suing Stan for maintenance, as we have noted before. But she might well have felt that her long journey with Stanley Jefferson had finally run its course, and accepted the rather shabby deal offered. According to Rock's account, the day Mae left, and Stan celebrated his 'freedom', Rock introduced him to a young actress on his payroll, Lois Neilson, who had, as we noted, appeared in one of Stan's 1918 Rolin comedies. According to Rock, they hit it off right away, and were married six weeks later. Since Stan's last Rock film was released in August 1925, and Stan and Lois were married on 23 August 1926, this stretches the six weeks beyond all reasonable bounds.

Whether Stan knew Lois Neilson before the break with Mae, or only renewed his acquaintance months later, is a matter lost in the recollective whirl. Hints that she acted in some of Stan's Joe Rock movies are not borne out by their credits. These reveal one Julie Leonard as a frequent female lead, and, in a still from *The Snow Hawk*, the first appearance of a lady later to be famous as an axiom of the Laurel and Hardy series – eighteen-year-old Anita Garvin.

Stan's films for Rock continued his ongoing personal workshop of gags, character, and situations, though the plots remain a mite threadbare. In *Mandarin Mix-Up* Stan plays a Chinese laundry worker, Sum Sap. This is a kind of continuation of Stan's work-themed films, but with a bizarre edge. Wafted into a dream by an opium-smoking companion, Stan dances off his bunk in slow motion, and falls into a Buddhist temple frequented by yellow-peril stereotypes with knives. There are some odd gags with pigtails – Stan ties two of his fellow workers' hair together and hangs a pair of pants over the span – an incomprehensible twist dressed as a cop, *à la* Chaplin's *Easy Street*, and the whole wraps up with the revelation that he was a white kid left in a pile of laundry. At the end, Stan does a soon-to-be famous scissors kick and run as he chases after the taxi out of which he's fallen. *Kinematograph Weekly* called the piece 'an irresponsible filler comedy'.

Stan followed this with a return visit to Rhubarb Vaselino in *Monsieur Don't Care*, a spoof on Valentino's *Monsieur Beaucaire* and the only one of the Rock movies still missing. But the next film shows Stan in top form. In *West of Hot Dog*, Stan is a tenderfoot travelling west on the stagecoach when Bad Mike holds it up. As

Stan is trying to drive the robbed stage on into town with the sheriff's daughter (Julie Leonard again), the horses bolt, and he is left with the reins. The film was shot in the autumn of 1924 at Universal Studios, as were most of the Rock films, and benefits from fine frontier sets. Stan is in town to claim an inheritance left by his uncle, but, at the lawyer's office, he finds two mighty tough hombres, who are also nephews of the deceased.

There follows one of Stan's finest gags. As he sits hesitant by the window, the two tough guys pick him up and throw him out into the street, on his head. He runs back in and closes the window, only to be thrown through the smashed glass, again. The third time he dives out of the window without being thrown. All three falls must have involved a dummy, but running the video version in slow motion repeatedly, there is only the most fleeting sign of the join where dummy Stan gives way to real Stan for the pratfall. The balcony outside the window is hung with sheets rippling in the wind, making the seamless join even more remarkable, akin to Keaton at his best in *Sherlock Junior*'s cinemagic transitions. It could not have been possible to do the stunt 'for real' – not even Keaton could have fallen twenty feet on to the back of his neck, let alone even the best pro stuntman. Larry Semon often performed such gags – courtesy of his stuntmen or dummies – but the seam almost always shows clearly.

The uncle has left all his property, including the Last Chance Saloon, to Stan, but 'in the event of your death' it goes to the others. There follow some vintage saloon gimmicks, and a shoot-out in a house in which Stan, dodging the bullets, causes the bad men to shoot each other as they appear suddenly through doors and windows. At the end, coyly turning away from the sheriff's daughter's outspread arms, he mistakenly mounts a cow and is tumbled down the path out of town.

In Stan's next film, *Somewhere in Wrong*, he edges closer to the routines that will define Laurel and Hardy, but not too close, for although the film begins with Stan and Max Asher as two bums hungry for a meal – a possible pre-run of Laurel and Hardy's *One Good Turn* of 1931 – Max is quickly dropped from the plot as Stan is taken in by the farmer's daughter after a run-in with the family dog over doughnuts. Stan is introduced in the film as 'a fierce, fiery, fearless, two-fisted loafer', but although he takes the initiative to steal the doughnuts, and pines after the pickings from the farmer's safe, his kindly instincts lead him to return the money he has stolen from the rich landlord to the farmer and his daughter, and save them from eviction. As he sees the daughter ungratefully embrace her dapper suitor, he exits the house with the first full instance of the Laurel face contorted in tears. It is not quite the real Laurel cry, but it's getting there.

It appears clear from Stan's Joe Rock films, where he is very much in control of his material, that he had no intention of becoming part of a double act. Joe Rock, who, like everyone in the comedy business, knew Babe Hardy at the time and had worked alongside him at Vitagraph, presents himself as the first in a long line of claimants to the honour of bringing Babe and Stan together, or at least trying to do so:

I tried hard [to get Stan to work with Babe]. Babe worked on some of the Jimmy Aubreys. But Stan wouldn't have him. And I said, 'Stan, why? Why?' He said, 'Because Babe's always trying to get a laugh. And if a heavy gets a laugh in the picture, it destroys his heaviness.'

Rock's shaky memory may have been conjuring this up, as Stan would be unlikely to say something so technically dubious, but it is fairly obvious that, having worked so hard to become a leading man in his own right, Stan was as loath as Larry Semon to allow his screen foils to rival him, although Larry always allowed Babe to shine. Rock was more reliable in his account of the nuts-and-bolts of Stan's productions:

SKRETVEDT: Did Percy [Pembroke] improvise when he was shooting the films?
ROCK: No . . . Percy was from the stage . . . and that was his specialty. He was good, he was fine, he was high class, he was clean, and a hell of a nice guy . . .
SKRETVEDT: I know that Tay Garnett did some titles on some of the films.
ROCK: Yes. Tay was a hell of a good fella to get the gag group together, and in line, you see. And he'd stick to a gag – you might have started it with a premise. Then you'd say, 'Wait a minute', and this one would say something, and it would go around, and the girl would keep taking notes . . .
SKRETVEDT: Did Stan sit in on the gag sessions at all?
ROCK: Oh, he was in everything! He wanted to see the daily rushes, and

he saw the cuts, he would stay – that was the good part about him – until he started not staying and not coming in the morning; he didn't care about the thing, because he was beginning to break his deal. You know, he was getting tough to work with . . . Babe, in any of his stuff, never gave a . . . all he would do is say, 'What time tomorrow? What's the business?'

The business, as far as Stan Laurel was concerned, was Joe Rock's somewhat creative financing. According to researcher Rob Stone, Rock was shooting each film in ten days but had in hand a month's budget for it from the distributor. Rock kept the difference, but Stan was being paid only for his ten days. This was the basis for Stan's growing disillusion with his long-term contract with Joe Rock.

Despite this, two of Stan's last movies for Rock were among the best in his solo period. *The Sleuth*, a two-reeler released in June 1925, had Stan revelling in the role of Webster Dingle – with Anita Garvin as the 'Other Woman' – donning a variety of disguises to unmask a cheating husband. His first disguise, as a maid, has the husband chasing him round the table, until the 'maid' leaps out of the window to a pratfall. Other disguises include the Sherlock Holmes cap and cloak, with pince-nez, a swell with a long moustache, and a death mask tied on his head backwards to scare the crooks the husband brings in. Stan's penchant for 'surreal' tricks is in evidence as he lurks outside a door with a panel through which a hand emerges to snatch his beard, then his hat. An arm then extends with a crooked finger inviting him. He comes nearer. It beckons again. He comes nearer, and is biffed with a fist. Researcher David Wyatt points out that this gag occurs, decades later, in Peter Sellers's and Spike Milligan's wacky *Running, Jumping and Standing Still Film*, and has even excavated a Sellers-narrated compilation film in which the Laurel gag occurs in a clip. Thus wisdom passeth on.

The film climaxes with an equally eccentric scene in which Stan, in drag, as the vamp to end all vamps, lures the ruffians to a punch-up in which they knock each other out, following which he bashes the husband with a vase. This is the first of a number of films in which Stan will revel in cross-dressing, culminating, with Babe, in the extraordinary *Twice Two* (1933).

Stan's last but one film for Rock was perhaps his strangest, *Dr*

Pyckle and Mr Pride, a spoof of John Barrymore's 1920 feature, *Dr Jekyll and Mr Hyde*. This is a very different Stan from any seen previously, enjoying a sojourn in the grand Victorian era in which his own roots lay. Stan's attraction to the theme of dual personality will prove to be central to many aspects of the movies he would make with Oliver Hardy. Stan's own life with Mae might well have caused him to reflect on the absurdities of a split public and private persona. Cavorting each evening on the stage with Mae, as perfect partners, only to return to the battleground of the bedroom, must have taken a heavy toll. We can imagine Stan feeling that lurking about as the sneering, cheerily evil Pride, the man who frightens all the women and steals an ice-cream cone from a child, was a good catharsis. If only we could split ourselves apart and live our separate schizoid personalities, we might not have to spend so much time dissembling . . .

Stan's last film for Rock, *Half a Man*, sees Stan regressing to the role of the manic idiot he had launched with *Nuts in May*. Son of a bankrupt fisherman – 'a simple child of nature – VERY SIMPLE,' says Tay Garnett's title – he leaves home only to end up on a boatful of young ladies who are shipwrecked with only Stan for male company. Stan's troubles with Mae are brutally reflected in the character of one rapacious ogress who ogles Stan and chases him, only to throw him off the cliff when the drifting male crew of the boat come ashore. The scenes of the rampaging man-killing women might have also been prompted by the release, in April 1925, of Buster Keaton's marriage-trauma epic, *Seven Chances*, in which Buster is chased by a horde of would-be brides. 'Promise you'll beware of women, you can't trust them!' is the advice given Stan by his mother at the start of the film, following her initial send-off: 'Son, y'gotta fare for yourself. The odds are against you.'

But the odds were narrowing all the time. Separated from Mae, and becoming estranged from Joe Rock and his financial shenanigans, Stan was ripe to be wooed back to Hal Roach. Warren Doanne, Roach's general manager, offered Stan an intriguing way to elide his contract with Rock. He was still legally tied to Rock as an actor, but his growing reputation as a constructor of comedy suggested an alternative role. And so in May 1925, with several of his Rock pictures still awaiting release, Stan rejoined the Hal Roach Studios as a writer and director, alongside F. Richard Jones,

Jimmy Parrott, Clarence Hennecke and Leo McCarey. His first commissions were two shorts starring Jimmy Finlayson, with George Rowe and other familiars – including a young actress who would become a cinema icon, Fay Wray.

The third film Stan co-directed, with Clarence Hennecke, was a standard spoof of a current romantic drama, *No, No, Nanette*, entitled, with great sagacity, *Yes, Yes, Nanette*. It, too, starred Jimmy Finlayson. But it also featured one of Roach's newest recruits – Oliver 'Babe' Hardy.

Mr Laurel – Mr Hardy, I presume.

OLIVER HARDYS HAPPY AGAIN

Laurel and Hardy were children . . . A little baby in a high chair has a spoon and hits himself with the spoon. He doesn't think that he hit himself. He looks round to see who did it . . . A child learning to walk, it falls a hundred times. If you did the same fall as he did, you'd break your spine . . . You don't teach a child to laugh, it teaches itself, it's an emotion – it comes. When you take a grown person, and do the same thing as you would do with a child, it becomes just as amusing. And that is the basis of so-called slapstick comedy.

Well, up to a point, and no further. All clowns regress to basic behaviour, from Grimaldi to Chaplin and beyond, but there is a great deal in their antics that hardly belongs in the cradle, not even in our day and age. What is perhaps most childlike, and most attractive, in Stan and Ollie, is that, like small children, they stick together even when events, and their own natures, test their solidarity to the utmost. It is no wonder that, in a time when close friendship between men can hardly be seen without a sexual aspect, Laurel and Hardy have been either 'outed' or adopted as a homosexual or gay couple. But this, too, was part of the repertory. Their innocence, in fact, never existed. The mask of childhood is their escape route from the poisonous arrows of the adult world's violence and fury. The child within, even away from California's touchy-feely ethics, never lies far below anyone's surface. The Bible tells us that when we grow older we put aside childish things, but it also infantilizes us all before the concept of God. The clown, by his or her nature, rips aside this veil of pretence and arrogance, and shows us the terrified infant in us all, the ghost in the biological machine, the naked ape dressed in civilization's clothes, the atheist in the priest's vestments, the fool behind the pose of the wise.

We do need to grow up, and grasp the external world, but we also need to balance the outer and inner realities. The God of the Old Testament said: know where you have come from and where you are going – a command to follow instructions. But the clown is nature's disobedient soul. You never know where we are going, but you face the unknown bravely, perhaps with the courage of ignorance, but with the utmost good will. This is the Fool's legacy – coincidentally, too, the legacy of ancient wisdoms . . .

Stan and Ollie proceed, in their march towards Judge Foozle, to cross the cemetery on the way to his home. This is no easy task, as a mysterious wind blows their hats off, leading to the first classic hat-switching scene in their *œuvre*. (And remember Stan's gags with hats, going back to *Mixed Nuts*?) The shadow of a goat tripping over a pile of cans sends them running like greased lightning, but the 'Tipton Slasher' has arrived before them. This is Noah Young, one of Roach's veterans, a champion weightlifter who, according to the lore, was turned down for the navy in the Great War because of the bad state of his teeth. He uses these dental resources to the utmost here, as he replaces the new butler hired by the Judge and proceeds to stalk the house armed with a long knife. Primal terror, as the far from fearless detectives are chased through the Judge's ornate chambers by Noah wielding a massive scimitar, after Stan has handcuffed Ollie by mistake. Reduced to a gibbering wreck himself by the sight of a devil mask that has become stuck on the back of Fin's head (remember Fin walking backwards in *Madam Mystery*?), the Slasher is apprehended and locked in a cupboard. The cops rush in and arrest the villain, law and order is restored, and Stan and Ollie saunter off, together.

Although Babe took command, in *Do Detectives Think?*, the character of Ollie was still not in his grasp. Perhaps Babe was too much the jobbing actor to reach within himself and find the key to unlock the door to his Aladdin's cave. He was perhaps still too tied to the straightforward concept: What's the business? What time do we start?

The answer to the first question was still: another Hal Roach story that seemed a good idea at the time – *Flying Elephants*, a prehistoric romp, along the lines of Buster Keaton's caveman episode of his first feature, *Three Ages*. As Randy Skretvedt has written: 'In *Flying Elephants*, Laurel and Hardy spend 90 per cent of the film doing solo turns, and when they finally do meet up, they try to kill each other. They appear to be as much of a team as Popeye and Bluto.' Well, that was not a bad act either. According to the annals, this piece of cinematic bric-à-brac was personally directed by Hal Roach (and not the credited director, Frank Butler) at a rocky site in Moapa, Nevada. Stan is the effeminate Twinkle Star, Babe is the macho Mighty Giant, and the said floating pachyderms appear in animated superimposition – achieved by opticals whiz-kid Roy Seawright – to illustrate the Mighty Giant's comment, 'Beautiful weather – the elephants are flying south.' As well they might, as there was precious little to do in Nevada in 1927, some years

Prehistory: Cave Stan and Ollie with maidens in *Flying Elephants*

before the sleepy railroad town of Las Vegas became a byword for razzle-dazzle.

The razzle-dazzle of the day was in fact in Tijuana, on the Mexican border, to which Hollywood's great and not-so-great gravitated when they wished to unload their newly acquired money. Babe Hardy was becoming no stranger to the culture that married earthly paradise to temptation. Gambling on the horse races was another little vice that could be accommodated in so large a physical frame. But Babe had good reason to drown his sorrows in some kind of leisure activity, beyond golf, as will soon be revealed.

For Stan, these were the happy years. Life with Lois was a tranquil breeze after the storms of Mae, and conception took place in the spring on the production of a new Laurel, little Lois, who would première on 10 December 1927. The fact that Stan's domestic calm coincided with the most important creative stage of his career might be significant, were it not for the fact that later tempests did not seem to diminish his capacity to turn out gags, to keep the ball rolling. The creative juices just seemed to run, independent of the local turbulence, but also, as we shall see, fed by it.

The summer of 1927 was a watershed for Roach, too, as he was consummating a long-desired divorce with his distributors, Pathé Exchange, and a new marriage to the giant MGM. As in all good American marriages, this was marked by a lawsuit, of Roach against Pathé, alleging unfair distribution policies and finagled accounts. Pathe counter-sued and all the lawyers lived happily ever after (or until 1932, when this particular dispute was settled). *Flying Elephants* was the last Laurel and Hardy film handled by Pathé, who held it back for release until way into 1928, by which time the team was well and truly launched.

The first MGM Laurel and Hardy release was *Sugar Daddies*, a kind of reprise of *Love 'Em and Weep* and another go for Jimmy Finlayson as a rich old lecher, whose roaming eye for the ladies leads him to marry women while drunk. In this case he has acquired not only a wife, Charlotte Mineau, but a gold-digging daughter, Edna Marian, and the wife's brother, Noah Young, who has exchanged his scimitar for a Colt 45. Stan is Fin's pince-nezed lawyer and Ollie, for a change, is the butler, as he was in *Slipping Wives*. The highlight is a scene in a funfair, with Fin and Co. being chased by Noah and Co., through the Tunnel of Fun and the Great Slide, which sweeps them into a heap. The film benefits from a handsome look provided by the young George Stevens, later to be a regular L&H lensman and, still later, distinguished Hollywood director – though he did begin his feature-helming career modestly, with *The Cohens and the Kellys in Trouble* (1933).

Tall oaks from little acorns grow.

Sugar Daddies was the last of Roach's forlorn attempts to miscast

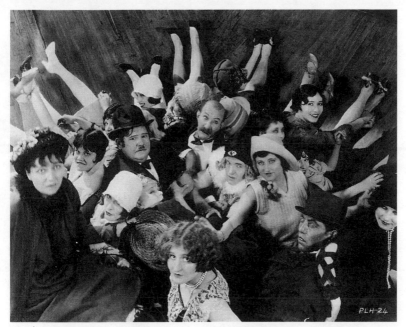

Ollie, Stan in drag and Jimmy Finlayson in *Sugar Daddies*

Stan and Babe, give or take a few later guest appearances, commencing with *Call of the Cuckoos*, a Max Davidson tale of a Keatonesque crazy house, in which they are tagged on to the plot, larking on the lawn with Charley Chase and Jimmy Finlayson, and doing a mock William Tell act looking very similar to that in Chaplin's *The Circus*.

In June 1927 the first comedy universally accepted as a full-blown Laurel and Hardy team film was shot. *The Second Hundred Years* was also the first film to benefit from full-blown huffing and puffing by MGM's publicity people, though they did not quite pitch it as just a Laurel and Hardy film, as we can see:

NEW STARRING TEAM UNCORKS RIOTOUS PERFORMANCE IN
FIRST PICTURE AS COMEDY DUO.
THE SUPER COMEDY ARRIVES!

Motion picture comedies have outgrown their infancy, and nobody is crying 'Keep Him a Baby Still.' The ancient humor dependent on custard pies, and ridiculous costumes now seems hopelessly stupid. It is the high standard set by such worthwhile comedies such as *The Second Hundred Years*, latest Roach M-G-M offering, now regaling crowds at the ____ theater that has educated the public to the point where the better type of humor is demanded.

In this funfection, Jimmy Finlayson, as a dignified [prison] governor, is largely responsible for the hilarious and hair-raising plot that engulfs the other members of the famous comedy trio, Oliver Hardy and Stan Laurel. Not the least pleasing feature of a notable supporting cast is a host of beautiful women, who are modishly gowned. Fred Guiol directed.

The inclusion of Fin in the comedy trio was a last-ditch attempt by Finlayson to maintain the star status he had been promised by Roach, but which was becoming eroded by the popularity of the other 'All-Stars'. Fin's frustration would soon lead him to leave the Hal Roach Studio and trawl for work elsewhere, but he was fated to return. The cast of beautiful women did not appear until later on in the picture, the modish dress of its first part consisting of the striped garments of the inmates of the state penitentiary, from which Stan and Ollie escape, having first tunnelled out uninspiringly through the floor of the warden's office. The exploits may have been hair-raising, but not for our heroes, who have been shaved to the roots. The step-marching prisoners may well have derived from a folk memory of Stan's of Fred Karno's ancient sketch of *Jail Birds*. Turning their uniforms inside out, the boys manage to leave the prison disguised as painters, whitewashing everything in sight. They then leap into a taxi in which two French police chiefs are on their way to the prison governor's mansion as guests of honour. Changing clothes again, and arriving in tux and sash, to their chagrin, back at the jail they've escaped, the boys proceed to kiss the butlers and ogle the women in true French style before eventually being caught out. A scene follows that will later be reprised and refined in *From Soup to Nuts*, in which Stan has to learn proper dinner etiquette and chases a cherry round a plate with a fork.

These society scenes may have been the point at which Oliver Hardy put the finishing touches to the character he was to play from then on. It would gel, to all accounts, in the next team film, *Hats Off*, the missing link, stubbornly evading all searchers, and appear full blown, and overtly presented, as a Southern Gentleman, in *Putting Pants on Philip*. The graceful social airs, the gaucherie clad in a repertoire of cautious smiles and finger twiddles, the mask of elegance concealing frustrated desire, all these at last have Oliver Norvell Hardy delving deep into his own roots and family history.

Remember Oliver Hardy senior, the father Norvell never knew? In the words of the reminiscing Dr H. R. Casey in the *Columbia Sentinel* of 1885:

This Falstaffin figure . . . as polite and graceful as a French dancing master, a popular ladies' man and is quite sure to kiss the babies about voting time . . . It is quite hard to resist that good, open, jolly, funful face, round as the full moon, and covered all over with smiles . . . evincing a very decided penchant for the good things of the table . . .

Unknown, but all too often dreamed of in the aftermath of mother Emmie's soothing tales, the missing and missed father whose name the boy took on as soon as he could express his independence of the Norvell–Tant clan.

And lo, he has returned from the dead! A little the worse for wear, if not necessarily in convict garb, but eventually settling for the worn jacket and tie and much battered derby hat. The Civil War had reduced the proud Southerner to a shadow clinging stubbornly to his perceived patrimony. The Universal War of pitiless reality against the fragile human species reduced Ollie to a wandering life, sometimes a vagrant, often freshly unemployed, but never losing sight of his essential dignity. Victimized by fate, he is further subject to the often infuriating antics of his bosom friend cum factotum, Stan.

He gazes at us, because he knows we all share his frustration. Life surely should be better than this. But he then shrugs, and turns back to the business of getting along with the next chore. He does not want our pity. He'll settle for our laughs. For we are laughing with him, not at him. We know he understands us as well, or better, than we understand him, and he represents our own follies, and our hopes.

CHAPTER TWENTY-ONE

Running Frantically through the Streets

'Exploitation Suggestions' from MGM's press sheet for *The Second Hundred Years*:

Get two men to impersonate Stan Laurel and Oliver Hardy as they appear in this picture. Attire them in convict suits as indicated in posters and lobby display cards. Have them run frantically through the streets in the neighborhood of your theater. Pin placards on their back announcing the showing of *The Second Hundred Years* at your theater. Imagine the attention this stunt will get!

Indeed. It is interesting to note that this gimmick is exactly the same as that used by Fred Karno to advertise his *Jail Birds* sketch thirty years earlier. It perfectly illustrates Charley Chase's adage that the best comics recycle gags that are fresh in the memory despite the fact that the public has forgotten them. (And it invites the question whether Stan's convict larks with Larry Semon in 1918's *Frauds and Frenzies* owed more to Stan's Karno-trained memory than to Semon's ideas – note that Stan had already made *No Place Like Jail* for Hal Roach a few weeks earlier.)

The Second Hundred Years marked the return of Leo McCarey, who would 'supervise' or direct the next eighteen Laurel and Hardy movies. These would include a fair number of their most classic titles, some of them unarguably masterpieces of the short comedy film: *Putting Pants on Philip*, *The Battle of the Century*, *The Finishing Touch*, *From Soup to Nuts*, *You're Darn Tootin'*, *Two Tars*, *Liberty*, *Wrong Again* and *Big Business*. That's quite a lot of masterpieces, and all shot in a sixteen-month period, between summer 1927 and December 1928! Speculation can add to the list the film preceding *Philip*, the 'Holy Grail of Laurel and Hardy movies', *Hats Off*.

Remade and revamped as *The Music Box* in 1932, *Hats Off* introduced the boys' most iconic setting, the grand flight of steps in the Silver Lake district of Los Angeles, between 923 and 937 Vendome

Whitewash in *The Second Hundred Years*

Street. Instead of a piano, the boys were carrying a washing machine up the steps, to sell to Anita Garvin at the top, only to discover she just wants them to post a letter for her. This missing film introduced one of the trademarks of the best silent Laurel and Hardy comedies, the grand finale of Mutual Assured Destruction – in this case, a massed ripping of hats which spread from the two protagonists to the entire street. This scene was shot, as were many subsequent finales, in Culver City's pristine centre, a small-town locale that would ironically become familiar to audiences around the world, from Santiago to Shanghai. The scene allegedly derived from an incident at one of the Roach lot's raucous parties, in which Mabel Normand pulled Leo McCarey's tie open and inspired him to go around the room pulling off everybody else's tie. Or so McCarey chose to tell the tale.

MGM once again went to town on promotion, sending out

trucks and buses plastered with posters for the film, advertising in Ralph's groceries and Owl's Drug Stores and putting vast billboards up all over the city. It all paid off, as the *Los Angeles Evening Herald* raved on 9 March 1928:

HATS OFF

This glorious slapstick occupies a subordinate position on the bill to *Tillie's Punctured Romance*, a feature-length attempt at humor, but it saves the day as far as entertainment is concerned. It is no exaggeration to say that the entire audience bordered on hysteria at the climax of this two-reeler. They were really laughing at the same gag used in the first Laurel and Hardy comedy. But the substitution of hats for pies proved enough of a variation in the recipe to secure an equal reaction.

In my opinion, Hal Roach has the most promising comedy team on the screen today in Laurel and Hardy. It is to be hoped he withstands the temptation to promote them into five-reel features, a horrible example of which is on the Metropolitan bill in *Tillie's Punctured Romance*.

The unfortunate supporting feature on this programme was, alas, W. C. Fields's last but one silent film for Paramount Pictures, co-starring Chester Conklin. The pies mentioned in the review referred to Laurel and Hardy's next but one movie, *The Battle of the Century*, released on 31 December 1927 – the release dates of these Roach films can be quite confusing, but the hats were definitely shot before the pies! In effect, the first Laurel and Hardy films came out in a burst at the turn of 1928, contributing to the sudden realization that comedy had obtained its true new heroes.

This was all the more gratifying to Roach and his new stars, since the greatest technical upheaval in the history of the motion-picture business had been signposted, in October of 1927, with the release of Warner Brothers/First National's *The Jazz Singer*. Al Jolson's wailing 'Mammy' marked the birth of the Talking Picture era. Jolson's atrocious tear-jerking would not kill the silent movie overnight, as studios pondered the cost of total re-equipping, from set to theatre, with the new sound equipment. Hal Roach would bite the bullet himself in October 1928, announcing a deal with the Victor Talking Machine company and predicting that 'at the Hal Roach Studios the most progressive strides will be made towards not only the perfect synchronization of short subjects but also the introduction of comedy through the spoken word'.

This left Stan Laurel and Oliver Hardy a full year and more to make their mark on the final phase of silent cinema comedy. Their last silent picture, *Angora Love*, was shot in March 1929 and released at the end of that year. By that time, not only the silent cinema, but the whole apparently non-stop party of America's 1920s, the age of the flapper and the flivver, the hot cha-cha and all-night dancing in speakeasies, had been brought to a juddering halt by the Great Wall Street Crash of October 1929. And even that did not stop our boys.

Many years later, Stan certified to his authorized biographer, John McCabe, that *Putting Pants on Philip* and *Battle of the Century* were the first two proper Laurel and Hardy movies, though as we have seen they came pretty far down the line. The point is that neither Stan Laurel nor Babe Hardy were much concerned to place landmarks, or make historical judgements, or see themselves in the same iconic light cast by their adoring fans. They considered themselves, to the end, two working actors who happened to have hit on an incredible streak of good luck, after years of daily grind. They were happy to recall the good times and airily dismissive of the bad.

The eponymous pants put on Philip have been discussed end-lessly by fans and critics, donned, undone, flapped in the wind and pressed into the service of any number of theories, potty or pro-found. The tale, as everyone knows, is of the respectable gent Piedmont Mumblethunder (Ollie), who goes to the dock to meet his nephew Philip (Stan), who has just come over frae the auld country, complete with sporran, tam o'shanter and kilt. Continually embarrassed, Piedmont has to cope with Philip's mad chases after a girl and his penchant to draw a crowd wherever he comes into public view. Long before Marilyn Monroe excited avid filmgoers by having her skirt blown upwards by a vent in the pavement, Stan made the good ladies of Culver City faint by standing above a shaft of air that firmly settled the question of whether Scotsmen wore anything under their kilts. Finally, determined to take no more, Piedmont drags Philip to the tailor to de-kilt him and measure him for trousers, setting off an early sample of a recurring Laurel and Hardy theme, the comic male near-rape and emasculation of Stan by Ollie – the symbolic kilt standing in for more than the delicate members of the audience might wish to contemplate, or as much as their imagination wishes to engage. As Ollie and the tailor wrestle the weeping Stan to the floor, the sexual innuendo is as clear as it will ever be in a Hollywood movie, comic or not. Walter Kerr wrote:

The fact that the assault is taken as homosexual and Laurel doesn't even know what homosexuality is is simply an indication that the once knowing and aggressive Laurel is becoming as childlike as Roach envisioned and Hardy already looked. Laurel the victim, Laurel the put-upon, Laurel the go-and-stand-in-the-corner booby is well on the way to being born.

But the fact that Philip has spent the first part of the film knowingly chasing women – and not, I suggest, because he thinks they carry lollipops under their skirts – does make us suspect his prepubertal innocence. Both Stan and Ollie know very well what they are up to: all the comedians knew, after years of traditional cross-dress training, how to get away with things the censor hated but the audience loved. Everyone winks and pretends to see what is convenient, but the clowns appreciate, despite their protests of innocence, the well of pain, embarrassment and confusion from which they draw so many laughs.

The finale, in which Piedmont and Philip stage a rival contest to chat up the flighty Dorothy Coburn, restages the gag from *Why Girls Say No*, shot in 1926, with Babe as a cop. Stan puts his kilt down over a puddle for the girl to walk over; she jumps over it; Babe elbows Stan aside before he can recover the kilt, steps on it, and falls into a six-foot hole. Cue the first of many fade-outs to Ollie's soaked and sorrowful face at the camera.

In *Battle of the Century*, whose title refers to the Dempsey–Tunney Heavyweight Champeenship fight of September 1927, Stan gets KO-ed by Noah Young after a pastiche of the famous 'long count' of the iconic brawl. (The referee keeps interrupting the count as Stan refuses to move back to the proper corner after he has knocked his opponent down by pure chance.) Somewhere in the sieve that is silent-film preservation the next five minutes or so of the film got lost, but Stan himself preserved the memory of it in an interview with Bill Rabe:

I'm just sitting there, one of those things . . . Gene Pallette comes along . . . he's selling insurance, cheap insurance. For a dollar, Hardy can insure me – for a broken arm he gets $150, for a broken back, two thousand . . . [Hardy] says, 'How much?' He says, 'For one dollar, you know, he's one of those fast guys.' So Hardy . . . takes out this phony insurance . . . so from then on Hardy's trying to get me hurt. See, he's walking me under ladders – of course, he gets the brunt of everything – brick drops on him. Tries to put me in front of a streetcar, another one comes along the other way and hits him . . .

This culminates in a banana joke, on which the film we have picks up, with Hardy trying to get Laurel to slip on the banana skin but instead bagging first a cop and then pie-vendor Charlie Hall. This leads to Stan and Ollie's most famous 'reciprocal destruction' sequence, the greatest pie fight of all time. In Stan's words:

There's a dentist, and a guy's with his mouth open when the pie comes in – you know, you never saw where it came from. But every gag was a belly laugh, you know, and before you know, it snowballed, and the whole town is eventually pied, I mean, the wagon [unintelligible, as Stan bursts into hysteria].

Both *Putting Pants on Philip* and *Battle of the Century* were directed by Clyde Bruckman, who had co-directed Buster Keaton in *The General* and was later to tangle both with Harold Lloyd and W. C. Fields. He, too, played his part in nudging our heroes along towards the roles that would become so well known.

Once both Stan and Babe had settled on the characters that made the Laurel and Hardy films work, and engage the audience, they locked them in, and stuck to their last, for the next thirty years. Like Chaplin, they had finally found masks that required no further development as characters, only a proper stream of situations, stories and gags that would test their capability to cope with the endless tasks and obstacles thrown in their way. This was the key to their recognition, throughout the world. Other comedians buckled under the strain: the Marx Brothers were soon tired of their unremovable masks, Groucho in particular; W. C. Fields became the character he had invented and his real self disappeared from view; Mae West got fat; Lloyd became too old to be the eternal glasses boy; Keaton could not convince the sound-era studios to allow him to grow under his own power; even Chaplin had to doff the tramp's costume when Adolf Hitler galvanized him into a more direct engagement with the terrors of the real world. But Laurel and Hardy stayed the same. The actors grew older, and Babe Hardy's battle with his own girth took its toll eventually, and entropy and the incompetence of the corporate studio system pressed upon them, in the fullness of time, but, for their legions of fans, they stayed the same. Everything else could disappoint: friends and spouses could be inconstant; time laid you traps of disappointment, hardship, injury, disease; economies could crumble; politicians deceive; wars ravage the earth; a thousand and one pinpricks could afflict you, and death lie ever smirking round the corner. But Laurel and Hardy stayed the same, and were regenerated, in the magic of television, video cassettes, and, in the words of publishers' contracts, 'any media yet to be invented between now and the end of the world'.

The comedy techniques of Laurel and Hardy have been analysed forwards and backwards, examined under microscopes and magnifying glasses. Without doubt the real miracle of the Great Leap into Immortality lies in the boys' achievement in bridging the painful transition from silent films to the talkies that left so many actors, comic and dramatic, beached like dying whales on the shore. Stan and Ollie's apparent bad luck in emerging as silent-movie stars at the very moment the silent cinema was doomed was turned into their greatest stroke of good fortune. Just why this occurred is one of those intangible things that can easily be a tautology: they succeeded because they succeeded. The audience, entranced, was just not willing to let them go. But plenty of popular stars – Keaton being the most prominent – were doomed by circumstances, or studio intransigence. Harry Langdon, making a succession of bad choices, disappeared almost completely, only to appear in a very different guise from his star status in Laurel and Hardy annals.

Walter Kerr defined what he called 'the second Laurel and Hardy turnaround' in the change of pace from comedy's customary frenetic rush to the more leisurely step of Ollie's graceful movements – 'the soothing guidance of a steady 2/4 beat, the mellifluous promptings of a chastely tuned pianoforte'. But of course we have seen that Babe himself did not develop that pace before the Teaming, and so we are back to the mystery of the guiding hand – not the single-minded insight of the lone genius, but the combined genius of the movie makers: Roach, McCarey, Stan and Babe. Writes Kerr, 'If the front man was slowed down by the delicacy of his nature, the second man, Laurel, had to be slowed further still, rendered all but inanimate as he waited for his master's cue. How, then, were the gags to be performed?' The answer, Kerr pointed out, was quite simple. They did not invent new gags, or do anything that comedians before them had not done; they stepped on the same banana skins, threw the same pies, crashed into cars and so forth, but:

They confessed to the joke . . . explained it most carefully, anatomized it . . . Here, you see, is Mr Hardy climbing out of bed to get a hot-water bottle for Mr Laurel, who has a toothache. Here, on the floor between the bed and the bathroom, is a tack. Here comes Mr Hardy, stately in his kindliness and blind to his peril. Here is Mr Hardy stepping on the tack, howling in pain and plucking it from his bare foot. Here is Mr Hardy throwing the tack away with infinite disgust. Here is Mr Hardy in the bathroom, filling the hot-water bottle, and returning to the bedroom. Here, once again, is the tack on the floor, exactly where Mr Hardy has thrown it . . .

And the inevitable follows. The joke was no longer a secret, lying in wait, it was 'a ritual through which the well-informed were courteously conducted, a ceremonious tour of well-marked terrain'.

This ritual is perhaps the most important element that enabled the popularity of Stan and Ollie in almost every country of the globe. Chaplin was a universal comedian, whose tramp character appealed across all frontiers. But Keaton and Lloyd, for example, were quintessentially American: their need for problem resolution through action – Keaton's tremendous chases; Lloyd's rush through life's perils to win true love – are defining icons of 1920s America, the urgent social climb, the necessity of speed. These are also individual values, the core of the American Dream. And many previous comedy teams, like Babe's own Plump and Runt, or Pokes and Jabbs, or Ham and Bud, were more often than not just two separate individuals, scrapping against each other for a place in the sun, typical marriages of inconvenience. Stan and Ollie, on the other hand, were two halves of an organic whole – once matched, they could not be split asunder. Together, they struggled through the obstacle course of ornery reality. Anyone, anywhere, in any country, could identify with this continual battle, which may be propelled forward by ambition, but which proceeds in a circular fashion back to the state of failure and helplessness from whence it often came. Speed is not of the essence – there is little point in rushing if one can proceed more sedately, and with the proper dignity, towards inevitable disaster.

When, in *You're Darn Tootin'*, Stan and Ollie are unable to walk down an ordinary street without falling down a manhole, their struggle for survival has been reduced to its most primal level. Watching these seminal scenes, we might pay attention to other crucial elements of the boys' movies – their crew of regular collaborators, who accompanied them throughout the Roach years. Richard Currier cut almost every film made at Roach, if one believes the credits, until late 1932, giving the Roach mob a certain rhythm that marked them out from their competitors. Principal cameraman George Stevens would remain on the team till 1931. In *You're Darn Tootin'* – whose cameraman, as chance would have it, was second stringer Floyd Jackman – the camera's contribution is marked in the way it precedes Stan and Ollie down the street in a close-shot and allows first Stan, then Ollie, to fall out of the screen while the other continues blithely for a while, looks back, and the camera dollies out to the long-shot of the fallen one in the hole, legs waving in the air, while he who remains upright glances long-sufferingly into the lens.

The ritual element is at its clearest in the great denouement of *You're Darn Tootin'*, when a long poke-in-the-eye kick-in-the-shins tit-for-tat between Stan and Ollie leads to the ripping of pants off every passer-by who crosses the screen, including, of course, the inevitable cop. The frenzy of debagging that convulses everyone repeats the follies of the great pie fight, but at a much more surreal pitch. The camera stands back and observes, almost neutrally, as utter madness grips the sidewalk on which Stan and Ollie have begun the sequence innocently attempting to ply their desperate trade of street musicians, to which they have been reduced after losing their jobs in the orchestra in the first part of the picture, and their accommodation in the second. Randy Skretvedt has written of this:

You're Darn Tootin' is the first clear statement of the essential idea inherent in Laurel and Hardy. The world is not their oyster: they are the pearl trapped in the oyster. Their jobs hang by rapidly unravelling threads. Their possessions crumble into dust. Their dreams die just at the point of fruition. Their dignity is assaulted constantly. At times they can't live with each other, but they'll never be able to live without each other. Each other is all they will ever have. That, and the hope of a better day . . .

The rituals were honed, perfected, and became second nature, as Laurel and Hardy meshed ever closer. In *The Finishing Touch*, two titles earlier than *You're Darn Tootin'*, the already rehearsed cadences of Stan's solo *Smithy* were honed with balletic precision. Instead of Jimmy Finlayson as foil Stan has Ollie, his match in house-building incompetence. The gag with the endless plank, with Stan at each end, is lifted straight out of *The Noon Whistle* and, instead of a tack, Ollie has a whole bucket of nails to step on, trip over, and swallow. Two external foils are provided by the ever fearsome Dorothy Coburn and another Roach regular, Edgar Kennedy. Every possible carpentry gag in the universe is dusted down and used, then played again. When Stan and Ollie's bickering releases the truck at the end to roll into the finished house and demolish it, we recognize the deep footprint of fate.

Precision, as all the great clowns knew, is everything when dealing with chaos. Stan has gone on record as stating that the Laurel and Hardy films were shot in chronological order – an unusual and, today, prohibitively expensive method. 'The only place I could do it was at Roach,' Stan declared. 'Anywhere else, they wouldn't go for that.' And of the scripts:

Well, we had a rough outline of a story. And we had lines, to motivate what we were going to do . . . or what the plot was about, naturally, but as far as the Laurel and Hardy scenes, those were worked out practically on the set . . . You rehearse a scene, and then try to improve it; if it looks OK, you shoot it, and if you think you can make it better, fine. Occasionally things would crop up and we'd kind of ad lib and do something else. But not too often. It was pretty well cut and dried. And we had a lot of mechanics. Sometimes they didn't work. Like an explosion where everything, the walls fell down, the drapes and all else, all that was wires and what have you, sometimes they got fouled up, sometimes in the middle of a scene a carpenter would come in the window and say, 'Did it work?'

One of the greatest of all mechanical challenges came in *Two Tars* (late 1928). Stan and Ollie are sailors on shore leave who pick up a couple of girls and have a wrestling match with a recalcitrant bubble-gum machine, watched over by shopkeeper Charlie Hall. This is merely flapdoodle to bring us to the grand part two of the

two-reeler in which the boys and their gals get stuck in a traffic jam caused by roadworks. The subsequent wreckage of vehicles would make any old or new Luddite proud. Here, at last, is America's pride and joy, the flivver, the Model T Ford and all its rattling offspring brought to a cataclysm of torn fenders, broken windshields, wrenched-off wheels and doors and entire chassis mangled to cartoon shapes. Never has tit-for-tat destruction looked more satisfying. Stan told interviewer Bill Rabe, who asked him, 'How many Model Ts did you have?'

Oh, we had them specially made. One in a half-circle that would go around and around, then we had one that was squashed up between two cars. It was tall, we were sitting high up in the air, up in the front seat. Then we had one that went into a railroad tunnel, and a train would come through at the other end, and we came out with the four wheels practically in line . . . There were no motors in them, you know, they were just breakaways; and we had one that was all fitted together, and you pulled wires and everything collapsed, at one time! [Stan laughs uproariously.]

In classic form, the thread of convention and civilization unravels, as one small insult begets another until all drivers and passengers are engaged in their orgy of mutual destruction. Not for nothing have Laurel and Hardy become metaphors of our social and political mores, as the clowns, without seeking to do more than amuse, peer more clearly into the mechanisms of our follies and just say, 'What if I pulled that small wire?' Down comes our fragile edifice of deception. And at the end, as the mangled cars go by, some up-ended, some wheelless, shouldered by their passengers, another bouncing and juddering down the road as if afflicted by vehicular ague, the two miscreants who started it all look on, collapse in mischievous laughter, and, as instantly, freeze into seriousness as the watching, helpless cop – whose own motorbike has already been flattened to a tin rag – wags his finger: 'You're going to pay damages for this!'

By now, our heroes are well established. They have long stopped being called Ferdinand Finkleberry, or Sherlock Pinkham, or Canvasback Clump. They are now fully ensconced on the screen as themselves, Mr Laurel and Mr Hardy. The masks have replaced the persons, and can address us directly, without subterfuge. There is nothing up our sleeve. We are naked in daylight. Like Popeye, we answer the existential question with the oldest answer of all: 'We yam who we yam.'

CHAPTER TWENTY-TWO

Full Supporting Cast: The Lot of Fun

Nineteen twenty-eight, the Hal Roach Studios: the 'Lot of Fun' as it was called, principally by its own publicists. Despite Roach's determination to pay his employees as little as possible, and keep them on contracts that served his interests – his insistence on separate contracts for Stan Laurel and Oliver Hardy was to be a bugbear for years to come – the alumni remembered those days with a golden glow. These were the years when they were encouraged to exchange ideas, to develop their own, to see themselves as collaborators in a unique project devoted to comedy and its rewards – the esteem of colleagues and audiences, not to speak of earning a living in a country where prosperity was soon to hit the buffers with a terrifying crash.

A surviving Hal Roach Studios 'datebook' might present a somewhat lackadaisical approach to the business of running a large enterprise with numerous projects and offshoots working away at the same time. The 'datebook' is a simple lined notebook with the entries scrawled in ink. The year 1928 begins with Monday, 2 January, entered as 'Holiday', then the main crew present on each location is listed:

Tuesday, 3 January
s–8   Kennedy, French, Driscoll, Powers, Ireland, McBurnie(?),
       Williams
       Laurel Hardy – stage
G–8   McGowan, Sandstrom, Jackman, White, Boshard
       Kids – stage
s–8   Hy East and Buddy
G–8   mule – Moore(?) + Blunt
G–8   Tony and Duke + Jiggs
G–8   Bob Sanders dog
       Harold Lloyd Co – on tread

Wednesday, 4 January
s–8   same as yesterday – stage

```
G-8    same as yesterday – stage
G-8    horse – Moore – Blunt
       mule – Jones
       ostrich – L.A.O. Farm
       Tony – Duke + Jiggs
       Bob Sanders – dog
s-8    Hy East + Buddy
       Harold Lloyd on tread
```

Roach still seems to have been churning out his animal pictures, though the short-lived *Dippy Doo-Dads* had been dumped. The summer entries recorded:

Monday, 2 July
```
L-13   Laurel and Hardy – Parrott, French, Black, Stevens, Hopkins,
       White, Collings(?)
G-14   Lloyd and Kids
```

This must refer to the shooting of *Two Tars*, which wrapped on 3 July, George Stevens having photographed the film, with Jimmy Parrott directing. On 8 August we have:

```
S-15   Parrott, French, Litefoot, Stevens, Davidson, L&H
L-14   nite retakes – cemetery
```

Clearly a reference to *Habeas Corpus*. At the same time, on floor S-15, the notebook records: 'Tony and dog.' On Thursday, 23 August:

```
L-15   Laurel & Hardy Stage 2
       McCarey – Scott – Black – McBurnie – White
S-15   Retakes using 2 goats
S-15   Retakes used our own goat
```

Friday 24 August
```
       Retakes using cow
```

And so forth. Roach was at this point, though still keeping his eye on the creative processes, more and more involved with the financial aspect. His distribution deal with Metro Goldwyn Mayer gave the studio a healthy balance sheet of current assets, posted on 28 July 1928, of $1,856,895 against liabilities of $215,826. Roach was still paying Stan no more than $33,150 throughout the year and Oliver a meagre $21,166.67. The second half of the year –

after Roach returned from a five-month round-the-world reconciliation tour with his wife, from January to May – was taken up with
Roach's plans to grasp the nettle of the new technology and re-
equip the studio top to bottom for sound. The *Los Angeles
Examiner* of 10 October 1928 reported:

By the terms of contracts just signed between Hal Roach and the Victor
Talking Machine company, the Hal Roach Studios in Culver City, Cal.,
will be allied for many years to come with the reproducing facilities of the
Victor organization . . .

Everyone in Hollywood was already hiring voice coaches,
dreading that their larynxes would cause the abrupt termination of
their movie careers. Anita Garvin remembered her fears on hearing
her first sound recording: 'I thought, "Oh my God! Here I am lisp-
ing all over the place! I'm finished, I'm finished!" But fortunately,
the next person in the scene did the same thing, so I knew it was
the soundtrack and not me.'

But these horrors still lay in the future, as 1928 continued its
crop of Stan and Ollie silent classics, wrapping up the year with
Liberty, Wrong Again, That's My Wife and *Big Business*, all shot
in a period of just over two months. The stock company was
forging forward at full speed.

By now, most of the regulars who would become familiar to
legions of Laurel and Hardy fans were in place, apart from Billy
Gilbert, who would appear in the talkies, and Mae Busch, who had
touched base with Stan and Ollie in *Love 'Em and Weep* and
would rejoin them in their first sound film, *Unaccustomed As We
Are*, in 1929. We have already been introduced to Anita Garvin,
who was also doing sterling work with Charley Chase, and was to
appear in three films teamed with another Roach starlet, Marion
Byron, in 1928 and 1929. A New Yorker, Garvin had toured with
the Ziegfeld show, *Sally*, and dropped off in California, appearing
in a few short films before her meeting with Stan at Joe Rock's. No
one can forget her coruscating performance in Stan and Ollie's
From Soup to Nuts, shot between *The Finishing Touch* and *You're
Darn Tootin'*, in which Anita, as the haughty society hostess, Mrs
Culpepper, who has been unlucky enough to hire our heroes as
waiters for her dinner party, chases a cherry around her plate with
a spoon while her tiara keeps slipping down over her eyes. This is

a reprise, as we have noted, of the dinner scene at prison governor Fin's house in *The Second Hundred Years*, but Anita is a more inspired choice as the cherry chaser. Her attempt to maintain her sang-froid in this struggle, while Ollie is performing serial pratfalls into the cake, is one of silent comedy's best moments. Note, in this scene, how the gag, again, is prefigured, with the family dog carefully placing a banana skin, in close-up, on the carpet, so that we know Ollie is due for the fall. In his next attempt to serve the cake, the banana skin is still present, and spotted by Stan, who, rather than remove it, places his hand over his eyes, while the inevitable once more occurs.

Anita's husband in the movie, Mr Culpepper, is played by Tiny Sandford, all-purpose heavy, cop, prison guard, waiter and general surly visage of authority. A very tall gentleman, six foot five inches without socks, Stanley J. Sandford was born in Osage, Iowa, and spent his formative years with the Daniel Frawley stage company in Seattle and Alaska. He appeared in films since at least 1910, and was said to have played the card player who has an altercation with Chaplin in his seminal short, *The Immigrant*, in 1917, though historian Glenn Mitchell notes the actor in question was in fact the much shorter Frank J. Coleman. History will remember Tiny Sandford best as the representative of Culver City's finest who sits in his car and notes every move of Stan and Ollie's destruction of Jimmy Finlayson's house and his reciprocal demolition of their car in *Big Business*. Every fresh outrage prompts a breathless take, a lurch forward, a lick of the pencil and a feverish new charge written down in the policeman's notebook. Like Anita Garvin, Sandford had one of the faces that have become attached as icons to the silent comedy, recognized by viewers who have long forgotten the name or the title of any movie in which they appeared.

Charlie Hall was another screen foil, as small in frame as Sandford was large. Another transmuted Englishman, he had been born in Birmingham in 1899 and was reputed to have come over the pond with Fred Karno, though there is no evidence that he ever worked for the Guv'nor. Despite claims that he had known Stan Jefferson way back when, all the signs are they met while Stan was working for Larry Semon. His first appearance in a Laurel film was in 1923, in *The Soilers*, and he also appeared in Stan's *Near Dublin* and beside Babe and Charley Chase in *Bromo and Juliet*. Apart from his role as a bit-part actor, Charlie was also a carpenter on the Roach lot and advertised for work as 'Comedy Relief and Characters' in the Hollywood film magazines. From late 1928, Hall was a regular in Laurel and Hardy movies, and was eventually to clock up forty-seven appearances in their films. In *Two Tars* he was inaugurated as the feisty and permanently aggrieved shop owner whose small world is always under threat by the forces of chaos who come tripping, in tandem, into his life. He had to wait until 1935 to get his on-screen revenge, in *Tit for Tat*, where the boys are foolish enough to have set up their electrical shop next door to his grocery, having already frivolously flirted with his wife in their previous movie, *Them Thar Hills*.

Another Charlie, and another Englishman, was Charlie Rogers, who played small parts in *Two Tars*, *Habeas Corpus*, *Double Whoopee* and several other Stan and Ollie films, but whose main contribution was as a gag writer said to be second only to Stan on the Roach lot, and as a director, who was to helm a few of the boys' mid-1930s shorts (*Them Thar Hills* and *Tit for Tat*, for two) and features – *Fra Diavolo*, *Babes in Toyland* and *The Bohemian Girl*. He had appeared with W. C. Fields in *So's Your Old Man*, in 1926, and had apparently met Stan a decade earlier, in the vaudeville period. Another, closer companion of Stan's vaudeville years who was employed in the boys' films, Baldy Cooke, is less recognizable to fans, but turns up in the periphery of such classics as *Two Tars* and *County Hospital*, where he dons the garb of a doctor, and *Perfect Day*, in which he appears as a neighbour.

Edgar Kennedy, on the other hand, was a more full-fledged foil, whose prodigious output stretched to performances in over two hundred short films and about a hundred features. Born in 1890 in Monterey, California, his early career see-sawed between singing in musicals and knocking out opponents in the boxing ring. His first film, according to the annals, predated even Oliver Hardy's – *Hoffmeyer's Legacy* – for Mack Sennett's Keystone in April 1913. Often a policeman (though not necessarily a Keystone Kopper), he romped alongside Ford Sterling, Fred Mace, Hank Mann, Mabel Normand, Mack Sennett himself and the newcomer, Charlie Chaplin, in 1914. In 1915 he became a regular foil for Fatty Arbuckle. A stint in features in the mid-1920s led to Roach, and his first role in a Laurel and Hardy film, *Leave 'Em Laughing*, in the classic cop role. Stan and Ollie have got themselves both laughing-gassed at the dentist and drive off, chortling uncontrollably. Edgar's efforts to get the traffic moving only reduce them to helpless fits of mirth, increased every time his furious face glares at them in incomprehension: 'You're practically in jail right now!' he grits at them, as his trousers fall over his ankles. Eventually despairing, he gets into the driver's seat, only to drive them promptly, laughing even louder, into a ten-foot water hole.

Kennedy was the movies' quintessential Irish cop, with his stubborn belief in the virtues of his own authority, despite it always being mocked by the world. He developed his trademark 'slow burn', the puffing of that balding, potato-like face and the narrowing of the eyes expressing the mounting rage against unsurmountable subversion, seen to great effect in his soft-drink-stall war with Harpo Marx in Leo McCarey's *Duck Soup*. But he was not just a pretty face, as the credits show us that, as 'E. Livingston Kennedy', he directed two of Stan and Ollie's finest silent shorts, *From Soup to Nuts* and *You're Darn Tootin'*.

Edgar's greatest ordeal was to come in the talkie picture *Perfect Day*, in which, as the grumpy uncle, he is loaded in the boys' car with his gouty, heavily bandaged foot hanging over the side, in preparation for the picnic that is not to be. Never was a foot subjected to so much hammering, smashing of car doors and general battery.

Kennedy was, in that film, a replacement for Jimmy Finlayson, who had rejoined the Roach lot after a few months spent looking for his fortune in other fields, namely Warner Brothers/First National. He rejoined Stan and Ollie for a small role in *Liberty*, as a shop owner whose gramophone records are smashed to smithereens in the usual manner (the triple-double-take in fine fettle), but he played the role for which he was undoubtedly welcomed into heaven in *Big Business*.

Selling Christmas trees in California – not in the summer, as some commentators have ignorantly alleged, as the film was shot over the Yule 1928 period, and the boys are wearing heavy coats despite the sunshine – Stan and Ollie, after a few false starts, arrive at Fin's house determined to make at least one sale this day. The subsequent mayhem, as Fin begins by snipping the tree up with shears and the boys tear the bell off his door jamb, represents the

Conflict resolution in *Big Business*, with Jimmy Finlayson
and Tiny Sandford

most perfect metaphor in the movies of the human condition of
short-sighted response. He does it to me; I'll do it to him. They
trash his house, pull up the trees in his garden, chop up his piano.
He reduces their car to metal shreds with his bare hands, dancing
on the wreckage. Conflict resolution is provided, as we have noted,
by Tiny Sandford, who, having asked the ritual 'Who started all
this?', prompts the combatants to tearful and seasonal reconciliation, only to find Stan and Ollie laughing at him behind his back.
End with chase into the distance, as Fin discovers the cigar he has
been handed by his enemies inevitably explodes in his face.

One of the funniest of all films, *Big Business* is capable of reducing
an audience, seventy years after its production on the Roach routine
schedule, to hysteria. Here the triple act is working at full steam, with
Fin as the perfect equal of Stan and Ollie, marking a solid triangle of
action–reaction–super-reaction. In tragedy, chaos is unleashed, and
pain and suffering ensue from folly. In comedy, pain and suffering
transform into cathartic relief. (That's as far as I intend to go about
why people find things funny.) And the rest is box-office history.

A host of other talents waltzed through Stan and Ollie's movies: Dorothy Coburn was the fist-waving nurse from the next-door sanitarium in *The Finishing Touch*, and the flighty flapper who causes Ollie to step in the puddle in *Putting Pants on Philip*. Vivien Oakland was a blond harridan wife who scared the bejasus out of many screen husbands. Viola Richard and Daphne Pollard did time as Stan's or Ollie's wives. Thelma Todd was about to come on board, as have noted. Stan and Ollie's last but two silent, *Double Whoopee*, featured eighteen-year-old Jean Harlow, a terrific addition to the Roach team who was soon to blossom in other gardens, as the glamour girl who gets her flimsy dress torn off by hotel doorman Stan by mistake. She made cameo appearances in both *Bacon Grabbers* and *Liberty*.

In *Liberty*, she played the girl who tries to get into a taxi only to find that Stan and Ollie are inside, desperately trying to change their trousers, a sight even the most seasoned flapper might frown at. Escaped from jail again, they have evaded the guards and leapt into the cab of a henchman who has brought them civilian clothes, only to find that when they have doffed their prison stripes, they have put on each other's trousers. The entire film then follows their endeavour to change their pants back, leading them into corners, alleyways and ultimately the lift in a construction site which wafts them aloft into the steel beams of the skeletal floors high above the city.

The whole film plays on an unspoken and unacknowledged running joke on the assumption by all the shocked passers-by that Stan and Ollie are homosexual lovers trying to have sex in public. As mentioned earlier, 'gender-bending' and gay, or 'pansy' effeminacy were standard ploys in vaudeville from time immemorial. The cleverness of *Liberty* is that Stan and Ollie's perfect innocence offers, again, a childlike simplicity in their continual embarrassment at being caught, literally, with their trousers down. Sex is not an issue, but a crab fallen in the backseat definitely is. As the boys twist and squirm, dancing the dance of the pull of gravity even higher above the streets than Harold Lloyd, they never lose touch with their essential characters, which underlie every gag and thrill.

As in Lloyd's *Safety Last*, no back-projection process shots were used. The studio construction crew built a three-storey set on top of the Western Costume Company building on South Broadway in

Liberty – caught with their pants down

Los Angeles. Randy Skretvedt quotes set designer Thomas Benton Roberts: 'The roof of the building was 150 feet, and we were working three storeys above that. Each time we changed the set-up for a shot, we'd have to move the camera platform around, and try to miss the flagpole on the corner of the building.' A safety platform was provided twenty feet below, but, director Leo McCarey told an interviewer in 1954, 'Babe said to Stan, "I'm going to show you that it's perfectly safe." And he jumped. Well, it wasn't safe.' The platform splintered, as well it would if Oliver Hardy landed on it, but a safety net below did the trick. According to Skretvedt's research, something must have gone wrong with the footage, because the records show the actors clambering about the set again in November, a month after the initial shoot. The re-shoot was directed by James Horne.

Leo McCarey was at the helm again for the boys' next masterpiece, *Wrong Again*, in which, playing stable hands, they mistake the report of a millionaire's missing painting, *Blue Boy*, as referring to the horse in their care. Luis Buñuel put a dead cow on a piano in his short *Un chien andalou* – shot in the same year as *Wrong Again* –

Liberty – on the high rise

in the name of art; Laurel and Hardy put a horse on a piano just for laughs. The result, in both cases, is surrealism, an artifice in the first example, a natural outcome of life's confusions in the second.

A mint moment of high acting skill derived from the English music-hall can be seen in an earlier sequence in the rich man's home, when the boys knock over a small nude statue and Ollie absent-mindedly puts the pieces back the wrong way. As Stan enters the room, he spots the strange figure, breasts pointing the same way as the buttocks, and pauses, finger poised, glancing, first at the statue, then up, quizzically, then back again, in a long series of 'takeums'. Ollie has already told him that the rich think differently, and everything is 'the other way' with them. Stan's face registers a whole gamut of questions, answers, considerations, bewilderment and finally acceptance that the strange desires and mores of people cannot be gauged. Life, for on-screen Stan, is an endless variety show of events and activities that cannot be fathomed: motivations that cannot be understood, objects that drop on your head for no apparent reason, streets with holes in them, furniture that is more often than not in the wrong place, vehicles with uncontrollable appendages, such as wheels, utensils and tools whose function is wholly mysterious, and social structures, such as employment, finances, or marriage, which have rules that are utterly occult and meaningless, and can be survived only moment by moment.

These affairs, off screen as on, were to cause both Stan and Babe grief, and set them challenges that were easier to face in the movies than in reality.

CHAPTER TWENTY-THREE

Multiple Whoopee, or Wives and Woes

Nineteen twenty-nine marked not only Laurel and Hardy's transition to sound movies, but also the resumption of marital crises, after the term of stability that followed the traumas of Stan and Mae Laurel, and Babe and Madelyn Hardy. With non-stop work on the Roach lot, a beautiful wife and a new-born bouncing baby girl, Lois junior, life appeared set fair for Stan. He and Lois moved into a large brick colonial-style house at 718 North Bedford Drive, plumb in Beverly Hills, with a proper nursery and even room for servants and a cook. According to legend, he bicycled to the studio in Culver City, but the distance suggests this is a doubtful claim. Lois appeared to settle for the role of homebody and mother, and the couple bought a St Bernard dog, to amuse the baby, or so they claimed.

It was about this time, according to Stan's biographer, Fred Lawrence Guiles, that, despite his domestic delights, Stan became involved with a minor actress named Alyce, or Alice, Ardell. This relationship, Guiles claims, drawing on the reminiscences of Stan's second wife, Virginia Ruth, née Rogers, lasted on and off for a decade. Miss Ardell does not, however, figure in the abundant cuttings of marital gossip and tittle-tattle that plagued Stan from the mid-1930s. The columnists did make freer merriment with wives than mistresses, being more cautious in print then than now, if no less gleeful about the tribulations of the rich and famous. On the surface, however, Stan was floating on the smooth currents of the best years of his career.

The first salvos in the new Laurel and Hardy Marriage Wars were fired on 24 July 1929 by Myrtle Hardy née Reeves:

OLIVER HARDY, FILM COMEDIAN, SUED FOR DIVORCE BY WIFE
Oliver Norvell Hardy, motion-picture actor, was charged with cruelty in a divorce complaint filed against him today by Myrtle B. Hardy.
Mrs Hardy alleged her husband made it a practice of staying away from home often for several days at a time and failing to give her any explanation.

He stated in the presence of others that he no longer cared for his wife and that the sooner he was given his freedom the better it would suit him.

The *Los Angeles Examiner* continued, on the 25th:

In her complaint . . . she asserted that Hardy came home late at night, 'bearing evidence of having been in close proximity to persons using powder and other cosmetics'. She also charged him with remaining away from home at night, frequently returning in an intoxicated condition.

Myrtle was getting her retaliation in first, for reasons that would soon become obvious. As is the case with domestic histories, one cannot with any certainty peer behind the net curtains of time, but it can't have been long after the Hardys' marriage in 1921 that Myrtle's drinking problem surfaced. By 1928, at least, she was a classic alcoholic, resorting to every trick in the book to conceal the bottles her husband diligently and wearily tried to clear out of the house. As Hardy's second wife, Lucille, reported, 'She even hid them behind the toilet.'

Oliver Hardy's second marriage had become a nightmare, as these dysfunctions are, for the addicted person as well as the partner, punctuated by rows, fits of drunken tears, and absences. There was no evidence that Babe had any other love interest at that time, and his absences were mainly trips to the casinos and racetrack of Agua Caliente, in Tijuana, to drown his sorrows by losing money. Signs that the pressure was building on Babe and affecting his relationship with other people can be found in an earlier cutting, from March 1929, which reported him being sued by fellow actor Tyler Brooke, who alleged that 'Hardy hit him with a billiard cue and broke his arm'. The incident took place at a pool hall at Sycamore Avenue and Cahuenga, and Brooke demanded $109,570. Hardy claimed Brooke had called him a 'son of a bitch', which he took as a slur on his mother.

On 17 September, the *Examiner* reported:

OLIVER HARDY, WIFE RECONCILED
Oliver Norvell 'Babe' Hardy, film comedian, and his wife, Myrtle Lee Hardy, have reconciled their differences. This was disclosed today when the dismissal of Mrs Hardy's divorce suit was filed in Superior Court. According to Attorney David H. Cannon, counsel for the wife, the couple have become reunited and are living together again.

This took the Hardys, mercifully, out of the public eye for a while, but their sorrows continued in private. Babe's inner life has always been a sealed book, the original mystery wrapped in an enigma, hidden behind those folds of flesh. Lucille Hardy's reminiscences, recorded in 1983 by Randy Skretvedt, and previously set out in letters to John McCabe in the late 1950s, soon after Babe's death, established the accepted image of a gentle giant, a man of extreme modesty, who saw his physical bulk as a hindrance and a burden, and sought to shrink into privacy. While his on-screen persona danced and sparkled in the sunlight, the man behind the actor's mask drifted in shadows. Lucille portrayed him with great affection, wielding spatula and spoon in the kitchen, humming over his spaghetti-stained apron, diligently whiling away the long evening hours following through his subscriptions to *Liberty* and the *Saturday Evening Post*, so he could catch up with the education he so woefully missed out on at school. Hardly the sort of man to hit Tyler Brooke with a billiard cue at the corner of Sycamore and Cahuenga.

Nevertheless, he was a gregarious man, as he had always been, from the time when being the life and soul of the party at school made the crucial difference between social acceptance and being jeered at as 'Fatty' in the yard. At Lubin and Vim, he had excelled in being part of the gang, and enjoyed the after-hours company of his work mates. At Roach, he often had to hurry home to Myrtle, fearful of what condition she might be in.

Stan and Ollie might be twins on the screen, and partners on the set, but in social life they did not meet often. Like most of the Hollywood colony, they lived a close distance from each other, but Stan's friends were almost all his show-business colleagues, past and present, the fraternity of the comedy world. Once, in April 1928, between filming *Should Married Men Go Home* and *Early to Bed*, Babe ventured out on a joint vacation with Stan, Charley and Jimmy Parrott, Charlie Rogers and a few more of the Roach crew, to Vancouver, in Canada, where, outside the US, the curse of Prohibition did not apply. Much convivial singing was assayed under the influence. With the Parrotts in attendance, one could expect nothing less.

Back at home, Babe's private life with Myrtle proceeded in its curious bubble. Our only insight into this intimate sphere is in the

241

form of anniversary and Christmas cards which were preserved by Myrtle and nestle in Randy Skretvedt's archive, the earliest of these, dating from 1927, handwritten:

For my precious on this our anniversary as our love grows stronger,
Your devoted,
Daddy – Babe Hardy

For Thanksgiving 1928, Babe writes:

To my dear angel,
These few flowers express just a slight idea of my love and devotion and with my darling's help and love I am going to in the next hundred years prove that I idolize my angel I love you my darling and actions will show,
Yours, Daddy, Our Anniversary

And she replies:

To my sweetheart,
Happy Thanksgiving Daddy Boy O mine. I am so thankful I have had you all these years may God be good enough to let us go through life together. I love you so, Oh I love my darling Daddy,
Your own honey girl,
On our seventh anniversary, may there be seventy more. And lots of little Hardys to carry it on,
Baby. 11–28–28

These poignant pointers into the heart and soul of Babe and Myrtle chide their reader with an uneasy sense of intrusion. These are the private moments of a couple, locked in their own turmoil, but yearning for a certain truth beyond sentimentality that they know they cannot grasp. There was no chance of lots of little Hardys, certainly not from this union. The relationship between 'Daddy' and 'Baby' did not allow for much else. These gushing emotions persist in the cards that Babe Hardy continued to send Myrtle in years to come, in the Rosewood Lodge sanitarium to which Myrtle eventually agreed to be committed to attempt to dry out. Tiny three-inch cards, from the gentle giant, with that rolling, rounded handwriting, the letters separated wide from each other and connected with elegant swirls:

I love you sweetheart – and think of you every second every minute every hour every day . . . Daddy

Just a thought to my precious that I love and adore.

Valentine greetings – to the sweetest little Baby in the world and the most wonderful wife and companion that any man could hope to love and cherish,
   Yours, Daddy. I love you angel.

Christmas 1931:

To my wife, lover, sweetheart and dream baby. I love you more than ever darling and as each day passes into years I will try and prove my self worthy of your sweet wonderful precious little body. I love you angel, now, tomorrow, next year and into eternity,
   Daddy

But it was not to be. Eternity can reside only in the movies, where real life is tempered with fantasies. And indeed, Stan's and Ollie's on-screen marriages provide a fascinating mirror to their real life débâcles. Given Hal Roach's penchant for domestic comedies, replete with non-stop marital infidelities and much running in and out of doors and pistol-packin' betrayed wives on the rampage, it was no surprise that Laurel and Hardy would reprise this standard act. It does, however, dent the image of the team as innocent children, and Stan's continual return to the 'married' pictures shows that he saw the 'childlike' element as an extremely malleable concept in the films.

The first of the 'Stan and Ollie with Wives' pictures was *Their Purple Moment*, filmed immediately after *You're Darn Tootin'*, in February 1928. This was their first joint film directed by Jimmy Parrott, who had been transferred from helming the short films of his brother, Charley Chase. Jimmy Parrott was very popular on the lot and, next to McCarey, he was considered the star-maker who could propel the team into the top ranks. This appointment, though worrying to Charley Chase, who inherited second-stringer Fred Guiol, demonstrated Hal Roach's commitment to enabling talent, as Jimmy was already known to have health problems that could lead to sudden absences from work. Jimmy was prone to nervous breakdowns, perhaps connected with his epilepsy, possibly due to a war injury – he was said to have been exposed to mustard gas in the Great War in 1917 or 1918. Later on, he developed an addiction to amphetamines, which led to a serious heart condition.

Coupled with brother Charley's heavy drinking, this made Roach all the more worried about the staying power of the Parrotts, and probably fed into his decision to place Laurel and Hardy in the top slot.

In the tradition of clowns, the domestic hearth was not the domain of happiness and tranquility. *Their Purple Moment* actually has a rare script attached, allowing us an opportunity to gauge the trip from page to screen. The script is not a thing of splendour, consisting of a mere five pages of closely typed exposition, with no credited author. It goes like this:

Open on title, 'Saturday afternoon, when all good husbands bring their pay checks home.'

Fade in on interior of Stan's home, his wife counting cigar coupons with a premium catalog nearby. She hears the bell, goes to the door and admits Stan.

Stan enters and kisses his wife on the cheek. She immediately starts pantomiming for his pay check. He hands it to her and she counts it quickly, then gets over that there is money missing. Stan hands her a phonograph record and pantomimes it cost $3.00. She looks at the record and discovers that it is 'Three O'Clock in the Morning'. She gets over that she doubts very much that the record cost that much. Stan gets over a suggestion of guilt, gives her a winning smile and exits.

Stan enters halls and comes to a picture of his grandfather, looks all around to see that he is not being watched. The wife appears from a door upstage, unknown to Stan, and sees him take a dollar from under his collar. He opens grandpa's coat, takes out a wallet, puts the dollar in it and replaces the wallet, then exits back to living room.

The wife makes a hurried entrance back to the living room and Stan wonders whether she saw him or not.

The doorbell rings and Stan admits Babe and his wife. He brings them into the living room and misses his wife.

Cut to Stan's wife substituting the coupons for Stan's money, which she puts into her apron pocket. She returns and nods to Babe's wife pleasantly and also to Babe. She also nods to Stan, but it is a menacing nod. Stan starts to acknowledge it, then wonders what's wrong. The two wives engage in conversation and the two boys ease over to one side.

Babe tells Stan that his wife caught him holding money out. Stan gets over that he was too slick for his wife, takes Babe into the hall and pulls out his wallet, taps it knowingly and puts it in his pocket. Stan speaks, whispered title to Babe, 'How are we going to get out?' Babe gets over he will tend to it.

And the scene is thus set. Wives, in Laurel and Hardy movies, were the modern version of the mythical Furies, ferocious harpies with cuddly or cute faces, ever on the watch for the inevitable betrayal, as the film's opening title, expanding on the script's version, has it: 'Dedicated to husbands who "hold out" part of the pay envelope on their wives – and live to tell about it.'

As in all silent movies, the eventual titles were written after the film was shot, and H. M. (Harley M.) 'Beanie' Walker was a past master at this. A sports columnist whose byline was 'The Wisdom of Blinkey Ben', he joined Hal Roach in 1916 as titler and head of the editing department. His signature is all over the intertitles of a host of Roach movies, including Charley Chase's *œuvre*, and almost all the Laurel and Hardy silent shorts. In *Their Purple Moment*, H.M.'s titles introduce Ollie as 'Just another husband', and the first exchange between Stan and Ollie is 'She's found my hide-out – she's a bloodhound!', to which Stan replies, 'My wife'll never find mine – I'm a weasel.' Of course, she already has.

One wonders what has brought these two husbands and their wives together in the first place. Babe's and Myrtle's real-life division into 'Daddy' and 'Baby' is inverted in the films to a relationship that seems more of 'Mammy' and 'Sonny'. Even in wooing the Other Women, two floozies stuck at the entrance to the night-club after their 'beaux' have been ejected for failure to pay their bills, Stan and Ollie bill and coo like a brace of awestruck pigeons. Babe twiddles his fingers, tie and hat and simpers like a ten-year-old about to stick his hand in the cookie jar. The pre-pubescent element does rear its head here. The stiffest erection seems to be of Stan's hair, standing on end as if struck by a bolt of lightning at one of Dr Walford Bodie's soirées. Having skived off on the pretext of a night at the 'bowling alley', Stan and Ollie have been spotted entering the den of sin by a gossipy neighbour, who rattles off to alert the wives. Stan and Ollie offer to pay the girls' bills, and Ollie airily instructs their cab driver to wait outside, while the meter ticks away. It is only within, having ordered big juicy steaks all round, that Stan and Ollie discover that the stuff in the billfold is the worthless 'cigar store' coupons substituted by Mrs Stan. The script reads:

Stan starts to suffer. He looks at Babe, sees him having a great time. The waiter returns with the four dinners. As he starts to serve them, the taxi

'Stan starts to suffer . . .' – the Laurel cry

driver enters with the meter. Babe greets him jovially and says, 'Another dinner!' Stan continues to suffer. Babe starts to eat and notices Stan sitting there. He asks Stan if he is sick. Stan shows him the wallet and passes it under the table to him.

Babe reaches under the table and opens the wallet. Without raising his head he does a lot of heavy thinking. He raises his eyes enough to see the waiter put a steak in front of the taxi driver, then comes up facing the lens with a woebegone look. He looks at Stan and whispers, 'What'll we do?' Stan gets over, 'I don't know.'

Silent scripts like this are a mere blueprint, a kind of nuts-and-bolts guide for the action. When the script baldly states, 'Stan starts to suffer', it can't convey the flow of emotions across Stan's face in close-up, as he looks in his wallet, looks up, baffled, looks back in the wallet, sees that nothing has changed, looks up again, and comes the Laurel cry, then another look, then the cry again, as the realization of the trap that fate has laid sinks in. Ollie, too, does the full range of soulful looks and gulps, as he tries to figure a way out of the impasse and, finally, when caught in the club kitchens between the Scylla and Charybdis of Tiny Sandford as the waiter and the wives, battleaxe Fay Holderness and chubby Lyle Tayo, can only come up with the lame 'We started for the bowling alley . . .', only to lapse into embarrassed twiddling. An inevitable mutual pie-ing ensues, with old stalwart Jimmy Aubrey, as the cook, upending the soup on Stan's head.

The original script has a quite different denouement, which was filmed but then deleted, making much of a minor element in the eventual film, a group of midgets who perform an act in the night-club. In the script, Stan and Babe dress as women and join the midgets in a 'Floradora Sextette' number. The wives and floozies – Kay Deslys and Anita Garvin in fine fettle, stiletto and Derringer poised in case of further boyfriend betrayal – gang up on them and chase them out of the club down the street –

Cut to the street: Stan and Babe as midgets come up to a cop. The cop picks Stan up, tickles him under the chin, and Stan pulls the cop's mustache. The cop sets Stan down and bows very politely as they exit.

As Stan and Babe go around a corner they see their wives coming out the entrance of the café. The wifes [sic] see them. The boys are standing over a sidewalk ventilator and their dresses fly up in the air. Several people watching this take it big.

As well they might. But we shall have to wait a few more years to see Babe and Stan in full-fledged double drag in *Twice Two*, filmed in November 1932. (The earlier silent *That's My Wife*, shot in Christmas 1928, features Stan as the ersatz Mrs Hardy, reprising some of his favourite flirtations.) By which time the real-life marital woes of both were racking up again.

Marriage and its pitfalls seemed nevertheless to be on the boys' minds in the early part of 1928, as their next film after *Their Purple Moment* returned to the theme, with *Should Married Men Go*

Home. This opened with an unusually blood-curdling title, more appropriate to Stephen King than H. M. 'Beanie' Walker: 'Question: What is the surest way to keep a husband home? Answer: Break both his legs.'

This time Ollie and wife Kay Deslys are in middle-class bliss, but the fly in the ointment is Stan who, in chequered golfing jacket and trousers is sauntering up the road to entice Ollie out to the golf course. 'He'll stay for hours! Don't make a sound!' Ollie tells Kay. But their attempts to hide are thwarted when Stan spots them at the window. This is a different Stan, a more adult pest than we have seen before, possibly reflecting an attempt by his creator to expand a little on the narrow sphere of action destiny had carved for his character. But this was a one-picture wonder. Once the boys get to the golf course – having been pushed out by Kay – things become a little more predictable, as two young girls, Edna Marian and Viola Richard, attach themselves on 'foursomes only' day. The golf scenes appear to be in the picture mostly to show off the Westwood and the Riviera golf courses, the latter a somewhat bleak landscape with oil derricks in the background. Edgar Kennedy is a golfer who loses his toupee in the rough, and the whole descends into a literal mud-slinging match, a poor sample of the ritual destruction. Wife Kay does not reappear, presumably pouting at home, and Stan is merely a single menace.

Four films further on, in *We Faw Down*, the boys are married again, this time to Bess Flowers and Vivian Oakland, and plotting on the sofa ('Our husbands are up to something,' muse the wives) to join the poker game downtown. This time the excuse to go is that their 'Boss' wants them over at the Orpheum Theater, but on the way they fall in the mud and are enticed, to dry their clothes, into the pad of floozies Vera White and Kay Deslys, the latter 'making whoopee' away from her hunky boyfriend, One-Round Kelly (played by heavy George Kotsonaros). Meanwhile the Orpheum Theater burns down and the wives, reading a dubiously instant newspaper headline, wait for the return of their husbands with smouldering eyes.

Fans will recognize an early rehearsal of the boys' later feature, *Sons of the Desert*, which will play this situation to much better effect. Here, Ollie's lame efforts to describe the Orpheum show to the wives ends in the entrance of Vera, holding up the jacket Ollie has left behind in her rooms. Exeunt Stan and Ollie, running down the street, as wife Bess follows with a shotgun. The final shot is another dry run for its use in a later feature, *Block-Heads* – as Bess fires, a cascade of adulterous men spills out of all the windows of the buildings on both sides of the street, a trouserless horde rushing panic-stricken into the fade-out.

This finale in itself carries all the contradictions between worldly wisdom and the childlike innocence that is supposed to be Stan Laurel's and Oliver Hardy's hallmark. Sexual panic, in fact, comes very early to Stan and Ollie. Prepubescent they may pretend to be – look at what Stan and Ollie think 'making whoopee' is in their upstairs scene with the two girlfriends, all poking in the ribs and neck, sticking out the tongue, ruffling the hair, and the ultimate rough stuff – pushing the girl off the chair. But they must still pay the adult price. Pursued by female nemesis, death lurks in the shadow of that innocence – although one should point out that taking a load of buckshot in the backside has only a cartoon result in silent-comedy movies. The entire point in comedy violence is, after all, to make pain virtual.

The filming done, the day's work over, Stanley and Oliver return to their homes. Stan's happy family life not quite yet shadowed. Oliver, walking up the driveway, dreading what he might find on opening his front door. Not the comic fall of a banana skin or a dislodged brick on the head but the melancholy sight of a wife sprawled on the sofa clutching a whisky bottle.

Not everything in life can be material for art, not even for the jobbing comedian.

CHAPTER TWENTY-FOUR

Unaccustomed As We Aren't

Stan and Ollie's last two silent films were filmed in February and March 1929, and released in the autumn and winter, with synchronized soundtracks of music and effects. *Bacon Grabbers* featured Edgar Kennedy as a grumpy householder and the boys as officers of the county sheriff's office trying to repossess his radio. In *Angora Love* the boys are followed by an escaped goat and try to hide it in their boarding-house room. Edgar Kennedy is the suspicious landlord, and this is one of the first films in which Stan and Ollie share a bed. Poverty, not sex, is the guiding principle here, although the finale has three little goat kids coming out from under the bed, to Stan's delight and Ollie's dismay.

In one scene, with Stan and Ollie sitting on the bed, Ollie picks up what he believes to be his own foot and massages the toes, with growing delight, until he realizes it is actually Stan's foot he is kneading, a nice example of the identity confusion Stan was so fond of exploring in all its facets. (He would repeat it in *Beau Hunks*, in 1931.) Just as W. C. Fields experienced great difficulty in having his own head in the right place when trying to put his hat on, so Ollie is so perfectly self-assured – and wrong – that he can mistake Stan's limbs for his own. The first source of a clown's delight, and confusion, like that of a baby, is his own body. Nothing, not even your corporal self, obeys your mind.

By the time *Angora Love* was released, in December 1929, sound had fully conquered Hollywood. The movies, having achieved an unprecedented fluidity of style and creative maturity in telling pictorial tales, were suddenly thrust back into the womb: the camera encased in its sound-proofed glass booths, the microphones struggling to pick up only the sounds they were supposed to, and actors with squeaky voices contemplating unemployment and ruin. The movie industry was lucky this clumsy transition, requiring the re-equipping of both studios and theatres, came just before the bubble of American prosperity burst in the Great Wall Street Crash of 25 October that defenestrated instantly bankrupt investors and ushered in the era of the Depression.

The last year of the boom, 1929, was in fact a good year for Hollywood, which saw its profits jump courtesy of the hundred million people who went to the movies every week. Profits of the major studios did not begin to nosedive until 1930 and 1931, while Roach himself declared net profits of $86,052.93 over the last thirty-four weeks to July 1930 on current assets of just under one million dollars. His early leap into talking comedies was a sound move. Stan Laurel, on the other hand, lost about $30,000 in the stock-exchange crash, a serious blow, given his total salary of $44,025 in 1929.

On 4 May 1929, Hal Roach Studios released the first talking Laurel and Hardy picture, *Unaccustomed As We Are*. It had started life as 'Their Last Word', which would have been confusing, as it was their first. The opening salvo goes to Ollie, who speaks the first words of Laurel and Hardy on screen, as the two are seen walking down the corridor of an apartment building towards Oliver's home:

OLLIE
First we're going to eat – we're going to have a great big
juicy steak with mushroom sauce, strawberries with a
whipped cream mixed down in the bottom of it, a cup of
coffee, with a big black cigar.

To which Stan ripostes, in his first on-screen words, 'Any nuts?'

They are then interrupted by Thelma Todd, making her Laurel and Hardy début, as neighbour Edgar Kennedy's wife, slinking from the doorway:

THELMA
Oh, good evening, Mr Hardy.

OLLIE
Good evening, Mrs Kennedy. (*Nodding towards Stan*) This is
my friend, Mrs Kennedy.

THELMA
Good evening.

OLLIE

(*Poking Stan to take his hat off*) I brought him home for dinner, Mrs Kennedy.

THELMA

Oh, how lovely of you, Mr Hardy.

OLLIE

How is Mr Kennedy?

THELMA

Oh, he's very well, Mr Hardy.

OLLIE

Is Mr Kennedy home, Mrs Kennedy?

THELMA

No, he isn't, Mr Hardy. I must be going. Good night, Mr Hardy.

OLLIE

Good night, Mrs Kennedy.

She exits into her apartment.

(*To Stan*) That was Mrs Kennedy.

Stan looks stumped.

Why, what's the matter?

STAN

(*Pause, then*) I was wondering who it was.

This exchange, with its ponderous, idiot-proof diction, may be only the boys' 'unaccustomed' status as deliverers of dialogue, but it also suggests their realization, and that of their screenwriter, 'Beanie' Walker, promoted from titling, that the very slow, self-conscious speech of early talkie actors was itself ripe for spoofing. Hardy's wife, who is expected to deliver on the 'great big juicy steak', is none other than Mae Busch, introduced by her strident off-screen voice yelling out, 'Whadaya-mean, "yoo-hoo"?' when Ollie coos into the kitchen. Of course, she has no intention of being cook–washer-up for Ollie and the 'bums' he brings home for dinner any longer, and launches into a full-blown tirade.

Stan, Ollie, 'Beanie' Walker or director Lewis R. Foster, whatever the creative combination, display an early grasp of the comic possibilities of the new-fangled medium. When Ollie puts on a record to drown Mae's speech, her rant takes on the staccato rhythm before she realizes she is dancing to a tune and breaks the disc over Ollie's head, storming out. Ollie promises Stan he'll prepare dinner himself – 'I'll cook you a meal like you've never eaten!' – but after tripping over Stan's feet comes out with the first utterance of the recurring 'Why don't you do something to help me?', followed by 'Set the table, that's easy, you don't need to use any brains to do that.' An invitation to inevitable folly. Lighting the stove, the two manage between them to cause an explosion that sets Thelma's dress on fire. Mae's approaching return prompts the boys to hide the undressed Thelma in a bedroom trunk. The scene is now set for Mae's attempted reconciliation, Ollie's speech about setting off for South America with the trunk, the intervention of neighbour Edgar Kennedy – of course, a cop – and subsequent shenanigans. The beating up of Edgar by his wife, then of Ollie, by Edgar, occurs largely off screen, with blood-curdling noises, and, in the finale, Stan waves Ollie goodbye and falls off screen down the stairs, crashing noisily floor by floor.

Even in their first talkie, Stan and Ollie realize that it is funnier to anticipate than to arrive at the joke itself, which is, more often than not, slight or banal. Nevertheless, *Unaccustomed As We Are* is an aberration, in its reliance on extended dialogue scenes. By their second sound movie, *Berth Marks*, the boys have returned to pantomime as the driving force of their craft. The story is slighter than slight: Stan and Ollie, two parts of a musical vaudeville act, are supposed to meet at the Santa Fe station to take a train to Pottsville, their next venue. This is the same location Stan used in one of his earliest Rolin solos, *Hustling for Health*, in 1919. An attendant's garbled announcement of train destinations provides an early sound gag, anticipating – or perhaps inspiring – the gobble-degook train announcement in Jacques Tati's *Mr Hulot's Holiday* twenty-three years later. Of course, Stan and Ollie manage to nearly miss their train, leaving their music sheets strewn along the track.

A full five minutes of the eighteen-minute film is taken up with Stan and Ollie trying to take their clothes off, having managed to climb together into their upper Pullman bunk. Some critics have found fault with this sequence, which carries on beyond reasonable bounds, with much repetition of Ollie's phrase, 'Can you quit crowding me?', and a long series of gasps, thumps, grunts, shushing, slapping and counter-slapping. Who in the end is undressing whom? Nightmares of entanglement in clothing seem to be a common feature of the human species since the perfect naked apes, Adam and Eve, got tangled in their fig leaves. The entire sequence can be perceived as a sweaty homosexual *Kama Sutra* gone terribly wrong, although it also conjures, once again, the frustrated conflicts of sibling children. At the end, having to de-train just as they have finally settled down to sleep, the boys are left in dishevelled underwear at their destination, Stan having left their sole remaining possession, the double-bass, in their bunk.

These early sound films were edited in silent as well as sound versions, with intertitles unseen, of course, in today's versions. Randy Skretvedt reports that the long Pullman sequence may have become unwieldy because of the length of time it took to shoot, a full three days, due to the 'giggle factor', the as yet unsolved problem of crew and cast collapsing into laughter in mid-shot. Cameraman Len Powers succumbed too:

Sometimes I can't do a thing for laughing as they start to ad lib . . . in *Berth Marks*, most of the funniest stuff was absolutely devised on the spur of the moment by Stan and Oliver. They got started and we couldn't stop them.

Sound kept setting the crew, who were used to being able to talk over the action, new challenges. Roach himself said, about the sound pictures he would occasionally still direct himself, 'just to keep my hand in',

When we ran the dailies, the projection room was packed. The first scene came on, and it was fine. At the end of the scene, somebody from off screen said, 'That's good.' And the next scene came on. At the end of the scene, somebody said, 'That's good' again. The third scene came on. The guy said, 'That's good' again. I jumped up and said, 'Stop the projection machine! I'm directing this picture, I'll decide what's good and what's bad. Now who the hell is it in this organization that decided they're gonna say whether it's bad or good?' And there was a lull. Finally . . . a script girl very quietly said, 'Mr Roach, that's you.'

The third Stan and Ollie sound short, *Men o' War*, returned the boys to full working order, in a sound variant of their characters in *Two Tars*. Once again, the boys are on shore leave and chatting up a couple of girls, played by Anne Cornwall and Gloria Greer.

'Soda, soda, soda. And what will you have, Stan?'

Jimmy Finlayson returns in his first sound role, mostly still silent but with a few measured lines, as a soda jerker, in a remake of a minor scene from *Should Married Men Go Home*. Stan and Ollie want to treat the two girls to drinks, but have only 15 cents, enough – they think – for three sodas, though the real cost of each soda is a dime. Spoken dialogue has now enabled one of Stan and Ollie's most iconic scenes, as Ollie tries to figure a way out of their dilemma:

> OLLIE
> (*To Stan*) I have an idea. When I ask you to have a drink,
> you refuse.

Crescendo of Stan looks and glances as he tries to figure this out. Ollie returns to the two girls at the counter, ticking off their orders –

> Soda, soda, soda. And what will you have, Stan?

> STAN
> (*Beaming*) Soda.

> OLLIE

(*Outraged*) Pardon me. (*Pulls Stan aside.*) Don't you understand, we've only got fifteen cents! Now when I ask you to
have a drink, you refuse! Do you understand?

Stan nods. Ollie returns to girls –

Soda, soda, soda. And what will you have, Stan?

STAN

Soda.

OLLIE

(*Desperate*) Just a moment please . . .

*Ollie pulls Stan aside, salvo of slaps, tugs; Stan pulls out one of Ollie's
chest hairs.*

Can't you grasp the situation? You must refuse!

STAN

But you keep askin' me!

OLLIE

(*Spelling it out patiently*) I'm only putting it on for the girls.

STAN

(*After long pause for dawning wisdom*) Oh!

OLLIE

And we've only got fifteen cents! (*Gestures thrice with five
fingers.*)

They return to girls, as Fin triple takes, watching.

Now let's see: Soda, soda, soda, and, my dear Stan, what
will you have?

STAN

I don't want any.

GIRL

Oh, general, don't be a piker!

STAN

All right, I'll have a banana split.

Kick, poke, push, finger in the eye, as Ollie tries to get his point across,
finally striding back to order the three sodas, having promised to
share his with Stan. 'And what flavour please?' asks Fin, the first

256

instance on film of that distinctive Scottish burr. 'Cherry, choco-late,' say the girls. Ollie twiddles his fingers and simpers terribly, before coming out with, 'Sassafras!' Only to be taken aside by Stan: 'I don't like frassassas . . .' Nevertheless, when the drink arrives, he bolts it all down behind Ollie's back and hands him an empty glass –

OLLIE

(*With look of cosmic pain*) Do you know what you've done?

Stan, with look of dire guilt, nods and cries.

(*Shaking his head*) What made you do it?

STAN

(*Crying*) I couldn't help it.

OLLIE

Why?

STAN

My half was on the bottom! (*Sobs uncontrollably on Ollie's shoulder.*)

Ollie, receiving the 30-cent bill, comes over all forgiving, allow-ing Stan to settle the bill. Then, *deus ex machina*, the slot machine beside the counter comes to Stan's aid. Amid a crescendo of fren-ziedly worried looks by Fin, Stan spends one of his precious coins, and is rewarded after a suitable pause and a dismayed Fin by a shower of coins. Double take and gulp by Finlayson, triumphant wave of the hands by Stan.

All human drama is here: desire, insolvency, distress, despair, hope against hope, faith against the odds, delusion, friendship invoked and betrayed, the unbridled power of the libido driving one to consummate delights even if one doesn't like frassassas. And in the end, despite it all – triumph, the fragile and always tempo-rary inheritance of the meek.

At this cusp of the curve between the dying world of the 'Roaring Twenties' and the new harsh awakening of the Depression years, Laurel and Hardy reigned supreme. The Marx Brothers released their first film, *The Cocoanuts*, in May 1929, but this barely qualified as a motion picture, being little more than a celluloid version of their Broadway hit revue of 1925. Mack Sennett, struggling to survive throughout the late 1920s, adapted with difficulty to the new medium, and retreated further and further from the limelight, enjoying a brief success in 1932 with his four shorts starring W. C. Fields. Fields himself did not unveil that groggy voice until 1930, with *The Golf Specialist*, a one-off released by RKO. Mae West was yet to hit first Paramount and then the world, in 1932. But throughout the early years of sound, Roach survived as the undisputed king of comedy. Both Our Gang and Charley Chase followed Stan and Ollie into the talkie age. In Charley's first sound film, *The Big Squawk*, released in May 1929, he played a saxophonist in a jazz band. A later film, *Great Gobs!*, featured four songs, two of them apparently sung by Edgar Kennedy, no less, though the soundtrack of the film has not been found.

Stan and Ollie continued to turn out classics throughout the years 1929 to 1932. Seven sound shorts in 1929 (plus a guest appearance in a portmanteau feature, *The Hollywood Revue of 1929*, along with Buster Keaton and a very young Jack Benny); seven shorts in 1930; seven in 1931; eight in 1932. Beside these there were other projects: the first Laurel and Hardy feature films, and the boys' first trip abroad as a team – a first sojourn across the ocean for Babe, and a belated and unusual homecoming for Stan.

Perfect Day, *They Go Boom*, *The Hoosegow* and *Night Owls*, all directed by Jimmy Parrott, rounded out the shorts of 1929. During the autumn, Stan and Babe were signed on to a feature-film fantasy, *The Rogue Song*, based on Franz Lehár's opera *Gypsy Love*, a vehicle for warbler Lawrence Tibbett. This was a typical MGM stew stirred by wunderkind Irving Thalberg. Randy Skretvedt summarizes it thus:

Yegor, 'the singing bandit of Agrakhan' (Tibbett) is an insurgent against the powerful Cossack soldiers. Ali-Bek (Laurel) and Murza-Bek (Hardy) are his sidekicks. Despite Yegor's hatred of the Cossacks, he falls in love with young Princess Vera, whose brother commands a Cossack region. Yegor and Vera alternately romance and berate each other, while the sidekicks provide comic relief.

This concoction is, alas, a lost film, another 'holy grail' for Laurel and Hardy enthusiasts, of which some two-strip colour segments featuring the boys have turned up in recent years. Given

Roach's distribution deal with MGM, he was obliged to lend his stars to the mother ship, but there is no sign that this enhanced their careers, despite the decent box office that the producers enjoyed. Lawrence Tibbett returned to the grand-opera stage.

The boys returned to *Night Owls*, an odd concoction loosely resembling Stan Laurel's all-purpose 'Nutty Burglar' vaudeville routine. Cop Edgar Kennedy has been reprimanded by his chief about the epidemic of unsolved robberies on his beat. Coming across vagrants Stan and Ollie sleeping on a park bench, he rousts 'em up and makes them an offer they can't refuse: to rob the chief's house themselves and afford Edgar a chance to square himself by catching them red-handed – it's either that or the rock pile. Jimmy Finlayson is the chief's suspicious valet and the boys make every conceivable kind of noise with knocked-over garbage cans, crashing windows, thrown bricks and shoes, and an inadvertently switched-on player piano.

This was the first Laurel and Hardy film to be shot in alternative foreign language versions – Spanish and Italian. Later films would add French and German versions. As our earlier clipping described, this involved Stan and Ollie learning lines in all these languages phonetically, with the aid of a voice coach, laboriously taking each shot in each language before proceeding to the next. The studio then added scenes, with appropriate actors either replacing the original supporting cast or in separate, additional scenes. In *Night Owls*, grumpy police chief Anders Randolph was replaced for the español by one E. Acosta, a Mexican customs official. Fin and Edgar Kennedy, on the other hand, had to sweat their way through the multilingual labyrinth. This procedure was very slow and costly, but Roach got rich returns from European and Latin American audiences. If the bugbear of comedians was the loss of their universal status with the death of the silent cinema, Stan and Ollie saw their popularity soar with audiences who accepted them as local heroes. Hal Roach told Randy Skretvedt some piquant tales about these foreign versions:

I get [to Argentina] and they [the foreign bookers] said, 'You've got to go to a theater and see this Laurel and Hardy picture.' Well, in every country, like in the United States, you have slang. So I go to the theater, and Laurel said something in Spanish, I don't know what the hell it was, and the audience roared with laughter! He had mispronounced a Spanish word, and the word he used meant 'to pee' . . . We had the same experience in Germany in a picture . . . where Laurel is in a Ford and Hardy is a cop. Laurel goes around and catches Hardy's suspenders and breaks them. Hardy's trying to wave the traffic through, and when he does this his pants go down . . . Right in the middle of this, they put in a German title which said, 'He looks like a washerwoman.' I said, 'What the hell, there's nothing funny in looking like a washerwoman.' Then they took me to the theater and the audience laughed like hell at this title. Then I found out there's a dirty saying in Germany about a washerwoman leaning over and somebody attacking her from the back.

So much for cultural confusion. Roach, in fact, is misremembering, as this is a scene from the silent short *Leave 'Em Laughing*, and the cop is Edgar Kennedy, not Babe. This serves as a warning about reliance on oral history as related by senior citizens in their twilight years, but the point still stands. When jokes travel, they sometimes arrive at strange destinations.

At the end of 1929 another interesting marker was set with the arrival at the Hal Roach Studios of Stan's old 'Guv'nor', Fred Karno, in person. In October, presumably just before the Wall Street Crash, Roach signed Karno on as a producer and writer at the studio. Roach recalled, 'I hired him after working with Chaplin and Laurel and always hearing them talk about Karno, Karno, Karno. I thought, hell, this guy must know a lot of gags. His business had gone to pot over in England, so I told him how much I'd pay him a week in salary, and paid his way over.'

Karno had indeed gone bankrupt in England in 1926, after a long run of self-imposed setbacks. Since 1912, not content with music-hall prowess, he had become obsessed with the building of a great luxury centre on Tagg's Island in the River Thames, to be named the 'Karsino'. Karno dredged the whole island and built a £70,000 hotel, gardens and greenhouses, as well as a £20,000 personal houseboat. The building proceeded despite the outbreak of the Great War in 1914, which transformed the centre into a kind of trysting place for army officers and their girls. Even the plum contracts Karno was still getting from the theatre circuits for his ongoing plays and revues could not save him from this financial folly. Litigation over purloined titles, and revelations about his overly lecherous private life and casting-couch prowess ground him down until his humiliating crash.

Nevertheless, Karno was still 'The Guv'nor', and people such as Paramount's Jesse Lasky wooed him with invitations to the US. Karno's biographer, J. P. Gallagher, claims that Karno was chased by a New York agent to write material for the Marx Brothers, an unlikely story if ever there was one. However, he did arrive in New York, only to find that Mr Lasky had 'gone to the Coast'. Hieing to Los Angeles and booking into the Roosevelt Hotel, Karno made directly for Charles Chaplin's studios and was fêted by his old employee, who put his publicity machine to work and alerted all the other American 'ex-Karnies' that their mentor was in town.

Doing the rounds of his old disciples, Karno gravitated soon enough to Roach and Stan Laurel. A number of publicity stills were taken of Karno with Stan and Babe, together with director Jimmy Parrott, on the set of *Night Owls*. Babe and Stan lie beside a garbage can, between the old master and the new. Stan looks delighted, Babe nonplussed, and Jimmy Parrott simmers in the right-hand corner. Karno, on the left, holds out his arms expansively.

But, as Roach related later, 'I never knew that he was just the businessman. He wasn't a writer. He just hired guys that were funny, and he hired other guys to write for them. He was only interested in management. I finally let him go. I wanted him to be a gag man.'

Part of the problem was that the United States and Britain were still two countries divided not only by an ocean but by a common language. Karno required an interpreter to explain to him such terms in Roach Studios scripts as 'They take it big'; 'He horns in on them'; 'He does a Brodie', or even 'They neck.' Karno's imperious nature and old-world hauteur did not go down well with the wise-cracking, somewhat 'low-class' Roach team. In February 1930, Roach and Karno parted company, and Karno returned to England soon after. Attempts to try his luck in British films with the Gaumont and Ealing companies fared no better, though about six short films, which remain obscure, were produced by him for the Hutton company. In 1936 he returned to the theatre with a show called *Real Life*, which revived his fortunes for a while. Still dogged, however, by financial troubles, he faded away, and the Music Hall Benevolent Society bought him a share in an off-licence situated in the aptly named Dorset village of Lilliput, where he died in 1941.

Laurel and Hardy's second film after the Wall Street Crash was *Blotto*, a strange addition to the soon-to-be-superseded genre of the 'Prohibition' movie. This, too, was rendered into other languages, the French version entitled *Une nuit extravagante* and the Spanish, *La vida nocturna*. One wonders what these foreign audiences made of the bizarre subterfuge that seems necessary to get a bottle of booze into a night-club. The film also presents one of the bleakest on-screen marriages in the entire Laurel and Hardy *œuvre*, that of Stan and Anita Garvin, as a positively lethal spouse. 'You've been pacing up and down here for the last hour,' she grates at Stan, as he waddles about the parlour with his curved pipe. 'What's on your mind?' 'Can I go out?' he asks in frustration. 'And what for may I ask?' 'I need fresh air!' claims Stan in desperation. But Anita is having none of this. 'Now sit down, and stop annoying me!' Stan settles down, unfolding the pages of the Hebrew-printed newspaper, the *Yiddishe-Velt*. (The headline, the new sharp video release of the film enables me to reveal for the first time, for all pedants, is of Lindbergh's solo flight to Paris. But Stan soon crumples this up and tosses it aside.)

Stan, of course, is awaiting a telephone call from Ollie, who wishes to entice him out to the newly opening Rainbow Club. But first, a whole flurry of mis-calls, with Ollie constantly forgetting the number he is trying to call: 'Oxford 0614!' (Stan's real-life phone number at the time.) The extant Spanish version allows us to see Stan and Ollie in foreign action, with Oliver pretty proficient at his Spanish twang and Stan having a harder time wrapping his Lancashire tonsils around it. As replacement Spanish wife Linda Loredo purrs at Ollie, '*Como está, señor Hardy?*' '*Estoy bien, señora Laurel,*' oozes Hardy.

Ollie persuades Stan to escape the bonds of matrimony by sending himself a telegram calling him out on 'important business', so he can swipe the wife's hidden liquor. But wifey is listening on the other line upstairs and replaces the drink with tea spiked with mustard, pepper and tabasco. This leads to one of Stan and Ollie's most sustained scenes of making something out of nothing, as they settle at their night-club table and surreptitiously pour themselves

Multiple wife trouble for the innocent spouse

their doses under the table. The result contorts Ollie into a complete spasm: '*Es un licor excelente!*'

Blotto was the first of Stan and Ollie's sporadic three-reelers, a
kind of halfway house towards the features. The Spanish version is
fully fifty minutes long, padded out to feature length – for financial
reasons – with extended night-club numbers. Jimmy Parrott, as
director, shares the laurels with Stan in this most minimalist of
Laurel and Hardy premises: just the two of them at a table breaking
into an extended laughing jag as the imagined effect of the booze
takes hold. Even spotting the wife glowering at a nearby table with
her newly bought shotgun fails to sober them, until she responds to
Stan's gasping chortle of 'We drank your liquor!' with the chilling
statement: 'That wasn't liquor. That was cold tea.'

The despair behind the laughter is seldom so close to the surface
as in this movie, when the night-club singer Frank Holliday renders
a kind of homily to all husbands drowning their marital betrayals
in speakeasies, Stan sobbing inconsolably while Ollie pats him
round the shoulder:

You made me what I am today,

I hope you're satisfied,
You dragged and dragged me down until
The soul within me died.

You shattered each and every dream,
You fooled me from the start,
And though you're not through – may God bless you,
That's the curse of an aching heart!

Anita chases Stan and Ollie out of the club, taking aim at the taxi whose driver they have hailed to drive them off to safety, and bringing the whole vehicle down with one shot, blowing it into a pile of scrap metal.

Estoy bien, señora Laurel, indeed!

CHAPTER TWENTY-FIVE

The Song of the Cuckoos

Consummate workaholics, Stan and Ollie were getting film after film in the can. *Brats, Below Zero, Hog Wild, The Laurel–Hardy Murder Case, Another Fine Mess, Be Big, Chickens Come Home* (a remake of the 1927 silent *Love 'Em and Weep*), *Laughing Gravy, Our Wife, Come Clean* . . . There was barely time to present señora Laurel, or señora Hardy, with excuses to unwrap the double-barrelled shotguns. The Roach factory was still going full steam ahead, as, in the outside world, the grip of the Depression tightened, the lines of the unemployed stretched longer and longer, and their embarrassing shanty towns, or 'Hoovervilles', proliferated in major cities. Ten years later, writer–director Preston Sturges would make *Sullivan's Travels*, in which a pretentious young director, played by Joel McCrea, ventures out from Hollywood into the world of the Depression's victims, only to find himself locked up in a chain gang, amnesic from a blow on the head. But even in jail, the showing of a comedy, in this case a Disney cartoon, brings a moment of relief and healing to the oppressed, and an epiphany for the would-be social reformer. Instead of making his projected epic, 'Oh Brother Where Art Thou', he will devote his life to comedy.

Sturges was the scion of the kind of family that would have employed Laurel and Hardy as butlers but would not have minded if they had served the salad 'undressed'. He saw the struggles of ordinary people from the outside, a maverick gadabout who managed, for a brief period, to pit his talent against the Hollywood system and win, moulding his own brand of stinging satire. Laurel and Hardy, on the other hand, were still labourers in the salt mines, blue-collar workers who had come up the hard way, and worked their comedy by experience and instinct. They had been tramps, sleeping on benches and goggling at the doughnuts in the kitchen through the outside window, long before these figures had proliferated in real life, to prick the conscience of the prosperous élite. In *One Good Turn*, shot in June 1931, Stan and Ollie appear openly as 'victims of the Depression', begging for food at the home of a kind old lady. Mistaking the amateur play the lady and Jimmy Finlayson (acting the villainous landlord) are rehearsing for the real thing, they vow to save her, and the usual embarrassments ensue. This was, incidentally, the first Laurel and Hardy film to feature Billy Gilbert, a stalwart huffing and puffing supporting actor who was to join the regular crew. A singer in his teens, and then vaudeville and stage actor, he was encouraged by Stan to join the Roach Studios, but never broke free of bit parts and character roles. Although he had been born in Louisville, Kentucky, he excelled in apoplectic foreigners, most explosively in Stan and Ollie's piano saga, *The Music Box*.

By now, the boys had the procedure for their productions down to a fine art. Asked 'What would a typical day's shooting schedule be like?', Hal Roach related to Randy Skretvedt:

ROACH: Laurel and Hardy as a rule rehearsed all morning. They seldom photographed in the morning. They would go through the scenes and see how they would play. If they played well, they might start photographing. If the scenes didn't play well, the gag man, with Laurel, would change them so that they would play . . . Laurel bossed the production. No question about that. And with any director that was directing Laurel and Hardy, if Laurel said, 'I don't like this idea', the director didn't say, 'Well, you're going to do it anyway.' That was understood. Many people who directed Laurel and Hardy weren't exceptionally great directors, but they got along well with Stan. Laurel worked hard. When they were making the picture he was working all the time to make the picture as good as he could. But unfortunately he had limitations as far as writing stories is concerned.

SKRETVEDT: Anita Garvin says that Stan had a very subtle way of working. He would actually direct the films without the director knowing it, by making suggestions.

ROACH: Well, it depended who the director was . . .

SKRETVEDT: How about, say, Leo McCarey?

ROACH: Oh, Leo McCarey, hell, Stan wouldn't open his mouth. He adored McCarey . . .

SKRETVEDT: Often, after a picture was previewed, if something didn't go over with the audience, you would recut or re-shoot different sequences. Weren't you concerned about the expense involved in doing this?

ROACH: On most every picture we did with Laurel and Hardy, we previewed the picture and then redid the picture afterwards . . . [On relying on the preview audience's reaction:] After sound came in . . . you had to judge the length of laughter before you talked. If the dialogue was furthering the story, then if the audience laughed over it and didn't hear the line, it didn't mean anything . . . There were many times when something had happened and it was funnier to the audience than you thought it would be. Therefore you would add to that sequence. And another time you would have a sequence that you felt was very funny, and the audience would miss it completely. So you would have to cut it out and put something else in.

SKRETVEDT: We know that Laurel contributed a great deal of gags to the team's films. Did Hardy ever contribute much in the way of gags?

ROACH: No, but the things that Hardy did himself were his. The tie, and his looking at the camera, and the way he did things individually, nobody told him. I never heard anybody, including Laurel, direct him in anything. They just told Hardy what to do and he did it . . . He was a hell of a good actor . . . I never saw Hardy at any time try to steal a scene from Laurel, and never saw Laurel try to steal a scene from Hardy . . . As far as working together on the set is concerned, that other team Abbott and Costello worked at our studio, and they used to fight like hell. But with Laurel and Hardy, when I fired Hardy, Laurel cried . . .

In 1930, however, nobody was firing anybody at the Roach Studios, and new talent was being brought in. *Brats*, in which Stan and Ollie doubled as their own offspring, featured special oversize sets to surround the infant boys. It also showcased a new musical title theme, the 'Cuckoo' (sometimes called the 'Ku-Ku') song, which had been first used in *Night Owls*. The composer was the twenty-five-year-old T. Marvin Hatley, an Oklahoma musician who was working at the KFVD radio station, located on the Roach lot. He was one third of the 'Happy-Go-Lucky' Trio, which also featured Vern Trimble and Art Stephenson. Stan told an interviewer:

We heard this one morning and we thought the tune . . . tickled us and we thought let's get a recording made of it and put it in one of our pictures at the opening and see what the reaction would be. The audience laughed at it. So I think Roach gave the guy fifty bucks for the rights.

This was another example of 'tall oaks from little acorns grow' because Hatley was to become the musical director at the Roach Studios, writing hundreds of scores for a host of films, progressing from shorts to features. He was a multi-talented, energetic and endearing man who, like his music, preferred to stay in the background.

Another musician, who scored most of Laurel and Hardy's sound shorts, was Leroy Shields, whose own music was often misattributed to Hatley. Hatley scored Laurel and Hardy's feature films from *Way Out West* to their last Roach project, and was nominated for an Academy Award for his scores for *Way Out West* and *Block-Heads*. He lived to a great age, and was befriended by many Laurel and Hardy fans.

Apart from the opening of Beethoven's Fifth Symphony, it is hard to think of another musical phrase that is so immediately recognizable and evocative as the few bars of the 'Cuckoo' theme. The music became so attached to the image that the studio later reissued all the pre-Hatley Laurel and Hardy sound films, rescored with Hatley's signature theme – the form in which they are seen today, in TV transmissions and videos.

Brats, 'Ku Ku' song apart, is a *tour de force* of Stan's perennial theme of split and confused identities, and further evidence, if any were needed, of his penchant for bizarre and unreal images. As little Stan and Babe scamper beneath Laurel and Hardy's big feet, one tends to wonder what strange conception has brought about this grotesque outcome. The original script called for a scene in which Big Hardy spanks little Stan over his knee, and Big Laurel punches little Babe in the chin, but this was too complex an effect to film. The entire thing appears as an over-elaborate metaphor of the idea of Stan and Ollie as children, the adults acting as childishly as the kids, the kids as painfully adult as their fathers. Delightful to some, to others it is an unsettling experience, more Dada than Daddy. On the plus side, we have a rare rendition of Oliver Hardy's singing voice with the lullaby 'Go to Sleep, My Baby', the mellow timbres of a long-abandoned career. It is no wonder that Stan ruins this poignant moment the instant he joins in himself.

Stan and Ollie's next film, *Below Zero*, featured the Depression in its full despondency. From its opening title – 'The freezing winter of '29 will long be remembered – Mr Hardy's nose was so blue, Mr Laurel shot it for a jay-bird' – this is perhaps the most melancholy and dark of all the boys' duo films. A partial remake of episodes from *You're Darn Tootin'*, it presents Stan and Ollie as street musicians in a most unconvincing snowstorm, Ollie on double-bass and Stan on harmonium. Their first effort to strum up business fails due to their setting up outside the obscured sign of the 'Deaf and Dumb

Below Zero – in the Depression dumps

Institute', a gag Stan had been using from time immemorial, possibly dating as far back as *Nuts in May*. Removed to another location, Ollie's soulful rendition of 'She's Your Tootsie-Wootsie in the Good Old Summertime' earns him a snowball in the face from surly street cleaner Charlie Hall. A blind man goes by and then stops as he spots a dollar dropped in the road. A pigeon lays an egg in the outstretched tin mug. A hatchet-faced woman (played by Blanche Payson) breaks the bass over Ollie's head and throws Stan's instrument into the path of a steel-wheeled truck. To cap it all, the billfold of money they later find in the street turns out to belong to the neighbourhood cop they've invited to dine with them in the nearby steakhouse. The diner itself, in echoes of Chaplin's seminal restaurant scene in *The Immigrant* – as well as a similar sequence from Stan's early solo, *Just Rambling Along* – features the inevitable thuggish waiters who beat up customers who can't pay.

Below Zero is almost impossible to laugh at, because Stan and Ollie's humiliations derive not from their familiar characteristics or errors, but from the exigent social reality. When Ollie is beaten and thrown out, and Stan tossed by waiter Tiny Sandford into a barrel of icy water, the 'freezing winter of '29' becomes less of a joke and more of a cry of unrelieved pain. The climactic gag, that Stan has swallowed the water in the barrel, and waddles into the fade-out with a massive distended belly like today's images of a malnourished child, can chill the blood, rather than tickle the funny bone. Once again, there are echoes of older films – of Jimmy Finlayson's gas-bomb-distended belly in Stan's *Madame Mystery*, floating above the ocean, but there is no albatross available to peck the stomach and send the afflicted man plunging back to earth.

Plunging back to earth does occur, repeatedly, in *Hog Wild*, the next Laurel and Hardy short, in which Mrs Hardy, Fay Holderness, makes Ollie go up on the roof to fix the radio aerial before he can be allowed to go out with Stan. (The main event occurring after an evocative domestic scene in which Ollie fumes about not finding his hat, which is on his head all the time, to the despair of his wife and the humiliating giggles of the maid.) Charles Barr quotes the famous critic Basil Wright's contemporary comments:

In this film, the attempt to fix a wireless aerial on the roof of Hardy's house precipitated Hardy off the roof into the goldfish pond at least five times. Each time, a different gag variation appeared, until the comedy passed into the realms of cutting, and the final fall was but a flight of birds and the sound of a mighty splash. Even Eisenstein would have been proud to do it.

High praise, and editor Richard Currier deserves all of it, despite the fact that the flight of birds is merely in the critic's imagination. This was an occupational hazard, in recounting Laurel and Hardy films from memory, through the haze of laughter, and trying to disentangle one film from another.

Hog Wild is an excellent example of the maturity reached by Stan and Ollie's comedy within just one year of their initiation into the talkie world. Although dialogue is central to the opening sequence of Ollie and his vanishing hat, the rest of the film relies almost solely on visual gags, give or take the inevitable crashes, crunches and cries as Ollie goes off the roof yet again. Unlike *Liberty*, in which the perils on the heights were of the surreal Lloyd-like school of spills and thrills, the balancing act on the slanted roof of the Hardy home is a comedy of everyday manners. Here the ritual of the pre-figured joke is at its most developed stage. From the moment Ollie, and then Stan, climb on the roof to fix the

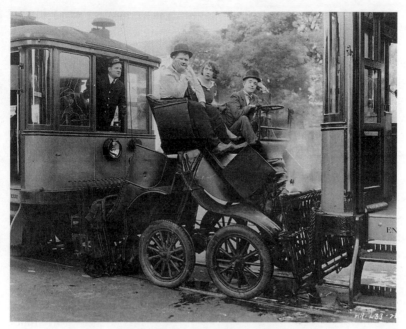

Modern transport in *Hog Wild*

aerial, the consequences are obvious, even to the most dimwitted child in the audience. Basil Wright may have been wrong about the birds, but the cutting – and the directing – ensure that, after Ollie's (or his stunt man's) first fall, there is no need to show those that follow, which are covered by the sounds of Ollie's desperate moan, the crash, and the splash rising to the rooftop. Stan, for his part, stands helplessly above, the wholly innocent instrument of the Fall. Once on the ground, in the pond, or in a pile of bricks, or in the fireplace, the Fallen remains in place silently, the glance of mortification to the camera at its most eloquent, Ollie gathering strength for the next futile effort. *Hog Wild* is the perfect exemplar of a great Laurel and Hardy principle: if at first you don't succeed, fail, fail again. Charles Barr, in discussing 1932's *The Music Box*, defined this as an inversion of the principle of the western: the Hero has a set task to do, and succeeds against all odds. Laurel and Hardy have a set task to do, and they fail. And yet – they always climb back up the ladder again.

For the climax of *Hog Wild*, Stan drives off with the ladder, with

Ollie still clinging to it, mounted on his car, into the busy Culver City traffic, tangling with streetcars before Ollie lands flat on his face. W. C. Fields was to present his own affectionate tribute to this kind of mad movie ride in his maternity hospital dash at the end of his last starring feature, *Never Give a Sucker an Even Break*, in 1941. But *Hog Wild* presents an exquisite topper, after Ollie's wife has rushed up to cry on his shoulder, not because he has almost been killed but because the radio has been repossessed. Slumped exhausted in the car, as Stan vainly tries to start it, firing the exhaust and honking the horn for good measure, the three are struck by a tram rushing up behind the stalled vehicle, as passers-by, including the traffic cop, cover their eyes. Cut to the last shot of the film – the flivver concertinaed between two trams, and, like a reject from the traffic chaos of *Two Tars*, being driven off into the fade-out.

After the successful run of shorts, how to create a topper for Laurel and Hardy's two- and three-reel hits? Hal Roach was reluctant to move from the world of shorts to comedy features. The two-reel format, he always declared, was the ideal length for a comedy idea. Stan, essentially, was in agreement – the old stalwart format of the vaudeville sketch was still the structure he was most attuned to. The days of the supporting short were not yet over, but the feature film, of course, provided a better income. Thus, after the lacklustre *The Laurel–Hardy Murder Case*, Stan and Ollie set to the production of their first feature-length film, *Pardon Us*, in the summer of 1930.

The story goes that the film, originally entitled 'The Rap', was planned as a short too, with Roach requesting MGM to allow him to shoot on the existing prison sets of their Wallace Beery jail saga, *The Big House*. MGM agreed on the proviso Roach loaned them Laurel and Hardy again, as in *The Rogue Song*, for their own uses, but Roach refused and built his own prison set, at such an expense that the only way to recoup it was to extend 'The Rap' to full length.

Whatever its origins, *Pardon Us* turned out to be a pot-pourri of recycled and previously unused ideas. Stan and Ollie are incompetent bootleggers who land in jail because Stan has sold a bottle of beer to a policeman, on the grounds that 'I thought he was a streetcar conductor.' Cue Ollie's: 'Well, here's another nice mess you've gotten me into.' Stan is in further trouble because of a chipped tooth which makes him follow every sentence with what sounds like a deliberate raspberry, an unwise course when up against the warden, and then against Stan and Ollie's most faithful heavy, plug-ugly convict Walter Long.

Confusion over Laurel and Hardy versions is particularly rife with regard to *Pardon Us*, which is listed variously as lasting 56, 61 and 63 minutes, the shortest being the extant US version and the longest existing in transmission of the British release. The latter includes an extended sequence of the boys' mid-film escape from the prison, hiding out in blackface in a community of plantation workers, who seem to be living way back when in a happy-go-lucky, if indentured, state. All the versions include the long take in close-up of Ollie rendering the sentimental ditty: 'Lazy moon, come out soon, make my poor heart be warmer . . . oh moon, don't keep me waiting here tonight, longing for my little lady love . . .' If Oliver Norvell Hardy ever sang with the minstrels, this is his heartfelt tribute. It is a poignant scene, ignored by many commentators, perhaps embarrassed by the unabashed racial patronizing of the entire episode.

The escape is foiled, when the warden and his daughter turn up in their car for a countryside jaunt and break down, calling on the two false cotton-pickers to assist them. Ollie's blackface is licked off by a dog and Stan pulls out the chewing-gum he has been using to fix his tooth, emitting the tell-tale raspberry. In a previous scene, Stan, or director Jimmy Parrott, or both, pull off a bold 'anti-cinematic' coup when Stan and Ollie are locked in separate solitary cells after pelting prison teacher Jimmy Finlayson with ink. The camera remains static on the exterior of the two locked cell doors, in the corridor, for a full two minutes, while Stan and Ollie's voices provide the following exchange from within:

STAN

Ollie, I wonder how long we're going to be in here.

OLLIE

Oh, about two months, I guess.

STAN

(*Pause for thought.*) That's a month apiece.

OLLIE

273

(*Muttering*) A month apiece! . . . You can take it from me, when I get out of here I'm going back on the farm. I can see it now – rows and rows of sweet corn swaying in the breezes, honey bees buzzing in the clover – and the smell of new-mown hay in the air.

STAN

Ollie.

OLLIE

What?

STAN

Did you say you can see all that?

OLLIE

Why, certainly.

STAN

That's funny, I can't see a thing, it's dark in here.

The uneasy mixture of boldness and derivative scenes, in an episodic structure, will be characteristic of the Laurel and Hardy features as they struggle to fill the longer slots. Returned to jail after their escape, a few more minutes are gained by reprising the dentist scene from *Leave 'Em Laughing* – Ollie getting his tooth pulled by mistake and Stan having the wrong tooth taken, leaving him with his dangerous rasp. The climax is a standard prison riot, with Stan handed Walter Long's hidden tommy-gun by mistake at the prison meal, leading to shots, mayhem, and the boys foiling the hard-core mutineers by sheer chance. Given their pardon by the warden for saving the day for law and order, they are told to start over where they left off. Prompting Stan's logical query, 'Can we take your order for a couple of cases?', the panic run from the enraged warden, and fade-out.

Following *Pardon Us*, Stan and Ollie returned to the factory production of their short works. The first of these, *Another Fine Mess*, was a talkie remake of *Duck Soup*, based once again on the primal Arthur Jefferson *Home from the Honeymoon* sketch. The mad owner of the house they hide in as butler and maid this time is Jimmy Finlayson, as the aptly named Colonel Buckshot, pursuing the two miscreants at the end as they escape dressed in a wildebeest skin, riding a tandem. Tangling with a streetcar in a tunnel, the bicycle and riders are shorn apart, each in his part of the skin, uni-cycling into The End.

The original writer of the sketch, back in Olde England, was not as charmed as most audiences by his son's continued expropriation of his act. In an interview for the British magazine *Picturegoer Weekly* in 1932, in which he was posed in a bowler hat 'to empha-size his likeness to his son', Arthur Jefferson commented that 'I sent him a little sketch of my own, which they filmed under the stupid title of *Another Fine Mess*, and I didn't like the American angle they got on it one bit.'

Stan's desertion of the home front to make his life and career in America clearly rankled with the elder Jefferson twenty years on. He talked about encouraging his son to 'give us a little bit more of what England expects and a little less of what America expects . . . But', the old man grudgingly accepted, 'I think he is going to get the chance to give what he wants to give, from what I can hear.'

Stan had made one brief trip to England in 1927, to see his family, but he had not then been a famous or even a recognizable star. His next trip, with Babe Hardy, would be a very different affair. But it would have to await a gap in the schedule.

Be Big, *Chickens Come Home* and *Laughing Gravy* bridged the pass from 1930 into 1931. The latter was a remake of the silent *Angora Love*, with Stan and Ollie hiding a dog, instead of a goat, from landlord Charlie Hall. The film was intended to be a three-reeler, but was cut down on release to two reels. The original finale of the film, extant in the foreign versions, was replaced in the US with a short scene in which, after the landlord's desperate attempt to catch them with the dog, 'Laughing Gravy', and evict them, a policeman arrives with a quarantine notice that says no one can leave the house for two months. Charlie exits and two shots are heard off screen. Stan, Ollie and cop doff their hats. But the replaced scene, restored from an unreleased English-language copy for the recent video re-release of the film, turns out to be a mint centrepiece of the fundamental Laurel and Hardy relationship. In this version, after the landlord has ordered them to quit the house, the boys pack in their room, Ollie muttering angrily to himself.

STAN

275

In bed with 'Laughing Gravy'

What's the matter?

OLLIE

What's the matter? You're the cause of me being in this
deplorable condition. You've held me back for years and I'm
sick of it.

*They continue packing. Knock on the door, and landlord Charlie delivers
Stan a letter, which says that he is 'the sole heir to your late Uncle's fortune – providing you sever all connections with* OLIVER HARDY, *whom
your Uncle felt is responsible for your deplorable condition'.*

(*Looking worried, then smiles*) What's that?

STAN

A letter.

OLLIE

Who is it from?

STAN

A friend.

OLLIE

276

What's it about?

It's about me.

OLLIE

Is it good news or bad news?

STAN

Yes and no.

OLLIE

What do you mean, 'yes and no'?

STAN

Well, 'tis, and 'tisn't . . . 'tisn't and 'tis . . .

OLLIE

You're getting on my nerves. Let me see that letter.

STAN

It's private.

OLLIE

(*Goes into a fuming sulk.*) Well, if it's private it's private . . .
Thank goodness it's not in my nature to hold out anything
on a pal . . . Once a friend always a friend. It's fifty–fifty
with a Hardy. But then, it takes all sorts of people to make a
world. It's all right. Don't worry, I won't complain. (*Turns
away, packing his shirt collars, chanting:*) You'll be sorry just
too late, when our friendship turns to hate, when our friendship turns to hate, you'll be sorry just too late . . .

Stan, worn down, flustered, turns and holds out the letter to Ollie.

What? Me read your letter? I should say not! . . . No Hardy
would read anyone's personal mail . . .

STAN

(*Turning away*) All right.

OLLIE

(*Grabbing the letter*) Oh, give me that letter! (*Begins reading, sees check.*) Oh, holding out on me! 'Twas ever thus . . .
(*Reads on, glances with a terrible guilt at the camera. His
face softens as he turns to Stan.*) Now I know why you
didn't want me to read it. I'm sorry of everything I said.
And I thought all the time it was you holding me back. Isn't

it funny. We never see ourselves as others see us. Well, you'd
better be going.

                              STAN
(*Tearful*) What's going to become of you?

                              OLLIE
Oh, don't worry about me. I'll be all right. Goodbye.

                              STAN
Bye.

                              OLLIE
And good luck.

Stan exits frame, goes to pick up suitcase and the dog, 'Laughing Gravy'.
Ollie steps up to him and takes the dog.

You're not going to strip me of everything, aren't you? It's
going to be lonesome enough without you taking the dog.
Goodbye.

                              STAN
Bye.

He turns. Ollie glances at us, with dog. Stan puts down his case, turns,
tears the letter and check to shreds.

                              OLLIE
(*Beaming*) My pal! And to think you're giving it all up for me!

                              STAN
(*Nods, then double take.*) For you? I didn't want to leave
Laughing Gravy.

Stan takes dog from Ollie. Ollie goes berserk, begins smashing every-
thing in sight. Fade-out.

Hidden from English-speaking fans for over fifty years, this
scene has a resonance that goes far beyond our two heroes. The
simple, tit-for-tat dialogue, in its deliberate slowness and its mono-
syllabic cadences, looks forward to the kind of dialogue modernist
playwrights, such as Harold Pinter and Samuel Beckett, derived
from the rhythms of ordinary, banal talk. In a later period, when
serious writers examined the way people hide their thoughts behind
their speech, some of the most influential voices of our time harked
back to the formulations of music-hall. Grimaldi and Dan Leno's

famous comic observations of everyday life and parlance echo into the present age. The Marx Brothers, and W. C. Fields, played with language, turned it about, stood it on its head, extracted all manners of unexpected, hidden meanings. But Stan and Ollie are completely devoid of subterfuge, on the one hand, and consumed with self-deception, on the other. They have the capacity to misunderstand the simplest things that human beings take for granted. Like an old married couple, they are locked into a 'co-dependency' in which each is the mirror image of the other. They may come from different ends of the earth, they may be ground down by misfortune, they may be physical, even temperamental opposites, but they partake in the purest form of the human principle that no man – or woman – is an island. We complement each other, a part of the whole. This, of course, may only be a dream, an aspiration, but everything is a dream – in the movies.

CHAPTER TWENTY-SIX

Chickens Come Home

The opening title of *Come Clean*, shot in May 1931, revealed that:

MR HARDY HOLDS THAT EVERY HUSBAND SHOULD TELL HIS WIFE
THE WHOLE TRUTH – MR LAUREL IS CRAZY TOO.

Two months before, the domestic troubles of Oliver Hardy had erupted into the public domain once again. The *Los Angeles Examiner* reported, on 31 March 1931: 'Wife of Hardy, Film Comedian, Paroled: Mrs Myrtle Hardy . . . yesterday was granted a parole on a charge of excessive use of stimulants by Superior Court Judge Thomas C. Gould, upon her promise to go to a private sanatorium for a cure.' This was preceded by a press report on 26 March, to wit:

COMEDIAN'S WIFE REPORTED MISSING FROM SANATORIUM
Suffering from a nervous breakdown, according to relatives, Mrs Oliver Hardy, twenty-eight years of age . . . was reported last night to have left the Rosemead Lodge Sanatorium at Temple where she has been undergoing treatment. Previously Mrs Hardy had wandered away from the home of her sister, Mrs Mary Pense of 2243 Ben Lomond Drive, Hollywood, where she had been under a doctor's care, and was located by police in Newport Hotel late Tuesday night.

There was more to Ollie's mournful gaze into the camera in his numerous movies than met the casual eye. A photograph taken in mid-1931 of Stan and Babe and their wives, Lois and Myrtle, in the audience at the Los Angeles Coliseum, portrays a poignant moment of truth: Stan and Lois are at the furthest end of the foursome, Babe and Myrtle between them; both wives are looking away from their tuxedo-clad spouses. Stan is smiling rather shyly at the camera, under an oversize bowler. Babe stares at us with a look of naked pain. Who knows more than actors how the camera can catch you unawares, if you doff your mask, and reveal more than you wish. Myrtle, in a thick white fur, looks regal, Lois elegant and unassuming. But Babe's gloom is a heavy clue to the turmoil that lurks below the well-dressed surface.

Within eighteen months of this image, Stan and Lois were also to part. The *Los Angeles Times* announced regretfully, on 16 November 1932:

Incompatibility, the greatest nemesis of marital bliss in Hollywood, has delivered another solar plexus blow. This time it is Stan Laurel, member of the famous comedy team of Laurel and Hardy. Yesterday the comedian with the funny face admitted he and his wife, formerly known to the screen as Lois Neilson, have separated and that divorce proceedings are contemplated by her.

In telling of his domestic rift, Laurel let it be known that everything in a comedian's life is not comedy, as generally believed.

'It was difficult for us to separate, but it was just one of those things,' he said. 'I felt badly about it and I know that Mrs Laurel did too. We got to a point where anything that either of us did didn't please the other and we got on each other's nerves. So there wasn't anything left for us to do.'

In fact Mrs Laurel had been Mrs Laurel for only a little over a year, since Stan had made the legal change of his name from Jefferson to Laurel only in August 1931. The press announced on the 8th of the month:

Stan Laurel, motion-picture comedian, finally became so tired of explaining to people that his real name was Arthur Stanley Jefferson, when he signed it on checks, that he went to Superior Judge McComb's court yesterday and had it changed. So Laurel is Laurel in legal matters as well as electric lights now.

A few months before, another, less marked, name change was registered, that of Babe's half-brother, Henry Lafayette Tante, known to family and friends, for reasons that have never been figured out, as 'Bardy'. Hankering after the good life of the actor, he had arrived in California around 1930, and was helped by Babe to find some jobs as an extra on the Roach lot. In 1931 he changed his name from Tante to Hardy. His sojourn in Los Angeles led, according to family tales, to a quickie marriage to a wealthy widow, appropriately named Frances Rich, who lived near Babe's home, but it hardly lasted a day, and he returned to Georgia to marry an old sweetheart.

According to the lore, Babe's mother, Emily, was also in Los

Angeles during this period. But there is no evidence that 'Miss Emmie' stayed for more than a few days at a time in California. Other family members who ventured west from Atlanta, for a much longer stay, were Margaret and Mary, Babe's nieces, the daughters of his sister Elizabeth and her husband Ira Sage. They too found work at the Roach Studios in minor walk-on roles. Emily Norvell-Tante-Jackson remained, most of the time, in Atlanta. The apocryphal tale, told by Lucille Hardy, has her living for six weeks in Los Angeles, at the Hollywood Hotel, provided with a car and a chauffeur. After this period, she decided she missed her friends back home and took the chauffeur and the car back to Georgia, never to return to California again. The date for this event varies wildly. It was, at any rate, a somewhat tortuous way for the Tantes and the Sages to maintain the fiction of Babe's closeness to his mother throughout his movie career. Madelyn might have been long gone, but she was not forgotten, and there is no evidence that Emily bonded in any way with Atlanta-born but luckless Myrtle. As mother Emily might well have said to her baby son, Norvell, 'Here's another nice mess you've gotten yourself into.'

By this time, indeed, there was another woman in Babe Hardy's life: Viola Morse, also Southern born, a divorcée with a little boy. She had become a close companion on Babe's outings to night spots or the gambling haunts and racecourses of Agua Caliente, Tijuana. She featured, though was not named, in Myrtle Hardy's second-time around divorce petition in July 1933, when Myrtle alleged, 'Recently Hardy took a woman to Agua Caliente and introduced her as his wife, Mrs Hardy complained, adding that the comedian often told acquaintances that he no longer cared for his wife, and "the sooner he got his freedom, the better for him".'

Few might blame poor Babe for that, although his little anniversary notes to Myrtle, in her sanatorium, remain filled with sugary declarations of love and affection, and the 'Daddy'–'Baby' exchanges continued. There can be little doubt that Babe loved Myrtle deeply, but found he could not remain both faithful and celibate in the face of her profound addiction.

The source of Stan's marital troubles with Lois is less obvious. Certainly Stan was a doting father to little Lois, and his home life appeared, on the surface, quite calm. Whether his roving eye for the pretty ladies was a serious threat or not before 1932 is a matter of choice of gossip. A more serious strain on the marriage was Lois's difficult second pregnancy of the winter and spring of 1929–30. A son, Stanley Robert Jefferson, was born on the evening of 7 May 1930, at the Hollywood Hospital, two months premature. The baby died, nine days old, on 16 May. Stan was devastated. He had just completed shooting *Hog Wild* and was due to commence *The Laurel–Hardy Murder Case* in mid- to late May. It is no wonder that the movie remains one of the weakest in the Stan and Ollie canon. In June, Stan had recovered enough to begin filming the feature *Pardon Us*. For Lois, however, there was no respite in work.

As usual, in the saga of artists, the role of the spouse becomes often obscured. Lois had given up her own career as an actress to be Mrs Stan Jefferson, then Laurel. Living in Hollywood, in the midst of the movie colony, the sacrifice was brought home every day. Stan's record with Mae, as with his vaudeville partners, bears witness to the strong argumentative streak in his personal character. In this matter, one might risk a little amateur psychology, in speculating on Stan's state of mind in this period. Looking at Stan's solo films, we were struck by the consistent effort to develop a certain type of comic character which was almost completely opposite to the Stan of the Laurel and Hardy we know: the brash, pushy, sometimes manic, sometimes downright aggressive boy-about-town, the type that initiates action rather than reacts. We can recall, from the beginning, young Stanley Jefferson's hesitancy and problems in deciding 'what kind of a comedian I wanted to be'. The shadow of Chaplin, and the long march from Chaplin imitation to his own brand. And then, when the characters of Stan and Ollie finally click, the critical 'turnaround' that Walter Kerr writes about, 'with Hardy as discreet but firm aggressor, and Laurel as deferential, if stunned tag-along'.

From 1927 on, Stan reined in his solo ambitions, and accepted his role as one half of a team – the instigating half, as planner, behind the scenes, but an equal half on the screen. We might surmise that the aggressive, pushy aspects of Stan Laurel would have to find expression somewhere, if they were suppressed where it mattered most to him – 'on stage'. And so perhaps it should not surprise us that Stan, at home, would be appreciably more of a trial to his real-life partner than he might be standing back on the roof of *Hog Wild* and causing Ollie to fall off by sheer circumstance.

'Unaccustomed as they were', and amid these brewing domestic storms, Stan and Ollie still managed to turn out more masterpieces throughout 1931 and into the summer of 1932. Their four-reeler, *Beau Hunks*, does not quite qualify, being an unadulterated delight only to those who do not mind their orientalism replete with barefoot towel-headed knife-packing tribesmen being foiled by spilled cases of sharp nails. James Horne replaced Jimmy Parrott as director and the standard does dip. However, Jimmy Parrott was back in the autumn for *Helpmates*, *The Music Box* and *County Hospital*, the latter introducing the immortal cry of 'Hard-boiled eggs and nuts!' and the previous two films constituting the highest point of Stan and Ollie's art.

In *Helpmates*, the pain of domestic strife is inverted to present Ollie's house as a graveyard of empty booze bottles, used food plates and ashtrays full of cigarette butts. This is the result, not of an addicted wife, but of a profligate husband. The opening shot reveals Ollie in close-up, berating the camera – his own image in the mirror, complete with ice-pack on sozzled head –

Aren't you ashamed of yourself? A man of your supposed intelligence . . . You took advantage of your wife's absence and pulled a wild party – and that's not all! You lost all of your ready money in a poker game. Could anything be more crass? More disgusting? There are times when I had high hopes for you, but that time is passed. I'll tell you what's wrong with you in two words: Im–possible!

A postman brings a telegram from the absent wife, who is due back from visiting her mother, at noon. Nothing to be done but to call up your pal Stan, roust him from bed and get him to help you clean up the house. The resulting destruction, a perfect metaphor in its use of the most ordinary props and objects, utilizes every single piece of household furniture to reduce both men and home to a shambles: pails of water, stacks of smashed dishes, facefuls of soot and flour, a bathroom plunger in the eye, a hoseful of water in the bedroom and the inevitably exploding kitchen stove. ('Do you realise that this is the only suit that I've got left? It's enough to make a man burst out crying.') For the topper, Stan lights a nice fire, helped along with a generous dolloping of petrol, and burns the whole house down. As both stand in the ruins, Ollie clad in the remains of his Masonic uniform, the sword bent, the black eye delivered by the wife at the railway station, Stan's parting shot, after a spectacular cry, is:

STAN
Well, I guess there's nothin' else I can do.

OLLIE
No, I guess not.

STAN
I'll be seeing you.

OLLIE
Goodbye . . . Would you mind closing the door. I'd like to be alone.

Left in the ruins, the skies open up over Ollie: the lightning forks; the monsoon pours down. Ollie picks a bit of lint off his trousers, with a resigned look, and fade.

Note a further milestone in the series of harridan wives, fulfilled here in one coruscating close-up of Blanche Payson, who looks as if twisting the heads off crocodiles would be her idea of a good time.

Another milestone, in the autumn of 1931, was the Depression catching up even with Hal Roach Studios, which began to cut staff, letting go such talents as cameraman George Stevens. Roach was in the bad books of the Bank of America for being wobbly on some of his loans and, at their insistence, a new, tough general manager, Henry Ginsberg, was appointed to run the studio. Stan had built a 'regular five-room bungalow' in order to burn it down for *Help-mates*, but this kind of extravagance was out of the question from now on. Anita Garvin told interviewer Randy Skretvedt:

Stan used to call Henry Ginsberg 'The Expediter'. He was always trying to get everything to work as quickly as possible. One day, Ginsberg came down to the Laurel and Hardy set to see how quickly things were moving along. Well, Stan . . . slowed everything way down, delaying everything as much as possible, until Ginsberg finally got the message and left.

Despite all this, *The Music Box* was created, around Christmas-time of 1931. Jimmy Parrott directed; Walter Lundin and Len Powers photographed; Richard Currier edited. 'Beanie' Walker wrote what there was of the dialogue. But there was not much of

Delivery accomplished – with Billy Gilbert and Gladys Gale in
The Music Box

that. *The Music Box* advances, in perfect motion, to the rhythm of
the time-honoured ritual. Gladys Gale is the woman who buys a
player-piano to surprise her husband on his birthday. 'THE LAUREL
AND HARDY TRANSFER COMPANY – FOUNDERED 1931' – motto:
'Tall Oaks from Little Acorns Grow' – is delegated to deliver the
crate, to 1127 Walnut Avenue, up the same steep flight of steps at
Vendome Street, Silver Lake, tried out by Charley Chase in *Isn't
Life Terrible* in 1925 and reprised by Stan and Ollie in the vanished
Hats Off, in 1927. Billy Gilbert is the apoplectic husband, Professor
Theodore von Schwartzenhoffen M.D., A.D., D.D.S., F.L.D., F.F.F.
und F., who tangles with them on the steps and wreaks his total but
self-destructive havoc on the player-piano at the end.

The Music Box won the Oscar for Best Short Subject (Comedy)
at the Academy of Motion Picture Arts and Sciences Awards in
November 1932. According to special-effects man Roy Seawright,
there really was a piano in the crate that Stan and Ollie hauled up
the steps and into the house. Certainly something was necessary for
the weight, but perhaps one might doubt the witness this time.

Although the film was, at base, a simple remake of a silent movie – already an established procedure for L&H – replacing the washing machine with a piano, it is difficult to think that no one involved was aware of the mythical underpinnings of this three-reel saga. Even a child knows that Sisyphus rolled a rock up the mountain again and again, despite possible vagueness about whether Sisyphus was a companion of Popeye. The ritual nature of the event is emphasized all the more when the boys have finally got the piano up to the top of the stairs, only to be told by postman Charlie Hall that they could have driven it up following the road around the hill. Ollie, exasperated: 'Now why didn't we think of that before?' He motions to Stan, and they both pick up the crate and carry it back down the steps to load on their wagon, to the chagrin, one assumes, of the not quite trustworthy equine, Susie.

It is not so much, the story is saying, the doing of the deed, but the manner in which it is done – as Ollie says to Stan in more than one movie, 'There's a right way and a wrong way of doing things.' And then they proceed to do the wrong.

The Music Box remains the best of the boys' 'blue-collar' films, and the favourite of many, including myself. In the midst of the Depression, it must have been salutary to ponder the image of such puffing, sweated labour, brought to nought by the beneficiary of the work, who proceeds to wreck the goods with an axe. Only 'The Star-Spangled Banner', emanating from the piano's 'Medley of Patriotic Songs', stays the destruction for a moment's frozen salute, before the axe continues to smash the piano to smithereens. When the wife arrives, tearfully explaining the nature of her gift, the Professor's rage turns to the most insincere repentance, which lasts only an instant before the pen he is given to sign the delivery note inevitably sprays ink in his face. Laurel and Hardy, however, have done their duty. Free Enterprise can proceed to the next job, such as rescuing the nation from its own follies.

After *The Chimp* and *County Hospital* (Ollie laid up with leg in plaster, Stan bringing the despised 'hard-boiled eggs and nuts! huh!'), the boys launched into their second feature-length picture, *Pack Up Your Troubles*, in May 1932. *Pardon Us* had been declared a 'laugh triumph' by the critics and the audiences had responded with coin of the realm.

A new director, George Marshall, was hired, and gave value for money by doubling as the movie's sinister heavy, the army cook with the sharp knife. (Raymond McCarey, Leo's brother, was credited as co-director, but did not direct much except second-unit scenes.) The script, however, stretched H. M. 'Beanie' Walker and his co-writers' capabilities to their breaking point. Stan and Ollie are two vagrants lifted off their park bench by the recruiting sergeant to serve their country in the Great War (much as the California Fire-Fighting Service sought to sweep them up in *Duck Soup*). In the Normandy trenches, their bosom friend, Eddie Smith, is killed, having left a small daughter (there is a vanished wife somewhere in the textual driftwood) in the hands of strangers back home. Most of the film is taken up with Stan and Ollie, after the war, searching the Los Angeles city directory for Smiths, in their attempt to find Eddie's own estranged parents and give the child a proper home before the villainous welfare man (Charles Middleton) carts her off to the orphanage. In the end, Grandad turns out to be the bank president (Richard Tucker) Stan and Ollie have tried to touch for a loan to finance their lunch-wagon business.

Pack Up Your Troubles was a popular film, but it marks the beginning of a process that was to change Stan and Ollie from the harder-edged survivors of a harsh world to the avuncular, cuddlier, softer personas that were to take over in future Roach films. Perhaps it was simply the times, which were about to change, in America, from the obtuse era of Herbert Hoover to the upbeat voice of Franklin Delano Roosevelt's New Deal – despite the continuing economic slump. Or perhaps it was our old enemy, the Hays Code, which would, in 1934, begin the fight to roll back the sassy, raucous, often anarchic cinema characterized by the Marx Brothers, W. C. Fields and Mae West. The chronology suggests, however, that Laurel and Hardy were softening their approach long before any external forces were biting, apart from the dour strictures of Henry Ginsberg, which hardly affected Stan's gags and plots.

At any rate, one can trace the origins of a gentler, more child-friendly tone in Stan and Ollie's output to the plot of their second feature. Toting cute four-year-old Jacquie Lyn with them as they search for Smiths in the city, Stan and Ollie are KO-ed by a brutish boxer, have an embarrassing moment with a black householder and reduce a society wedding to chaos (W. C. Fields stalwart Grady

Sutton takes the fall as the wrong Eddie almost left holding the baby), before the final chase by the Welfare heavies and happy ending. Reviews were mixed, *Variety* complaining that the film was 'inanely obvious', while the *New York Times* conceded that 'there are several good bits while Laurel and Hardy are in uniform', which is pretty damning to the last two-thirds of the picture.

Stan and Ollie were not too upset by these reviews, as they came after an event that transformed their perception of their work's impact on the world outside Hollywood. One more two-reeler, *Scram*, was shot immediately after the feature, before Stan and Babe set off on a well-earned vacation.

Scram returned, perhaps in relief, to the more hot-blooded Hal Roach world of drunks, ill-tempered judges and jaunty women, introducing a new member of the stock company, Arthur Housman, whose drunken cameos were apparently achieved by the Stanislavsky method of complete immersion in the role. This did not, according to the lore, affect his professional competence, as far as turning up on time and staying afloat during the relevant takes was concerned, though chronology suggests that his death in 1942, at the age of fifty-two, indicates that one cannot mix fantasy and reality too closely, too often, without paying the price.

Scram wrapped in early July, and soon afterwards, on 12 July, Stan and Babe took a train from Los Angeles, bound for New York and an ocean liner, which would take them east, on their first tour abroad.

CHAPTER TWENTY-SEVEN

A Very Good Boy

From the *New York Times*, 30 July 1932:

FIGHT TO GREET ACTORS
Thousands at Glasgow welcome Laurel and Hardy
Nine persons went to hospitals and many others were less seriously hurt in a wild crush of several thousands at Central Station today to greet Laurel and Hardy, the Hollywood movie team, who came to spend the weekend. Police were unable to control the mob and the comedians almost lost their coats when enthusiastic souvenir hunters tried to snatch buttons.

Some persons were thrown over a stone balustrade by the crowding enthusiasts and others were run down by a tramcar. Laurel wept with emotion. Each of the comedians said he had never seen such a welcome.

Stan and Babe had not initially intended to travel together – their social lives, as we have noted earlier, were not closely entwined. But Stan had long planned another trip to visit his father and family, and Babe had read about the fair golf courses of Scotland, and so the idea of a joint trip was born. Myrtle travelled with Babe, on a last-ditch attempt to patch up their marriage, and distance him from Viola Morse. Two family friends, Dr and Ethel Falconer, accompanied them. Lois Laurel remained behind, perhaps weary of trying to keep up appearances.

It was supposed to be a private vacation, but the MGM publicity department had other ideas, and their British branch scheduled and announced a month of Laurel and Hardy films to run from 25 July. The press was wired the details and right at the start of the trip, as the entourage changed trains in Chicago, both press and public closed in *en masse*, to Stan's and Babe's great surprise. In New York, they were driven down Broadway past cheering crowds, followed by churning newsreel cameras, in an all-but-ticker-tape send-off.

When they arrived at Southampton, on board the *Aquitania*, on 23 July, the first intimation of their global fame hit Stan and Ollie

290

forcefully. Thousands of fans gathered on the dock, waving and cheering, and whistling the 'Cuckoo' song. In the mêlée, Stan ran up and down, looking for his Dad, who finally materialized, with his second wife Venetia. The party battled aboard the train for London's Waterloo station, where thousands more fans waited with the same refrain.

Repairing to the Savoy Hotel, they were caught by the newspapers again, and the *Daily Sketch* recorded the family reunion, quoting the ever dominating Arthur Jefferson:

'A good boy, a very good boy. Success hasn't spoiled him . . .' 'He's still the same kid,' said his sister. The boy hung his head modestly. [Stan was aged forty-two. Ed.] 'Seems to me', said Jefferson, 'that comedians are born, not made.'

'You said a lot, Dad,' said the boy.

'I always go to see him in the pictures,' Mr Jefferson added. 'In our home in Shields in the old days I could see he had something in him. Always being funny, he was . . . What I say is, what's bred in the bone . . .'

Two thousand people turned up at the Empire Theatre in Leicester Square, mobbing their car, for a personal appearance by the boys. On 27 July, they broadcast on the BBC. Everywhere they went, the wild enthusiasm was repeated. Their homecoming, to the North of England, to Tynemouth, Newcastle and North Shields, was a triumphant return of local heroes, with Babe adopted in equal status with Stan. Stan tried to visit his old childhood home in Dockwray Square, but a tide of people kept him from the door. The *Shields Hustler* wrote, 'What struck us all was Stan's sweet naturalness. Success hasn't spoilt him, as it does so many people. He has not developed a swelled head, and his old friends in North Shields were glad of that.'

In Edinburgh, the crowds were equally large, but respectful, and the local Playhouse was showing *Laughing Gravy*. The appearance of the real Laurel and Hardy evoked enormous applause. It was not until they arrived in Glasgow, at the Central station, that the full impact of Laurel-and-Hardy-mania, as reported in the New York press, broke through. Were it not for the police, the crowd might have torn their adored idols apart.

Today we are used to the sight of famous people travelling with bodyguards, re-routing traffic to avoid the potentially lethal crush of their adoring fans. A near riot had occurred at Rudolph Valentino's funeral, but at least the star was dead at the time. For Stanley Jefferson of Ulverston and Oliver Norvell Hardy of Harlem, Georgia, to be so treated, as worshipped icons, and this not in excitable America, but in the sedate United Kingdom (albeit in fierier Scotland), was a staggering experience for both, and totally unexpected. For years they had been ploughing their furrow, rising through the ranks of comedy performers, to find what they chiefly regarded as job security at the Hal Roach factory. They were aware of their status, as bankable actors. But world fame, on this scale, was a revelation.

The British press continued to record their progress, as they left Glasgow for Preston, *en route* for their next stop in Blackpool:

GREAT WELCOME AT BLACKPOOL; ATTEMPT TO DODGE CROWD
Four limousines sped through the quiet streets of Blackpool from Preston this afternoon and approached as unassumingly as possible the entrance to the Hotel Metropole.

But the efforts of their 'freight', the famous Laurel and Hardy, of Hollywood, to travel incognito, was naturally doomed to failure.

There had been no official announcement of the time or place of arrival, but thousands and thousands of Blackpool's Bank Holiday-makers stood in a seething mass in Talbot Square to greet them.

Special police precautions for dealing with the crowd were organized during the morning by the Chief Constable . . . Whilst in Blackpool, probably tomorrow morning, the comedians are anxious to visit the children at the Chronicle Cinderella Club's sunshine home at Rossall . . . 'For many of the children here it will be the greatest event in their life,' the matron had told me.

At Preston a little girl presented them with a piece of Lancashire cheese, a gift inspired by a scene in *The Rogue Song*, and in Blackpool they had to shake endless hands: 'I must have shaken hands at least ten thousand times since I arrived in England,' Stan told a reporter for the Lancashire *Daily Post*, 'and my partner has an even greater record.' From Blackpool the tour moved on to Manchester, where they were mobbed again, and also visited the home of an old colleague of Babe's from Vim days, Bert Tracy, whose mother served them afternoon tea. Leeds followed, where, once again, the *Yorkshire Evening News* reported:

'Gosh! But this is great. Real Yorkshire hospitality, I'll say.' Thus spoke Stan Laurel . . . when he could find time to say anything at all after he and Hardy had reached the Queens Hotel following a vociferously hearty welcome from a large crowd at the Leeds New Station this afternoon . . .

'We never thought it would be anything like this,' Laurel said to a *Mercury* reporter . . . 'We came over for a quiet vay-cation, a run around the country-side, in a car, looking up old friends . . .' Instead of his being free to see them, they have to come to see him; as did Mr and Mrs Shaw, his uncle and aunt, and their daughter, with whom he used to spend holidays at Batley . . . Only once have the two comedians been able to walk abroad – at Blackpool, where they stole out at 1:30 in the morning for sticks of rock. 'Gee, we'd a swell time,' Hardy said . . . Middle impression of Laurel and Hardy: 'A couple of really good fellows.'

And so it went on, from Leeds to Sheffield, the echoes of 'their great delight at the warmhearted Yorkshire welcome' ringing in their ears –

The question of lunch brought up the subject of Yorkshire puddings, and it was a treat to see the smile of anticipation on Laurel's face at the mention of this delicacy. After his marriage to his American wife, one of his first domestic duties was 'to teach her to make Yorkshire pudding', he said.

The newspapers also found time to talk to Mrs Hardy: 'My husband is just a big, shy boy,' Myrtle told the reporters. 'He would like to spend his holiday taking quiet rides into the country.'

Mrs Hardy thinks there is nowhere in the world like California. She lives in Beverly Hills among the stars and knows almost all of them. 'I haven't met Garbo, but then so few people have; but I know most of the others,' she told me. 'You are bound to come up against them sooner or later.'

Stan regaled the press with sage words about comedy, telling the *East Anglian Times*:

The slapstick of today is more refined than the slapstick of twenty years ago. It has more point. Its wit is sharper and its capers are more extravagant. Slapstick more closely approximates to the daydreams of childhood than any other form of screen entertainment. The antics of the funny men in the custard-pie comedies are an exaggeration of those which keep children in the heights of laughter. You may not see the similarity at first, but on thinking it over the resemblance is very definitely there. The come-dian who knocks down the policeman is the small child rebelling against authority. The custard-pie is the symbol of revolt – revolt against an igno-rant world of grown-ups which cannot appreciate that the dirty puddle at the end of the garden path is really the most romantic of lakes, on which there are boats to be sailed and bridges to be built . . .

Stan's and Babe's final appearance of their British tour was back in London, keeping a unique rendezvous at the Walpole Cinema in Ealing. Arthur Jefferson, then resident near by at Colebrook Avenue, had promised, the year before, that he would introduce his son and Oliver Hardy to the local audience if ever they visited England. Reported the *Middlesex County Times*:

'My hope has been realized,' said Mr Jefferson in his introductory remarks, 'and I am enabled to get them to express their appreciation of the loyalty you have shown to the Laurel and Hardy films . . . They have returned from a wonderful tour in provincial centres, where their reception has been indescribable. They are dog tired and fagged out, but neverthe-less, to keep faith with us all . . . they have come here tonight.'

The hefty Hardy then tripped forward (literally) in his inimitable style and stumbled up the platform, followed closely by his partner, little Laurel, who assumed his famous asinine expression upon being pushed forward to face the audience . . . They kept up their clowning for several minutes, and then Mr Hardy became a little more serious.

'May I say a word or two,' he said, 'to express my feelings at being received like this – a stranger in a strange land. I have not had a finer friendship for anyone in my life than I have had for Stan Laurel in the last few years. He is as great a pal as my own mother. I had not met his father until tonight, but I knew what to expect – a great guy.' (Laughter and applause.)

'You may not realize what a wonderful feeling it is to be received as we have been,' said Mr Laurel . . . 'It is a great moment to have with me here tonight my dear old Daddy to share my success.' (Applause.)

Mr Hardy: Our father! (Laughter.)

He thereupon gave Mr Jefferson a semi-serious embrace.

Having lost a father as a baby, Hardy gained a new one forty years later, if only temporarily, in Ealing. It was a strange moment, for all concerned, and one that, luckily, they took in jest, before, once again, leaving the theatre and facing the adoring crowds outside.

CHAPTER TWENTY-EIGHT

Busy Bodies and Devil's Brothers

Stan and Ollie returned to the United States at the beginning of September, exhausted after their busy vacation, and having cut short a trip to Paris that promised more of the Glasgow station treatment. By 24 September they were on the Hal Roach lot again, in their element, before the camera.

The first film after the tour was *Their First Mistake*, a two-reeler that has driven commentators and critics into paroxysms of inflated analysis. This is the movie in which Stan prompts Ollie to adopt a baby, after Mrs Ollie – who else but Mae Busch – has stormed out over his continual neglect of her in favour of Stan. The boys are left with the baby when they are served papers from Mae suing Ollie for divorce, and Stan for alienating his affections.

Cultural critic Jonathan Sanders has gone to town over this, calling the film 'a subtle Utopian fantasy of personal relationships, in which Ollie's desire for a male friend/lover, a wife and a child are all satisfied by one person – Stan'. Well, subtle it certainly ain't! As Ollie and Stan are in bed with the babe, which is crying out to be fed, Ollie's outraged looks crescendo as Stan unbuttons his nightshirt, only to subside in relief when Stan pulls out the bottle. In the next scene, Ollie, half asleep, thinks he is feeding the baby from the bottle when it's really Stan sucking at the teat.

Theories of 'feminization', 'cross-gender reversal', 'mock eroticism' and the like suck furiously at this synthetic nipple, perhaps to nourishing effect. But given the events in both Stan's and Babe's personal lives, one might wish to gaze on the strange goings on in the on-screen Hardy household in a slightly different light: the extent to which life and art are intertwined in the creative progenitor's head – i.e., in Stan's fertile brain. The record shows that the boys' regular dialogue writer, H. M. 'Beanie' Walker, had resigned in July 1932, two months before *Their First Mistake* was prepared. The film has no writing credit attached, and we can safely assume Stan's authorship. For someone who kept saying that he had no

Gender-bending in *Their First Mistake*

interest in 'art', and was a comedy gagster and storyteller pure and simple, he was certainly ratcheting up a high number of projects in which his personal troubles and extremely adult anxieties about identity and survival in the real world of 'grown-ups' figured again and again. Stan keeps returning to the idea of Stan and Ollie as children acting out adult themes and relationships. The smallest child can laugh at Stan and Ollie's exposure of the often arbitrary nature of the adult presumption of authority.

Like many comic characters of the 'golden age of comedy', Laurel and Hardy might well be strangers who have arrived on our planet as extra-terrestrial visitors from a place where other rules apply. They are constantly dumbfounded, as we have noted before, by the strange social strictures that human beings place on themselves. Grown men are supposed to marry, so they do, co-habiting uneasily with the females of the species that society has provided for this mysterious purpose. Children are part of this design, but quite how they are to be engendered is a matter that, quite literally, the Motion Picture Code forbids to be revealed. In *Brats*, they are created by the magic of special effects and outsize sets. In *Their First Mistake*, they are obtained from some off-screen agency, ever ready to hand over an infant when Oliver Norvell Hardy knocks on the door. In fact, as Randy Skretvedt reveals, in the original script of the movie, in a scene filmed but deleted, Mrs Hardy returns to reconcile with her husband, toting her mother and two more babies, having reached the same conclusion as Stan about the means required to re-invigorate the marriage. But Stan's cut opted to end with the boys left holding the baby. The wife is written out of the tale.

It doesn't need much imagination to connect Stan's estrangement from Lois, his complex guilt feelings about the little girl, Lois junior, and, more traumatically, the painful memory of his short-lived baby son, to the strange plot line of *Their First Mistake*. The fact that the dead child had been named Stanley Robert Jefferson made the tiny ghost even more potent. Like all the great clowns, Stan Laurel took his pain and forged it into his comic sword. Babe's own suppressed desire for children from his blighted marriage to Myrtle winds powerfully into these images. Babe has, indeed, only Stan to nurture. The other battle is already lost.

In an age in which male friendships cannot be seen without their sexual aspect, in the world since Sigmund Freud, sex looms everywhere. But what remains erect, for Oliver Hardy, is not his penis, but his dignity. The echoes of the Old Southern gentleman do not fade. In a society in which one has lost everything, in which the old cause is – perhaps even rightly – despised, the man of refined sensibility retains not only an idea, perhaps absurd, of the proper form but, more than that, a fiery sense of loyalty. As we have quoted him from the cut scenes in *Laughing Gravy*: 'Once a friend, always a friend. It's fifty–fifty with a Hardy.' For Stan, the Lancashire lad, it may be not as simple. You stick by your pal, but he does remain, even in your own eyes, something of an enigma. The Self always presupposes the Other, even though you might not always be able to tell which is which. And if you have a father as domineering as Arthur Jefferson, who calls you a 'boy' at the age of forty-two, you have good cause to doubt your adult status.

Stan and Babe returned to the hearthside genre in their next but one film, *Twice Two*. This, too, has inspired the modern critics to wax eloquent yet again about feminization and 'gender ambiguity', but is, quite simply, our old vaudeville standard, the drag act, this time *à deux*. Laurel and Hardy play themselves and their wives as well: Babe doubles as Mrs Laurel and Stan as Mrs Hardy. The women are the sisters of the men, which gets over the genetic problem. Babe is Oliver Hardy, M.D., Brain Specialist – a somewhat unlikely story. Stan is his 'Associate Advisor'. It's their anniversary and Ollie wants to go out to celebrate but Mrs Laurel insists the wives will make a meal. The cake ends up on Mrs Stan's head and Stan is sent out to the corner store with fifteen cents to buy strawberry ice-cream. The man behind the counter is Baldy Cooke, Stan's old vaudeville partner. Stan spends the coins calling home every time he is told the shop hasn't got the right flavour, before being informed he's in the wrong shop for ice-cream anyway.

Twice Two is the last Laurel and Hardy film to feature this level of full-scale drag, although Stan appears as a maid in the later *A Chump at Oxford*, and harridan wives continue to feature prominently in the 1930s *œuvre*. It was also the last Laurel and Hardy film to be directed by Jimmy Parrott, who left the studio soon afterwards. His drink and drug problems were making him more and more of a liability at a time of ruthless staff cuts. Even though Stan and Babe were the Roach Studios' best assets, their salaries were docked by manager Henry Ginsberg for their 1932 vacation, despite the fact that MGM made enormous publicity from the tour: Stan lost over $19,000 and Babe $15,000 from their pay cheques. A Roach Studios note assesses that Mr Laurel's salary for 1932 would have been $123,566.67, and Mr Hardy's $102,416.67, had they not gone on tour. (Note those pesky 67 cents again!)

To put things in perspective: in January 1932 Roach himself set off from El Paso airport on a 20,000-mile South American flight with a pilot, James Dickson, and MGM executive Arthur Loew, ostensibly to break some flying record, and possibly to escape from the persistent stories about his divorce from Mrs Hal Roach. He continued flying throughout the spring and early summer – at a time when the rest of Hollywood was feeling the brunt of the deepening Depression – having a go at Charles Lindbergh's transcontinental record in June and landing with pilot Dickson at Los Angeles airport on 15 July 'aboard his low-winged plane, *Spirit of Fun*, after a sky jaunt across the continent'. (On 22 September 1932, Dickson landed Roach's Lockheed Orion plane in the streets

Oliver Hardy as Mrs Laurel – *Twice Two*

of Wilmington, at the junction of Broad and D Streets, setting yet
another aerial record. But Roach was back at work by then.)
During this entire period, therefore, Henry Ginsberg was left *in situ*
to transform the Hal Roach Studios into the Not-A-Lot-Of-Fun-
At-All. So mean was Ginsberg to his chief stars that he actually
asked editor Richard Currier to sneak down to the lot and see
whether the boys were just 'fooling around' on the set rather than
performing their profitable chores. Currier refused, and was promptly

added to the roster of old hands peremptorily fired. He had worked for Roach for twenty-two years.

Ginsberg's hostile attitude to Stan and Babe probably arose from the strange accounting procedures at the studio, which posted an increasing loss on Laurel and Hardy pictures, from $25,000 during 1930–31, to over $166,000 in 1931–32 and $140,000 in 1932–33. How this was arrived at, despite the duo's growing popularity, is a mystery that could make not only Stan stand still and scratch his head.

Stan and Babe were indeed continuing to fool around, but to great artistic, if not financial benefit. *Towed in a Hole*, shot between *Their First Mistake* and *Twice Two*, was a return to vintage mayhem, with Stan and Ollie as vendors of 'Fre–esh Fish! Caught in the ocean thi–is mo–orning!' ('Crabs a Specialty.') They decide to buy a boat, so they can catch their own merchandise and cut out the middle man, and most of the film is a leisurely romp around the damage two men can do to each other while fitting up an old tub. Ollie (after a long bout of mutual water drenching): 'Can't we stop this quarrelling? That's why we never get anyplace. Let's put our brains together so that we can forge ahead. Remember: united, we stand; divided, we fall.' And into the mud puddle he goes.

This was the boys' last film with director George Marshall, who, in *Variety*'s modern parlance, 'ankled', and went off to become one of Hollywood's most versatile craftsmen, directing W. C. Fields, Bob Hope, and soldiering on into the era of Dean Martin and Jerry Lewis, as well as directing dramas and westerns. His last film was *Hook, Line and Sinker*, a 1969 Jerry Lewis vehicle which finally convinced him to hang up his spurs.

Despite the accountants, logic and public demand required that Laurel and Hardy should escalate their output, and continue their move from the declining domain of short pictures to feature films. The exigencies of the Depression were forcing distributors to offer two features for the price of one at their theatres, and the standard fare of a newsreel, short and full feature was being superseded.

The chosen script for Stan and Ollie's next full-length foray was *Fra Diavolo*, an adaptation of a nineteenth-century comic opera by Daniel Auber, commissioned from writer Jeanie McPherson. Thelma Todd and Jimmy Finlayson were hauled on board, and the helm was seized by Hal Roach himself, re-invigorated by his flights around the continent, and possibly in lieu of the other directors Henry Ginsberg had unwisely kicked out. Charles Rogers was drafted in to direct the comedy sequences; Art Lloyd and Hap Depew were behind the camera, and Bert Jordan and William Terhune took over the slicing from exiled Dick Currier. Dennis King was to play the singing bandit of the title.

Stanlio and Ollio are two amateur hold-up men in a Ruritarian-style eighteenth-century Italy who are captured by the real bandit and, managing to avoid being hanged, are adopted as his personal servants. An early script version introduces them, in an Ollie monologue much shortened in the finished film:

OLLIO

(*Regarding their two little bags of cash*) Wouldn't it be terrible if we should lose our wealth? Think of the years we've slaved and toiled, gone without the necessities of life, stinted, scrimped and saved; frozen to death in the winters, sizzled in the summers, deprived ourselves of food – starved! Shunned by society, looked down upon as if we were the scum of the earth! And we went through it all together – just you and I. Now we have our reward. From now on we can settle down for the rest of our lives and live off the fat of the land!

Of course, they are immediately robbed by a highwayman and Ollio adopts Stanlio's idea that they should become bandits themselves. As Stan explains:

STANLIO

If we become rich, we could rob the poor and . . . give them to the bandits . . . We could start right at the top and get to the bottom in the easy way without working hard any more. We can't go wrong. It's the law of conversation. As you cast your bread on the waters, so shall ye reap.

Their first attempts, naturally, fail, as they are too soft-hearted to rob the poor, and the story continues from there. When they try and rob Diavolo himself, unaware who he is, the bandit offers to spare Stanlio if he will hang Ollio. Stan's query to Ollie if he prefers to be buried or stuffed prompts the usual outraged glances, but when the tree breaks both are spared and begin their proper career.

Both Stan and Babe were worried that their image might suffer by being wrenched away from their normal outfits and derby hats and put into period costume, complete with tufty wigs. But the film, when eventually released in May 1933, after a preview which caused it to lose over twenty minutes of Roach's own plot-based footage, and a change of US title to *The Devil's Brother*, was a hit, both at home and abroad. Laurel and Hardy were considered to have adapted well to the slowed-down rhythms of a fully fledged feature, and their comedy sequences were highly praised, despite some mutterings about the clumsiness of the remaining Roach footage and the musical numbers. Hal Roach responded in 1970 to a query by interviewer Anthony Slide:

SLIDE: Looking at *Fra Diavolo* today, there seem to be two different stories taking place on the screen – the comedy with Laurel and Hardy and the opera.
ROACH: That was the intent of the thing; you didn't have to go on for an hour and a half just doing funny things. You just can't be funny that long.

But you can still be in character, and this was the success of *The Devil's Brother*, that the characters could sustain the audience's interest even if the structure of the comic business was altered. And so Stan and Ollie's 'kneesie-earsie-nosie' game, a childish knee-slap, nose- and crossed ear-pull, can delight (or annoy) whatever the costume, and whatever the setting of the story.

    The Devil's Brother (or *Bogus Bandits*, or *Virtuous Tramps*, to cite more of its titles) retains an old-world charm, the old world being pre-jazz show business, the once ubiquitous theatrical environment of operettas and old-style musicals. Stanlio and Ollio both partake of Stan's Harlequin-like mutinous servant, but these are mischievous knaves rather than the destructive imps whose place at the steering wheel of a Model T Ford is merely the prelude to mass mayhem. The film continues the mutation of Stan and Ollie into the lovable scamps that would make them the firm friends of any child who set eyes on their movies. *Fra Diavolo* was, my hazy memory suggests to me, the first Laurel and Hardy film I ever saw, and the lilting call of the singing bandit still transports me back further than I would usually wish to go.

    In 1933, however, and long before my time, Stan and Babe were not finished yet with short films, and churned out another four before their next feature. *Me and My Pal, The Midnight Patrol, Busy Bodies* and *Dirty Work* were all filmed between March and August 1933, presumably under the eagle eye of Henry Ginsberg, who saw to it there would be no slacking. *Me and My Pal* is another curiosity in the 'marriage' series, with Hardy this time as a businessman about to marry an oil magnate's daughter, and Stan as the best man who brings as a wedding present a jigsaw puzzle which diverts everyone from the nuptials. Stan and Ollie were still not completely ready to leave the adult world of hard satire on the themes of matrimony, prosperity, ambition and social climbing. The infuriating jigsaw puzzle, with its missing piece, plays against the Depression's dizzying rise and fall of financial prospects, with an impassioned radio voice stating about Ollie's stocks: 'News flash: after a sensational rise today in the stock market, the Great International Horsecollar Corporation took a tremendous crash and failed. This will mean the loss of millions to its investors. More good news later.' Stan ripostes to Ollie: 'Don't worry, prosperity's just around the corner.' The missing piece of the puzzle is finally found but Ollie, by now totally enraged, kicks the entire jigsaw to pieces.

In *The Midnight Patrol*, Stan and Ollie are inept policemen in a kind of blueprint of an idea that would blossom much later in the TV age as 'Car 54 Where Are You?' To wit: 'Calling car thirteen: look out, boys, somebody's stealing your spare tyre. That is all.' Finding a burglar in mid-job Stan first apologizes for interrupting his work and then Ollie serves him a ticket and begins haggling over the date of his appearance at the station – 'I can't make it Tuesday, I'm having my hair cut.' Alerted to a prowler at 24 Walnut Avenue, they follow a suspect they see trying to break into a house, in fact the home-owner who has been locked out, trying to get in again – with expected results.

Busy Bodies is one of the boys' best films and a vintage swan-song of the most effective gags emanating from the old-time slapstick days. From its first sunlit scene of Stan and Ollie driving down a pleasant palm-lined Californian avenue it evokes a paradise lost. Ollie: 'What a beautiful morning! Turn on the radio and let's have some music.' The tune of 'Smile When the Raindrops Fall' wafts up. Ollie: 'Gee, it's great to have a good job to go to. It just

Modern carpentry in *Busy Bodies*

makes the whole world bright. Why, even you look bright this morning.' Stan smiles, then does his mystified take.

The boys turn up at their place of work, the sawmill, where they proceed to muck around with wood. Stan has returned to the good old days of *The Noon Whistle*, and his set of 'proletarian' work films – *Pick and Shovel*, *Collars and Cuffs*, *Oranges and Lemons* and *Smithy*. Every gag that can be pulled with woodwork is pulled. The boys run into a plank carried past, several times. Ollie gets stuck in a window frame. Stan tears the back off Ollie's trousers with a plane. Ollie hits him with a bending saw. Stan glues a brush on to Ollie, then tries to cut it off, leaving Ollie with an Amish-type beard, which he proceeds to shave in the old barbershop routine. As a topper, Ollie falls into the saw works and is pushed through the flue, propelled parabolically out through the air in a sight gag reminiscent of Larry Semon at his best. Finally, chased by foreman Tiny Sandford, the boys get in their car and drive into a band-saw, which cuts the Model T Ford in two.

Early reports that the band-saw scene was shot straight, without special effects, are incorrect, according to Randy Skretvedt. Roy Seawright, the Roach effects man – presumably too indispensable for Henry Ginsberg to sack – explained that it was partially achieved with a travelling matte: 'a travelling split-screen. We had one half go through first, then we introduced the other half.' And then the Model T, neatly sawn in half, with Stan on one side and Ollie on the other, wobbles forward, and collapses.

A short cameo appearance in an 'Our Gang' film (*Wild Poses*) and *Dirty Work*, a routine chimney-sweep tale, rounded off the year's crop of two-reelers. But work had already begun, and cameras were ready to roll, on Stan and Ollie's next major feature outing. Three scribes, Frank Craven, Frank Terry and Byron Morgan, hammered together the foundations and basic structure through the summer of 1933. Stan and Roach comic Glenn Tryon firmed up the comic material. (Glenn Mitchell points out that the probable source was a *risqué* comedy of that year – *Convention City*.) Veteran director William A. Seiter, who had begun his movie life as a Keystone Kop for Sennett, had directed about fifty films in the 1920s, and would in five years' time take charge of the Marx Brothers least-fortunate vehicle, *Room Service*, was engaged to helm the picture. Shooting began on 2 October 1933 and was completed three weeks later.

And thus *Sons of the Desert* was born.

The Exhausted Rulers

Synopsis (from the Campaign Book of *Sons of the Desert*, issued by MGM):

Sworn to attend the annual convention of their lodge in a distant city, Laurel and Hardy are forced to accomplish their purpose by subterfuge because of the strenuous objections of Hardy's wife.

Oliver pretends he is deathly ill. A veterinarian friend of Stan's . . . prescribes a trip to Honolulu as the only sure cure. Mrs Hardy begs Stan to accompany her husband as she herself detests sea voyages.

The two conspirators leave, ostensibly for Honolulu, but in reality for the convention city, where both gleefully enter all 'Sons of the Desert' social activities. The first evening, while carousing in a night-club, they are joined by a delegate from Texas, Charley Chase. The trio become great pals and when Chase learns that his new-found friends are from Los Angeles, he decides to call, via long-distance telephone, a sister who lives there. He introduces Hardy to her over the phone. During the flirtatious conversation Hardy takes down her number. A second glance tells him it is his own and that the semi-familiar voice on the other end of the wire has been his wife . . .

The two arrive home decked out with leis and strumming ukes . . . they are horrified to find their wives gone and a newspaper on the table headlining the sinking of the ship on which they were supposed to be returning from the islands. According to the newspaper story . . . the rescued passengers are due to arrive the following day on another boat. Realizing their predicament, the boys start for a hotel to spend the night, only to see both wives entering the front gate of their adjoining homes. In desperation, Stan and Oliver climb on to the roof, where they spend the night, despite a heavy rain . . .

And so forth to the denouement . . .

From the original script, dated 28 September 1933, and recently found hidden in an archival censorship file:

FADE-IN:
INT. LODGE ROOM OF THE SONS OF THE DESERT. NIGHT. FULL SHOT.

A weird and eerie shot of the dimly lighted assembly hall of the lodge which gives us an opening atmosphere of ghostly mystery.

Camera shooting from behind and slightly above the Grand Master of the lodge, a large, iron-jawed man of about fifty, who is standing behind the small table on the raised dais. The lodge members, all in business suits, but each wearing a broad sash with an attached sword, are standing in a half-circle, facing the Grand Master. There is an air of suspense and almost grim seriousness reflected in their faces. The Grand Master is speaking in a heavy and very dramatic voice:

> GRAND MASTER
> This Oasis must face this situation with determination. Every
> man must be accounted for. Every man must do his part.
> There must be no weaklings in our midst. We must put our
> very hearts and souls into this great undertaking.

As he speaks, the camera trucks slowly past him until it centers on a close shot of Laurel and Hardy. They are standing in the half-circle of lodge members. Their faces are strained and tense as they listen to the words of the Grand Master with their eyes nearly popping out.

> GRAND MASTER'S VOICE
> (*Coming over scene*)
> There *must* be no thought of failure. We *must* stand shoulder
> to shoulder.

Laurel and Hardy move closer together.

> We *must* work. We *must* sacrifice. The weak *must* be helped
> by the strong.

Laurel looks appealingly at Hardy.

> For, gentlemen, this, the oldest lodge in the great Order of
> the Sons of the Desert, must be represented one-hundred-per-
> cent strong in our annual convention at Decago next week.

As the Grand Master pauses, there is a terrific round of applause. Hardy is nearly beating his hands off. Laurel doesn't applaud. Babe gives him a sharp nudge, forcing him in a weak applause, which is obviously half-hearted and against Stan's wishes.

Close on Grand Master. He holds up his hands for silence, then contin-ues dramatically:

> We will now take the oath. And remember – once taken, this
> oath has never been broken by *any man* – down through the

centuries of time in the history of this fraternal organisation. If any member is doubtful of his strength to keep this solemn pledge, he should step out of line *now*.

Close on Laurel and Hardy. Stan, looking very bewildered and uncertain, starts to step out of line. Babe yanks him back, glaring at him. Stan makes a vague gesture of futility.

(*Coming over scene*)
Do you all solemnly swear to be present at this, our 487th annual convention at Decago?

Close shot on members. Pan shot. The members cross their arms and join hands. Camera pans past several members, each saying in turn: 'I do.'

Camera pans to Laurel and Hardy. Babe says with great determination:

HARDY
I do.

Laurel stands in meek silence. Hardy gives him a vicious dig in the side with his elbow, Stan blinks and says in a timid voice:

LAUREL
Me too.

INT. TAXI. NIGHT. PROCESS SHOT.
Babe and Stan are seated in the taxi, their arms still crossed and hands clasped. Stan looks deeply worried. Babe suddenly notices their clasped hands and immediately breaks the grip.

HARDY
Well, now what are you worrying about?

LAUREL
I'm worrying because I'm worried about if my wife will let me go to the convention.

HARDY
(*Impatiently*) Of course she will let you go. Didn't you swear you were going?

LAUREL
(*Mournfully*) That's what's worrying me. I haven't asked her if I could go.

HARDY
(*Disgustedly*) Do you have to ask her everything?

308

Well, if I didn't ask her, I wouldn't know what she wanted
me to do. (*Nods emphatically.*)

HARDY
I never realized such a terrible condition existed in your
family. (*Boastfully*) You should pattern your life after mine.
I go places – do things – and then tell my wife.
(*Grandiloquently*) A man should be the king of his own
castle.

We can see how faithfully Stan and Babe adhered to the script
by viewing the final film. The Grand Master, played by John Elliott
with appropriate authority and menace, the high-contrast lighting,
the dialogue, are all almost word for word as in the text. There is
no ad libbing here. The scene has been enhanced in the directing by
having Stan and Babe enter the hall late, after the Grand Master's
speech has begun, disrupting all the delegates until they settle in
their chairs. The scene in the taxi between Stan and Ollie is played
verbatim as written. The same applies to the 'Honolulu plot'
sequence, in the Hardy home. As the synopsis notes, Laurel and
Hardy live behind adjacent doors, with two bell buttons and two
cards side by side: one presenting MRS AND MR STANLEY LAUREL
and the other, MR OLIVER HARDY AND WIFE. The quack doctor –
Hardy: 'Why have you brought a vetanarian?' Stan: 'I didn't think
his religion had anything to do with it' – played by Lucien
Littlefield, insists, according to the pre-arranged plan:

DOCTOR
I'm sorry, Mrs Hardy – but a voyage to Honolulu is the *only*
cure for your husband.

HARDY
I won't go to Honolulu. If you can't go, sugar – I'll just stay
home and suffer. (*More deep groans.*)

MRS HARDY
(*Firmly*) You'll do nothing of the kind. If the doctor says you
must go to Honolulu, you'll do just as he says.

Laurel enters the shot, looking bewildered at Babe's protests.

But I can't go alone. I've got to have somebody to take care
of me.

Mrs Hardy looks at Stan, and gets a bright idea.

MRS HARDY
Perhaps Stanley would be kind enough to go with you.

HARDY
(*Feigning surprise*) I never thought of that! (*Looks up at
Stan.*) Will you go with me, Stanley?

LAUREL
Where?

HARDY
(*Covering his impatience*) Why, to Honolulu, of course.

LAUREL
But I can't go.

HARDY
(*Controlling himself with an effort*) Why?

LAUREL
I'm going to the convention.

*Hardy almost leaps from his chair, then remembers and drops back with
a groan.*

HARDY
What do you mean – *you're going to the convention?*

LAUREL
(*Blandly*) Well, I forgot to tell you. I asked my wife and she
said I could go. (*Nods and grins.*)

Hardy sinks back in the chair with an exasperated moan.

HARDY
(*Disgustedly*) That settles it! I'm not going to Honolulu!

MRS HARDY
(*With firm determination*) Oh, yes you are, Ollie dear. You're
going to Honolulu – if you have to go alone.

Hardy glares up at Laurel.

HARDY
All right! If I have to go to Honolulu alone – *he's going with me!*

Sons of the Desert sums up all the themes of the Laurel-and-Hardy-and-Their-Wives genre. Once again, Mae Busch has been engaged to play Ollie's wife, having transformed from brunette to peroxide blonde. In Stan's corner, the haughty and tall Dorothy Christie came in at the last moment as a replacement for the original choice, Roach regular Patsy Kelly.

After so much critical speculation about these strange double marriages, it is worth pointing out that the battle of the sexes played out in so many of Stan and Babe's movies, and brought to the boil in *Sons of the Desert*, had been a staple of American popular culture since before the First World War – as well as an old favourite theme of the English music-hall.

In my previous volume on W. C. Fields I drew attention to the comic strips of Bud Fisher's 'Mutt and Jeff' and George McManus's 'Bringing Up Father' as exemplifying the hen-pecked husband and the harridan wife. Mutt and Jeff, in 1918, a decade before Stan and Babe are in full flight, play cards together while Mutt's wife is out, and when she comes back Jeff has to hide in the stove. Mutt's mother-in-law lights the stove while Mutt is berated for hiding in the bed with his clothes on: 'Up to the attic for you, you freak,' says Mrs Mutt, brandishing a rolling pin. 'You can't be trusted for a minute.' Jiggs, the hero of McManus's strip of the same year, is locked in the house by his wife when she goes out to the opera.

We have surmised the early influence on Babe of the *Happy Hooligan* (in lieu of the non-existent Helpful Henry), and both he and Stan would have been totally familiar with these characters, which were syndicated for years. The grumbling wives of the W. C. Fields sketches were presented on the stage in the mid-1920s *Ziegfeld Follies*, and there are countless other samples. As we have seen, Roach's silent films returned again and again to the themes of errant husbands and angry wives.

But the period leading up to the shooting of *Sons of the Desert* was a crucial one in the history of both Stan's and Babe's private lives. In June 1933 the Myrtle–Babe conflict came to the boil again, and this time it was Babe who threw in the towel. On 20 June he filed for divorce, charging that 'his wife, Myrtle Lee Hardy, went on periodic, liquor-drinking sprees'. Babe filed on grounds of 'mental cruelty', charging that 'many times his wife would leave home for a long period and that when he found her "she was in an

exhausted and bedraggled condition due to intoxicating liquors".'
The suit further alleged that 'during these occasions she repeatedly
insisted on driving one of the actor's automobiles. This caused
great mental stress, it was alleged, due to the fact that it was feared
that she might kill or injure herself or others.'

A few weeks before this, Lois sued Stan for divorce, the pair
having been separated since November 1932, soon after Stan
returned from the British tour. Lois claimed, according to the *L.A.
Times*, that 'Laurel would ignore her and the fact that he had
attained renown as an actor made his attitude unendurable and
caused her to suffer embarrassment'.

In fact, during the spring of 1933, while Stan had been on a
yachting trip together with his future director, Bill Seiter, he had
met a young vivacious woman called Virginia Ruth Rogers at
Catalina Island. This relationship blossomed through the year,
watched anxiously by Roach corporate lawyer Ben Shipman, ever
nervous of developing scandal.

In July, the Babe–Myrtle follies spun into a new phase with
counter-claims by Myrtle against Babe. Myrtle's sister, Mary
Hunter née Reeves, filed suit, alleging that she had been beaten up
by Hardy – 'a large and powerful man, weighing more than 300
pounds' – who, she said, struck her several blows on the face. She
claimed $500,000 damages, adding, in defence of her sister, that
Hardy was a profligate gambler, who had lost $30,000 in one day
at the races in Agua Caliente in 1931, and more recently had
dropped $3,000 on roulette and had daily losses of $100 to $175
'wagering on golf and cards'. The 'other woman', presumably
Viola Morse, was also cited as proof of Hardy's misdeeds.

Then, in August, an unlikely miracle was reported by the Los
Angeles papers, which announced that both Laurel and Hardy had
patched up their 'family rifts'. Cooed the reporters:

The dove of peace is hovering above the Roach comedy team of Laurel and
Hardy. Stan Laurel, with radiant face, said yesterday that he and Mrs
Laurel, who has filed a divorce complaint against him, have become
reconciled, are living together again, and she will drop the proceedings. He
credited their baby Lois, now five years of age, with having led them
together into the old paths of happiness again. 'And', he said, 'the Hardys
are doing the same thing.'

This balmy state of affairs continued into October, as *Sons of the Desert* began shooting. The press announced:

Hardy announced that he and his wife were back together again, both very happy about it, and that 'both of us realized we made a very bad mistake in parting'.

In Ollie's on-screen words: 'I made a *faux pas* . . .' But no such luck for Mr and Mrs Laurel. On 10 October the Los Angeles *Daily News* reported:

STAN LAUREL TOO OFTEN GONE; WIFE AWARDED DIVORCE
Mrs Laurel was granted the decree after a brief hearing before Superior Judge Walter S. Gates without contest on the comedian's part.

'Mr Laurel would leave home apparently for no reason at all,' Mrs Laurel began. 'He would be gone for one, two and three days at a time, and would come back without any explanation whatever. Many times he said he didn't care for me any more.'

A property settlement was agreed 'whereby Laurel promised to provide substantially for the support of his wife and their daughter, Lois, age five. The agreement . . . gave Mrs Laurel custody of the child and title to the couple's former home, 718 North Bedford Drive, Beverly Hills.'

Some time later, Stan moved in with Virginia Ruth Rogers, chaperoned, it seems, by his old friends Alice and Baldy Cooke. Stan and Ruth would be married, at Agua Caliente, early in April 1934, with alimony issues still unresolved.

With all these shenanigans, it is amazing that *Sons of the Desert* emerged so fresh, so light-hearted, its marital plot a catharsis of the real-life pain that so directly affected its heroes. Indeed, think of the fun of escaping from the domestic wars into the raucous party of the Chicago convention – the early coyness of naming the actual city disappears in the final print. Given Oliver Hardy's Masonic links, we might speculate as to his often unsung role in discussing plot line and details, though MGM's press Campaign Book is at pains to emphasize that '*Sons of the Desert* is a very funny burlesque of an imaginary fraternal order. There is nothing mean or spiteful in it and nothing to which any intelligent group of officers of local lodges in your town can take exception.' One wonders if

Party time with Charley Chase in *Sons of the Desert*

they are referring to the merry scenes in the night-club, in which the revellers whack unsuspecting newcomers to the club over the bottom with a traditional double-pronged 'slapstick'. The usual constraints on dealing with the imbibing of intoxicants had suddenly disappeared with the repeal of Prohibition earlier in the year. The Campaign Book enthused:

Liquor repeal and its many aftermaths is front page news in all wet states. Repeal is still so new . . . that people are getting a kick out of everything pertaining to their alcoholic freedom. Play dates around New Year have a double chance of planting above half-tone strip [four photos of Stan and Ollie demonstrating 'How Not to Open a Bottle' with a hammer] or using it as a bottle wraparound by stores or places licensed to sell wet goods.

The atmosphere of mad abandon is exemplified in the film by Charley Chase, who described his role as the kind of 'Goodtime Charley' you run into at parties, 'easily recognized by his peculiar characteristics and mannerisms. He is the fellow who slaps you so hard on the back that your false teeth are jarred loose. He slips up behind you and slips ice down your neck. His voice is the loudest . . .'

As indeed it is, as Charley introduces himself as 'Texas, ninety-seven!' and proceeds to squirt Ollie in the eye with his buttonhole and wields the slapstick with the cackling cry of 'Oh, isn't it a darb!!!'

The character was so obnoxious, and so at odds with the amiable clown he played in most of his own short pictures, that Charley was said to have prevented his teenage daughters from seeing the film at the time. But it demonstrates the strengths that 'All-Star' Roach regulars could bring to each other, if the studio so decreed. Alas, it was a one-off, though Stan and Babe were to reciprocate by appearing in cameo roles in a later Chase two-reeler, *On the Wrong Trek*, in 1936. The 'Goodtime Charley' role was as poignant for Chase as the marital plot was for Stan and Babe, as his own drinking problems were souring his relationship with his own long-suffering wife, BeBe. The repeal of Prohibition was certainly not good news in the Chase home.

In the movie, the convention scene cuts back to the wives discovering to their horror that a storm has sunk the ship on which their husbands were supposed to be sailing back from Honolulu, and they rush off to the docks, distraught, to find out more news. Entering a cinema to calm their nerves, they are then stunned to see a newsreel report of the lodges' convention in Chicago, replete with footage of the husbands they feared are drowned cavorting in the fraternity's parade. The parade, the film's most complex and much planned segment, was originally to have been a much longer sequence, to include a scene of mass mayhem on bicycles, with Stan and Ollie, as set out in the script, but omitted from the film:

FADE-IN: EXT. STREET. DAY. COMPOSITE SHOT OF PARADE ATMOSPHERE. *A trick shot of the gayly decorated electroliers, buildings draped with flags and bunting, bands, marching feet, and banners which read:* WEL-COME SONS OF THE DESERT. *Over this we hear the sound of gay band music and of people cheering and shouting.*

LAP DISSOLVE: EXT. STREET. CHICAGO. MED. LONG SHOT.
On the parade of the Sons of the Desert – a very impressive view of the marching bands, drill teams, and the picturesquely uniformed ranks of the parading conventioneers.

CUT TO: MED. SHOT ON BICYCLE SQUAD
Mounted on decorated bicycles, the crack team from the Los Angeles lodge is going through a series of intricate formations, each move cued by the blast of a whistle. A band is marching behind the squad.

Laurel and Hardy, resplendent in their brilliant uniforms, are riding at the head of the bicycle squad. A large, oblong banner which covers nearly half the width of the street is fastened to poles on the front of their bicycles. They are doing whatever cycling stunts that the length of the banner will permit.

The parade continues, until Stan and Ollie manage to crash their own bicycles into the formation, and all 'pile up in a terrific mess'. This scene was to precede the night-club segment and the 'Honolulu Baby' number, at the end of which the boys bicker and are thrown out by the club's bouncers. As they try and get back in, a heavy light-globe falls on Babe's head and Stan throws another globe through the night-club's window, blind to the policeman standing just behind him. Stan and Ollie end up in jail, in another omitted sequence:

INT. TANK CELL IN JAIL. MED. SHOT
The cell is packed with tramps and drunks of all descriptions. Stan and Babe are sitting dejectedly on a bench in the background.

A dirty looking bum leans into the shot and leers at Stan and Babe.

                              TRAMP
          What did youse guys get?

                               BABE
          (*Mournfully*) Ten days.

                               STAN
          That's nearly a week.

                              TRAMP
          (*Disdainfully*) Aw, you can do that standin' on your head.

Stan looks up quizzically and begins to scratch his head.

MED. CLOSE ON DOOR TO CELL
A turnkey opens the door.

Come on, you guys! All out!

The prisoners line up and march out, each receiving a mop, pail or other cleaning equipment. Stan and Babe come up to the turnkey. He hands Stan a broom and Babe a plumber's suction plunger.

INT. JAIL CORRIDOR. CLOSE SHOT
On prisoners' feet as they shuffle along.

DISSOLVE TO: EXT. STREET. SHOOTING ON LOW MARCHING FEET
Over the dissolve we hear the bands playing the marching songs of the convention.

CAMERA PANS UP
The drill teams and conventioneers are marching down the street on their way to the depot. The crowd on the sidewalk is waving and calling: 'Goodbye!' And above one unit of the parade we see a banner which reads: FAREWELL CHICAGO.

CUT TO: EXT. JAIL CLOSE ON BARED [sic] WINDOW
Laurel and Hardy heads are framed in the window as they mournfully watch their comrades marching away.

We hear a band playing: 'California here I come.'

The music grows louder, and then fades into the distance. Stan and Babe begin to tearfully sing the words of the song.

Fade-out.

Both these scenes were cut before the filming began, presumably to save time and money, and remain recorded only on the page.

At the finale of the film, when Stan and Ollie have climbed up from the attic to the roof to escape their wives, who keep hearing sounds above them, a swift downpour and a precipitate descent down a drainpipe, watched by the neighbourhood cop, bring them to a tearful doorstep reunion. The wives have made a bet: which one of the husbands will tell the truth about their escapade. Ollie fails the test, insisting that, in Stan's phrase, they 'ship-hiked' from the stormy waters so as to arrive a day before their rescue boat was due to dock, and adding, 'Why, it's too far-fetched not to be the truth, isn't it, Stanley?' 'It's imposterous,' agrees Stan. But under pressure from icy Dorothy Christy, Stan wilts and begins the famous cry. Stan confesses and is led off, practically at gunpoint, only to be fêted and even allowed to smoke for his honesty. Ollie remains, as Mae Busch stockpiles every plate and pot in the house, for a splendiferous bout of crockery smashing over his head. Stan, hearing the noise, rings the doorbell and appears in his dressing-gown, puffing on his cigarette. 'What did your wife say?' Ollie asks. 'She said honesty is the best policy,' Stan replies, and exits, singing 'Honolulu Baby', only to be conked by a saucepan hurled by off-screen Ollie.

If only real life were as straightforward as that.

.

Babes in Toil-land

Sons of the Desert marks the high point of Laurel and Hardy's film career. Its iconic status has been affirmed by the great fan club bearing its title, founded by John McCabe and Al Kilgore in 1965, with Stan's explicit blessing just before his death. Modelled on the film's imaginary order, the organization would have a Grand Sheik, a Vice-Sheik (in charge of vice), a Grand Vizier, a Sub-Vice-Vizier (in charge of sub-vice) and several hundred Board Members-at-Large, who would all 'sit at an exalted place at the annual banquet table'. Today, this order has Tents throughout the world, demonstrating the abiding power of Stan and Ollie to attract enthusiasts into the twenty-first century.

But immortality was the last thing on the minds of Stan Laurel and Oliver Hardy in the new year of 1934. Despite the good reviews of their latest feature, released at the end of December 1933 (*Hollywood Reporter*: 'It has nothing to do with the desert, but plenty to do with real genuine laughter'), and solid box office, which was to place the film among the ten top-grossing pictures of the year, the name of the game at Roach was still survival under the stern Ginsberg regime. Hal Roach himself was often an absentee landlord: he spent much of the autumn of 1933 heading an organizing committee to build a 2-million-dollar non-profit racetrack in southern California, 'a sporting proposition, for sportsmen only, and if the commercial angle enters into it, we will drop the entire matter'. In October, he pulled out of the project, only to pull back in again early in the new year, with a new set of partners. Later in the spring of 1934 he set out in a luxury yacht to Alaska with new York financier E. F. Hutton. In June, on a hunting trip to the Frozen North, he bagged six Alaskan bears – two grizzlies and four black bears. The hunting party also bagged a New York sportsman, David McCullogh, who was shot by mistake. Something tells us Mr Roach was getting a little jaded with the day-to-day business of making motion pictures.

Stan and Babe were to make another seven short pictures, interspersed with the features they were now committed to as a full-time job. *Oliver the Eighth, Going Bye Bye, Them Thar Hills, The Live Ghost* and *Tit for Tat* were shot in 1934. *The Fixer-Uppers* and their very last short, *Thicker than Water*, were shot in 1935. Before all these, the boys also appeared in an MGM *mélange, Hollywood Party*, in which they assayed an egg-breaking battle with voluptuous Lupe Velez.

By this time, the talkies were in full bloom in Hollywood, and everyone had forgotten silent pictures. But spoken dialogue, which added a new dimension to movies, also added new problems and obstacles. Apart from the universality of comedy, which Stan and Babe laboriously extended by means of their foreign versions, there was also the issue of censorship, and the new restrictions of the formalized Hays Code. Even Laurel and Hardy could not escape the attention of the eagle eye of Colonel Joy and Joseph Breen of the Motion Picture Producers and Distributors Association. As early as 1931, objections had been made to the Foreign Legion spoof *Beau Hunks*, when Baron Valentin Manderstamm, representing the French government, took umbrage at the line: 'The Legion is hell on earth and in heaven.' The line was cut out.

Sons of the Desert was generally approved by the Board, but various states objected to certain scenes. In Pennsylvania, they demanded elimination of the 'scene of Laurel slapping woman on posterior with wooden slapper'. In British Columbia they didn't like Laurel's running pun on being like 'two peas in a pot'. (Ollie: 'Pod! Po-dah!') In Quebec, the censors demanded the elimination of 'all scenes of girls wiggling their hips while dancing wherever shown'.

But this was small beer. Throughout the world, censorship was rife and often inexplicable. *Bonnie Scotland*, of 1935, was rejected outright in Bohemia and Moravia for reasons that were not divulged, but might have had something to do with men wearing skirts. In Lithuania, they demanded the deletion of the scene in which 'Laurel sits on Hardy's lap'. *The Bohemian Girl*, released in 1936, caused Japan, Sweden and Norway to 'delete scenes of Gypsy kissing'. Hungary deleted scenes in which 'Hardy, awkwardly and for comedy effect, holds up and attempts to rob a gentleman', and Latvia decreed: 'Delete scene of Laurel's wife hitting him and Hardy's wife striking him on head with a spoon.' *The Bohemian*

Girl was banned outright in Nazi Germany, for dealing sympathet-ically with Gypsies, who counted with Jews as a pariah people. Later on, there would be objections from Germany to the scenes of Stan and Ollie capturing a whole German battalion single-handed in *Pack Up Your Troubles*. In Fascist Spain, too, the latter movie was rejected on its re-release in 1940.

Compared to others, Laurel and Hardy had little trouble with the Hays Code, particularly as the subject matter of their movies had already become tamer by the time the new, 'improved' Code began to bite. Nevertheless, even as tame a creature as *Babes in Toyland*, the next Laurel and Hardy feature after *Sons of the Desert*, attracted some unease:

Internal memo, from 'EEB' to 'Doug', 2 August 1934:

Doug,
This starts off grand and would be a delightful thing, especially for children.

However, I worry about the gruesome, frightening effect of BOGIELAND. They would just scare an impressionable kid to death and make him have nightmares. I think the studio should give careful thought to that.

There is a shot of Stan in a wedding gown (he is impersonating BO-PEEP). The wedding gown is torn off and he stands in a pair of long, lacy underpants. What about this?

Babes in Toyland, despite its fairy-tale theme, was a troubled film for Stan and Babe. After the success of *Fra Diavolo*, Hal Roach was looking for another musical comedy, and had bought the rights to Victor Herbert's operetta, first performed in 1903. We do not know if Stan had a hand in this decision, but the idea might well have tickled his fancy due to its similarity to his earliest stage appearance, as 'Golliwog Number Two', in Levy and Cardwell's *The Sleeping Beauty*, of 1907, in which Wee Georgie Wood's toys came alive and performed the old tale.

Hal Roach, as usual, due to his extraordinary longevity, had the last word, in 1981, giving his version of the developing trouble to interviewer Randy Skretvedt:

I had worked so hard on *Babes in Toyland*. I worked like a sucker on that thing . . . The [original] show was vignettes from different fairy-tales, but it had no story line. So after I bought the property in New York, I came back on the train, so I would have time to write a story for it. I stayed alone in my room and wrote all the way, and I had what I thought was a hell of a story. Hardy was supposed to be the Pieman, and Stan Laurel was Simple Simon. You remember, 'Simple Simon met the Pieman going to the fair . . .' The Pieman says, 'Where's your penny?' and Simple Simon says, 'I haven't any.' Well, now it's with Laurel and Hardy . . . The finish was that the heavy, who was a spider turned into a man, wants to destroy Toyland and puts hate into the wooden soldiers. The wooden soldiers come out to destroy Toyland, but Laurel and Hardy find out that they're put together with glue, and water kills glue, and by putting water on the wooden soldiers they save Toyland.

The only snag was that when Roach proposed this tale to Stan, Laurel, according to Roach, turned it down, saying, 'We can't work without the derby hats, they're our trademark.' (Roach forgot that they had already made *Fra Diavolo* in period gear.) Roach related:

We argued for about two weeks. *Babes in Toyland* was a big property, and I was paying real dough for it. I worked so hard on this thing, and I was disgusted in the light of this opposition, that I just said, 'Enough, I'm out of the thing completely. Go make the picture.' I never paid a bloody bit of attention to what they did, and it was a flop. It didn't even get the cost back. And I know that the story that I had written would've gone very well. Could've been one of the biggest pictures in the business.

Once again, we have Roach's selective memory rewriting history. The movie did very well on its release towards Christmas 1934, and attracted rave reviews. 'Never has the talking screen attempted such splendid fantasy so successfully,' warbled the L.A. *Examiner*. 'Every youngster', wrote Andre Sennwald in the *New York Times*, 'ought to find a ticket for *Babes in Toyland* in his Christmas stocking.' The *Examiner* reported from the front line that 'a seven-year-old assured me with delight sparkling in her eyes that *Babes in Toyland* is "Keen!"' And yet Roach's bitterness lasted for over forty years. In 1970, he told Anthony Slide:

They brought these goons in from the forest to destroy Toyland, and the Parent Teachers Association of America condemned the picture because that would scare children. Instead of being a picture for children, it was condemned! Laurel just couldn't take it that somebody else was writing the story.

Clearly, it was more a case of Roach not being able to take it that his employee threw his version of *Babes* in the trash. This was a defining moment, oddly enough for so innocent a project, in the

Mounting silliness in *Babes in Toyland*

growing acrimony between the studio boss and his creative workers. Even someone as non-worldly-wise as Stan Laurel would have been seething by 1934 at the fact that his contribution to the company's profits was not recognized in a better contractual and financial deal, and that he still needed to fight tooth and nail to maintain artistic control. The irony is that when we watch the movie that became the straw that broke the camel's back, some of us might have the distinctly odd feeling that, in fact, the boss was right. The plot line he outlined to his autumn-years interviewers does seem markedly more coherent and promising than the clumsy ragbag that *Babes in Toyland* actually is, given the test of time.

In the event, we have Stan and Ollie not as Peter Pieman and Simple Simon, but as Ollie Dee and Stannie Dum, workers at the toy factory, who misinterpret Santa's order of six hundred one-foot high toy soldiers as one hundred six-foot ones, thus driving the Toymaker into a most unseasonable bate. Ollie and Stannie live in a shoe with Mother Peep, whose daughter, Bo, has, of course, lost her little fluffy friends. Other fairyland creatures, the cat with the fiddle, the three little pigs and so forth, prance about in costumes fitted to appeal to the toddler public. Villain of the piece is Silas Barnaby, who, like the desiccated heavies in Stan solo movies, threatens to evict the Peeps for lack of mortgage payments.

Henry Brandon, né Kleinbach, who played Barnaby, came hot foot from a stage engagement as the wicked landlord in *The Drunkard*, a spoof revival of an old nineteenth-century play first produced by none other than the Great Barnum, and which was lampooned by W. C. Fields in his nostalgia-fest, *The Old Fashioned Way*, just released in July 1934. Brandon simply transferred this character to Barnaby.

The result is indicative of the problem with *Babes in Toyland*, if we compare Silas Barnaby to W. C. Fields's evil on-screen Squire. Fields is all pastiche and flummery, the ham actor in his perfect element. Brandon plays Silas Barnaby straight. There is nothing funny about his character. Indeed there is nothing funny about anything in *Babes in Toyland* when Stan and Ollie are off screen. In *Fra Diavolo*, the plot line itself is frothy, with Thelma Todd and Jimmy Finlayson leading the tale of medieval frolics. *Babes in Toyland* has a cast of lead balloons. Bo Peep's lover, Tom-Tom, played by Felix Knight, has to assay lyrics like 'Don't cry, Bo Peep, don't cry/To find your sheep we'll try', and the supporting players heave and hum like a fancy-dress party that has swallowed something rum in the punch. The marching wooden soldiers who defeat the Bogeymen are a fine example of stop-motion photography, but the Bogeymen, whom Roach justly hated, are perhaps the most uncomfortable quasi-racial stereotypes (hairy apelike creatures with fangs and African style loin-strips) that have ever graced a Hollywood film. What was Stan thinking of?

In his eternal innocence, it seems that Stan was prone to be led astray, not by external influences but by his own unconscious – the font of his 'surreal' comedy style. While coming from such different traditions, both Stan and Babe shared an essential trait of functioning by gut emotions: if they felt something was right they acted on that feeling, in life as in their actors' personas. Intellect and emotions weave a complex web in any actor's work, but instinct was the overwhelming factor in Laurel and Hardy's own 'method'.

Stan, more than Babe, applied this principle in his off-screen life too, and it was to lead him into increasing tangles as the marriages and divorces proliferated. These were scripts it was not possible to rewrite, or change on the set. On the screen, his judgement of individual scenes, of building the gags, of deploying the character, was, in most cases, very fine. But as future works were continually to demonstrate, he struggled with the structure of the longer films. Carrying the elements of the comedy sketch successfully into features was to be a continual dilemma, but, like the on-screen Stan and Ollie, Stan Laurel was no quitter.

Hal Roach, on the other hand, went on record later to say that this was the moment when he gave up on Laurel and Hardy. 'When I let Laurel and Hardy go,' he told Randy Skretvedt, 'it had nothing to do with money. I said I didn't want to make any more pictures with them.' Roach, as usual, was telescoping his history here, since that break was yet some years in the future. But, after a quarter of a century in the business, he was becoming more and more impatient and less amenable to the kind of give and take, and the creative freedom that had characterized the original 'Lot of Fun'. One might add that the record shows that, on 9 August 1934, just as *Babes in Toyland* started filming, Hal Roach was in the Good Samaritan Hospital in Los Angeles, having his appendix cut out. He was just about to take off in his private plane for a non-stop flight to New York. Two days later his wife and daughter were injured in a car crash, and, on 14 August, Stan Laurel himself tripped and fell off a platform on the set, tearing ligaments in his right leg. The production was postponed, during which time Henry 'Silas Barnaby' Brandon got into a drunken brawl and ended up in jail for a week. Other actors caught the bad-luck bug, among them jovial Kewpie Morgan, playing Old King Cole, who reportedly ruptured his stomach by laughing continuously in repeated takes. To cap it all, Babe Hardy had his tonsils removed just after the end of the shoot.

If *Sons of the Desert* was a high point, *Babes in Toyland* marked another watershed for Laurel and Hardy – the moment at which they became firmly established as the special idols of children, more than of adult comedy fans. While the critic might see the process of the 'infantilization' of Stan and Ollie as the symptom of a decline, in commercial terms Stan and Babe were ensuring their recognition well into the next generation. Like the Jesuits, comedians too can gain a lifelong loyalty once the heart and mind of a child is won over. If your first memory of comedy is, or includes, Laurel and Hardy, as my own experience, it tends to be indelible. Despite Roach's mutterings about the Parent Teachers Association, Laurel and Hardy became, from then on, fit for all ages, as wholesome as apple pie. The betrayed wives, chasing their drunken and philandering husbands out of the night-club with shotguns, fade into the screen background, only to emerge, more than metaphorically, in the real life of the men behind the masks. But the two figures prancing towards us on the screen, to the refrain of the village blacksmith beating out the 'Cuckoo' tune, have shucked off their shady past. They have become, as they wished to be, eternal children, marching bewildered into the chaotic world, with an eager determination to make good. 'From the moment I saw them on the screen,' said the master of *The Goon Show*, Spike Milligan, 'I knew they were my friends.'

The irony is that at this magic moment, when Stan and Ollie partook of the Elixir of Life and rejuvenated, their best work already lay behind them. After *Babes in Toyland*, they were to make four more short films, and eighteen more features, of which a handful can stand out as classics. They were to become even more famous than they ever were, to become icons, their images pressed out in dolls, cards and posters. They were to become characters in comic magazines and, later still, in TV animation. They were to be used and misused in newspaper cartoons to make political points about a whole variety of national and international policies. They were to represent a certain kind of human folly, often at a great remove from the characters they had laboured to etch out on the screen. But, as they rose, so did they fall. It was a strange and contradictory destiny, which they bore, as ever, with fortitude. As Stan says to Ollie in *Oliver the Eighth*, defending himself against a charge of dereliction of duty, 'I couldn't help it! I was dreaming I was awake and then I woke up and found myself asleep!'

In the movie, it has all been, in fact, Oliver's dream. In reality, it is all a bit more like a sequence in Luis Buñuel's *The Discreet Charm of the Bourgeoisie*, or a painting by Magritte, or one of the strange graphic panels by Max Ernst, or George Herriman's Krazy Kat strips, in which contradictions shimmer with their own inner, perfect logic –

They dreamed our dream, and we dream theirs.

PART THREE

'We Faw Down':
On the trail of the lonesome mimes

'Nice Weather We Had Tomorrow...'

By 1934, the Hollywood studios had recovered from their worst Depression blues, and were producing, on average, about fifty movies each per year. Metro Goldwyn Mayer, in any case, had been least hit by the massive dip in profits that battered the other major studios in the first years of the decade. The studio that had 'more stars than there are in heaven' had the added asset of the young Irving Thalberg, registering hit after hit. From *Grand Hotel* in 1932 he continued to *Queen Christina* in 1933, and films such as *Mutiny on the Bounty* and *David Copperfield*, in 1935, would maintain MGM's firm lead. Hal Roach Studios, nestling in the crook of MGM's distribution arm, was in a pretty comfortable, if at times pungent position.

Since Stan and Ollie's dark vision of the winter of 1929 in *Below Zero*, Franklin D. Roosevelt's New Deal was beginning to grapple with the economic slump, although tens of millions were still unemployed. Apart from allowing Americans to drown their sorrows in drink legally, the government passed a raft of reforming legislation, aimed at putting the country back to work.

With a bit of luck, no longer would Laurel and Hardy have to hang about on the pier, as they did in *The Laurel–Hardy Murder Case*, dreaming of the inheritance Stan might get from his Uncle Ebeneezer. (Stan would have known that Ebenezer was the first name of Charles Dickens's Scrooge, and scant cash could be expected from that source . . .)

In *Oliver the Eighth*, shot between December 1933 and January 1934, Stan returned to the somewhat unimaginative dream framework of the 'Murder Case', in another display of the morbid element that kept popping forth from Stan's mind. Stan and Ollie are both barbers, owners of the Laurel and Hardy Tonsorial Parlor. They spot an advertisement: 'Wealthy young widow, with huge fortune, wishes to communicate with congenial young men – object matrimony.' Both decide to answer the ad, but Ollie cheats Stan and mails only his own letter, hiding Stan's, who finds it later and follows Ollie to the lady's sinister mansion. The widow, played of course by Mae Busch, is, unbeknownst to the boys, a serial murderess, who has already cut the throats of seven previous Olivers, as a revenge for Oliver Number One, who had jilted her on the eve of her wedding.

The dark recesses of Stan's mind are not that difficult to fathom, and the primitive Bogiemen less puzzling to appreciate if we recall the direct thread leading from his 1930s persona to Arthur Jefferson's era of the Victorian theatre. The cheap peals of artificial thunder on the soundtrack of the 'Murder Case' can hark back to little Stanley Jefferson's home theatrics at Dockwray Square, North Shields. One might even speculate about the absent mother, the constant attraction of the young man towards strong-willed women, the pre-pubescent on-screen Stanley, and a whole raft of Freudian factors which could form the basis of several decades of therapy. But Stan's only therapy was the fleshing out, on film, of the ghosts, imps and angels of his imagination. In *Oliver the Eighth*, the dominating spouse stalks the corridors of her Dracula-like castle noisily sharpening two massive knives. We all know that it is not the throat, but another part of the male anatomy she is after.

Later in 1934, W. C. Fields was to release *It's a Gift*, his own meditation on the American marriage as a series of small, continual skirmishes. But Fields was lampooning a real world, whereas Laurel and Hardy were steadily retreating into a world of pure fantasy. The widow's lair is a fairy-tale castle, with a mad butler who entices Ollie with a game of invisible cards. Dinner is invisible too, a nightmare pretence of empty plates, ladled air and imaginary wine, marked with the insistence of totally proper etiquette. Thirty-seven years later, Luis Buñuel's aforementioned movie, *The Discreet Charm of the Bourgeoisie*, would present us with a very similar scene, in the name of high surrealist art.

'Nice weather we had tomorrow,' the crazy butler comments to the guests, an encapsulation of Stan's underlying philosophy. Time means nothing. The child is ever present in the adult. The consequences of actions cannot be grasped by the person who lives only for the moment. Echoing Chico Marx, Stan answers Ollie's query in the 'Murder Case', 'Where were you born?', with the self-evident 'I don't remember. I was too young to know.' 'Mr Laurel', the opening title of *Hog Wild* reminded us, 'never had a memory to lose.' As we have noted, Stan the man had the best memory in the business. But Stan the mask was a blank sheet, a *tabula rasa*, and upon it, we can write our own tales . . .

Oliver the Eighth marked another curious milestone in Stan's life, the death of his younger brother, Teddy, Everett Jefferson, on 17 December 1933, in a freak accident, suffering a heart attack while under 'laughing gas' in a Los Angeles dentist's chair. This was not, alas, unlike Ollie's slumbers in the barber's chair, a dream, and filming was stopped over the Christmas period. Teddy had joined Stan in America some time in the 1920s, but details of his progress from then on have been sketchy. He had long given up any involvement in show business, and at the time of his death was a chauffeur for the manager of the Ambassador Hotel. According to Stan's new wife-to-be, Ruth, Stan made the funeral arrangements but avoided the services, hosting friends for drinks at his rented home afterwards, in a 'traditional' wake.

*

Aside from the comic and tragic shadows, 1934 found Stan and Babe performing their own quota of good deeds, cheering up sick war veterans at a hospital in San Fernando as part of a scheme of movie-star visits. The burdens of fame now required them to fend off their fans, and the dossiers of the Hal Roach Studios bulge with their responses to the many letters sent by well-wishers requesting their autographs, or cables calling for personal appearances and endorsements:

On 29 June 1934:

LAUREL AND HARDY = CARE HAL ROACH STUDIOS = 500 KIDS PLAYING NITE BALL IN POMONA NEED YOUR HELP TO FINISH NEW BALL FIELD WE WANT YOU FELLOWS TO PITCH FOR OPPOSING TEAMS OF LOCAL BUSINESS MEN IN COMIC GAME NIGHT OF JULY 11TH WEDNESDAY . . .

To which Sam B. Cohen, director of Advertising and Publicity at the studio, answers with sincere regrets.

J. B. Goodrich, of the photo studio of the same name, sends a snapshot of a baby which, at six months, is the image of Babe Hardy, receiving in turn a letter from the same Sam B. Cohen, affirming that 'the resemblance is very striking and Mr Hardy had much pleasure in showing the picture to his friends and associates'.

But unlike some stars, who revelled in the spotlights of public acclaim, or, like Eddie Cantor, threw themselves into a variety of good works with boundless energy, Stan Laurel and Babe Hardy remained what they always had been, jobbing actors anxious to keep on working. This proved continually problematic for Stan, with Hal Roach. Two of the boys' best short films, *Them Thar Hills* and its sequel *Tit for Tat*, both with Mae Busch and Charlie Hall as their foils, straddled the filming of *Babes in Toyland*, along with *The Live Ghost* and *The Fixer-Uppers*, minor additions to the canon. Looking at the happy antics of Stan and Ollie on mountain vacation or as the new electrical suppliers, trading blow for blow with grocer Charlie, one would think that all's right and normal, at least in the Laurel and Hardy world. But this was a period of intense conflict between Stan and his increasingly impatient employer.

The trouble erupted in March 1935. Stan and Babe were already contracted to begin another feature film, provisionally entitled 'McLaurel and McHardy', based on a story known as 'Kilts', written by Roach scenarist Frank Butler. This evolved into a merry romp with Stan and Ollie in the British Indian Army. But on 16 March the *New York Herald Tribune* announced from Hollywood:

LAUREL AND HARDY BREAK
Little Stan Fights with Hal Roach, Refuses to Sign Contract

L.A. March 15: Producer Hal Roach announced today that Laurel had declined to continue under contract because he and Roach disagreed about screen story matters. Hardy will continue under the Roach colors.

Variety gave a more detailed account, citing Laurel as saying that he had been called into manager Henry Ginsberg's office and told that his contract was terminated. The background story was that Stan refused to sign a new long-term contract under terms dictated by the studio. The boss had obviously decided that spending three days and nights on a train writing a Laurel and Hardy story only to have it thrown out by his employee was a humiliation too far. The studio also announced, ratcheting the pressure up further, that Laurel and Hardy would be replaced by a new series called 'The Hardy Family', featuring Babe Hardy, Patsy Kelly and Our Gang's Spanky McFarland.

Hal Roach remembered this spat with his usual selectiveness, telling Anthony Slide in 1970:

After the *Babes in Toyland* thing, we made one more picture – I forget. But their contracts were coming to a conclusion, so I just didn't renew them. Seventy-five per cent, 80 per cent of their basic plots were mine. Now we were gone from two-reelers and were into feature pictures, and Laurel in story construction was just impossible.

No less a figure than Hollywood's poison gossip queen, Louella Parsons, weighed in, on 24 March 1935, on Roach's side, giving her own personal angle:

I might have thought that Stan was trying to cover outbursts of temperament, which I had been told were the cause of the break, if Oliver Hardy hadn't been just as vociferous in his denial that he and Stan had ever had a serious quarrel. The trouble then, simmered down, is with Hal Roach, who during the days that Stan Laurel was separated from his wife had to put up with a good deal of annoyance and inconvenience. Stan was fighting the alimony question with the first Mrs Laurel and for months he held up pictures at the Roach Studios. He insisted time and time again that unless his alimony differences could be settled satisfactorily he would never make another picture. Consequently in those days Hal was kept in a constant state of upset and the studio lost thousands of dollars.

Things looked bleak for the future of Laurel and Hardy. But on 5 April the *New York Times* reported:

LAUREL AND HARDY REUNITED

Hollywood April 4: Stan Laurel, who had 'story trouble' with Hal Roach, producer of the comedian's pictures, patched up the difficulties today and signed a new contract. Oliver Hardy, his team-mate, was all smiles as Laurel, who writes the gags for all their films, emerged from Roach's office with the announcement that they were to go to work at once on a picture.

The Los Angeles *Examiner* added:

The famous duo will start work immediately in 'McLaurel and McHardy', the comedy feature in which they were playing last month when Laurel's contract was cancelled by the studio after a dispute over the script. 'There had been a veritable deluge of telegrams and letters from all parts of the world demanding that Laurel be again teamed with Hardy,' producer Hal Roach explained. 'All our troubles have been ironed out, and Laurel said he was "mighty pleased" with his new contract. And so are we.' Despite their film separation, Laurel and Hardy have continued their personal friendship.

Therein, without doubt, lies the key. Although Roach had little social contact with Stan, he played golf regularly with Babe at the Lakeside Country Club, and Babe would have been sure to convey his feelings. Despite being an instinctive avoider of conflicts – Babe was still desperately trying to avoid the final break with Myrtle – he clearly realized that 'The Hardy Family' would be no substitute for the partnership that had propelled him from years of supporting roles to stardom, and job security. A very public show of support, at the Coconut Grove club, at which Stan and Babe walked in arm in arm, was a clear signal to the studio. ' "We're pals," said Laurel. "Pals," stated Hardy firmly', according to the next day's press (28 March). Stan's friend and one-time manager, impresario Claude Bostock, hurried to Hollywood from New York to settle the contractual dispute. Hal Roach retreated, unbowed, biding his time to strike again. The boys proceeded with 'McLaurel and McHardy', soon to be retitled *Bonnie Scotland*.

Bonnie Scotland is one of the Laurel and Hardy later features that has stood the test of time, mostly because fans forget the

swathes of turgid plot in which the inheritance of one Angus Ian McLaurel goes to Lorna McLaurel (played by June Lang), on the proviso she goes to live in India with her guardian till she reaches the age of twenty-one. Stan and Ollie, not having learned the lesson of Uncle Ebeneezer (or even of Stan the presumptuous inheritor in

1924's *West of Hot Dog*), turn up for the reading of the will, to find Stan has inherited only the old man's snuff box and a set of bag-pipes 'blown at Waterloo'. Trying out the snuff, they fall in the river (Ollie sneezing the river away in proper mythological manner) and end up in their lodgings with shrunken pants and no money. All they can look forward to is a return to the jail they escaped from in America, but they vow to go to a state with no 'exposition laws'. Hieing to a tailor's to be fitted for a new, and cheap, suit of clothes, they end up in an army recruiting station by mistake and get signed on for their Colonial duty.

The memorable part of *Bonnie Scotland* consists of another bout of classic larking with Sergeant 'Leatherpuss' (Jimmy Finlayson), and their dance while assigned to pick up the camp litter, to the regimental band's 'One Hundred Pipers'. We expect the nimbleness of vaudeville-trained Stan Laurel, but not the grace and finesse of 300-pound Hardy – obviously inherited from Oliver senior, the 'Falstaffin' Georgian who had been in his day as 'polite and graceful as a French dancing master'. It is one of the essential moments of Laurel and Hardy, as the boys twirl and pirouette, till, chased by Finlayson, they dance themselves into the barrack's jail. The rest of the film, a kind of rehash of *Beau Hunks*, with Indian 'natives' instead of Arabs, who are routed with beehives instead of nails, is standard Hollywood guff, the stereotyped sins of the age.

Bonnie Scotland was shot in May and June 1935, and previewed in late July. In the first week of July, Stan and Babe, with their now regular director, James W. Horne, proceeded to shoot their very last short movie, *Thicker than Water*.

It is their two-reel swan-song. Ollie is married again, this time to diminutive Daphne Pollard, another Australian actress. Stan is the lodger who hasn't paid the rent, and Fin the skinflint who demands payment for the couple's installment-plan furniture. A verbal money-go-round patter enlivens the somewhat dour proceedings, and Ollie sets out with Stan to pull his total savings of $300 out of the bank to pay off the furniture debt. Detouring to an auction with the enticing sign 'We Are Actually Giving Things Away Today' (Stan and Ollie as consumerism's greatest suckers), they end up bidding for a grandfather clock on behalf of a nice lady who asks them to keep the bids going while she hurries home to get more cash.

Having bid the lot up against each other – Ollie to Stan: 'What are you bidding against me for?' Stan: 'Well, *you're* bidding against *me*' – they end up spending the entire stash. Moments later the clock is demolished by a truck as they try to haul it across the road – and back at home nemesis beckons. Wife Daphne climbs on a chair to brain Ollie with a frying pan, and he ends up in hospital. A doctor who seems to be moonlighting from a Universal horror movie arranges an emergency blood transfusion from Stan to Ollie, but their blood gets mixed, and they emerge from the operating room physically exchanged: Stan has Ollie's moustache and voice, bossy mannerisms and tie-twiddle, and Ollie, clean-shaven and childish, does the Laurel cry.

They walk away down the corridor together, manifesting, once again, Stan's eternal identity crisis, in its most potent form.

CHAPTER THIRTY-TWO

Bohemian Girls

Oliver Hardy might well have wished to change places with Stan in the summer of 1935, as he had to park Myrtle once again in the Rosemead Sanitarium. Babe was becoming used to living a double life – apart from his screen character – dealing with his moribund marriage and at the same time wooing Viola Morse. The Los Angeles *Examiner* reported early in July that Oliver and Myrtle Hardy, accompanied by her sister, Mary, as chaperon, were sailing to Honolulu where, the paper claimed, the 'rotund motion-picture comedian is going to become a sugar-plantation owner, suh!' Nothing much came of this, and while Myrtle submitted to her umpteenth drying-out period, Babe drove to the Seattle racetrack, in his new eight-cylinder roadster, did some fishing, and then returned to start work on the next Laurel and Hardy feature, *The Bohemian Girl*.

This was yet another operetta, based on an 1843 work by Michael W. Balfe, a gypsy tale set in seventeenth-century Bohemia, or at least the Hollywood designers' idea of it. Filming took place through October and November. An extant letter survives, written by Babe to Myrtle at Rosemead, after the end of the shooting, dated 23 November 1935. It was another of Babe's annual anniversary notes, accompanying a gift. The three handwritten pages are the longest sample we have of Babe's languid, mostly unpunctuated scrawl:

Dear little girl,
I was so pleased to get your sweet letter and invitation today at 4:30 I don't think it advisable to see you as it would make matters worse from [for?] that day I am going to the [illegible] but have gotten you a little something which I hope you will like and particularly the misconception on the inside I will be with you always in mind and heart as you are never out of my mind I would have written you before, but your letter is the first that I knew you could receive mail there. Regardless of the future dear do try and be the strong sweet little baby that you will

always be in your daddy's heart. Have been working awfully hard there
has been so much silliness on this picture Stan was laid up for 2 ½
weeks Mae Busch for 4 weeks it seems we have been at it for a year –
Happy anniversary dear and I hope you will like what I have gotten for
you I will send everything to the house Wed morning – be sweet, think
sweet and know that my devotion has never changed and never will but
we must go up hill and not back so [consequently?] why that next time
must be the time – I love you darling everlasting.

DADDY

The silliness referred to here was yet more squabbles and
alarums behind the scenes of *The Bohemian Girl*, which was
supposed to be co-directed by Hal Roach and James Horne, with
the former covering the dramatic scenes and the latter the comedy
with Stan and Babe. In the event, Roach was too preoccupied with
studio business, and the directing credits list James Horne and
Charlie Rogers as the culprits. Stan was preoccupied too. On 28
September, he hied off to Florence, Arizona, to marry Virginia Ruth
née Rogers for the second time, as the first wedding, on 3 April in
Tijuana, had technically preceded his formal divorce from Lois.

Filming eventually began in October, then was suspended due to
Stan catching flu, and proceeded after his recovery, by fits and
starts. Production troubles did not end, however, with the film's
wrap. The movie was previewed on 11 December, but a few days
later tragedy struck actress Thelma Todd, who had played the
Queen of the Gypsies. On 16 December 1935, she was found dead
at the wheel of her car in the garage of her home, killed by carbon-
monoxide poisoning.

Thelma Todd had been a fixture of the Roach Studios for many
years, and her colleagues were shocked and distraught. Roach,
however, was more worried about the impact of negative publicity,
fuelled by the intense press interest, with juicy rumours of suicide
or murder and revelations of Thelma's business and personal
affairs, which included a failed marriage to a henchman of mob
boss Lucky Luciano. (For a controversial summation of this celebrated Hollywood mystery, see the author's *Monkey Business: The
Lives and Legends of the Marx Brothers*.) Most of Thelma's scenes
were cut from the film, leaving her with one dubbed song, and
another actress, Zeffie Tilbury, was brought in to re-shoot
sequences of the Gypsy Queen as a much older woman.

Perhaps someone should have read the film's fortune beforehand, given the plot, which has Stan and Ollie as itinerant fortune-tellers and thieves, in a gypsy community which has parked its caravans on the land of an intolerant, gypsy-hating nobleman, Count Arnheim.

The Bohemian Girl is a curious film, in the context both of Stan's and Babe's private lives, and the real Europe that was darkening overseas, still far from Hollywood's gaze. The film was a big hit in France, but was banned in Germany, then firmly under Hitler's regime. One cannot suspect writers Charlie Rogers, Jimmy Parrott, Charlie Hall and Stan, let alone producer Roach, of any political intentions in their choice of this particular tale. But it is a fact in the chronology of history that, on 15 September 1935, a few weeks before the film began shooting in Hollywood, the German Reich had passed the Nuremberg Laws which disenfranchised all citizens 'not of German blood' – with particular effect on Jews and Gypsies. A tale of racial intolerance, set in feudal Central Europe, was bound to be seen a little differently in Paris and Berlin than in New York and Beverly Hills.

From the point of view of Laurel and Hardy, rather than that of Reichsminister Josef Goebbels, the story provided an opportunity to tweak their familiar characters in an unfamiliar setting. Even without its inadvertent contemporary echoes, the tale has its dark undertones. Gypsy Ollie is married to a shrewish wife, Mae Busch, who cuckolds him openly with her handsome lover, Devilshoof. The Gypsies are perceived as romantic (and costumed to the gills), but their profession of theft is heavily flouted. In an inversion of the normal Stan–Ollie relationship, Stan is the proficient thief and Ollie the dunce. Stan Laurel has taken advantage of a brief escape from the bowler hats and modern dress to resurrect the more aggressive, if not as manic, figure of the solo Laurel films. The plot involves Mae and her lover abducting the only child of the ruthless Count, whose soldiers have humiliated and whipped Devilshoof. Ollie returns to find the little girl playing outside his own caravan, prompting the following exchange with Mae:

OLLIE

Whose kid is that?

MAE

It's none of your business.

340

What do you mean it's none of my business? I demand to
know who she is.

Well, if you must know, she's yours.

Mine? (*Beaming*) Well, why didn't you tell me before?

Because I didn't want her to know who her father was till
she was old enough to stand the shock.

Soon after, Mae has ridden off with her lover and Ollie's stash of
stolen jewels, leaving him holding the baby and a note stating baldly:
'Thanks for the jewels. I am leaving you forever. P.S. You are not
the father of that child. Your wife.'

There is a bitter irony in Stan's comic twisting of the knife in the
wound of his partner's painful marriage and childlessness. Note
that it is a long time since Laurel too had a wife, in the movies.
Stan's morbid streak was more evident than ever in the denouement
of the movie, when, twelve years having passed, and the child
grown up to be a beautiful woman who calls Ollie 'Daddy' and
Stan 'Uncle', the Gypsies camp again in the domain of Count
Arnheim and all three are captured by the Count's villainous
Captain Finlayson. The girl is about to be flogged when the Count
recognizes her by her medallion and birthmark. But Stan and Ollie
are dragged off to the torture chamber, from where they are rescued only by the girl's pleas halfway through the gruesome process:
Ollie has been stretched on the rack and walks forth ten feet high,
and Stan has been crushed in a cage and emerges as a midget, with
stunted legs.

This was a glaring example of the kind of ending Hal Roach did
not like, and would try to eliminate, when he finally had the chance
to wrest control from Stan. But in the short run he was still
embroiled in much bigger and more complex problems concerning
the future of his studio. Early in 1936 the disliked Henry Ginsberg
was elbowed out and Roach's personal friend, David Loew, son of
one of MGM's founders, Marcus Loew, became general manager.
Stan's conflicts with Roach, however, were not solved. There

were several sore points, all involving both power and money. Roach had Stan and Babe Hardy signed to separate contracts, and so could play on the threat of terminating one and keeping the other – a ploy he had already tried in March 1934. Stan proposed a joint contract, but was rebuffed. Stan was guaranteed approval of stories and directors, but had no ownership whatever of the movies. Everyone in the business looked with envy to Chaplin, who owned his films, and self-financed them. Stan and Babe were working for flat salaries, Stan receiving $75,000 per picture, and Babe still signed to a weekly fee. At the end of the day, despite 'story approval', Stan had no legal recourse if the studio decided to recut his films against his will. He was Roach's employee, albeit the goose that laid the golden eggs.

But the goose can still end up in a pie.

As a concession, Roach allowed each of the next two Laurel and Hardy films to be billed as 'A Stan Laurel Production'. Not much power was ceded, but Stan's injured pride was soothed a little. The problematic operettas were shunted aside, and more contemporary material, allowing a return to the jackets and bowlers, and more prominence, rather than supporting roles, for Laurel and Hardy, was chosen. The result was *Our Relations*, based on 'The Money Box', a short story by the British writer W. W. Jacobs.

If one Stan and one Babe were popular, Stan may have thought, how couldn't we clean up with four of us? In *Our Relations*, Stanley and Oliver are respectable, if rather dim, members of society, properly married, but with a secret: twin brothers, Alf and Bert, who were supposed to have been hanged after taking part in a mutiny on the high seas. They swear never to reveal the family black sheep to their wives. But, unbeknownst to them, Alf and Bert are very much alive, on their docked ship, eagerly anticipating shore leave.

As supporting cast, Jimmy Finlayson has evolved, or rather devolved, from a manic foil with a life and motivation of his own to a scrounging cheat who swindles them out of their cash. The ship's captain entrusts them with a task: to take charge of a package he is awaiting and bring it to him on shore. The package is a valuable pearl ring, but of course our lads lose it in the course of events, leaving it as surety for an unpaid tavern bill.

A great deal of confusion arises from the hustling in and out of the two pairs of twins, who are constantly being mistaken for each other and punished for each other's misdeeds. Yet again, Stan finds a visual metaphor for his theme of identity confusion and split personality, the two fun-loving sailors being the alter egos of their socialized twins. As with Jekyll and Hyde, internal complexities are externalized in different bodies, and as with the Prince and the Pauper, the clothes make the man, or men. Indeed, there is a great deal of disrobing and re-robing in the movie, with Alf and Bert, at one point, stuck in a police station wearing bedclothes ('like those fellows we saw in Singapore'), mistakenly addressed in Arabic by another turbanned fellow in the line.

Special-effects wizard Roy Seawright kept the two sets of Laurel and Hardys apart for most of the picture, and brought in process photography to show them together only for a few key shots at the end. Had Stan thought a little more deeply, he might have realized that this in itself would cause problems in the over-elaborate plotting required to keep the muddle going to feature length. Once again it was demonstrated that, though the features were popular, they lacked the economy and drive of the shorts.

One wishes, against the grain of reality, that extended process photography might have enabled the two Stans and the two Ollies to confront each other in more scenes, well before their joint appearance at the end. There can be so much that one *Doppelgänger* might say to another, the complaints, indeed the possible misunderstandings that could occur between the selves directly, rather than through a mechanistic confusion. But the writers ran out of ideas. Towards the end an unnecessary twist of the plot introduces a band of crooks who try to force Alf and Bert to disclose the whereabouts of the pearl ring they have inadvertently passed on to their twins, by encasing their feet in cement bowls and threatening to throw them off the dock. As they teeter like weighted dolls for what seems an eternity, they are eventually rescued by their brothers and all march off, two by two. 'That Laurel is the dumbest thing I ever saw,' says Ollie to his twin Bert. 'The other one is too,' agrees Bert, before they both step off the end of the dock and thrash about in the sea, watched by the two Laurels, stopped short right on the edge.

Our Relations had been an elaborate production at all levels, and boasted better than average sets and photography. The lighting cameraman was Rudolph Mate, a veteran of the German Expressionist cinema who had also been the cameraman of two of Carl Dreyer's greatest films, *The Passion of Joan of Arc* (1928) and *Vampyr* (1932). One of his first assignments in Hollywood had been *Dante's Inferno*, earlier in 1935. Mate was and remained a great craftsman, but he was a strange choice for Stan and Ollie, and some friction was reported, due to the classic dramatic lighting he set up for them, modelling their faces in light and shadow. Like Greta Garbo, they required a flat light that made their faces somewhat unreal. At the ages of forty-six and forty-four, it was of some importance that the wrinkles of real life should not show.

By the summer of 1936, storm clouds were a-gatherin' on the horizon of the private lives of both Stan and Babe, although their next film, a comic western, was already scripted, by a quadrille of Charles Rogers, Jimmy Parrott, Vernon Jones and Felix Adler. Its original title had been 'You'd Be Surprised', but that turned out to be claimed by another studio. Two more titles, 'Tonight's the Night' and 'In the Money', were offered and relinquished, before the film gained its natural title, *Way Out West*.

The film was shot between the end of August and the beginning of November, and the results are there for posterity, for all of us to enjoy. But the shooting of the film coincided with the breaking of the matrimonial storm, a combination of the worst that screen wives Anita Garvin, Mae Busch, Daphne Pollard *et al.* could dish out to their recalcitrant husbands.

The first shots were fired across the barricades this time by Stan's new wife, Ruth Laurel. This was a marriage that had not seemed to gel at all, despite having taken place twice. In early September, soon after the commencement of the shoot of *Way Out West*, Stan and Ruth separated. A few days later she filed a suit for maintenance. The shoot itself was punctuated by the usual spats between Stan and Hal Roach. Stan's lawyer and agent Ben Shipman, who was previously Hal Roach's attorney, made a deal for four new Stan features with Roach, containing an unusual 'morals' clause, stating that Laurel agreed 'to conduct himself with due regard to public conventions and morals, and . . . will not commit any act or thing which will tend to degrade him in society, or bring him into public hatred . . . or prejudice the producer or the motion-picture industry . . .'

No sooner was the ink dry on this than disaster struck, from a wholly unexpected direction, though Stan might have had intimations of trouble long before the matter became public. The Los Angeles *Examiner*, which had been following the progress of Ruth Laurel's suit, reported, on 1 November:

Matrimonial difficulties of Stan Laurel, film comedian, increased yesterday when a second woman appeared, claimed Laurel as her husband, filed a separate maintenance action against him, and demanded a share of his property.

She is Mrs Mae Laurel, who, in her complaint, prepared by Attorneys S. S. Hahn and W. O. Graf, asserts she became Laurel's common-law wife in New York in 1919 and that they lived together until he left her in 1925. Already pending against Laurel is a separate maintenance suit filed by Mrs Virginia Ruth Laurel, his present wife. He has filed a cross-complaint, asking a divorce.

This was the drumroll of fate indeed, the tightening of the vice of the Bohemian torturers. Virginia Ruth was claiming $1,000 a month alimony, $10,000 attorneys' fees, court costs and a division of the community property, which included a $25,000 home at Glenbar Drive, furnishings valued at $10,000, two cars, a $9,000 yacht, $33,000 cash in banks, life annuities of $70,000 and Laurel's earnings, placed at $200,000 a year. Mae Laurel, weighing in, claimed she was practically destitute, currently earning $55 a month on a Federal sewing project, having lost her previous employment on a Federal theatre scheme. She asked for $1,000 a month separate maintenance, $1,000 attorneys' fees and half of the community property.

On 6 November, just as shooting was completed on *Way Out West*, the *Examiner* noted:

LAUREL WOES BEFORE COURT
And Comedian Cannot Go Fishing
Woes of Stan Laurel, film comedian, were heaped sky-high yesterday and laid on the table before Superior Judge Caryl M. Sheldon by the actor's attorney, Jerry Geisler, who said that his estranged wife, Mrs Virginia Ruth Laurel, is trying to collect a £9,000 fee for her attorney, Roger Marchetti, from him; another woman has sued him for support contending she is his common-law wife, and – to make matters worse, he can't even 'get away from it all' by indulging in his favorite pastime, swordfishing, because Mrs Laurel has tied up his yacht with an injunction . . .

Perils of matrimony – Oliver and Myrtle Hardy, 1936

Four days later, lightning struck in the same place, as Babe Hardy was hit by a new petition from Myrtle, filing for $2,500 a month separate maintenance, and, in the words of the *Examiner*:

She charges her rotund husband with extreme mental cruelty, and declared they separated last July. Her complaint stated: 'On the night of October 11, 1935, my husband went to a woman's apartment at 2:25 a.m. He carried bottles of liquor with him. At 3:45 he came out.'

Mrs Hardy was also represented by Attorney Roger Marchetti. The wives were ganging up – life following art with a vengeance!

On the 16th, Hardy filed an affidavit, rebutting Myrtle's charges and telling in detail of 'habitual intemperance on the part of Myrtle Lee Hardy, her retirement to a sanitarium on several occasions, and of several "escapes" from these institutions'. Mrs Hardy, not to be outdone, claimed, 'Hardy had wrongfully and fraudulently caused her to be confined in a sanitarium against her will.' The couple admitted to having 'separated and become reconciled "eight or ten times"'. The Judge, nevertheless, ordered Oliver Hardy to pay the thousand bucks monthly maintenance, and $7,500 to maestro Marchetti.

On the same day, Mae Laurel appeared before Superior Judge
Dudley S. Valentine armed with a 'book of memories', a scrapbook
of theatrical cuttings 'harking back to the days when Mrs Laurel
and the film star were teamed together in vaudeville as "Stan and
Mae Laurel"'. On her arrival in court she was served with a document from Stan denying the common-law marriage ceremony
alleged to have taken place in 1919. On the 18th, Stan appeared in
court in person, offering the explanation we have cited earlier, in
discussing the events at the time:

'It was the gentlemanly thing to do.'

In a sotto voice, Stan Laurel, rubber-faced comedian, yesterday gave
this as an explanation of the fact that for many years he introduced his
vaudeville partner, Mae Laurel, as his wife, although they never went
through a wedding ceremony. Laurel, who followed his present theatrical
partner into alimony court by one day, admitted to Superior Judge Dudley
S. Valentine that he lived as man and wife with the auburn-haired actress
until 1925.

This story would run and run. It is still a mystery where Mae
Laurel came from and how she had been living since she was
hustled out of town by Stan and Joe Rock. The 1935 Los Angeles
Directory lists her as resident at 4276 South Hoover, which means
she must have been in the area at least from 1934. The possibility
that the entire 'packed off to Australia' tale is a myth cannot be
ruled out. Mae could have taken her settlement and sailed away
anywhere, or ended up in New York, where she might well have
had vaudeville friends. News of Stan's fame might have rankled for
a long time, and reports of matrimonial troubles brought her
buzzing like a bee to the honey. Her tale of the Federal employment
projects evokes the harsh Depression years. Poor Mae. In the event,
as we noted earlier, she could not prove the common-law marriage, and had to settle out of court, in December 1937, for a sum
that was not disclosed.

The apparent coincidence of the Spousal Invasion following so
soon after Roach's 'morals' clause suggests that the volcanic
eruption was preceded by seismic shifts charted by Stan's colleagues, and his employer, for some time. Fred Lawrence Guiles,
'unauthorized' Stan biographer, reported a great deal of disquiet
surrounding both Stan's extra-marital philandering and allegations

of drunken binges that threatened to get out of hand. Most of these revelations come from the memories of Ruth Laurel, who cannot be seen as an impartial observer, given the turmoil of her multiple separations from and remarriages with Stan, and, like many senior citizens' recollections, her chronology is somewhat impaired. Guiles paints Ruth as an old-fashioned 'lady of the nineteenth century', content to be a home-maker, but not to indulge Stan's mood changes, occasional tantrums and his roving eye. The obscure mistress, Alyce Ardell, was still, it is alleged, much in evidence throughout the on-again off-again marriages. Mrs Lillian Burnett, one of the Laurels' cooks, told Guiles that 'Ruth had a lady detective, a woman named Beulah Siep, staying with her'.

Guiles claims Ruth had a history of miscarriages, during a previous marriage, and she spoke of adoption, though nothing was done about this. Little Lois became a favourite weekend companion, and would remain a close friend of Ruth's until her death in 1976. Tales of Beulah Siep's Marlowesque adventures, following Stan to various rendezvous around Los Angeles, particularly with one of a pair of nineteen-year-old twin sisters living in Downey, to whom he allegedly gave an $8,000 diamond bracelet, can be found in Guiles's book. None of these escapades featured in the well-covered press reports of Stan's marital troubles (and the Downey diamond tale sounds a lot like an extrapolation from *Our Relations*). But, fictional or not, rumours or tales of these kinds of shenanigans must have inspired Hal Roach's peculiar contractual demands.

The Laurel–Hardy Matrimony Case lingered well into 1937, with gloomy results for Stan and Babe. Although Ruth's divorce suit was initiated, it was not followed through, at this point, though the Los Angeles *Examiner* reported that the couple were divorced 'the day before Christmas' 1936. On 5 February, the paper wrote that Stan and Ruth were 'reconciled and are motoring to New York, Mr Laurel's attorney, Roger Marchetti, announced yesterday'. How Mr Marchetti became the husband's, as well as the wife's attorney, is another part of this befuddling jigsaw, if it is not just another incidence of bad journalism. 'Mrs Laurel', said the *Examiner*, 'won a default divorce after she had withdrawn a separate maintenance suit in which she charged the comedian with improper conduct with another woman and also asserted that he beat and kicked her.'

A later extended article, in the *American Weekly*, in 1938, drew a broader, if more slanted, picture of the Stan Laurel matrimonial follies, reporting Stan's explanation to Ruth of his erratic behaviour to her in a quoted letter:

I don't think I could ever love again like I loved Lois. She killed all my illusions. I tried to get over it but I couldn't . . . When Lois divorced me it unbalanced me mentally and I made up my mind that I could not be happy any more. I met and married you in that frame of mind and the longer it went on the stronger it became. That's why I left you – with the insane idea that Lois would take me back. After I left you I found definitely that she wouldn't. I realized the terrible mistake that I had made. I do want to come back to you and start all over again. I want a little home with you and a baby.

Assuming that this is a genuine missive and not a complete invention of the anonymous writer, it reveals a greater identity between Stan Laurel on and off screen than might previously have been thought. Its strange logic closely resembles the incoherent monologues that Stan offers Ollie when asked to 'tell me that again', after suggesting some apparently straightforward course of action.

Be that as it may, the 'third honeymoon' proceeded, but was short lived, for the *Examiner* reported on 27 April 1937 that Stan and Ruth had separated again. In a total paradox, Ruth requested that her original interlocutory divorce decree be set aside, so that grounds could be laid for fresh litigation, not based on the original suit. Now it was not only Stan who was scratching his head in disbelief.

Three days earlier, on 24 April, Oliver Hardy finally threw in the towel and filed suit for divorce against Myrtle. The case was not contested, and was formally granted on 18 May. Press photographs of Babe in court on the day show his baby face marked with a glum melancholy that is far from comic, as he testified to Superior Judge Joseph Vickers that Mrs Hardy had 'suffered a nervous ailment and refused to adhere to treatments given her'. 'Did she say she no longer cared for you, and wanted to get a divorce?' lawyer Ben Shipman asked him. Hardy replied simply, 'Yes.'

With all this going on, it is a miracle, and a tribute to Stan's and Babe's sheer professionalism, that *Way Out West* appears to us as the elegant, light, perfectly performed confection that it is. As two wanderers in the Wild West, Stan and Ollie look totally relaxed and at ease as they are first seen, traversing the classic frontier landscape, Stan leading their mule while Ollie is pulled behind, reclining on a pannier. The plot, with Stan and Ollie as two prospectors bringing the deed to a dead friend's goldmine to his daughter whom they have never seen, was later purloined for the Marx Brothers' 1940 feature, *Go West*. Jimmy Finlayson is the villainous saloon owner of Brushwood Gulch, who knows the girl in question (Mary Roberts, played by Rosina Lawrence) is his kitchen skivvy but plots with his wife Lola to have her impersonate Mary Roberts and get the deed.

Unlike some of the earlier, and most of the later Laurel and Hardy features, the plot is simplicity itself, which allows space for the boys to develop their episodic routines. These include two of the most famous moments in the entire L&H canon, their dance to the Avalon Boys' old cowboy song, 'At the Ball, That's All', and their rendition, at the bar, of 'The Trail of the Lonesome Pine', with Stan shifting into Chill Wills's bass voice for a while before being smacked on the head with a mallet by Ollie and seguing into the voice of Rosina Lawrence. Neither of these sequences was in the original script, and they were a serendipitous addition to the charm of the story. ('The Trail of the Lonesome Pine' was issued as a single record in Britain in 1975, and was placed Number Two in the hit charts of that year. Anything can happen in show business.)

In the previous scene, as Stan and Ollie dance, swaying and tangoing to the rhythm of an old turn-of-the-century tune, they touch the core of their distinct appeal to all ages, all creeds and nationalities – the sheer joy of an untramelled freedom to express oneself, for no apparent reason, in a crowded street, among strangers. We seldom do it, but we know, in the often perplexing, annoying, harsh or plain humdrum progress of life, that we should. Laurel and Hardy are there to do it for us. They are, at root – although often themselves confined, suppressed, or apparently socialized – free spirits, imps of the perverse.

Randy Skretvedt, in his thorough listing of all Stan and Babe's movies, includes, as ever, a detailed account of the changes in the film from script to screen. In the original text, when Stan and Ollie are introduced to the pretending-to-be-distraught fake daughter, Lola, Ollie says, 'Your father made us a very solemn promise before

Carefree against the odds in *Way Out West*

he . . . he went away.' Stan corrects him, 'He didn't go anyplace, he died.' Ollie: 'I was only trying to find a tender way of telling her that her father is deceased.' Stan: 'Yes, he was so deceased that he died.' In the film, this has become the snappier and more surreal:

> LOLA
> Tell me about my dear, dear Daddy. Is it true that he's dead?
>
> STAN
> Well, we hope he is. They buried him.
>
> LOLA
> Oh, it can't be! What did he die of?
>
> STAN
> I think he died of a Tuesday. Or was it Wednesday . . .

Stan's old-world formulations confuse the new. In another script change, the original version has the boys, after being thrown out of town by the sheriff, who is in cahoots with Fin, sneak back in, disguised as cigar-store Indians, only to be chased by the real redmen through the town. In the movie, this is omitted, and the boys reprise the block-and-tackle routine from *The Music Box*: trying to haul Ollie, anchored by the mule, on to the saloon's second floor balcony, only to end up with Ollie crashing into the cellar and the mule landing on the balcony instead.

The film is full of gags, all manner of funny business and robust characterizations. One of its finest scenes has Ollie trying to squeeze a locket over his neck and head to present to the grasping false heiress, only to endure a long disrobing session with Stan trying to help him retrieve it from whatever fold of his clothing it has fallen into, while Fin and Lola fume in frustration. In another, Ollie reminds Stan, after they have been evicted from the town the first time, that Stan pledged to eat his, Ollie's, hat if they didn't recover the deed. In an obvious reference to (or theft of) Chaplin's famous boot-eating sequence in *The Gold Rush*, Stan ties a napkin round his neck and proceeds to salt the hat and eat it with relish. When Ollie tries to take a bite of the hat, he spits it out instantly. It's only Stan who can make reality fit his deepest fantasies.

In the finale, Stan, Ollie and Mary, having foiled Finn and Lola and reclaimed the deed, stroll off down the western trail. Mary reveals that she would like to go home to the South. Ollie is delighted: 'You're from the South? Well, fan ma brow, I'm from the South, too.' 'I'm from the South, too,' Stan chips in. Ollie is disgusted: 'South of what, suh?' 'South of London,' says Stan. And so they proceed, singing together 'We're Going to Go Way Down in Dixie'. As they cross the stream that separates the town from the wilderness, Ollie falls into the same hole in the river bed he has fallen into before, while Stan and Mary continue onwards. There was, as yet, no way back to Dixie, for Babe.

CHAPTER THIRTY-THREE

Believe It or Not – Stan and Hal Go Off the Rails

In 1937, Ripley's famous 'Believe It or Not' series entered Laurel and Hardy into its canon of peculiar and significant facts:

Believe It or Not: Oliver Hardy weighs nearly twice as much as Stan Laurel (303 to 167lb), but Stan Laurel earns nearly twice as much as Oliver Hardy (in 1935 Laurel was paid $156,266, Hardy $85,310).

Whatever happened to the 67 cents? The year 1937 was hard for both Stan and Babe. In November of the previous year, they had made a guest appearance in a Roach musical, *Pick a Star*, just after *Way Out West*, and in the midst of their court extravaganzas. Their next feature, *Swiss Miss*, was not begun until the last days of December 1937. For twelve months, Stan and Babe were off the screen.

Reports of the break up of the team continued. The studio announced that Hardy would make a solo appearance in a movie called *Road Show*, which was then postponed. Stan was said to be staging a 'one-man sit-down strike' by refusing to sign his new contract. In March, Stan filed papers to establish his own company, 'Stan Laurel Productions', with a starting capital of $100,000. But Babe had still two years of his contract to run with Roach, so no Laurel and Hardy films could be produced under this heading. Some said Stan was forming his company only to tie up his personal funds, so they could be safe from the alimony-seeking wives. Randy Skretvedt reports that Stan signed a deal with producer Jed Buell to produce low-budget westerns, featuring singing cowboy Fred Scott, and three of these were actually made before Buell left to produce a western starring midgets, called *The Terror of Tiny Town*, which figures to this day in lists of cinema turkeys. But Stan did not, it appears, follow Buell down this road.

Babe Hardy, for his part, had a brief respite from wife trouble once the divorce from Myrtle was granted. But, in another of these strange parallels with Stan, he too was shaken up by a claim from

353

the past, with the appearance of a flurry of telegrams from Hardy Wife Number One, Madelyn née Saloshin, emanating from New York City. The first, of 19 July, was sent to Oliver Hardy Care of Hal Roach Studios: 'URGENT YOU DELIVER MESSAGE TO OLIVER HARDY CONDITION SERIOUS MUST GO TO HOSPITAL OPERATION DELAYED FATAL PLEASE HELP 35 WEST 64 RUSII = MADELYN HARDY'.

Babe might have had some advance warning of this blast from a long-suppressed past, as John McCabe has reported Madelyn staking a claim, from New York, to fifteen years' back alimony in 1936. According to McCabe, attorney Ben Shipman settled with her lawyer for an undisclosed sum. Be that as it may, the new spate of telegrams came at a time when Babe was enmeshed in two other worrying entanglements. The first concerned a dubious investment in an Alaskan Oil Drilling company called Iniskin, and the other involved his offer to sign a bond for a golfing buddy, John Montague, alias La Verne Moore, who turned out to be wanted for a roadhouse robbery seven years earlier. Montague had, it appears, been a one-time house guest of Hardy's, but it is unclear what other commitments Babe might have had to the man dubbed 'Mysterious Monty', or, even more intriguingly, the 'Garbo of golf'. Monty did have a capacity for making friends in Hollywood, as Bing Crosby was another of his defenders.

On 20 July the directors of Iniskin invited Oliver Hardy by wire to attend a dinner at which 'MOTION PICTURES OF OPERATIONS WILL BE SHOWN AT UPLIFTERS COUNTRY CLUB MONDAY JULY 26 … WIFE = WIVES INVITED'. We do not know if Babe attended, but he certainly would have been *sans* wife. On the 21st another wire came in from Madelyn: 'REGARDING OUR WIRE JULY 19TH OLIVER HARDY HAL ROACH STUDIO … MADELYN HARDY SENDER IS ASKING FOR AN IMMEDIATE ANSWER OR REASON PLEASE ADVISE.'

These wires were passed to lawyer Ben Shipman, who did not seem to take any action, as 26 July brought another plaintive cry: 'MUST BE OPERATED ON AT ONCE ULCERS VERY SERIOUS NEED HELP TO GET IN TOUCH WITH BABE HARDY AT ONCE DELAY FATAL'. And on 30 July: 'MADELYN HARDY VERY SICK AND DESTITUTE MUST BE OPERATED NEEDS IMMEDIATE HELP DO WHAT YOU CAN WIRE 35 WEST 64 CARE MCCARTHY MABEL'.

Again we do not know what response was made to these pathetic calls, but the dossier shows that no fatality took place, as, on 21 June 1938, a year later, Madelyn was still sending telegrams: 'MADELINE HARDY NEWYORKCITY IS ASKING FOR IMMEDIATE ANSWER TO HER TELEGRAM TO YOU DATED JUN 20TH. MAY WE HAVE THE ANSWER PLEASE? WESTERN UNION TELEGRAPH COMPANY'.

These were not the only family begging letters that Babe was receiving, as his ageing mother, Emily, was also prone to sending urgent wires, as Babe's response in a telegram of 26 August 1936 reveals: 'MRS E HARDY 1392 PEACHTREE ATLANTA GEORGIA – IMPOSSIBLE TO MAIL CHECK BEFORE TENTH WILL HAVE IT THERE PROMPTLY ON TENTH LOVE AND KISSES TO ALL – OLIVER'.

Despite sending his mother sums of money there is no evidence that Babe visited her or his family in Georgia at any time during his career in Hollywood. One might have thought that being a local boy made good might have tempted him to a homecoming of some sort, but, whatever the temptation, it was resisted. Dixie remained, despite the poignant ditty that ended *Way Out West*, a fondness of the heart, what we might today call a 'virtual' loyalty.

These archival snippets, like pieces of an incomplete jigsaw puzzle, reveal aspects of a familiar messiness in the conduct of our subject's affairs. Did Babe send money to Madelyn? She certainly survived the first crisis, though we do not know about the second, as we do not have a date of Madelyn's death, and this is our last glimpse of her in the annals. (A possible sighting is one Madeline Hardy, died in June 1941, but she was listed as aged forty-seven – ten years younger than Madelyn Saloshin.)

In September 1937, it was the turn of Hal Roach himself to be in the headlines, in a manner that brought his entire studio into serious disrepute. Trouble was brewing for a while, over his proposed plans to make a deal with an Italian producer to produce opera films with Italian actors and American crews. The only problem was the producer in question was Vittorio Mussolini, son of the Fascist Duce, Benito Mussolini. On 12 September the press reported:

HAL ROACH GOES ITALYWOOD
Partner with Duce's Son in Films
Rome, September 11: Hal Roach of bathing beauty and film comedy fame, and Vittorio Mussolini, Il Duce's flying son, announced tonight formation of an equal partnership for production of motion pictures. Dictator

Mussolini's gigantic new cinema city in Rome, which he hopes will some day rival Hollywood, will be used for production.

This was a particularly naïve and stubborn move on Roach's part. Italy's Fascist government was by no means ostracized in the United States, and many professed admiration for its famous capacity to 'make the trains run on time'. Even the Jewish Eddie Cantor visited Mussolini in Rome, in 1934, to campaign for American actors to be allowed to act in Italian movies. But in October 1935 Italy invaded the nominally independent Ethiopia, annexing the country in 1936, amid great bloodshed and the bombing of civilian populations. Ethiopia's exiled Emperor, Haile Selassie, travelled to Europe and America, gaining League of Nations support for his cause. The Jews of Hollywood's studios, seeing the alarming parallels between Italy's rampant militarism and the anti-Semitic policies and re-armament of Nazi Germany, were resolutely opposed to any friendly deals with Rome. Ironically, in Italy too there were voices against a movie deal between Fascismo and Roachismo. The powerful film censor, Luigi Freddi, cautioned the Duce against a joint production of such titles as *Rigoletto*, *Tosca*, or *Aida*:

Has anyone thought that each of these films might be rejected by the censors in Italy? Is it really possible that today anyone would think of producing a *Rigoletto* – that brutal story of a petty provincial tyrant who exploited and abused his subjects . . . with all the political consequences that such a film might have on the mass of people who go to the movies? . . . Is it really possible that in an Italy that claims to be stabilizing moral standards for relations between the white race and the coloured race anyone should think of producing an *Aida*, which . . . extols the marriage between a white man and a Negress whose father only lacks the backing of a League of Nations in order to appear as the Negus?

That took care of Verdi. But Roach, the hard-nosed business-man, understood little of this kind of thinking, which helps us appreciate why as innocent a movie as *The Bohemian Girl* was seen to be subversive by Fascists. On 24 September, Vittorio Mussolini, having arrived in New York City, boarded the TWA sleeper plane for Los Angeles, accompanied by Hal Roach, two other Italian film functionaries, and one C. L. Willard, 'State Department representative'. The *New York Herald-Tribune* reported,

Elaborate precautions were taken to insure Mr Mussolini's safety, and 100 policemen were on hand at the airport. The T.W.A. management disclosed that for forty-eight hours before the take-off mechanics had constantly guarded the plane in which Mr Mussolini was to fly.

The American government was certainly keen on helping young Vittorio along. But Hollywood, bless its heart, cold-shouldered Baby Duce, and even in the Roach Studios, Roy Seawright recalled to Randy Skretvedt, there were hostile voices: a favourable comment on the foreign guest gained Seawright a lambasting by a diminutive actor named Sammy Brooks, who shouted at him, 'How could you condone a man who just dropped bombs on all those black people in Ethiopia? What kind of an American are you?'

Vittorio had to save face by being called back to Rome by his father on urgent national business, flying out on 6 October and missing a slap-up dinner at the Bel-Air Country Club. To compound his woes, Roach was sued by a Dr Renato Senise in Los Angeles, who claimed he was the authorized representative to discuss Italian co-productions with MGM. Louella Parsons stated firmly, 'Hal Roach, who brought the young Mussolini here to learn the film business, will not be making pictures in Italy.'

And when Louella wrote it, so it was.

At about the time Roach was wooing Vitto M. in Rome, Virginia Ruth Laurel was making another of her convoluted divorce suit manœuvres in court via Attorney Marchetti, and even Marchetti himself had to admit, 'You can never tell, however, when the Laurels are going to decide to try married life again, so there may be a change in plans between now and December.'

The Ruth–Stan wars were to prove small beer in comparison with what was to come. But Stan was mercifully tied up, during the autumn of 1937, in scripting the boys' long-delayed new feature, and in December cameras finally rolled on *Swiss Miss*.

Roach, despairing of making *Rigoletto* in Rome, had patched up his latest spat with Stan and agreed to a four-picture deal with 'Stan Laurel Productions'. The first in line, originally titled 'Swiss Cheese', retained an operatic background, led by Walter Woolf King, refugee from the Marx Brothers' *A Night at the Opera*, testing his tonsils with the old yodelay-hee-ho. He played the famous

357

composer who arrives at the Alpen Hotel, where men are men, albeit in short trousers. The long garments are worn by the singer's wife, Anna, played by blond, toothsome Della Lind, aka Grete Batzler. Even longer garments, if moth-eaten, are worn by Stan and Ollie, American mousetrap salesmen who have come to Switzerland because, according to Stan, there must be more mice where they make the most cheese. Selling their entire stock to a crooked cheese vendor, who pays them with a useless Bovanian banknote, they proceed to dine on the proceeds and insult the chef who fails to provide Ollie with apple pie, only to find they have to work their bill out in the chef's kitchen, with each broken dish earning them another day's labour.

The film is amiable enough, if simple minded, with its main plot consisting of wife Anna trying to prove to her husband, who feels her status as a singing star overwhelms his composing, that she can play an ordinary person that a peasant, i.e. Stan or Ollie, can fall in love with. Naturally Ollie falls in love at the first eyelid flutter. His condition is neatly diagnosed by Stan: 'That sloppy look on yer face . . . you're in love – L-U-G-H – love.'

The main set piece of the film is an attempted reprise of *The Music Box*, with Stan and Ollie required to transport the composer's piano across a narrow rope bridge to a tree house, as a performing ape – actor Charles Gemora in a monkey suit left over from *The Chimp* – ambles across the bridge towards them. This is amusing, up to a point, as Stan and Ollie trying to haul a real crate up a real flight of steps in a real place is funny, while Stan and Ollie puffing and panting before a painted backdrop in a fantasy setting is considerably less jocund.

The boys' matrimonial and industrial disputes have begun to tell on their appearance: Ollie is appreciably heavier, presumably having indulged in massive comfort-eating, and Stan looks puffy and strained, not surprising considering what he was experiencing off screen. Anita Garvin appears in a tiny role at the beginning as a Tyrolean wife who beats them on the head with a frying pan, and Eric Blore, familiar from so many 1930s 'screwball' comedies, adds a touch of twisted class.

A number of reprised gags and situations attest to a certain weariness – Stan and Ollie being chased by a chef round a kitchen table, the ape hurling a crutch after them at the end, knocking them cold at a vast distance – an old Hal Roach staple. Roach was said to have cut a number of sequences, making the film incoherent in parts, and the omission of a set-up of a bomb in the piano that will go off if a certain key is played makes a nonsense of Stan crashing about the keys while the boys teeter on the studio bridge.

Teetering on and then clinging to the broken rope bridge were, however, apt metaphors for the latest episode in The Slap-Happy Marriages of Stan Laurel, which unfolded just as the film began shooting. The first rumblings of this phase of the saga were noted by the press just after the New Year of 1938:

STAN LAUREL WEDS SINGER
Yuma, Arizona, Jan 1. Stan Laurel, film comic, was married here today at a predawn ceremony to Vera Ivanova Shuvalova, Russian singer. With final divorce papers received only yesterday from his former wife, Virginia Ruth Laurel, the actor and his fiancée entrained from Los Angeles and arrived here to be married by Judge Ed M. Winn. Laurel met his new wife when auditioning singers for his latest picture.

With familiar impulsiveness, Stan swept Vera Ivanova, more commonly known by her second name, Illiana, off her feet, or, as she was a somewhat substantial lady, she might have swept him up, and the couple yodelled off to Yuma, Arizona, another centre for quickie nuptials.

Unfortunately for Stan, but to the delight of the newspapers, ex-wife Virginia Ruth, getting wind of this 'elopement', followed hot on their heels, and in the colourful description of the *American Weekly*, which summed up these capers in 1941 –

Virginia arrived in the courtroom a moment too late. Justice of the Peace Ed Winn (not the comedian, one comedian in the case was enough) was just uttering the last syllables of 'I pronounce you man and wife.'

'You can't do that!' Virginia shouted to the assemblage. 'Stan's and my divorce isn't final yet. This isn't legal!'

Legal or not, it had been done and, while Justice Winn was explaining as much to the distraught second wife, Stan and his third escaped to a local hotel. Virginia is said to have followed them and picketed the bridal suite.

Despite these shenanigans, the press reported that 'Stan managed to preserve his new wife from the clutches of his old by smuggling her back to Los Angeles in a baggage car'.

Life had finally come to resemble a Stan and Ollie two-reeler in

Funny Mr. Laurel Who Keeps On Getting Married

Lois

Virginia Ruth

Illiana

Mae

The Laurel–Hardy Matrimony Case – assorted claimants

full flow. But who was Vera Illiana Ivanova Shuvalova? She claimed, as of course she would, to be a Russian countess, an escapee from the Red Hell of Bolshevism. Her attendants at the wedding were named as 'Countess Sonia Belikovich', who sounds like an escapee from the cast of Stan's old solo short *Frozen Hearts* (remember Mae Dahlberg as Princess Sodawiski?), and Roy Randolph, a dancing master. These two would continue to be constant companions of Illiana in her Hollywood carousings, attached like barnacles to a shipwreck. Illiana stated in court she was a native of Georgia, not Norvell Hardy's Southern state but the Caucasian mountain nation. She gave her age as twenty-eight. Stan admitted to journalists he had never been able to pronounce his bride's family name, and the marriage licence simply made do with 'Illiana'.

Suits and injunctions followed like legal confetti, and the ubiquitous Roger Marchetti was kept occupied full time, as Ruth went on the warpath. On 22 January, Stan obtained a court order instructing that 'she must not invade the "honeymoon apartment" of her ex-mate; she must not harass him at the studio or molest him in public; she must not interfere in any way with his private and business life, Superior Judge Emmet H. Wilson ruled'.

Well, at least they had got away from Ed Winn. Or perhaps not, since newspapers later reported that Stan and Illiana had returned to Yuma to conduct the marriage again without ex-wifely interruptions, although Superior Judge Goodwin I. Knight ruled on 11 February that the original marriage to Illiana was legal. Then, on 25 April, a third marriage ceremony was held, in accordance with the rites of the Russian Orthodox Church. This took place at a private address, 455 Beverwil Drive. Witnesses were Sergei Malavsky and Sergei Jemoff, both residents of Hollywood, California. A press photograph was published, showing Stan and Illiana holding the hem of the bearded priest's robe, while the witnesses hold two crowns above the not-so-newly-weds' heads. Everyone in the picture looks a bit stunned, as if they have each been brained with the mallet Ollie wielded to castrato effect in *Way Out West*.

The only logical explanation of Stan's marriage to Illiana has to be that he completely took leave of his senses. At the exact moment when he most required a respite, a pause for reflection in his personal life, not to speak of a clear mind to engage with the movie he was actively shooting at that time, Stan compounded his woes almost beyond measure.

All three previous companions in Stan's life had obvious qualities. Mae was talented in her own right. Lois was both talented and warm, with a not-quite-infinite patience for Stan's erratic nature. Virginia Ruth had what the Hollywood studios used to call 'warmth and charmth'. Illiana appeared to be, not to put a fine line upon it, nuts. The press decided she conformed to the worst stereotype of the 'gold-digger', a woman without resources who latches on to a rich man. The bizarre floozies played by Kay Deslys and Vera White in *We Faw Down* come to mind. Clearly there was a lot of billing and cooing, ruffling of the Laurel hair, teasing of the chin and other more satisfying physical endearments that Illiana was adept at supplying.

She was, from the start, a noted Hollywood lush. On 13 April, four months into the marriage, she was up before the judge and released on $500 bail after driving a rented automobile in a reckless manner, striking two parked cars on Beverly Drive and then crashing into a tree within a block of her home. She lambasted the judge, blaming the hire-car company for leasing her the car without first ascertaining whether she had a licence, or knew how to drive.

On 2 May, Illiana was found guilty of drunk and disorderly charges and released on $250 bail after being arrested for 'causing a disturbance in a Russian café, where she allegedly shouted that the film colony should be Hitlerized'.

We can only speculate about the life that led Illiana to become the nightmare spouse and souse of Beverly Hills. She was a widow and, it became known later, though Stan presumably knew this from the start, she had a son from another previous mate, though not, it was alleged, the dead husband. Like so many whom life has dealt several bad hands, she covered her hardships up with reckless carousing. In physique, she was a hefty blonde, not dissimilar to Mae Dahlberg. In home life, she seemed to be a combination of on-screen Anita Garvin, Mae Busch, and a female version of the chefs who chase Laurel and Hardy around kitchen tables with knives.

If this was an attack of temporary insanity for Stan, it was compounded by the complaints he made about Virginia Ruth's alleged harassment: He claimed that Ruth was invading his privacy by calling out fire engines on spurious missions to his new married quarters – presumably Illiana's home in Beverly Hills. As the *American Weekly* described this colourfully:

Firemen would run all over the premises shouting: 'Where's the fire?' Police cars appeared in answer to calls to quell a disturbance. Once in a while, just for variety, it would be an ambulance with uniformed attendants carrying a stretcher and looking for the 'victim'. Worst of all was the occasion when a mortician's carriage rolled slowly into the driveway and an individual as sad-faced as the comedian himself asked if he could pick up the body.

As a result of all this, the newlyweds moved up town, to North Hollywood.

For her part, Illiana complained, when the inevitable divorce suits were filed barely one year later, that Stan had insisted on taking his other ex-wife, Lois, along with them on their honeymoon cruise, to chaperone Stan's by now ten-year-old daughter, little Lois. The previous wives were always butting in on their life, stopping by 'for a cup of tea or what-not', and rows would often ensue, in one of which, Illiana was to allege, she took a knockout punch (we don't know if this was swung by Stan, Ruth or Lois) and landed in hospital for three days. In counter-claim, Stan related an incident in which he was falsely arrested for drunk driving, but was driving erratically because he 'asserted that she threw sand in his eyes . . . He did not explain why, at that time, he was attired in only socks and shorts, but who would question a comedian's whim and anyway it might have been a hot day.'

The fiasco was capped by Illiana's lurid tale, related in the divorce court, that Stan had 'beat her many times, threatened to kill her with a gun and to cut her throat with a safety razor blade, and on at least one occasion, was apparently all set to bury her alive'. The press loved this story, which was related with relish:

Looking out of the window, she saw her husband digging a hole in the back yard of their North Hollywood home. With pardonable feminine curiosity she asked him what the hole was for. Turning his ever-solemn countenance upon the former Countess he replied in sepulchral tones:

'To bury you in, Shuvalova.'

The wife of a common, unfunny man would hardly have taken this threat seriously. But this wife of one of the country's star jokesters took him at his word and took it on the run as fast as her nimble dancer's legs would carry her.

She also alleged that said comedian had already once before hit her with the said shovel, 'approximately five feet in length, the blade of which was of metal', and therefore she was in fear of her life.

Mr Laurel, according to the *American Weekly*, had a tale of his own:

'She phoned me from the studio one afternoon that she would be late and asked me to cook the dinner and I did,' he said. 'But she didn't come. I kept the dinner back until it was pretty well spoiled when she finally showed up in a taxi. She looked at the dinner which wasn't much to look at any more and suddenly remembered that she had to go right back to the studio and must take our car. When I forbade it she tried to sock me with the skillet and then the telephone but missed with both barrels, after which we raced for the keys in the car, and I won.'

The car was near a sand pile, which accounts for the sand-in-the-face episode. You can't make this sort of stuff up – although one should be cautious, since the anonymous writer of the *American Weekly* may well have done just that in the details. (The alliteration between 'Shuvalova' and 'shovel' does raise a strong suspicion.) Clearly, though, there was constant mayhem in the Laurel–Shuvalova household, and the untimely 'morals clause' in Stan's contract with Hal Roach was ticking explosively away in the wings.

Amazingly, once again, in the midst of all this domestic chaos Stan and Babe made another feature, *Block-Heads*, rightly regarded as the last but one Laurel and Hardy classic. The film was scripted quickly during May 1938 and shot in one month, in June. Randy Skretvedt writes that Stan and Babe had been planning a film set on Devil's Island, for which Stan wanted to cast Illiana as the female lead. The story proved difficult to develop, and Roach wanted a quick film shot cheaply. Babe suggested an extended remake of the first Laurel and Hardy sound picture, *Unaccustomed As We Are.*

Block-Heads is set up with a sequence in the Great War's trenches in France. As the troops, Ollie included, go over the top, the commanding officer orders Stan to stay and guard the post until relieved from duty. In the turmoil of battle the trench is abandoned, but Stan remains, faithfully marching up and down, as the war ends, and long after. Twenty years later Stan shoots at a passing plane, and the pilot lands to reveal to the 'Block Head' that the war has long been over. 'Everything's been kinda quiet round here lately,' Stan agrees. (An irony the film-makers couldn't know: Stan would have had to wait only a little over a year for war in Europe to resume . . .)

Back in the U.S. of A., Ollie is getting all cuddly with his wife of one year, played by Minna Gombell (Mae Busch was not cast for some reason), who has an unsettling facial and temperamental resemblance to Stan's Illiana. Meanwhile, next door, pretty blonde Patricia Ellis is awaiting the return of her big-game hunting husband, Billy Gilbert. Ollie reads in a newspaper about some fellow in the Soldiers' Home who was found in France, having failed to realize the war's been over for twenty years. 'I can't imagine anyone being that dumb,' says Ollie; then double-taking at the picture, 'Oh yes I can!'

At the Soldiers' Home, Stan plays a gag variation on the joke in *White Wings*, when he stood with his leg folded on a fire hydrant, and a passer-by, mistaking him for a legless war veteran, gave him a coin. Here he forsakes the hard wood bench for the soft seat of a wheelchair vacated for the moment by another inmate. Sitting with his leg folded under him, he recognizes Ollie, giving rise to the poignant exchange –

OLLIE

You haven't changed a bit.

STAN

Neither have you too. You know, if I hadn't have seen you I never would have known you. Gee I'm glad to see you.

OLLIE

I'm glad to see you too.

STAN

Have you missed me all this time?

OLLIE

I certainly have.

STAN

I missed you too . . . This is just like old times, you and I being together . . . You remember how dumb I used to be?

OLLIE

Yeah.

STAN

Well I'm better now.

OLLIE

Well I'm certainly glad to hear it.

Ollie wheels Stan in the wheelchair towards his car, having promised to take him home for some luscious cooking by the wife, and even proceeding to carry him in his arms when another soldier reclaims the wheelchair. Only when they have already tumbled out of the car does Ollie realize Stan can walk normally –

OLLIE

Why didn't you tell me you had two legs?

STAN

Well, you didn't ask me.

OLLIE

Get in the car!

STAN

(*Mumbling*) Well I've always had 'em . . . I don't know . . .

OLLIE

You're better now! Huh!

The rest of the film is a succession of gags surrounding the original two-reel material: Ollie brings Stan home; the wife walks out in disgust; Ollie and Stan manage to blow up the stove; the neighbour's wife comes in to help; the boys hear Mrs Hardy coming back and hide Mrs Gilbert in a trunk. Et cetera. Jimmy Finlayson appears in an earlier scene in a cameo as a stuffed shirt who has a fight with Ollie, egged on by Stan who rushes about telling all and sundry in the apartment building, 'There's going to be a fight.' There are a number of 'magical' Stan gags in the film – lighting an invisible pipe with his thumb, pulling down the shadow of a blind on a stairway wall, and producing a glass of water from his right jacket pocket and blocks of ice from his left. A total trouble-making imp, Arlecchino to the core, Stan has recast himself as the

Block-Heads – the walking wounded

very spirit of perversity, a self-lacerating transfer from unconscious to ego of the role he was compelled to play, by his inner demons, in his tumultuous private life.

At the end, pompous hunter Billy Gilbert, discovering his wife in the trunk, pursues the boys down the flights of stairs with his rifle, reprising the finale of *We Faw Down*, as they run down an alley between two buildings and Billy's shot brings a cascade of adulterous men climbing desperately out of the windows on either side.

In Stan's original script, there was to be a different shot: Stan's and Ollie's heads mounted as trophies on Billy's wall, Stan weeping as Ollie glares at him, in the traditional 'here's another nice mess you've gotten me into'. But Roach, despiser of Stan's trick ideas, managed to get this little coda deleted.

A fair amount of recutting, previewing and retakes were undertaken after the film wrapped initially. Roach was unhappy with the film, with his insubordinate star and his increasingly public and lurid private life, with allegations of drinking and absences from the set, and with the whole Laurel and Hardy *œuvre* in general. Times had moved on. Even humour was different, with Hollywood rocking to the laughs of the audiences of screwball comedies with mainstream stars such as Cary Grant and Katharine Hepburn, films such as *The Awful Truth* (1937) and *Bringing Up Baby* (1938), movies with masterly directors: Leo McCarey (long gone from Roach's menagerie) and Howard Hawks. Hal Roach saw his type of comedy becoming dated, and was preparing to move on, towards dramatic features, like *Of Mice and Men*, and *Captain Fury*, to be produced in 1939.

Block-Heads was ready for release in August 1938, when, on the 6th, its director, John G. Blystone, who was helming his second Stan and Ollie picture, after *Swiss Miss*, fell dead of a heart attack. This increased the feeling of continual bad luck plaguing the Laurel and Hardy unit. On 12 August, Roach told Stan's lawyer Ben Shipman that he was cancelling the Stan Laurel contract. The newspapers announced the news on 17 August 1938 – Stan Laurel had been fired.

Stan had been right: There was going to be a fight. But it was not Oliver Hardy who was going to be biffed with a briefcase and left unconscious in the street – it was him.

Hardy Without Laurel, Laurel Without Hardy

Among the scribes listed in the credits of *Block-Heads*, there was a new name added to the Stan and Ollie stock company: Harry Langdon. Charlie Rogers, Felix Adler and Arnold Belgard were joined by this veteran of the silent-comedy era, who was once considered the equal of Chaplin, Keaton and Lloyd, but had blown his career away in much the same manner as the deceased Larry Semon. Born in Council Bluffs, Iowa, in 1884, he was another of the stalwart body of vaudevillians who trod the stage along with Mae West, W. C. Fields, and Stan Jefferson-Laurel. Sennett gag man Frank Capra brought him into the movie fold, in 1923, and Capra co-wrote Langdon's first feature, *Tramp, Tramp, Tramp*, directed by Harry Edwards, and directed his second, *The Strong Man*, both in 1926.

By then Langdon had left Sennett for First National (the company later to be merged with Warner Bros), hoping to control his own work. He was a unique clown, a grown man in baby face, a kind of victim of arrested development who staggered from folly to folly. Historian David Thomson, commenting about his screen character, writes, 'Imagine Laurel without Hardy, imagine Laurel preoccupied with the loss, and you are surprisingly close to Harry Langdon, not just in looks but in the self-absorbing dismay.'

Langdon had benefited, in his two Capra-directed pictures (the second was *Long Pants*, in 1927), from the input of a film-maker who was later to define his own powerful brand of Hollywood satire. But he looked around him and saw his rivals, Chaplin, Keaton *et al.*, controlling their own destiny and using directors as traffic cops, to keep the machinery going. A proud and stubborn man, he rowed constantly with Capra – as with many other colleagues – and fired him when *Long Pants* was completed. Langdon directed his next three movies on his own, but none were of stature, and his prospects diminished. The coming of sound was a catastrophe for him. Warner Brothers did not renew his contract, and he turned up at the Hal Roach Studios in 1929, to join the All-Stars list of performers. He starred in a handful of shorts for Roach, but then moved to other companies – Educational, which was also a dubious haven for Buster Keaton after MGM, and later to Columbia Pictures. Like Keaton, Langdon became a hired hand, a gag man for other comedians.

Having freed himself, or so he thought, from Stan Laurel, Roach lost no time in making sure that the shorn partner, Oliver Hardy, was not left to eke out the few months of his contract still left to run playing golf and betting on horses. Within days of terminating Stan's contract the studio announced that Harry Langdon had been signed to replace him in a series of films teamed with Oliver Hardy to be 'based on important novels'.

This turned out to be the usual Hollywood hyperbole, as the property Roach had in mind was a short story called 'Zenobia's Infidelity' by H. C. Brunner. 'Adapted for the screen' by Norman Blackburn, it was to star Roland Young as a country doctor 'who loses caste with his patients after treating an elephant burned in a circus fire'. But Roach soon earmarked it as his first Langdon and Hardy picture.

In the event, the film went through a number of name changes before it emerged at its preview in February 1939 as 'It's Spring Again', although the studio announced, for some reason, that it would be released as 'We, the People'. Somewhere along the line, this title too fell away and the film was released in May as *Zenobia*.

Condemned as a curiosity, although well reviewed at the time, *Motion Picture Herald* even acclaiming it as a '"must see" on any theatregoers' list', *Zenobia* has lingered in relative obscurity for decades, before being restored as part of the ongoing Laurel and Hardy revival.

It is, in fact, a relatively handsome production, designed by Charles D. Hall, who art-directed Chaplin's *The Gold Rush* and *Modern Times* as well as some of the cinema's greatest horror classics – *The Phantom of the Opera*, *Dracula*, *Frankenstein* (and his *Bride*), *The Black Cat*, etc. Photography was by the veteran Karl Struss who had cut his camera teeth with Cecil B. de Mille. The producer for Hal Roach was Eddie Sutherland, whom Roach for some reason hated intensely, but who had directed four movies with W. C. Fields (*It's the Old Army Game*, *Tillie's Punctured*

Romance, *International House* and *Mississippi*). The director was Gordon Douglas, who had made 'Our Gang' films for Roach and was to go on to become one of Hollywood's most prolific directors, although titles such as *I Was a Communist for the F.B.I.* (1951), *The Fiend Who Walked the West* (1958) and *Call Me Bwana* (1963) do not add lustre to his portfolio.

Corey Ford wrote the screenplay, but we do not know the amount of input he had from the co-stars. Langdon clearly had a hand in it somewhere, though the film affords few chances for comic gags. The intriguing thing for us, in the context of Oliver Hardy, is the setting of the film in Mississippi of 1870, a bright black-and-white world of the genteel South, untouched by the real-life ravages of the Civil War. Babe Hardy was cast as Dr Emery Tibbitt, a warm and kindly doctor in a small Southern town. He has a wife, not the skillet-wielding harpy of Stan's traditional ilk, but an amiable scatterbrain, played by Billie Burke, one-time stage star and the widow of impresario Florenz Ziegfeld. There is a daughter, Mary, played by Jean Parker, who has a fiancé, Jeff Carter, played by James Ellison, who in turn is burdened with a blue-blood mother (Alice Brady) who won't let her boy marry into this lowly jobbing family. Meanwhile, a circus show has come to town, whose only apparent featured performer appears to be snake-oil vendor Professor J. Thorndyke McCrackle – Harry Langdon – whose second fiddle is his performing pachyderm, Zenobia.

Dr Tibbitt's home also includes two black servants, and a little boy, Zeke, played by Philip Hurlie. The servants are played by Hollywood's two prime purveyors of the black image in American cinema of the 1930s – Hattie McDaniel and Stepin Fetchit.

At last, Oliver Hardy has returned to Dixie, in a role he takes on gladly. Here is an opportunity for Babe to show he can be an actor with a wider range than the iconic Ollie, the elegant buffoon. One cannot watch Dr Tibbitt without seeing the mask behind the mask, our familiar Oliver Norvell Hardy. But there is another Oliver Hardy here too – an alter ego that might have developed had Norvell taken another pathway in life. The kindly doctor is not just an apple-cheeked darling, he is a man of principle, who treats his poorer patients gratis, and forgoes the fat fee he might earn by playing along with the hypochondriac fantasies of the rich Mrs

Zenobia – Dr Tibbitt with Zeke, played by Philip Hurlie

Carter. Dr Tibbit's guiding light is the Declaration of Independence, framed on his wall, with its bold assertion that 'all men are created equal', with the right to 'life, liberty and the pursuit of happiness'.

A fine sentiment, but one which leads the good doctor, Mr Hardy, and the movie, into confusion when the story seeks to apply the rubric, not only to the love marriage of the rich boy and the less rich girl, but to the relationship between the kindly master of the house and his black servants, namely the little boy, Zeke. When the boy asks why just because his skin is black he can't mix with the white folks at the grand party, he gets a somewhat embarrassed lecture by Dr Tibbitt on the black pills and the white pills in the medicine cabinet, which are each good for something, but in a different way. This little homily, which would have been familiar in apartheid South Africa, is then contradicted by Dr Tibbitt showing the boy the Declaration of Independence, and offering him a quarter if he can learn it all by heart.

This split personality lies at the heart of all the – admittedly not very many – Hollywood films of the 1930s that dealt with racial themes or included black characters, mostly as comic relief. Film historian Donald Bogle, in his provocatively named *Toms, Coons,*

Mulattoes, Mammies and Bucks, traces the history of the black American performers who broke into the Hollywood mainstream by representing the racial fantasies of whites – and mainly white liberals – about black people. Hattie McDaniel and Stepin Fetchit were the most prominent of this small group. For years, in film after film, Hattie McDaniel portrayed the ubiquitous black mammy, humanizing the stereotype with the force of her ebullient personality. She would follow *Zenobia* with her role in *Gone with the Wind*, which was to win her the first Oscar awarded to a black performer for her performance as Vivien Leigh's faithful servant. In *Zenobia*, too, she bustles around, ruling her kitchen and bossing poor Stepin Fetchit around.

Stepin Fetchit – born as Lincoln Theodore Monroe Andrew Perry in 1902, in Florida – was the most fascinating, and to many appalling, example of the dehumanization of the black man in Hollywood movies. In his shambling gait, and mumbling, incoherent speech, he was the archetypal Jim Crow, a comic character beloved of whites, a travesty to black Americans. Behind the mask there was an extremely skilful actor, who had developed his bizarre character as a deliberate parody. The man himself lived the high life on his increasing salaries, owning six houses, twelve cars, employing sixteen Chinese servants and flaunting $2,000 cashmere suits. He had, Bogle reports, 'a champagne-pink Cadillac with his name emblazoned on the side in neon lights'. But as time passed, and black pressure groups protested ever more vociferously about Hollywood's racist portrayals, he went out of fashion, and faded into obscurity – though he lived on until 1985.

Hattie McDaniel used to say to her detractors that she had a choice, either to earn $7,000 a week playing a black maid, or $7 a week being a black maid. These actors, courting ridicule and resentment, opened a door that would, in a later generation, enable actors such as Sidney Poitier to burst through and shrug off the stereotype. But, in the 1930s, there was little else.

The writers who gave Dr Tibbitt his two scenes with the boy Zeke seemed to recognize this problem, if only to elide it, as Zeke, at the end of the movie, recites the Declaration of Independence pat, to a beaming Tibbitt and a gathering audience of white townspeople. Hollywood always wanted to have its cake and eat it. Oliver Hardy clearly relished this role. Observe, in the party scene, how he dances elegantly with his 'daughter', bringing to life that other Oliver Hardy, the Falstaffian and avuncular town politician, the elegant dancer and kisser of babies. For the one and only time in his life, Babe captures and presents on screen his loving tribute to the father he never knew, whose name he always carried with pride.

All men are created equal, but some are created more equal than others. This was a principle that Oliver Hardy was temperamentally inclined to hold true. Many commentators on Laurel and Hardy have found this aspect of Hardy's patrimony uncomfortable, and the issue of race has lead many to tread warily around this aspect of his background. The facts are, as we have seen, that Norvell Hardy was born into a racist community, scarred by the trauma of civil war. His first marriage, bitterly though it ended, demonstrated that he was able to resist racist strictures in the choices he made about his own private life. He could not wholly escape being a product of his environment, and he was not a man inclined to deeply held political views. But I believe we can take his onscreen homily to the Declaration of Independence as a heartfelt commitment – given that its framers themselves were the owners of slaves . . .

With such a problematic heritage, Oliver Hardy flourished to become an actor who gave pleasure to millions of people, regardless of colour, creed, nation or even language. The clowns transcend, or fade away. The fate of Stepin Fetchit is a sombre reminder of the limitations of a comedian who chooses a mask defined by others. The lasting comic is the one who finds a way to exemplify, even with an invented character, in the deepest sense, the aphorism 'to thine own self be true'.

Characterization alone could not, however, save *Zenobia* from a dire box-office fate. The teaming of Hardy and Langdon was a failure. Even in the few scenes they share, they are simply two actors exchanging lines. There is no 'chemistry', and none enabled by the script, which awkwardly connects the social travails of the Tibbitt family with the tale of the good doctor being called out to treat a patient at the nearby circus, only to find Professor McCrackle's elephant, Zenobia, moaning and twitching about her stall. The plot line then has Zenobia taking a shine to Hardy, following him about everywhere, ruining whatever social life he has left, and causing Langdon to sue him for stealing his elephant's affections. The haughty Mrs Carter subsidizes this claim, to ensure her son can't marry the disgraced doctor's daughter. All this is quite silly, and the court scenes, with Harry Langdon fluffing his pre-pared speech in the witness box and Babe Hardy having to plead his case from outside the window, as the elephant keeps following him inside, lack any proper humour or cohesion. At the end, it turns out that Zenobia's ailment was pregnancy, and Professor McCrackle shoos his two happy pachyderms off to their home in the circus, while Mrs Carter realizes her selfishness and consents to the marriage.

There was no follow-up to *Zenobia*, although the Hollywood trade press did announce that a second Langdon–Hardy movie, the ubi-quitously titled *Road Show*, was pending. Roach did not need to wait for box-office returns to realize that there was no future for this team. Nor did he need any opinion polls to know the public wanted Laurel and Hardy. Roach had capped a long series of dis-putes with his distributors, MGM, by switching to United Artists in a deal made in May 1938, and United Artists was far from ecstatic at the prospect of a Langdon–Hardy series. Reluctantly, Roach proceeded to mend his fences with Stan Laurel, who had, in the meantime, sued the studio for $700,000 damages for breach of contract.

On 8 April 1939, Roach and Laurel agreed to settle their differ-ences, and Roach, still resisting a joint contract for Stan and Babe, signed a short-term one-year contract with each, to produce, not full-length films, but four 'streamliners', 40-minute films that exhibitors could book as supporting features.

The first of these was *A Chump at Oxford*, which was shot in June 1939, but not released until early in 1940. The movie exists in two versions, as additional scenes were shot in September to make the film a full feature for European sales. It is this 63-minute ver-sion that has now been restored.

The added section comes at the beginning, in a self-contained episode that recycles the 1928 silent short *From Soup to Nuts*. Stan and Ollie, looking for work, overhear a call at the employment agency for a maid and butler at short notice. In his last reprise of his cross-dress maid outfit, Stan turns up with Ollie to face Anita Garvin once again as haughty Mrs Vandervere and Jimmy

Finlayson as her husband. 'What a strange looking person!' says Anita, looking Stan up and down. 'What do you expect on a few hours' notice?' ripostes Stan.

The boys proceed to wreck the Vanderveres' dinner party, with Ollie reseating everybody in an endless musical chairs and Stan, having scoffed the left-over wine, again serving the salad undressed. Fin chases them out with a rifle, but bags a cop in the behind by mistake.

The original 'streamliner' then picks up the tale, with Stan and Ollie as two 'white wings' street cleaners, sitting down to their lunch outside the door of a bank:

OLLIE

Well, here we are at last, right down in the gutter. I wonder what's the matter with us? We're just as good as other people, yet we don't seem to advance ourselves. We never get any place.

STAN

You know what the trouble is, don't yer. We've never had no education. That's what's the matter, you see. We're not illiterate enough.

OLLIE

I guess you're right.

It's nice to be back with the familiar voices once again. But Stan and Ollie used to lament their fate far less in the old days. It was just the way things were. In a harsh world, who could expect better? We know, however, that behind the masks Stan and Ollie have come a long way, overcoming many hurdles and difficulties, only to face more obstacles. Or at least – that was the reality in Stan's life. On 25 April 1939, he had finally filed for divorce from Illiana, retaliating to a suit she had herself initiated on 28 December 1938, citing mental anguish, indifference, drunkenness and violence. One of her complaints was that Stan had taken his first wife, Lois, on their honeymoon cruise, and they had ridiculed Illiana's singing. For this insult, Illiana demanded $1,000 per week alimony. Her suit was dismissed on 13 April, and Stan promptly filed his own. On 17 May, he obtained a divorce by default, which suggests that Illiana could or would not turn up to contest the case. Stan therefore proceeded to shoot *A Chump at Oxford* with at least some measure of relief.

Back to the film. While Stan and Ollie eat their lunch on the sidewalk, carelessly tossing wrappings and a banana skin on the pavement, a robbery is taking place inside the bank behind them. The bank president has been tied up by an armed desperado who is making his escape with the cash. Running out, he slips on the banana skin, gets entangled with Stan and Ollie as they innocently try to help him up, and is arrested by the cops. The president, in gratitude, offers the boys anything their heart desires. They want to go to night school. But the president packs them off for the best education money can buy – over the ocean, at the University of Oxford.

The Oxford scenes of the film were shot on the Roach lot, providing one of the most cheesy and unconvincing English backlot experiences in a long line of cheesy Hollywood backlots. A cast of potato-mouthed exiles playing Oxford students, including a very young Peter Cushing, plot to make the visiting Yanks the butt of a series of practical jokes. As part of this 'Royal Initiation', they lead them first into a maze with their suitcases, and then show them to 'their' quarters, which are in fact the Dean's personal digs. Smoking and drinking merrily in the Dean's bed, the boys are soon discovered and engage in a soda-spurting, pillow-fighting battle with the bewhiskered worthy, before the students' plot is unmasked.

The students, enraged at Ollie 'snitching' on their plot, gang up on the Yanks, marching in phalanx and intoning solemnly, 'Fee Fi Fo Fum, we want the blood of an American . . .' But this awkward caper is only a prelude to the completely unexpected final sequence of the picture, Stan's transformation, after being slugged on the head by a falling window, into the long-lost and legendary Oxford all-round athlete and scholar, Lord Paddington. This *deus ex machina* is introduced by a valet, Meredith (played by Forrester Harvey, an Irish actor who played Cockneys in Hollywood), who tells Stan, before the window crashes down, that he is a dead ringer for the said Lord, who disappeared years before after a knock on the head and has never been seen since.

Stan's performance, as he suddenly becomes Lord Paddington, is a startling revelation of the range we might have expected from Stanley Jefferson-Laurel had he undertaken any other roles, in the talkies, apart from the eternal Stan. Transformed into an arrogant upper-class fop, he takes command immediately: 'Good gracious, Meredith, why don't you fix that window, it hit me right on the cranium. Where's my tea and crumpets? Hurry! Silly old bounder . . .' The students, who all rush in at this moment to evict the snitchers, are met with 'What is the meaning of this vulgar intrusion?' and a demonstration of Lord Paddington's singular mannerism of wiggling his ears ferociously, before throwing the intruders bodily, one by one, out of the window, ending with the astonished Ollie.

As Ollie returns, battered and bruised, this apotheosis of Stan's identity crisis is played out in a most affecting scene:

STAN
Meredith, who is this coarse person with the foreign accent?

MEREDITH
Mr Hardy, meet Lord Paddington.

OLLIE
Stan, don't you know me?

STAN
Know you? Why I never saw you before in my life.

OLLIE
Don't you remember? We used to sweep the streets together!

STAN
Sweep the streets? How dare you? How dare you make such
slurring remarks? Meredith, show this common person the
egress, and eject him forcibly.

But in the next scene Ollie is still *in situ*, though the price of his inclusion in Stan's world is to have become his servant. With as much dignity as he can muster, he brings Lord Paddington his tea tray, in a room lined with a mass of sporting trophies. Lord Paddington is attired in his dressing-gown, jauntily chewing on a long cigarette-holder, monocle screwed into his eye:

STAN
Oh, good morning, Fatty.

A Chump at Oxford – Stan as Lord Paddington

OLLIE

Good morning, your lordship. Tea, your lordship.

The Dean enters. Stan gestures to Ollie.

STAN

Don't stand there like a dummy. Get a chair for the Dean.
(*To Dean*) Pardon my valet being so horribly stupid. He's
not quite broken in yet. Rather thick as it were.

DEAN

Why do you tolerate him?

STAN

Oh, I don't know. He's got a jolly old face, you know. Breaks
the monotony, and helps to fill up the room and, uh, besides,
he's someone to talk to, you understand.

The Dean has come to ask Lord Paddington to help the visiting
Professor Einstein, from Princeton, who has been having some
trouble with his theory. Stan would be delighted to do so, and the Dean
leaves the room. Stan is left facing an indignant Ollie, who has been
double-taking and fuming throughout the previous exchange –

STAN

By the way, Fatty, I've noticed that you're getting terribly
sloven. You don't seem to have the dignity becoming of a
lackey. Pull in your stomach. Throw your shoulders out.
Chin up – both of them. Now walk around, snap into it,
make it brisker, brisker, chins up . . .

Ollie walks about with tray and slips on skate, smashing to the floor.

Now look what you've done, clumsy.

This is the last straw for Ollie, who goes berserk, throwing
things around, yelling at Stan, 'I've had enough of this! Why I knew
you and I had more brains in my little finger than you had in your
whole carcass – even with your overcoat on!' Stan talks through all
this tirade, muttering, 'You're a witty old stick in the mud, aren't
you, Fatty –' 'Don't call me Fatty!' yells Ollie. 'I'm through, I've
never been so humiliated in all my life – and one more thing too –
I didn't like that double-chin crack!' 'I was only trying to help you
out, really old dear.' Stan wags his cigarette-holder nonchalantly.
'My goodness, what a *faux pas* . . .' But he is interrupted by the
student crowd outside singing, 'For he's a jolly good fellow!'
Peering out of the window, Stan is conked again by the sash. This
leads us to the final poignant moment:

OLLIE

(*Rushing back into the room having stomped out*) Get
another boy! Goodbye! (*Stomps out again.*)

STAN

(*Returned to normal*) Hey, Ollie, where are you going?

OLLIE

Back to America for me! (*Rushes out again.*)

STAN

Hey, Ollie . . . (*Mumbles and cries.*)

Ollie turns back, startled.

OLLIE

Stan! You know me!

STAN

Of course I know you! What's the matter, you got one of
those dizzy spells?

380

Ollie comes up, laughs, embraces Stan, halts a moment, touching his double-chin with exasperation, then laughs again, and hugs the astonished Stan. The End.

Stan and Babe were not to know it, but their strange confrontation in the trophy room of the ersatz Lord Paddington was to be another swan-song, of a kind. It is, in the history of Laurel and Hardy, the last great exchange, the last tit-for-tat dialogue that will resonate in the hearts and minds of fans. A *Chump at Oxford*, minor undertaking though it appeared at the time, provides the last vintage moments of comedy in which Stan and Ollie are seen in their prime. It may be happenstance, or it may not, that Stan, at key moments, dreams up – or develops, with his writers – significant, metaphoric pieces of business, gags and lines that express the constant tension implicit in the teaming of these two disparate characters. The forces that threaten to break them apart are powerful – physical incompatibility, temperamental differences, separate ambitions, divergent personal prospects, clashing needs and desires, falling window sashes, and a social world that constantly erodes the ties that bind a pal to a pal. Stan may have denied, repeatedly, as if warding off accusations of some unmentionable disease, the definition of his trade as an art. But, in film after film, the evidence reveals the high artistry of the fine delineation, the multifold variations on the theme of the endurance of friendship against every possible encumbrance.

Words of more than one syllable, I know, but not all of us can be as dumb, and as smart, as Stan Laurel at one and the same time.

CHAPTER THIRTY-FIVE

'Something wholesome, something tender . . .'

Laurel and Hardy were to make only one more film for Hal Roach, *Saps at Sea*, released in 1940. Before this, and immediately following the shooting of the main sections of *A Chump at Oxford*, they shot an independent feature, released by RKO in October 1939, *The Flying Deuces*. An ex-Broadway producer named Boris Morros arranged a 'loan-out' of Laurel and Hardy from Roach, as soon as the Laurel–Roach contract dispute had been settled in April. A writer, one Alfred Schiller, wrote an outline story based on a French comedy film called *Les aviateurs*. Mr Schiller, however, was not familiar with the work of Laurel and Hardy, which, one would have thought, might have been spotted beforehand as a handicap. In the event, Stan spent two months with trusted co-writers Charlie Rogers, Harry Langdon and Ralph Spence, hammering out a workable script from the dross.

By this point, Stan had achieved a modicum of stability in his private life, following the break with Illiana. The whole course of events of the past year had, however, left its mark. Soon the press was reporting that Stan Laurel was making sure he would be immune to 'any further blisskrieg invasions' by building a huge fence around his house at 20213 Strathern Road, in Reseda in the San Fernando Valley, whence he had escaped from Ruth's rousting of the fire brigades to interrupt his Russian tryst. It was to become a seven-foot-high, foot-thick wall made of red brick, described as 'Stan's new barrier against alimony wars . . . against sharpshooting process servers; against blue-clad forces of the law; against pencil-and-pad armored newspaper men, and against the brazen-equipped curious'. The estate was henceforth known as 'Fort Laurel', within which '"General" Laurel . . . enjoys only peace and quiet – with even an unlisted telephone – and is in complete command over his faithful troops of servants'.

Despite this protection, Illiana continued to lob counter-suits for alimony over the wall, while her own problems continued unabated.

She was being sued by the rental company whose car she had wrecked in April 1938, an offence for which she spent five days in jail in January 1939. There were several further arrests for drunken behaviour, and eventually an unusual judgment was made by Judge Cecil D. Holland, who gave her a 60-day sentence for 'intoxication', suspending 45 of them on the condition that she promised to leave the State of California for a year, 'for the protection of our police'. But even elsewhere, on the East Coast to which she then repaired, she continued to fall foul of the law in petty offences, such as passing bad cheques in dress shops in Atlantic City, New Jersey.

Stan, nevertheless, was optimistic, at the start of his attempt to build his house of bricks, rather than of straw, about his new beginning free of the wars with Hal Roach. Babe, too, was relieved to be able to continue the Laurel and Hardy series. He greatly enjoyed his different role in *Zenobia*, but he had, like all show people, a healthy respect for the verdict of the box office, and could see that Langdon-and-Hardy was a doomed franchise. In the event, *The Flying Deuces* turned out to hold a special gift for Babe, in a wholly unexpected way.

The Flying Deuces is a poor film, although it does contain a few semi-vintage L&H sequences. The best are in the opening episodes, which find Stan and Ollie on vacation in Paris. In Schiller's script (perhaps echoing *Sons of the Desert*), they were part of an American Legion beano, and had gone to Monte Carlo to bet at the Casino. In the movie, Stan is planning to go home, so he and Ollie can resume their jobs at the 'fishmarket in Des Moines', but Ollie has fallen in love with one of the waitresses at their hotel. He has given his portrait and some candy to the flirtatious Georgette, along with a poem not very different from Babe's real-life anniversary odes to Myrtle:

> Roses are red, candy is sweet,
> This is something I sent you to eat.
>
> OLLIE

Here is Ollie in Love, all blushing and simpering, writhing in the coils of *amour*. Unfortunately, Georgette is married to a dashing Foreign Legion officer, François, who turns up to claim his conjugal kiss. Ollie is devastated, taking his candy and flowers back to his hotel room, while Stan, ingenuously, tries to console him:

> STAN
> Don't worry about it. You'll get over it all right.
>
> OLLIE
> To think that this would happen to me, just at a time in my life when I needed something real, something wholesome, something tender.

384

Why don't you try a nice fat juicy steak?

This leads to an argument, in which Ollie wants to be left alone, and Stan bridles, 'Don't talk to me like that after all the hospital I've given you . . . I've waited on you with your hands and feet . . . If I felt as bad as you I'd go and drown myself.'

Ever suggestible, Ollie takes up this proposal of a way out of his woes, and we next find them on the banks of the river, Ollie tying a rope around both himself and Stan and attaching it to a stone. In an awkward piece of plotting that seems to have been omitted from later British prints of the film, newspaper headlines have previously revealed that a man-eating shark has escaped from the aquarium into the Seine. The ensuing dialogue has echoes of the old-style routines, but reveals a certain hard-hearted humour in the lines Stan has projected into Ollie's mouth, as Ollie insists that Stan should jump in the river with him, and Stan demurs –

OLLIE
So that's the kind of a guy you are. After all I've done for you you'd let me jump in there alone!

Stan is still unconvinced.

Do you realize that after I'm gone that you'll just go on living by yourself, people would stare at you and wonder what you are and I wouldn't be here to tell them – there'd be no one to protect you. Do you want that to happen to you?

STAN
I didn't think about that. I'm sorry if I hurt your feelings, Ollie. I didn't mean to be so dispolite.

After all these years, the relationship has become pretty bleak, a desperate symbiosis, with an almost mythological ethos – that only death can finally prove friendship. There follows a strange exchange on reincarnation, a belief Stan was said to have held off screen as well as on: perhaps a symptom – along with the Byzantine third nuptials with Illiana – of a personal search for spirituality, long distanced from his Methodist roots, or perhaps more simply of more mundane Hollywood celebrity dabblings in occult flimflam.

'What would you like to be when you come back?' Stan asks Ollie, trying to delay the final jump. Ollie reflects and decides he might like to be a horse – the choice playing on Babe's love for the gee-gees. Stan declares, 'I'd rather come back as myself, I always got along swell with me.' Life and art, once again intertwined.

All this fine talk interrupts the plunge long enough for François, whom the pair have not yet met, to come down the steps to remonstrate with them and suggest that, if he wants to get over a girl, Ollie should join the Foreign Legion.

The rest of the film recycles the plot of *Beau Hunks*, along with bits of *Bonnie Scotland*. Charles Middleton is the ruthless Saharan camp commandant, and Jimmy Finlayson is a double-taking prison guard. Stan and Ollie are made to wash endless laundry, which they finally set alight by mistake as they decide to leave, and are hunted down and charged with desertion. While trying to escape from the camp, the boys pause for some unearthly reason by a Legion band so that Ollie can sing a couple of verses of 'Shine On, Harvest Moon'. This attempt to reprise *Way Out West* only emphasizes what a well-plotted film that was compared with the current flabby project. The boys head for the camp's airfield, where a plane lands, bringing Georgette. Ollie embraces her but François arrives, and the boys are captured. Condemned to be shot as deserters at sunset, Stan comments, 'I hope it's cloudy tomorrow.'

In their jail cell, Stan pulls the strings from his bed and plays it as a harp, Harpo Marx style, while Ollie fumes beside him. An anonymous hand throwing a stone with a message informs them there is a tunnel under the cell. And the inevitable escape and chase follow, into the commander's quarters, around the yard, and back to the airfield, where the boys commandeer a plane and fly off in a crying panic.

At the film's finale, Stan produces one of his most morbid endings. The plane crashes and Stan climbs from the wreckage to see Ollie's ghost, with angel wings, waving goodbye to him as it rises into the sky. He walks alone, down a country pathway, a tramp forlorn, shorn of his better part. Ollie's voice calls to him from behind a hedge. Stan turns. It is a horse, with Ollie's moustache and Ollie's hat between its ears. 'Ollie, is that really you?' Stan asks.

'Well, here's another nice mess you've gotten me into.'

But Stan embraces the horse around the neck, fondly. It is not, after all, the clothes that make the man.

*

When *The Flying Deuces* was previewed, in September 1939, the world outside had been plunged into crisis. In Europe, Nazi Germany had invaded Poland, and Great Britain and France were at war with Germany. The only response in Hollywood, at that immediate moment, was the commencement of the shoot of Charlie Chaplin's provocative anti-Fascist comedy, *The Great Dictator*. The realization that the United States could not remain neutral was slow in coming. America was not yet at war. Fort Laurel was being constructed to keep out ex-wives, not Nazi or Japanese invaders. The world of Laurel and Hardy was still self-contained.

But Ollie in Love proved to be a serendipitous theme, during the summer and autumn of 1939. During the making of *The Flying Deuces*, Babe met a vivacious thirty-year-old script continuity girl, Lucille Jones, Texan-born, who had joined the film-making colony after living in Phoenix, Arizona. At the time she was living with her mother in Los Angeles. Lucille recalled the circumstances of that first meeting, in her 1983 interview with Randy Skretvedt:

I had been working in the writing department, for Sol Lesser, for several years, then . . . Lesser did a retrenchment and I was let go, with several others, and I started doing free-lancing for one or two studios, and one day I got a call from the guild – Boris Morros, and they wanted me to call him, so I did, and it was a Laurel and Hardy picture. Well I had never done comedy . . . but I thought it would be a challenge . . . They hired me so I went to work the following Monday and met Stan and Babe for the first time . . .

My first encounter with Babe . . . I went over to tell him after the master shot had been taken, and we were going in for the close shot or two-shot, I saw that Babe's hat was in the wrong hand, and the cane and gloves were – nothing was right – and his stance . . . so I walked over to him and said, 'Mr Hardy, in the last shot your cane and your hat were in . . .' He said, 'It's all right, my dear, I know how it was.' I thought, oh, this is really going to be a chore, I'm not gonna have any fun on this picture. I found out how wrong I was because the minute they were ready to shoot . . . everything went back as it should be. And he was always that way. He was a great study. I never had any problems, he really did know. He was a very like-able person. This was July 1939, and we were married next March, so I guess we got along all right.

Babe did not make any romantic advances towards Lucille for quite a while. He was still involved with 'fiancée' Viola Morse, his

387

companion to the casinos and the racetracks, although she was kept, most of the time, out of the public eye. She finally hit the headlines on 9 February 1940, when the Los Angeles *Examiner* reported a vehicle accident in which she drove a car under the influence of sedatives, hit three other cars at Sepulveda and Wilshire and ended up in the emergency ward:

SELF-STYLED FIANCÉE OF OLIVER HARDY HITS 3 CARS

Recovering from the effects of eighteen sleeping tablets and an automobile collision, Mrs Viola Morse, self-styled fiancée of Oliver Hardy, comic behemoth of the screen, was in St Vincent's Hospital yesterday . . .

She declared she was engaged to marry Hardy . . . but had quarreled with him recently and had just returned from Honolulu . . .

Associates of Hardy, who is away from Hollywood at present, his whereabouts unknown to his employers, said it was a fact that the actor had introduced Mrs Morse to his friends as his fiancée, but they knew nothing of any wedding plans. On the other hand, Hardy's attorney, Benjamin Shipman, asserted that 'Mr Hardy is not engaged to marry anyone.'

Whether this was technically true or not, Lucille related that Babe had proposed to her towards the completion of the shooting of the boys' next, and last, Roach movie, *Saps at Sea*, in December 1939. In the previous few months, he had been attentive, asking after her welfare, and otherwise treating her very much as Ollie might, though perhaps not with as much tie-twiddling and coy simpering as onscreen. 'I just thought he was naturally polite,' Lucille recalled. Her first inkling of any special feelings on his part came when she was laid up at home for a few days after tripping on a carpet on the lot and hurting her head. Roses, candy and get-well cards from Hardy were delivered to her bedside. A few days after she returned to work, she was typing up some script revisions when Babe Hardy came and asked to talk to her, pacing the floor as he said, 'I just can't contain myself any longer. I want to tell you the longer I know you the more impressed I am. Don't take this the wrong way, but it would make me the happiest man in the world if you would be my wife.'

Babe was being premature even then, for his divorce from Myrtle had not yet been finalized to the last jot of the law. It was only on 25 February 1940, two weeks after Viola Morse's accident, that the final decree was issued, three years after the original interlocutory judgment. Obviously in anticipation of this Babe had broken the news of the new love in his life to Viola, who did not take it well. In fact, her life was probably saved, after her eighteen sleeping pills, by her foolhardiness in driving forth down Wilshire Boulevard and landing herself in the hospital, where she was promptly treated.

Oliver Hardy and Lucille Jones were married in Las Vegas on 7 March 1940. They 'eloped', together with Lucille's mother and other members of her family, but keeping the wedding plans secret from colleagues and the press.

This was Babe's third and lasting marriage, and Lucille remained with him to the end. Her recollections are the only direct information we have of Oliver Hardy's intimate life, albeit close to the end of a long career. Lucille related:

We celebrated our wedding anniversary weekly, monthly and yearly. We were married at 4:35 on Thursday, March 7, so we celebrated every week at 4:35. We met, no matter where we were – if he had to be away, he sent me a cable on Thursday, even in mid-ocean, in '47 [*when Lucille was laid up in the hospital*], he called me from mid-ocean on the telephone in the hospital . . . If he was in the studio, he'd wait for the scene to break and then phone me . . .

With Lucille, Babe settled down to a life of domesticity. He was a natural homebody, shying away from social occasions, restricting his comedy to the screen and never being 'the life of the party'. He used to sit and watch people, Lucille said, just as he had as a child in Miss Emmie's boarding house in Milledgeville: 'He couldn't just go up and start talking to a stranger, he had to be approached . . . he was a good listener . . . He said to me, "People think I'm smarter than I am, but I'm not at all, you know that . . ."' Even at the age of forty-eight, Babe felt keenly the lack of a proper education, despite the fact that he had not stopped the MGM publicists producing a biography that claimed him as a law graduate of the University of Atlanta. He would make up for this by reading magazines, gaining a smattering of knowledge of many things, keeping up with current affairs. Despite their totally apolitical façade, both Babe and Stan were, like most of Hollywood's actors (apart from the ever contrary W. C. Fields and his coterie) devout fans of Franklin D. Roosevelt and the New Deal, a party loyalty they preserved into the post-war period, supporting Truman, and then Adlai Stevenson. But these were private beliefs. In religion, both were iconoclasts, and Babe remained a freethinking Mason.

Lucille described a typical day in Babe's life during the period of his post-Roach movies:

He was an early riser . . . up by 5:30 or 6 o'clock. He'd go into the kitchen and make the coffee and orange juice . . . very seldom ate breakfast . . . Go over his lines, drive to the studio. [He used to have a] custom-made Packard, but gave it up during the war . . . bought a used Mercury from a policeman . . . [When he finished work] he'd stop off for a drink some-place, usually at the Beverly Hills Hotel . . . then he'd come home, if it was still light he'd go out to check on the chicken house, on the vegetable gar-den . . . then we'd have dinner, and then we'd read the script for the next day's work . . . I would prompt him, read the other parts . . . then he'd go to bed early, maybe listen to the radio . . . he liked Jack Benny, George Burns, Eddie Cantor . . .

The backyard farm became more prominent in Babe's and Lucille's lives as the war and its shortages continued. They kept chickens, ducks, turkeys, a cow that had to be returned as it ate the fruit off the trees, and on one occasion two pigs, who were kept for meat but became household pets, following Babe around like dogs and nuzzling him, so that he couldn't bear to have them butchered. Way in the past, he had enjoyed quail hunting, but his only foray into big game, with colleagues Guy Kibbee and Douglas Dumbrille, was short-lived when he killed a deer and, in Lucille's words, 'felt like a criminal. He never hunted after that.'

'In the eighteen years I was married to Babe,' related Lucille, 'we went to one film. Gary Cooper was in it . . . *Sergeant York* . . .' Normal theatre seats were too uncomfortable for Babe, and on that occasion there were box seats which could accommodate his great bulk. There was a small theatre at home, with a proper screen and 35mm double-projectors, at which Babe, Lucille and guests would watch rented films, and also Laurel and Hardy pictures. He would, Lucille said, never go to the premières of his and Stan's movies, but wait for Stan or others to report back to him. Like many actors who claim not to care about such things, he read the reviews of the films assiduously.

Babe continued to be anxious about his bulk, and remained

uncomfortable with his own body. Lucille said, 'He didn't like to see himself on the screen, and he was self-conscious about his weight, his size.' During their marriage he tried several times to lose weight, but would then say, 'What the hell, I make a living on account of my size, what am I doing to myself? Trying to get myself out of work?' There could be no danger on that account, as Babe ballooned even larger as the years went by.

'He'd get up in the morning,' said Lucille,

and he'd get out of the shower, and he'd walk in and he'd look at himself in the mirror and he'd look at me and say, 'Do you love me?' And I'd say, 'Of course I love you, don't be silly.' [And he'd say,] 'How can you love a big fat slob like me?' I'd say, 'Don't talk about my husband like that.' I knew that it was deep inside, because he'd do that so often . . .

He was optimistic about life. Always trying to improve himself. He was always saying that he wouldn't look back on life. 'Cause he said he had an unhappy life all his life – his sister [Elizabeth] said he was always sad . . . It was partly frustration, because he wanted to do more than he felt capable of doing, maybe that was it . . .

The echoes of the derisive cries of 'Fatty' in the playground never quite faded away.

Before marriage to Lucille, however, Babe had another divorce to attend to, with Hal Roach, as soon as Stan and he completed their last movie for their long-time mentor, the aforementioned *Saps at Sea*. This was a low-key end – with a high-key theme – to a partnership that had lasted fourteen years.

To the film's credit, it has a welcome absence of the romantic entanglements that stretched out previous thin feature material. In structure, the film is two three-reelers strung together. In Episode One, Stan and Ollie are testers at the Sharp and Pierce Horn Manufacturing Company, an impossibly shrill environment that drives Ollie into a nervous breakdown. There follows a transitional scene with a stuck horn in their car, which prompts Stan to knock the engine out, and a convalescence at home with a visit by Doctor Finlayson – the last appearance by Fin in a Laurel and Hardy movie. Fin's medical examination involves checking Ollie's lungs with a rubber device that inflates to breaking point, and then explodes. Stan and Ollie's apartment, and that of the neighbour across the corridor, is all topsy-turvy, the plumbing crossed with the wiring, a radio-playing fridge, and a frost-encrusted wireless. The cause of this, it turns out, is cross-eyed Ben Turpin, who is the super in the basement, but the film wastes the asset of this vintage eccentric in a single, static shot. The episode wraps with a visit by Stan's music teacher, whipping up a fine trombone cacophony which goads Ollie into a new hysterical fit. The film's best gag then ensues, with Ollie dangling by the telephone out of the window, and Stan rushing downstairs with a mattress to put on his car, which, driven backwards, smashes into the lobby, leaving Ollie to fall to the ground.

Episode Two. The doctor has ordered a sea voyage, but Ollie cannot abide the ocean, so they rent a boat tied to the dock. They also bring on board a goat (shades of *Angora Love*), as Doc Finlayson has prescribed goat's milk. Here the film runs out of ideas, as all the script can come up with is the old escaped-killer gambit, Rychard Cramer playing the standard heavy, with whom they are stuck in mid-ocean after the goat has chewed the rope tying the boat to the quay. The thug bosses them around, ordering them to fix him a meal, which they make 'synthetic', with lamp-wick bacon and talcum-powder biscuits. Wise to them, the killer makes them eat the stuff themselves. At his wit's end, Stan remembers the trombone he has brought on board to practise, and which Ollie has cast aside. A few notes suffice to make Ollie go crazy, beating the killer senseless just as the coastguard cutter rolls up. To demonstrate the wheeze, Stan plays a few more notes to the coast-guard captain, driving Ollie to violence again. In the last shot, they are led by the captain, smashed trombone round his neck, to the cells, to be locked up with the thug they've just caught.

Thus endeth an era, as the end credits appear to the strains of the old saw, 'There's no place like home.' Before the film was completed, in fact very soon after shooting began, Stan and Babe formally filed papers for the incorporation of their own company: Laurel and Hardy Feature Productions. Attorney Ben Shipman was the third director of the company, and its treasurer.

The team had contracted to make four 'streamliners' for Roach, but had instead produced only the one, and one full-length feature. The deal, however, was for one year only, and the contract expired on 5 April 1940, one month after the marriage of Babe and Lucille.

It was, all round, a new start for Laurel and Hardy. Both Stan and Babe were upbeat, despite the drums of war sounding in the real world, off the screen. They were not to know that it was also a drumroll that signified the beginning of their own saga's end.

CHAPTER THIRTY-SIX

The Fox and the Huns

Nineteen forty was a strange year in America. Franklin Delano Roosevelt was nearing the end of his second term as President. The Depression was still a reality for millions of citizens, though there was hope for a better economic future. The radio and the cinema newsreels brought sombre news of the war in Europe: in the spring the Nazi forces occupied Denmark and invaded Norway, Belgium and the Netherlands. There was a new Prime Minister in Great Britain, Winston Churchill, soon to lead a wartime coalition. In June Italy joined the war on the German side, and the Germans occupied Paris. In the autumn Japanese armies occupied Indochina, and Japan, Germany and Italy made a three-power 'Axis' pact in Berlin. In November Roosevelt was elected for an unprecedented third term.

But still, America was not at war. Isolationists and interventionists fought on the battleground of public opinion, but it was not until March 1941 that Congress passed the Lend–Lease Act, which enabled Roosevelt to help Britain's war effort. Hollywood, in particular, was all atwitch about the dangers of US involvement. The Jewish moguls of the big studios, Mayer, Cohn, *et al.*, bent over backwards for fear of an anti-Semitic backlash in a country still rife with racial prejudice. In any case, the studios, MGM in particular, were still doing business with Germany. The exception was Warner Brothers, who had, in 1939, produced Anatole Litvak's somewhat lurid tirade, *Confessions of a Nazi Spy*. The Production Code still held, even in 1940, that the movie industry was bound by impartiality not to urge America to go to war.

On the other hand, Hollywood was being renewed, as it had always been, by a new influx of foreign refugees who joined the movie colony. Fritz Lang, Otto Preminger and Curt Siodmak were among many who fled Nazism during the 1930s and were to make their mark on the movies. Most significant of all, perhaps, a young Viennese, Samuel (later Billy) Wilder, arrived in 1934 and established a name as a screenwriter, not least of a movie directed by an older German immigrant, Ernst Lubitsch: *Ninotchka*, with Greta Garbo, made in 1939. Wilder was to carve out his own niche as Hollywood's most sophisticated satirist.

The jokes were changing, even if the urge to laugh in the face of dire reality was as powerful as ever. Another satirist, Frank Capra, having left the silent world of Harry Langdon, had prospered in the talkie era. Capra's *It Happened One Night* (1934) wrote the rules for a new genre of romantic comedy. His second Oscar winner, *Mr Deeds Goes to Town* (1936), perfectly expressed the Depression-driven dream of the common man beating the established bureaucracy. The pure clowns, W. C. Fields, the Marx Brothers, and Laurel and Hardy, faced competition, not only from screwball comedies, but from the bleak comedy of contemporary life.

Born in the 1880s and 1890s, the great vaudevillian clowns were all now in their late forties or early fifties. W. C. Fields, the elder anti-statesman of comedy, was sixty years old in 1940, the year of *The Bank Dick*. By now, there were other contenders for the clown's thrones, upstarts of one kind or another. The Ritz Brothers, Al, Harry and Jim, had been making comedies since 1934. Audiences, if not the critics, liked them. Two major stars of radio, Bing Crosby and Bob Hope, released their first joint movie, *The Road to Singapore*, in 1940. And another comedy team, coming out of late vaudeville and Broadway revue, Bud Abbott and Lou Costello, had made an unnoticed film called *One Night in the Tropics* in 1940, and were about to shoot a film that would kick-start their own successful career, *Buck Privates*, released in 1941.

Other contemporaries of Stan's and Babe's had long dropped out of the running. Buster Keaton was making a series of forgettable shorts and was about to join Harry Langdon on the begging circuit ekeing out a living as a hired gagman. Harold Lloyd had virtually retired after 1938's *Professor Beware*, only to return for a swan-song in Preston Sturges's ill-fated *The Sin of Harold Diddlebock* (aka *Mad Wednesday*) in 1947. Chaplin was following his own star into the brave provocation of *The Great Dictator*, which premièred in October 1940, and he would not make another film until *Monsieur Verdoux*, in 1946.

But Stan and Babe did not feel defeated. The final divorce from Hal Roach appeared to both as the harbinger of a completely new start. For the first time, they had their own production company. They could now work for themselves, and make their own deals with other studios. Their enthusiasm was not dampened by the lack of a rush of employers following their declaration of independence. Babe's new marriage, and Stan's preoccupation with constructing Fort Laurel, made them amenable to the inevitable lull. In the interim, they performed a sketch, 'How to Get a Driver's License', at a Red Cross Benefit in San Francisco on 22 August 1940. The audience's response was so satisfying that Ben Shipman arranged for a nationwide tour of the act, which took them from the West to the East Coast, from September to December that year. In Omaha, they were given the key to the city, but the city managers had to reclaim it in embarrassment because they had promised it to their next visitor of that day, Republican presidential candidate Wendell Willkie. The boys, in any case, rooted for Roosevelt.

The direct contact with the fans revealed to Stan and Babe just how popular they remained with the public. Stan was cheered up enough to have another go at his on-again off-again marriage with Ruth, which was announced by the press in January 1941:

'Fort Laurel has fallen,' beamed Film Comedian Stan Laurel last night as he brought a bride to his high-walled 'retreat from blondes' at 20213 Strathern Road, Reseda.

For drama and impact his announcement hardly vied with the tidings of Paul Revere or the message to Garcia. The collapse of the Laurel Maginot Line was fairly apparent to all concerned Saturday when Stan remarried the third of his four wives, Virginia Ruth Laurel, in Las Vegas, Nevada.

However, Mrs. L. Nos. 3 and 5, a shapely blonde with aquamarine eyes, made it official by giving the fort's main caserne a quick once-over and decided to redecorate the whole she-bang.

WE'LL GET ALONG SWELL

'It happened suddenly,' Stan explained his newest romance, 'like heart failure, or strike one. We hadn't seen each other for a year when Virginia called me up a few nights ago. I invited her out to the fort, and first thing we knew we had decided to do it all over again.'

The Reverend Albert C. Melton, of Las Vegas's Immanuel Community Church, performed the ceremony in the aptly named 'Hitching Post'. The hitching took place just in time, for Stan was sued only one month later by his ex-bodyguard, 'Tonnage' Martin, a six-foot-two, 395-pound geezer who had the dangerous task of interposing himself between Stan and Illiana, and was now claiming back salary of $2,700.

Longer-lasting help was, however, now on hand, as gossip queen Louella Parsons announced on 24 April 1941, during a visit by Stan and Babe to Mexico City:

Laurel and Hardy, who have been away from the screen too long, are booked to do 'Forward March', an Army comedy for Twentieth Century Fox. Señor Fat and Señor Thin, as they are called by their Mexican fans, were so popular in Mexico City that it opened all of our eyes to what these two comics mean to movie-goers all over the world.

Stan and Babe were in Mexico to attend a film festival, but also on an appropriately quixotic quest to make a deal for a Laurel and Hardy version of *Don Quixote*. This might well have been what Charley Chase called a 'darb', but the intriguing promise never was fulfilled. Instead, they had to make do with a hearty handclasp from the Mexican Foreign Minister, who said, 'The wit of such artists as Laurel and Hardy, Joe E. Brown and Mischa Auer has brought smiles to faces frowning under the weight of care and worry of life itself.' Darryl F. Zanuck appeared to agree, as he brought out his gold signing pen and put his moniker on the dotted line. The publicity directors of Fox explained the matter thus:

In the spring of 1941, Twentieth Century Fox was looking for comedians so that the studio might participate in the vogue for slapstick comedy, a result, probably, of war psychology. Laurel and Hardy were caught on a personal appearance tour, without film contractual obligations, and, in June, were signed to make two pictures a year for the next two years.

A familiar biography of Stan and Ollie, appended to this press release, ended curiously with a final tally of 'Measurements: Laurel – Height: 5 feet 9 inches; Weight: 160 pounds; Hair: Blond; Eyes: Blue. Hardy – Height: 6 feet 1 inch; Weight: 293 pounds; Hair: Brown; Eyes: Brown.' This was presumably to demonstrate that Fox had got something substantial for its money.

Twentieth Century Fox had long been a somewhat maverick company. The original Fox company, founded by film pioneer William Fox in 1913, was making about seventy films a year by 1917, covering the whole gamut of forms and genres – westerns with Tom Mix and Buck Jones, children's tales, steamy romances with Theda Bara. In the 1920s, directors such as Raoul Walsh, William Wellman and John Ford added lustre to the company, and in 1927 it enabled German director F. W. Murnau to make his Expressionist masterpiece, *Sunrise*. The talkies brought musicals with Shirley Temple and Alice Faye. In 1931 the studio reorganized itself, splitting into an 'A' and a 'B' unit, with the former handling a smaller number of prestige products, and the latter grinding out cheaper genre product, like the popular 'Charlie Chan' detective series, starring the most un-Chinese Warner Oland of Sweden, and its spin-off, the shorter-lived Japanese 'Mr Moto', played of course by a Hungarian *émigré*, Peter Lorre. The 'B' unit also employed the Ritz Brothers. In 1935, with founder Fox already out of the picture, a merger with Twentieth Century Pictures created the studio Laurel and Hardy now joined.

In 1941, the 'B' unit was headed by Sol Wurtzel, a dry veteran who had been with the company almost from its inception. He knew exactly what he wanted – cheap and fast pictures that would play as second features. Spare the trimmings; churn the sausages out of the machine; shoot first and don't ask any questions. The choice of a first comedy for the newly signed team was dictated by the principle of box-office precedent: Abbott and Costello had just made a big hit for Universal with *Buck Privates*. Fox's response: shoot a 'Buck Privates' for Laurel and Hardy.

The post-Roach features of Laurel and Hardy have always been a sore point for their many fans, involving much argument over the beer mugs and chicken fries. John McCabe, in his classic *Mr Laurel and Mr Hardy*, first published in 1961, dismisses the entire *œuvre* from 1941 to 1945 with barely a page, saying, through obviously gritted teeth, 'To evaluate the results as charitably as possible, these films should not have been made.'

Other aficionados have been even more charitable, none more so than Desert Son Scott MacGillivray, whose book, *Laurel and Hardy from the Forties Forward*, gives chapter and verse, from soup to nuts, of the despised Fox and post-Fox product. This tells us a great deal about a neglected period, but does not make Stan and Babe's 1940s movies any more delightful to sit through.

In one sense, the Fox contract and its consequences can be said to prove, in painful hindsight, Stan Laurel's lack of a solid business sense. McGillivray claims that Stan was not aware, when Ben Shipman made the deal, that he and Babe would end up in Fox's 'B' unit. If 'twere so, 'twere a grievous fault, and grievously did Stan suffer for it. Given the apparent vogue for 'slapstick' declared by Fox, the boys might have been snapped up by another studio – Universal, which had the new franchise of Abbott and Costello, or Paramount, which had the first Hope–Crosby 'Road' movie. But this evades the issue – that Stan and Babe were the stars of yesteryear, in a business that, then as now, fetishized the upcoming and the new.

Fox hired Laurel and Hardy precisely because they could get a tried brand on the cheap. After the first movie, the fee for each film, paid to Laurel and Hardy Feature Productions, was stabilized at $50,000 a picture, not, even in those days, a massive amount if it had to be split three ways with Ben Shipman and cover the company running costs.

Stan's major miscalculation, however, lay in a more technical area. The very size of the Fox operation, and its rigid bureaucratic structure, made it a very different working environment from the Roach lot. Lois Laurel told author McGillivray how she was taken aback, as a young teenager, at the procedures she had to go through to visit her father on the Fox set:

They'd give me a temporary badge, which you'd turn in when you left, and I was escorted to the sound stage. I was told I wouldn't be wandering around . . . where at Roach I'd be in the barbershop and down to see 'Our Gang', I could go where I wanted or fall in the lake.

At home, both Stan and Babe complained that the scripts written for them often made little sense. The Fox 'B' system was to assign writers, give the actors their texts, and tell them to get on with it, as quickly as possible. Lucille recalled how Babe would sit shaking his head in the evenings when he went over his lines, reading something out to her, and saying, 'You know I [my character] wouldn't say that . . .' But, as Stan claims to have found out too late, they were hired as actors, with no formal approval of story or direction. All real control had slipped away.

The problems are evident from the first ten minutes of the first

Laurel and Hardy Fox film, *Great Guns*. Stan and Babe are house servants of a young millionaire, Dan Forrester (played by Dick Nelson), who has been convinced by his relatives and doctor that he is a helpless victim of a mass of allergies, and is too weak to function in the real world. He receives a Draft Board summons, and passes his medical tests, so his faithful minions, Stan and Ollie, enlist with him, to protect him from any harm.

Stan and Ollie as loyal gardener and chauffeur? Surely not! But these characters are perfectly happy to be servile, revelling in their inferior status. Wherever they go, they act stupidly, and are met with jeers and insults. But does the worm turn? Not a millimetre. Once a worm, always a worm, seems the motto of the script of *Great Guns*.

The idea men at Fox, and their handmaiden, writer Lou Breslow, had come up with a firm proposition to change the boys' previous characters. No longer would they be grotesque children in adult form, imps of the perverse, the forces of chaos. Now they were to be 'realistic' characters, albeit exaggerations, but of recognizable types. This was to be followed both in word and substance: even the white, clown-like make-up that exemplified Stan and Ollie as the public knew them was to be changed for the more realistic look. The adult children were now to show their age.

The results, which should have been foreseen by the writers, and director Monty Banks, of silent-movie fame – whose last movie enterprise this was – were quite dire: The only way for Stan and Ollie to be realistic and yet still remain the same dumb innocents was to make them appear simply stupid, practically retarded persons. Gone is the Stan that once said to Ollie, 'You know how dumb I used to be? Well, I'm better now.' These idiots are too dumb to know that they're dumb, or ever were. When lectured by the bullying sergeant, Ollie in uniform says, 'Maybe they'll put me in the Intelligence Corpse.' The sarge, pointing to Stan: 'Brother, you're with him now.'

On it goes, the parade of imbecility, wooden supporting actors and hackneyed scenes. To pep things up, the writers supplied Stan with a pet crow, Penelope, who follows them wherever they go and is the mechanism that eventually saves the day when the boys are taken captive during army manœuvres. The entire army background is, in fact, embarrassingly anachronistic, with the troops

Reborn in the Fox-hole – *Great Guns*

practising their cavalry prowess and breaking bucking broncos, displays of riding going along with stock shots of tanks, a somewhat lacklustre preparation for the defence of the nation. Very soon, indeed, America would be at war, and the horses would have to be left in the stables.

The lack of the old stock company is felt very keenly. Gone is Jimmy Finlayson; gone are the harpy wives, Mae Busch *et al.*; gone is the apoplectic Billy Gilbert, replaced by one Ludwig Stossel as the young millionaire's quack Dr Schickel. One blast from the past is old silent-film star Mae Marsh, in a small role as the young man's Aunt Martha. The cast list includes one Alan Ladd, as a customer in the army photo shop, slowly climbing the lower rungs of the ladder, and romantic interest is provided by sassy Sheila Ryan as the photo-shop girl from whose embrace the boys try and rescue young Dan. There are no 'Great Guns' in the movie, apart from some stock shots of cannon fire. The whole enterprise is more like a shower of squibs.

Despite all the above, the movie was a success for the Fox company and for Stan and Babe. Box office was excellent and *Variety*, which had often panned Laurel and Hardy when they were doing their best work, declared that *Great Guns* was 'as good as any Laurel and Hardy have made . . . The gags run riot, and the characteristic Laurel and Hardy antic has a lot of elbow room for a hilarious workout . . .'

The Fox Press Book went to town on promotion, under the log-lines of: 'THEY'RE DRAFT-DAFFY! THEY'RE DRILL-ERIOUS! YOUR FAVORITE NITWITZ WILL BLITZ YOUR BLUES AWAY!' and 'LOOK WHAT THE DRAFT BLEW IN!' The publicists invited theatre owners to –

Draw a bead on the army! Near an army camp? Then slant your campaign to affect the soldiers' attention. This is a picture about them, and they will find plenty to laugh and cheer about . . . fire your gun at the Laurel and Hardys in your camp – those poor fellows who are always getting into trouble . . . have the boys write you letters about the funniest adventures of these misfit soldiers. Limit these letters to fifty words or less, and let the writer of the best entry attend the opening night of 'Great Guns' as your guest together with three of his buddies . . .

It is not difficult to see how the looming shadows of war made both soldiers and civilians hungry for anything that would take their minds off what was just around the corner, especially if it featured old favourites. Many of the soldiers would have been weaned on Stan and Ollie. We should remind ourselves of the very different circumstances in which films were seen by audiences more than half a century ago. Where today we can endlessly reprise old classics on video and even newer media, where the 1950s and 1960s brought television to almost every home, and film buffs could run 8mm or 16mm movies in makeshift home theatres, the audience of the wartime 1940s could, in the main, see their old favourites only if they were featured in a new film. Re-releases were rare. Today we are used to the word 'memory' meaning a device that preserves texts, images, sounds. In the 1940s, memory was still all in the mind. And so even a bad or indifferent Laurel and Hardy movie was better than no Laurel and Hardy movie at all.

A more direct contribution to army morale was made by Stan's and Babe's personal appearances at army camps around the country. In November 1941, they went further afield, on a 'Flying Showboat' tour, to entertain troops in Puerto Rico, Antigua, Trinidad and British Guyana – the Caribbean 'theatre of operations'. Flying with Stan and Babe in a fleet of F-18s were Chico Marx, John Garfield, Ray Bolger, Jane Pickens and Mitzi Mayfair. This tour gave rise to an incident recorded by the FBI and quoted in my volume on the Marx Brothers, as it was filed under the name of Chico Marx. A 'morale officer', one Colonel Justin G. Doyle, reported a comment overheard in a Miami Hotel room, in which Mr Oliver Hardy and Mr Stan Laurel referred to their fellow touring actors Chico Marx and John Garfield as 'the two Communists'. The po-faced 'morale officer' was probably unaware of a concept called 'irony', as contemporary photographs show the whole troupe in comradely mood with the troops. But the military's fear of subversion, espionage, and what was becoming known as 'fifth columnists' was already part of the suspicious culture that would six years later spawn the rebirth of the dormant 'House Un-American Activities Committee', and wreak havoc among Hollywood's liberals.

The 'Flying Showboat' tourers returned to Los Angeles towards the end of November. On 7 December, the Japanese bombed Pearl Harbor, and on 8 December the United States declared war on Japan. On 11 December Germany and Italy declared war on the United States. America was in the war now, with a vengeance . . .

In January Stan and Babe embarked on another countrywide tour of their 'Driving License' sketch, appearing in cities from Chicago to Boston. On 20 February, Babe contracted laryngitis and the boys had to shelve the tour soon after and head back to base. When they returned, Lou Breslow had a brand new script waiting for them, based on a story by co-writer Stanley Rauh. Originally titled 'Pitfalls of a Big City', it eventually found its way into the world under the title A-Haunting We Will Go.

No one can find any rhyme or reason for this, as there is no haunting in the movie. Rather it is a tale of gangsters and skullduggery, with Stan and Ollie as vagrants who are being run out of town, and take on a job to deliver a coffin to a sanitarium run by a crooked doctor. Unknown to them the coffin contains the criminals' very live pal, Darby Mason, who has to get to Dayton, Ohio, to claim an inheritance without being caught by the cops. At the train depot the coffin gets mixed up with the casket of a stage magician, Dante. On the train, Stan and Ollie get hustled by a couple of petty crooks who sell them a fake money-expanding device. Too stupid to see the con, Stan and Ollie order huge meals in the dining car, and are rescued from the dire consequences of trying to pass the fake money by the generous Dante. In return, Stan and Ollie don silly costumes and become Dante's helpers in his act. Much havoc and confusion ensue on stage with the wrong casket; the crooks turn up and threaten our heroes; a corpse turns up in the coffin; Stan has vanished somewhere among the stage props; a detective turns up to unravel the murder; almost everybody gets caught up in a lion's cage, and Ollie finally finds Stan, magically miniaturized inside Dante's stage egg.

This senseless farrago was directed by veteran Alfred L. Werker, who had directed some not too terrible westerns in the 1920s and 1930s, and passable dramas, such as 1934's *House of Rothschild*. (His last movie would be *The Young Don't Cry* in 1957, with Sal Mineo.) Comedy was, alas, not his forte. Dante the Magician was an authentic stage act but the maestro was not a comfortable screen performer. The supporting performances were wooden, the dialogue below the standard of the weakest 'B' movie, and the direction somnambulant at best. The miniaturization of Stan, however, might be seen to represent another terrible moment of self-knowledge for the man who had hatched so many great gags in a career stretching back for over twenty-five years, only to end up laying this egg.

What had gone wrong? And was there some real saving magic that could put things right, even at this late stage?

CHAPTER THIRTY-SEVEN

Nothing But Trouble

If the verdict on Stan Laurel's and Oliver Hardy's post-Roach films is that they 'should not have been made', it invites the question of what else could two screen comedians who had dedicated their lives to making comic movies do, having reached the not so very advanced ages of fifty-one and forty-nine? Where other performers of equivalent fame might have put away a sizeable nest egg for their twilight years, Stan's and Babe's cupboards were relatively bare. Stán had multiple alimony headaches, and Babe too was trying to wrestle with new claims for over $21,000 from Myrtle, a total of weekly payments of $250 purportedly unpaid since 1939.

To make things worse, the taxman was breathing heavily on his trail, suing Oliver Hardy in September 1941 for a total of $96,757 accruing from as far back as 1934. It was no consolation that said taxman, Nat Rogan Esq., was also targeting other Hollywood miscreants, namely Victor McLaglen, Raoul Walsh, ZaSu Pitts and Peter Lorre, albeit for much smaller sums. Myrtle's alimony case would drag on, unbelievably, into 1948, when Babe turned to Superior Judge Paul A. Eyman and symbolically turned his pockets out to show them empty, in court.

And so, though it would be rash to say of Oliver Hardy that he might face starvation, or eviction from the ranch-like home on Magnolia Avenue, neither he nor Stan could afford to stop working. *A-Haunting We Will Go* was shot in March and early April 1942 and Stan and Babe braced themselves for a third round with Fox's blinkered executives, although no immediate offer of a third film was forthcoming. As the boys' contract with Fox was non-exclusive, Ben Shipman began scouting for other studios that might offer a better deal, with a little more input accepted from Stan. In the interim, Stan and Babe joined the 'Hollywood Victory Caravan', a trainload of Hollywood's best and brightest, including Groucho Marx, Bing Crosby, Jimmy Cagney, Cary Grant, Claudette Colbert, Pat O'Brien, Merle Oberon, Joan Bennett,

Olivia De Havilland, Bob Hope and Bert Lahr. They opened in Washington on 30 April after a grand dinner with the President and Eleanor Roosevelt at the White House, and then toured a dozen cities, coast to coast, closing in San Francisco on 19 May.

The boys returned home to some crumbs of good news. The two movies with Fox, which posterity has panned so thoroughly, had actually pulled Laurel and Hardy back into the ranks of bankable stars. MGM, noting box-office receipts, began reissuing some of the 1930s short films as supporting programmes in the 1941–42 winter season. Scott McGillivray quotes an open letter from a theatre owner in Lyons, Nebraska, to MGM:

Everyone wants comedy and music to help them forget the hardships and heartaches brought them by the war. All studios should go all out on national defense and do their part to help America laugh. Keep our boys in uniform in good spirits as well as the folks at home and they will whip the Axis to its knees.

MGM obliged, and invited the old boys back for a reunion with their old mentors, if not with Roach himself, who was taking a break from his own movie business to join the army. In July 1942 he joined the Photographic Division of the Signal Corps, based in the old Paramount studio in Astoria, Long Island, with the rank of major. At the end of August, Hal married a new twenty-nine-year-old wife, Lucille Prin, his estranged former wife, Marguerite, having died at the age of forty-five, in March 1941.

In December Stan and Babe began filming their MGM comeback film, *Air Raid Wardens*. Stan was optimistic, as old pal Charlie Rogers had been brought in to augment the script already prepared by writers Martin Rackin, Howard Dimsdale and Jack Jevne. A fifth scribe, MGM staffer Harry Crane, was brought in to toss the salad. Another old acquaintance, Edward Sedgwick, who had directed Stan and Babe in a cameo appearance in the Roach mêlée *Pick a Star*, in 1937, was hired to direct the picture. Even better, in prospect, old hand Edgar Kennedy was brought in as one of the heavies. The whole enterprise seemed pretty promising.

Alas, the promise is not fulfilled. Film critic Wanda Hale summed up the feeling of many tried and true aficionados in the New York *Daily News*:

Unless Metro Goldwyn Mayer finds it worthwhile to take more pains with

Laurel and Hardy vehicles, *Air Raid Wardens* should end all Laurel and Hardy comedies.

Those are plain words, and hard, but, due to goshawful gags and situations and this team's now tiresome slapsticks, their latest, at the Rialto Theater, is pathetically unfunny. Remembering the times when I was among those who enjoyed Laurel and Hardy's monkeyshines, I look sadly at their earnest efforts to amuse in this new number. You can only laugh at the absurdity, the hopelessness of *Air Raid Wardens*. And certainly not heartily.

We are in Huxton, 'just a small town', with small ordinary people, apart from the town banker, J. P. Norton, a pompous skinflint, with his snobbish wife. Dan Madison, editor of the local paper, is rallying the town to play its part in the civil defence of the nation in time of war. Laurel and Hardy are the town ne'er-do-wells, who have failed in business after business, from fertilizers, to a pet shop, and now a bicycle shop, which they are closing to go to 'fight the Japs'. But they are rejected by all the services, and return, dejected, only to find that a brutish Edgar Kennedy, and his wheedling boss, Donald Meek, are taking over their shop to sell radios. What they don't know, yet, is that Meek is a front for a group of Nazis who are planning to blow up the nearby magnesium plant just outside the town, under the cover of a civil-defence exercise.

Even as the titled air-raid wardens poor Stan and Ollie can't hack it. In a minor mock exercise, they rough up the banker and land him in hospital, after disrupting Dan Madison's important town meeting by trying to conceal a dog in Ollie's pants. (Note that stuffing an animal down Ollie's buttocks seems to be a recurring motif in these films, as Penelope the pet crow had found her way there in *Great Guns*.) Once again, Stan and Ollie are not the ebullient clowns they once were, but the village idiots, self-pitying of their own limitations: 'I guess we're not smart like other people, but at least we can do something for our country – we can do anything that Uncle Sam wants us to do.' Eat your heart out, Forrest Gump! It seems Uncle Sam doesn't even want them to be air-raid wardens, so instead they snoop around their old shop and, suspicious of the new boss, follow him to an abandoned house, Moonbeam Inn, on Highway 51, which is a 'nest of Nazi spies'. So cosy is the nest that it even has a portrait of Adolf Hitler on the wall. Of course, they rout the Nazis and summon the citizens to the magnesium plant, where the villains are captured.

Air Raid Wardens – 'Gone to fight the Japs'

One feels trapped in a nightmare, in which familiar icons, old friends we have grown to love, like Edgar Kennedy, blunder about in a fog of incomprehension, looking not so much like professional comedians as like sumo wrestlers lost in a fog. Eddie Sedgwick, a contemporary of Babe's, had been directing movies since 1921. He directed Buster Keaton's last two silent pictures, *The Cameraman* (1928) and *Spite Marriage* (1929). Himself an old vaudevillian, who had performed in a family act, 'The Five Sedgwicks', with his parents and twin sisters, he should have been an ideal partner for Stan in this attempt to regain the passions of old. But there is no passion in *Air Raid Wardens*. An air of ineptitude and fatigue hangs over it all.

Once again, however, we, along with Wanda Hale, are confounded by box-office profits. Another critic, Theodore Strauss of the *New York Times*, noted 'a house densely packed with soldiers, sailors, family parties, and small fry aged three to thirteen . . . the folks in the Rialto pews are laughing their heads off . . .'

The august Library of Congress screened the film, as part of a policy of appraising all war-related movies, to check their content in terms of national security. They logged it as 'tiresome throughout'. But still the audiences paid cash to see it.

Reasons are not difficult to find. War anxiety is an easy phrase to utter, but if one looks at the events impacting on the American public during this period we can gauge just a little of its full meaning. During 1942 US forces fought fierce battles in the Philippines, the East Indies (Java and Timor) and the Pacific islands that became household names – Midway, Guadalcanal. Thousands of American troops were killed. Families who had last seen their sons, husbands, fathers at the end of 1941 had to face the terrible fact that many would never return. Worst of all, there seemed no end in sight, as the Japanese armies held stubbornly on to their gains. It may be unseemly to pass from such distressing matters to the antics of clowns, but, *in extremis*, clowns are sometimes all we're left with, when the pain has gone so deep.

And so Stan and Ollie continued to cavort on screen, and the studios continued to offer them employment in indifferent projects that amply served their modest commercial purpose. Twentieth Century Fox was ready to resume business with the boys, proposing two scripts that fell by the wayside, a story entitled 'Me and My Shadow' about Laurel and Hardy running a Coney Island wax museum (replete with so many Nazi spies and sub-plots that even Sol Wurtzel declined to produce it), and an 'Untitled' project set in a Swiss sanitarium where the news of World War II had not penetrated. Nevertheless, the Gestapo turned up anyway. Instead of these, the studio plumped for a non-wartime picture written by old hired hand Scott Darling, to be directed by another old-timer, director Malcolm St Clair, who had worked with both Buster Keaton and Rin Tin Tin, and had gained a reputation in the early 1920s as a master of sophisticated social comedies. Both Stan and Babe got on with him very well, and were delighted to work, after so much disappointment, with a craftsman who appeared to be on their wavelength.

The result was *Jitterbugs*, probably the best, among a bad bunch, of the post Hal Roach features. No Nazis, no fifth columnists, no army uniforms. Just Stan and Ollie, motoring down a hot desert road, pulling behind their jalopy a caravan emblazoned with 'LAUREL AND HARDY, THE ORIGINAL ZOOT SUIT BAND – A SYMPHONY

IN A NUTSHELL'. And a sop to current events: 'WE PLAY FOR VICTORY'.

They run out of gas, and some familiar bickering ensues, with Ollie reproaching Stan for always saying he's sorry and Stan replying, 'I'm sorry that I'm sorry, but if you're sorry you can't help being sorry' – a statement about the boys' circumstances that may have meant more than it seemed to. After they have unsuccessfully tried to flag down passing trucks, a car draws up with a cheerful young man, Chester, who is delighted to help them, demonstrating his own 'Eighth Wonder of the World' – a gasoline pill, which transforms water to petrol. Of course the boys are too dumb to recognize this is a con. All proceed to the nearby town, where Stan and Ollie are roped in by Chester to use their band – a cornucopia of mechanically played instruments, with Ollie on trumpet – to advertise his fake pills. The scam is rumbled, and the boys escape, but not before Chester has become entangled with a fair blonde, Susan, played by Vivian Blaine.

There follows a complicated plot involving crooks who have cheated Susan's aunt out of $10,000 and a plan by Chester, transformed by love into an honest beau, to get her back the money by playing the con men at their own game. These complex plots were always the downfall of the Fox pictures. Smart writers, like the Roach mob, or other vintage comedy scribes, knew that the best plots to wrap round comedians were simple confections, the flimsiest pretexts to allow the comics to do their stuff. Even as sophisticated a mainstream maven as George S. Kaufman knew, when faced with the Marx Brothers, that the best way to highlight them was to construct the clearest, merest plot lines, as he did masterfully with *The Cocoanuts* and *Animal Crackers*. No one can fail to grasp the plot of *Sons of the Desert* or *Way Out West*. But the Fox writers smothered Stan and Ollie with twists and turns that were both convoluted and badly thought out.

The best of *Jitterbugs* is the subterfuge wherein Stan and Ollie arrive at the New Orleans hotel where the crooks are quartered, Ollie breezing in with a ten-gallon hat and a broad Southern accent as 'Colonel Waterson Bixby, of Leaping Frog, Amarillo, Texas', and Stan being introduced as 'my valet, butler and general factotum, Potts'. Ollie is all smiles and elegant posturing as, for only the second time in his acting career, after *Zenobia*, he is able to act out his fantasy of the Harlem politician, Oliver Hardy senior. Stan wears a pince-nez, a kind of memory, possibly, of some of his roles in his solo period, such as *West of Hot Dog*. Ollie flirts with the con lady Dorcas as part of the master plan to entrap the crooks, downing his brandy 'to the fairest flower in the garden of Southern womanhood!' (Stan, of course, is trapped under the bed.) They dance, a brief moment of elephantine grace: 'Colonel, you dance divinely!' 'It must be the Gypsy in me! Kiss me, my little dove!'

There are even some quotable lines by Stan in the script, notably a good old-fashioned Stanism: 'You know, Ollie, I was just thinkin'.' 'About what?' 'Nothing. I was just thinkin'.' And at a later stage, Stan is made to impersonate Susan's Aunt Emily, in a reprise of the once common Laurel drag acts, dropping the guise of the idiot for a short sequence to assay a shrewd and somewhat sassy old maid. The writers, alas, omitted to supply a logical explanation for this sudden burst of lucidity. Or perhaps Stan took over at that point.

Stan's daughter Lois bore witness that both Stan and Ollie enjoyed working on *Jitterbugs*, huddling with Mal St Clair and Scott Darling at the end of each day's filming, going over the next day's lines, providing a proper input. It was a big change from the previous Fox titles, when Stan and Babe would be handed a finished script a couple of days before the shoot and told to get on with it. One can see that Babe, on screen, is very much at ease, revelling in the part within the part of Colonel Bixby. Stan does not look as comfortable, though he is much more at ease than in any other wartime film. The 'realistic' make-up, however, still renders him a somewhat puffy, middle-aged man trying hard to regain his paradise lost.

The end of the film may contain another comment of Stan's about his professional life: As the boys make their final moves against the crooks on a showboat moored to the dock, the boat floats off, on a highly unconvincing set of near-misses with process-shot ships in the New Orleans harbour. The crooks are foiled, and Chester kisses Susan, but the irate mobsters are still after Stan and Ollie, who dive overboard, thrashing in the water, and then sinking from sight at the final fade-out, with a parting cry from Ollie: 'We're going down for the third time!'

It was not, however, the final dunking, as there were still four more sinkings to come. *The Dancing Masters*, released in November 1943, was a product of the same team as *Jitterbugs*, director Mal St Clair and Scott Darling, but the script is, alas, stupefying. Starting with a not so bad idea, of Stan and Babe as masters of a dancing academy for young ladies, the story then descends into another wartime farce, involving the romantic male lead (Bob Bailey as Grant Lawrence), an engineer who is developing, in his free time at the munitions factory, a marvellous invisible ray. His lady love, Mary (played by Trudy Marshall), has drawn the short straw and got Margaret Dumont for her mother, though there is nothing useful for the Marx Brothers' great foil to do but flutter her arms and twitter inanely. The plot puts Stan in the position of demonstrating the death ray, wearing a walrus moustache and bearing the moniker of the non-English-speaking Professor Fendash Gorp.

Given Stan's closeness to Mal St Clair, there is no way he can escape totally from responsibility for this confusing mishmash, though he was not responsible for the segments reprising routines in old Laurel and Hardy shorts which were inserted in the movie by Fox executives: the auction scene from *Thicker than Water*, where Stan and Ollie use their savings to buy a grandfather clock, which is then wrecked by a truck, and a sequence at the end, where Ollie tries to raise money on an insurance policy on Stan he has bought from a couple of crooks at the beginning of the movie, by getting Stan to have an accident. This first turned up in the truncated silent *Battle of the Century* – Ollie trying to make Stan slip on a banana, only for everyone but Stan to slip on it. Here, Ollie tries all manner of subterfuges in vain, culminating in a trip to the beach to get on the rollercoaster, by way of a madcap – and dreadful process-shot – ride on a driverless bus. (Remember a similar scene in Ollie's 1926 solo, *A Bankrupt Honeymoon*? The bus gets on to the rollercoaster, but at Fox's 'B' budgets the resulting model coach ride is merely embarrassing, rather than comic or thrilling. A small aside for Hollywood talent-spotters: Robert Mitchum rolls along lankily as one of the crooked insurance vendors in the earlier scenes of the film. (This was, unbelievably, his fifteenth appearance in the movies.)

The Dancing Masters was followed by *The Big Noise*, once again with director Mal St Clair and writer Scott Darling. This has been long considered by the fans as the worst Laurel and Hardy film ever, and later earned inclusion in Harry Medved's and Randy Dreyfuss's 1978 compilation, *The Fifty Worst Movies of All Time*. Stan and Ollie are janitors in a detective agency who pick up a call from an eccentric inventor who wants two dicks to guard his latest invention, a super-bomb which will win the war. Meanwhile the usual motley crooks are out to steal the weapon, and Stan and Ollie get away with the bomb hidden in a concertina. One pointless thing leads to another and they end up in a plane which the army happens to be about to use for target practice. Up over the ocean, the plane is shot full of holes and they parachute out. On the way down Ollie spots a Japanese submarine. Stan drops the bomb and bags the Jap sub. The finale has Stan and Ollie seated on a buoy while Stan plays a tunesome ditty ('Mairzy Doats') on his concertina, accompanied by a shoal of dancing fish.

To try to sugar this bitter pill, St Clair and Darling inserted in the course of the movie several bits and pieces of old Laurel and Hardy routines: the upper-berth scene from 1929's *Berth Marks*, a sinister woman sleepwalking with a knife *à la Oliver the Eighth*, echoes of the long 'goodbyes' from *A Perfect Day*, and so forth. But the film could not be saved, and even the reviewers began deserting the sinking ship – Howard Barnes, in the New York *Herald-Tribune*, declaring that 'from any comic consideration, it represents the last stop on a dead-end street'.

But Stan and Ollie were a long time a-dying. Sol Wurtzel bowed out of producing with *The Big Noise*, and the studio, perhaps uneasy at the depths to which the Laurel and Hardy product had plummeted, sat on the film between April and October 1944, when it was finally released. In the interim, Stan and Ollie returned again to MGM, to take up a project that had been proposed soon after the release of *Air Raid Wardens*, but had been put aside.

The resulting film was released as *Nothing But Trouble*, and MGM archives, handed to the Academy of Motion Pictures Arts and Sciences library, enable us to chart a case history of one of these late Laurel and Hardy affairs. It is a sad chronicle.

In the beginning, there was a story outline, dated 7 July 1943, from director-to-be Sam Taylor, who had, believe it or not, co-directed five of Harold Lloyd's best silent features, from *Safety Last*

413

through to *The Freshman*, and then returned to direct Lloyd in *The Cat's Paw*, in 1934. He had worked with John Barrymore, Norma Talmadge, Mary Pickford and Douglas Fairbanks, but had stopped directing after 1935. This experienced and capable man produced the following:

This is merely a rough outline of a story idea, with very few 'plot' ramifications, since, in a Laurel and Hardy comedy, only enough 'story' is needed to tie together the 'gag' sequences.

It is proposed to treat this idea entirely as a *satire* on the present civilian wartime situation in which it is almost impossible to get help of any kind, either business or domestic . . . The picture will unfold exclusively from the viewpoint of Laurel and Hardy, two likeable but *very* stupid bums who haven't held a job in ten years, and who suddenly find their services at a premium – with employers fighting madly to give them a job and to *keep* them on the job.

We will open with a series of signs in downtown shop windows: 'Stenographer Wanted – Salary No Object' . . . 'Dishwasher Wanted – Good Salary and Half our Profits' . . . 'Bank President Wanted – No Questions Asked' . . . Laurel and Hardy are walking past these signs, convinced in their typically humble manner that there is no use in *their* applying for a job, because they've never in their lives held on to one longer than a day or two . . .

On 14 July one of the assigned writers, Robert Halff, presents his own treatment for this project, which the studio has named 'The Home Front':

Laurel and Hardy become employed as butler and cook in the home of Talbot Bullock, manufacturer of autogiros [helicopters]. Bullock is working on a device whereby he can speed up production of these planes. It is his belief that, in addition to manœuverability and ability to land on a small area, these planes may also achieve a speed of one hundred miles or more. As the story unfolds Mrs Harry Foster, a neighbour, attempts to get the servants by flirting with them. This leads to several amusing sequences. Finally she succeeds in securing Laurel and Hardy to work for her.

When the Bullocks re-employ the boys, Laurel and Hardy mix the bubble bath and the gelatin. After Mr Bullock is frozen in the bath tub he begs his wife to allow him to fire them and in a dramatic scene she acquiesces. Laurel and Hardy leave, first wrapping their lunch in the blueprints for the speed-up device. When, on a park bench, they realize their error, and also know that these are the plans that Mr Bullock was to take on a trip with him. They decide to get them back as quickly as possible. In doing so they get in the helicopter with which Mr Bullock has been experimenting and go in search of him. While in the helicopter they are in great danger and become involved in a series of gag episodes before they can finally return the plans to the manufacturer.

Instead of sacking Mr Halff, the managers of the Fox scenario department attached several other writers to him, and, on 31 July, an outline of a composite script was logged, credited to Halff, Wilkie Mahoney, Harry Crane and none other than Buster Keaton, roped in to earn his keep at Metro. This commences:

Ollie and Stan, who haven't done a lick of work in the past six years, are still innocently living in the Depression Era when jobs were scarce and labor plentiful. They decide to try their luck in an employment agency. The place is jammed – with frantic employers looking for help. When it becomes known that the boys want jobs, they are mobbed. Escaping into the next room, they are virtually kidnapped by Margaret Bullock, a charming society woman who smuggles them down the fire escape and out into her car. Returning home in triumph, she flaunts her two men servants in her envious neighbour's faces. Evie, the pretty blonde next door, is already scheming how to steal away the coveted servants . . .

This version introduces Mr Bullock, who has a model of his fabulous 'microcopter', which Laurel and Hardy mistake for a toy and give to some kids on the street. As the hired help, Stan and Ollie 'serve dinner, pulling every sort of boner imaginable' (shades of *From Soup to Nuts*), 'falling over themselves to give Evie the best of everything and ending up wrecking the joint and squashing a gooey cake over the enraged McAtee's head'. (Mr McAtee is, in this tale, the President of the International Aeronautical Association.)

Laurel and Hardy then fight a duel over Evie:

After all these years, their paths must sever – because of a woman! For Hardy, in his characteristically pompous manner, decides that there is only one *honorable* thing to do. Like the knights of old, they must fight a duel to determine which of them shall win her hand. Laurel, of course, cannot even comprehend what Hardy is talking about and fails utterly to understand why he should shoot him. Hardy, on the other hand, also feels quite miserable about killing his pal – and their resultant 'duel' should have a tinge of heart interest as well as offer splendid opportunities for another sequence of gags . . .

In the course of the duel, Ollie's pants are to be set on fire, but Evie's husband arrives, and Stan and Ollie escape in the micro-copter – no longer, one assumes, a child's toy:

The machine speeds through the air, skimming roof tops, careening crazily while the boys experiment frantically with gadgets and levers. They have all kinds of wild adventures in which at the last moment they are accidentally saved from disaster. Set for a landing over the Zoo, Ollie throws down a rope and Cheeta, a trained chimpanzee, climbs up and over the side of the cockpit . . .

Buster Keaton was given the assignment of producing gag sequences for this skylark, and the archived script contains a segment of four blue pages setting out his section of the script:

MEDIUM SHOT OF SHIP SKY BACKGROUND
Ollie pulls Stan into the ship, and helps him get the rope off of his wrist.

CLOSE-UP STAN'S HANDS
With the rope off, he throws it down in the bottom of the microcopter. We can see that his suspender buttons on the front of his pants have been scraped off, and the two ends of his suspenders are dangling free.

CLOSE-UP STAN AND OLLIE

OLLIE
What did the man say you did to make this thing go down?

STAN
(*Crying*) I don't know.

OLLIE
What's this?

He pulls out a bunch of web scraps, and on the end is a pack parachute. He turns to Stan.

Here, put this on and you can chute down to safety.

STAN
What? And leave you behind? I couldn't do that. You take it.

OLLIE
No, I wouldn't leave you here, either, so we'll try to land the ship the best we can . . .

LONG SHOT
Microcopter flying over the heart of the city.

MEDIUM SHOT
The ship drifts alongside a tall building.

OLLIE
Get ready to jump into that open window.

Stan climbs up, but just as he jumps, the ship moves forward so that Stan lands flat up against the building on a narrow ledge, and has a hard time keeping his balance.

Get to that window, and I'll throw you the hook.

MEDIUM SHOT STAN
As he tries to edge along the ledge, his pants start falling. With a little difficulty, he reaches the window, only to find it closed and locked. Starting back for the other window, which is opened, he is still having trouble with his pants and is keeping his balance. He finds that the best way to do it is to turn and face the building. Suspenders now hang from the back of his pants. As he eases up to the edge of the opened window, a lady is there to look him right in the face. A strong gust of wind blows his suspenders in over the window ledge. The lady slams the window shut, and the suspenders are caught in the jam. Stan makes one feeble attempt to open the window. He squirms around with his back to the building, facing Ollie.

OLLIE
I'll see if I can get any closer. Get ready to jump!

The wind keeps blowing Stan back . . . Stan falls and catches the undercarriage, catches the rope and swings on it . . . Stan struggles up, but now 'Tarzan's pet ape is hanging on to the end of the hook.' [??] monk ends up in the control seat with Stan and Babe slid back to the rear –

With nobody now at the controls, the ape takes command.

CLOSE-UP OLLIE AND STAN

STAN
Do you think we could reason with him?

OLLIE
I guess there is nothing to do but try.

They both start easing forward. Ollie stops.

> I have it. If we are nice to him, maybe he'll let us put that
> chute on him, and we can drop him out . . .

But Stan is yanked out by the chute . . . Ollie, looking back, screams.
The ape applauds.

CLOSE-UP STAN
Just dangling.

This is the only sample we have of a text written by Buster
Keaton for use in a Laurel and Hardy movie. It may even have been
funny, in execution. We will never know, because none of it is in
the movie. The 'microcopter' scenes were probably considered too
expensive to shoot, or 'Tarzan's pet ape' Cheeta was not available
for hire, or perhaps, by the time the movie went into production,
well over a year later, the MGM executives figured that Stan and
Ollie had done none too well with eccentric gadgets in the interim.
So poor Buster's scene hit the trash.

What eventually got shot, in the fall of 1944, was a typically
nondescript concoction. The opening gambit of the *'very* stupid
bums' who don't know the Depression is over remains, with Stan
and Ollie touting an album of all the Laurel and Hardy ancestors
who were, like them, chefs and butlers. Their 'kidnapping' by the
society lady, renamed Mrs Hawkley, was preserved, but the daft
duel was dropped. All that is left of the zoo is a scene in which the
boys, having forgotten to buy a steak for the Hawkley dinner, try
to steal a cut of meat from a caged lion. The 'microcopter' plot has
been replaced with flimflam about an exiled boy king, Christopher,
who dreams of being an ordinary American kid, and whose treach-
erous uncle, Prince Saul, wants to assassinate him. Stan and Ollie
come across the boy in a park and take him in, assuming he is an
orphan.

Stan and Ollie get sacked by Mrs Hawkley, and end up in a
mission hostel with the boy, but he is recognized and restored to the
wicked uncle. Stan and Ollie are arrested for kidnapping but then
released and invited to serve at an official reception, where Prince
Saul plans to get them to serve the boy a poisoned canapé. Stan and
Ollie mix up the plates, and the boy king discovers the plot. The

Nothing But Trouble – two cooks with the wrong recipe

villain forces young King Christopher, Stan and Ollie on to a window ledge, where they dangle above the city traffic, screaming in terror, before being rescued by the cops. No ape is on hand to applaud.

By the time *Nothing But Trouble* was released, in March 1945, the war in Europe was almost over, and Stan and Ollie had shot their last film for the Fox company, *The Bullfighters*, at the end of 1944. The film was set in Mexico City, to capitalize on Señor Fat and Señor Thin's popularity in Latin America, but it was shot entirely on the Fox lot and the climactic bullfight was a pick-and-mix of studio sequences, stock bullfight newsreels, and crowd shots from Fox's own 1941 Rouben Mamoulian film, *Blood and Sand*. Mal St Clair and Scott Darling officiated again, with another cock-eyed plot of Stan and Ollie as detectives from Peoria chasing a female thief, Larceny Nell, who fall foul of a bullfight tycoon they once sent to jail for twenty years, but he turned out to be innocent, and has vowed to skin them alive if they ever cross his path again. (Shades of Walter Long in *Going Bye Bye* . . .) The connecting plot point is that Stan is a dead ringer for the world-famous Barcelona bullfighter Don Sebastian, whom he is blackmailed into impersonating in the bullring. It was far from an original idea – Eddie Cantor had impersonated one 'Don Sebastian II' in the bullring twelve years earlier in his musical comedy, *The Kid from Spain*. But that had been directed by Leo McCarey, photographed by Gregg Toland, with 'ensembles' by Busby Berkeley . . .

The Bullfighters was released officially on 18 May 1945, eighteen days after Adolf Hitler died in his bunker in the ruins of Berlin, and nine days after the war ended in Europe. American soldiers were still fighting in the Pacific, and the real Big Noise of the Bomb that would end the war was still to be heard, three months ahead, in Hiroshima and Nagasaki. A moment in which even the clowns would have to hold their silence.

At the end of *The Bullfighters*, the wronged ex-convict, Muldoon, catches up with Stan and Ollie and carries out his threat, wielding his long knife. In perhaps the most gruesome of the boys' trick endings, Stan and Ollie stand, their familiar heads perched on clanking special-effects skeletons, as they clatter their bare bones towards the camera –

OLLIE
Well, here's another nice mess you've gotten me into.

STAN
(*Weeping*) Well, I couldn't help it . . .

OLLIE
Come on, let's get back to Peoria, where we belong.

CHAPTER THIRTY-EIGHT

Any Old Port

And Peoria welcomed them back. One would forgive anyone, among the Allied nations, for a tremendous sense of fatigue, as well as elation that the terrible years of war were over. Those who grieved, grieved, and the business of peacetime began to pick up, slowly. After so much sacrifice, people hoped to prosper, as the great burst of war industries had turned back the Depression. Yet there was a foreboding in the air, an unease about unfinished conflicts, the icy tendrils of what would become known as the Cold War drifting from the European fault line across the Atlantic.

There was a new sombreness in the movies too. Amazingly, during the war years, a new, more brash satire had flourished under the baton of one man, Preston Sturges, who directed his string of witty comedies from 1939 to 1944, including *Sullivan's Travels*, *The Miracle of Morgan Creek* and *Hail the Conquering Hero*, all stinging comments on the state of American manners, mores and patriotic posturing. But post-war audiences were fickle, and Hollywood struggled to find themes and stories that would appeal to a nation that had been thrust violently out of its shell into a global dominance.

Brazen comedians like Abbott and Costello ruled the comic roost, and would continue to do so, well into the 1950s. The Three Stooges was another team that thrived, with a continual stream of shorts from Columbia Pictures. But the font of Laurel and Hardy had run dry.

In hindsight, one can see this was inevitable. Stan and Babe could not continue churning out films of the calibre of their wartime output much longer, however loyal the audiences. The deal with Twentieth Century Fox had called for ten films over five years, but the five years had gone by with only six titles, and although the Fox bosses were ready to churn on, Stan and Babe decided to call it a day.

For Stan and Babe, personally, the after-effects of the Fox films (and the two MGM in-betweens) were somewhat different, reflecting their own distinct roles. As an actor, whose input to the films was mostly restricted to influencing character and gags, Babe Hardy could have gone on indefinitely, had the opportunity arisen. Among the post-Roach films, there are those in which he looks tired and demoralized, such as *Air Raid Wardens*, and others where he is as good as his old self, as in *Jitterbugs*, but in all cases he continued to be the consummate professional, always ready to give of his best. Stan, on the other hand, as the master of the blueprints, the maker of scenes and structures, the one-time director–writer, was much more damaged by the loss of control and the humiliation of having to give in to inferior talents. We need only to look at him on the screen, sometimes literally staggering through a routine that he knows is hackneyed, vulgar, demeaning or downright stupid, speaking lines that reflect the dumbness of the scenarist, not the character, to realize how painful the experience was. At times, he looks like an anguished puppet who knows there is a greater dummy than him jerking the strings, but knows also that the audience sees only his performance. He does his best, but who more than him understands that if the spirit is not there, the flesh will fail.

In his personal life, the war years of Stan Laurel are a kind of hiatus. Although Stan had remarried Virginia Ruth, for the third time, in January 1941, it appears that, once again, their married life was tempestuous, and the new bliss did not last very long. In June 1943, suing for maintenance of $765 a week, Ruth claimed that she and Stan had actively separated on 31 May 1941, after barely five months of marriage. Superior Judge William S. Baird heard her claim grounds of 'general cruelty', which in Hollywood could mean anything from domestic abuse to failing to feed the family dog. In later years, Ruth told biographer Fred Lawrence Guiles that she had had a disastrous wisdom-tooth extraction, which led to a chronic infection that made Stan lose all romantic interest in her. Ensconced behind the high walls of Fort Laurel, who knows what personal blights festered away. One can only point at the absence of allegations, or newspaper gossip, concerning any other Laurel entanglements until the end of the war as negative evidence that Stan and Ruth might well have been loath to cut the cord yet again.

The only other person close to Stan in the period immediately following the third estrangement of Ruth appears to have been a companion cum valet, Jimmy Murphy, an old variety friend who was employed by the Laurel and Hardy company and accompanied Stan on his night-club jaunts around Los Angeles. Murphy related in later years that he had once had his teeth knocked out in a rowdy argument defending Stan during one of these soirées, and had them replaced with dentures inscribed 'Property of Laurel and Hardy Productions', which, Glenn Mitchell reports, 'should be returned if he left their service'. Historian Mitchell also reports, intriguingly, that Stan had his own teeth fixed in the early 1940s, and his shy, tight-lipped smile in all the previous *œuvre* was most likely due to the terrible state of his chompers. This would put the dental 'raspberry' joke, in *Pardon Us*, in a more personal context . . .

Louella Parsons, who kept a watchful eye on all things Hollywood, and who was said to have passed the Fox executives malicious gossip about Stan and Babe because they didn't send her presents for Christmas, reported on 18 September 1943, that

Stan's current wife, Virginia Ruth, the one he married, divorced and remarried three times, is in the Cedars of Lebanon Hospital waiting to have an operation. Dr Krahulik, who is to operate, said it was necessary to have Stan's approval, since they were only separated but still legally man and wife. Roger Marchetti, Mrs L.'s attorney, asked Stan to sign the papers, which up to last night he had refused to do, his reason being that he couldn't find his lawyer and he never signed any paper without his lawyer seeing it first.

Even the minor maintenance suit dragged on in the courts, until Ruth's attorney, who may have made more money out of Laurel and Hardy than the comedians themselves, dropped it on her behalf in May 1945, stating that 'my client is ill and the worry of this suit has so upset her that she has decided to dismiss it'. Apparently the court had ordered Stan to pay $300 a month and $3,000 attorney's fees, but the contest had rolled on. Finally, at the beginning of January 1946, Ruth asked for a divorce from Stan. This was granted in Las Vegas on 30 April, and a week later Stan married Wife Number Four, Ida Kitaeva Raphael, in Yuma, Arizona, the favourite venue for Hollywood stars marrying Russian blondes.

Stan and his new wife met, so the tale goes, at one of the Russian restaurants which Stan had frequented with Illiana, and to which he was drawn by a kind of nostalgia, these venues being relatively safe to visit since Illiana had been literally run out of town in 1940. According to continuing press reports, Illiana was thereafter engaged in shaking up the East, rather than the West Coast, announcing a string of prospective marriages, to an artist, an attorney, and then to James B. Long, said to be a seaman and brother of the late Governor Huey Long of Louisiana. In November 1941 Illiana was put under mental observation after trying to leap out of the window of a New York theatrical agent, Eugene E. Fouvan, and, the poor man related to the police, insisting on singing to him. '"She just keeps on singing," he complained. "That's a lie," said Illiana, and burst into "When Irish Eyes Are Smiling".' She was promptly taken to Bellevue.

In the event, Ida Kitaeva Laurel turned out a very different samovar of tea from Illiana, despite the similar circumstances of the nuptials. These took place at 5 a.m. on 6 May after a night drive to Yuma, where,

routed out of bed by the couple, Justice of the Peace R.H. Lutes . . . performed the ceremony before hastily rounded up witnesses. The sixth [sic] Mrs Laurel was the widow of 'Raphael – the World's Greatest Concertina Virtuoso', who died several years ago. An opera singer, she has played in several films, most recently for Preston Sturges.

Notably, in *Hail the Conquering Hero*, as the singer ready to bawl out the anthem at the welcoming ceremony for fake war hero Eddie Bracken. She also had a small role in Sturges's ill-fated Harold Lloyd movie, eventually released as *Mad Wednesday*.

Stan's marriage to Ida lasted to the end of his life. At long last, he had a stable home environment. In any case, his days of carousing around the available watering holes would soon be over for reasons of health, as Stan was diagnosed with the early symptoms of diabetes. The unflagging energy that had characterized his working life was curtailed now, and he had to take things more easily.

Babe's marriage to Lucille was still prospering, the weekly wedding anniversaries still celebrated. Lucille told her interviewer, Randy Skretvedt, that the intimations of mortality had crept into Babe's and Stan's thinking during their earlier films at Fox: 'For the first time they began to feel that the world was passing them by, they began to feel their age. The idea of age had never occurred to them before, and they suddenly became conscious of that.'

Nineteen forty-six was a fallow year. Stan spent several months developing a script with writer Sam Locke, but no information has emerged about it. Stan's determination to settle down at last, with Ida, and 'no more divorces', was cemented by their selling Fort Laurel and settling in a modest house off Mullholland Drive. They were rewarded with an abrupt falling off of press interest and a drying up of the Louella Parsons type coverage. Stan was becoming a private citizen at last, and this was a welcome balm.

Babe tended his chickens and read his magazines. Lucille said, 'They still planned to go on filming, but didn't see the possibility of getting on with it.' Requests came in for participation in a radio show. Babe passed the proposed scripts to Stan, deferring as ever to his partner's judgement. Stan passed them back, saying, 'It's not for us, it's no good.' And nothing came of that either. (Two earlier radio projects, a skit with Edgar Kennedy in 1943, and a pilot for a 'Laurel and Hardy' show in 1944, had been recorded, but not followed up.)

Late in 1946, a job offer suddenly came from an unexpected source. Over the sea, in England, a great thirst for entertainment had sprung up after the end of the six years of war. The wartime Laurel and Hardy films were released to an audience that remembered Stan and Ollie in their prime, from the pre-war years. Val Parnell, manager of the Palladium Theatre in London, planned to bring over a set of American acts, and a young impresario, Bernard Delfont, thought immediately of Laurel and Hardy. Finding out that they had a written and rehearsed stage act ready made, the 'Driver's License' sketch, he contacted Ben Shipman in Los Angeles.

Stan, at first, was reluctant, the humiliations of the Fox and two last MGM films fresh in his mind. Perhaps he also dreaded seeing the damage done to his home country by the bombing and the rigours of the war. But it would be, he must have realized, his last chance to see his father alive, A.J. being at that time eighty-four years old. Late in 1946, both Stan and Babe signed the contracts.

Just before they were about to embark for New York and the sailing east, Lucille Hardy was struck down by a long-standing back ailment that required her to go in for hospital treatment on 2 January. Babe was distraught, but Lucille urged him to honour his contract. In the event, she joined Babe, Stan and Ida in England, towards the middle of the tour.

On 10 February 1947, Stan Laurel and Oliver Hardy docked at Southampton, aboard the *Queen Elizabeth*. Once again, as in 1932, the crowds turned out in force. At Waterloo station, thousands of fans crammed the railway station and, in the mêlée, Babe was separated from Stan and Ida and had to take a bus on his own, to the Savoy Hotel. The following morning, the visitors had their first taste of British post-war ritual, the line to get their ration cards.

The winter of 1947 was the fiercest Britain had seen for decades – snow, ice, winds and shortages, particularly of coal, which increased the misery. Arthur Jefferson and Stan's sister Olga were snowed in inland, at Grantham, Lincolnshire, and so the family reunion had to be postponed. Stan and Babe were to rehearse their sketch in London, but to open in Newcastle and Birmingham, before playing the London Palladium in March.

Up north, in his long-forsaken native habitat, Stan was shepherded by the mayor of Tynemouth to the former Jefferson family home at Dockwray Square in North Shields. On their previous visit, crowds had prevented Stan from getting near the house, but this time the square was empty. The bleakness of the surroundings, and the war damage evident everywhere, made for a gloomy homecoming. Nothing could have been a greater contrast to the new world of sunny California, from which Lucille, recovering from her operation, reported to Babe that the temperature was 27 degrees.

The welcome from the fans, however, was as warm as ever. Our indefatigable local hero, A. J. Marriot, in his *Laurel and Hardy: The British Tours*, has documented the trip of 1947 (and the others) to the last wave, handshake and cup of tea. From Newcastle to Birmingham, to London, then Dudley, and Liverpool, Morecambe and Blackpool, Glasgow, Skegness, Edinburgh, Hull.

Lucille Hardy remembers the trip as initially based on a two-week appearance at the Palladium, but in the event Stan and Babe spent nine months in Britain. In Glasgow the welcome surpassed any they had seen before, as the local *Evening Citizen* recorded:

No wonder Oliver Hardy blew most of his 'Thank you' kisses to the gallery at the Glasgow Empire last night. The whistles, yells, and cheers of welcome were loud enough to be heard at Charing Cross, and the audience just wouldn't let them go. Taken critically, the sketch is quite ordinary and some of the jokes are very familiar. But who wants to be critical with old friends like Laurel and Hardy?

Writer A. J. Marriot adds a further quotation from the *Citizen*'s reporter, Robert Hewitt:

If there's one thing I dislike it's snobbishness. And I'm sorry to say I've seen it shown by quite a few stars, some of whom refuse to mix with other artistes on the bill, and walk past stage crews as if they didn't exist . . . Let me tell you what a pleasure it is to meet Laurel and Hardy. Backstage I've found them to be probably the most unassuming, modest and friendliest top o' the bill stars who ever walked through the stage door. For them the stagehands would do anything. Every evening before they go, the Hollywood pair wander around at the back of the stage chatting to the lads. As one stagehand says, 'They're just a couple of regular guys.'

Stan was happy as a small boy to revisit the Metropole Theatre, where he had run about as the manager's son, taking tickets, doing all the errands and making up his mind that the stage would be his future. Glasgow was equally happy to adopt Stan as a local hero, an honorary Scot, despite his English, Lancastrian birth. The most famous Scottish star, Harry Lauder, who had been a vaudeville headliner when Stan was still in short pants, came backstage and invited the visitors to his home, Lauder Ha', at Strathaven. The boys obliged, and were photographed clowning about on the grounds of the old veteran's manse. Two nights later, Stan and Ollie turned up on the stage in kilts, having been serenaded on the occasion of a belated 'happy birthday' tribute to Stan.

On went the triumphal journey, in a balmy June, to Skegness, where Stan and Babe played the Butlin's holiday camp, and judged the local beauty competition. Then on to a longer reunion with Stan's father and his sister Olga, who with her husband, Bill Healey, was running the Plough Inn at Grantham. By this time, one assumes, the grand old man of the northern theatre circuits was past addressing his famous son as 'the boy', though no journalists were on hand to record this last reunion, a son's farewell to a previous century's champion of the cultural heritage of the 'common' people.

This was the longest period Oliver Hardy had ever spent away from the United States, and he too began to see himself as an honorary Scotsman. From his mother's tales he had gathered his maternal grandfather, Thomas Edward Norvell, had been an Edinburgh man who had studied at the university in Scotland's capital, but he found no evidence of this, which was not surprising, as Thomas Norvell had in fact been born in Georgia, as we have seen. But it is not difficult, given the general adulation, to appreciate why Babe would wish to put down virtual roots in the country that had nurtured his second half's, Stan's, creative life.

By June, Lucille had joined the touring party, and the two couples continued through the summer, and into the autumn, swinging back to London at the end of September, where they were given a banquet at the Savoy by the variety artists' organization, the Water Rats. Veteran English comedians Will Hay and Lupino Lane were on hand to toast the guests of honour. The tour then swung on, by ship to Denmark, Sweden and France, where more fans mobbed the Gare du Nord to cheer Stan and Babe into Paris. Then back to London for the Royal Variety Performance of 3 November, an annual show attended by the British monarch, a fixture since 1912.

Even as another winter closed in, Stan and Babe were reluctant to return home to uncertain prospects, lingering tax demands and the tag ends of the eternal alimony wars. They returned to Paris, at a time of great political turmoil involving constantly failing governments and a strong challenge from unionized workers and a powerful Communist Party. A General Strike made normal business in Paris impossible, and jokes were not the order of the day. As there was no public transport, the Laurel and Hardy troupe had to be ferried north out of Paris, in a hired Belgian bus, sneaking the bacillus of comedy in the dead of night across the border to Brussels. A special show, billed as the 'Hollywood Parade', but built around the 'Driver's License' sketch, played various Belgian towns and cities through the first week of January 1948.

Stan and Babe returned to the United States separately, Babe sailing directly from Antwerp and Stan returning to England for another two weeks, spending more time with his family. The two couples had not, in fact, spent all their time together during their British tour, sleeping, on occasion, at separate hotels. Gossip related that the wives were not always on the best of terms. They were, Lucille related, temperamentally different, Lucille being an energetic early-riser, whereas Ida Laurel tended to be a 'night person', staying up into the small hours, even cleaning the house well after midnight, and sleeping in till noon. This could have been a wise course, as the tour was gruelling, even without the winter glooms and political upheavals, a heavy schedule for much younger performers, let alone our somewhat grown-up boys.

When Stan and Babe returned to the US, they had been away for an entire year. During their absence a certain veneer of innocence had been stripped away from American life. The euphoria that had followed Victory in Europe and Japan had evaporated, and given way to the chill winds of a 'Cold War' with a new implacable enemy, the expansionist Soviet Union. The frostbite had spread over the country, from Washington to sunny Los Angeles, where the House Un-American Activities Committee was uncovering subversive threats at the heart of Tinseltown. Like two Rip Van Winkles, Stan and Babe had missed the entire brouhaha of the Committee hearings, the denunciation of Hollywood's 'Commies' by Ginger Rogers's mother, the interrogation of those who would become known as the 'Hollywood Ten' – Alvah Bessie, Herbert Biberman, Ring Lardner, Dalton Trumbo et al. – the hearings spreading even unto Leo McCarey, who wriggled out of a tight spot by declaring that none of his movies had ever made any money in Russia. 'Why not?' asked the Committee's chief investigator, Robert Stripling. 'I have a character in there they didn't like,' said McCarey, referring to his recent hit movies Going My Way and The Bells of St Mary's. 'Who, Bing Crosby?' asked Stripling. 'No,' replied McCarey, 'God.'

Apart from the strange FBI memo previously quoted about their 1941 Caribbean tour, we have no direct evidence of Stan and Babe's thinking about the Hollywood witch-hunt period – their absence had also covered the founding of the pro-free speech Committee for the First Amendment which encompassed luminaries from Humphrey Bogart to Groucho Marx. Babe did confide in a Hearst columnist, Henry McLemore, a fellow Southerner and member of the Lakeside Country Club, that his experiences in Europe – probably referring to the midnight run from Paris – had made him aware of the dangers of Communism at close hand. This had not, however, altered his domestic affiliations – both he and Stan, Lucille reports, were staunch supporters of Harry Truman for the 1948 presidential elections, against the Republican Thomas E. Dewey.

Unsurprisingly, these were not good times for comedy. Bing

Crosby and Bob Hope made no 'Road' movies between 1947 and 1952. Abbott and Costello made three movies in 1948, the aptly named *The Noose Hangs High*, the execrably titled *Abbott and Costello Meet Frankenstein* and *Mexican Hayride*. The Three Stooges were still Stooging. Danny Kaye made one movie, *A Song Is Born*, in 1948, though he had appeared in the seminal *The Secret Life of Walter Mitty* the year before. It was an appropriate metaphor for the desire to be someone else, somewhere else. Around the corner, the first Jerry Lewis–Dean Martin film, *My Friend Irma*, would soon loom, in 1949.

In this context, and with Stan now diagnosed as a full-blown diabetic, it seemed the boys would go their separate ways. Ida took over the daily care of Stan in his illness. Babe was building back the 90 pounds he had lost in the austerity-struck British Isles. Early in 1949, Babe took on a small role, as the town mayor, in a charity production by the Hollywood actors' Masquers Club of Maxwell Anderson's First World War play, *What Price Glory*. The play was performed for the Military Order of the Purple Heart, to benefit war veterans, under the direction of John Ford. Three of Ford's stock movie actors starred: John Wayne, Maureen O'Hara and Ward Bond. This led to Oliver Hardy's first solo part without Stan in a movie since 1939's *Zenobia* – a supporting role with John Wayne in Wayne's own production of *The Fighting Kentuckian*, a drama of post-Revolutionary America of the early nineteenth century.

The film was shot in the summer of 1949, and gave Babe a late opportunity, once again, to demonstrate his skill as a character actor in his own right. As Willie Paine, he plays a kind of Sancho Panza to Wayne's Don Quixote – John Breen, a soldier of a Kentucky militia regiment heading home after five years of service. In Mobile, Alabama, Breen falls in love with the daughter of an exiled French general. The inevitable villain is a riverboat mogul who has cheated the French exiles of their land. There is a great deal of ridin', marchin', shootin' an' posturin' with buckskins and coonskin caps. Babe clearly made an effort to be Willie Paine, and not Ollie, apart from one comic scene with surveyor's instruments in which he moves back and falls in a stream. In one elegiac scene he sits under a tree, musing about back home, slyly trying to dissuade John Wayne from getting entangled in the French girl's affairs. In an echo from the jail sequence in *Pardon Us*, Willie says:

I was thinkin' about Kentucky. The grass is knee high to a yearling. The blue jays are peckin' at the persimmons and everything is peace and quiet. Ma's bakin' bread so you can smell it all through the house. Down in the barn Pa's sittin' up with an old red mare that's groanin' way down deep. Tomorrow mornin' the neighbours'll come ridin' in to see the new foal.

BREEN

It's no use, Willie, they got my neck bowed.

WILLIE

Why can't we jest stop this foolishness and sit under a tree? The sun ought to feel mighty good on a bowed neck.

It is an easy scene to lampoon, but Oliver Hardy plays it straight, conjuring a might-have-been of a Walter-Brennan-type character that could have graced a peck of old classics. In the event, Babe might have been prepared to lie back under the Hollywood tree, with the sun on his bowed neck, except that post-World-War California required a little more resources for livin' than the new foal in the barn. So Babe picks up his musket and marches off with the Duke, joining the serried ranks of militiamen, stomping down the road and singing their old song:

> We have six hundred miles more to go!
> We have six hundred miles more to go!
> And if we can just get lucky
> We can wind up in Kentucky,
> We have six hundred miles more to go!

CHAPTER THIRTY-NINE

Utopias and Unpromised Lands

Oliver Hardy's last solo appearance in a movie was an uncredited cameo in a Frank Capra picture, *Riding High*, released in April 1950 (a remake of Capra's own 1934 film *Broadway Bill*). Bing Crosby played a racetrack lover who is told to give up his obsession if he wants to marry a rich heiress. Babe appears at the racetrack as a sucker who buys a tip from hustlers Raymond Walburn and William Demarest and then spoils the trick by shouting out the name of the tipped horse, 'Doughboy!', so loudly that everyone bets on it, including Walburn. When Doughboy finishes last, Babe is carried out on a stretcher, still calling out plaintively, 'Doughboy! Doughboy!'

Another might-have-been – seeing Babe in the company of Capra's best stock actors, though this was a late, waning Capra. It was fitting, however, that Babe bowed out of character-acting guying his own late lamented love of the nags. But soon after the shooting of the movie, a new opportunity presented itself for that prospect so devoutly sought, but almost despaired of, by both Stan and Babe – to make another Laurel and Hardy film.

Hindsight allows us to make judgements that could have been only guesswork at the time. Both Stan and Babe had the example of their dismal wartime movies to warn them of potential, if not inevitable, hazards. But Stan, even in his reduced, health-battered state, could not let go of the holy grail of the independent production, free of meddling studio bureaucrats, restrictive budgets, and the bondage of Fox's 'B' unit. The catalyst for the new project was an American financier, George Bookbinder, who realized that the European release of the last batch of Laurel and Hardy movies, which had been held up by the war, had created a special thirst, away from the United States, for a brand new feature. Both French and Italian film producers were eager to get their industries going again, and co-production deals were attracting government subsidies in both countries. Both the will, and the way, were there.

Ollie's last stand-alone – in Frank Capra's *Riding High*

And thus *Atoll K*, or *Utopia*, was conceived.

The tale has been oft told, and the diligent Randy Skretvedt has given a blow-by-blow account of the production of the film in *Laurel and Hardy: The Magic Behind the Movies*, so a brief account should suffice.

The question fans might ask is why, given the prospect of an independent L&H production, the movie's godfather, Mr

Bookbinder, did not turn to Stan to suggest a script. The necessities of the co-production, however, required a multi-national cast, and a story to fit. Mr Bookbinder brought in a Mr Paul Kohner, an agent with European contacts, who roped in his brother Frederick, who had co-written some scripts with a fellow scribe, Albert Mann-heimer. Paul Kohner already had a story concept, courtesy of one Leo Joannon, a French writer–director whose credits included *Adieu le copain* (1930), *Six cent mille francs par mois* (1932), *Alerte en Méditerranée* (aka *SOS Mediterranean*, 1938), *Document Secret* (1945) and so forth. He was a man of experience, but not, alas, with comedy, still less with American comedians.

The movie was supposed to prop up the American comedians with the French comic star Fernandel and the Italian clown Toto. In the event these worthies dropped out. So did Tim Whelan, first candidate for director, leaving Joannon with the chair and the megaphone. Actress Simone Simon, too, was an early casualty. Frederick Kohner arrived in France only to find he had co-writers, Rene Wheeler and Pierro Tellini, thus providing three languages, albeit not common to the three scribes.

Stan and Ida arrived in Paris in April 1950, but had to hang around waiting for the writers to figure out how to communicate with each other. The budget was no problem – Skretvedt estimates the film cost $2m., an astonishing sum in those austerity days for such a project. After three months a bizarre screenplay emerged about Stan being swept up from his California home by a typhoon that lands him on a Pacific island, which soon becomes a magnet for all the world's forces when it is found to be chock-full of ura-nium. In this early version, Ollie is washed ashore inside a grand piano. Hearing there was a script available, Babe and Lucille washed up aboard the RMS *Caronia*, in June, only to be whisked off for a Laurel and Hardy revival in Rome. Eventually Stan read the script in Paris and pronounced it 'rubbish'. He summoned a veteran gagman, Monty Collins, and began rewriting. By August the script was ready to roll.

Or so it seemed. The filming, which took place in Marseilles and at Cap Roux, off Cannes, was dogged by more multilingual obstructions. Leo Joannon arrived with Erich-von-Stroheim-style pith helment and puttees, and turned out to be completely impos-sible. He was indecisive to the point of incompetence, and his command of English was too poor for any meaningful communication. Stan called over his veteran friend, director Alf Goulding, from England, to 'supervise' the chaos, but was stuck with Joannon because of French union rules. Stan and Babe had to struggle not only with the director and the script, but with Fernandel replacement Max Elloy and Toto replacement Adriano Rimoldi, who had no comic flair at all. Instead of Simone Simon there was Suzy Delair, who was pretty, but not prominent.

To cap it all, both the stars became exhausted by an extreme heatwave, which affected their health. Stan developed a prostate problem, which caused him to be checked in to hospital in Paris, but he insisted on returning to the location, where the catering gave him dysentery. His weight plummeted, and he became virtually a walking wraith, a terrible sight to see on the screen.

Due to the vagaries of film distribution, which landed it in the public domain, *Atoll K* became, ironically, one of the most available Laurel and Hardy titles for many years, rather than suffering its deserved fate, which was to have been lost in the climactic on-screen storm that sinks the atoll and almost everyone on it.

The principle behind the film, potentially, was promising. In a post-war world, contemplating the smoking ruins caused by fanatical nationalism, intolerance and militarist frenzy, it was no bad idea to present a story of a group of stateless people, who sail off to a desert island where they proclaim themselves free of all laws, passports and taxes, only to find that commercial interests bring the full fury of the world's states down on them. It might even have been good for some laughs. It might even have been a reasonable vehicle for Laurel and Hardy, universal clowns. Perhaps it was tragic, rather than pathetic, that this kernel of an idea whose time had come was so profligately wasted.

Be that as it may, the product speaks, or rather stutters, for itself. *Atoll K* lurches from moment to moment like a drunk who has long forgotten the way home. The opening scene, set in London, has Stan and Ollie entering a lawyer's plush office to be greeted with large piles of money inherited by Stan, which are immediately reduced to a rump by the three lawyers clawing back their fees and a plethora of inheritance and other taxes. The scene then shifts to the dock at Marseilles, where Stan and Ollie claim a boat to go to a South Seas island, these being the two remaining items of the

435

Endgame – marooned on Atoll K

estate. Meanwhile a stateless man, Antoine, who has been shuttled around the world because he has no passport which would allow him to land, is caught hiding in a cage of monkeys. Stan and Ollie take charge of the boat, and Antoine becomes their cook. Another stateless man, Giovanni, stows away. The engine is lost, but Ollie's great trousers waft them on as a sail.

A storm lands the travellers on the eponymous atoll, where another waif, Cherie, has landed to escape her boyfriend, a ship's captain. Meanwhile, surveyors have found uranium on the island, and the refugees set up their own taxless state, with Ollie as president. Somehow, from somewhere, the world's riff-raff descend on the atoll, overthrow the 'government' and build a gallows to hang our heroes. Another storm erupts and the atoll sinks, as per script, leaving the boys, adrift on the gallows platform, to be rescued by Cherie's amorous captain. The boys finally reach their real island, where officials intervene again, confiscating all their supplies, along with the island, as taxes. And, for the last time: 'Here's another nice mess you've gotten me into!' 'I couldn't help it . . .!' and Laurel cry.

Weep, indeed, for the frightful vision of what was once the comic glory of the motion picture. Ollie is at his heaviest, and has totally lost the graceful movement he could summon even in the worst Fox films. Stan looks at death's door, as he almost was, since a makeshift clinic had to be set up for him on set, with Ida in constant attendance. The film is further marred by the almost universally bad acting, and direction, of all the supporting players, excluding Max Elloy, who is competent, if not more than that. Speaking different languages, the players were then dubbed, execrably, so that entire swathes of dialogue appear to be out of synch. As Stan himself wrote, in commenting to a fan who had written him in 1962 saying he had just seen *The Big Noise* – 'NUFF SAID!'

Atoll K trickled out into distribution, playing in France and Italy at the end of 1951 and in Great Britain, retitled *Robinson Crusoeland*, in 1952. It was not shown in the US until 1954, entitled *Utopia*, and then cut from 98 to 82 minutes, eliminating some dross with the romantic leads. It was, in another irony, the longest Laurel and Hardy film, and by far the most painful to experience, despite more gallantry from fans who insist it has its funny moments.

Stan and Babe returned to the United States in the spring of 1951, both taking time off for recovery. Despite the pain, they put a brave face on their project, announcing to the press that

they have another Edith Piaf or Marjane in Suzy Delair, they're booking her for night-club appearances before bringing her to Hollywood for their next comedy . . . Come September, Laurel and Hardy return to Europe to star in a revue that will tour the principal cities of Italy. These zanies are so popular in that country that their old hit, *Fra Diavolo*, made twenty years ago, is in its third month at a movie house in Rome.

This was the greater irony, that as Stan's and Babe's prospects for a return to filming faded, their star was rising again in the east, a cinematic phoenix crowing from the ashes. The new medium, television, still available only in a minority of homes, began to recycle their repertoire. A TV distributor, Regal Films, obtained the rights to Hal Roach's releases, including those he had bought back from United Artists and MGM in 1944.

Neither Stan nor Babe received any payments of 'residuals' in these screenings, having been mere employees of Roach. But at least viewers could now see them in their prime, rather than in their decline. These reissues also had the side effect of creating more Laurel and Hardy titles than actually existed, as feature films and old 'streamliners' were chopped up into shorter episodes, with new titles such as *Where To Now* and *Horn Hero* hacked out of *Saps at Sea*, and *Block-Heads* shrunken into a two-reeler entitled *Better Now*. *Sons of the Desert* became *Fun on the Run* and *Way Out West* became *The Whacky West*, both chopped to 20 minutes. *Bonnie Scotland* became three separate shorts. *Fra Diavolo* was cut in four.

Television aside, Hollywood had become a new world, with the old studio system practically dismantled and the industry itself chopped up into smaller players. There was no way back in for those whose *modus operandi* had been to find powerful backers who would give them their small corner of a larger ranch where they could grow their own modest yield. Stan and Babe's last offer, an RKO Technicolor musical entitled *Two Tickets to Broadway*, to be produced by Howard Hughes, lapsed because they were delayed in shooting *Atoll K*, and the film was eventually made with variety stars Smith and Dale. The only two tickets on offer were not to Broadway or Hollywood, but, again, sent by Bernard Delfont, for another tour of the British theatre circuits.

Utopia would indeed prove to be Stan Laurel and Oliver Hardy's last movie. From now on, there would be a bitter-sweet irony – the cyclical nature of Stan's and Babe's unfolding fates: for Stan, to return again, as the mainstay of his life and living, to the status of a jobbing vaudevillian, playing variety sketches on the stage; for Babe, ending up on the stage he had occupied only hesitantly in his earliest days, and that as a singer, not an actor. Now both were reprising the roots of comedy, the oldest form of the clown's profession, as travelling troubadours.

It took Stan and Babe the better part of nine months to recover from the sinking atoll. By the end of 1951, they felt well enough to embark on the transatlantic crossing, and face an arduous programme of personal appearances. On 28 January 1952, they disembarked from the *Queen Mary*, at Southampton, on the coldest day of the year.

The tour of 1952 was to be the first of two tours of Britain and Ireland undertaken by Stan and Babe, with their wives, Ida and Lucille, in the early 1950s. The second tour would commence in the autumn of 1953. Both trips involved specially written sketches, which Stan put together from the old repertoire.

The first, called 'On the Spot' or 'A Spot of Trouble', was a revision of the two-reeler *Night Owls*, of 1929, featuring Stan and Ollie as two tramps caught on a railway-station bench by a cop, who agree to rob a house and be arrested by him so he can get into his chief's good graces. We may recall this was the movie whose set Fred Karno visited when he came to the Hal Roach Studios, and note the faint echoes of Stan's primal 'Nutty Burglar' sketch, performed almost forty years before with the Hurleys, and Alice and Baldy Cooke. It was not a sketch that contained great dialogue (extended text can be found in John McCabe's *The Comedy World of Stan Laurel*) apart from the usual 'Here's another nice mess you've gotten me into.'

Leslie Spurling, rather than Baldy Cooke, played the cop in the 1952 tour, which touched all the bases covered in 1947 and then some, opening at Peterborough and proceeding to Glasgow, North Shields, Newcastle, Sunderland, Hanley, Leeds, Nottingham, Shrewsbury, Edinburgh. Another regular member of the touring team was Bert Tracey, the very same Bert Tracy who had acted with Babe four decades before, with the Vim company, in Jacksonville, Florida. Long back in his native England, and out of a job, he was taken on by Babe and Stan as their dresser.

One reunion that could not take place was with Stan's father, Arthur Jefferson, as A.J. had passed away peacefully at his daughter Olga's home in Barkston, in January 1949. He had lived to see his son world famous, an actor acclaimed beyond the wildest dreams of either father or son. But still it seemed that the old benefactor of the theatre arts and of the northern English working classes could never wholly endorse his son's adoption of the clown's mask, and of the vulgar esteem of Hollywood. From beyond the grave, he still seems to be muttering, 'What about the home and the hearth?'

After Edinburgh, the tour turned back south, to Birmingham and Southampton, then north again to Liverpool, and across the Irish Sea to Dublin. The local *Evening Herald*, quoted by A. J. Marriot, offered a detailed description:

On to the stage strode a little man wearing a broad benign grin, a pair of big baggy trousers, a battered bowler, and carrying what once upon a time might have been a respectable-looking violin case. The crowd roared with delight, only to break into a howl of mirth a moment later when he was followed by a somewhat large gentleman, with a worried countenance, and a gleam in his eye that spelled trouble for the little man with the benign grin. Yes, it was Dublin's welcome for those famous comedians, Laurel and Hardy. Personally I found them much more entertaining in person than in celluloid. In two short scenes they managed to convey their genius for the trade which has kept them in the forefront for so long.

Ireland was obviously in love with Stan and Ollie, as the movie, *Atoll K* (screened as *Robinson Crusoeland*) was being shown in Dublin at the time. Crowds besieged both the theatre and the hotels they stayed in, so that, in Belfast, they became known, according to the *Belfast Telegraph*, as 'the prisoners of Room 113'. This might well have had to do with both the heroes' exhaustion, as Babe and Lucille took off for a week's vacation while Stan checked in to the Musgrave and Clark Clinic in Belfast. A. J. Marriot has interviewed a nurse at the clinic, Nancy Jane Reid, who recalled that Stan, painfully thin,

seemed to be always writing. I thought perhaps he was writing a book, or the script for his show. He was a very nice writer. His room was at the end of the building. It had a big window which looked out on to a nice lawn, and a tall chestnut tree. He used to sit and look out quite a bit, watching the birds.

Nurse Reid also testified that Stan's diabetes did not keep him from feeding an old habit – hiding chocolates and sweets under his pillow. Other than that, she said, 'he was a real gentleman'.

The 'boys' continued, after Stan's two-week convalescence, to Sheffield, Brighton, Manchester – where they partied with Noël Coward – Rhyl, Bradford, Coventry and towns and cities in the south of England and Wales, wrapping up in Cardiff at the end of September. By the end of this heavy schedule they were really worn out, described as 'totter[ing] on to the stage' at the Theatre Royal in Portsmouth, but never losing their grace and delight at meeting with the fans and signing endless autographs. The tour, remained, however, resolutely provincial. Stan and Babe's only appearance in London was in the audience of a show starring a new young comedian, Norman Wisdom, whom they greeted backstage. Then they returned, in October 1952, aboard the *Queen Elizabeth*, to New York.

*

The second tour, launched eleven months later, began with an event that became a late part of the Laurel and Hardy mythology. Immigration laws prevented Babe, as an American citizen, from working in Britain before a full year had elapsed from his previous departure, but he could work in Northern Ireland, provided he entered overland from the Republic of Eire. This was the cause of the docking of Laurel and Hardy at the small port of Cobh, in southern Ireland, on 9 September 1953. Although there was no official advance publicity, everyone in the town knew that Stan and Ollie were coming. Children and adults crowded the dock, and all the ships and boats in the harbour sounded a welcome by every noise, hoot and blare they could muster. As the visitors struggled through the throng and into the town, its cathedral's bells tolled the 'Cuckoo' song, moving Stan and Babe to tears.

This time round, Stan was in relatively good shape, compared to the previous year, but Babe was considerably slowed down. His weight was well over 300 pounds, and the old well-timed moves were much curtailed. Critics noted that 'the old magic doesn't shine so brightly'. Nevertheless, their new sketch, 'Birds of a Feather', delighted the fans.

As whisky tasters – 'the more we drink, the more we earn' – Stan and Ollie soon end up in a room marked 'MENTAL WARD – COUNTY HOSPITAL', Ollie having proclaimed himself 'happy as a lark' and fit to fly with the birds, thus depositing himself out the window and into an offstage river. This plot line enabled Babe to play the rest of the sketch in bed with an ice-pack and his arm in a sling – echoes of the 1932 short, *County Hospital*. Remembering 'hard-boiled eggs and nuts', Stan has brought Ollie a couple of eggs and 'a nice onion and jam sandwich'. Ollie: 'I can't eat that.' Stan: 'You always said you liked jam, and you liked onions too.' Ollie: 'I do, but not together!'

The sketch then gets increasingly surreal as a nurse comes in to read Ollie's chart, which says, 'For the attention of Dr Berserk. Patient thinks he's a bird. Advise immediate frontal lobotomy and dissection of the cerebellum.' Dr Berserk, says the nurse, always operates successfully, 'even if the patient dies'. A character dressed as a caricature undertaker enters, measuring Ollie. The boys decide to escape, through the stage window, but then Ollie gets back in bed for the nurse. Dr Berserk enters and asks who's the patient. Ollie points to Stan.

I'm not the patient. He's the one who's insanitary.

How dare you make such a statement? Why I've never seen
you before in my life . . . My name is Ticklebottom.

Then what are you doing here?

I came to visit a relative and got in this room by mistake.

The doc is ready to let Ollie go, but the nurse intervenes, and,
finding the two eggs Stan has brought Ollie, produces them as
evidence he still thinks he is a bird, since he has laid these eggs. The
doctor gives Ollie a potion to determine 'what kind of bird you
think you are, a canary or a buzzard', and the sketch wraps with
Ollie chirping, and two pigeons, covered in eggshells, emerging
from his bedside cabinet. As the script says: 'All take it big. Very
loud chirping sounds. Pandemonium reigns.'

As the last text ever performed by Stan and Babe, 'Birds of a
Feather' is a strange artefact. One might expect to find it on the
music-hall stage, c. 1890, rather than in the British post-war variety
circuit of 1953. It was the last gasp of Stan's old, incorrigible lik-
ing for bizarre, non-realistic ideas. For the last time, the albatross
hovered over Jimmy Finlayson's belly, pecking at the gas-filled
abdomen, before everyone plunges back to earth, and the pricks
and kicks of encroaching mortality.

The tour proceeded from Ireland to England, opening at
Northampton, then Liverpool and Manchester before touching
down in London, at Finsbury Park and Brixton. Newcastle and
Birmingham were next on the list. It was at Birmingham that a
young American student, John McCabe, caught up with the performance and dared to go backstage, initiating a long and friendly
discourse with Stan, which was to lead to McCabe's seminal 1961
book, Mr Laurel and Mr Hardy, and to the worldwide Sons of the
Desert. Leo Brooks, another youthful American fan, later Tent-dweller
and Stan and Ollie scholar, caught the show in February 1954. A
new generation, which was to spark off the Laurel and Hardy
revivals of the 1960s and 1970s, was girding itself for the task.

But even on this 'revivalist' tour the sense of decline was present. As in 1952, there were no bookings at major London West End theatres. The last venue of the tour was at the Palace, Plymouth, opening on 17 May 1954. The local *Evening Herald* reported that

Laurel and Hardy . . . look a little older, and are not as boisterous as they used to be – perhaps because Oliver Hardy was suffering from a chill and had to have penicillin treatment before the act last night – but all their old cleverness and that delightful craziness is still there.

The boys were scheduled to play Swansea, and close their tour there, on the 24th. But the opening show at Plymouth was the last. On the 18th, Babe had to cancel his appearance due to illness, and the doctors diagnosed that he had suffered a mild heart attack. The curtain stayed down, and Stan spoke to the local press about his own sorrow at disappointing the fans, saying, 'I am completely lost without Hardy. We do comedy sketches – situations. I am not a gag man.'

Within a few days, Oliver Hardy was fit to travel, but not to perform. The rest of the tour, which had been planned to continue for some months, was cancelled. On 30 May Stan and Babe and their wives took ship from Hull, aboard a merchant vessel, the SS *Manchuria*, bound on a tropical route across the Atlantic, towards Vancouver, via the Panama Canal. Twenty days later the ship docked at Los Angeles, unloading its by now fragile cargo.

It was the last tour of Laurel and Hardy. The final home visit of Stanley Jefferson, and the farewell performance of Stan and Ollie on stage or cinema screen.

CHAPTER FORTY

Twilight of the Vauds

Old actors never die, if their images remain. Before the cinema enabled us to preserve their best moments – as well as their worst – we could only guess at the impact great names of the past had on their audiences: David Garrick, the clown Grimaldi, Herbert Beerbohm-Tree, Sarah Bernhardt, Dan Leno, Little Tich, though of the last of these we have some flickering snippets of the motion pictures in their infancy. The past is still the most distant of countries, even though the movies have enabled us to view some of its quaint and outlandish customs. As for what happened off screen, we still have to grope away from the limelight, in the often misty memories of oral testimony, and into the archival records. As the story advances towards us in time, our heroes themselves step back into the shadows, celebrated as a kind of majestic absence.

A sombre sample of this retreat into the gloaming is Stan Laurel's and Oliver Hardy's last dedicated public appearance, in Ralph Edwards's television show, *This Is Your Life*, aired live on 1 December 1954. A particularly ghostly apparition, preserved on fuzzy kinescope versions, this shows Stan and Babe being ambushed by the camera in their room at the Knickerbocker Hotel – to which they were inveigled by Bernard Delfont and Ben Shipman – and invited over to the El Capitan Theater on Vine Street, a block away, from where the show was being transmitted.

In the event, it took longer than expected to get the slow-moving Oliver Hardy to the theatre, causing one of those embarrassing moments of live television in which a desperate presenter all but dies on air as he attempts to ad lib his way through a *faux pas*. 'Fifty million of your fans are eager to see your lives unfold,' burbles Edwards, though Stan and Babe seem noticeably less keen, having looked forward to a quiet night in their hotel room. A bedraggled crew of old acquaintances is then trooped on, the most lively of whom are Leo McCarey and Stan's daughter Lois. Stan graciously receives one Roland Park, who posed with him in his first public photograph at the celebration of the relief of Mafeking in Dock-wray Square in May 1900, and who reminisces about Stan's first comedy appearances in his Dad's ill-fitting long-tailed coat. Babe fails to recognize an elderly lady who is introduced as Mrs Horne, aka Alicia Miller, but she remembers him as a permanently happy and singing child in Milledgeville: 'Instead of carrying my books, I carried his so that he could dance and sing all the way [to school].'

Stan and Babe were rewarded for their graceful patience, and a spot of on-screen hat switching, with a book of the proceedings, a 16mm sound projector, two pairs of cuff links, and some gew-gaws for the wives, who turn up at the end, to round off the surprise. It is, all in all, a depressing sight, and Stan was said to have com-plained, afterwards, about being caught unawares. As ever, he was well aware that in order to be the Stan Laurel the fans called for, Stanley Jefferson had to prepare his act.

Plans to revive Laurel and Hardy were still not completely aban-doned. A BBC radio show, entitled *Laurel and Hardy Go to the Moon*, was scripted by British writers Denis Gifford and Tony Hawes, but this launch fizzled out when Babe's ill-health forced the curtailment of the 1954 tour. A series for television was suggested in 1954, and in 1955 a series of one-hour colour films, under the general heading of *Laurel and Hardy's Fabulous Fables*, was pro-posed for production with Hal Roach junior, who took over his father's studios in Culver City. Roach senior had been transform-ing his studio for television production since 1950, and was an early prophet of its eventual dominance, but he could not compete with the networks. The best deal he could get in television was from his son, who bought the whole shebang from his Dad for a reputed $10,000,000.

The absolutely final public appearance by Stan and Ollie was as a filmed insert in a 1955 BBC programme celebrating the British variety organization, the Water Rats. Stan and Ollie reminisced about music-hall and ended with a farewell to their fans. It was, indeed, the last goodbye.

In June 1955, before the BBC recording, Stan suffered a minor stroke, which temporarily paralysed his left side. Although he was to make a good recovery from this setback, any further TV projects were shelved.

The vital organs were a major concern for Babe too, since his

British illness. In 1956, he became so worried about the impact of his excess weight on his heart, that he underwent a crash diet, which reduced his weight by 150 pounds. From a massive 350 pounds, he shrunk to 210, with the result that, apart from having to shop for new outfits, he was physically completely transformed: The last photograph of Stan and Babe together, in 1956, shows a recognizable smiling Stan, but beside him stands a stranger, relatively trim, with flabby flesh replacing his double chins, thin silvery hair and a rictus of a smile. The Ollie that we knew for so long has disappeared completely, in accordance with doctors' orders and, with his vanished poundage, gone were any prospects of a revival of the act that depended so strongly on the physical contrast between the two.

John McCabe reports that friends of Stan and Babe who attended the last photo-shoot were so visibly upset by the total change Babe had undergone that he was terribly perturbed by their reaction, and became a virtual recluse from that day.

It is mightily ironic that Babe, who was always so self-conscious of his own weight and self-perceived ugliness, would suddenly appear shocking to his friends when he had, after a lifetime, suddenly shed the obesity that was the source of his pain. He must have been deeply touched, on his foreign tours, by the adulation with which both he and Stan were received, particularly in Britain and in Ireland. But it probably never occurred to Oliver Hardy that his fans actually considered him beautiful. Our classical standards of beauty are, of course, difficult to shake, but many might agree, I think, that Oliver Hardy's inner qualities, that intangible charisma that makes us empathize with his long, despairing gaze at us in his moments of humiliation and folly, rendered him enchanting in body as well as soul. It is far from the sexual allure of a James Dean, but it still works its charms. Babe, the professional actor, was so used to the camera pointing at him, that he took it for granted as a tool of his trade. But it is, as it has ever been, a magical lens, which transforms frogs into kings.

Babe's last few months of mobility were spent in a kind of seclusion, with only Lucille, Stan and Ida, Ben Shipman and a handful of close friends seeing him. On the morning of 14 September 1956, he suffered a massive and crippling cerebral stroke. The press announced:

Ex-Film Comedian Oliver Hardy, sixty-four, was admitted to St Joseph's Hospital, Burbank, early yesterday after having suffered a stroke at his 5429 Woodland Avenue home in Van Nuys. Hospital physicians have termed his condition 'poor'.

In the following days the newspapers reported a slight improvement, but he remained in the hospital for the next month. On 7 October, he was 'taken off the critical list', and, on the 13th, he was released in the custody of Lucille and a team of special nurses. Lucille brought Babe to her mother's, Mrs Monnie L. Jones's, home in North Hollywood. He was totally paralysed apart from minor movements of his left arm and leg, and could not speak. At some point, according to letters Stan later wrote to one of his regular fan correspondents in England, a cancer set in, which shrunk the once great frame even further, to less than 120 pounds, and he had 'no hope for recovery'.

Even in this terrible time, with death hovering, the mundane troubles of the clown did not cease. Lucille related that a process server, sent by Myrtle in her incessant campaign for an acceptable alimony settlement, came one day in January 1957 to the door. On being informed of the circumstances of the 'defendant', the appalled man withdrew with apologies.

Stan himself was still in recovery from his own stroke, and his distress can be easily imagined. He asked to see Babe if he ever became lucid, and Lucille called him whenever hope beckoned. But Stan could only sit by Babe's bed, trying to communicate in pantomime, trying to respond to the ever-so-slight fluttering of his partner's eyes and fingers. The two wives left them to conduct whatever telepathic moments could be conjured up from the past.

Babe died, after a series of convulsive strokes, on the morning of 7 August 1957, at 7.25 a.m. Cause of death was recorded as 'Acute Cerebral Vascular Accident'. Lucille told the press:

It was a blessing for Oliver. He is finally out of his suffering, and he did not suffer at the end. Oliver suffered another stroke Sunday, and a third, Tuesday, sent him into a coma from which he did not emerge. His heart just stopped beating.

An anonymous cutting in the University of Southern California's Doheny Library files preserves this tribute, from the day after:

447

We mourn the passing of Oliver Hardy as the loss of a great American artist in that most difficult and rare of all dramatic achievements: the ability to make people laugh.

His medium was slapstick, in which the authentic masters are very rare indeed. For here the comedian must understand deeply the pathetic smallness of the human ego, its unconquerable vanity and extreme fragility.

To do this demands insight, humility and creative impulse. Performers without these qualities often succeed in what passes for sophisticated humor. But the supreme talent for generating the curative tonic of guffaws is reserved to the great clowns alone.

Oliver Hardy was unquestionably one of these.

He has left us the priceless legacy of resounding ridicule – devoid of malice – at pretension, false pride and conceit.

We accept it with the strange feeling that this is the first time Oliver Hardy couldn't make us laugh.

A freethinker to the last, Oliver Hardy was given full Masonic rites at Pierce Brothers Beverly Hills Mortuary, at 1 p.m. on 9 August. The body was then cremated and the ashes interred in the Garden of Hope, the Masonic section of North Hollywood's Valhalla Memorial Park.

Stan did not attend the funeral, apparently on doctors' orders. The press quoted him as stating, 'What is there to say? He was like a brother to me. This is the end of the history of Laurel and Hardy.'

Ida and Lois junior attended, to support Lucille, along with Ben Shipman, and a small group of old-timers: Jimmy Aubrey, Joe Rock, Dick Cramer – the hard-faced judge from *Scram* – Babe London – Ollie's fiancée in *Our Wife* – Clyde Cook and Andy Clyde. Cameraman George Stevens joined Hal Roach and producer Harry Joe Brown, along with Babe's Hollywood friends Adolphe Menjou and Wallace Ford. It was a select crowd, which represented two generations of Hollywood's old guard.

And a great silence falls, in the Californian summer, as the survivor gathers his thoughts. Stan had moved from the small house he had bought with Ida in North Hollywood to a large house in Santa Monica (at 1111 Franklin Street), with seven rooms and twenty-four windows with venetian blinds, lawns and gardens. This house turned out to be too much to manage for two elderly retired people (Stan's daughter Lois had married an actor, Randy Brooks, in

1948), and in the summer of 1957, Ida and Stan moved to a one-bedroom apartment at 25406½ Malibu Road, forty feet from the ocean waves. From this address, and from the Santa Monica apartment at which he would spend his last years from 1958, 849 Ocean Avenue – a complex named 'Oceana' – Stan sent out a mass of letters to fans far and wide, but with a particular soft spot for those in his old home region.

Since 1952, during the British tour of that year, Stan had been corresponding with a Mr and Mrs Short, in Northumberland, England, who had caught Stan and Babe's act at the Empire Theatre, Newcastle. The Shorts had sent Stan and Ida carnations, and he replied directly from the Empire, Nottingham, and kept writing them for the next twelve years. In 1957 the Shorts sent Stan a photograph of one of the old Theatre Royals and Stan answered, on 17 May:

I remember the old theatre that was on the same site which my Dad was running, it was a very run-down affair – benches instead of chairs, sawdust on the floors, cement stairs to the gallery, gas was the only lighting it had, it used to play old-time melodramas and was nick-named 'The Blood Tub'. Anyway it used to do a wonderful business and the place was always packed . . . [Later] he invested a great deal of money & the new Theatre Royal was erected, the most modern theatre of its time – electric lighting, the floors were carpeted, tip up red velvet chairs etc. . . . Even had a nursery with nurses in attendance to take care of the children so the parents and others in the audience wouldn't be disturbed during the performance . . .

These memories, and the echoes of the old days of music-hall, are recurring themes in many of these letters, some written to very old friends who had surfaced from even pre-Karno days. Trixie Wyatt, who had shared the stage with Stan in his first paid theatrical performance as the Golliwog Ebeneezer in Levy and Cardwell's *The Sleeping Beauty*, in 1907, was the recipient of one of Stan's responses to a Babe Hardy condolence letter, dated 26 August 1957: 'Thanks for your sweet letter 18th inst. Yes, it was very sad about my dear partner Mr Hardy passing on . . . I shall miss him terribly . . . God bless him.' Stan adds a comment about the situation in England, as seen from Los Angeles: 'My sister told me about all the strikes going on over there – the world is unsettled, trouble everywhere, it's shocking, everybody so restless & unhappy &

fighting each other. Things have sure changed from the happy times we knew.' Stan was blotting out, nostalgically, all those shoeless miners' children his Dad had to clothe out of his own pocket, but it was certainly a happier time when one was seventeen rather than a health-battered sixty-seven.

On 16 May 1959, Stan wrote again to Trixie Wyatt, replying to her information about one of the old Empire theatres being up for sale: 'Yes, I'm afraid Variety is a thing past now. The TV medium of entertainment has taken its place, it costs less than going to the theatre & you avoid bad weather conditions & having to queue up possibly to see a poor show . . .'

Stan's letters, unlike those of W. C. Fields or Groucho Marx, were not vintage samples of the clown's wit seeping into the private as well as public life, but casual affairs, friendly notes to people who made contact with him as person to person, devoid of pretension or affectation. To another corresponding couple:

Dear Vic and Gladys,
Enclosed: Tape – symphony orchestra – thought you'd enjoy it . . . Got a big kick out of Tommy Gibson's gag re the Castor oil – incidentally, it's possible your dog is troubled with 'WORMS' not piles . . . You should check on this right away Vic.
    The swelling dept. has finally gone away but am still bothered with the diabetic business – I finally decided to go into hospital for a thorough examination – the cost of the room alone is $35 per day, so can only afford a few days – am hoping no more than a week . . . This 'Digitalis' I understand is very fine medicine – frankly don't know what it is but it sounds to me like an Indian Magician – 'THE GREAT DIGITALIS' who eats a bale of hay with the aid of a toothpick!! . . . Take care – God bless. As always –
                                                                                STAN

This letter was written in July 1964, and Stan had already vented to the Shorts his sad thoughts about the assassination of President Kennedy on 22 November 1963. So much had occurred and was occurring that was strange and alien to the jobbing comedian who had set out with the Fred Karno company to the 'New World' on 22 September 1910. In 1910 the Model T car was only two years old, and its wooden body was not replaced by metal until 1911. Demonstrations were taking place for women's suffrage, which would not be granted till 1919. Broadway star Marie Dressler moved hearts with her song, 'Heaven Will Protect the Working

Girl'. The *Ziegfeld Follies* of 1910 featured new recruits Fanny Brice and Bert Williams. William Howard Taft was President. Hollywood was a sleepy town, and even D. W. Griffith's Biograph company had barely began shooting some motion-picture shorts in California. Far from the madding crowd, the young 'electrician' Oliver Norvell Hardy was goggling at his nightly movie diet at the Electric Theater in Milledgeville, Georgia. Life was indeed simpler then, if as precarious for many people.

Facing the perils of modernity, Stan and Ollie had given us their view of a planet-busting bomb in their Fox feature, *The Big Noise*: an eight-inch round ball which can be hidden inside Stan's concertina, a thing of musical fakes and alarums. The Manhattan Project, Trinity, Hiroshima, Bikini Atoll (rather than Atoll K) and the H-Bomb were matters far beyond the purview of Laurel and Hardy. How would Oliver have greeted the Civil Rights movement of the mid-1960s, the battle for emancipation of those his father had fought and bled to hold down? Certainly the New South today claims him as its own, and we might be sure Babe, with his longing for reconciliations, would have embraced the New South. The saga of Laurel and Hardy is nothing if not the tale of everyman's survival amid the twists and turns of fortune.

Stan Laurel lived the twilight years that illness had not granted Babe Hardy. Many of his contemporaries came to pay homage to the man who lived modestly in a Santa Monica apartment and was listed in the phone book like any other citizen. Some who came calling felt he was a forgotten figure, embittered at the way fame had touched him but not left much in the way of the recognition that should have been his due. Others found a man full of life and fun, with that infectious giggling laugh that was his trademark, happy to be alive in the face of the ailments that fate had thrown like so many banana skins to trip up his fragile body.

Comedians and celebrities who felt they owed him a great debt visited and paid court to their crown prince – Danny Kaye, Peter Sellers, Dick Van Dyke, Dick Cavett, Jerry Lewis. The French mime Marcel Marceau, whom Stan had seen in Paris in 1950, during the preparation of *Atoll K*, was another adoring visitor. Randy Skretvedt reports that Jerry Lewis offered Stan $100,000 a year to be his comedy consultant, but Stan politely declined. Though not wealthy, between his own bank balance and Ida's, he had enough for his needs – although the above letter of 1964 does show that by then he was counting the dollars, if not the pennies. Most likely Stan knew he could not fulfil the professional needs of a hungry performer in a new, perturbing age.

Nevertheless, his mind continued to turn over, thinking about new ideas, new gags, innovations found in unlikely places. In a 1963 letter to his friends Vic and Gladys he writes:

Glad you got a few laughs out of 'MAD' magazine. Interesting about the 'TARZAN ROPE' idea – should be attractive to the kids if you can find some means to demonstrate it to them . . . Enclosed some more gadget ideas (was in the Sunday paper ad section) . . .

From one generation to another – one can see how *Mad Magazine*'s Alfred E. (Wot Me Worry?) Neuman could have been a cheeky child of Stan Laurel . . . Earlier on, in 1961, two events gave Stan a well-deserved feeling that the world had not entirely passed him by. John McCabe's long gestating book, *Mr Laurel and Mr Hardy*, was finally published and enabled the new generation to read about the clowns they were enjoying on their TVs. Stan had maintained contact with McCabe, delighted that someone was interested in writing about his art, not just his troubled private life. In the 1950s, and into the 1960s, however, there remained many difficulties in finding prints of the pre-talkie Laurel and Hardys. Another enthusiast, Robert Youngson, who specialized in restoring old newsreel footage and silent films, produced a compilation film, in 1960, entitled *When Comedy Was King*, including segments from films starring Chaplin, Keaton, Langdon, Fatty Arbuckle, the Keystone Kops and a host of others, and ending on Stan and Ollie's *Big Business*. This was a precursor of several more compilations, but the first to concentrate on Stan and Ollie's *œuvre*, *Laurel and Hardy's Laughing '20's* (1965), appeared too late for Stan to appreciate.

The second event that gave Stan satisfaction in 1961 was the vote of the Academy of Motion Picture Arts and Sciences to award him an honorary Oscar for his life's work. Stan was not well enough to attend the ceremony – his eyes were suffering from a periodic haemorrhaging – and Danny Kaye accepted the award for him.

Another 1961 landmark was a business deal for a television animation series, based on the Stan and Ollie characters, to be produced by Larry Harmon. This was far from the first time Stan and

Ollie had been cartooned – four Mickey Mouse shorts of the 1930s had featured their caricatures, and Mickey's actual creator, Ub Iwerks, also drew them in four separate works. (The earliest Iwerks were *Movie Mad* (1931) and *Soda Squirt* (1933). The first Disneys were *Mickey's Gala Premiere* (1933), and *Mickey's Polo Team* (1936). Full cartoon details can be found in Glenn Mitchell's *The Laurel & Hardy Encyclopedia*.) Stan and Ollie dolls were already rife throughout the land. The Larry Harmon series was to become one of television's most oft repeated shows.

Ordinary people, as well as celebrities, would be received cordially in the Oceana apartment, overlooking the sea. A cat can look at a king, and can surely share a bowl with the court jester, whose legacy belongs to the world. This classless approach was certainly something Stan inherited from his egalitarian father.

In 1962, Stan wrote to the Shorts:

Thanks for your nice letter 9th inst. The news report that I lost an eye is greatly exaggerated, I had a haemorrhage in my left eye a few months ago . . . I still have sight but of course it's weak – anyway am not discouraged – if it was good enough for Lord Nelson, it's quite good enough for me!!!

Lord Nelson, of course, looked out to sea through his blind eye and said he did not see the signal to cease battle. Stan sat in his chair and looked out to the Pacific Ocean, thinking what thoughts we cannot tell. Certainly his nostalgia for things gone by suggests he thought a lot about the old times. Many would like to think that he was mulling over and over in his mind new ideas for comic situations and gags that could be used in Laurel and Hardy movies, movies that could no longer be made, except inside the clown's still fertile brain. Although the drugs he was taking, and his illnesses, affected his moods, there is no evidence that his mind was anything but alert, well up to the end. He surely followed the rancorous events that overtook his old stamping ground, the Hal Roach Studios, which went into terminal crisis during 1962. In December the entire lot was sold to a real-estate company, and soon after the studios themselves were completely demolished. Everything was torn down, the administration buildings, the screening rooms where so much work in progress was viewed, the sound stages where Charley Chase, Thelma Todd, Jimmy Finlayson, Max Davidson, Clyde Cook, Stan and Babe and a host of others had cavorted, where such as Leo McCarey and George Stevens had learned their trade. All fell to the wrecking ball of development, and crumbled into dust.

It was perhaps no wonder that the blood rushed into Stan Laurel's eyes and refused to let him see. The clown who could not comprehend why the world was full of anger and strife would not have wished to look on at the full-scale war that a Democratic President, Lyndon Johnson, would unleash on far-off Vietnam. On the other hand, he missed the satisfaction granted to his contemporary, Groucho Marx, in seeing his old work widely revived and enjoyed by young and old alike – the old clowns rediscovered as prescient imps of a perverse and absurd cosmic flow. He might have looked on amazed as the boys and girls beat their tambourines in the jingle-jangle mornings of their self-declared 'Age of Aquarius', of which he and Ollie too would be among the patron saints. And he would have been astonished and bemused at persons, such as myself, who claimed him for art, despite his oft repeated statement: 'I mean, we were just two-reel comics. That wasn't art.'

Oh yes it was!

But even the old routines of music-hall have their mortality. On 23 February 1965, 'The Great Digitalis' finally failed to deliver his regular magic trick. At 1.45 in the afternoon, felled by a massive heart attack, Stan Laurel died. Like his partner, he had also been stricken by a cancer, of the palate, in his last months. Later press reports said his last words were a joke, to the nurse who was preparing an injection. 'I'd much rather be skiing than doing this.' The nurse: 'Oh, Mr Laurel, do you ski?' Stan: 'No, but I'd much sooner be skiing than what I'm doing now.'

Right at the end, Stan's fears were those of a small child, befitting the clown who most preserved the child's world to his end. The doctor's names for the dark angel who wielded the scythe were 'Myocardial Infarction, Massive (Posterior), Arteriosclerosis, Atherosclerosis (Advanced 12 Years); also Diabetes Mellitus – Brittle.'

The shell was indeed brittle, but the content remained. In the corporeal world, no one was left to say to Stan, 'Here's another nice mess you've gotten me into.' And he was no longer there to respond with the cry, the puckering of the face and the plaintive lament of 'I couldn't help it!' But as he flew up, flapping those flying deuces' wings the special-effects men had put on his partner twenty-five years before, we can be sure there was a familiar, large-bodied spectre to meet him, up above, tapping his great feet and shaking his head with a fatalistic resignation.

'You took your time,' Ollie might have said, sighing.

'I was coming straight away, but something happened . . .' says Stan.

'Well, come on and help me get through this gate,' says Ollie. 'It's so simple, even you can do it.'

And one might add the final notation of Stan and Ollie's last sketch: 'All take it big. Very loud chirping sounds. Pandemonium reigns.'

And CURTAIN.

Going Bye Bye

The Church of the Hills in Glendale, on 27 February 1965, must have looked like a house full of live ghosts. Buster Keaton was there, and Andy Clyde and Clyde Cook, and the studioless Hal Roach, and Roach stalwarts Patsy Kelly and Babe London. Joe Rock and Leo McCarey stood by as the second half of the grand act was eulogized. 'The halls of Heaven must be ringing with divine laughter,' said Dick Van Dyke.

Others had already departed. Jimmy Finlayson died on 9 October 1953, also of a heart attack. He lived alone, but breakfasted every morning with an old friend, actress Stephanie Insall, at her home. When he didn't arrive one morning she called, to find him dead. A fellow Mason, his funeral rites were held at the same Masonic Chapel as Oliver Hardy's. Old stalwarts Mack Sennett, Billy Bevan, Hank Mann and 'Snub' Pollard were on hand to say farewell to Fin. Of them, only veteran Keystone Kopper Hank Mann was alive at Stan Laurel's death. Hank outlived Stan by six years.

Jimmy Aubrey, the oldest of all the old-timers, born in 1887, lived on till 1984. Billy Bletcher, another great survivor, of Vim vintage, died, aged eighty-five, in 1979. Of the ladies, Dorothy Coburn, who made Babe fall in the mud hole in *Putting Pants on Philip*, and Anita Garvin, peerless at chasing a cherry round a plate, were long lived, the former checking out aged seventy-two, the latter handing in her plate at the ripe age of eighty-eight in 1994. Billy Gilbert died of a stroke aged seventy-eight in 1971. Charlie Hall had preceded Stan, departing in 1959. Edgar Kennedy had bowed out even earlier, aged fifty-eight, in 1948. Tiny Sandford, the cop with the triple takes and the useless notebook in *Big Business*, checked out in 1961. Charlie Rogers succumbed to a traffic accident in Los Angeles in 1960. Leo McCarey survived Stan by four years. Joe Rock died in 1984.

Of all the survivors, Hal Roach was the most stubborn. Like Adolph Zukor, the Hollywood pioneer who clung to the vital force until 1976, aged a hundred and three, Roach battled on, to have many a last word. When the press announced that Roach had died, aged one century, in 1992, it might equally have proclaimed, 'Hal Roach Resumes Production', or 'Hal Roach Set to Break New Flight Record.' The man who had started out driving trucks in Alaska in the kind of environment Charlie Chaplin was to lampoon in *The Gold Rush* had survived almost to the threshold of the twenty-first century, to the brink of the Internet age. He was single-minded, ambitious, politically naïve, but in tune with the mass audience's hunger for comedy. His was, indeed, a fabulous life, in the course of which he had created a consistent world, a comic legacy that has not been surpassed.

As for the personal partners:

Lucille Hardy remarried, to a retired business man, Ben Price, and lived on until 1986. Myrtle Hardy, despite her continued alcoholic condition, survived to the age of eighty-six, and gave up the ghost in 1983. Of Madelyn Hardy's date of death we have no verifiable record, as she faded out of the tale with her plaintive telegrams of the late 1930s.

Virginia Ruth Laurel appears to have remarried three times since her marriages to Stan Laurel, hitching up with Messrs Block, Gates and White (consecutively); the last named signed on in 1960. She died in 1976, Stan's daughter Lois remaining close to her to the end. According to John McCabe, Mae Dahlberg, still calling herself Laurel, died at the Sayville Nursing Home in New York State in 1969. A year earlier, he had interviewed her and received the tale of the laurel leaves of Scipio Africanus. 'That's how he got his name,' she insisted. 'It was that simple.'

Sic transit gloria mundi.

Ida Kitaeva Laurel died in 1980, aged eighty-two. She had continued living in the Oceana apartment in Santa Monica, standing guard over Stan's memory.

Stan's first wife, Lois, was the last to depart, at the age of ninety-four, in 1990. She was resident with her daughter at the time.

The merry-making Illiana's fate is less certain. Where she went, whom she married, divorced, remarried, drove crazy, remains outside our tale. A San Francisco death certificate records the decease of a Vera I. Ivanova on 7 February 1994. Her birth is noted as 6 November 1897, which would make her just over ninety-six years of age, another strange affirmation (which might have delighted W. C. Fields) of the preservative powers of alcohol.

And so they have all departed, both stars and supporting cast, leaving behind the usual jigsaw puzzle of memories, oral and inscribed. But beyond the memories there are the works, the living art of the movies, which the actors, technicians and producers churned out for fun and profit. Just two-reelers, Stan Laurel insisted, and a dash of feature films, made in the exigencies of ongoing business. At most, he would concede, a craft.

All the comedy practitioners of old saw it the same way. Working men and women, they turned up in the morning for their call and did the job they knew best how to do. None – not even Chaplin – aspired to the pretension of an Eisenstein or a Stanislavsky who would write books explaining the methodology of the film director or the actor. At most, they would propose some general rules of thumb, like a brief exchange between Stan and Oliver quoted in a *Sight and Sound* article by film historian David Robinson in 1954:

STAN: Keep a semblance of belief, however broad. Let your gags belong to the story: you must have a reason to motivate everything.
OLIVER: The fun is in the story situations which make an audience sorry for the comedian. A funny man has to make himself inferior . . .
STAN: Let a fellow try to outsmart his audience and he misses. It's human nature to laugh at a bird who gets a bucket of paint smeared on his face even though it makes him miserable.
OLIVER: A comedian has to knock dignity off the pedestal. He has to look small – even I do by comparison. Lean or fat, short or tall, he has to be pitied to be laughed at.
STAN: Sometimes we even feel sorry for each other. That always gets a laugh out of me – when I can feel sorry for Babe.
OLIVER: Me too, when I can feel sorry for Stan.

In our day, we have become very wary of that emotion – pity, an old centrepiece of the idea of compassion which has been philosophized into an out-dated oblivion. We are not allowed to feel pity for our fellow humans, lest we be accused of feeling superior to them. In a world that worships equality – in theory, if not in practice – the object of pity now more often rejects it, demanding not an emotion, but the delivery of a material compact. This may well be the apt shape of our political requirements in the 'global village'.

458

But the clowns have always frolicked in that part of our existence that material needs alone cannot satisfy. Unlike priests, rabbis, mullahs, or any kind of pastor, the clowns offer no succour in certainty, no solution or balm in an afterlife. In the here and now, they offer themselves, as sacrificial spirits, as objects of that part of our compassion that can realize the common flaws in us all. In Stan and Ollie we can pity ourselves without the reproach of self-aggrandizement. A king can look back at a cat. None of us can be totally certain that we can walk down the street without falling in the manhole. It's funnier if it happens to them than to us. Cruelty, too, is a part of comedy, but it is cauterized, with comedy's fire. It is no wonder that the early Christians forbade the sacraments to actors, who usurped the role of spiritual mentors. Nor that comedy is the most proscribed form of social comment in any dictatorship, past or present. Chaplin's lampoon of Hitler might have been disproportionate in the light of the horrors unveiled after the act, but it was a necessary element of the removal of fear. Once a tyrant is laughed at, and booed in the street, as Romania's Ceauşescu was in his last day of power, nothing is left but retreat and the fall.

If I appear to have made extravagant claims for comedy, it is because, in my own life, as, I am sure, in many others', comedy has had a major part in buoying up the spirits against the inevitable setbacks of life. Like Preston Sturges's ambitious but innocent movie director, Sullivan, my travels take me back to those earliest moments when funny things happened on a silver screen, and could be relied on to continue happening.

They appear to be trivial, and the comic practitioners, as always, eschew anything other than the urge to amuse and entertain. But remember that the great artists of our age, who are garlanded with radiant and detailed tributes, the Picassos, the James Joyces, the Pinters and Becketts, have all lauded, and been touched by the movie clowns of our times. In Samuel Beckett's seminal modern play, *Waiting for Godot*, first performed in 1955, two tramps, Vladimir and Estragon, are waiting along a country road –

ESTRAGON
I told you I wasn't doing anything.

VLADIMIR
Perhaps you weren't. But it's the way of doing it that counts,

the way of doing it, if you want to go on living.

ESTRAGON

I wasn't doing anything.

VLADIMIR

You must be happy too, deep down, if you only knew it.

ESTRAGON

Happy about what?

VLADIMIR

To be back with me again.

ESTRAGON

Would you say so?

VLADIMIR

Say you are, even if it's not true.

ESTRAGON

What am I to say?

VLADIMIR

Say, I am happy.

ESTRAGON

I am happy.

VLADIMIR

So am I.

ESTRAGON

So am I.

VLADIMIR

We are happy.

ESTRAGON

We are happy . . . What do we do now, now that we are
happy?

VLADIMIR

Wait for Godot.

Stan and Ollie knew all about waiting. Waiting on street corners,
on park benches, on the wharf, in cramped boarding rooms, in cus-
tomerless shops, at the employment office, in jail. Opportunity, and
prosperity, is always just around the corner . . .

460

Battered by an incomprehensible world, Stan and Ollie may be burdens to each other, but they are yoked together by the mysterious force of friendship. As they dance off into the sunset, realizing that all they were waiting for was each other, we can hear the echoes of Ollie's plea in *Towed in a Hole*: 'Here we are, two grown men, acting like a couple of children. Why, we ought to be ashamed of ourselves . . . Let's put our brains together so we can forge ahead! Remember: united we stand; divided we fall!'

And let the pratfalls go on.

Notes on Sources

Abbreviations

AJM   A. J. Marriot personal collection
AMPAS   Academy of Motion Picture Arts and Sciences, Los Angeles
FHA   Family History Archive, Mormon Church, Los Angeles, via
           David Rothman
FLP   Free Library of Philadelphia Theater Collection
LCM   Lord Chancellor Manuscripts, British Library, London
NYPA   New York Library of the Performing Arts, New York
RS   Randy Skretvedt personal collection
USCHR   University of Southern California, Hal Roach Collection

Prologue: 'No thoughts of any kind . . .'

xi   'Dear Friends', Jenny Owen-Pawson and Bill Mouland, *Laurel Before Hardy* (Westmoreland Gazette, Kendall, 1984)
xiii   'humor, in any form', USCHR, cuttings

PART ONE: TWICE UPON A TIME . . .

1   Once Upon a Clown

3   'The Censor frowns', Petronius, *The Satyricon* (Penguin Books, 1969), 151

4   'an impudent race of buffoons', R. J. Broadbent, *A History of Pantomime* (1901; rp The Citadel Press, New York, 1965), 62; 'He is a mixture of wit', ibid., 119

5   '[He] is an odd and fantastical being', ibid., 121–2; 'uses his folly as a stalking horse', etc., Beryl Hagill, *Bring on the Clowns* (David & Charles, 1980)

6   'an entertainment of the People', W. MacQueen Pope, *The Melodies Linger On, The Story of Music Hall* (W. H. Allen, 1951), 3

7   'I came into the world a mere child', etc. Dan Leno, *Dan Leno, Hys Booke, A Volume of Frivolities, etc.* (Greening & Co., 1904), 14

8   'BARONESS: Oh! That my first husband', etc. Gyles Brandreth, *The Funniest Man on Earth, the Story of Dan Leno* (Hamish Hamilton, 1977), 36

463

2   Fathers and Sons: Stanley

13 'previous to the raising of the curtain', *Consett Guardian*, 12 August 1892, AJM

14 'It seemed to have a profound effect', *Auckland Chronicle*, 28 October 1892, AJM; 'I told him never to darken my doors', *The World's Verdict* (1893), LCM

15 'JACK: I love you as I have never loved', *The Orphan Heiress* (1895), LCM; 'SAMMY: Yes sir, bring the macaroni', *The World's Verdict*, LCM

16 'The vestibule gives one the first real idea', [local press], 9 February 1900, AJM

18 'Work in the shipyards', *Shields Daily News*, 21 May 1900, AJM

19 'As Stan grew older', John McCabe, *The Comedy World of Stan Laurel* (Moonstone Press, Beverly Hills, California, 1990), 2

20 'Not a bit', *Picturegoer* (1932); AJM, cuttings

21 'his good lady', *Victualling Trades' Review*, 15 August 1901, AJM

3   Sons and Fathers: The Road Diverges

23 ''Oneymooners! Poor deluded creeter', etc., *Home from the Honeymoon* (1905), LCM

24 'Very soon Stan's number', John McCabe, *The Comedy World of Stan Laurel* (Moonstone Press, Beverly Hills, California, 1990), 11

25 'I removed my make-up', A. J. Marriot, *Laurel and Hardy, The British Tours* (A. J. Marriot, Blackpool, 1993), 18

26 'EBENEEZER: Ya! Ya! Ya!', *Sleeping Beauty*, LCM

27 'HAROLD: I say, Percy', *The House That Jack Built*, LCM; 'SCENE 3: Scotland Yard office', *Her Convict Lover* (1908), LCM

28 'SON: Bring me a ladder quick', *Amateur Fire Brigade* (1908), LCM; 'Mr Stanley Jefferson . . . is a first-rate', *Todmorden Herald*, AJM, cuttings

29 'ANGEL: I come from Arkansas', *Alone in the World* (1909), LCM

4   Fathers and Sons: Ollie – War and Peace

33 'Captain Joshua Boyd', etc., Thomas Earl Holley, *Company K, Ramsey Volunteers, the 16th Georgia Infantry Regiment, Army of Northern Virginia, Confederate States of America, the Officers, the Battles & a Genealogy of its Soldiers* (Wolfe Publishing, Florida, 1995), 14, 21, 246

35 'Oliver Hardy, Columbia's active and efficient', *Columbia Sentinel*, 25 April 1885; courtesy of Charles Lord, Grovetown, Georgia

5   Mother and Son: The Boarding House Boy

38 'The spirit of the gay nineties', Louise McHenry Hickey; *Rambles Through Morgan County* (Morgan County Historical Society, 1971)
39 'where real balls were given', ibid., 22
43 'There's very little to write about me', etc., John McCabe, *Mr Laurel and Mr Hardy* (Signet, New York, 1968), 41, 43

6   We Are Fred Karno's Army: What Bloody Use Are We?

49 'Her most important part', *Victualling Trades' Review*, AJM, cuttings
50 'I just didn't know what kind of comedian', A. J. Marriot, *Laurel and Hardy, The British Tours* (A. J. Marriot, Blackpool, 1993), 23; 'I was originally one of the "submerged"', etc., J. P. Gallagher, *Fred Karno, Master of Mirth and Tears* (Robert Hale, 1971), 23
53 'Mr Fred Karno . . . during a performance', *Era*, April 1897; 'a humorous donkey' ibid., 9 January 1897; 'The first scene represents', etc., ibid., 1 February 1896
55 'an original pantomime burlesque', etc., ibid., 10 January 1903
56 'The contriver of this clever sketch', ibid., 26 March 1904; 'Surely, guv'nor, you don't seriously intend', etc., Edwin Adeler and Con West, *Remember Fred Karno, The Life of a Great Showman* (John Long, 1939)
57 'we'll turn you out anything theatrical', etc., *New York Morning Telegraph*, 7 October 1906
58 'A gentle-voiced little man', Marriot, op. cit., 27

7   In the Temple of the Magic Light Beams

59 'A well-equipped picture exhibition', *New York Times*, 10 January 1909
61 'I always asked a man to get my ticket', 12 July 1911
62 'a real novelty, being a classical comedy', *New York Dramatic Mirror*, 16 April 1910
63 'I saw some of the comedies', John McCabe, *Mr Laurel and Mr Hardy* (Signet, New York, 1968), 43
67 'the Jew who raped and murdered', *New York Times*, 18 August 1915

8   Wow-Wows in Wonderland

69 'At ten o'clock on a Sunday morning', Charles Chaplin, *My Autobiography* (Pocket Books, New York, 1966), 120

70 'We had a lot of fun in those days', etc., John McCabe, *Mr Laurel and Mr Hardy* (Signet, New York, 1968), 27
71 'ARCHIE: Has the last train gone', *Skating*, LCM, 1909
72 'ARCHIE: I'm going to have a bath', etc., *The Wow Wows*, LCM
73 'Chaplin will do all right for America', *Variety*, 8 October 1910
75 'This class of pantomime must not be confused', *New York Mirror*, 22 September 1906
77 'We lived uptown', etc., Chaplin, op. cit., 127, 128

9   Rum 'Uns a-Roamin'

79 'The setting is a city square', John McCabe, *Mr Laurel and Mr Hardy* (Signet, New York, 1968), 29
80 'Then, like a couple of silly schoolgirls', A. J. Marriot, *Laurel and Hardy, The British Tours* (A. J. Marriot, Blackpool, 1993), 32
82 'We were playing *A Night in an English Music Hall*', etc., David Robinson, *Chaplin, His Life and Art* (Paladin, 1986), 96
84 'I wrote this act', John McCabe, *The Comedy World of Stan Laurel* (Moonstone Press, Beverly Hills, California, 1990), 16
86 'We are faced with a hero of shifting loyalties', Fred Lawrence Guiles, *Stan: The Life of Stan Laurel* (Michael Joseph, 1980), 53; 'We all got together to do our own three-act', McCabe, *The Comedy World of Stan Laurel*, op. cit., 18

10 Babe: 'All Broken Out with the Movies'

89 'Jacksonville is all broken out with the movies', Richard Alan Nelson, 'Movie Mecca of the South', *Journal of Popular Film and Television*, vol. 8, no. 3 (fall 1980), 38, NYPA
91 'Life-Motion pictures may be given', Joseph P. Eckhardt, *The King of the Movies: Film Pioneer Sigmund Lubin* (Farleigh Dickinson University Press, Associated University Presses, New Jersey and London, 1997), 30
92 'Overacted at times', quoted in Rob Stone with David Wyatt, *Laurel or Hardy: The Solo Films of Stan Laurel and Oliver 'Babe' Hardy* (Split Reel, Temecula, California, 1996), 3; 'a comedy that's about on the par', ibid., 3
93 'Jack Burns and Billy Hale', Lubin Bulletins, FLP
94 'Babe Hardy, the funniest fat comedian', Stone and Wyatt, op. cit., 29
99 'While Babe generally disliked New York City', ibid., 104

11 Vim and Vigour – or Straddling the Home Plates

102 'PLAY BALL: SOME BASEBALL', etc., RS, cuttings, undated

104 'Dear Halle', USCHR; 'Ethel, Hiram Gothrock's daughter', Rob Stone with David Wyatt, *Laurel or Hardy: The Solo Films of Stan Laurel and Oliver 'Babe' Hardy* (Split Reel, Temecula, California, 1996), 117

111 'A public is supposed to last seven years', Brian Anthony and Andy Edmonds, *Smile When the Raindrops Fall, The Story of Charley Chase* (The Scarecrow Press, Lanham, Maryland, 1998), 88

12 The Laurel Wreath of Scipio Africanus – and Other Tall Hollywood Tales

113 'I can remember just how Stan', John McCabe, *The Comedy World of Stan Laurel* (Moonstone Press, Beverly Hills, California, 1990), 25

115 'Last week a harmless steamroller', Rob Stone with David Wyatt, *Laurel or Hardy: The Solo Films of Stan Laurel and Oliver 'Babe' Hardy* (Split Reel, Temecula, California, 1996), 400

116 'A two-reel comedy number', ibid., 402

117 'the films were pretty bad', ibid., 405

13 Just Rolin Along – Commence the Hal Roach Story

119 'A.S.: How did you get', *The Silent Picture*, no. 6 (spring 1970), NYPA

120 'When I was very young my grandfather', FLP; 'When I started my own company', ibid.

121 'We'd go out in a park', Tom Dardis, *Harold Lloyd: The Man on the Clock* (The Viking Press, New York, 1983; Viking Penguin, 1984), 35

122 'Mack was almost 100 per cent physical', *Screen Actor Hollywood*, winter 1987, 11, NYPA

126 'Much of the attraction centers', Rob Stone with David Wyatt, *Laurel or Hardy: The Solo Films of Stan Laurel and Oliver 'Babe' Hardy* (Split Reel, Temecula, California, 1996), 411

14 Flips and Flops: The Larry Semon Show

128 'Larry Semon, star comedian', quoted by George A. Katchmer

132 'You introduced her as Mrs Mae Laurel', *Los Angeles Examiner*, 19 November 1936, USC cuttings; ROCK: He [Stan] always wanted Mae', RS

134 'He would go to the cutter', ibid.

135 'Miss Myrtle Reeves', etc., RS

136 'cruel, inhuman and barbarous manner', etc., FHA

137 'COMEDIAN MARRIES', RS

15   Their First Kiss: 'Put 'em both up, insect, before I comb your hair with lead . . .'

142   'We had no studio', Rob Stone with David Wyatt, *Laurel or Hardy: The Solo Films of Stan Laurel and Oliver 'Babe' Hardy* (Split Reel, Temecula, California, 1996), 421
144   'Humor, in any form', USCHR
146   'Father throws suitor', Stone, op. cit., 296

16   The Handy Man

150   'Had she played the character parts', Joe Rock interview, RS
152   'Every now and then', etc., Rob Stone with David Wyatt, *Laurel or Hardy: The Solo Films of Stan Laurel and Oliver 'Babe' Hardy* (Split Reel, Temecula, California, 1996), 435
153   'consisted of one little open-air stage', Brian Anthony and Andy Edmonds, *Smile When the Raindrops Fall, The Story of Charley Chase* (The Scarecrow Press, Lanham, Maryland), 44
157   'James Finlayson had an excellent opportunity', *New York Dramatic Mirror*, 22 May 1912, NYPA

17   Somewhere, Over the Rainbow . . .

163   'one of the best comedies', Rob Stone with David Wyatt, *Laurel or Hardy: The Solo Films of Stan Laurel and Oliver 'Babe' Hardy* (Split Reel, Temecula, California, 1996), 315
165   'Larry was second only to Stan', John McCabe, *Babe: The Life of Oliver Hardy* (Robson Books, 1989), 52
168   'Dear Mr Doane', 7 April 1924, USCHR
169   'I had given Stan', etc., Joe Rock interview, RS
173   'SKRETVEDT: Did Percy [Pembroke]', RS

18   Into the Home Stretch: The Reluctant Suitors

178   '. . . a little wisp of a woman', Brian Anthony and Andy Edmonds, *Smile When the Raindrops Fall, The Story of Charley Chase* (The Scarecrow Press, Lanham, Maryland, 1998), 77
179   'We were together in fifty pictures', ibid., 78
181   'He started playing the piano', *Richmond News Leader*, 22 May 1940, NYPA; 'On still another occasion', ibid.; 'Anything I do would have to have humor', *New York Herald Tribune*, 31 November 1937, NYPA
183   'Stan used to laugh more', Clyde Cook interview, RS
184   'Gentlemen, I wish to inform you', 29 December 1926, USCHR
185   'One of the strangest sequences', 24 July 1926, reproduced in

Randy Skretvedt, *Laurel and Hardy, The Magic Behind the Movies* (Past Times Publishing, Beverly Hills, California, 1996), 46

186 'His sales talk dies a natural death', USCHR

187 'comedy burlesque of cowboy ways', Rob Stone with David Wyatt, *Laurel or Hardy: The Solo Films of Stan Laurel and Oliver 'Babe' Hardy* (Split Reel, Temecula, California, 1996), 550

PART TWO:

THE GLORY DAYS – 'TALL OAKS FROM LITTLE ACORNS GROW'

19 The Fruits of Toil

193 'HARD WORKERS WINNING OUT', *Wheeling* [West Virginia] *News*, 22 December 1929, RS

199 '. . . the secret . . . which lay in a reversal', Walter Kerr, *The Silent Clowns* (Knopf, New York, 1980), 322

200 'JIM: Clear as daylight', etc., *Home from the Honeymoon*, LCM, 1905

202 '"How about taking this guy"', RS; 'LAUREL AND HARDY TEAM UP', reproduced in Randy Skretvedt, *Laurel and Hardy, The Magic Behind the Movies* (Past Times Publishing, Beverly Hills, California, 1996), 75

20 From Babe to Ollie: The Metamorphosis

209 'Laurel and Hardy were children', interview with Anthony Slide, NYPA

210 'In *Flying Elephants*', Randy Skretvedt, *Laurel and Hardy, The Magic Behind the Movies* (Past Times Publishing, Beverly Hills, California, 1996), 90

213 'NEW STARRING TEAM', MGM press release, RS

21 Running Frantically through the Streets

216 'Get two men', MGM press release, RS

218 'HATS OFF', *Los Angeles Evening Herald*, 9 March 1928; RS

220 'The fact that the assault', Walter Kerr, *The Silent Clowns* (Knopf, New York, 1980), 327; 'I'm just sitting there', etc., RS

222 'the soothing guidance' Kerr, op. cit., 329

223 'They confessed to the joke', ibid., 330

224 '*You're Darn Tootin'* is the first clear statement', Randy Skretvedt, *Laurel and Hardy, The Magic Behind the Movies* (Past Times Publishing, Beverly Hills, California, 1996), 117

225 'The only place I could do it', etc., RS

22   Full Supporting Cast: The Lot of Fun

228   's–8 Kennedy, French', etc., RS
230   'By the terms of contracts', *Los Angeles Examiner*, 10 October
       1928; USCHR; 'I thought, "Oh my God!"', Randy Skretvedt,
       Laurel and Hardy, The Magic Behind the Movies (Past Times
       Publishing, Beverly Hills, California, 1996), 157
236   'The roof of the building', ibid., 137

23   Multiple Whoopee, or Wives and Woes

239   'OLIVER HARDY, FILM COMEDIAN', *Los Angeles Examiner*, 24 July
       1929, USCHR
240   'In her complaint', ibid., 25 July 1929, USCHR; 'Hardy hit him
       with a billiard cue', ibid., 13 March 1929, USCHR; 'OLIVER
       HARDY, WIFE RECONCILED', ibid., 17 September 1929, USCHR
242   '*For my precious on this our anniversary*', etc., RS
244   'Open on title', etc., typescript, RS
245   'Stan starts to suffer', ibid.
247   'Cut to the street', ibid.

24   Unaccustomed As We Aren't

254   'When we ran the dailies', interview with Hal Roach, RS
258   'Yegor, "the singing bandit"', Randy Skretvedt, *Laurel and Hardy,
       The Magic Behind the Movies* (Past Times Publishing, Beverly
       Hills, California, 1996), 180
259   'I get [to Argentina] and they', RS
260   'I hired him after working with Chaplin', ibid.
261   'I never knew that he was just the businessman', ibid.

25   The Song of the Cuckoos

266   'ROACH: Laurel and Hardy as a rule', RS
267   'We heard this one morning', ibid.
270   'In this film, the attempt to fix', Charles Barr, *Laurel and Hardy*
       (Studio Vista, 1967), 133
275   'I sent him a little sketch of my own', etc., *Picturegoer*, 1932, AJM

26   Chickens Come Home

280   'Wife of Hardy, Film Comedian', *Los Angeles Examiner*, 31
       March 1931, USCHR
281   'Incompatibility, the greatest nemesis', *Los Angeles Times*, 16
       November 1932, AMPAS; 'Stan Laurel, motion-picture comedian',
       unsourced, 8 August 1931, AMPAS

282   'Recently Hardy took a woman', *Los Angeles Examiner*, 6 July 1933, USCHR

285   'Stan used to call Henry Ginsberg', Randy Skretvedt, *Laurel and Hardy, The Magic Behind the Movies* (Past Times Publishing, Beverly Hills, California, 1996), 227

27 A Very Good Boy

290   'FIGHT TO GREET ACTORS', *New York Times*, 30 July 1932, NYPA

291   'A good boy', *Daily Sketch*, 24 July 1932, quoted in A. J. Marriot, *Laurel and Hardy, The British Tours* (A. J. Marriot, Blackpool, 1993), 46

292   'GREAT WELCOME AT BLACKPOOL', undated, RS; 'I must have shaken hands at least', ibid. (also AJM)

293   'CAR MOBBED', *Yorkshire Evening News*, 4 August 1932, RS; 'We never thought it would be', *Leeds Mercury*, 4 August 1932, RS; 'Their great delight at', etc., RS, cuttings; 'The slapstick of today', *East Anglian Times*, undated, RS

294   'My hope has been realized', *Middlesex County Times*, undated, RS

28 Busy Bodies and Devil's Brothers

295   'a subtle Utopian fantasy', Jonathan Sanders, *Another Fine Dress: Role-Play in the Films of Laurel and Hardy* (Cassell, London and New York, 1995), 160–61

298   'aboard his low-winged plane', *Los Angeles Examiner*, 16 July 1932, USCHR

302   'SLIDE: Looking at *Fra Diavolo*', interview with Anthony Slide, NYPA

29 The Exhausted Rulers

306   'Sworn to attend the annual convention', RS; 'FADE-IN', script extracts from *Sons of the Desert*, MPPDA file, AMPAS

311   'Up to the attic for you', *The Smithsonian Collection of Newspaper Comics* (Smithsonian and Harry Abrams Press, Washington and New York 1978), 47; 'his wife, Myrtle Lee Hardy', *Los Angeles Examiner*, 21 June 1933, USCHR

312   'Laurel would ignore her', *Los Angeles Times*, 25 May 1933, AMPAS; 'a large and powerful man', cutting, 1 July 1933, AMPAS; 'The dove of peace is hovering', cutting, 3 August 1933, AMPAS

313   'OLIVER HARDYS HAPPY AGAIN', *Los Angeles Examiner*, 3 October 1933, USCHR; 'STAN LAUREL TOO OFTEN GONE', *Daily News*, 10 October 1933, AMPAS; '*Sons of the Desert* is a very funny burlesque', RS

30 Babes in Toil-land

319 'sit at an exalted place', John McCabe, *Mr Laurel and Mr Hardy*
(Signet, New York, 1968), 161
320 'scene of Laurel slapping woman', etc., *Sons of the Desert*
MPPDA file, AMPAS
321 'Doug, this starts off grand', ibid.; 'I had worked so hard', RS
322 'a seven-year-old assured me', *Los Angeles Examiner*, 29
December 1934, USCHR; 'They brought these goons', RS
325 'When I let Laurel and Hardy go', ibid.

PART THREE: 'WE FAW DOWN'
ON THE TRAIL OF THE LONESOME MIMES

31 'Nice Weather We Had Tomorrow . . .'

332 'LAUREL AND HARDY = CARE HAL ROACH STUDIOS', USCHR;
'the resemblance is very striking', ibid.
333 'LAUREL AND HARDY BREAK', *New York Herald Tribune*, 16
March 1935, NYPA; 'After the *Babes in Toyland* thing', interview
with Anthony Slide, NYPA; 'I might have thought', *Los Angeles
Examiner*, 24 March 1935, USCHR
334 'LAUREL AND HARDY REUNITED', *New York Times*, 5 April 1935,
NYPA; 'The famous duo will start work immediately', *Los
Angeles Examiner*, 5 April 1935, USCHR

32 Bohemian Girls

338 'rotund motion-picture comedian', *Los Angeles Examiner*, 21 July
1935, USCHR; '*Dear little girl, I was so pleased*', RS
344 'to conduct himself with due regard', Randy Skretvedt, *Laurel and
Hardy, The Magic Behind the Movies* (Past Times Publishing,
Beverly Hills, California, 1996), 325
345 'Matrimonial difficulties of Stan Laurel', *Los Angeles Examiner*, 1
November 1936, USCHR; 'LAUREL WOES BEFORE COURT', *Los
Angeles Examiner*, 6 November 1936, USCHR
346 'She charges her rotund husband', *Los Angeles Examiner*, 10
November 1936, USCHR; 'habitual intemperance', etc., ibid., 18
November 1936
347 'It was the gentlemanly thing to do', ibid., 19 November 1936
348 'Ruth had a lady detective', Fred Lawrence Guiles, *Stan: The Life
of Stan Laurel* (Michael Joseph, 1980), 152; 'reconciled and are
motoring', *Los Angeles Examiner*, 5 February 1937, USCHR
349 'I don't think I could ever love', *American Weekly*, 1938, NYPA;

'suffered a nervous ailment', *Los Angeles Examiner*, 19 May 1937, USCHR

33 Believe It or Not – Stan and Hal Go Off the Rails

353 'Believe It or Not', cuttings, NYPA
354 'URGENT YOU DELIVER', 19 July 1937, USCHR; 'REGARDING OUR WIRE', 21 July 1937, ibid.; 'MUST BE OPERATED ON AT ONCE', 26 July 1937, ibid.
355 'MADELINE HARDY NEWYORKCITY', 21 June 1938, ibid.; 'MRS E HARDY', 26 August 1936, ibid.; 'HAL ROACH GOES ITALYWOOD', *Los Angeles Examiner*, 12 September 1937, USCHR
356 'Has anyone thought', Edward Tannebaum, *Fascism in Italy, Society and Culture 1922–1945* (Allen Lane, 1973), 278
357 'Elaborate precautions were taken', *New York Herald-Tribune*, 25 September 1937, NYPA; 'How could you condone a man', Randy Skretvedt, *Laurel and Hardy, The Magic Behind the Movies* (Past Times Publishing, Beverly Hills, California, 1996), 334; 'Hal Roach, who brought the young Mussolini', *Los Angeles Examiner*, 7 October 1937, USCHR; 'You can never tell, however', ibid., 15 September 1937, USCHR
359 'STAN LAUREL WEDS SINGER', 2 January 1938, cutting, NYPA; 'Virginia arrived in the courtroom', etc., *American Weekly*, 1941, NYPA
361 'she must not invade', *Los Angeles Examiner*, 22 January 1938, USCHR
362 'causing a disturbance', *Variety*, 3 May 1939, NYPA
363 'Firemen would run all over the premises', *American Weekly*, 1941, NYPA; 'Looking out of the window', ibid., 1939
364 'She phoned me from the studio', ibid.

34 Hardy Without Laurel, Laurel Without Hardy

370 'who loses caste', etc., *New York Times*, 2 August 1938, NYPA

35 'Something wholesome, something tender . . .'

382 'Stan's new barrier against alimony wars', *Los Angeles Examiner*, 2 September 1940, USCHR
383 'for the protection of our police', cutting, 24 February 1940, NYPA
387 'I had been working', Lucille Hardy, audiotape interview with Randy Skretvedt, RS
388 'SELF-STYLED FIANCÉE', *Los Angeles Examiner*, 9 February 1940, USCHR; 'I just thought he was naturally polite', etc., Lucille Hardy, ibid.

389 'We celebrated our wedding', etc., ibid.
390 'He was an early riser', etc., ibid.

36 The Fox and the Huns

396 'Fort Laurel has fallen', *Los Angeles Examiner*, 13 January 1941, USCHR
397 'Laurel and Hardy, who have been away', ibid., 25 April 1941; 'In the spring of 1941', press release, Twentieth Century Fox company, AMPAS
398 'To evaluate the results', John McCabe, *Mr Laurel and Mr Hardy* (Signet, New York, 1968), 142
399 'They'd give me a temporary badge', Scott MacGillivray, *Laurel and Hardy, From the Forties Forward* (Vestal Press, Maryland, 1998), 8
402 'THEY'RE DRAFT-DAFFY!', *Great Guns* press book, MGM, RS

37 Nothing But Trouble

406 'Unless Metro-Goldwyn-Mayer', cutting, NYPA
408 'a house densely packed with soldiers', ibid.
413 'from any comic consideration', ibid.
414 'This is merely a rough outline', MGM file, *Nothing But Trouble*, AMPAS; 'Laurel and Hardy become employed', ibid.
415 'Ollie and Stan, who haven't done', etc., ibid.
416 'MEDIUM SHOT OF SHIP', etc., ibid.

38 Any Old Port

423 'should be returned', Glenn Mitchell, *The Laurel and Hardy Encyclopedia* (B. T. Batsford, 1995), 85; 'Stan's current wife', *Los Angeles Examiner*, 18 September 1943, USCHR; 'my client is ill', ibid., 24 May 1945, USCHR
424 'She just keeps on singing', ibid., 12 November 1941, USCHR; 'routed out of bed by the couple', ibid., 7 May 1946, USCHR; 'For the first time they began', etc., Lucille Hardy, audiotape interview with Randy Skretvedt, RS
426 'No wonder Oliver Hardy', etc., A. J. Marriot, *Laurel and Hardy, The British Tours* (A. J. Marriot, Blackpool, 1993), 122
429 'Why not?', etc., Otto Friedrich, *City of Nets, a Portrait of Hollywood in the 1940s* (University of California Press, 1997), 319

39 Utopias and Unpromised Lands

437 'they have another Edith Piaf', *Los Angeles Examiner*, 2 June 1951, USCHR

439   'On to the stage strode', A. J. Marriot, *Laurel and Hardy, The British Tours* (A. J. Marriot, Blackpool, 1993), 186

440   'seemed to be always writing', ibid., 188

40   Twilight of the Vauds

447   'It was a blessing for Oliver', *Los Angeles Examiner*, 8 August 1957, AMPAS

448   'We mourn the passing of Oliver Hardy', USCHR; 'What is there to say?', *Herald and Express*, 7 August 1957, AMPAS

449   'I remember the old theatre', Jenny Owen-Pawson and Bill Mouland, *Laurel Before Hardy* (Westmoreland Gazette, Kendall, 1984), 119; 'Thanks for your sweet letter', AJM

450   'Yes, I'm afraid Variety', ibid.; 'Dear Vic and Gladys', ibid.

452   'Glad you got a few laughs', ibid.

453   'Thanks for your nice letter 9th inst', Owen-Pawson and Mouland, op. cit., 131

454   'I'd much rather be skiing', cutting, 26 February 1965, NYPA

Epilogue: Going Bye Bye

456   'The halls of Heaven', *Los Angeles Times*, 27 February 1965, AMPAS

458   'STAN: Keep a semblance of belief', David Robinson, *Sight and Sound*, July–September 1954, 42

459   'ESTRAGON: I told you', Samuel Beckett, *Waiting for Godot* (Faber and Faber, 1965), 60

Chronology

1841   5 December, Georgia: birth of Oliver Hardy senior
1860   Birth of Emily Norvell
          Askrigg, Yorkshire: birth of Margaret Metcalfe
1862   Darlington: birth of Arthur Jefferson
1884   Ulverston: marriage of Arthur Jefferson and Margaret
          Metcalfe
1890   16 June, Ulverston: birth of Arthur Stanley Jefferson
          3 December: marriage of Oliver Hardy senior and Emily
          Norvell Tant
1892   18 January, Harlem, Georgia: birth of Norvell Hardy
          22 November, Madison, Georgia: death of Oliver Hardy
          senior
1897   Jefferson family move to North Shields, near Newcastle
1898   Norvell Hardy in 1st Grade school in Madison, Georgia
1900   Emily Hardy and family move to Milledgeville, Georgia
          20 May: young Stan Jefferson's first public appearance at
          Relief of Mafeking parade in North Shields
1901   Arthur Jefferson takes over Metropole Theatre in Glasgow
1906(?) First stage performance of Stan Jefferson at Glasgow
          Britannia Theatre
1907   Norvell Hardy enters Georgia Military College
          Stan Jefferson plays the Golliwog Ebeneezer in Levy and
          Cardwell's *The Sleeping Beauty*
1908   Stan Jefferson plays bit parts in Arthur Jefferson sketches
          Norvell Hardy attends Young Harris Mountain College
1909   Stan Jefferson joins Fred Karno company
1910   Norvell Hardy, now naming himself Oliver Norvell Hardy, is
          running the Electric Theater in Milledgeville
          22 September: Stan Jefferson, with Charles Chaplin and others
          of the Fred Karno company, embarks to the United States
1911   summer: Stan Jefferson leaves Karno troupe and returns to
          England
1911–12 Stan Jefferson in double-act, The Barto Brothers, playing *Rum*
          'Uns from Rome
1912   spring(?): Stan Jefferson plays Holland with The Eight Comicques

1912	18 September: Stan Jefferson embarks again with Karno troupe for New York
	Oliver Norvell Hardy leaves Milledgeville for Jacksonville, Florida
1912–13	Oliver Hardy as singer in Jacksonville and Atlanta Georgia
1913	17 November: Oliver Norvell Hardy marries Madelyn Saloshin in Macon, Georgia
	November: Charles Chaplin leaves Karno troupe for Hollywood
1914	9 May: last sighting of Karno company in current US tour
	Oliver and Madelyn Hardy in Jacksonville, Florida
	21 April: release of first film featuring Oliver 'Babe' Hardy, *Outwitting Dad*, for the Lubin company
	summer: Stan Jefferson joins Edgar and Ellen Hurley to form The Three (or Four) Comicques
1914–15	Oliver Hardy continues making films with Lubin company, then with other companies in New York, returning to Jacksonville, Florida, to join the Vim company
1915	February: first sighting of Stan Jefferson's new act with Edgar and Ellen Hurley, The Keystone Trio
	autumn(?): formation of new Stan Jefferson Trio with Alice and Baldwin Cooke
1916–17	Stan Jefferson Trio plays the boondocks
	Oliver Hardy continues making films in Florida
1917	Stan Jefferson meets Charlotte Mae Dahlberg
	April: first appearance of Stan and Mae Laurel
	June: Stan Laurel shoots his first film, *Nuts in May*, in Hollywood
	September–October: Stan Laurel shoots four films for Nestor/L-KO Pictures
	October: Oliver and Madelyn Hardy move to Hollywood, California
	Oliver Hardy continues film career (see Filmography)
1917–22	Stan and Mae Laurel continue vaudeville circuit act
1918	June–July: Stan Laurel shoots four films for Hal Roach Rolin company
	summer: Stan Laurel begins working with Vitagraph and other film companies (see Filmography)
1921	January or February: Oliver Hardy and Stan Laurel appear together for the first time in *The Lucky Dog*
	November: Oliver Hardy divorces Madelyn Hardy
	25 November: Oliver Hardy marries Myrtle Reeves

1925	Oliver Hardy and Stan Laurel separately sign contracts with Hal Roach Studios
1926	23 August: Stan Laurel marries Lois Neilson Ozmun
	September: Stan and Ollie appear in *Duck Soup* for Roach
1927	June: Stan and Ollie shoot first official Laurel and Hardy movie, *The Second Hundred Years*
1929	March–April: Stan and Ollie shoot first Laurel and Hardy sound movie, *Unaccustomed As We Are*
1931	August: Stan changes his name officially from Jefferson to Laurel
1932	July–August: Stan and Ollie's first British stage tour
1935	Stan Laurel divorces Lois
	3 April and 28 September: Stan Laurel marries Virginia Ruth Rogers in two ceremonies
1937	Oliver Hardy initiates divorce with Myrtle Reeves
	Stan Laurel's divorce-court battles with Virginia Ruth
	24 December: Stan's divorce decree issued
1938	1 January: Stan Laurel marries Vera Ivanova Shuvalova (Illiana)
	late January and 25 April: two further marriage ceremonies with Illiana
1939	May: Stan Laurel divorces Illiana
1940	February: Oliver Hardy's divorce with Myrtle is finalized
	7 March: Oliver Hardy marries Lucille Virginia Jones
1941	January: Stan Laurel remarries Virginia Ruth
1946	April: Stan Laurel re-divorces Virginia Ruth
	6 May: Stan Laurel marries Ida Kitaeva
1947	February–November: Stan and Ollie's second British stage tour
1952	February–September: Stan and Ollie's third British stage tour
1953	October–
1954	–May: Stan and Ollie's last British stage tour
1957	7 August: Death of Oliver Hardy
1965	23 February: Death of Stan Laurel

Filmography

With so many film credits, solo and duo, only a listing of Stan's and Ollie's early output is possible here. For a full filmography the reader should refer, at the bare minimum, to Rob Stone's *Laurel or Hardy: The Solo Films of Stan Laurel and Oliver Hardy*, and Randy Skretvedt's *Laurel and Hardy: The Magic Behind the Movies* (see Bibliography), which rack up to over 1,000 pages in total. The following is a basic guide:

Oliver 'Babe' Hardy

Solo output as actor

LUBIN COMPANY

1914
Outwitting Dad, Casey's Birthday, Building a Fire, He Won a Ranch, For Two Pins, The Particular Cowboys, A Tango Tragedy, A Brewery-town Romance, The Female Cop, Good Cider, Long May it Wave, His Sudden Recovery, Who's Boss, The Kidnapped Bride, Worms Will Turn, The Rise of the Johnsons, He Wanted Work, They Bought a Boat, Back to the Farm, Making Auntie Welcome, The Green Alarm, Never Too Old, A Fool There Was, Pins Are Lucky, Jealous James, When the Ham Turned, The Smuggler's Daughter, She Married for Love, The Soubrette and the Simp, The Honor of the Force, Kidnapping the Kid, She Was the Other, The Daddy of Them All, Mother's Baby Boy, The Servant Girl's Legacy, He Wanted His Pants, Dobs at the Shore, The Fresh Air Cure, Weary Willie's Rags

1915
What He Forgot, They Looked Alike, Spaghetti and Lottery, Gus and the Anarchists, Cupid's Target, Shoddy the Tailor, The Prize Baby, An Expensive Visit, Cleaning Time, Mixed Flats, Safety Worst, The Twin Sister, Who Stole the Doggies?, A Lucky Strike, Matilda's Legacy, Capturing Bad Bill, Her Choice, Cannibal King, What a Cinch, The Dead Letter, Avenging Bill, The Haunted Hat, Babe's School Days, Edison Bugg's Invention, A Terrible Tragedy, It Happened in Pikersville

EDISON COMPANY

It May Be You, Not Much Force, Poor Baby, Clothes Make the Man, The Simp and the Sophomores

WHARTON FILMS (ITHACA, NEW YORK)

The Bungalow Bungle, Three Rings and a Goat, A Rheumatic Joint, The Lilac Splash

MISCELLANEOUS NEW YORK FILMS

Ethel's Romeos (Casino Star/Gaumont), *Fatty's Fatal Fun* (Starlight/ Pathé), *Something in Her Eye* (Novelty/Mutual), *A Janitor's Joyful Job* (Novelty/Mutual), *The Crazy Clock Maker* (Wizard/World Film Corp.)

VIM COMEDIES

1915
The Midnight Prowlers, Pressing Business, Love, Pepper and Sweets, Strangled Harmony, Speed Kings, Mixed and Fixed, Ups and Downs

1916
This Way Out, Chickens, Frenzied Finance, A Special Delivery (first Plump and Runt film), *Busted Hearts, A Sticky Affair, Bungles' Rainy Day, One Too Many, Bungles Enforces the Law, The Serenade, Bungles' Elopement, Nerve and Gasoline, Bungles Lands a Job, Their Vacation, Mamma's Boys, The Battle Royal, All for a Girl, Hired and Fired, What's Sauce for the Goose, The Brave Ones, The Water Cure, Thirty Days, Baby Doll, The Schemers, Sea Dogs, Hungry Hearts, Never Again, Better Halves, A Day at School, Spaghetti, Aunt Bill, The Heroes, Human Hounds, Dreamy Knights, Life Savers, Their Honeymoon, The Tryout, An Aerial Joyride, Sidetracked, Stranded, Love and Duty, The Reformers, Royal Blood, The Candy Trail, The Precious Parcel, A Maid to Order, Twin Flats, A Warm Reception, Pipe Dreams, Mother's Child, Prize Winners, The Guilty Ones, He Winked and Won, Fat and Fickle* (last three directed by Babe Hardy)

1917
The Boycotted Baby, The Other Girl, The Love Bugs, A Mix Up in Hearts, Wanted a Bad Man (all four directed by Babe Hardy)

KING BEE
(with Billy West as Chaplin impersonator)

1917
In Jacksonville, Florida: *Back Stage, The Hero, Dough-Nuts, Cupid's Rival, The Villain*; in New York and New Jersey: *The Millionaire, The Goat, The Fly-Cop, The Chief Cook, The Candy Kid, The Hobo, The Pest, The Band Master*; in Hollywood, California: *The Slave*

1918
In Hollywood, California: *The Stranger, His Day Out, The Rogue, The Orderly, The Scholar, The Messenger, The Handy Man, Bright and Early, The Straight and Narrow, Playmates, Beauties in Distress, He's In Again, Married to Order*

L-KO STUDIOS

1918
Business Before Honesty, Hello Trouble, Painless Love (all three directed by Charles Parrott), *The King of the Kitchen, Distilled Love* (released 1920)

1919
The Freckled Fish, Hop the Bellhop, Lions and Ladies, Hearts in Hock

VITAGRAPH PICTURES

1919
With Jimmy Aubrey: *Soapsuds and Sapheads, Jazz and Jailbirds, Mules and Mortgages, Tootsies and Tamales, Healthy and Happy, Flips and Flops, Yaps and Yokels, Dull Care* (with Larry Semon), *Mates and Models, Squabs and Squabbles, The Head Waiter* (with Larry Semon), *Switches and Sweeties, Bungs and Bunglers, Dames and Dentists, Maids and Muslin*

1920
Squeaks and Squawks, Fists and Fodder, Pals and Pugs, He Laughs Last, Springtime, The Decorator, The Stage Hand (with Larry Semon), *The Backyard, His Jonah Day, The Trouble Hunter*

1921
The Nuisance, The Mysterious Stranger, The Blizzard, The Tourist [*The Lucky Dog* (with Stan Laurel, for G. M. Anderson)]
With Larry Semon: *The Rent Collector, The Bakery, The Fall Guy, The Bellhop, The Sawmill*

1922
The Show, A Pair of Kings, [*Fortune's Mask* (drama feature); *The Little Wildcat* (drama feature)], *Golf, The Agent, The Counter Jumper*

1923
No Wedding Bells, The Barnyard, The Midnight Cabaret, The Gown Shop, Lightning Love, Horseshoes

1924
Trouble Brewing, for Larry Semon independent productions: *The Girl in the Limousine, Her Boy Friend, Kid Speed*

1925
The Wizard of Oz

ARROW PICTURES

1925
With Bobby Ray: *Stick Around, Rivals, Hey Taxi, Hop To It, They All Fall*; with Billy West: *Fiddlin' Around, The Joke's On You*

HAL ROACH STUDIOS

1925
Wild Papa, Neptune's Stepdaughter, Isn't Life Terrible (with Charley Chase, directed by Leo McCarey), *Should Sailors Marry* (with Clyde Cook), *Yes, Yes, Nanette* (directed by Stan Laurel and Clarence Hennecke, with Jimmy Finlayson), *Wandering Papas* (directed by Stan Laurel, with Clyde Cook), [*The Perfect Clown* (independent Larry Semon feature)], *Laughing Ladies*, [*Stop, Look, Listen* (independent Larry Semon feature, released 1926)], [*The Gentle Cyclone* (Fox feature, directed by W. S. Van Dyke, as Sheriff Bill)]

1926
[*A Bankrupt Honeymoon* (Fox release, two-reeler)], *Madame Mystery* (directed by Stan Laurel and Richard Wallace), *Say It with Babies, Long Fliv the King, Thundering Fleas, Along Came Auntie* (writer: Stan Laurel), *Two Time Mama, Bromo and Juliet, Crazy Like a Fox, Galloping Ghosts* (writer: Stan Laurel), *Be Your Age, The Nickel Hopper*

1927
Crazy to Act, Why Girls Say No (writer: Stan Laurel), *Honorable Mr Buggs* (co-writer: Stan Laurel), *Should Men Walk Home?, No Man's Law, Fluttering Hearts, Baby Brother, Love 'Em and Feed 'Em*

1928
Barnum and Ringling, Inc., Hollywood Handicap (MGM release)

As co-writer

For producer Howard Hawks: *Quicksands*, 1923

Later films without Stan Laurel

Zenobia
Hal Roach/United Artists, produced by A. Edward Sutherland, directed by Gordon Douglas, written by Corey Ford (based on a story by Walter DeLeon and Arnold Belgard), photography: Karl Struss, edited by Bert Jordan, art director: Charles D. Hall, music by Marvin T. Hatley, special effects by Roy Seawright
With Oliver Hardy (as Dr Tibbitt), Harry Langdon, Billie Burke, Stepin Fetchit, Hattie MacDaniel
Released May 1939

The Fighting Kentuckian
Produced by John Wayne, directed by George Waggner, story by George Waggner, photography: Lee Garmes, art director: James Sullivan
With John Wayne, Vera Ralston, Philip Dorn, Oliver Hardy (as Willie Paine)
Released October 1949

Riding High
Produced and directed by Frank Capra, screenplay by Robert Riskin
With Bing Crosby, Collen Gray, Charles Bickford, William Demarest, Raymond Walburn, James Gleason, Ward Bond, Oliver Hardy (as Horse Player)
Released April 1950

Stan Laurel

Solo films

1917
Nuts in May (Stanley Comedies/Bernstein Productions)

UNIVERSAL, NESTOR AND L-KO

1918
Phoney Photos, Hickory Hiram, Whose Zoo, O It's Great to Be Crazy

ROLIN – HAL ROACH

1918
Do You Love Your Wife, Just Rambling Along, Hoot Mon, No Place Like Jail, Hustling for Health

VITAGRAPH PICTURES

1918
Huns and Hyphens, Bears and Bad Men, Frauds and Frenzies (all with Larry Semon)

1921
The Lucky Dog (with Oliver Hardy; Sun Lite series/Reelcraft, produced by G. M 'Bronco Billy' Anderson)

AMALGAMATED PRODUCING (G. M. ANDERSON)

1922
A Weak-End Party, The Handy Man, The Egg, The Pest, Mixed Nuts (released 1925), *Mud and Sand*

1923
When Knights Were Cold

HAL ROACH STUDIOS

1923
Under Two Jags, The Noon Whistle (first film with Jimmy Finlayson), *White Wings, Pick and Shovel, Kill or Cure, Collars and Cuffs, Gas and Air, Oranges and Lemons, Short Orders, Save the Ship, A Man About Town, Roughest Africa, Scorching Sands, The Whole Truth, Frozen Hearts, The Soilers, Mother's Joy*

1924
Smithy, Zeb vs. Paprika, Postage Due, Brothers Under the Chin, Wide Open Spaces, Rupert of Hee Haw, Short Kilts

JOE ROCK

1924
Detained, Mandarin Mix-Up, Monsieur Don't Care, West of Hot Dog

1925
Somewhere in Wrong, Twin, Pie-Eye, The Snow Haw, Navy Blue Days, The Sleuth, Dr Pyckle and Mr Pride, Half a Man

1925

As director: *Chasing the Chaser, Unfriendly Enemies, Yes, Yes, Nanette* (with Oliver Hardy), *Moonlight and Noses*

1926

As director: *Wandering Papas* (with Oliver Hardy), *Wise Guys Prefer Brunettes, Get 'Em Young* (co-director, co-writer, appears as Summers, the Butler); as writer: *Starvation Blues, Don Key (Son of Burro), Your Husband's Past, What's the World Coming To* (appeared in as Man in Window), *Dizzy Daddies, Wife Tamers, Madame Mystery* (co-directed), *Never Too Old* (co-directed), *The Merry Widower* (co-directed), *Raggedy Rose* (co-wrote, co-directed), *Along Came Auntie* (with Oliver Hardy), *Should Husbands Pay* (co-directed); as co-writer: *The Nickel Hopper* (with Oliver Hardy), *On the Front Page* (appears as Dangerfield)

1927

As actor: *Seeing the World* (bit part), *Eve's Love Letters* (writer)

1928

As actor: *Should Tall Men Marry*

The Duo Films of Stan Laurel and Oliver Hardy

Before 'Laurel and Hardy'

HAL ROACH STUDIOS

1926

45 Minutes From Hollywood
With Glenn Tryon, Theda Bara, Our Gang

1927

Duck Soup
Based on *Home from the Honeymoon* by Arthur Jefferson, directed by Fred L. Guiol

Slipping Wives
Supervised by F. Richard Jones, directed by Fred L. Guiol

Love 'Em and Weep
Directed by Fred Guiol; with Mae Busch, James Finlayson, Charlotte Mineau, Charlie Hall, Vivien Oakland

Why Girls Love Sailors
Directed by Fred Guiol; with Viola Richard, Anita Garvin

With Love and Hisses
Directed by Fred Guiol; with James Finlayson, Anita Garvin

Sailors Beware
Directed by Hal Yates; with Anita Garvin, Lupe Velez

Do Detectives Think
Directed by Fred Guiol; with James Finlayson, Viola Richard, Noah Young

Flying Elephants
Directed by Frank Butler; with James Finlayson, Viola Richard, Dorothy Coburn

Sugar Daddies
Directed by Fred Guiol; with James Finlayson, Noah Young, Charlotte Mineau, Edna Marian

[*Call of the Cuckoos*]
(supporting part in Max Davidson comedy)

Laurel and Hardy Comedies
(All credited as produced by Hal Roach)

SILENT SHORTS

1927

The Second Hundred Years
Directed by Fred Guiol; with James Finlayson, Tiny Sandford, Ellinor Vandeveer

Hats Off
Supervised by Leo McCarey, directed by Hal Yates; with James Finlayson, Anita Garvin, Dorothy Coburn

Putting Pants on Philip
Supervised by Leo McCarey, directed by Clyde Bruckman; with Dorothy Coburn, Harvey Clark, Sam Lufkin

The Battle of the Century
Supervised by Leo McCarey, directed by Clyde Bruckman; with Noah Young, Eugene Pallette, Charlie Hall, Sam Lufkin

1928

Leave 'Em Laughing
Supervised by Leo McCarey, directed by Clyde Bruckman; with Edgar Kennedy, Charlie Hall, Viola Richard, Dorothy Coburn

The Finishing Touch
Supervised by Leo McCarey, directed by Clyde Bruckman; with Edgar Kennedy, Dorothy Coburn

From Soup to Nuts
Supervised by Leo McCarey, directed by E. Livingston Kennedy; with Tiny Sandford, Anita Garvin, Edna Marian, Ellinor Vanderveer

You're Darn Tootin'
Supervised by Leo McCarey, directed by E. Livingston Kennedy; with Otto Lederer, Agnes Steele

Their Purple Moment
Supervised by Leo McCarey, directed by James Parrott; with Anita Garvin, Kay Deslys, Fay Holderness, Tiny Sandford, Lyle Tayo, Jimmy Aubrey

Should Married Men Go Home?
Supervised by Leo McCarey, directed by James Parrott; with Edgar Kennedy, Kay Deslys, Viola Richard, Edna Marian, John Aasen

Early to Bed
Supervised by Leo McCarey, directed by Emmett J. Flynn

Two Tars
Supervised by Leo McCarey, directed by James Parrott; with Thelma Hill, Ruby Blaine, Edgar Kennedy, Charlie Hall

Habeas Corpus
Supervised by Leo McCarey, directed by James Parrott; with Richard Carle, Charlie Rogers

We Faw Down
Directed by Leo McCarey; with Vivien Oakland, Bess Flowers, Kay Deslys, Vera White, George Kotsonaros

1929

Liberty
Directed by Leo McCarey; with James Finlayson, Jean Harlow, Jack Hill

Wrong Again
Directed by Leo McCarey; with Del Henderson, Josephine Crowell, Harry Bernard, Sam Lufkin

That's My Wife
With Vivien Oakland, Charlie Hall, William Courtright, Jimmy Aubrey

Big Business
Supervised by Leo McCarey, directed by James W. Horne; with James Finlayson, Tiny Sandford, Lyle Tayo

Double Whoopee
Directed by Lewis R. Foster; with Jean Harlow, William Gillespie, Charlie Rogers, Tiny Sandford, Captain John Peters, Rolfe Sedan

Bacon Grabbers
Directed by Lewis R. Foster; with Edgar Kennedy, Jean Harlow, Harry Bernard

Angora Love
Directed by Lewis R. Foster; with Edgar Kennedy, Charlie Hall

SOUND SHORTS

1929

Unaccustomed As We Are
Directed by Lewis R. Foster; with Thelma Todd, Mae Busch, Edgar Kennedy

Berth Marks
Directed by Lewis R. Foster; with Harry Bernard, Charlie Hall, Baldwin Cooke

Men O' War
Directed by Lewis R. Foster; with Gloria Greer, Anne Cornwall, James Finlayson, Harry Bernard

Perfect Day
Directed by James Parrott; with Edgar Kennedy, Kay Deslys, Isabelle Keith

They Go Boom
Directed by James Parrott; with Charlie Hall, Sam Lufkin

The Hoose-Gow
Directed by James Parrott; with James Finlayson, Tiny Sandford, Dick Sutherland, Ellinor Vanderveer

1930

Night Owls
Directed by James Parrott; with Edgar Kennedy, James Finlayson, Anders Rudolph

Blotto
Directed by James Parrott; with Anita Garvin, Tiny Sandford, Frank Holliday

Brats
Directed by James Parrott (Laurel and Hardy double act)

Below Zero
Directed by James Parrott; with Tiny Sandford, Frank Holliday, Blanche Payson, Bobby Burns, Leo Willis

Hog Wild
Directed by James Parrott; with Fay Holderness, Dorothy Granger

The Laurel–Hardy Murder Case
Directed by James Parrott; with Fred Kelsey, Del Henderson, Dorothy Granger, Tiny Sandford, Frank Austin

Another Fine Mess
Directed by James Parrott; with Thelma Todd, James Finlayson, Charles Gerrard

1931

Be Big
Directed by James Parrott; with Anita Garvin, Isabelle Keith, Charlie Hall, Baldwin Cooke

Chickens Come Home
Directed by James W. Horne; with Mae Busch, James Finlayson, Thelma Todd, Norma Drew

[*The Stolen Jools*]
(Promotional short for National Variety Artists fund raiser for tuberculosis sanitarium at Saranac Lake, New York. Released by Paramount and National Screen Service, and in England as *The Slippery Pearls*; with Buster Keaton, Our Gang, Joe E. Brown, Edward G. Robinson, Joan Crawford, etc.)
(Stan and Ollie as detectives drive Eddie Kane to home of Norma Shearer, and their car disintegrates in front of the house.)

Laughing Gravy
Directed by James W. Horne; with Charlie Hall, Harry Bernard and 'Laughing Gravy'

Our Wife
Directed by James W. Horne; with Babe London, James Finlayson, Charlie Rogers, Blanche Payson, Ben Turpin

Come Clean
Directed by James W. Horne; with Mae Busch, Gertrude Astor, Charlie Hall, Tiny Sandford, Linda Laredo

One Good Turn
Directed by James W. Horne; with Mary Carr, James Finlayson, Billy Gilbert, Dorothy Granger, Snub Pollard

1932

[*On the Loose*]
(Brief guest appearance in Thelma Todd–Zasu Pitts short, directed by Hal Roach, with John Loder, Charlie Hall, Billy Gilbert)

Helpmates
Directed by James Parrott; with Blanche Payson, Robert Callahan, Bobby Burns

Any Old Port
Directed by James W. Horne; with Walter Long, Harry Bernard, Jacqueline Wells, Charlie Hall, Bobby Burns

The Music Box
Directed by James Parrott; with Billy Gilbert, Lilyan Irene, Charlie Hall, Sam Lufkin, William Gillespie, Gladys Gale
Oscar winner for 'Best Short Subject (Comedy)' for 1931–32
(Trivial note: Randy Skretvedt reports counting a mere 131 steps at location of Vendome Street, Silver Lake district.)
'Tall Oaks From Little Acorns Grow.'

The Chimp
Directed by James Parrott; with Billy Gilbert, James Finlayson, Charles Gemora, Tiny Sandford

County Hospital
Directed by James Parrott; with Billy Gilbert, William Austin, May Wallace.
('Hard-boiled eggs and nuts!!')

Scram
Directed by Raymond McCarey; with Arthur Housman, Vivien Oakland, Rychard Cramer

Their First Mistake
Directed by George Marshall; with Mae Busch, Billy Gilbert, George Marshall

Towed in a Hole
Directed by George Marshall; with Billy Gilbert

1933

Twice Two
Directed by James Parrott; with Charlie Hall, Baldwin Cooke, the voices of May Wallace and Carol Tevis

Me and My Pal
Directed by Charles Rogers and Lloyd French; with James Finlayson, Eddie Dunn, Bobby Dunn, Frank Terry, James C. Morton

The Midnight Patrol
Directed by Lloyd French; with Frank Terry, Eddie Dunn, Frank Brownlee

Busy Bodies
Directed by Lloyd French; with Charlie Hall, Tiny Sandford

[*Wild Poses*]
(Cameo appearance in short with Our Gang and Franklin Pangborn]

Dirty Work
Directed by Lloyd French; with Lucien Littlefield, Sam Adams

1934

Oliver the Eighth
Directed by Lloyd French; with Mae Busch, Jack Barty

Going Bye Bye
Directed by Charles Rogers; with Walter Long, Mae Busch

Them Thar Hills
Directed by Charles Rogers; with Mae Busch, Charlie Hall, Billy Gilbert

The Live Ghost
Directed by Charles Rogers; with Walter Long, Mae Busch, Arthur Housman, Charlie Hall

491

1935

Tit for Tat
Directed by Charles Rogers; with Charlie Hall, Mae Busch, James C.
Morton, Bobby Dunn

The Fixer-Uppers
Directed by Charles Rogers; with Mae Busch, Charles Middleton, Noah
Young, Arthur Housman

Thicker than Water
Directed by James W. Horne; with James Finlayson, Daphne Pollard,
Bess Flowers, Charlie Hall

1936

[On the Wrong Trek]
(Cameo appearance in Charley Chase short, with Rosina Lawrence)

LAUREL AND HARDY FEATURES

[The Hollywood Revue of 1929]
(Compilation feature, with Jack Benny, Joan Crawford, Buster Keaton,
etc.; produced by Harry Rapf, directed by Charles F. Riesner.)

The Rogue Song
MGM, 1930. Two-colour Technicolor, 115 minutes. Missing film
Produced by Irving Thalberg, directed by Lionel Barrymore, story by
Frances Marion and John Colton (based on *Gypsy Love* by Franz
Lehár), photography by Percy Hilburn and C. Edgar Schoenbaum
With Lawrence Tibbett, Catherine Dale Owen

Pardon Us
MGM, 1931. 56 minutes
Produced by Hal Roach, directed by James Parrott, photographed by
George Stevens, edited by Richard Currier, dialogue by H. M. Walker,
sound by Elmer Raguse
With Walter Long, Wilfred Lucas, Tiny Sandford, James Finlayson,
Charlie Hall, June Marlowe

Beau Hunks
MGM, 1931. Four reels
Produced by Hal Roach, directed by James W. Horne, photographed by Art
Lloyd and Jack Stevens, edited by Richard Currier, sound by Elmer Raguse
With Charles Middleton, Broderick O'Farrell, Harry Schultz, 'Abdul
Kasim K'Horne'

Pack Up Your Troubles
MGM, 1932. 68 minutes
Produced by Hal Roach, directed by George Marshall and Raymond McCarey, photographed by Art Lloyd, edited by Richard Currier, sound by James Greene
With Donald Dillway, Jacquie Lyn, James Finlayson, George Marshall

The Devil's Brother (*Fra Diavolo*; also *Bogus Bandits*)
MGM, 1933. 90 minutes
Produced by Hal Roach, directed by Hal Roach and Charles Rogers, photographed by Art Lloyd and Hap Depew, edited by Bert Jordan and William Terhune, adapted by Jeanie MacPherson from Daniel Auber's 1830 comic opera *Fra Diavolo*, sound by James Greene, musical director: LeRoy Shield
With Dennis King, James Finlayson, Thelma Todd, Henry Armetta

Sons of the Desert
MGM, 1933. 68 minutes
Produced by Hal Roach, directed by William A. Seiter, story by Harry Craven, photographed by Kenneth Peach, edited by Bert Jordan, sound by Harry Baker, dance director: Dave Bennett, song 'Honolulu Baby' by Marvin Hatley
With Mae Busch, Dorothy Christie, Charley Chase, Lucien Littlefield

[*Hollywood Party*]
(Cameo appearance in egg-breaking battle with Lupe Velez, in portmanteau film with Jimmy Durante, Charles Butterworth, Eddie Quillan, etc. Produced by Harry Rapf and Howard Dietz, music by Rogers and Hart, and others.)

Babes in Toyland
MGM, 1934. 79 minutes
Produced by Hal Roach, directed by Charles Rogers and Gus Meins, screenplay by Nick Ginde and Frank Butler (adapted from the musical comedy by Victor Herbert and Glen MacDonough), photographed by Art Lloyd and Francis Corby, edited by William Terhune and Bert Jordan, sound by Elmer Raguse, musical director: Harry Jackson
With Charlotte Henry, Felix Knights, Henry Brandon, Florence Roberts, William Burress

Bonnie Scotland
MGM, 1935. 80 minutes
Produced by Hal Roach, directed by James W. Horne, screenplay by Frank Butler and Jeff Moffitt, photographed by Art Lloyd and Walter Lundin, edited by Bert Jordan, sound by Elmer Raguse

With June Lang, William Janney, Anne Grey, James Finlayson, Daphne
Pollard, David Torrence

The Bohemian Girl
MGM, 1936. 70 minutes
Produced by Hal Roach, directed by James W. Horne and Charles
Rogers, no screenplay credit (based on the opera by Michael Balfe),
edited by Bert Jordan and Louis McManus, sound by Elmer Raguse,
musical director: Nathaniel Shilkret
With Mae Busch, Antonio Moreno, Jacqueline Wells, James Finlayson,
Thelma Todd, Darla Hood

Our Relations
MGM, 1936. A Stan Laurel production for Hal Roach Studios.
74 minutes
Directed by Harry Lachman, screenplay by Richard Connell and Felix
Adler, adapted by Charles Rogers and Jack Jevne (suggested by *The
Money Box* by W. W. Jacobs), photographed by Rudolph Mate, special
effects by Roy Seawright, edited by Bert Jordan, sound by William
Randall, music by LeRoy Shield
With Daphne Pollard, Betty Healy, James Finlayson, Alan Hale, Sydney
Toler, Iris Adrian, Lona Andre

Way Out West
MGM, 1937. A Stan Laurel Production for Hal Roach Studios.
65 minutes.
Directed by James W. Horne, story by Jack Jevne and Charles Rogers,
screenplay by Charles Rogers, Felix Adler and James Parrott, photo-
graphed by Art Lloyd and Walter Lundin, special effects by Roy
Seawright, edited by Bert Jordan, sound by William Randall, music by
Marvin Hatley, art director: Arthur Royce
With James Finlayson, Rosina Lawrence, Sharon Lynne, Stanley Fields,
Vivien Oakland

[*Pick a Star*]
(MGM, 1937. 70 minutes)
(Cameo appearance in Hal Roach production with Patsy Kelly, Jack
Haley, Rosina Lawrence, etc.)

Swiss Miss
MGM, 1938. 72 minutes
Produced by Hal Roach, directed by John G. Blystone, story by Jean
Negulesco and Charles Rogers, screenplay by James Parrott, Felix Adler
and Charles Melson, photographed by Norbert Brodine and Art Lloyd,
special effects by Roy Seawright, edited by Bert Jordan, sound by

494

William Randall, musical director: Marvin Hatley, music arranger:
Arthur Morton, songs by Phil Charig and Arthur Quenzer
With Walter Woolf King, Della Lind, Eric Blore, Charles Judels,
Ludovico Tomarchio, Charles Gemora

Block-Heads
MGM 1938. 58 minutes
Produced by Hal Roach, directed by John G. Blystone, story and screen-
play by James Parrott, Charles Rogers, Felix Adler, Harry Langdon and
Arnold Belgard, photographed by Art Lloyd, special effects by Roy
Seawright, edited by Bert Jordan, sound by Hal Bumbaugh, music by
Marvin Hatley
With Minna Gombell, Patricia Ellis, Billy Gilbert, James Finlayson

A Chump at Oxford
United Artists, 1940. 42- and 63-minute versions
Produced by Hal Roach, directed by Alfred Goulding, story and screen-
play by Charles Rogers, Felix Adler and Harry Langdon, photographed
by Art Lloyd, special effects by Roy Seawright, edited by Bert Jordan,
sound by William Randall, music by Marvin Hatley
With Forrester Harvey, Wilfred Lucas, Forbes Murray, Eddie Borden,
Charlie Hall, Peter Cushing

The Flying Deuces
Released by RKO Radio Pictures, 1939. 69 minutes
Produced by Boris Morros, directed by A. Edward Sutherland, story and
screenplay by Ralph Spence, Alfred Schiller, Charles Rogers and Harry
Langdon, photographed by Art Lloyd, aerial photography by Elmer
Dyer, edited by Jack Dennis, sound by William Wilmarth, musical
director: Edward Paul
With Joan Parker, Reginald Gardiner, Charles Middleton, James
Finlayson

Saps at Sea
United Artists, 1940. 57 minutes
Produced by Hal Roach, directed by Gordon Douglas, story and screen-
play by Charles Rogers, Felix Adler, Gill Pratt and Harry Langdon,
photographed by Art Lloyd, special effects by Roy Seawright, edited by
William Ziegler, art director: Charles D. Hall, sound by W. B. Delaplain,
music by Marvin Hatley
With James Finlayson, Rychard Cramer, Eddie Conrad, Harry Bernard

Great Guns
Twentieth Century Fox, 1941. 74 minutes
Produced by Sol M. Wurtzel, directed by Monty Banks, screenplay by Lou
Breslow, photographed by Glen MacWilliams, edited by Al de Gaetano,
sound by W. D. Flick and Harry Leonard, musical director: Emil Newman
With Dick Nelson, Sheila Ryan, Edmund MacDonald, Russell Hicks,
Ludwig Stossel

A-Haunting We Will Go
Twentieth Century Fox, 1942. 67 minutes
Produced by Sol M. Wurtzel, directed by Alfred L. Werker, story by Lou
Breslow and Stanley Rauh, screenplay by Lou Breslow, photographed by
Glen MacWilliams, musical director: Emil Newman
With Harry A. 'Dante' Jansen, John Shelton, Sheila Ryan, Don Costello,
Elisha Cook junior

Air Raid Wardens
MGM, 1943. 67 minutes
Produced by B. F. Zeidman, directed by Edward Sedgwick, screenplay by
Martin Rackin, Jack Jevne, Charles Rogers and Harry Crane, photo-
graphed by Walter Lundin, music by Nat Shilkret, art direction: Cedric
Gibbons, Harry McAfee
With Edgar Kennedy, Jacqueline White, Horace McNally, Donald Meek

Jitterbugs
Twentieth Century Fox, 1943. 74 minutes
Produced by Sol M. Wurtzel, directed by Malcolm St. Clair, screenplay
by Scott Darling, photographed by Lucien Andriot, art directors: James
Basevi, Chester Gore, musical director: Eric Newman
With Vivian Blaine, Robert Bailey, Douglas Fowley, Lee Patrick, Anthony
Caruso

The Dancing Masters
Twentieth Century Fox, 1943. 63 minutes
Produced by Lee Marcus, directed by Malcolm St. Clair, screenplay by
W. Scott Darling (based on a story by George Bricker), photographed by
Norbert Brodine, art directors: James Basevi, Chester Gore, musical
director: Eric Newman
With Trudy Marshall, Robert Bailey, Margaret Dumont, Charles Rogers,
Daphne Pollard

The Big Noise
Twentieth Century Fox, 1944. 74 minutes
Produced by Sol M. Wurtzel, directed by Malcolm St. Clair, screenplay
by W. Scott Darling, photographed by Joe MacDonald, art directors: Lyle
Wheeler and John Ewing, musical director: Emil Newman
With Arthur Space, Doris Merrick, Veda Ann Borg, Robert Dudley,
Esther Howard, Bobby Blake

Nothing But Trouble
MGM, 1945. 70 minutes
Produced by B. F. Zeidman, directed by Sam Taylor, screenplay by
Russell Rouse and Ray Golden (contributors to early scripts: Robert
Halff, Wilkie Mahoney, Harry Crane and Buster Keaton), photographed
by Charles Salerno junior, edited by Conrad Nervig, art directors: Cedric
Gibbons, Harry McAfcc, sound by Douglas Shearer and Thomas
Edwards, music score by Nathaniel Shilkret
With David Leland, Henry O'Neill, Mary Boland, Philip Merivale

The Bullfighters
Twentieth Century Fox, 1945. 69 minutes
Produced by William Girard, directed by Malcolm St. Clair, screenplay
by W. Scott Darling, photographed by Norbert Brodine, art directors:
Lyle Wheeler and Chester Gore, musical director: Emil Newman
With Richard Lane, Ralph Sanford, Margo Woode, Carol Andrews,
Edward Gargan

Atoll K
1951. 98 minutes
Released in UK as *Robinson Crusoeland* in 1952. 82 minutes
Produced by Raymond Eger for Franco London Films S.A., Films E.G.E.,
Films Sirius and Fortczza Film, directed by Leo Joannon, screenplay by
John Klorer, Frederick Kohner, Rene Wheeler and Piero Tellini, director
of photography: Armand Thirard, art director: Roland Quignon, edited
by Raymond Isnardon, music by Paul Misraki
With Suzy Delair, Max Elloy, Adriano Rimoldi, Luigi Tosi

ADVERTISING/PROMOTIONAL FILM

The Tree in a Test Tube
1943; one-reel colour
Produced by US Department of Agriculture, Forest Service, directed by
Charles McDonald, photographed by A. H. C. Sintzenich, narrated by
Pete Smith and Lee Vickers
Stan and Ollie demonstrate the various kinds of wood products which
form part of everyday life.

Bibliography

The Crucial Reference Books

McCabe, John, with Al Kilgore and Richard Bann, *Laurel and Hardy*, W. H. Allen, 1975

Marriot, A. J., *Laurel and Hardy: The British Tours*, A. J. Marriot, Blackpool, 1993

Mitchell, Glenn, *The Laurel and Hardy Encyclopedia*, B. T. Batsford, 1995

– *The A to Z of Silent Film Comedy*, B. T. Batsford, 1998

Skretvedt, Randy, *Laurel and Hardy: The Magic Behind the Movies*, Past Times Publishing, Beverly Hills, California, 1996

Stone, Rob, with David Wyatt, *Laurel or Hardy: The Solo Films of Stan Laurel and Oliver 'Babe' Hardy*, Split Reel, Temecula, California, 1996

Biographies

Guiles, Fred Lawrence, *Stan: The Life of Stan Laurel*, Michael Joseph, 1980

McCabe, John, *Mr Laurel and Mr Hardy*, Signet Books, New York, 1968

– *The Comedy World of Stan Laurel*, Moonstone Press, Beverly Hills, California, 1990

– *Babe: The Life of Oliver Hardy*, Robson Books, 1990

Other Books on Laurel and Hardy

Anobile, Richard J., *The Best of Laurel and Hardy* (aka *A Fine Mess*), Michael Joseph, 1975

Barr, Charles, *Laurel and Hardy*, Studio Vista, 1967

Bergan, Ronald, *The Life and Times of Laurel and Hardy*, Green Wood, 1992

Brooks, Leo M., *The Laurel and Hardy Stock Company*, Blotto Press, Hilversum, 1997

Crowther, Bruce, *Laurel and Hardy, Crown Princes of Comedy*, Columbus Books, 1987

Everson, William K., *The Films of Laurel and Hardy*, Citadel, 1967

Forbes, Stanton, *If Laurel Shot Hardy the World Would End* (thriller), Doubleday and Co., New York, 1970

Gehring, Wes D., *Laurel and Hardy, a Bio-Bibliography*, Greenwood Press, 1990

Grant, Neil, *Laurel and Hardy (Quote Unquote)*, Parragon Publishing, 1996

Kaye, Marvin, *The Laurel and Hardy Murders* (thriller), Dutton, New York, 1977

McFerren, Robert, and Joan Jones , *Laurel and Hardy in Big Quizness*, Plumtree Publishing, 1997

McGarry, Annie, *Laurel and Hardy*, Chartwell Books, Secaucus, New Jersey, 1992

MacGillivray, Scott, *Laurel and Hardy: From the Forties Onwards*, Vestal Press, Maryland, 1998

Maltin, Leonard (ed.), *The Laurel and Hardy Book*, Curtis, 1973

Owen-Pawson, Jenny and Bill Mouland, *Laurel Before Hardy*, Westmoreland Gazette, Kendall, 1984

Owst, Ken, *Laurel and Hardy in Hull*, 1956

Sanders, Jonathan, *Another Fine Dress: Role-Play in the Films of Laurel and Hardy*, Cassell, London and New York, 1995

Scagmetti, Jack, *The Laurel and Hardy Scrapbook*, Jonathan David, New York, 1982

Scott, Allen Nollen, *The Boys: The Cinematic World of Laurel and Hardy*, McFarland, 1989

Wilson, Colin, *The Laurel and Hardy Theory of Consciousness*, Robert Briggs Association, 1986

Selected Books on Film, Film Comedy and Comedians

Anthony, Brian and Andy Edmonds, *Smile When the Raindrops Fall: The Story of Charley Chase*, The Scarecrow Press, Lanham, Maryland, 1998

Bergman, Andrew, *We're in the Money: Depression America and its Films*, Elephant, Chicago, 1992

Bowser, Eileen, *The Transformation of Cinema 1907–1915 (History of the American Cinema*, vol. 2), University of California Press, 1994

Chaplin, Charles, *My Autobiography*, Simon and Schuster, New York, 1964

– *My Life in Pictures*, Grosset and Dunlap, New York, 1975

Dardis, Tom, *Harold Lloyd: The Man on the Clock*, The Viking Press, New York, 1983; Viking Penguin, 1984

Durgnat, Raymond, *The Crazy Mirror – Hollywood Comedy and the American Image*, Faber and Faber, 1969

Eckhardt, Joseph P., *The King of the Movies: Film Pioneer Siegmund Lubin*, Farleigh Dickinson University Press, Associated University Presses, New Jersey and London, 1997
Everson, William K., *The Films of Hal Roach*, Museum of Modern Art, New York, 1971
Friedrich, Otto, *City of Nets: A Portrait of Hollywood in the 1940's*, University of California Press, 1997
Kerr, Walter, *The Silent Clowns*, Knopf, New York, 1980
Lahue, Kalton C. and Sam Gill, *Clown Princes and Court Jesters, Some Great Comics of the Silent Screen*, A. S. Barnes and Co., New Jersey and London, 1970
– *Mack Sennett's Keystone: The Man, the Myth and the Comedies*, A. S. Barnes and Company, Thomas Voseloff Ltd, 1971
– *World of Laughter: The Motion Picture Comedy Short 1910–1930*, University of Oklahoma Press, 1972
Louvish, Simon, *Man on the Flying Trapeze: The Life and Times of W. C. Fields*, Faber and Faber, London; W. W. Norton, New York, 1997
– *Monkey Business: The Lives and Legends of the Marx Brothers*, Faber and Faber, London, 1999; St Martins Press, New York, 2000
Maltin, Leonard, *The Great Movie Comedians: From Chaplin to Woody Allen*, Crown Publishers, New York, 1978
Mast, Gerald, *The Comic Mind, Comedy and the Movies*, University of Chicago Press, 1979
Musser, Charles, *The Emergence of Cinema: The American Screen to 1907 (History of the American Cinema*, vol. 1), University of California Press, 1994
Robinson, David, *Chaplin, His Life and Art*, Collins, 1985; Paladin, 1986
– *The Great Funnies*, Studio Vista, 1969
Ross, Steven J., *Working-Class Hollywood, Silent Film and the Shaping of Class in America*, Princeton University Press, New Jersey, 1998
Sennett, Mack, with Cameron Shipp, *King of Comedy*, Doubleday and Co., New York, 1954
Sklar, Robert, *Movie-Made America: A Cultural History of American Movies*, Vintage Books, New York, 1994
Slide, Anthony, *Early American Cinema*, Zwemmer/Barnes, 1970

Books on Music-Hall and Theatre

Adeler, Edwin and Con West, *Remember Fred Karno: The Life of a Great Showman*, John Long, 1939
Arliss, George, *On the Stage*, John Murray, 1928

Brandreth, Gyles, *The Funniest Man on Earth: The Story of Dan Leno*, Hamish Hamilton, 1977

Broadbent, R. J., *A History of Pantomime*, 1901; republished by The Citadel Press, New York, 1965

Busby, Roy, *British Music Hall: An Illustrated Who's Who from 1850 to the Present Day*, Paul Elek, London and New Hampshire, 1976

Cheshire, D. F., *Music Hall in Britain*, Farleigh Dickinson University Press, 1974

Felstead, S. Theodore, *Stars Who Made the Halls: A Hundred Years of English Humour, Harmony and Hilarity*, T. Werner Laurie, 1947

Hagill, Beryl, *Bring on the Clowns*, David and Charles, 1980

Leno, Dan, *Dan Leno, Hys Booke: A Volume of Frivolities, etc.*, Greening & Co., 1904

Leslie, Peter, *A Hard Act to Follow: A Music Hall Review*, Paddington Press, 1978

Mellor, G. J., *The Northern Music Hall*, Frank Graham, Newcastle, 1970

Pope, W. MacQueen, *The Melodies Linger On: The Story of Music Hall*, W. H. Allen, 1951

Slide, Anthony, *The Vaudevillians: A Dictionary of Vaudeville Performers*, Arlington House, Westport, 1981

Acknowledgements

Plaudits and thanks to all those who have helped to make this book happen: first and foremost the gurus of Stan and Ollie studies: Randy Skretvedt in sunny California; Leo Brooks in Texas; Rob ('Solo') Stone in Los Angeles and his London counterpart, David Wyatt; A. J. Marriot in wildest England, master of the early life of Stan Laurel. All have given of their time and energy and enabled access to their archives. Thanks also as ever to Glenn Mitchell, master of the A-to-Zs of classic film comedy, who has been kind enough to fact-check this tome. Any remaining errors are, of course, my own responsibility, as are my speculations, interpretations and analyses of Stan and Ollie's art and lives, in particular my comments on marital matters, concerning which Glenn wishes to demur from my excessive fondness for old news cuttings. Genuflections to the usual suspects in archival nirvanas: Rod Bladel and staff at New York Public Library of the Performing Arts; staff of the Special Collections of the Margaret Herrick Library at the Academy of Motion Picture Arts and Sciences in Los Angeles; Ned Comstock of the University of Southern California; Geraldine Duclow and staff of the Theater Collection of the Free Library of Philadelphia; staff at the British Film Institute Library and Westminster Reference Library; staff at the British Library's Manuscript Division. David Rothman, Genealogist First Class of California, once again dug and delved for nuggets. Thanks also to Marion Grave and staff at the Laurel and Hardy Museum in Ulverston, and to the good people of Harlem, Georgia: Dave Carlsen and family for their hospitality, and the organizers of the annual Oliver Hardy Day. Special thanks to Charles Lord of Grovetown and Marshall Williams of Madison, Georgia, graceful guardians of the local lore. Thanks too to Anthony Slide, Armond Fields, John Cooper, Rick Mitz, Walter Donohue, Richard Kelly and staff at Faber and Faber, who have endured my 'Why don't you do something to *help* me?' for far longer than should be humanly necessary. And yet again luv to Mairi, whose tolerance for the 'Cuckoo' song and other comical clangs and clamours has been tested far beyond the bounds of duty.

Index

Note: Page references in *italics* are to illustrations

Abbott, Bud 267, 395, 398–9, 421, 430
Abrams, Charles 108
Academy of Motion Picture Arts and
    Sciences
  awards 286, 452
  library 413
Adams, Ed 35
Adeler, Edwin 50, 54, 56
Adler, Felix 344, 369
An Aerial Joyride 106
A-Haunting We Will Go 403–5
Air Raid Wardens 406–8, *408*, 422
Alexander, Frank 145
Alkali Ike 63, 197
'All-Star Comedies' 184, 189, 199, 203,
    206, 213, 315, 370
Alone in the World 28–9, 49
Along Came Auntie 188
Amalgamated Producing (company) 138,
    143
Amateur Fire Brigade 22, 28
An American Count 62
American Film (company) 61
American Lifeograph (company) 60
American Weekly 349, 359, 363–4
Anderson, G. M. ('Broncho Billy') 138,
    142–3, 148, 152
Anderson, Gilbert 61
Anderson, Maxwell 430
Angora Love 219, 250, 275
Another Fine Mess 23, 274–5
anti-Semitism 66–7, 165, 340, 394
Arbuckle, Roscoe ('Fatty') 64, 94, 97, 110,
    197, 205, 232
Ardell, Alyce 239, 348
Arlecchino 198, 366
Arling, Charles 116
Arliss, George 12
Armat, Thomas 90
Armstrong, Billy 143
Armstrong, John 156

Arnold, Lucille 115–16
Aronson, Max 61
Arrow Pictures 166–7
Asher, Max 172
Astor, Gertrude 184
At the Music Hall 63
Atlanta 45–6, 65–7, 101, 282
Atoll K 433–40, 436
Aubrey, Jimmy 110, 133–6, 173, 197, 247,
    448, 456
audience participation 60
Austin, Albert 69
Austin, William 203
The Awful Truth 182

Babes in Toyland 321–5
Bacon Grabbers 250
Bailey, Bob 412
Balboa (company) 135
Ballard, Wave 34
A Bankrupt Honeymoon 187, 200–201,
    412
Banks, Monty 400
Banks, Ted 82, 85
Bara, Theda 183–4, 398
Bard, Wilkie 50
Barnes, Howard 413
Barr, Charles 270
Barrymore, John 174–5, 414
Barrymore, Lionel 184
The Battle of the Century xiii, 160, 218–21,
    412
The Battle Royal 105
Batzler, Grete 358
Baum, Frank 163
Bearden, J. W. 42
Bears and Badmen 130
Beau Hunks 284, 320, 386
Beckett, Samuel 278, 459
Beery, Wallace 272
The Beggar's Opera 6

Belgard, Arnold 369
Belikovich, Sonia 361
Bell, Charley 56
Bell, Spencer 164
The Bellhop 146
Below Zero 268–70, 269
Ben My Chree 80–81
Bennett, Joan 405
Benny, Jack 258
Benton Roberts, Thomas 236
Berkeley, Busby 420
Bernstein, Isadore 115
Berth Marks 126, 253–4, 413
Bevan, Billy 158, 456
Big Business xi, 156, 231, 233, 234, 456
The Big House 272
The Big Noise 412–13, 451
The Big Parade 143, 177
Billboard 60, 62, 78, 84
Biograph (company) 61, 91, 451
'Birds of a Feather' 441–2
Birth of a Nation 90
Bischoff, Samuel 149
Blackburn, Norman 370
Blackpool 292–3
Blackton, Stuart 63
Blaine, Vivian 410
Bletcher, Billy 110, 456
Block-Heads 159, 268, 364–8, 367, 369, 438
Blood and Sand 150, 420
Blore, Eric 358
Blotto 262–3
Blystone, John G. 368
Boer War 18–20
Bogart, Humphrey 429
Bogle, Donald 372–3
The Bohemian Girl 320–21, 338–41, 356
Bolger, Ray 403
Bond, Ward 430
Bonnie Scotland 320, 334–6, 335, 386, 438
Bookbinder, George 432–4
The Bootblack 15, 49
Bostock, Claude 84–5, 87, 334
Bostock, Gordon 84–5
Bowers, Billy 91, 94, 100
Brady, Alice 371
Brandon, Henry 324–5
Brats 110, 267–8, 296–7
Breen, Joseph 320
Breslow, Lou 400, 403
Brice, Fanny 451
Brigadoon 30
Bright and Early 111

Broadbent, R. J. 4–5
Brook, Sam 182
Brooke, Tyler 182–6, 198, 240–41
Brooks, Leo 33, 36, 43, 442
Brooks, Randy 448
Brooks, Sam 156, 168, 357
Broughton, Lewis 157
Brown, Harry Joe 448
Browning, Tod 177
Bruckman, Clyde 221
Brunner, H. C. 370
Buck Privates 395, 398
Buell, Jed 353
The Bullfighters 419–20
Bunny, John 63, 197
Bunty Pulls the Strings 157
Buñuel, Luis 236–7, 326, 331
Burke, Billie 371
Burnett, Lillian 348
Burns, Bobby 100, 104
Burns, George 131
Burns, Neal 116
Burstein, Louis 100, 104, 108–9
Busch, Mae 123, 184, 204–5, 230, 252–3, 295, 311, 330, 332, 340–41, 401
Business Before Honesty 133
Busted Hearts 107
Busy Bodies 158, 303–4, 304
Butler, Frank 167, 210, 332–3
Byron, Marion 230
Byron, Roy 93

Cagney, Jimmy 405
Calhoun, Alice 147
Call of the Cuckoos 213
Campbell, Herbert 8, 49, 52
Cantor, Eddie 332, 356, 420
Cappello, Bill 156
Capra, Frank 182, 369, 395, 432
Cardwell, J.E. 25, 449
Carney, Augustus 63, 72
Carroll, Lewis 8, 44
Carter, Jimmy 32
Caruso, Enrico 45
Casey, H.R. 35, 215
Cash, Morny 49
The Cat's Paw 414
Cavett, Dick 451
Ceausescu, Nicolae 459
Ceder, Ralph 178
censorship 14, 54–5, 105, 146, 220, 288, 320–21
Chadwick, Helene 138
Chaney, Lon 177–8

506

Chaplin, Charlie 7, 50, 56, 58, 63, 69–87
  passim, 70, 97, 107, 116, 125, 128,
  143–4, 152, 163, 177, 197–8, 209, 221,
  223, 261, 269, 342, 352, 387, 459
  imitations of 109–11, 117, 121–4, 133,
  283
Chaplin, Sydney 57, 82, 125
Chase, Charley 123, 154, 167, 178,
  180–82, 188, 205, 213, 216, 230, 243,
  258, 286, 306, 314–15, 314; see also
  Parrott, Charles
Chevalier, Albert 7
Chickens 104–5
The Chief Cook 109
childlike quality in acting 208–9, 220, 235,
  249, 296, 326, 461
Christie, Dorothy 311
A Chump at Oxford 298, 375–81, 379
Church of the Hills, Glendale 456
Churchill, Winston 394
City Lights 185
Clifford, Nat 126
Clothes Make the Man 98
clowns and clowning 3–9, 54, 297, 395,
  409, 448, 459
Clyde, Andy 448, 456
Cobb, Ty 47
Cobh 441
Coburn, Dorothy 220, 225, 235, 456
Coburn Minstrels 43–4
The Cocoanuts 177
Cody, Buffalo Bill 61, 86
Cohen, Joe 107
Cohen, Sam B. 332
Colbert, Claudette 405
Coleman, Frank J. 231
Collars and Cuffs 159
Collins, Monty 434
Columbia Pictures 370, 421
Come Clean 280
comic strips in newspapers 96
Confessions of a Nazi Spy 394
Conklin, Chester 64, 85, 218
Conti, Albert 205
Conway, Jack 138
Cook, Clyde 123, 182–4, 448, 456
Cooke, Alice 86–7, 313, 439
Cooke, Baldwin ('Baldie') 86–7, 232, 298,
  313, 439
Coolidge, Calvin 177
Cops 130
Cornwall, Anne 255
Costello, Lou 267, 395, 398–9, 421, 430
Courtwright, William 203

Coward, Noël 440
Cowley, Thomas 113
Crackles, Billy 82
Craig, George 57
Cramer, Dick 448
Cramer, Rychard 392
Crane, Harry 406, 415
Craven, Frank 305
The Crazy Clock Maker 99–100
The Crazy Cracksman 86–7
Crazy Like a Fox 180
Crazy to Act 188
Crosby, Bing 354, 395, 399, 405, 430, 432
Crossley, Syd 202
Cubin, Bill 11
'Cuckoo' theme 267–8, 291, 326, 441
Culver, Harry 154
Culver City 123, 154, 168, 217, 230, 272,
  445
Cummins, Samuel 108
Currier, Richard 202, 224, 270, 285,
  299–300
The Curtain Pole 62
Cushing, Peter 377
Cuthbert, Edith 52

Dahlberg, Mae 87–8, 113–18, 131–3, 142,
  150–52, 156, 159–62, 168–71, 175,
  186–7, 283, 345, 347, 362, 457
D'Albrook, Sidney 167
The Dancing Masters 412
Dandoe, Arthur 69, 78–9
Daniels, Bebe 120
Daniels, Mickey 169
Dardis, Tom 120–21
Darling, Scott 409–13, 420
datebooks 228–9
Davidson, Max 182, 213
Davies, Marion 152
A Day at School 107
De Haviland, Olivia 405–6
The Dead Letter 62
Dean, Martha 109
Dean, Priscilla 204
Delair, Suzy 435, 437
Delfont, Bernard 425, 438, 444
Demarest, William 432
Depew, Hap 301
Depression years 265–8, 285, 287, 298,
  303, 329, 415
Deslys, Kay 247–8, 362
The Devil's Brother 302; see also Fra
  Diavolo
The Devil's Passkey 205

507

Dewey, Thomas E. 429
Dickson, James 298
Dimsdale, Howard 406
The Discreet Charm of the Bourgeoisie 326, 331
Dix, Richard 138
Do Detectives Think? 208, 210
Do You Love Your Wife? 123
Doane, Warren 168, 175
Dr Jekyll and Mr Hyde 174–5
Dr Pyckle and Mr Pride 174–5
A Dog's Life 125
Double Whoopee 235
Douglas, Gordon 371
Doyle, Justin G. 403
Dressler, Marie 450
Dreyfuss, Randy 413
The Drunkard 324
Duck Soup 23, 181, 198–202, 233, 274, 288
Dull Care 134
Dumbrille, Douglas 390
Dumont, Margaret 412
Durfee, Minta 64
Dwan, Dorothy 163–5, *164*

Early Birds 55–6
Easy Street 56
Eckhardt, Joseph P. 94
Éclair (company) 61
Edinburgh 291
Edison (company) 91–2, 98
Edwards, Harry 369
Edwards, Ralph 444
The Eight Comicques 80
Eisenstein, Sergei 458
Elder, T. C. 7
Elliott, John 309
Ellis, Patricia 365
Ellison, James 371
Elloy, Max 435, 437
The Era 53–4, 56, 81
Ernst, Max 326
Essanay (company) 61, 63, 83
Ethel's Romeo 99
Evans, Owen 116
Eve's Love Letters 187
Evolution of Fashion 83
An Exile's Lover 62

Fairbanks, Douglas 414
Falconer, Dr and Ethel 290
The Fall Guy 146
fans of Laurel and Hardy xii–xiii, 332, 396,

426; *see also* Sons of the Desert (fan club)
Fatty's Fatal Fun 99
Faye, Alice 398
Fazenda, Louise 158
Federal Bureau of Investigation (FBI) 403
Fernandel 434
Fields, W. C. 63, 99, 143, 177, 196, 218, 221, 250, 258, 272, 279, 288, 300, 324, 331, 389, 395, 449
The Fighting Kentuckian 430–31
The Finishing Touch xii, 158, 225
Finlayson, Jimmy xi, 156–61, 168–9, 176–7, 182–4, 187–9, 198, 204–13 *passim*, 214, 231, 233, 234, 255–9 *passim*, 266, 270, 273–4, 300, 324, 336, 341–2, 350, 352, 366, 375–6, 386, 391–2, 401, 442, 456
First National (company) 218, 369
Fisher, Bud 311
Fitzgerald, F. Scott 177
Flowers, Bess 248–9
The Flying Deuces 382–7, *383*
Flying Elephants 210–12, *211*
'Flying Showboat' tour 403
Foolish Wives 205
For His Sake 22
Ford, Corey 371
Ford, John 177, 398, 430
Ford, Wallace 448
foreign language versions of films 259–60
'Fort Laurel' 382, 387, 396, 422, 425
Fortune's Mask 147
45 Minutes from Hollywood 189
Foster, Lewis R. 252–3
Fouvan, Eugene E. 424
Fox Film Corporation 167, 187, 201, 205, 398–402, 405, 410–11, 419–20; *see also* Twentieth Century Fox
Fra Diavolo 300–302, 322, 324, 437–8
Frank, Leo 66–7
Frauds and Frenzies 130, 216
The Freckled Fish 133
Freddi, Luigi 356
The Freshman 177, 413–14
Freud, Sigmund 297
From Soup to Nuts 16, 161, 214, 230, 233, 375
Frozen Hearts 5, 160–61
Fun on the Tyrol 80

Gale, Gladys 286
Gallagher, J. P. 50, 261
Garbo, Greta 344, 395

Garfield, John 403
Garnett, Tay 173, 175
Garvin, Anita 171, 174, 182, 206–7, 217,
    230–31, 247, 262–6, 285, 358, 375–6,
    456
Gas and Air 159
Gay, John 6
Geisler, Jerry 345
Gemora, Charles 358
The General 221
The Gentleman Jockey 26
Get 'Em Young 185, 198
Gibson, Ethlyn 109
Gifford, Denis 445
Gilbert, Billy 230, 266, 286, 365, 367, 401,
    456
Gilbert, John 143
Gillespie, William 123, 156, 182
Gillstrom, Arvid 109
Ginsberg, Henry 285, 288, 298–305 passim,
    319, 333, 341
The Girl in the Limousine 163
Girl Shy 188
Gish, Lillian 151
Glasgow 290–91
Go West 177
Goebbels, Josef 340
The Gold Rush 177, 352
Gombell, Minna 365
Gone with the Wind 94
Goodrich, J. B. 332
Goodwin, Harold 187
Goulding, Alf 118, 435
Grant, Cary 182, 368, 405
Grant, Katherine 156, 159, 168
The Great Dictator 387, 395
The Great Game 157
Great Guns 400–402, 401, 407
Greed 143
Greer, Gloria 255
Gregory, Ena 161
Griffith, D.W. 21, 61–2, 91, 177, 451
Griffiths, Charles 69
Grimaldi, Joseph 5–6, 54, 209, 279, 444
Guiles, Fred Lawrence 86–7, 132, 239,
    347–8, 422
Guiol, Fred 198, 203, 213, 243
Gus and the Anarchists 97

Habeas Corpus 183, 229
Haddock, William 61
Hahn, S. S. 132
Haile Selassie 356
Hale, Creighton 189

Hale, Wanda 406–8
Half a Man 175
Halff, Robert 414–15
Hall, Charles D. 370
Hall, Charlie 221, 225, 231–2, 269, 275,
    287, 332, 340, 456
The Handy Man 148, 197–8
Happy Hooligan 96, 311
Hardy, Catherine and Samuel 33
Hardy, Cornelia 33–6
Hardy, Elizabeth 36–7, 59, 65–6, 282, 391
Hardy, Emily 36–47, 65, 68, 101, 281–2,
    355
Hardy, George M. 35
Hardy, Jesse 33
Hardy, John 33
Hardy, Lillian 35
Hardy, Lucille 45–6, 103, 134, 145,
    240–41, 282, 387–91, 399, 424–9, 434,
    438, 440, 446–8, 457
Hardy, Madelyn 64–8, 98, 101, 134–8, 282,
    354–5, 457
Hardy, Mamie L. 35
Hardy, Myrtle 101–2, 134–8, 165, 239–42,
    280, 282, 290, 293, 297, 311–12, 334,
    338, 346, 349, 384, 388, 405, 447, 457
Hardy, Oliver senior 33–9, 42, 215, 336,
    374
Hardy, Oliver
    acting ambitions 145
    appearance 41, 45–6, 79, 358, 390–91,
        446
    birth 30–31, 37
    choice of names 43, 48, 94
    Christmas cards sent 242–3
    comedy techniques 222–7
    consistency in characterisation 221–2
    contracts with Hal Roach 342, 392
    cross-dressing 107, 109
    death 447
    film acting technique 96
    first appearance in film 68, 91–2
    first film as director 106
    first work with Stan Laurel 140–42, 176,
        182, 189, 202–3, 208, 219
    gambling 211–12, 240, 312
    home life with Lucille 389–90
    job as projectionist 47–8, 59, 64
    last performance 443
    last television appearances 444–5
    love of music 40–41, 45, 47
    Masonic connections 108, 313, 390, 448
    passion for golf 165, 290, 334
    racial attitudes 67, 374

509

reliance on instinct 324
salary 195, 229, 298, 353
schooling 41, 43, 46–7
sense of isolation 67
tours to Britain (1952 and 1953–4)
    438–43
visits to Europe (1932 and 1947) 290–94,
    425–9
Harlem, Georgia 30–32, 36
Harlequin 4–5
Harlow, Jean 235
Harmon, Larry 452–3
Harris, Joel Chandler 41
Hart, William S. 177
Harvey, Forrester 377
Hatley, T. Marvin 267–8
Hats Off 214, 216, 218, 286
Hauber, Bill 129
Hawes, Tony 445
Hawks, Howard 138, 368
Hay, Will 428
He Wanted Work 94
The Head Waiter 134
Healey, Bill 427
Hello Trouble 133
Helpmates 126, 284–5
Hennecke, Clarence 175–6
Hepburn, Katharine 368
Her Boy Friend 145, 206
Her Convict Lover 22, 27
Herbert, Victor 321
Herriman, George 326
Hersholt, Jean 138
Hewitt, Robert 427
Hey, Taxi! 167
Hickey, Louise McHenry 38
Hickory Hiram 116–17
Hilarity 53–4
Hiller, Louis 108
His Majesty's Guests 57
Hitler, Adolf 177, 340, 407, 420, 459
The Hobo 110
Hog Wild xv, 270–72, 271, 283, 331
Holderness, Fay 247, 270
Holley, Thomas Earl 33–4
Holliday, Frank 263
Hollywood Revue of 1929 258
'Hollywood Ten', the 429
'Hollywood Victory Caravan' 405
Home from the Honeymoon 22–4, 27, 198,
    274
Hook, Line and Sinker 300
The Hoose-Gow xiii–xiv
Hoot Mon! 126

Hoover, Herbert 288
Hope, Bob 300, 395, 399, 405–6, 430
Horne, James 236, 284, 336, 339
Horseshoes 147
Hotaling, Arthur 89, 91, 94–5, 97
Houdini 196–7
The House That Jack Built 26–8, 49
House Un-American Activities Committee
    429
Housman, Arthur 289
Hughes, Howard 438
Hughes, Raymond 109
Hungry Hearts 105
Huns and Hyphens 129, 159
Hunt, Caroline C. 36
Hunter, Mary 312, 338
Hurley, Edgar and Ethel ('Wren') 82–6, 439
Hurlie, Philip 371
Hurlock, Madelaine 203
Hustling for Health 126
Hutton, E. F. 319

The Immigrant 231, 269
Ince, Thomas 154
Iniskin (company) 354
Insall, Stephanie 456
The Iron Horse 177
Isn't Life Terrible? 167, 180, 286
It Happened One Night 395
It's a Gift 331

Jackman, Floyd 224
Jackman, Fred 178
Jackson, Jackie 109
Jacksonville 89, 91, 97–8, 100, 64–8, 103–8
    passim
Jacobs, W. W. 342
Jail Birds 53–5, 216
Jameson, L. S. 55
Jamison, Bud 125–6
Jaxon Films 106
The Jazz Singer 218
Jefferson, Arthur 12–28, 20, 49–50, 57, 81,
    144, 148, 198, 200, 274–5, 291, 294,
    297, 425–7, 439
Jefferson, Arthur Stanley *see* Laurel, Stan
Jefferson, Edward 17
Jefferson, Gordon 13, 17, 25, 80
Jefferson, Joseph 12
Jefferson, Madge 12–14, 17–18, 22, 48, 144
Jefferson, Olga 17, 25, 81, 291, 426–7, 439
Jefferson, Stanley Robert 297
Jefferson, Sydney 17
Jefferson, Teddy 331

Jemoff, Sergei 361
Jenkins, C. Francis 90
Jeske, George 159
Jevne, Jack 406
Jimmy the Fearless 58, 71–2, 79
Jitterbugs 409–11, 422
Joannon, Leo 434
John Jasper's Wife 14
Johnson, Lyndon 454
Jolson, Al 218
Jones, Buck 398
Jones, F. Richard (Dick) 175, 182, 202–3
Jones, Lucille *see* Hardy, Lucille
Jones, Monnie L. 447
Jones, Vernon 344
Jordan, Bert 301
Journal of Popular Film and Television 89
Joy, Colonel 320
Joy, Leatrice 109
Joyce, James 459
Julian, Rupert 177
Just Nuts 121
Just Rambling Along 123, 125, 154, 269

Kalem (company) 89
Kalma 84
Karno, Fred 50–58, 70–84 *passim*, 123, 142, 197, 216, 231, 260–62, 439
Karno, Fred junior 69
Kaufman, George S. 410
Kaye, Danny 430, 451–2
Keaton, Buster 77, 110, 129–30, 144, 163, 175, 177, 207, 221–3, 258, 370, 395, 408, 415–18, 456
Kelly, Patsy 311, 333, 456
Kennedy, Edgar 225, 232–3, 248–53, 258–60, 406–8, 425, 456
Kennedy, John F. xi, 450
Kerr, Walter 208, 220, 222–3, 283
Kerrigan, J. Warren 120
Keystone Kops 158
Keystone Studio 63–4, 82, 97, 122, 197, 205, 232
Keystone Trio 85–6
Kibbee, Guy 390
The Kid 163
Kilgore, Al 319
Kill or Cure 159
King, Dennis 301
King, Walter Woolf 357
King Bee Film Corporation 108–9
The King of the Kitchen 133
Kingsley, Grace 137–8
The Kiss Was Mightier than the Sword 62

Kitchen, Fred 76
Klaie, Rick 53
Knight, Felix 324
Kohner, Paul 434
Kotsonaros, George 248
Krahulik, Dr 423
Kruger, Paul 55
Ku-Klux-Klan 67
Ku-Ku song 267–8; *see also* 'Cuckoo' theme

Ladd, Alan 401–2
Laemmle, Carl 116
Lahr, Bert 405–6
Lakeside Country Club 165, 334, 429
Lane, Lupino 428
Lang, Fritz 394
Lang, June 335
Langdon, Harry 165, 222, 369–71, 374–5, 382, 384, 395
Lasky, Jesse 261
Lauder, Alex 156–8
Lauder, Harry 50, 52, 427
Laughing Gravy 275–6, 276, 291, 297
Laurel, Ida 423–30 *passim*, 434–8, 446–9, 457
Laurel, Illiana 359–64, 376, 382–4, 423–4, 457
Laurel, Lois 171, 187, 212, 239, 280–83, 290, 297, 312–13, 362–3, 376, 399, 457
Laurel, Lois junior 239, 282, 297, 312–13, 348, 363, 411, 444, 448, 457
Laurel, Mae *see* Dahlberg, Mae
Laurel, Stan
 apolitical stance 144
 appearance 79, 123, 358
 argumentative streak 283
 birth 11–12
 childhood 15–17
 choice of name 88, 113–14, 457
 comedy techniques 222–7
 consistency in characterization 221–2
 contracts with Hal Roach 342, 344, 348, 368, 375, 392
 correspondence with fans 332, 449–50
 cross-dressing 114, 174, 206, 375
 crying on screen 161, 173, 185–6, 198, 246, 367–8
 death 454
 drinking 131–2, 347–8
 early performances 18–19, 23–9
 feeling for the theatre 117–18, 438
 first appearance in film 88, 115–16
 first trip to America (1910–11) 69–78

511

first work with Oliver Hardy 140–42, 176, 182, 189, 202–3, 208, 219
lack of business sense 399
last performance 443
last television appearances 444–5
reliance on instinct 324–5
salary 195, 229, 298, 353
schooling 18, 22
tours to Britain (1952 and 1953–4) 438–43
use of scripts 187, 247
visits to Europe (1932 and 1947) 290–94, 425–9
Laurel, (Virginia) Ruth 132, 239, 312–13, 331, 339, 344–9, 357–63, 396, 422–3, 457
Laurel and Hardy, local names for xii
Laurel and Hardy Museum, Ulverston 11–12
The Laurel–Hardy Murder Case 283, 329–30
Lawrence, Ed 93
Lawrence, Rosina 350
Leave 'Em Laughing 232–3, 260, 274
Leeds 293
Leno, Dan ix, 7–8, 10, 49–50, 52, 76, 197, 279, 444
Leo, Ted 80
Leonard, Julie 171–2
Lesser, Sol 387
Levering, James 94
Levy, Harold B. 25–6, 449
Lewis, Jerry 300, 430, 451
Liberty 233, 235–6, 270
Lightning Love 147, 177
Lindbergh, Charles 177, 298
Linder, Max 63
Linthicum, Dan 120
Little Tich 7, 50, 76, 444
The Little Wildcat 147
Littlefield, Lucien 309
Litvak, Anatole 394
L-KO Motion Picture Kompany 116, 133
Lloyd, Art 301
Lloyd, Harold 77, 110, 120–27 *passim*, 121, 123, 143–4, 154, 163, 177, 188, 207, 221, 223, 235, 270, 395, 413–14
Lloyd, Marie 7–9, 50, 52
Lobach, Marvin 159
Locke, Sam 425
Loew, Arthur 298
Loew, David 341
London 291, 294, 440
London, Babe 448, 456

London by Day and Night 14–15
Long, James B. 424
looks to camera 207, 267
Lord, Charles 35–6
Lorre, Peter 398, 405
Los Angeles Examiner 322, 334, 345–6, 348, 388
Los Angeles Times 87, 114–15, 281
'Lot of Fun' 228, 325
Louis, Will 98
Love 'Em and Weep 204–5
Love in a Tub 52
Lubin, Siegmund 89–91, 97
Lubin (company) 62, 68, 89–98 *passim*, 197
Lubitsch, Ernst 395
The Lucky Dog 139–43, 182, 189
A Lucky Strike 98
Lundin, Walter 285
Lusitania 78
Lyn, Jacquie 288

McCabe, John xii, xiv, 19, 29, 43, 46, 63, 70–71, 79, 83–6, 101, 113, 165–6, 202, 219, 241, 319, 354, 398, 439, 442, 446, 452, 457
McCarey, Leo 123, 168, 175, 178–82, 187, 179, 198, 202–3, 206, 216–17, 236, 243, 266, 368, 420, 429, 444, 456
McCarey, Raymond 288
McCrea, Joel 265
McCullogh, David 319
McDaniel, Hattie 94, 371, 373
MacDonald, J. Farrell 138
Mace, Fred 64
McFarland, Spanky 333
MacGillivray, Scott 398–9, 406
MacGowan, Robert 155
McIntosh, Burr 99
Mack, Hughie 128
McKee, Raymond 91, 98
McLaglen, Victor 405
McLemore, Henry 429
McManus, George 311
Macon, Georgia 65–6
McPherson, Jeanie 300
MacQueen Pope, W. 6
Mad Magazine 452
Madame Mystery 183–4, 210, 270
Madison, Georgia 37, 40–41
The Madisonian 38–9
Magritte, René 326
Magruder, Cornelia 33–6
Magruder, George Milton 34
Mahoney, Wilkie 415

Maid to Order 107
Malatesta, Fred 183
Malavsky, Sergei 361
Mamoulian, Rouben 420
A Man About Town 160
Manchester 292
Mandarin Mix-Up 171
Manley, Harry 51
Mann, Hank 456
Mannheimer, Albert 434
Marchetti, Roger 345–6, 348, 357, 361, 423
Marian, Edna 212, 248
Marriot, A.J. xv, 80–81, 87, 426–7, 439–40
Marris, Edward 26
Marsh, Mae 401
Marshall, George 123, 201, 287–8, 300
Marshall, Trudy 412
Martin, Dean 300, 430
Martin, 'Tonnage' 397
Marx, Chico 3, 331, 403
Marx, Groucho 7, 82, 405, 429, 450, 454
Marx, Karl 6
Marx Brothers 177, 181, 203, 221, 257–8, 261, 279, 288, 305, 350, 395, 410
Masquers Club 430
Mate, Rudolph 343–4
Mayfair, Mitzi 403
Me and My Pal 303
Medved, Harry 122, 413
Meek, Donald 407
melodramas 61
Melroyd, Frank 69
Melton, Albert C. 396
Men o' War 254
Menjou, Adolphe 448
Merrick, Mollie 193
Metcalfe, George and Sarah 13, 17
Metcalfe, Madge see Jefferson, Madge
Metro (company) 152, 415
Metro Goldwyn Mayer (MGM) 143, 212–13, 217–18, 229, 258–9, 272, 290, 298, 306, 313, 320, 329, 375, 394, 406–7, 413, 418, 421
Middleton, Charles 288, 386
The Midnight Patrol 303
Milledgeville, Georgia 41–7, 102–3, 445
Miller, Alicia 445
Miller, Rube 117
Milligan, Spike 174, 326
Mineau, Charlotte 212
Minster, Amy 69
Mr Deeds Goes to Town 395
Mr Hulot's Holiday 253

Mitchell, Glenn xv, 106, 108, 231, 305, 423, 453
Mitchum, Robert 412
Mix, Tom 61, 398
Mixed Nuts 115, 125, 148–9, 198, 210
Modern Times 78
Moffat, Graham 157
Monsieur Beaucaire 171
Monsieur Don't Care 171
The Monster 177
Montague, John 354
Montgomery, Earl 132
Moonlight and Noses 182
Moore, La Verne 354
Morgan, Byron 305
Morgan, Kewpie 325
Moriarty, Dennis 32
Morrison, Ernie 123
Morros, Boris 382, 387
Morse, Viola 282, 290, 312, 338, 387–9
Mother's Joy 161
Motion Picture Herald 370
Motion Picture Patents Company 60, 91
Motion Picture Producers and Distributors Association 320
Moving Picture World 116, 127, 133
Moyer, Frances Ne 91
Mud and Sand 149, 151, 152
Mumming Birds 56, 58, 63, 74, 133
Murnau, F. W. 398
Murphy, J. A. 93
Murphy, Jimmy 422–3
Murray, Charlie 64
The Music Box xi, 30, 180, 266, 271, 285–7, 286, 352, 358
music-hall 6–9, 50, 54–6, 74–6, 107, 195, 197, 278–9
The Musical Ranch 62
Mussolini, Benito 177, 356
Mussolini, Vittorio 355–7
Myers, Harry 185, 198

The Navigator 163
Near Dublin 169
Neilson, Lois 123; see also Laurel, Lois
Nelson, Dick 400
Neptune's Stepdaughter 167
Nestor Comedies 117
Never Give a Sucker an Even Break 272
New Adventures of J. Rufus Wallingford 99
New Deal 288, 329, 389
New York Dramatic Mirror 62
New York Herald Tribune 333
New York Morning Telegraph 57

New York Times 59, 289, 334
The Nickel Hopper 186
A Night at an English Music Hall 56, 74–8,
  82
A Night in a London Club 74, 81
Night Owls 259, 261, 267, 439
Ninotchka 395
No Mother to Guide Her 131
No, No, Nanette 176
No Wedding Bells 146
The Noon Whistle 156, 158–9
Normand, Mabel 63–4, 85, 97, 123, 151,
  182–6, 205, 217
Norvell, Emily *see* Hardy, Emily
Norvell, Susan 40
Norvell, Thomas Edward 427–8
Norvell, Thomas Benjamin 36
Nothing But Trouble 413, 418–19, 419
Nottingham Theatre Royal 49
Novello, Arnold 118
Nuts in May 88, 115–16, 148
The Nutty Burglars 84–5, 439

Oakland, Vivien 184, 188, 235, 248
Oberon, Merle 405
O'Brien, Pat 405
O'Connor, Flannery 41
Oglethorpe, James 33
O'Hara, Maureen 430
Oland, Warner 398
Olcott, Sydney 89
The Old Fashioned Way 324
Olive, Sarah E. 35
Oliver Hardy Festival 30, 32
Oliver the Eighth 326, 329–31, 413
On the Front Page 186, 198
On the Wrong Trek 315
One Good Turn 265–6
One Too Many 105
O'Neill, Frank 58
Oranges and Lemons 159
The Orphan Heiress 14–15, 198
Oscars 286, 452
'Our Gang' films 123, 154, 169, 178, 258,
  305, 371
Our Relations 342–4
Outwitting Dad 68, 91–2

Pack Up Your Troubles 287–8, 321
Paige, Mabel 95–6, 100
Painless Love 133
Pallette, Gene 220
Palmer, Fred 69
Palmer, Muriel 69

pantomime 25–6, 49–50, 55, 75–6, 253
The Paperhanger's Helper 166
Paramount (company) 399
Pardon Us 272–4, 283, 287, 423, 430–31
Parent Teachers Association of America 322
Park, Roland 444–5
Parker, Jean 371
Parkinson, Harry 19
Parnell, Val 425
Parrott, Charles 110–11, 123, 133, 154–5,
  178–9, 184, 241, 244; *see also* Chase,
  Charley
Parrott, Jimmy 111, 123, 125, 154–5, 175,
  178, 184, 186, 188, 194, 229, 241–4,
  258, 261, 263, 273, 284–5, 298, 340,
  344
Parsons, Louella 333–4, 357, 397, 423, 425
The Patchwork Girl of Oz 163
Pathé (company) 212
Patterson, Adolph Dahm 45
Payson, Blanche 269, 285
Pembroke, Percy 155, 159, 168–9, 173, 178
Pense, Mary 280
The Perfect Clown 164, 165
Perfect Day 233, 413
The Pest 148, 149
Petronius 3
Phagan, Mary 66–7
The Phantom of the Opera 177
Phoney Photos 116
Picasso, Pablo 459
Pick and Shovel 159
Pick a Star 353
Pickard, Albert 24
Pickens, Jane 403
Pickford, Mary 132, 151, 414
Picturegoer Weekly 275
The Pilgrim 204
Pinter, Harold 278, 459
Pitts, ZaSu 405
pity 458–9
Playmates 110
'Plump and Runt' 104–6, 223
Poitier, Sidney 373
Pollard, Daphne 235, 336–7
Pollard, Harry ('Snub') 110, 118, 122,
  154–5, 159, 456
Potel, Victor 63
Powers, Len 254, 285
The Precious Parcel 106
Preminger, Otto 394
Preston 292
Price, Ben 457
Prin, Lucille 406

Prohibition 131, 314–15
Punctured Romance 218
Putting Pants on Philip 189, 202–3, 214,
    219, 221, 456

Quicksands 138

Rabe, Bill 220, 226
Rackin, Martin 406
Raffles, the Dentist 87
Raggedy Roses 185
Ramish, Adolph 115
Randall, Harry 49
Randolph, Anders 259
Randolph, Roy 361
Raphael, Ida Kitaeva 423; *see also* Laurel,
    Ida
Rauh, Stanley 403
Rawlinson, Herbert 204
Ray, Bobby 166–7
Raynor, Dan 83
Reed, Bob 80
Reeves, Alf 69, 74, 78, 81–2
Reeves, Billy 56, 58, 76, 97, 197
Reeves, Maggie Lee 137
Reeves, Mary *see* Hunter, Mary
Reeves, Myrtle *see* Hardy, Myrtle
Regal Films 437
Reggie's Engagement 62
Reid, Hal 28, 49
Reid, Nancy Jane 440
Reijnhoudt, Bram 80
Rhodes, Cecil 55
Rich, France 281
Rich, Lillian 186
Richard, Viola 206, 235, 248
Riding High 432, 433
Rimoldı, Adriano 435
The Rink 71
Ritchie, Billie 57, 110, 155, 197
Ritchie, Charlie 100
Ritz Brothers 395, 398
RKO (company) 382
Roach, Hal (and Hal Roach Studios) 110,
    118–27, 121, 142, 152–62, 167,
    175–84, 187, 189, 196, 199–213, 218,
    225, 228–30, 243–5, 251, 254, 258–61,
    266–7, 272, 281–2, 285, 289, 295,
    298–302, 311, 319–25, 329, 332–4,
    339–44, 348, 355–9, 364, 368, 370,
    375, 377, 384, 391–2, 395, 406, 448,
    453–6
Roach, Hal junior 445
Roach, Marguerite 406

The Road to Singapore 395
Robbins, Jess 138, 142
Roberts, Arthur 7
Robey, George 7, 50, 76, 197
Robinson, David 458
Robinson Crusoeland 437, 440
Rock, Joe 129, 132–4, 150, 155–6, 162,
    168–75, 184, 189, 202, 230, 347, 448,
    456
Rock, Louise 169–70
Rockne, Knute 177
Rogan, Nat 405
Rogers, Charlie 232, 241, 301, 339–40,
    344, 369, 382, 406, 456
Rogers, Rena 116
Rogers, Virginia Ruth *see* Laurel, (Virginia)
    Ruth
The Rogue Song 258, 272, 292
Rolin (company) 110, 120–23, 126–7
Room Service 305
Roosevelt, Eleanor 406
Roosevelt, Franklin Delano 288, 329, 389,
    394, 396
Ross, Budd 109
Rothman, Dave 65, 136
Roughest Africa 160
Rowe, George 159, 161, 168, 176
Ruge, Billy 104–6
Rum 'Uns from Rome 3, 79–80
Running, Jumping and Standing Still Film
    174
Rupert of Henzau 168
Russell, Lillian 45
Ruth, Babe 64, 177
Ryan, Sheila 402

Safety Last 144, 154, 163, 235, 413
Sage, Elizabeth 101
Sage, Ira 65, 44, 282
Sage, Mary 43
Sailors, Beware! 207
St Clair, Malcolm 409–13, 420
Sally of the Sawdust 177
Saloshin family 65–6; *see also* Hardy,
    Madelyn
Sanders, Jonathan 295
Sandford,, Stanley J. ('Tiny') 182, 231, 234,
    247, 269, 304, 456

Saps at Sea 382, 391, 438
Sargent, Epes Winthrop 94–5
Saturday to Monday 55
The Sawmill 129, 145
Schiller, Alfred 382, 384

Scipio Africanus Major 113, 457
Scopes, John Thomas 177
Scorching Sands 160
Scott, Fred 353
Scram 289
Seaman, George and Emily 69
Seawright, Roy 153, 210, 286, 304–5, 343, 357
The Second Hundred Years 213, 216, 231
Second World War 402–3, 409, 420–21
Sedgwick, Edward 406, 408
Seiter, William 305, 312
Selig Polyscope (company) 61, 89
Sellers, Peter 174, 451
Semon, Larry 110, 127–37 *passim*, 142, 145–7, 146, 159, 163–6, 164, 172, 177, 207, 216, 304
Senise, Renato 357
Sennett, Mack 62–4, 76, 82, 110, 122, 125, 158, 167, 178, 182, 188, 197, 205, 258, 305, 369, 456
Sennwald, Andre 322
The Servant Girl's Legacy 95
Seven Chances 130, 175, 177
Sewall, Bob 52
Seymour, Clarine 124
Shah of Iran 56
Shaw, George Bernard 50
Shaw, John 17
Sheffield 293
Sherlock Junior 172
Shields, Leroy 268
Shipman, Ben 312, 344, 349, 354, 368, 388, 392, 396, 399, 405, 425, 444, 446, 448
Shoddy the Tailor 97
Short, Mrs and Mrs 449, 453
Short Kilts 168
Short Orders 159
Should Married Men Go Home? 247–8
Should Tall Men Marry? 187
The Show 129
Siep, Beulah 348
Simon, Simone 434
The Simp and the Sophomores 98
Siodmak, Curt 394
Sjostrom, Victor 177
Skating 58, 71
Skretvedt, Randy xiv, 132–3, 137, 169, 173, 183, 202, 207, 210, 224, 236, 241–2, 254, 258–9, 266–7, 285, 297, 304, 321, 325, 350, 353, 357, 364, 387, 424, 433–4, 451
slapstick 122, 181–2, 293, 399, 448

Slaton, John 67
The Slave 109
Sleeper, Martha 184
The Sleeping Beauty 25–6, 321, 449
The Sleuth 174, 206
Slide, Anthony 119, 302, 322, 333
Slipping Wives 204–5
'slow burn' of comedy 181
Smith, Albert 63
Smith, Eddie 288
Smithy 169
The Snow Hawk 169, 171
Soapsuds and Sapheads 133
Society Secrets 179
The Soilers 161
Something in Her Eye 99
Somewhere in Wrong 172
Sons of the Desert (fan club) xii, xiv, 32, 319, 442
Sons of the Desert (film) 108, 248, 305–20, 314, 410, 438
Spaghetti and Lottery 97
Spaulding, Captain 196
Spence, Ralph 382
Spitzer, Nat 108
'split reels' 92
Spuds 165
Spurling, Leslie 439
Squeaks and Squawks 133–4
The Stage Hand 134
Stanislavsky, Konstantin Sergeyevich 458
Stepin Fetchit 371, 374
Stephenson, Art 267
Sterling, Ford 63–4, 158
Sterling, Mirta 148
Stevens, George 212, 224, 229, 285, 448
Stevenson, Adlai 390
Stewart, Roy 121
Stick Around 166–7
Stone, Rob xiv–xv, 92, 99, 104, 106, 108, 115–16, 123, 126, 131, 138–9, 148, 174
Stop, Look and Listen 165
Stossel, Ludwig 401
Strauss, Theodore 408
Stripling, Robert 429
Stroheim, Erich von 143, 195, 205
Struss, Karl 370
Stull, Walter 100, 104
stunts 129–30, 145–6, 172
Sturges, Preston 265, 395, 421, 424, 459
Sugar Daddies 212–13, 214
Sullivan's Travels 265
Sunrise 398

surrealism 149, 174, 184, 224, 237, 270, 324, 331, 351, 441
Sutherland, Eddie 370
Sutton, Grady 288–9
Swain, Mack 64
Sweet, Harry 169
Swiss Miss 353, 357–9

Taft, William Howard 451
Talmadge, Norma 414
Talmadge, Richard 129
Tant, T. Sam 36–7
Tante, Henry Lafayette ('Bardy') 281
Tati, Jacques 243
Taylor, Sam 413
Tayo, Lyle 247
television 437
Tellini, Pierro 434
Temple, Shirley 398
The Terror of Tiny Town 353
Terry, Frank 126, 305
Thalberg, Irving 258, 329
That's My Wife 247
Their First Mistake 295–7, 296
Their Purple Moment 243–5
They Bought a Boat 93
They Looked Alike 97
Thicker than Water 336–7, 412
This Is Your Life 444–5
This Way Out 104
Thomson, David 369
The Three Stooges 421, 430
Thundering Fleas 188
Tibbett, Lawrence 258–9
Tilbury, Zeffie 339
Tilley, Vesta 7, 50
Tit for Tat 232
Todd, Thelma 184, 235, 251, 253, 300, 324, 339
Toland, Gregg 420
Toto 118, 122, 434
Towed in a Hole 300, 461
The Tower of Lies 177
Tracy, Bert 103, 105, 292, 439
'The Trail of the Lonesome Pine' 350
Trimble, Vern 267
Trouble Brewing 147
Truart Pictures 165
Truman, Harry 429
Tryon, Glenn 123, 184, 188–9, 305
Tucker, Richard 288
Tumbleweeds 177
Turpin, Ben 143, 158, 392
Twentieth Century Fox 397, 409, 421

Twice Two 174, 247, 297–8, 299
Two Tars 225, 229, 232, 272
Two Tickets to Broadway 438
Tysall, Ted 52

Ulverston 10–12
Unaccustomed As We Are 230, 251, 253, 364
Under Two Jags 156
Unfriendly Enemies 177
The Unholy Three 177
United Artists 375
Universal Studios 63, 115–20, 178–9, 399
An Unwilling Burglar 22, 84
Ups and Downs 107
Utopia 437–8

Valentino, Rudolph 149, 292
Van Dyke, Dick xii, 451, 456
Variety 73, 87, 289, 333, 402
vaudeville 196–7, 272, 438
Vaughan, Kate 14
Velez, Lupe 320
Verdi, Giuseppe 356
Victor Talking Machine (company) 218, 230
Vidor, King 143, 177
Vim Comedies 100–109 *passim*
The Virgin of Stamboul 178
Vitagraph (company) 63, 127–8, 132–4, 137, 145, 147

Waite, Malcolm 206
Waiting for Godot 459–60
Walburn, Raymond 432
Walker, H.M. ('Beanie') xv, 142, 198–9, 204, 245, 252–3, 285, 288, 295
Walker, Whimsical 82
Wallace, Richard 183
Walsh, Raoul 398, 405
Wandering Papas 182
Wanted – A Bad Man 107
Wardell, Nancy 17
A Warm Reception 107–8
Warner Brothers 218, 369, 394
Water Rats 428, 445
Waters, Dale 32
Watson, Tom 67
Watson's Beef Trust 77
'The Wax Works' 80
Way Out West 268, 344, 349–52, 351, 386, 410
Wayne, John 430
We Faw Down 248, 362, 367

The Weak-End Party 148
The Wedding March 205
Weissberg, Roy B. 108; *see also* West, Billy
Weldon, Harry 76
Wellman, William 398
Werker, Alfred L. 404
Werner, Arthur 108
West of Hot Dog 171
West, Billy 108–11, 117, 133, 166–7
West, Con 50, 54, 56
West, Mae 221, 258, 288
West, Roland 177
westerns 61, 271
Wharton, Leopold and Theodore 98
What Price Glory 430
Wheeler, Rene 434
Whelan, Tim 434
When Comedy Was King 452
When Knighthood Was in Flower 152
When Knights Were Cold 152, 153
White, Jack 170
White, Leo 109
White, Vera 248–9, 362
White Wings 159, 365
Whiting, Dwight 121
Whose Zoo? 117
Why Girls Love Sailors 205–6
Why Girls Say No 188–9, 220
Wife Tamers 184
Wild Papa 167
Wilde, Oscar 50
Wilder, Billy 394–5
Wilhelm, Emperor 55
Willard, C.L. 356
Williams, Bert 69, 451

Williams, C. Jay
Williams, Earle 147
Williams, Marshall 35, 39
Williams, Percy 28
Willkie, Wendell 396
Wilton, Robb 49
Wisdom, Norman 440
With Love and Hisses 206–7
Wizard Comedies 100
The Wonderful Wizard of Oz 163
Wood, Wee Georgie 26, 49, 321
Wooden Wedding 180
Woolfe, Frank 157
The World's Verdict 14–16
The Wow-Wows 58, 71–4, 81
Wray, Fay 176, 180, 205
Wright, Basil 270–71
Wrong Again 236
Wurtzel, Sol 398, 409, 413
Wyatt, David xv, 174
Wyatt, Trixie 449–50

Yaps and Yokels 136
Yes, Yes, Nanette 176, 182
You're Darn Tootin' xi–xii, 160, 224, 233, 268
Young, Noah 123, 156, 210, 212, 220
Young, Roland 370
Youngson, Robert 452

Zanuck, Darryl F. 397
Zenobia 370–75, 372, 384
Ziegfeld, Florenz 76, 371
Ziegfeld Follies 177, 311, 451
Zukor, Adolph 456–7